D1563411

Bourgeois Society in
Nineteenth-Century Europe

BOURGEOIS SOCIETY IN NINETEENTH-CENTURY EUROPE

Edited by
Jürgen Kocka and Allan Mitchell

BERG

Oxford / Providence

English Edition
first published in 1993
by Berg Publishers Limited
Editorial offices:
150 Cowley Road, Oxford, OX4 1JJ, UK
221 Waterman Street, Providence, RI02906, USA

English Edition © 1993
Originally published as *Bürgertum im 19. Jahrhundert*
Translated from the German by permission of the publishers
© 1988 by Deutscher Taschenbuch Verlag, Munich

Library of Congress Cataloging-in-Publication Data
Bürgertum im 19. Jahrhundert. English. Selections.
    The Bourgeois society in nineteenth-century Europe / edited by
Jürgen Kocka and Allan Mitchell.
        p.   cm.
    Translated selections from: Bürgertum im 19. Jahrhundert.
    Includes index.

    1. Middle classes—Germany—History—19th century.   2. Middle
classes—Europe—History—19th century.   I. Kocka, Jürgen.
II. Mitchell, Allan.   III. Title.
HT690.G38882513   1992
305.5'5' 09409034—dc20   91–17753
                                                              CIP

British Library Cataloguing in Publication Data
A CIP catalogue record for this book is available from the British library.

ISBN 0 85496 414 2

Printed in the United Kingdom by WBC Bookbinders, Bridgend.

Table of Contents

List of Tables

| Preface to the English Edition

Ever since the late eighteenth century, European society has been undergoing a transformation in which the most dynamic element has been the middle class. Defining this social category, however, remains a conundrum. Exactly what persons are considered to be middle-class? What characteristics do they share? Are they defined by a common culture? What really distinguishes them from others? What has been their collective impact within the European community of nations that has evolved over time?

These are some of the issues discussed in this anthology, which is the product of a cooperative project at the Zentrum für Interdisziplinäre Forschung (ZIF)(the Institute of Advanced Studies) at the University of Bielefeld. The forty or so fellows who gathered there in 1986–1987, comprised a diverse group from twelve European countries plus Israel and the United States, and from nine different academic disciplines – history, literature, law, anthropology, political science, sociology, psychology, art history, and economics.

The full results of this complex undertaking have been published in a three volume German edition from which we have now selected seventeen representative essays for translation.* Although many other worthy contributions were thereby omitted, the reader can at least gain an impression of what the Bielefeld project entailed and what conclusions it reached.

In weekly seminars, evening lectures, special conferences and informal contacts, members of the Bielefeld group presented and discussed the progress of their individual research. Three aspects of the general topic were kept constantly in view: (1) the specific characteristics of the middle-class social types as well as the common denominator that afforded them social cohesion; (2) the extent to which middle-class values and interests altered the texture of nineteenth century European society; and (3) the national differences that emerged in the irregular development of a European pattern. It was in the third of these three contexts that there arose an unavoidable question about the 'peculiar course' (*Sonderweg*) of German history. The comparative

---

* J. Kocka (ed.), *Bürgertum im 19. Jahrhundert. Deutschland im europäischen Vergleich*, 3 vols. (Munich, 1988).

framework of the Bielefeld project was ideal for a thorough airing of this problem, which has in recent years attracted a large body of historical literature concerning the responsibilities of the *Bürgertum* for the uniquely violent phenomenon of German fascism.

Because German was ordinarily the common language at the ZIF, the operative vocabulary among the scholars resident in Bielefeld tended to be Central European in origin. Thus, a difficulty has been created by translating the concept of *Bürgertum* into English. Clearly the term "middle class" cannot be considered fully equivalent, because it too broadly includes the ranks of small businessmen, office clerks, typists, and other such service personnel who are relegated by the German language to the *Kleinbürgertum* (petite bourgeoisie).

Bürgertum should be understood as a more elitist social category (excluding both the nobility and high Catholic clergy and the majority of the *Kleinbürgertum*). Within that range the rich German vocabulary permits us to distinguish between the *Wirtschaftsbürgertum* – entrepreneurs and managers in industry, commerce, banking, and business – and the *Bildungsbürgertum* – including lawyers, judges, doctors, professors, Protestant clergy, engineers, scientists, and academically trained civil servants. At the same time, we should note that German nomenclature does not establish a precise distinction between the French expressions *bourgeois* and *citoyen* (citizen). *Bürger* may mean either or both. Like the English usage of 'burgher', moreover, that word may convey the notion of a city-dweller. The addition of another German prefix further widens the category of citizenship in question to the sphere of the nation-state (*Staatsbürger*).

Since the conceptual differences between the countries under investigation reflect important differences in the historical experience of their middle classes, we were confronted with the editorial dilemma either to attempt linguistic uniformity by translating critical terms such as *Bürgertum*, *bourgeoisie*, *borghesia*, etc. straightforwardly into 'middle class', thereby losing the subtleties of historical semantics, or to preserve the linguistic peculiarities, in each case by doing without translation and creating obstacles to the volume's readability.

We finally went for a compromise which to a large extent was suggested by the contributors' use of language. The German *Bürgertum*, French *bourgeoisie*, and Italian *borghesia* remained untranslated since those terms carry far-reaching social, cultural and political implications which differ significantly from the content of the English term 'middle class'. However, we did translate the corresponding adjectives *bürgerlich*, etc. into 'bourgeois'. Not to do so, we felt, would have unnecessarily reduced the volume's readability.

There was strong consent among the authors that the term 'bourgeoisie' which today appears to be fairly established in the historiographical discourse of the English speaking world should be used only to refer to the bourgeoisie in the 'classical' or 'narrow' sense of the word, namely the upper layers of the mercantile, financial, industrial and propertied middle classes. Finally, the term 'middle classes' has served as a general and comprehensive characterisation of the phenomena under investigation.

One major question of the Bielefeld research group was: to what extent did the middle classes influence or indeed determine an informal system of dominant social values in nineteenth century Europe? Despite its manifest untidiness, this line of investigation could not be ruled out by members of the research team, who were bound to inquire into the ramifications of middle-class lifestyle in philosophy and literature, art and architecture, gender relationships and family structure, dress and diet, school and play, and a host of other activities. By including only a limited selection of essays, of course, this anthology is unable to convey a complete sense of such diversity, for which one must refer to the German edition.

The Bielefeld project shows that the study and writing of social history has become an international enterprise. Yet it also demonstrates national differences persist. This volume provides an analysis of the European experience from a largely German perspective, but each instance has its obvious cultural idiosyncrasies, and that historical variety remains. In their formulation and viewpoint, therefore, the essays in this volume undoubtedly reflect their preponderantly Germanic origin. Still, few scholars left the Bielefeld project after several months of intellectual exchange without a strong conviction that nineteenth-century Europe did, after all, constitute a higher unity of which the middle class was an indivisible and vital element.

Among the many people and institutions that have sustained this project, we want particularly to thank Gus Fagan and Adam Tooze for the first draft of the translation and Adam Tooze and Kati Koerner for the final corrections; Allan Nothnagle for doing the index; Bernd Dornseifer for his assistance in editing; and the Zentrum für Interdisziplinäre Forschung in Bielefeld for its hospitality and support of the publication of this volume.

Berlin, June 1992
JÜRGEN KOCKA AND ALLAN MITCHELL

1 | EUROPEAN SOCIETY AND THE MIDDLE CLASSES

1 | The European Pattern and the German Case

Jürgen Kocka

The period which began with the Revolution of 1789, and which ended with the First World War, is often described as the century of the middle class. What does this mean? What was special about the middle class, which allegedly stamped its character on that century? What did its greatness consist of, what its much cited failure? Bourgeois society (Bürgerliche Gesellschaft) is still today, for some, the object of powerful criticism, from a variety of directions. For others it continues to be a model of a free and rational society that is still worth striving for and whose potential has still not been realised, or it is something belonging to the past, present only in mournful recollection. How does one explain this ambivalence? Is it true that German society in the nineteenth century, compared with the other countries of Europe, was characterised by a special lack of *Bürgerlichkeit*, a deficit that continued to shape Germany's history into the twentieth century?

The Precarious Unity of the Bürgertum

It is difficult to translate the German *Bürger* and related concepts into English. *Bürger* has at least three different levels of meaning which overlap and intermix both in the common and in the scholarly use of the word. It is initially used to describe the urban burghers of the late medieval and early modern period, a corporate group with specific legal privileges, lifestyles and status, which set it apart from the towns-men and the rural population. Since corporate distinctions between town and countryside, and between burghers and other townsmen took a relatively long time to disappear in nineteenth-century Central Europe, this traditional meaning of *Bürger* has survived, though in a continually weakened form.[1] Secondly, particularly with respect to

Notes to Chapter 1 can be found on page 33.

3

the late eighteenth, nineteenth and twentieth centuries, *Bürger* refers to those who belong to the *Bürgertum,* a social formation which included the *'Wirtschaftsbürgertum'* (businessmen, entrepreneurs, capitalists, managers and *rentiers*) and what is often called the *'Bildungs-bürgertum'*[2] (lawyers, judges, academically trained civil servants, ministers, journalists, engineers and so on). Usually the nobility, the petty bourgeoisie, the lower and working classes, the peasants, artists, the military, and the Catholic clergy were not included in the concept of *Bürgertum.* Sometimes *Bürgertum* in this sense can be translated without qualification as 'middle class'.[3] But 'middle class' in contrast to *Bürgertum,* usually includes the lower middle class (*Kleinbürgertum, Mittelstand*), and frequently excludes the bourgeois elites. The third meaning of *Bürger* is that of 'citizen', and the adjective *bürgerlich* can be translated as 'civil' or even 'civic'; *bürgerliche Gesellschaft* can be translated as 'civil society'. While the German language seems to differ from most other European languages in that it does not clearly differentiate between *bourgeois* and *citoyen,* this ambivalence cannot be regarded as simply a question of semantics. It rather points to the interconnection between the rise of the middle classes and the rise of civil society in late eighteenth- and nineteenth-century Central Europe, a connection which may not exist any more today, but which survives on the semantic level.

In the second half of the nineteenth century the *Bürgertum* came to approximately four per cent of the economically active population in Germany, and together with their families, about five per cent of the whole population (with a small upward trend).[4] It is to this small minority that the term *Bürgertum* in the present volume refers.

What were the defining attributes of the *Bürgertum* in the late eighteenth, nineteenth and twentieth centuries? What were the characteristics shared by businessmen, *rentiers*, doctors, lawyers, clergy and others, which distinguished them from other social categories not belonging to the *Bürgertum*? What was the common denominator and what were the *differentia specifica* of the *Bürgertum,* and how did they change over time?

Certainly, the *Bürgertum* cannot be seen as a class in a Marxist or Weberian sense, since it included self-employed and salaried persons, and, more generally, persons with very different market positions. Also, in contrast to the burghers of the late medieval and early modern period, the nineteenth-century middle class cannot be seen as a corporate group (*Stand*) either, since it was not characterised by specific legal privileges. Rather, there are two plausible and compatible arguments with respect to the unifying and defining characteristics of the *Bürgertum*.

It is generally more likely that individuals form social groups with some cohesion, common understanding and a potential of collective action if there is tension and conflict with other social groups. By setting oneself apart from others, one gains identity. This is well known from the history of classes. The same holds true with respect to the Central European *Bürgertum* as it emerged as a post-corporate supralocal social formation in the second half of the eighteenth and the first part of the nineteenth century. Entrepreneurs and capitalists, professors, judges, journalists, ministers and high-ranking civil servants differed in many respects, but they shared a critical distance from the privileged aristocracy and absolute monarchy. By stressing the principles of achievement and education, work and self-worth, the concept of a modern, secularised, post-corporate, self-regulating, enlightened 'civil society' emerged, which was supported by many *Bürger* and which opposed the privileges and despotism of the *ancien régime*. It was a complicated and multifaceted process with many exceptions. Still, the different sub-groups of the emerging *Bürgertum* were to some degree united by their common opponents: the nobility, unrestricted absolutism and religious orthodoxy. On this basis, they developed common interests and common experiences, and a certain degree of shared self-understanding and common ideologies emerged. The *Bürgertum* constituted itself as a social group or formation, which encompassed different occupational groups, sectors and class positions.

In the course of the nineteenth century this line of distinction and tension lost much of its structuring power, without fading away altogether. This was due to the gradual destruction of the legal privileges of the nobility, the rise of constitutional government and increasing *rapprochements* between the upper grades of the middle classes and parts of the nobility. Simultaneously, another line of distinction and tension comes into play, which had not been altogether absent around 1800, but which became more manifest, more clearly perceived by contemporaries and even dramatised in the second third of the nineteenth century: a line of demarcation setting the *Bürgertum* apart 'from below', from the lower classes, the emerging working class and 'small people' in general. This category of people included master artisans, small merchants, inn-keepers and clerks, frequently lumped together as 'petty-bourgeois' and distinguished from the *Bürgertum* proper. In spite of the many and great differences between late nineteenth-century industrialists, merchants and *rentiers*, lawyers and higher civil servants, professors, high school teachers, scientists and others, they usually shared a defensive-critical distance from 'the people', the 'working class' and the labour movement, and this meant much with respect to self-understanding and life-style, social alliances and political commitments at that time.[5]

A distinctive middle class formation such as the *Bürgertum* was therefore less likely where a strong tradition of aristocratic dominance was absent (as in the USA), where the gap between nobility and the higher echelons of the middles classes was bridged and integrated early (as in eighteenth-century England), and where the integration of the upper strata of the middle class and the nobility into a new composite elite was followed by a marked weakening of the tension so that both 'social fronts' faded away (as in most of Europe today). The existence of a distinctive middle class depends on constellations, which vary over time and place; the national differences of sociological conceptualisation reflect these variations. Against this background it becomes understandable why the discourse on the middle class is by and large a continental European phenomenon, why it is so difficult, for instance to translate *Bürgertum* into English, and why the growing German language literature on the history of the *Bürgertum* does not have a real parallel in the Anglo-American world.[6]

The second means of defining the *Bürgertum* refers to its culture. According to this view the *Wirtschaftsbürgertum* and the *Bildungsbürgertum* shared a specific respect for individual achievement on which they based their claims for rewards, recognition and influence. They shared basically positive attitudes towards regular work, a propensity towards rational lifestyles, and a fundamental striving for independence: individually or on the basis of associations and self-governed initiatives. Emphasis on education (rather than on religion) characterised middle-class views of themselves and the world. Simultaneously, education (*Bildung*) served as a basis on which they communicated with one another, and which distinguished them from others who did not share this type of (classical) education. There was much respect for scholarly pursuits (*Wissenschaft*) and a particular aesthetic appreciation of music, literature and the arts.

For bourgeois culture a specific ideal of family life was essential: the family was a purpose in itself, a community held together by emotional ties and basic loyalties. Dominated by the husband and father, it was an inner sanctum protected from the world of competition and materialism, from politics and the public, a sphere of privacy (although not without servants, whose work made it possible for the middle-class mother to give sufficient time to the cultural dimensions of family life, including the transmission of the 'cultural capital' to the next generation). Bourgeois culture could flourish only in towns and cities. There had to be peers with whom one could meet in clubs and associations, at feasts and at cultural events, something that a rural environment could not really offer. If one sees the cohesion and the specificity of the *Bürgertum* as defined by its culture, one appreciates the importance of symbolic forms in the daily life of the *bürgerliche*: table manners and conventions, the quotations from the classical literature, titles, customs and dress.[7]

Bourgeois culture claimed universal recognition. In contrast to aristocratic or peasant cultures, it had an in-built tendency to expand beyond the social boundaries of the *Bürgertum* and to imprint the whole of society. The *Verbürgerlichung* of other social groups was an essential element of bourgeois culture. The school system, the workplace, public life, and, finally, the sphere of organised leisure were the most important arenas in which bourgeois culture could express its hegemonic force and its attractiveness. In the long run, it spread widely and as a result – to the extent that this happened – bourgeois culture ceased to define the *Bürgertum*. The more clearly a whole society was imprinted with bourgeois culture, the more difficult it became to identify a specific *Bürgertum*. This is the situation in most Western countries today. Consequently, the concept of *Bürgertum* has developed as a major tool for analysing social developments from the late eighteenth to the first part of the twentieth century, but it is less helpful and indeed marginal for the analysis of present-day society.

On the other hand, there were (and are) obstacles preventing an easy spread of bourgeois culture beyond the *Bürgertum*. For, in order to participate fully in the values and practices of bourgeois culture, certain economic and social conditions have to be fulfilled. One needs a stable income clearly above the minimum. Life must be relatively secure economically; without security there can be no long-term planning which is needed to build up a systematic, rational and disciplined conduct of life. Within the family, the wife and mother as well as the children must be, to some degree, set free from the necessities of work and from the compulsion to contribute to the family's income – impossible in all lower-class and many lower-middle-class milieus. Again, the availability of servants appears to be central. Bourgeois culture cannot flourish without plenty of *space* (functionally specialised rooms in the house or apartment) and *time* for cultural activities and leisure. In order to take part in the game of culture and to obey its rules, such conditions had (and have) to be fulfilled, which were (and are) beyond the reach of the majority. This explains why the bourgeois status of most of the petty bourgeoisie was highly precarious and questionable, and why peasants, workers and lower-class persons in general did not qualify as *Bürger* at all. A tension between universalist claims and limited accessibility was (and is) typical for bourgeois culture, and the degree to which it spread beyond the social boundaries of the *Bürgertum* has varied in the course of history.[8]

Again the historical, context-related nature of the *Bürgertum* becomes clear. A specific culture contributed to its constitution, a culture neither ubiquitous nor uniform which presupposed urban milieus, and did not exist everywhere. It emerged from the eighteenth-century Enlightenment and it inherited its ideals of autonomy, work discipline and community from the corporate world of the burghers in the towns of the early modern period. Where the influence of the Enlightenment had been weak and autonomous burgher traditions absent, as in Eastern Europe and in most non-European parts of the world, a coherent and distinct social formation such as the *Bürgertum* was less likely to emerge.[9] On the other hand, the more widely spread and general a bourgeois culture becomes within a given society, the less powerful it is in defining a specific social group, and the more difficult it becomes to discern a clearly identified phenomenon like the *Bürgertum*.

While entrepreneurs, capitalists, managers, lawyers, ministers, doctors, administrators and other professionals may exist in all highly differentiated modern societies, they crystallise into a more or less coherent and distinctive social formation only under specific historical circumstances which emerge and then disappear. To study the *Bürgertum* means to study processes of its formation and devolution. The degree to which such a social formation existed differed from country to country, and from period to period. This opens up interesting avenues for comparative research.[10]

Bürgertum and Civil Society

As mentioned before, the term *Bürger* refers not just to the inhabitants of towns, and to those persons belonging to the social formation discussed in the previous section, but also includes in its meaning the notion of *Staatsbürger* (citizen). As a German author wrote in 1792: 'The word *Bürger* in German has more worth than the French *bourgeois*...and it has more because for us it signifies two things at the same time which, in French, have different names. On the one hand, it means a member of *bürgerliche Gesellschaft* – that is the French *citoyen*; it also means the non-noble inhabitant of a town, who lives from a certain industry or trade (*Gewerbe*) – and that is *bourgeois*'.[11]

In the public discussion of the late eighteenth century, a discussion carried out mainly by the *Bürgertum* and strongly influenced by the Enlightenment, there developed the concept of *bürgerliche Gesell-schaft*(civil society), signifying a future social order in which the idea of *Staatsbürger* wold develop to full fruition. *Bürgerliche Gesellschaft* signified a model of an economic, social and political order that would make real for all the principle of legally regulated individual freedom by overcoming absolutism, privileges of birth, and clerical manipulation. It was a model that would organise human social life according to the standard of reason, and which would organise the economy on the basis of legally regulated competition, and that would distribute opportunity according to the standard of achievement and merit. The state power would be, on the one hand, limited by law and constitution, while, on the other hand, it would be subject to the will of the mature citizens by means of electorally appointed, representative bodies. Art, science and religion would be permitted a large degree of autonomy.[12]

Bürger means bourgeois as well as citizen, and the adjective *bürgerlich* means both bourgeois and civil at the same time. This semantic ambiguity points to a real historical relationship. Firstly, at the time when the model of *bürgerliche Gesellschaft* (civil society) began to emerge, there existed an inner link between this model and the *Bürgertum* which was also in the process of formation. Bourgeois interests demanded the creation of civil law and a constitutional state (both central elements of the model of civil society); this involved not just the protection of property and capital,[13] but also the need for legal security and autonomy as preconditions for bourgeois culture and the ability to plan one's life.

Members of the emerging *Bürgertum* – professionals, academics, educated civil servants, merchants and other *Bürger* – were overrepresented in the lodges and reading societies in which the ideas of *bürgerliche Gesellschaft* were discussed and propagated, in the late eighteenth and early nineteenth century, brought the *ancien régime* to an end and prepared the way for *bürgerliche Gesellschaft*. While the details are complicated, there was without doubt a clear affinity between bourgeois culture and early liberalism which, in turn, did most to implement the programme of civil society.[14]

The relationship between civil society and *Bürgertum* can be discovered if one considers who was excluded from citizenship. It is interesting to see how the lexica and critical writings of the pre-1848 period saw the *Bürger* (in the sense of bourgeois) as the core of *Staatsbürger* and began to make his appearance no longer as a subject of the state, but as a *citoyen* with the right of participation, when full *Staatsbürgerschaft* (citizenship) became a practical possibility.

In response to the practical question of how to establish the preconditions for full rights of participation (such as passive and active voting rights), the *Krug'sche Lexikon* of 1827 suggested rationality and independence. This excluded the following from full *Bürgerrecht* (civil rights): women, 'because of their natural occupation, which binds them to the house and makes them dependent on the male; wage-earners, because of their dependence on the employers; the poor, because they depend on the charity of others' as well as the 'feeble-minded and the insane'.[15]

In the view of liberal spokesmen, and as established by most voting legislation, full citizenship rights were linked to property or education, which means they were virtually restricted to the *Bürgertum*, plus some other segments of society, including land owning peasants and farmers, and better-off parts of the lower middle classes. The restrictive voting rights that existed until the First World War in large parts of Europe, especially at the community level, acted as a constant reminder to the propertied and educated parts of the middle class that they belonged together and that they were not part of 'the people' and distinct from the working class. The socialist and conservative critics of liberalism found much justification when they attempted to reveal, under the fine ideological surface of the citizen, the naked self-interest of the bourgeois.[16]

The relationship between *Bürgertum* and *bürgerliche Gesellschaft* also becomes clear when we ask what it was that one had to do in order to fully belong to this *bürgerliche Gesellschaft*. The history of the Jews in Germany demonstrates that the achievement of full civil rights (*Staatsbürgerrechte*) went hand in hand with the ascent into *Bürgertum*. Without the latter it was difficult to achieve the former. The demand for full equality as citizens was a demand that the Jews could raise and gradually achieve only when they had become *bürgerlich* in their language and education, social manners and customs, their hygiene and their manner of dress.[17]

The same mechanisms were at work in the attempts of the movement for the emancipation of the workers, a movement which, until the First World War, had only limited success because the proletarian way of life was a barrier to full *Verbürgerlichung* in that it made entrance into bourgeois culture very difficult.[18] Clearly, the semantic relationship between *Bürger* and *Staatsbürger*, and between *Bürgertum* and *bürgerliche Gesellschaft* was no accident of linguistic history.

The concept *bürgerliche Gesellschaft* had, and in the opinion of many still has, a utopian component. A central element of this model of human social life is, in fact, a promise or, better still, an expectation which has, up to now, only been partly fulfilled. The critique of *bürgerliche Gesellschaft* is as old as *bürgerliche Gesellschaft* itself.

Early critics, bearing the experience of the French Revolution in mind, pointed to the dangers of hubris and terror which could lie hidden in a radical Enlightenment programme when and if it were physically enacted. Others condemned the fundamental contradiction peculiar to the model of a bourgeois society, especially if one were to attempt to translate it into reality; this criticism was given its classic expression by socialist and communist commentators and became a historical force in the labour movement. The conservative critique, which was older still and no less perceptive, also wanted to reveal the *bourgeois* behind the *citoyen*. In addition, the conservatives complained about the destruction and damage done to the world of tradition by a bourgeois world which was constantly changing and always on the search for something new.

To this can be added Nietzsche's critique of bourgeois philistinism, and the Youth Movement's rejection of what was typically bourgeois, mechanical and moderate, around and after 1900. Fascism must be understood as the most radical rejection of *Bürgerlichkeit*, as a product of its crisis, no matter how helpful many *Bürger* were in its ascent and victory, and in spite of the fact that it was not the *Bürger* who were primarily affected by its destructive consequences. At the present time a renewed scepticism about progress and a rejuvenated critique of civilisation are sharpening one's awareness of the 'dialectic of enlightenment', of the costs of western rationalisation and of the dark underbelly of *bürgerliche Gesellschaft*.

What has traditionally been the most effective critique of bourgeois society, the Marxist critique, takes as its starting point the conflict between capital and labour, between the bourgeoisie and the proletariat. Its basic argument can be briefly summarised.

As already discussed, the most important rights of self-realisation and participation in bourgeois society were linked to property as the guarantee of individual independence, and to education as the precondition to participation in public discussion and decision making. It soon became clear, however, that there was a contradiction between a universal claim and social reality, which did not develop, as the early liberals had hoped, in the direction of a social *juste milieu*, a society of more or less equal and, to a certain extent, bourgeois individuals (or families) without major differences in property or education. On the contrary, what developed, with capitalism and the industrial revolution, with the concentration of capital and large-scale factories, were new forms of dependence, new inequalities and an enormous potential for conflict.

As inherited privileges and absolutist control were overcome on the road to bourgeois society, the latter developed into a class society in which the bourgeoisie occupied the dominant position. Economic inequality and dependence now shaped the whole spectrum of economic, political, social and cultural life with even greater force than had been the case in pre-bourgeois times. The free and self-regulating mechanism of the market and competition continued to intensify these socioeconomic inequalities and dependencies with self-destructive consequences; from this self-destruction there would at some stage emerge a better, post-bourgeois, socialist society.

The attractive power of Marxist interpretation has declined. The widespread disappointment with socialism in recent decades provides a reason to approach this kind of critique of bourgeois society with caution. In the light of newer critique of the 'project of modernity', anti-capitalist socialism appears as merely a continuation of *Bürgerlichkeit* by other means. In addition, a more careful investigation clearly shows that, at least in Germany, the kind of unambiguous domination by the bourgeoisie, such as is claimed by this critique, never existed.

Most importantly, as a result of this critique which, when adopted by the socialist labour movement, developed into a real challenge, bourgeois society undertook self-corrective measures which, by introducing changes, were able to ensure its survival. Property and education were abandoned as conditions for political participation, democratisation took place, the welfare state emerged, and new mechanisms for dealing with and regulating class conflicts were invented.

In the relation between the *Bürgertum* and the working class, however, opportunities and limits of bourgeois societies become very clear. The ability of the working-class movement to carry out effective anti-bourgeois politics was due, in part, to the way in which this movement had been influenced and shaped by bourgeois traditions whose dynamic it adopted for itself and adapted to its own needs. The bourgeois *Verein* (association), however, could not simply be transferred into the non-bourgeois milieu of the developing working class. The emerging working-class movement had to make use of non-bourgeois strategies in order to win for itself a share of *Bürgerlichkeit*. But, at the same time, in the dialectical relation of bourgeoisie and proletariat there was something new which sought to push beyond the repertory of bourgeois society, in the direction of a post-bourgeois social model: the strike as an anti-bourgeois strategy, internationalism and solidarity as post-bourgeois basic values.[19]

With the more traditional criticism of bourgeois society along Marxist lines and stress on class discrimination becoming less important, increasing attention has recently been paid to the effect of the rise of bourgeois society on gender relations. The basic facts are disturbing enough, in that the bourgeois emancipation of humanity was largely for the benefit of its male half. In many respects, the legal, political and social inequalities between men and women increased during the nineteenth century. On the other hand, there was, in the latter part of the century, an improvement in the education of women. Emancipatory claims were developed, and there emerged a mainly bourgeois women's movement which exerted pressure for equality in important areas and which, although it was weak, paved the way for that emancipatory drive which has become clearly visible in the late twentieth century.[20]

There was some dispute, however, as to whether the emancipation of women, which began somewhat timidly in the nineteenth century, made progress decades later and is today still incomplete, followed from central principles of bourgeois society, or whether the full emancipation of women would of necessity lead to the collapse of the basic pillars of bourgeois society. The first view is supported by the fact that two components of bourgeois societies, the dynamic of the market and that of education, make in the long run no distinction with respect to gender. The universal character of bourgeois demands for individual freedom and equality tends ultimately to cause the erosion of all inherited privileges, whether it be that of class, race or gender. On the other hand, it is clear that the resistance to equal rights and equal opportunities for women did not disappear with the implementation of the basic principles of bourgeois society during the nineteenth century. In fact, there was an opposite tendency. The early women's movement came up against the same kind of stiff resistance as did the workers' movement. Just as the latter appeared as a threat to property, the former appeared as a threat to the family and, in the eyes of opponents, may have appeared as the greater threat.

The resistance to gender equality was a consequence, in systematic terms, of two basic principles that were (and still are) inherent in bourgeois societies: on the one hand, increasing social differentiation and specialisation (a precondition of performance and efficiency) and, on the other hand, the great importance attributed to the family as the locus of reproduction and self-realisation.

With the differentiation of social spheres (for instance, production, family, politics) and their internal specialisation (the increasing number of different life-long careers, increasing qualification requirements, professionalisation) individuals became increasingly and continuously tied to forms of specialised activity. This involved a more thorough and reinforced differentiation of roles between those engaged in economic activity and in education, between domestic and non-domestic labour, between production and reproduction, between men and women. It is also clear that the family in bourgeois societies is the principal institution for ensuring economic, social and cultural continuity from one generation to the next and it is precisely in bourgeois societies, unlike in the pre-bourgeois period, that the family has also become the sphere of compensation for the deprivations and losses suffered in the economic and in the public sphere.

Here was a basic contradiction between different principles of bourgeois society which was not overcome in the nineteenth century. It was the contradiction between the universal promise of freedom, responsibility and equal opportunity on the one hand, and its demands on the family and its requirement of ever-increasing productivity and specialisation on the other.

Alongside traditions that were age-old, deeply ingrained and only very gradually weakening, this contradiction contributed to the fact that, during the nineteenth century, the social inequality of men and women continued to exist and even grew worse while, at the same time, the opposition to this inequality increased. An awareness of this contradiction developed and it became a spur to action which gradually, and much later – in the twentieth century and at a much higher level of activity – led to fundamental changes in gender relations and promises to lead to more. Like the labour movement (although much later and, up to now, much weaker) the women's movement, which has actively promoted this process, has been able to call on some of the basic principles of bourgeois society. Seen in this way, the emancipation of women appears as a delayed consequence of the dynamic set in motion with the transition to bourgeois society.[21]

Rise and Decline: Stages in the History of the Bürgertum

What can be said about the beginning, the stages of development and the end of the phenomenon that is here under discussion? There are no sharp dividing lines; change was part of normality. In a very approximate and summary fashion, one can divide the 'century of the middle class' into three main periods.

Rise

The first phase extended from the last decades of the eighteenth century to the 1840s. It was a period characterised by the erosion of older inequalities (and of the laws supporting them) associated with the old corporate world of the *Stände* (estates); this erosion was prepared by the anti-corporate interventions of 'enlightened absolutism' during the pre-revolutionary period, given greater impulse by the 'reforms from above' at the beginning of the century (although there were great differences between the territory left of the Rhine, the Rhine Federation, Prussia and Austria) and carried through with some hesitation between 1815 and 1848. This first phase witnessed a cultural revolution: the Enlightenment of the eighteenth century, advancing secularisation and, the product of both of these processes, the neo-humanist educational reform at the beginning of the nineteenth century which had widespread effects in the decades that followed with new universities and new schools being established.

The institutional transformation of absolutism made slow and limited, but important, progress through the legal codes of the late eighteenth century, the constitutionalism of southern and central Germany during the early part of the nineteenth century, the shift of power from the autocracy to the bureaucracy in Prussia. The development of a political state apparatus, at the level of the individual states, continued to make progress in spite of the efforts made against it by the national movement in the follow-up to the French Revolution and the Napoleonic challenge. Pre-industrial capitalism was making rapid advances, evident from the expansion of proto-industrial cottage industries, the transformation of the old crafts, and the extension of the domestic market for commodities, labour, land and capital.

These were the decades in which the new *Bürgertum* emerged and began to evolve, when the conception of *bürgerliche Gesellschaft* was developed and its principles established, particularly during and after the reforms at the beginning of the nineteenth century. For the emerging *Bürgertum*, a primary concern was to distance itself from the old powers, especially from the nobility. Within the *Bürgertum* itself it was the *Bildungsbürgertum* (predominantly officials) rather than the *Wirtschaftsbürgertum* which was dominant. The latter was as yet relatively undeveloped with strong regional differences and without much power or respect. Those basic elements of *bürgerliche Gesellschaft* which were introduced, largely by means of government-initiated reforms and on the basis of many compromises with the old powers, were generally welcomed by the German *Bürger*. Their goals, however, went much further than this. They wanted a more consistent limitation of what were still absolutist powers of government; fundamental restriction of the still existing aristocratic privileges; national unity; bourgeois participation in public life in all its forms; and the application, in the economy, in society and in the activities of the state, of bourgeois standards of work and achievement, property and education. The slow development of *bürgerliche Gesellschaft* lagged behind the expectations of the German *Bürgertum*, which still found itself in a phase of advance and offensive.[22]

Culmination and Turning Point

The second phase lasted from the 1840s to the 1870s. These three decades were witness to a threefold crisis: the social conflict (pauperism and industrial revolution), the constitutional struggle (which ended in compromise) and the unification of the nation by means of 'blood and iron'.

The breakthrough of industrial capitalism, which took place during this period, shifted the balance within the *Bürgertum* in favour of the industrial-manufacturing bourgeoisie whose wealth, social standing and influence increased significantly. The *Bildungsbürgertum* and the *Wirtschaftsbürgertum* now had a more equal status, and their contacts and interactions intensified, while the distancing of both from the petty bourgeoisie increased. With the social crisis of the 1840s, the revolution of 1848/49, the final emergence in the 1860s of the working-class movement and the democratic-socialist critique of those decades, it was the social front against the lower social orders that now assumed primary importance in bourgeois self-awarenesss − all the more so as aristocratic privileges and corporate remnants continued to crumble during the period. Many of the bourgeois demands for unity, freedom, rights and political participation were being fulfilled. Never before or after did the liberals have as much influence as they did during the 1860s and 1870s. The *Verbürgerlichung* of the economy, of society and of culture continued to make rapid progress, even though the profound changes of those decades took place under the guidance of the Prussian state.

Although monarchic-bureaucratic-military domination was not really broken by a consistent parliamentarism, and there was no genuine abolition of aristocratic privilege, this period saw the *Bürgertum* – reasonably integrated internally, its separation from other social groups and classes relatively clear, culturally on the offensive and politically liberal – at the high point of its development, a high point which turned out, at the same time, to be a turning point.[23]

The Bürgertum on the Defensive

This phase lasted from the 1870s to the First World War. Within the firm framework of the Empire and the constitutional monarchy, a powerfully-developing capitalism increasingly penetrated the web of economic and social relations. Industrial growth was irregular and subject to crises but, in general, it advanced with extraordinary success; large-scale industry in particular became increasingly more important. Science and technology became a driving force of social change. There was a massive expansion of the working class and of the new white-collar layer. Simultaneously, the agricultural population decreased, the number of small independent producers shrank, class tensions increased, and state intervention in the economy and in society became gradually more intensive.

In many respects this was *bürgerliche Gesellschaft*. It was based on an undeniable capitalist, dynamic economy of entrepreneurs, on competition and on free market. It guaranteed individual rights, formal equality and well-codified civil law. Constitutional government, political participation, a relatively free and varied press, a functioning sphere of public life, relative autonomy of education, science and art – all of those elements corresponded to the model of bourgeois society described above. So did the flourishing associations (*Vereine*), the well developed local self-government and the thoroughly bourgeois family ideal, anchored in family law and in the rhetoric of the period.

On the other hand, the German Empire was not a fully developed *bürgerliche Gesellschaft*. There were two groups of limitations. Firstly, a large number of pre-bourgeois elements were retained. Although work and achievement could lead, in typically bourgeois fashion, to well-being, social status and power, and although large sections of the nobility appropriated for themselves bourgeois standards in education and economic life, aristocratic privileges were clearly maintained. Aristocrats retained privileged access to power via the Court, the second chambers, the officer corps and the diplomatic service, and maintained their control of rural administration. The constitutional compromise of 1871 blocked a consistent parliamentarisation of the political system. The thoroughly un-bourgeois prerogatives of the army in the Constitution corresponded to an un-bourgeois high esteem for military customs, titles and values in the hierarchy of prestige and in everyday life, criticised by many contemporaries as 'social militarisation'.

State intervention in the economy and society slowly intensified, and this helped to reinforce once again the old tradition of bureaucratic control from above, a feature that had characterised German society from the period of absolutism, particularly in Prussia. This tradition stood opposed to the demand for autonomous self-government, appropriate to the model of *bürgerliche Gesellschaft*. The Liberal, Friedrich Naumann, was not entirely without justification when he complained, in 1909, about this 'industrial society in the political apparel of an agrarian state. Our political situation is a little bit like the situation where a modern factory is being built in what were old farm buildings. The most modern machinery stands under the old roof beams, and iron girders are drawn through mud walls'. From a liberal point of view, the political structure, with its old pre-bourgeois relics and its new un-bourgeois elements, was preventing the German *Bürgertum* from becoming *Staatsbürger* in the full sense of the word. That is what the liberal historian Theodor Mommsen meant when he wrote in his Testament in 1899 that he had always wanted 'to be a *Bürger*'. But he continued: 'that is not possible in our nation…'.

The second source of limitations which hindered a full realisation of *bürgerliche Gesellschaft* arose from its being viewed critically by the *Bürgertum* which had hitherto been its principal supporter. Its achievements included the early democratisation of voting rights in Reichstag elections, the mobilisation of broad layers of the population by social movements and mass parties, the spread of school education and an increase in living standards from the 1860s onwards. As a consequence, opportunities for self-realisation, for freedom and for political participation, contained as a promise in the programme of a *bürgerliche Gesellschaft*, actually spread beyond its original base of support. This was in keeping with the claim to universality contained in the model of *bürgerliche Gesellschaft*. However, these developments were not always to the satisfaction of the *Bürger*, who recognised this democratisation as a double-edged sword and as a potential threat.

The *Bürgertum* had itself changed. New types of *Bürger* were added (managers, experts, functionaries), and the boundary between the *Wirtschaftsbürgertum* and the *Bildungsbürgertum* became less marked, in terms of background, education, communication and mobility. The traditional social barrier between the *Bürgertum* and the nobility became much less significant, without disappearing altogether. What increasingly came to distinguish the *Bürgertum* was its separation from the classes and strata below it, the less educated and less propertied strata, the *Mittelstand*, the workers and the 'people' in general. Nationalism changed, after the 1870s, from being a somewhat 'left-wing' to a primarily 'right-wing' ideology. The decline of party liberalism was evidence not only of the fact that its basic principles had, in the meantime, become common political property, but also of the fact that an increasingly exclusive and defensive *Bürgertum* became less and less liberal, in the Wilhelmine period.

There was a gradual weakening of the belief in progress which had been typical of the *Bürgertum* in its progressive-emancipatory phase. It continued to manifest its energy and capacity for innovation in its economic, technological, scientific and cultural activities. But it remains true that this bourgeois society, at the beginning of the twentieth century, was, from the political and social point of view, far removed from the period of its early breakthrough and, thereby, far removed also from the utopian elements with which it had started. The still unfulfilled elements of this programme – parliamentarisation, the universalisation of human rights, freedom and participation, emancipation and tolerance – were now the demands of sections of the labour movement, in strong opposition to the majority of *Bürgertum*.[24]

'The bourgeois epoch is finished. What will come now, nobody knows', wrote Kurt Tucholsky in 1920.[25] Such opinions were numerous in the 1920s and 1930s,[26] and there are some historians who tend to support this view.[27] Others see the 1950s as a kind of 'renaissance of bourgeois society' – after the disaster of the Third Reich and before the reform movements of the 1960s delivered an alleged new blow.[28]

It seems that the decline of the *Bürgertum* was already well under way before the First World War; the crisis of the 1920s and, finally, fascism and the Second World War deeply discredited and fundamentally destroyed it. Of course, social formations like the *Bürgertum* do not suddenly disappear; they change slowly, are overlaid by other new formations and new fronts. It is only gradually that the concept loses its objective content. Remnants of this social formation certainly still exist today. For present-day analysis, however, the concept of *Bürgertum* is no longer really useful, in view of the complete disappearance since 1945 of the aristocratic-bourgeois dividing line, the declining importance, in recent decades, of the bourgeois-proletarian divide and the ever-increasing diffusion – perhaps also 'dilution' – of bourgeois culture in our century. Today there is a tendency to speak rather of upper, middle and lower classes, of 'elites', of 'ruling classes', or of smaller social groupings.

Is it meaningful to use the concept of *bürgerliche Gesellschaft* in the context of the present situation in the industrially advanced western countries? Certainly, for polemical reasons, this concept is often used in Marxist analysis. But in the present volume, the concept is not employed in this way. There is no doubt also that certain central elements of what is meant by the concept of *bürgerliche Gesellschaft* continue to exist in the western countries today, including the market economy, civil law, the legal and constitutional state with its representative institutions. Other elements of the model have greater reality today than they did in the Wilhelmine period because certain feudal, military and late-absolutist limitations of *Bürgerlichkeit* have, in the meantime, been destroyed.[29] Other elements of the model, created under the influence of the Enlightenment, continue to exist only as promises for the future.

But one could also defend the view that the continuous growth of the socially interventionist state has penetrated and bureaucratically transformed the market organisation of the economy, the system of social relations and the autonomy of social units to such an extent that *bürgerliche Gesellschaft* is no longer appropriate as a characterisation of such a system. After all, the self-organisation of the economy and society, far removed from the state, was a central feature of those societies in the in the nineteenth century that we describe as *bürgerlich*. The bourgeois family too, so central to the system in the nineteenth century, has undergone important changes. One could name other fundamental discontinuities as well. And the distance has only increased between what we might still want to call *Bürgertum* today and those elements that remain from *bürgerliche Gesellschaft*. The gap between *Bürgertum* and *bürgerliche Gesellschaft*, which began to open during the Wilhelmine Reich, has become much wider. It might be more appropriate, therefore, to confine our usage of the concept *bürgerliche Gesellschaft* to the period 1789–1914.

The German Situation Compared with other European Countries

The previous section divided the development of German bourgeois society between the late eighteenth and early twentieth century into three main periods: a long period of ascent and offensive that lasted into the 1840s; a short phase of culmination and turning point from the 1840s to the 1870s; a period of increasing defensiveness and exclusivity that lasted until the First World War. Since then the dominant tendency has been a dissolution of the contours of *Bürgertum* as a social formation.

These stages do not appear to be something peculiar to Germany.[30] Under different circumstances, with different nuances and with certain deviations in time, similar processes took place in other European countries.

The Wirtschaftsbürgertum

In comparison with western Europe, the German *Wirtschaftsbürgertum* – capitalists, business people, entrepreneurs, merchants etc. – developed late; in comparisons with eastern and southern Europe, however, it appeared to be powerful and by no means backward. This comes as no surprise; it simply confirms what has been the classical view.[31] What may be less well known is the fact that in the economically more backward regions of Europe, particularly in Poland, the Czech and Slovak areas, Hungary and Russia, the owners of capital, entrepreneurs and managers were often foreign nationals: frequently Germans and unassimilated Jews. This national 'externality' of the bourgeoisie in eastern, east-central and probably also in south-eastern Europe made them, as a rule, extremely dependent on the government of the country and, at the same time, incapable of giving strong support to the various national movements, which in western Europe could usually rely on bourgeois support.

This national externality was at the root of a deep division between the business people and the intelligentsia, petty bourgeoisie and, in some cases, the nobility. In Russia and Poland, for example, these latter groups were part of the national majority. This division created severe obstacles on the path of developing a comprehensive formation similar to the *Bürgertum*, in the central and western European sense of the term. In this, as in many other respects, Germany was unequivocally part of the West.[32]

The *Wirtschaftsbürgertum* was much more internally integrated, less fragmented and more clearly separate from both academics and professionals as well as from the nobility than was the case in either England or France at the same time. Although regional entrepreneurial groups existed in the German territories, the sharp division between the capital and the provinces, such as existed in England and France, was not to be found in Germany. There was also no sharp division, as in England, between long established merchants and the newly emerging manufacturers.[33] The fact that the *Wirtschaftsbürgertum* was more enclosed and demarcated may be linked to its smaller weight relative to the other bourgeois strata and to the fact that it was confronted unlike in the West, in Sweden or in Switzerland, with an early-established, self-conscious and sometimes somewhat anti-capitalist *Bildungsbürgertum*.

The Bildungsbürgertum

There still remains some doubt about the usefulness of the concept *Bildungsbürgertum*. Is this neologism not merely a retrospective and artificial construction of historians? What social reality corresponded to this concept in the nineteenth century?

The common denominator and the common bond of the *Wirtschaftsbürgertum* can be described unequivocally: common interests based on the ownership of the means of production and their role as employers shaped their experience, created cohesion and brought about a willingness for joint action, sometimes in common interest organisations and pressure groups. I have already attempted to describe the much more fragile, much weaker common denominator of the *Bürgertum* as a whole, namely, common social opponents and a shared culture. The formative effect of education itself, however, and with it the constitutions of an identifiable *Bildungsbürgertum*, is less clear. What common interests were created by a common education? Did common education lay the basis for a capacity for collective action? It is doubtful. Around 1900 the educated and professional middle class in Germany found themselves in all the different political camps. There seems to have been no political option at all which would have been incompatible with the education of the *Bildungsbürger*. This seems to have been true even in the extreme situation of 1933.

In addition, the distinction between *Wirtschaftsbürgertum* and *Bildungsbürgertum* is sometimes unclear and problematic; their area of intersection increased during the course of the nineteenth century. As more entrepreneurs acquired an academic education, the number of those who were at the same time *Wirtschaftsbürger* and *Bildungsbürger* increased.[34]

Nevertheless, the concept has become to some extent an established one in the German historical literature. The international comparison also seems to show that something like the *Bildungsbürgertum* carried more weight and took clearer shape in the German, Austrian and Italian territories than was the case in western, eastern or northern Europe.

This becomes very clear in the comparison with England.[35] In nineteenth-century England it was businessmen, bankers and other entrepreneurs rather than solicitors, judges, church ministers, doctors or civil servants who were dominant. In the early decades of the century, the latter groups were considered more as part of the old order; they did not have access to a common academic education and therefore were not able to develop, on such a basis, a self-awareness that transcended particular careers. It is true that towards the end of the century formal tertiary education became gradually more important in England, but this was a whole century later than in Germany and occurred in a different form. It comes as no surprise, therefore to find that in England the term 'professionals' was used instead of some equivalent of *Bildungsbürgertum*. The conceptual basis of the 'professions' referred to what was specific to the various specialisations rather than to a general educational background as suggested by the concept of *Bildungsbürgertum*.[36]

A *Bildungsbürgertum* was also not to be found in eastern Europe; there is no equivalent term in the Slavic languages. Of course, a dominant *Wirtschaftsbürgertum* was also absent; what was really lacking, however, something which was important in Germany and Austria, was the cohesiveness of higher officials, professional academics and other intellectuals, a cohesiveness due to strong, common educational background in academic institutions which had developed quite early in Germany and Austria.

One element missing in eastern Europe was the mixture of absolutism and Enlightenment from which central European officialdom developed in the late eighteenth century. In addition, as a result of foreign domination, educated people in eastern Europe generally had no access to positions in the higher levels of administration; education was not given particular prominence in the modernisation process. If we compare members of the *Bildungsbürgertum* with Norwegian, Czech, Slovak and Finnish 'intellectuals', we can see the higher social origins of the German academics, their tendency to recruit from among their own ranks and their greater distance from the people. The teachers, priests, lawyers, doctors and technicians in these smaller countries of eastern-central, eastern and northern Europe had more social distance and a more critical attitude towards the bourgeoisie and the bureaucracy than was typical of the *Bildungsbürgertum*. In these countries one tended to use, and still uses, the term 'intelligentsia'.[37]

If we extend the comparison to France, where, until the 1870s, there was no tradition similar to the German integrated and non-specialised university system, and where there existed an intelligentsia (without civil servant status and not necessarily connected with the university) rather than a *Bildungsbürgertum* (educated at government controlled universities and including civil servants), then the peculiarity of the central European situation seems to be confirmed. On the one hand, a certain amount of economic backwardness and, as a result of this, no dominance of the *Wirtschaftsbürgertum*; on the other hand, a very specific educational and university tradition, rooted in the Enlightenment and in neo-humanism, and linked with a very specific bureaucratically-influenced variant of state-formation.

This was the central European (but not Swiss) background to the development of the *Bildungsbürgertum* which became influential and self-conscious.[38] As several articles in this volume make clear, the neo-humanist principle of education had a special influence on the culture of the *Bürgertum* and gave it a specific coloration.[39]

Catholic/Protestant Divisions

The particular religious-confessional situation that existed in Germany also had an influence on the history of the *Bürgertum*. The consequences of secularisation and – later on – the separation from Austria included a Catholic backwardness in education, which was much discussed in the nineteenth century and which improved only very slowly, under-representation of the large Catholic minority in officialdom and among entrepreneurs, and a low proportion of Catholics in the *Bürgertum* in general. This had less to do with any peculiarities of Catholic teaching per se than with the history of Catholicism in Germany, where it suffered a series of defeats.

This special situation of German Catholicism becomes very clear when we compare its history with the very different history of bourgeois society in Catholic France. It is clear that confessional conflict in Germany, which became increasingly sharp after the middle of the century, weakened the German *Bürgertum*. It produced inter-bourgeois conflict and coalitions which crossed the borderlines between different social classes on the basis of a common religion, thus setting a limit to the *embourgeoisement* of the economy, society, the state and culture. The Catholic-Lay conflicts in France may have had a similarly divisive effect on French bourgeois society, while in England the differences between the many non-conformist groups and High Anglicanism tended to separate the entrepreneurial and manufacturing bourgeoisie from the rest of society and to unify it to some extent.[40] As far as Germany is concerned, we are less well informed about the Catholic *Bürgertum* than about their reformed and Lutheran counterparts.

Relationship with the Aristocracy

The 'feudalisation thesis' has long dominated the critical historiography of the *Kaiserreich*. This thesis maintains that there was a political domination of aristocratic (or half-aristocratic, namely *Junker*) ruling groups over the *Bürgertum*. As a result of social rapprochement or even fusion of aristocratic groups with sections of the *haute bourgeoisie* (through marriage and other social contact and an imitation or adoption of aristocratic values and lifestyles) the rich bourgeoisie ceased thereby to represent a genuinely bourgeois culture. 'Feudalisation' is said to have been more acute in Germany than in other western societies during the same period and there was specifically in Germany an ascertainable lack of *Bürgerlichkeit*.[41] This thesis has not gone unchallenged.[42]

The thesis is undoubtedly right in pointing to a fundamental shift in the social self-location of the *Bürgertum*; the aggressive distancing of itself from the old powers, especially from the nobility, became increasingly less important in the course of the second part of the century, while a defensive barrier against the proletariat and the lower orders became increasingly marked. The thesis correctly points to a number of turning points in German history where the *Bürgertum* was defeated or had to accept a curtailment of its demands: the revolution of 1848/49, the constitutional conflict in Prussia in the early 1860s, the restructuring of power in the late 1870s. However, it often interprets these events too exclusively as bourgeois defeats and gives insufficient consideration to the fact that they were also compromises between the bourgeois movement and the old powers in which both sides made concessions, achieved some gains and came closer to each other.

The thesis is also correct in pointing to decisive aspects of the power structure of the *Kaiserreich* in which, in reality, aristocratic forces carried a lot of weight and hindered the rise of the *Bürgertum* to political rule. There is no doubt that ennoblement, marriage links and other close social contacts between the *Bürgertum* and the nobility were much more frequent in the Wilhelmine Reich than they had been in the pre-March period. One should also not forget that the privileged large estate owners east of the Elbe (the Junkers) were in fact the product of a fusion of the nobility and parts of the bourgeoisie which took place after the beginning of the century, when it became possible to purchase the estates and a large number of wealthy bourgeois became estate owners. For example, no-one could doubt that the lifestyle of Friedrich Alfred Krupp at Hügel (near Essen) in the 1890s more closely resembled the lifestyle of the nobility than that of his father, Alfred, who in the pre-1848 period had still lived in a house next to the steel plant in Essen.[43]

However, the shrinking distance between the nobility and the upper middle class and the increasing intermingling of sections of the aristocracy and *haute bourgeoisie*, creating a new elite, were pan-European phenomena (apart from Switzerland, which was more like America in this respect). National peculiarities manifested themselves in the degree and form of this interleaving of both social groups. Briefly, one can identify three peculiarities in German development, a development which was increasingly being determined by Prussia.

Firstly, the *Bürgertum* (at any rate, the *Wirtschaftsbürgertum*) had to share more political power with the nobility than was the case in England or France (not, however, in Poland, Hungary or Russia). It ought to be borne in mind that for much of the time after the basic compromises of the 1860s and 1870s there were no sharp differences between the goals of the *Bürgertum* and those of the nobility, and *Bürgertum* was able to manage quite well with this division of power.

Secondly, this intermingling of the aristocracy and the top bourgeois strata took place in England, France and Italy in circumstances when the bourgeoisie was already more powerful than in Germany, Austria, Russia and the rest of eastern-central Europe. In France the old aristocratic 'estate' did not survive the Revolution; the aristocrat-ic-*haut bourgeois* elite of notables was a result of this impetus towards *embourgeoisement* which was lacking in non-revolutionary Germany. In Italy the early patrician aristocracy did not have the same kind of relationship to landed estates and monarchy that characterised large part of the German aristocracy, nor, as a result of foreign domination, did it possess the' same kind of traditions of political rule as did the German-Prussian nobility. In northern Italy feudalism came to an end early, as it did in England and France, unlike east of the Rhine, where it continued much longer and was partly responsible for the much sharper division between town and countryside and, thereby, between the *Bürgertum* and the nobility. In England the division between the aristocracy and the bourgeoisie had been blurred for a long time; titles were inherited only by the oldest son and the rural nobility were already exhibiting a more commercial orientation and a slightly urban mentality.[44]

Finally, the comparison demonstrates, and this is perhaps the most surprising result, that aristocratic-*haut bourgeois* symbiosis in Germany was not only less advanced than is suggested by the feudalisation thesis, but also less advanced than it was in France and England. In terms of marriage patterns, mobility, legal status, political influence, perhaps also in terms of career and private conduct of life, *Grossbürgertum* and aristocracy in Germany, at the end of the nineteenth century and the beginning of the twentieth century, differed more sharply from each other than was the case in western Europe, in Italy and in parts of eastern-central Europe.[45]

Limitations to the Influence of the Bürgertum

In Germany, at least until the First World War, the wealthier members of the *Bürgertum* had fused with sections of the nobility to form a new composite elite to a much lesser extent than in France, England and in other countries. As suggested by the history of the concept briefly discussed earlier, the *Bürgertum* in Germany in the late nineteenth and early twentieth century was a more clearly delineated social formation than it was in the neighbouring countries, with the exception of Austria and, probably, Italy.

It would be wrong, however, to see this as indicating a special strength of the *Bürgertum* in Germany; quite the reverse, in fact. The tendency towards universalisation was a feature of bourgeois culture, in Germany as elsewhere. This culture was attractive and strong and it shaped German society in the nineteenth century far beyond the borders of the *Bürgertum* itself.

In an international context, however, at least in a comparison with western Europe, the relatively clear external boundaries of the *Bürgertum* corresponded to its relatively small influence and its relatively weak capacity to act as a formative force with respect to the rest of society. Just as the nobility in Germany linked up with the *haute-bourgeoisie* to a much lesser extent than in England and France, so also the *Bürgertum* in Germany succeeded less than the French *bourgeoisie* in influencing the petty bourgeoisie.[46] A German-Swiss comparison sees to show that white-collar employees (*Angestellte*) in Switzerland were more closely integrated into the *Bürgertum* of that country than was the case in Germany.[47]

It is still unclear whether the *embourgeoisement* of the working class in Germany before 1914 was more limited than in western Europe, but it probably was.[48] The impressive size, by international standards, of the labour movement and the sharpness of the 'class line' in Wilhelmine Germany would seem to point in this direction. The German division between town and country remained relatively sharp, much more so than in Sweden, France, England and, perhaps, Poland; this was also an obstacle to the extension of *Bürgerlichkeit*. And although liberalism in Germany was, by international standards, relatively bourgeois in character,[49] this was ultimately an indication of the relative inability of the Bürgertum to persuade the lower and working classes to embrace its principles. Apparently the relatively clear identity of the German *Bürgertum* corresponded to its relatively meagre success in bringing about a general *embourgeoisement* of German society.

Bureaucracy and the Relationship of the Bürgertum with the State

The *Bürgertum* and *bourgeois* culture in Germany and Austria, by comparison with other European countries, were characterised by a specific relationship to the state.

In the eighteenth century in particular, and in the first half of the nineteenth century, various types of academically qualified officials constituted the active core of *Bildungsbürgertum*. Until the 1870s, solicitors and notaries in Prussia were middle-ranking state officials and ministers in the Protestant churches had quasi-official status. Although the independent *Wirtschaftsbürger* and professionals became increasingly powerful in German society from the middle of the nineteenth century, officialdom continued to maintain its socially interventionist state, its functions and its significance increased.

This peculiar position of civil servants within German society can be seen in their very high numbers, in the high level of social respect accorded to them, their political power, their relative autonomy and in their *esprit de corps*. State-approved education and qualifications, a secure if not necessarily highly-paid position, proximity to power and to the state, a claim to serve the public interest and to know better what this was than any other private person – this was the characteristic public image of middle and higher-ranking officials.[50]

Numerous entrepreneurs attempted to distance themselves sharply from this type of official. They were involved with business and with the search for profitability, prepared to take risks and be innovative, accustomed to competition and capable of getting things done, concerned about their individual independence and proud of their property and achievement. German industrialisation took place in keeping with the rules of capitalism, certainly not under the direction of government officials. Again and again one finds examples of bourgeois criticism of the excessive manipulations of the state and its bureaucracy.[51]

Nevertheless, it seems that conformity to state direction and adaptation to the bureaucratic mentality were much more widespread among German entrepreneurs than was the case in the other western countries. Bureaucratic models, derived from public administration, shaped the major private economic organisations, (such as those involved with the development of the railway system and large-scale industrial enterprises), to a much greater extent than was to be found in France, England or the USA.[52] The bureaucratic title of *Kommerzienrat* (Commercial Councillor) was much sought after among Prussian entrepreneurs. It was granted only after extensive investigation and represented a state seal of approval which increased one's social standing, creditworthiness and prospects of business success. This act of the state created an upper layer from among the mass of entrepreneurs, who accepted this. Friedrich Naumann spoke in 1900 of a generation "in which one would rather be called Herr Kommerzienrat than Herr Baron". The suffix -*rat* (councillor) suggested the widely sought equality of rank with higher officialdom.[53]

Only seldom did German entrepreneurs demand an extreme laissez-faire policy. On the contrary, they expected a lot from the state. A collective orientation came more naturally to them and was more to their advantage; they held less firmly than their English colleagues to the principle of individual independence, which, in any case, could have been an obstacle to the rapid process of industrialisation. The gradual, very early and successful transition to an interventionist state after the 1870s met with little resistance from the big employers' organisations. Cartels and corporations were usually created with state assistance. Some commentators have used the phrase 'organised capitalism'. The typical difference between entrepreneurs and officials, therefore, was moderated earlier and faster than in other countries.[54]

Processes of professionalisation took place everywhere in Europe (and North America) during the nineteenth century. Clearly distinguishable specialist careers were created, the members of which had specialist and usually university education, on the basis of which they demanded monopoly control over whatever service it was they offered. They claimed autonomy for themselves and created successful organisations for the purposes of professional self-administration and defence of their interests. This process was similar in the different countries, but in Germany, much more unequivocally than in any other country, this professionalisation of careers was based on state-provided and state-regulated university education.

To a much greater extent than their English colleagues, for instance, German, and especially Prussian, doctors could rely on state regulations which excluded non-professional or only semi-professional competitors from the market as *Kurpfuscher* (quacks). Unlike their English, Swiss or Italian colleagues, spokespersons for professional organisations in Germany had recourse to a well-placed higher official whenever they wanted to justify demands connected with their status.[55]

Numerous other examples of the state-orientation and bureaucratic flavour of the German *Bürgertum* and German bourgeois culture could be given. German liberalism seldom argued in an anti-governmental manner and, unlike French liberals, German liberals offered little resistance to the regulating and interventionist social state.[56] The bureaucratic and statist character of the Prussian-German type of development is exhibited most clearly in an international comparison of constitutional and legal systems, from the absence of a revolutionary basis for constitutionalism and the early development of administrative law to the blocked parliamentarisation of the *Kaiserreich*.[57]

In addition to the social bureaucratisation evident in many areas of life there was added, after the foundation of the Reich in 1871 which boosted the status of the army, a kind of 'social militarisation'. Indications of this can be seen, for instance, in the continued importance attributed to 'reserve officer' rank in what was otherwise a very bureaucratically organised hierarchy of qualifications, and also to the duel, which died out in England after the middle of the century but which in Germany remained a central element of the code of honour subscribed to by both the nobility and the *Bürgertum*.[58] Admittedly, the figure of Diederich Hessling in Heinrich Mann's novel *Der Untertan* was an overstated, satirical exaggeration. The combination of monarchic-authoritarian subject mentality, north-German bourgeois dynamism, aggressive patriotism and inhibited narrow-mindedness in private life, was certainly not stereotypical of the Wilhelmine *Bürger*. But in what European capital other than Berlin could this character have been so convincingly portrayed?

It is important, however, not to overlook the fact that this German, thoroughly bureaucratic bourgeois culture also contained great potential for progress. It was the achievement of qualified officials, for instance, that the bourgeois self-administration of German cities at the end of the century became a model for American and British reformers who, although they had a less bureaucratic background, were full of admiration for what had been achieved.[59] The German organisation of technological and scientific research, which reached the high point of its worldwide influence during the Wilhelmine period, had been brought about primarily by bourgeois officials, by official *Bürger* using bureaucratic methods.

When one considers that smallpox was practically eliminated in Germany quite early on by means of a smallpox inoculation programme organised 'from above' by the state, while at the same time in France, where liberal resistance to the state prevented similar measures being taken, around 100,000 people died of smallpox, then one gets an impression of the strength of that 'bureaucratic tradition', that tradition of 'reform from above', which was so characteristic of German development and of the *Bürgertum*. This tradition enabled the Reich to become the pioneer in constructing a welfare state.[60]

This state-orientation and bureaucratic character were the decisive features which distinguished the German variant of *Bürgerlichkeit* from that of the other European countries – sometimes to its advantage, sometimes to its disadvantage. Or were this state-orientation and bureaucratic character an expression of the limits of *Bürgerlichkeit*? This was more or less the view of Max Weber, who was fascinated by Germany's bureaucratic state but linked this to the weakness of the *Bürgertum* and its culture. He ridiculed the titles, the concern about career security to be found even among the students, his colleagues' inclination to favour state-oriented strategies of social reform, which he also saw as a sign of social bureaucratisation and bourgeois weakness. And is it not the case, in fact, that the social figure of the official remains in a somewhat contradictory relationship with the ideal of the independent *Bürger*, standing on his own two feet and organised in his own associations? Many contemporaries in the nineteenth century saw it in precisely this way.

If we go through the definitions of *Bürger* and *Bürgertum* in the encyclopedias and writings of the nineteenth century, we will see that quite often the official was not reckoned to be part of the *Bürgertum*; this is in sharp contrast to modern historiography with its concept of the *Bildungsbürgertum*. In the linguistic usage of the time there were tensions between the concepts of *Beamte* (official) and *Bürger*.[61] And not without reason. If the capacity for responsible self-regulation and the rejection of state manipulation and welfare are part of the idea of a true *bürgerliche Gesellschaft*, then the state-oriented character of the German *Bürgertum* represented a sensitive limit of its *Bürgerlichkeit*.

It would certainly be incorrect to speak in general terms of a 'lack of *Bürgerlichkeit*' as a characteristic of German development in the nineteenth century. Compared with developments in eastern Europe, many things in Germany appear as a model of *Bürgerlichkeit*. If in addition, in a comparison with western, southern and northern Europe, we take into account the strong self-government of the cities, civil law, literature, science, general education and many other things, then there is no question about German *Bürgerlichkeit*.

There are a variety of peculiarities in Germany's development and they cannot all be subsumed under one category. Limitations and achievements, deficits and abundances were often mixed, as is evident in the brilliant and fascinating phenomenon of the *Bildungsbürgertum*, a phenomenon one will search in vain to find elsewhere in Europe. The position of the *Bürgertum* in the tense relationship between Catholicism and Protestantism is a subject that still needs to be studied more closely.

The *Bürgertum* as a whole, however, in spite of its inner fragmentation and its lack of sharply defined boundaries, had a clearer shape in Germany in the nineteenth century than elsewhere. The feudalisation thesis, in its traditional form, needs to be modified. The core of the *Sonderweg* thesis, however, survives. The relationship between the *Bürgertum* and the nobility manifested certain peculiarities which pointed to the former's weakness. Its relatively clear boundaries as a social formation corresponded to a relative weakness in its capacity to influence and integrate the rest of society. This was the origin of a number of specifically unbourgeois features of bourgeois society in Germany during the period of the Wilhelmine Reich. The bureaucratic aspects of German *Bürgerlichkeit* were the product of its most critical limitations.

Notes to Chapter 1

1. Cf. M. Walker, *German Hometowns. Community, State and General Estate 1648-1871* (Ithaca N.Y., 1971).

2. On the development of the concept, cf. U. Engelhardt, *'Bildungsbürgertum'. Bergriffs- und Dogmengeschichte eines Etiketts'* (Stuttgart, 1986); for a report on the literature, see G. Hübinger, 'Politische Werte und Gesellschaftsbilder des Bildungsbürgertums', *Neue Politische Literatur* 32 (1987), pp. 189–220.

3. This is the decision of Eric Hobsbawm in his paper in this volume.

4. For Prussia 1846/49 and 1871, see Tables 1 and 4 in J. Kocka, 'Zur Schichtung der preussischen Bevölkerung während der industriellen Revolution', in W. Treue, (ed.), *Geschichte als Aufgabe. Festschrift für Otto Büsch* (Berlin 1988), pp. 357–390. 1895 estimates based on *Statistik des deutschen Reiches* NF, vol. 104 (1897), pp. 608, 622; vol. 114 (1898), pp. 3 F. – There is no complete consensus as to the meaning of *Bürgertum*. Sometimes, particularly with respect to the early nineteenth century, self-employed and better-off artisans, small retailers, inn-keepers and similar categories are included. But during the course of the nineteenth century, as the bourgeoisie became more important, putting their own stamp on the concept of '*Bürger*', these small independent operators moved to the margins of *Bürgertum* and began to be described as '*kleinbürgerlich*' (petty bourgeois) or '*mittelständisch*' (lower middle class). Cf. Heinz-Gerhard Haupt's paper in this volume. Sometimes white-collar employees are regarded to be part of the *Bürgertum*. Cf. J. Kocka, *Die Angestellten in der deutschen Geschichte 1850–1980. Vom Privatbeamten zum angestellten Arbeitnehmer* (Göttingen, 1981). Artists and military officers are borderline cases, as well. A survey of definitions can be found in H. Henning, *Das westdeutsche Bürgertum in der Epoche der Hochindustrialisierung 1860–1914. Soziales Verhalten und soziale Strukturen. Part. 1: Das Bildungsbürgertum in den preussischen Westprovinzen* (Wiesbaden, 1972), pp. 5–14. Other works include A. Meusel, 'Bürgertum', in *Handwörterbuch der Soziologie* (Stuttgart, 1959), pp. 90–99; A. Meusel, 'Middle Class', in *Encyclopaedia of the Social Sciences (1933)* vol. 9 (1967), pp. 407–415; L. Beutin, 'Das Bürgertum als Gesellschaftsstand im 19. Jahrhundert', *Blätter für deutsche Landesgeschichte* 90 (1953), pp. 132–165; H. Freyer, 'Bürgertum', in *Handwörterbuch der Sozialwissenschaften* vol. 2 (Göttingen, 1959), pp. 452–456; E. Fraenkel, 'Bürgertum', in E. Fraenkel and K. D. Bracher (eds.), *Staat und Politik* (Frankfurt, 1971), pp. 65–72; H. A. Winkler, 'Bürgertum', in *Sowjetsystem und demokratische Gesellschaft* vol. 1 (Freiburg-im-Breisgau 1966), columns 934–953; P. N. Stearns, 'The Middle Class, Towards a Precise Definition', *Comparative Studies in Sociology and History* 21 (1979), pp. 377–396; E. Nolte, *Was ist bürgerlich?* (Stuttgart, 1979); H. Lübbe, 'Aspekte der politischen Philosophie des Bürgers', in R. Vierhaus, (ed.), *Bürger und Bürgerlichkeit im Zeitalter der Aufklärung* (Heidelberg, 1981), pp. 35 ff.; St. Strasser, *Jenseits des Bürgerlichen. Ethischpolitische Meditationen für diese Zeit* (Freiburg, 1982); A. Daumard, *Les bourgeois de Paris aux XIXe siècle* (Paris, 1970), p. 352.

5. The best synthesis of German history dealing with such issues is H.-U. Wehler, *Deutsche Gesellschaftsgeschichte*, vols. 1 and 2 (Munich, 1987). – The following decades are discussed in R. Rürup, *Deutschland im 19. Jahrhundert 1815–1871* (Göttingen, 1984); Th. Nipperdey, *Deutsche Geschichte 1866–1918*, vol. 1 (Munich, 1990). The relations between nobility and bourgeoisie in England, France, Germany, and Russia in W. Mosse's paper in this volume.

6. English and American authors usually see little reason to treat businessmen, professionals, and civil servants as a single category. If there is the need for a comprehensive concept that include the different groups, then there is a tendency to use terms such as 'elites', 'the rich', or similar categories. The term 'middle class' is becoming more frequent, particularly in studies with interest in cultural historical aspects. But 'middle class' and '*Bürgertum*' are not synonymous concepts. Cf. St. M. Blumin, 'The

34 | *Jürgen Kocka*

Hypothesis of Middle-Class Formation in Nineteenth-Century America. A Critique and Some Proposals', *American Historical Review* 90 (1985), pp. 299–338; M.P. Ryan, *Cradle of the Middle Class*. *The Family in Oneida Country, New York, 1790–865* (Cambridge, Mass., 1981); J. S. Gilkeson, *Middle-Class Providence, 1820–1940* (Princeton, 1986). – L. Davidoff and C. Hall, *Family Fortunes*. *Men and Women of the English Middle Class 1780–1850* (London, 1987). Also see the titles quoted by E. J. Hobsbawm in his paper in this volume. An excellent survey of the American literature: T. Göbel, 'Ärzte und Rechtsanwälte in den USA 1800–1920. Der schwierige Weg zur Professionalisierung', *Geschichte und Gesellschaft* 16 (1990), pp. 318–342.

7. Cf. the contributions of M. R. Lepsius, T. Nipperdey and H. Bausinger to J. Kocka (ed.), *Bürger und Bürgerlichkeit im 19. Jahrhundert* (Göttingen, 1987); W. Kaschuba's paper in this volume. P. Bourdieu, *La distinction. Critique social du jugement* (Paris, 1979); E. François (ed.), *Sociabilité et societé bourgeoise en France, en Allemagne et en Suisse 1750–1850* (Paris, 1986); F. H. Tenbruck, 'Bürgerliche Kultur', in: F. Niedhardt et al. (eds), *Kultur und Gesellschaft* (Opladen, 1986), pp. 263–285.

8. The contributions of Haupt and Eisenberg in this volume deal with limits to the accessibility of bourgeois culture for other social groups.

9. On the Polish situation: W. Dlugoborski, 'Das polnische Bürgertum vor 1918 in vergleichender Perspektive', in Kocka (ed.), *Bürgertum im 19. Jahrhundert* vol. 1, pp. 226–299. On Russia: M. Hildermeider, *Bürgertum und Stadt in Russland 1760–1870. Rechtliche Lage und soziale Struktur* (Cologne, 1986).

10. The notion of 'Bürgertum' seems to be most appropriate with respect to the central and western part of the European continent, also Italy. For a survey of the German literature: J. Kocka, 'La bourgeoisie dans l'histoire moderne et contemporaine de l'Allemagne: recherches et débats récents,' *Le mouvement social* 136 (1986), pp. 5–27; on France: A. Daumard, *les bourgeois et la bourgeoisie en France depuis 1815* (Paris, 1987); also see H. Kaelble's paper in this volume. On Italy: P. March and R. Romanelli (eds.), *Borghesie urbane dell'ottocento, Quaderni storici* 56 [1984]; M. Meriggi's paper in this volume; the essays by R. Romanelli and M. Meriggi in J. Kocka and A.M. Banti (eds.), *Borghesie europee dell'ottocento* (Venezia, 1989), pp. 69–94, 161–186. On the *Bürgertum* in Austria, Switzerland, and Hungary cf. ibid. the contributions of E. Bruckmüller/H. Stekl, A. Tanner and G. Ránki. In addition on Central and Eastern Europe: V. Bácskai (ed.), *Bürgertum und bürgerliche Entwicklung in Mittel- und Osteuropa* 2 vols. (Budapest, 1986).

11. C. Garve, 'Versuche über verschiedene Gegenstände aus der Moral, der Literatur und dem gesellschaftlichen Leben', (1792) quoted from M. Riedel, 'Bürger, Staatsbürger, Bürgertum', in O. Brunner et al. (eds), *Geschichtliche Grundbegriffe. Historisches Lexikon zur politisch-sozialen Sprache in Deutschland*, vol. 1 (Stuttgart, 1972), pp. 672–725, 701.

12. Cf. U. Haltern, 'Bürgerliche Gesellschaft. Theorie und Geschichte'; *Neue Politische Literatur* 19 (1974), pp. 472–488; 20 (1975), pp. 45–59; U. Haltern, 'Entwicklungsprobleme der bürgerlichen Gesellschaft', *Geschichte und Gesellschaft* 5 (1979), pp. 274–292; U. Haltern, *Bürgerliche Gesellschaft. Sozialtheoretische und sozialhistorische Aspekte* (Darmstadt, 1985); R. Rürup, 'Judenemanzipation und bürgerliche Gesellschaft in Deutschland' (1968) in R. Rürup, *Emanzipation und Antisemitismus* (Göttingen, 1975), pp. 11–36; R. Rürup, *Deutschland im 19. Jahrhundert 1815 bis 1871* (Göttingen, 1984), pp. 101 ff.; D. Grimm, *Recht und Staat der bürgerlichen Gesellschaft* (Frankfurt, 1987); Th. Nipperdey, *Deutsche Geschichte 1800–1866, Bürgerwelt und starker Staat*(München, 1983), pp. 255 ff.; H.-U. Wehler, 'Wie bürgerlich war das Deutsche Kaiserreich?', in Kocka, *Bürger und Bürgerlichkeit*, pp. 243–280. J. Keane (ed.), *Civil Society and the State. New European Perspectives* (London, 1988); J. Keane, 'Despotismus und Demokratie. Über die Unterscheidung zwischen bürgerlicher Gesellschaft und Staat 1750–1850', in Kocka (ed.), *Bürgertum im 19. Jahrhundert* vol. 1, pp. 303–339. J. Habermas, *Strukturwandel der Öffentlichkeit. Untersuchungen zu einer Kategorie der bürgerlichen Gesellschaft* (Neuwied, 2nd ed. 1965).

13. Cf. C. B. Macpherson, *The Political Theory of Possessive Individualism. From Hobbes to Locke* (London, 1971).

14. As to liberalism and *Bürgertum* see the articles by Langewiesche and Mitchell in this volume. J. J. Sheehan, 'Wie bürgerlich war der deutsche Liberalismus?' in D. Langewiesche (ed.), *Liberalismus im 19. Jahrhundert. Deutschland in europäischem Vergleich* (Göttingen, 1988), pp. 28–44. For lodges and reading societies: R. van Dülmen, *Die Gesellschaft der Aufklärer. Zur bürgerlichen Emanzipation und aufklärerischen Kultur in Deutschland* (Frankfurt, 1986). – An excellent synthesis: J. J. Sheehan, *German History 1770–1866* (Oxford, 1989). The affinity of liberalism and *Bürgertum* is over-stressed in L. Gall, *Bürgertum in Deutschland* (Berlin, 1989) – basically a history of the southwest German '*Wirtschaftsbürgertum*', particularly the history of the Bassermann family.

15. W. T. Krug, *Allgemeines Handwörterbuch der philosophischen Wissenschaften nebst ihrer Literatur und Geschichte* vol. 1 (Leipzig, 1827), p. 346. Likewise, Pierer, *Encyklopädisches Wörterbuch* vol. 4 (1835), pp. 483f.

16. Cf. Lorenz von Stein, *Geschichte der sozialen Bewegung in Frankreich von 1789 bis auf unsere Tage* vol. 1, 1842 (Darmstadt, 1959), p. 476 – The references in the works of Marx and Engels are legion. Df. for example, section 1 of the *Manifesto of the Communist Party*, (numerous editions, also in K. Marx and F. Engels, *Selected Works* (London, 1968); also 'Class Struggles in France 1848 to 1850', in Karl Marx, *Surveys From Exile, Political Writings* vol. 2 (Harmondsworth, 1973), pp. 35–142; F. Engels, 'Socialism' Utopian and Scientific', in Marx/Engels, *Selected Works*, pp. 399–433. From the conservative side, H. Wagener criticised the 'transformation of the old honourable organised *Bürgerstand* and its increasing dissolution into the modern *Bürgertum* on the one side and into the proletariat on the other . . . '. *Staats- und Gesellschaftslexikon* vol. 4 (Berlin, 1860), p. 366.

17. For details, see the paper by Volkov in the present volume.

18. Lack of independence, market-dependent insecurity, the manual character of labour, small income, cramped living conditions and the need for all members of the family to contribute to the family income – these were the factors which stood in the way of a real *Verbürgerlichung* of the workers in the nineteenth century.

19. The paper by Eisenberg in the present volume demonstrates the specific relationship that existed between the *Vereinsprinzip* (association principle) and *Bürgertum* and argues that the *Verein* (association), this bourgeois achievement, corresponded much less to proletarian needs and possibilities than has often been assumed. Also important to see H. Zwahr, 'Konstitution der Bourgeoisie im Verhältnis zur Arbeiterklasse. Ein deutsch-polnischer Vergleich', in Kocka (ed.), *Bürgertum im 19. Jahrhundert* vol. 2, pp. 149–186.

20. Cf. the article by Bogel in the present volume. Also U. Frevert (ed.), *Bürgerinnen und Bürger. Geschlechterhältnisse im 19. Jahrhundert* (Göttingen, 1988). For greater detail on the view presented here, see J. Kocka, 'Einige Ergebnisse', *ibid,* pp. 206–209; with a different emphasis: U. Gerhard, 'Andere Ergebnisse', *ibid.*, pp. 210–214.

21. On the general theme: U. Frevert, *Women in German History. From Bourgeois Emancipation to Sexual Liberation* (Oxford/New York, 1989).

22. The best surveys are to be found in Wehler, *Deutsche Gesellschaftsgeschichte* vol. 1, pp. 202–217; vol. 2, pp. 174–240. Cf. also H. -U. Wehler, 'Bürger, Arbeiter und das Problem der Klassenbildung 1800–1870. Deutschland im internationalen Vergleich', in J. Kocka (ed.), *Arbeiter und Bürger im 19. Jahrhundert. Varianten ihres Verhältnisses im europäischen Vergleich* (Munich, 1986), pp. 1–28; R. Rürup, *Deutschland im 19. Jahrhundert 1815–1871* (Göttingen, 1984), pp. 85–109; R. Vierhaus, 'Der Aufstieg des Bürgertums vom späten 18. Jahrhundert bis 1848/49', in Kocka, *Bürger und Bürgerlichkeit*, pp. 64–78; W. Ruppert, *Bürgerlicher Wandel. Die Geburt der modernen deutschen Gesellschaft im 18. Jahrhundert* (Frankfurt, 1981). In addition O. Dann (ed.), *Lesegesellschaften und bürgerliche Emanzipation. Ein europäischer Vergleich* (Munich, 1981): U. Im Hof, *Das gesellige Jahrhundert. Gesellschaft und Gesellschaften im Zeitalter der Aufklärung* (Munich, 1982); H. Müller, *Vernunft und Kritik. Deutsche Aufklärung im 17.*

und 18. Jahrhundert (Frankfurt, 1986); B. Lutz (ed.), Deutsches Bürgertum und literarische Intelligenz 1750–1800 (Stuttgart, 1974): H.H. Gerth, Bürgerliche Intelligenz um 1800. Zur Soziologie des deutschen Frühliberalismus (Göttingen, 1976); J. Reulecke, 'Städtisches Bürgertum in der deutschen Frühindustrialisierung', in M. Glettler et al. (eds.), Zentrale Städte und ihr Umland (St. Katherinen, 1985), pp. 296–311. L. Gall distinguishes a period of ascent until 1848/49, a phase of increasing exclusivity in the Bürgertum until the 1880s/1890s, and a phase of renewed opening after that: L. Gall, 'Die Stadt der bürgerlichen Gesellschaft – das Beispiel Mannheim', in Forschungen zur Stadtgeschichte. Drei Vorträge, Gerda Henkel Lecture (Opladen, 1986), pp. 55–71. Wehler, however, puts the decisive caesura in the development of the Bildungsbürgertum in the 1870s. Cf. H.-U. Wehler, 'Deutsches Bildungsbürgertum in vergleichender Perspektive. Elemente eines "Sonderwegs"?,' in J. Kocka, (ed.), Bildungsbürgertm im 19. Jahrhundert Part IV (Stuttgart, 1989), pp. 215–237.

23. Besides the works of synthesis by Wehler, Nipperdey, Rürup and Sheehan quoted in the notes 5, 12 and 14 above, cf. L. Beutin, 'Das Bürgertum als Gesellschaftsstand im 19. Jahrhundert', in Gesammelte Schriften zur Wirtschafts – und Sozialgeschichte (Cologne, 1963), pp. 284–319; J.J. Sheehan, German Liberalism in the Nineteenth Century (Chicago, 1978), ch. 3–4; H.A. Winkler, Preußischer Liberalismus und deutscher Nationalstaat (Tübingen, 1964); H.A. Winkler, Liberalismus und Antiliberalismus. Studien zur politischen Sozialgeschichte des 19. und 20. Jahrhunderts (Göttingen, 1979), pp. 11–80; S. Na'aman, Der Deutsche Nationalverein. Die politische Konstituierung des deutschen Bürgertums 1859–1867 (Düsseldorf, 1987).

24. Cf. Wehler. 'Wie bürgerlich', pp. 243–280, with a comment by D. Blackbourn, pp. 281–287; G.A. Craig, Germany 1866–1945 (Oxford, 1978), Chaps. 5–8, H. Rosenberg, Große Depression und Bismarckzeit. Wirtschaftsablauf,Gesellschaft und Politik in Mitteleuropa (Berlin, 1967); H.-U. Wehler, The German Empire 1871–1918 (Leamington Spa, 1985), F. Stern, The Politics of Cultural Despair: Study of the Rise of the German Ideology (Berkeley, 1961); Stern, The Failure of Illiberalism. Essay on the Culture of Modern Germany (New York, 1972). From another perspective, but with a discussion of Bürgertum, see M. Stürmer, Das ruhelose Reich. Deutschland 1866–1918 (Berlin, 1983). The quotation from F. Naumann, Werke, vol 3 (Cologne, 1964), p. 45; the frequently used Mommsen quotation from A. Heuss, Theodor Mommsen und das 19. Jahrhundert (Kiel, 1956), p. 282. Cf. L. Beutin, 'Das Bürgertum', pp. 284–319; K. Vondung, (ed.), Das Wilhelminische Bildungsbürgertum. Zur Sozialgeschichte seiner Ideen (Göttingen, 1976); M. Doerry, Übergangsmenschen. Die Mentalität der Wilhelminer und die Krise des Kaiserreiches (Weinheim, 1986); K.H. Jarausch, Students, Society and Politics in Imperial Germany, The Rise of Academic Illiberalism (Princeton, 1982).

25. Politische Texte (Reinbeck, 1971), p. 104.

26. Cf. H. Heller, 'Rechtsstaat oder Diktatur?', (1929) in H. Heller, Gesammelte Schriften vol. 2 (Leiden, 1971), pp. 443–462; R. Smend, 'Bürger und Bourgeoisie im deutschen Staatsrecht', (1933) in R. Smend, Staatsrechtliche Abhandlungen und andere Aufsätze (Berlin, 1968), pp. 309–325, 324; 'The Bourgeois epoch is coming to an end and we are standing before the closed gates of a new and different era. Our bourgeois past has turned subjects into citizens. It has created the idea and the type of the German Bürger and has thereby given to the future a significantt political and moral inheritance. Today it does not look as if the youth were of a mind to enter into that inheritance . . . They have no feeling for the Bürgertum's particular virtues, its particular mixture of commitment and humane moderation. This mixture has been a distinguishing feature of liberalism, which is too much maligned today'.

27. Cf. H. Mommsen, 'Die Auflösung des Bürgertums seit dem späten 19. Jahrhundert', in Kocka, Bürger und Bürgerlichkeit, pp. 288–315.

28. H.–P. Schwarz, Die Ära Adenauer. Gründerjahre der Republik 1949–1957 (Wiesbaden, 1981), p. 445; also p. 417: 'Twilight of Bourgeois Culture'.

29. Cf. J. Kocka, '1945: Neubeginn oder Restauration?', in C. Stern and H. A. Winkler (eds.), *Wendepunkte deutscher Geschichte 1848–1945* (Frankfurt, 1979), pp. 141–168.

30. The rest of this article is based on the contributions to the three volumes of Kocka (ed.), *Bürgertum im 19. Jahrhundert*, only some of which could be translated for this volume.

31. Cf. A. Gerschenkron, *Economic Backwardness in Historical Perspective* (Cambridge, Mass., 1962).

32. These results are based on the contributions of G. Ránki, W. Dlugoborski, E. Kaczynska and H. Zwahr in the collection quoted in note 30 above.

33. Cf. the articles by Cassis, Hobsbawm, Kaelble and Tilly in the present volume. A good example of a study of regional entrepeneurship is H. Henning, 'Soziale Verflechtungen der Unternehmer in Westfalen 1860–114', *Zeitschrift für Unternehmensgeschichte* 23 (1978), pp. 1–30.

34. On the political heterogeneity of the *Bildungsbürgertum* around 1900, cf. R. vom Bruch, 'Gesellschaftliche Funktionen und politische Rollen des Bildungsbürgertums im Wilhelminischen Reich', in Kocka (ed.), *Bildungsbürgertum* (see note 22 above), pp. 146–179.

35. Cf. the paper by Hobsbawm in the present volume.

36. Cf. J. Kocka, '"Bürgertum" and professions in the nineteenth century: Two Alternative Approaches', in M. Burrage and R. Torstendahl (eds.), *Professions and Theory in History. Rethinking the Study of Professions* (London, 1990), pp. 62–74.

37. Cf. N. Koestler, 'Polnische Intelligenz als sozialgeschichtliches Problem. Ein Bericht über die polnische Forschung', *Jahrbücher für Geschichte Osteuropas* 31 (1983), pp. 543–562. The concept 'intelligentsia' sometimes is used in a narrower sense, for instance by Th. Geiger, *Aufgaben und Stellung der Intelligenz in der Geschichte* (Stuttgart, 1949), pp. 4ff., 12f, (distinguishes academics, the educated and the intelligentsia – the latter working in the field of creative culture). Generally, however, the term 'intelligentsia' seems to have a wider meaning than *Bildungsbürgertum* and includes middle and lower-ranking white-collar employees. Lenin, for instance, wrote of '. . . all of the educated, the professions, the brain workers, as the English say, as distinct from the manual labourers'. See also J. Kuczynski, *Die Intelligenz. Studien zur Soziologie und Geschichte ihrer Größen* (Cologne, 1987), pp. 21–25. The concept of 'intelligentsia' does not contain the notion, as does *Bildungsbürgertum*, of a closeness to the other bourgeois groups, but it does suggest a greater openness to the petty bourgeoisie and the people. The concepts 'intelligentsia' and 'intellectuals' are more easily associated than *Bildungsbürgertum* with the notion of critique (including critique of *Bürgertum*). On the concept of 'intellectuals' see D. Bering, *Die Intellektuellen. Geschichte eines Schimpfwortes* (Berlin, 1982) with a lot of evidence about the use of the word in France and Germany since the late nineteenth century, including the workers' movement; O. Pascal and J. -F. Sirinelle, *Les intellectuels en France de L'Affaire Dreyfus a nos jours* (Paris, 1986); Ch. Charle, *Naissance des 'intellectuels', 1880–1900* (Paris, 1990).

38. That this was more true of the late eighteenth and early nineteenth century than of the late nineteenth and early twentieth century has already been mentioned above. In the late nineteenth century the *Bildungsbürgertum* was confronted with the rise of the bourgeoisie and with industrialisation and was probably increasingly fragmented, not least because of increasing specialisation that pushed general education into the background. See the introduction to Conze and Kocka (eds.), *Bildungsbürgertum*, pp. 25f.

39. See the paper by Frevert (on the duel in England and Germany) in the present volume; and the papers by M. Kraul and Steinhauser in the collection quoted note 30 above.

40. Cf. the papers by Hobsbawm and Kaelble in the present volume. Also M. Baumeister, *Parität und katholische Inferiorität. Untersuchungen zur Stellung des Katholizismus im Deutschen Kaiserreich* (Paderborn, 1987); A. Rauscher, (ed.), *Katholizismus,*

Bildung und Wissenschaft im 19. und 20. Jahrhundert (Paderborn, 1987); C. Bauer, 'Der deutsche Katholizismus und die bürgerliche Gesellschaft', in C. Bauer (ed.) *Deutscher Katholizismus. Entwicklungslinie und Profile* (Frankfurt, 1964), pp. 28–53; D. Blackbourn, *Class, Religion, and Local Politics in Wilhelmine Germany. The Centre Party in Württemberg before 1914* (Wiesbaden, 1980); J. Mooser, 'Katholik und Bürger? Rolle und Bedeutung des Bürgertums auf den deutschen Katholikentagen 1871–1913', unpublished thesis, Bielefeld, 1986.

41. The 'feudalisation thesis' (1904) in M. Weber, *Gesammelte Aufsätze zur Soziologie und Sozialpolitik* (Tübingen, 1924), p. 390; much evidence in F. Zunkel, *Der rheinisch-westfälische Unternehmer 1834–1879* (Cologne, 1962): H. Rosenberg, 'Die Pseudo-demokratisierung der Rittergutsbesitzerklasse,' (1958) in H. Rosenberg, *Machteliten und Wirtschaftskonjunktur* (Göttingen, 1978), pp. 83–101; H.-J. Puhle, *Agrarische Interessenpolitik und preußischer Konservatismus im wilhelminischen Reich 1893–1914* (Bonn, 1975); Wehler, *Kaiserreich*, pp. 129 ff.; G.A. Ritter and J. Kocka (eds.), *Deutsche Sozialgeschichte 1870–1914* 3rd ed (Munich, 1982), pp. 67f. G. N. Isenberg, 'Die "Aristokratisierung" der bürgerlichen Kultur im 19. Jahrhundert', in P. U. Hohendahl and P.M. Lützeler (eds.), *Legitimationskrisen des deutschen Adels* (Stuttgart, 1979), pp. 233–244; with emphasis on the long-term consequences H. A. Winkler, *Revolution, Staat, Faschismus. Zur Revision des historischen Materialismus* (Göttingen, 1978), pp. 117.

42. A critical view is presented in D. Blackbourn and G. Eley, *The Peculiarities of German History* (Oxford, 1984), especially pp. 228ff.; H. Kaelble, 'Wie feudal waren die deutschen Unternehmer im Kaiserreich?', in R. Tilly, (ed.), *Beiträge zur quantitativen deutschen Unternehmensgeschichte* (Stuttgart, 1985), pp. 148–174; D. L. Augustine Perez, 'Heiratsverhalten und Berufswahl in den nichtagrarischen Multimillionärsfamilien in Deutschland vor 1914', unpublished thesis, FU Berlin, 1983, pp. 63ff. The general European occurrence of the phenomenon is emphasised by A.J. Mayer. *The Persistence of the old Régime* (Princeton, 1981).

43. Cf. D. Baedeker, Alfred Krupp. *Die Entwicklung der Gußstahlfabrik in Essen* (Essen, 1912); T. Buddensieg (ed.), *Villa Hügel. Das Wohnhaus Krupp in Essen* (Berlin, 1984); W. Brönner, *Die bürgerliche Villa in Deutschland 1830–1890* (Düsseldorf, 1987).

44. See W. Mosse's paper in the present volume. On the adaptability and the strength of the English nobility see H.-C. Schröder, 'Der englische Adel', in A. von Reden-Dohna, (ed.), *Der Adel im bürgerlichen Zeitalter* (Wiesbaden, 1988).

45. Cf. especially Cassis and Kaelble in the present volume.

46. Cf. Haupt, in the present volume.

47. Cf. M. König's contribution to the collection quoted in notes 30 and 5.

48. Cf. Kaelble, in the present volume.

49. Cf. D. Langewiesche (ed.), *Liberalismus im 19. Jahrhundert. Deutschland im internationalen Vergleich* (Göttingen, 1988); and his contribution to the present volume.

50. Cf. O. Hintze, 'Der Beamtenstaat,' (1911) in O. Hintze, *Soziologie und Geschichte* (Göttingen, 1964), pp. 66–125. The prominent position of officials in the German *Bürgertum* is demonstrated in many regional studies. See for instance H. Bühler, *Das beamtete Bürgertum in Göppingen und sein soziales Verhalten1815–1848* (Göppingen, 1976), p. 28; 'Academically educated officials seldom married daughters of *Wirtschaftsbürger*, for such liaisons did not correspond to what contemporaries considered the quasi-corporate pride (*Standesbewußtsein*) of an academically educated official'. Cf. also D. Wegmann, *Die leitenden staatlichen Verwaltungsbeamten der Provinz Westfalen 1815–1918* (Münster, 1969).

51. Cf. Zunkel, 'Beamtenschaft und Unternehmertum beim Aufbau der Ruhrindustrie 1849–1880', *Tradition* 9 (1964), pp. 261–276; Gall, *Bürgertum*.

52. Cf. J. Kocka, *Unternehmensverwaltung und Angestelltenschaft am Beispiel Siemens 1847–1914* (Stuttgart, 1969); J. Kocka, 'Eisenbahnverwaltung in der industriellen Revolution, deutsch-amerikanische Vergleiche', in H. Kellenbenz and H. Pohl, (eds.), *Historia Socialis et Economica* (Stuttgart, 1987), pp. 259–277.

53. According to the results of a DFG research project on the history of Commercial

Councillors in Prussia, led by O. Büsch and myself. I am grateful to Karin Kaudelka-Hanisch for the preparation of this information.

54. Cf. the article by Tilly in the present volume. Also H.A. Winkler (ed.), *Organisierter Kapitalismus. Vora.ussetzungen und Anfänge* (Göttingen, 1974); G. A. Ritter, 'Entstehung und Entwicklung des Sozialstaates in vergleichender Perspektive' *Historische Zeitschrift* 243 (1986), pp. 1–90; G. Schmidt, 'Liberalismus und soziale Reform. Der deutsche und der britische Fall, 1890–1914', *Tel Aviver Jahrbuch für deutsche Geschichte* 16 (1987), pp. 212–238.

55. Cf. C. Huerkamp, 'Ärzte in Deutschland und England. Gemeinsamkeiten und Unterschiede des ärztlichen Professionalisierungsprozesses im 19. Jahrhundert. unpublished manuscript, Bielefeld, 1986; C. Huerkamp, *Der Aufstieg der Ärzte im 19. Jahrhundert.Vom gelehrten Stand zum professionellen Experten. Das Beispiel Preußens* (Göttingen, 1985); H. Siegrist's contribution to the collection quoted in notes 30 and 5 above.

56. Cf. the articles by Mitchell and Langewiesche in the present wolume.

57. Cf. A. Ferguson, *Versuch über die Geschichte der bürgerlichen Gesellschaft*, ed. by Z. Batscha and H. Medick (Frankfurt, 1986) see the editors' introduction, especially pp. 30ff. E. Fraenkel, *Deutschland und die westlichen Demokratien* (Stuttgart, 1964); G.A. Ritter, *Deutscher und britischer Parlamentarismus. Ein verfassungsgeschichtlicher Vergleich* (Tübingen, 1962).

58. Cf. the paper by Mosse and Frevert in the present volume.

59. Cf. J. Reulecke, 'Formen bürgerlich-sozialen Engagements in Deutschland und England im 19. Jahrhundert', in Kocka, *Arbeiter und Bürger*, pp. 261–286.

60. On the differences in the treatment of smallpox and tuberculosis in Germany and France, see the paper by Mitchell in this volume. On the structural conditions and some other consequences of the 'bureaucratic tradition' so characteristic of German development, see J. Kocka, 'Capitalism and Bureaucracy in German Industrialisation before 1914', *Economic History Review*, Second Series, 33 (1981), pp. 453–468.

61. Cf. M. Weber, *Wirtschaftsgeschichte* (Munich, 1923), p. 271: 'Finally, we understand *"Bürgertum"*, in a class (*ständisch*) sense, as referring to those layers who are lumped together by the bureaucracy, by the proletarians and, in any case, by all outsiders as people of property and education; entrepreneurs, rentiers and all those persons who have an academic education and possess, as a result, a certain class (*ständisch*) standard and social prestige'. Other examples can be found in Henning, *Das westdeutsche Bürgertum*, pp. 23, 31. For Weber's critique of bureaucratisation, see his *Gesammelte Aufsätze zur Soziologie und Sozialpolitik* (Tübingen, 1924), pp. 390, 413ff.; further material in W. J. Mommsen, *Max Weber und die deutsche Politik 1890–1920* (Tübingen, 1974), pp. 17, 94, 179ff.

2 | Liberalism and the Middle Classes in Europe

Dieter Langewiesche

The terms 'liberalism' and 'middle class' (*Bürgertum*) delin-
eate two richly variable phenomena that played a major
part in shaping the political and social development of Europe in the
nineteenth century.[1] In the idea of civil society (*bürgerliche Gesellschaft*)
they shared a common, apparently unifying goal: liberalism as both a
network of political and social models with the ideal of a self-respon-
sible person at its centre, and liberalism as a political movement of the
middle classes striving for a society of independent citizens. Although
this widespread formula correctly summarises the basic belief of
European liberalism, concrete historical research is required to see
how this regulatory idea was given theoretical content in specific situations, and who attempted to put this idea into practice. Any interpretation or generalised concept of liberalism remains historically
blind in view of the wide spectrum covered by the concept since its
emergence at the beginning of the nineteenth century. And it is only
in its concrete historical development that we can acquire an adequate
understanding of *Bürgertum* as a specific form of socialisation of the
middle layers of society.

Such an understanding of liberalism and *Bürgertum* as a historical
process may complicate the task of determining their volatile relationship throughout the course of the nineteenth century. It certainly
increases the difficulty inherent in making any historical comparisons.
In the analysis that follows, German liberalism will serve as the base-
line for comparisons. This should make it possible to deal with the
question of German peculiarity (*Sonderweg*), one of the key ideas discussed in this volume, without prejudging the conclusion through the
choice of countries with which Germany is to be compared. The situation in Britain, France, Italy, Hungary, and occasionally Spain, the
Netherlands and Russia will be looked at. Germany will not be put

Notes to Chapter 2 can be found on page 65.

prematurely in that special niche on the axis of East-West modernisation to which it is generally relegated in studies of 'Germany's deviation from the West'.

Out of the multitude of possible comparative perspectives three are chosen here: (1) Under what political conditions did liberal movements and organisations emerge and develop? (2) Who joined these movements and against whom were they directed? (3) Which political and social models characterised liberalism? In each of the three major areas of investigation, what has to be looked at in a comparative perspective is long-term development and change. Was there a basic current of pan-European liberalism from which the history of German liberalism deviated?

Conditions and Patterns of Activity

Liberals wanted to be politically effective. Thus, it would be appropriate to assess them primarily according to their political actions. The forms of action available to them differed significantly in each European country and changed fundamentally throughout the course of the nineteenth century. Until the middle of the century, revolution belonged to the pattern of action of the middle classes, but not to that of the liberals. That divided them sharply from the middle-class democrats and republicans. European liberals, at best, became "revolutionaries against their will" (Th. Schieder), using, albeit with a bad conscience, the revolutionary movements which they had neither wanted nor created for their own limited reform goals. If a revolution was unavoidable (a section of continental European liberals did not fundamentally exclude this as the worst of all reform possibilities in the period before 1848), then they sought to end the revolutionary process as quickly as possible by legalising it: alterations not by revolutionary right, but as a result of constitutional change defined by parliament.

Liberal policy, in other words, always aimed at an institutionalisation of conflicts, and regulation of them by means of rational discussion. Liberals rejected violent forms of collective action, such as were practised by the popular classes with the occasional support and participation of some middle-class groups, until the middle of the century. They were among the most decisive defenders of the state's monopoly of force that they nevertheless wanted to see regulated and limited by law. Their rejection of force as a political means drew a sharp dividing line between them and the left, which made them appear during revolutionary periods as part of the conservative alliance in support of the status quo.

This rejection, however, was not simply a consequence of the social fears of the *juste milieu*, but rather a result of their modern commitment to the constitutional state. The liberal model aimed at achieving institutionalised and legally guaranteed political participation. The demands were directed both against the absolutist state that denied any form of political participation, and also against any other form of force as political instrument, including force 'from below'.

In order to be politically effective, liberalism needed a public and institutional forum. Where these did not exist, or where liberals were excluded from them, a liberal movement was either unable to develop at all or was forced to go underground. Going underground contradicted the reasons underlying its self-conception and left it incapable of asserting itself effectively against competition from the left. Thus the strength or weakness of liberalism was also a reflection of the maturity of public institutions and of the public sphere in state and society. Britain and Russia provide examples of the existing extremes.

The Initial Phase of Democratisation

In Britain, very favourable circumstances existed for the development of a liberal movement at the beginning of the nineteenh century.[2] Liberalism's scope for action in Britain provides us with an appropriate standard of comparison, enabling an assessment of the different national types of European liberalism and of the position that German liberalism occupied within this spectrum. British liberalism developed earlier and more successfully than any of its continental counterparts, and therefore served as a model for European liberals. Broadly speaking there were three general characteristics that account for the uniquely favourable circumstances of British liberalism during the first two-thirds of the nineteenth century:

First, the revolution of the seventeenth century had led to a national state, and a system of rule in which the central position was occupied by Parliament. Government was formed by the majority in Parliament, and it was the latter that decided upon the central problems of the country. As the power of political decision making became concentrated in Parliament, the emerging political currents had to increasingly pursue aims relevant to the whole nation and to display willingness to compromise. Both of these factors extended the scope of action for liberals.

Secondly, counterbalancing the central Parliament was not the state bureaucracy, which was very weak in comparison to the continental European states, but, the powerful decentralised bodies of local government. British society administered itself through these bodies with a relatively large degree of autonomy and distance from the centre. To this extensive decentralisation of political decision making one must also add the organisational diversity in religious life. The forms of self-government, as well as conceptions of order developed and practised here, had importance far beyond the confessional sphere. It was for this reason that the British parties were influenced by religion to a large degree. The liberals found their support mainly outside the Anglican church, especially among the nonconformists but also among sections of the Catholic community. It was only in the late nineteenth century that these confessional bastions of British liberalism began to lose importance, as other social factors became more important in political attitudes.[3]

Third, the central socioeconomic processes on the road to modernity got under way in Britain earlier than they did on the continent - population growth, agrarian revolution, industrial revolution and the beginnings of urbanisation. Society began to change at a point where an instrumentarium of intervention did not yet exist such as was developed, to different degrees, in other European states during the course of the nineteenth century. British liberalism profited from this lead in two ways: the higher level of social self-organisation particularly favoured those political organisations in which the independent individual was the core of political belief; secondly, the mobilisation of society strengthened those who were considered representatives of progress. This mixture of concentration of power in Parliament with strong local self-organisation and a weak state bureaucracy, of social change and religious tradition promoting pluralism and individualism created political possibilities for British liberalism during the first two thirds of the nineteenth century that did not exist, on a comparable scale, on the continent.

A national parliament existed in France, but there was no parliamentary practice comparable with that existing in Britain.[4] A two-party system had not developed in France, and after the July Revolution of 1830, government ministers placed greater value on their personal contacts with the king than on the unclear relation of forces in parliament. The extent to which large sections of middle-class society felt themselves excluded from this kind of governmental practise became clear in the revolution of 1848, when even the *bour-geoisie* declined to support the '*bourgeois* monarch'.

The conditions in parliament made it impossible for French liberals to create a clear profile for themselves as a distinct political group with claims to national leadership. The preconditions for local and regional self-organisation on the British pattern were lacking in France. Hemmed in between the influence of the central administration, on the one hand, and on the other by the thin layer of leading notables whose importance began to diminish only in the 1840s, the liberals had very few opportunities to anchor liberalism socially, either as an idea or as a practice in local and regional politics. On this level, liberalism confronted a stronger competitor, republicanism, which had constituted itself as the real 'party of the people' after the French Revolution. The existence of a strong *parti du peuple* to the left of, but open towards, the liberals limited the integrative power of liberalism and therefore its political scope for action.

Compared with Britain and with the countries of southern and central Europe liberalism in France occupied, in one respect, a peculiar position. It was difficult for liberalism to make itself recognisable as an independent and distinct political current at a local, regional or national level. This difficulty existed in the public political sphere in the nineteenth century and still proves troublesome for the historian today. This led to a 'conceptual confusion' that continues to divide historians over which political currents should be regarded as liberal.[5] This indeterminateness at the same time enabled the liberals to exhibit a very high degree of flexibility that secured – until the First World War – a key position in the parliamentary coalitions between the middle-class parties.

In spite of all these differences, the development of both British and French liberalism was decisively influenced, from the beginning, by the existence of a national state which was unquestioningly accepted by all political forces. In contrast, the scope of action for Italian, German and Hungarian liberalism during the first two-thirds of the nineteenth century was determined, above all, by the fact that the nation either had no national state, or in the case of Hungary, had its national independence limited by the supra-national Habsburg monarchy within which it remained constantly under threat.

In Hungary, from around 1830, a strong liberal movement developed which was solidly rooted in the state institutions as well as in Hungary's leading social stratum, the nobility.[6] This created an extremely favourable scope for political action for Hungarian liberalism. It also makes Hungarian liberalism especially rewarding for a comparative analysis, because it does not conform to the traditional image of middle-class liberalism. In its social origins it was completely non-bourgeois, but at the same time it was committed to the model of 'civil society' while being politically organised in estates.

Hungarian liberals had no access to the upper echelons of the Habsburg state. Nevertheless, they were successful in making use of the dual nature of the political order that had always acted as a limit to the extension of absolutist power in Hungary. The central bastion of the nobility's strength was the *Komitate* (county administration), where it had been able to retain for itself a very high degree of self-administration. On this basis, the estates were able to survive periods in which the Hungarian Diet was not convoked. When, in the 1820s, the Diet once again considered proposals for reform, the aristocracy used their experience of self-administration to initiate a broad discussion. Informal circles prepared resolutions, which, after detailed discussions in local assemblies, were defended by deputies in the Diet.

During the decade before the revolution of 1848, the sphere of public political debate was extended significantly as a large number of associations, actively developing political objectives, were supported by newspapers and by the first party-like organisations. However, what constituted the potential effectiveness of the reform policies of aristocratic liberalism was the superior position of the nobility in the estatist institutions. Therefore, what emerged around 1830 from a policy of estatist self-organisation was an aristocratic reform movement that was well informed about western and central European liberalism, and that had adopted its models.

Although groups with quite different goals began to appear in the 1840s, no political competition for Hungarian liberalism emerged from the left. This accounted in large part for its willingness, during the revolutionary years of 1848 and 1849, to see the Hungarian monarchy replaced by a parliamentary state with a civil society based on legal equality. The fact that the Habsburg monarchy in the post-revolutionary period attempted to dismantle the bastions of Hungarian self-administration was one of the key experiences that determined Hungarian political life and, thus, the development of liberalism after the compromise (*Ausgleich*) with Austria in 1867.

Italian liberalism emerged under completely different conditions.[7] The legitimacy of the old order had disintegrated during the Revolutionary and Napoleonic era, and the dynastic restoration of 1815 was unable to restore this legitimacy. Social demands for participation could no longer be suppressed, but no state institutions were opened up to them; and where chambers of deputies did exist, as in Lombardy-Venice, they remained without influence. The response of society to this policy of state denial was to take part in non-state and sometimes in anti-state activities. Italy became the classical country of secret leagues and sects, putsches and attempted revolutions. But aspirations for reform also gave rise to more newspapers and journals, associations and scientific congresses, even kindergartens and schools.

No united political movement stood behind these activities. One can distinguish two major currents. First, there were the democrats who found a charismatic leader in Mazzini and who developed, from the 1830s, a unitary-republican program that could only have been put into effect by means of revolutionary force against the various state dynasties. The second were the liberals (*moderati*), who tried to work with the dynasties, as well as with the governments. Until 1848 their main goal was not unification but reform of the individual states on the basis of the existing order, and according to the pattern of western Europe. However, with their failure to achieve these reforms the liberals began in the 1840s to place more of their hopes in a future national state.

This division between the republican democrats and the monarchist liberals continued during the revolutionary years of 1848 and 1849. Their common defeat prepared the way for a post-revolutionary liberalism that brought together the *moderati* and the moderate wing of the democrats. This new liberalism became the main pillar of the Italian national movement. Only now, after the failure of the revolution, did Italian liberalism obtain that institutional locus of action that had existed in Britain, France, Hungary and in other states during the first half of the century, namely, parliament. This was the case, at first, only in Piedmont-Sardinia, which under the leadership of Cavour and supported by the liberal national movement, became the unifying power in Italy. With the emergence of the national state, created gradually after 1859, Italian liberalism came to the end of a phase in which institutional circumstances had kept its development behind that of the liberal movements in the other western European states.

In the light of the developments in Europe that we have examined so far, there is no basis for speaking of a *Sonderweg* of German liberalism.[8] Like the Italian *moderati*, German liberals demanded, first of all, reforms within the individual states. After the 1840s, the liberal constitutional movement became a broad national movement that outgrew the liberal spectrum to the same extent that elite nationalism developed into a mass nationalism. The democrats began, both organisationally and programmatically, to distinguish themselves from the liberals, although this division did not manifest the same intensity that had been reached in France and Italy.

It was not until the revolutionary years of 1848–1849 that the competition from the left became strong; the liberals, at that precise moment when they took over ministerial office, began to feel their scope for action limited by fear of an uncontrolled revolutionary overthrow of the entire political and social order. But this too was not a German peculiarity. Something similar happened in Italy and France, and to a lesser degree, in Hungary.

Until the revolution, the conditions of action for the liberals in the various states of the German Confederation differed to such an extent that one is tempted to see all the different European situations reflected here, except, of course, the extremes. Russian conditions did not exist in Germany. The British model was achieved only in 1848, and even then the German aristocracy, under the pressure of revolutionary events, accepted liberal ministers and a parliamentary form of government only partially and for a short time. Until that time, the German spectrum ranged from the complete rejection of central parliamentary bodies and the maintenance of the old estatist corporations to parliaments that approached the modern representative idea and demonstrated very high levels of competence.

As elsewhere in Europe, liberalism in the German confederation found its centres wherever the ruling system allowed some form of institutional participation. This included, in addition to parliament, the local organs of self-government. Their significance for the development of German liberalism has yet to be studied, but the present state of our knowledge would seem to suggest that, in this instance as well, German conditions represented a middle position in comparison to the rest of Europe. Self-government was not as distant from the state as it was in Britain, but in spite of the extension of state control during the reform era at the beginning of the nineteenth century, it was more developed in Germany than it was in Italy or France. This may have contributed to the fact that German liberalism had more support in the wider population than was the case in France or Italy. Self-government at local government level was also important in Hungary, but it was, of course, limited to the aristocracy.

The issue of religion and the extent of confessional self-administration seems to have been of only marginal significance for the early development of liberalism in Europe. The conflict between liberalism and Catholicism, which restricted the liberal scope of action after the 1850s, cannot be projected back into the pre-revolutionary period. The turning point was the revolution of 1848/49, when secular and religious models came into open conflict. Until then, liberalism and Catholicism had proven to be quite compatible. In Italy a section of the liberal movement had even hoped that the pope would provide an integrative force for a federal nation-state. This hope was similarly disappointed in 1848. In Germany the revolutionary years also repre-sented the beginning of an alienation between liberalism and Catholicism that was not to be overcome again. Until 1848, the German situation, once again, occupied a middle position between the confessionally homogeneous states and the confessional hetero-geneity in Britain.

German liberals found support from the self-administered bodies of Protestantism, but not to the same extent as the British did from the non-conformist groups. The Protestant churches of Germany remained state churches whose institutional freedom of movement was limited by the state authorities.[9] The hope of a section of pre-1848 liberals of finding in the Protestant *Lichtfreuden* and in the German Catholics a free-church bastion such as existed in Britain was fruitless. After 1848, German liberalism became a purely Protestant phenomenon, which did not mean that the Protestant church became liberal. Unlike in the Catholic states and in Britain, the Protestant church in Germany promoted the orientation of liberalism towards the state. This may have been a situation peculiar to Germany. Nonetheless, one has to emphasise that within the broad spectrum of institutional conditions of action in which European liberalism devel-oped in the first two thirds of the nineteenth century, a German *Sonderweg* cannot be discarded.

Parliamentarism and Democratisation

In the last three decades of the nineteenth century, political condi-tions in the countries under consideration changed fundamentally. Germany and Italy became nation-states. In 1867, Hungary acquired a form of state autonomy within the Austro-Hungarian dual monarchy. This nationalisation of the area of political action, within which national centres of decision making now existed everywhere in west-ern, southern and central Europe, was linked to a fundamental societal change that completely transformed the conditions of political action. This general trend of development, affecting all areas of life, could be described as a democratisation of the opportunities for participation.

There were changes in nutrition and hygiene, housing and life-expectancy, education and information. The opportunities for people to have a share in progress were extended everywhere while the demand for participation grew even more rapidly.

To be politically effective, it was essential to become attuned to this dynamic. The success of European liberals in doing so varied considerably from one country to another. Their ability to assert themselves in the political 'mass market' depended largely on the institutional structures available to them in each country.[10] There were two factors which were decisive: the extent of democratic franchise and the degree of parliamentarisation.

That voting rights should be graduated or limited by social criteria was part of the political creed of European liberalism. The citizen who was to be given full voting rights should be economically secure and educated. For most people, this liberal ideal of the citizen was not more than a model for the future, the achievement of which was the task of each individual. In the present, however, it acted as a filter that excluded the majority of the population and entrusted them into the care of those who, through property and education, were equipped to participate in political life. This liberal programme was put forward in the revolution of 1848, but the defeat of the revolution put an end to hopes of a democratic franchise. Only in France were voting rights preserved, and here they were used, first and foremost, to give electoral legitimacy to Bonapartist rule. Only in the new reformist climate of the 1860s could attempts be made again to further extend civil society by means of a more democratic franchise, and to allow greater participation in political power through parliamentarisation.

With respect to the institutional conditions of political activity, the 1860s were a turning point. This decade also marked the beginning of a particular path of development (*Sonderentwicklung*) in Germany that distinguished it not only from the West, but also from Italy and Hungary. Universal male franchise in Germany (1867/71) opened the path to democratisation without full parliamentarisation. In other European states, developments proceeded in the opposite direction: first came parliamentarisation, and then a gradual democratisation of participation in the election of parliament. Only in France did both coincide in 1871 – democratic male suffrage was maintained when the Bonapartist regime was replaced by a parliamentary republic – while both were absent in Russia. The Russian reforms of the 1860s were not really part of the eighteenth and early nineteenth century

European drive towards reform in those years but were more in the European tradition of bureaucratic-absolutist modernisation.[11]

This German type of thorough politicisation of society without parliamentarisation created very unfavourable conditions for the development of liberalism. The liberals had to deal with a highly organised political 'mass market' without being able to dampen or integrate competing interests. This situation meant that the options available to the German liberals were quite different from those available to the British, French, Italian and Hungarian liberals who, during the period before the First World War, participated in government either some of the time (Britain, France) or all of the time (Italy and Hungary). Both politically and socially, this blocked parliamentarisation limited the intergrative power of German liberals. Their weakness at the level of the Reich was not compensated for by the better opportunities for institutional participation that existed in individual states such as Baden and Bavaria, and in the cities.

Of course, contemporaries could not foresee this particular path of development which began in the 1860s, although they recognised quite clearly the epochal significance of the Prussian constitutional conflict for the future development of the political system: monarchy or parliamentary rule, military or constitutional state. German liberals perceived the situation quite clearly.[12] The fact that they could not determine the outcome of this conflict was neither their fault, nor the fault of the German national movement led by them. It was the creation of the German national state out of three wars that limited the scope of action for the liberals. These were not civil wars, but wars between states. Neither parliament, nor national public opinion determined their course. As wars of unification they were, in fact, welcomed by the majority of the German nation who demanded from their parliamentary representatives a willingness to compromise so as not to endanger the desired goal of a German national state.

The first elections in the North German Confederation and in the Reich demonstrated beyond question that little room for manoeuvering was left to parties that demanded more than Bismarck and the German sovereigns were willing to give. German liberals, regardless of whether they belonged to the left wing or to the National Liberal wing, placed their hopes in the future, believing that they would later be able to recover to their own advantage the basic constitutional measures that were cut off by military means in 1867 and 1871. The next decade seemed to confirm their hopes. 1866 saw the beginning of the 'liberal era', one of the most significant reform periods in modern German history. As Max Weber, one of the most perceptive left-liberal critics wrote retrospectively in 1917, it was to this period that 'we owe most of the Reich institutions that still stand the test today'.

The liberals had hoped that the failure to establish proper parliamentary institutions in 1867 and 1871 could be gradually corrected later, but these hopes were dashed in 1878/79 with the so-called 'second' or 'internal foundations of the Reich'. Now the liberals, especially the National Liberals, appeared as the ones who had been duped. It had been their willingness to compromise that made it possible to create the modern institutions of the national state, but this impressive reform achievement had not been crowned with the coveted parliamentarisation. By the end of the 1870s, the rapprochement of the conservatives and political Catholicism with the *kleindeutsch* national state, previously rejected by both, had progressed to the point where Bismarck could rely on their assistance in resisting the attempt of the liberals to acquire government power in Prussia and in the Reich. The failure of their plans for gradual parliamentarisation represented more than just a failure of liberal policies; it reinforced Germany's special development (*Sonderentwicklung*) on the road to modern statehood.

The conflicts that accompanied this development in Germany existed on a similar scale in Italy, Hungary and the western European states, but the failure of parliamentarisation prevented German society from taking the necessary steps to regulate these conflicts politically. The blocked opportunity for participating in government not only weakened the integrative capacity of the German political parties, it also displaced the contours of what could be considered 'progressive'. These contours were much more complex in Germany than in the other European states under consideration. Those who like the left liberals, demanded political reforms, rejected state social reforms because these would only strengthen the power of the unreformed state over society. Those who, like the National Liberals cooperated more willingly with the semi-parliamentary state and its conservative power elite, were more receptive to the social policy initiatives of the state. In Germany, it was this distance from, or closeness to, the state that created socio-political divisions cutting across the left–right political spectrum. It was only after the turn of the century that these complex divisions began to break down, divisions that made it difficult to construct an effective opposition.

European liberalism now entered the last phase of its development before the First World War.[13] The need for a policy of state social welfare, the increasing organisation and differentiation of social interests and the emergence of imperialism as a new form of mass ideological integration forced European liberals to undertake the difficult task of changing their traditional social models. The Germans carried out this task no worse than their European neighbours. Whereas the latter were able to translate their ability to adapt to new social conditions into new forms of government activity, this possibility was still barred to the German liberals. The retarded parliamentarism of the German Reich radically restricted the political effectiveness of the liberals' program for state and society, to a much greater extent in Germany than in the other western European states, or in Italy and Hungary.

Supporters and Opponents

With its idea of the 'citizen', political liberalism created 'the vision of a classless society'[14] – a promise for everyone striving for a society of free and equal individuals. This was directed, first of all, against the *ancien régime* and all of its privileged benificiaries. However, the front line shifted somewhat in the course of the nineteenth century as the ideal of 'civil society' was given legal, social, political and cultural content. The history of European liberalism can be seen as the continued attempt to promote such a development while also seeking to guide and restrict it. Who exactly supported and opposed liberalism was something that varied considerably over time and among the different European states. But, as a general rule, one could say that the more that nineteenth century society accepted the liberal idea of civil society, the more this ideal lost its integrative power. As the social restrictions built into its fundamental ideas began to be removed, the groups supporting it became socially more restricted. Liberalism became more 'bourgeois', but the bourgeoisie did not become more liberal. Even when liberalism became a predominantly bourgeois class movement, the bourgeoisie was not united behind it, not even in its majority. The *embourgeoisement* (*Verbürgerlichung*) of liberalism was accompanied by a de-liberalisation of the middle classes – a process that reached its high point after the First World War but which had in fact begun before the war.

Before the existence of modern large-scale organisations it is difficult to find precise data about the support for political ideas and movements in different social groups. If we look at the leading circles in parliaments and governments, we see that there was great variety within the European states with respect to social origins. This is not surprising, in view of the differences in social development in each country. However, in no sense did the liberals break with tradition. Their rejection of abrupt revolutionary change was an indication of this, as were their social models and the social origin of their leading circles. Until beyond the middle of the nineteenth century, the industrial bourgeoisie were not part of these circles.

Even in Great Britain, the pioneer of industrialisation, only 21 percent of Liberal members in the House of Commons between 1859 and 1874 were great industrialists. More than half of them owed their social position to the ownership of landed property, had enjoyed an aristocratic upbringing and led aristocratic life-styles.[15] In Hungary, it was the nobility alone that could participate in politics. It was here that the idea of 'bourgeois society' found its strongest base after 1830, supported also by the emerging group of (mostly Jewish) merchants. Liberal ideas were entertained by the urban middle class society in the towns, which remained rather traditional and distant from politics.[16] In Spain, likewise, the liberal parliamentarians and members of government in office after 1834, came mainly from the nobility with a minority coming from the military elite and from the commercial bourgeoisie. The industrial bourgeoisie of Catalonia, in contrast, were not politically active.[17]

In pre-constitutional Italy, the liberal movement was based on a modernising elite as well. Again it had its origins in the top social layers – the nobility, the educated professions and the bourgeoisie. Among the latter, merchants and agrarian capitalists were predominant, while the industrial bourgeois played no role. In Risorgimento Italy, a mixed group of middle-class and aristocratic origins in which the political elite (the nobility, officials, military) and the cultural elite predominated, promoted liberalism as an ideology of development. It was an ideology built around the western European model, but this vision of the future was nevertheless, not a vision of the industrial state.[18]

In both France and Germany the leading liberal political circles were more middle-class than in the other countries under consideration. This is confirmed by the data for the national assemblies elected in Frankfurt and Paris in 1848 on the basis of extensive democratic male suffrage.[19] The nobility played no role, but there were major differences with respect to the social make-up of the middle classes involved. In Franfurt the major group came from the *Bildungsbürgertum* (educated and professional middle classes). Most of them were active in the state service, a high proportion were also active on left of the political spectrum. In Paris, on the other hand, it was landowners and shareholders who made up the dominant group (around 30 percent, compared with 14 percent in Frankfurt). Active entrepreneurs in trade and industry played only a minor role in both France (11 percent) and Germany (8 percent).

The amazing effectiveness of the liberal model and the high degree of sociopolitical integrative power that early liberalism manifested would not have been possible without this anchorage of the early liberal leading circles in the socially dominant layers of their society. Liberal spokesmen were not upstarts of uncertain social rank. They were men with a respectable social background, held high in public esteem. When they demanded change, it was as if the whole weight of tradition stood behind such a demand. This imparted a certain stability to change. It could be trusted because it had been praised by the members of 'respectable society'. A 'bourgeois' liberalism would not have been able to achieve this.

Liberalism was the innovative section of respectable society – this characterisation of the early liberal leaders is, of course, an abstraction that ignores important differences among the various European countries. Bourgeois-aristocratic features of the leading liberal circles may mean different things in Britain and Italy. In Britain, it points to the openness of the aristocracy, which, because of its rules of inheritance, was constantly pushing a section of its membership into the middle class. It also points to the prominent position of Parliament, whose political weight attracted the social elites. In Italy, the bourgeois-aristocratic alliance was created primarily in opposition to Habsburg rule, which, directly and indirectly, was a burden on Italy and kept both nobility and bourgeoisie in a state of political impotence. The fact that the nobility in northern Italy had become an agrarian capitalist class much earlier made this cooperation with bourgeois strata easier. In Germany, this kind of bourgeois-aristocratic symbiosis was not a possibility. The landowning aristocracy was economically too insecure and insufficently modern. Within the existing political order, political cooperation with the middle classes would not have increased their political power. The German aristocracy set its hopes on an alliance with the monarchy, not with the middle classes.[20]

This form of estatism was a general feature of German development and it also characterised the development of early liberalism. Liberal leaders in Germany were part of the state service to a much greater extent than was the case in other European countries. In Great Britain, occupying an official position in the civil service was incompatible with holding a seat in Parliament. In the French National Assembly of 1848, public officials made up 20.5 percent of the deputies. Of these, only 12.6 percent were permanent officials. In the Frankfurt parliament, however, the number of deputies permanently employed in the service of the state was 50.9 percent, with the overall proportion of state officials being 55.8 percent. In the chamber of deputies in Württemberg, to pick another example, 20 percent to 50 percent of the deputies between 1820 and 1868 were state officials. There was, in addition, a proportion of municipal employees (as much as 21 percent), while a further 25 percent to 33 percent consisted of local officials who, although they came from a variety of professions in part were also employed in the public sector and usually worked under the supervision of the state.

This strong link between state bureaucracy and the elected chamber was also typical for the Frankfurt parliament. In France, however, the elected deputies had much stronger links with the associations and interest organisations. In Germany, these types of social organisations functioned more as compensation for the fact that the state either denied or limited the opportunities for political participation.[21]

Different views about the extent to which officials should be considered part of the bourgeoisie can be found in contemporary as well as recent historical opinion. There can be no doubt that the top levels of the state bureaucracy in Germany, whose reforms did much to break up traditional society, played an important role in the emergence of civil and bourgeois society in Germany.[22] What is also clear is the high proportion of officials in the leading circles of German liberalism at that time. Socially, they were a highly respected section of the *Bildungsbürgertum* (educated middle classes), and they showed themselves to be much more capable than all other social groups in giving general expression to the participatory demands of the time without breaking with the traditional political and social order. This was still basically the situation in the late nineteenth century.

Between 1874 and 1912, the proportion of *Bildungsbürger* with an academic background among the National Liberals in the Reichstag declined only slightly, from 86 percent to 70 percent (the proportion among the left liberals was 10 percent lower). There was a greater decline in their proportion in the civil service: from 47 percent to 24 percent. This may have been a consequence of the process of *embourgeoisement*. The greatest increase was in the representation of the educated and professional middle class who were not employed in the service of the state. The proportion of the bourgeoisie rose only slightly, from 12 percent to 16 percent for the National Liberals and from around 10 percent to 19 percent for the left liberals.[23]

During the same period, the bourgeois character of the parliamentary leadership of British liberalism was greatly strengthened. During the period 1859 to 1874, the proportion of Liberal members of the House of Commons whose social position depended on the ownership of land was 49 percent; in 1914 it was only 6 percent. During the same period the figure for the proportion of the bourgeoisie rose from around 30 percent to 40 percent. There was no comparable shift in the social composition of Conservative members. In 1892, 28.5 percent of Conservative members represented landed interests (Liberals 8.1 percent) while 25.9 percent represented the industrial and financial bourgeoisie (Liberals 44.2 percent).[24] In Italy, as in Germany, the social transformation led to the educated and professional middle class playing a leading role in the national parliament, while entrepreneurs and bankers in the two decades before the First World War, still had only 5 to 7 percent of the parliamentary seats.

However, in contrast to Germany, the proportion of public officials was quite low, only 7 percent, while professionals, especially lawyers had almost 50 percent of the seats.[25] In Hungary, the process of embourgeoisement did not remove the nobility from its leading role in parliament, but it did have the effect of binding them even more strongly to the liberal model of a 'bourgeois society' which was promoted by the lower house with a flood of reform laws.[26] In the Netherlands, as in Germany, officials had a strong position in parliament and in the liberal parliamentary group, but here a more advanced stage of parliamentarisation coexisted with a less democratic franchise.[27]

Thus the process of embourgeoisement of liberal leading circles varied greatly in the different countries of Europe. There was no standard path. Nonetheless, as far as the national-state phase of this process is concerned, one is justified in speaking about a special path of development (*Sonderentwicklung*) in Germany. It seems that only German liberalism, after the foundation of the national state, was subject to this massive double pressure from above and below, a double pressure that confronted the emancipatory movement of civil society with a 'mass democracy' before the parliamentarisation of state power had taken place. This contributed to a very great extent to the fact that liberalism's power of social integration declined earlier in Germany than in the other European states under consideration. There were, of course, other factors at work that can be summarised only briefly here.

In the period before the foundation of the Reich, German liberalism was not just one party among others. It was the incorporation of the national movement. Everyone who desired a *kleindeutsch* national state felt themselves to be part of this movement which extended far beyond the milieu of the liberal middle classes. But, as this exceptional situation came to an end during the 1870s, the liberals were reduced to the status of ordinary parties, although they still received as much as 25.9 percent of the popular vote in 1912 (1871: 46.6 percent; 1881: 37.8 percent). It was a process of normalisation that gave the liberal parties and their supporters a more bourgeois social profile. There were three main reasons why this process began earlier and developed at a more rapid pace in Germany than in the other European states.

Firstly, following the establishment of the *kleindeutsch*-Protestant Reich , the Catholic population was lost to the German liberals. This meant that the liberals were denied access to nearly one third of the Reich's population without, at the same time, being able to win a monopoly of Protestant votes. They had to compete with the conservatives for the Protestant middle-class vote and with the Social Democrats for the Protestant working-class vote. The Social Democrats were the only party able to expand their vote at a rate (1871: 3.2 percent; 1912: 34.8 percent) that kept up with the rapid expansion in electoral participation (1871: 50 percent; 1912: 84.9 percent). It was social democracy, not liberalism, that benefited most from the increasing secularisation of German society. In France and Italy, on the other hand, the secular-Catholic conflict helped to stabilise liberalism and the republican left. Whereas these confessional and social divisions were already deeply rooted in Germany during the period of the foundation of the Reich, they developed much later in Holland and reached a high point there only after the First World War. Nothing comparable existed in Britain. The nonconformist churches, although weakened, remained a base of support for the Liberals. Because of the Irish question, they also had the support of the Catholics, although in 1866 they lost support of some members of the House and of some voters who opposed Home Rule for Ireland.[28]

Secondly, until the 1830s, liberalism was an integrative movement with a wide social field of potential support. The majority of liberal supporters, however, came from the middle classes. Only in countries where there was no numerically significant and politically competent middle class, for instance in Hungary and to a lesser extent in Spain, did other social classes come to the fore, especially the nobility. Apart from these exceptions, not only with respect to its social model, but

also with respect to the wider social milieu that it integrated politically, European liberalism was a middle-class movement. The 'middle
strata' were the core of liberalism.

Liberalism had its widest social appeal in those countries where it
provided unchallenged leadership for the national movement. In this
period of nation building, these were both socially and politically the
most powerful movements of the nineteenth century. This was especially true of Germany. Right into the era of the foundation of the
Reich it was the liberals who were the main organisers and thinkers
of the national movement. As such, they were able to attract all the
social strata that constituted the political public sphere, in particular
the urban middle and working classes. However, the revolutionary
period of 1848/9 revealed to them the fact that they would lose their
leading role as soon as the national state that they envisaged came into
being. It was then, for the first time, that a differentiated political
party spectrum began to emerge in which middle-class democrats and
working-class organisations began to compete with the liberals, pushing them more and more into a narrower bourgeois milieu without
restricting them entirely to such a milieu. This process, already visible
in 1848, was irreversible after 1871.

In Italy, and even more so in France, the liberals had to compete
with the republicans and democrats for a recruiting ground to which,
in Germany, the liberals alone had access. Liberalism in these countries was, therefore, to a much greater extent concentrated among the
propertied and educated middle class. This was particularly true for
France, while post-revolutionary liberalism in Italy, through its links
with a section of the democrats, had access to the social groups that
supported the democrats, including the craftsmen and the lower social
orders of the cities.[29]

Thirdly, at the end of the nineteenth century liberal parties everywhere confronted the same central problem: social change had created previously unknown differences within the middle classes and had
brought into being a rapidly expanding and politically active working
class. As a result of these developments, European liberalism was
nowhere able to sustain its earlier power of social integration. It was
most successful in Hungary, where the liberal-dominated attempt to
create a national state remained an unresolved task of the future.
Parties formed themselves around the central issue of political life in
Hungary, relegating all other lines of political division to secondary
importance. Along with the restrictive suffrage, this secured the politically leading role of the liberals in Hungary.[30]

German liberals did not fail in the face of the new problems of integration, but they were less successful than their European neighbours. To understand why a comparison with Great Britain, Germany's principal competitor for the leading position among the industrial states, remains useful as far as party political competition for middle-class electoral support is concerned, it is worth emphasising once again that one should not underestimate the importance of the differences between the political systems and their institutions, nor the role played by religion.

In the German Reich, both liberals and conservatives competed for the support of the Protestant middle class, while Catholic society was inaccessible to both. In Britain, however, conservatives and liberals each had a distinctive base of support: the Anglicans supported the Conservatives while the non-conformists and Catholics clung to the Liberals. These confessional ties made a greater homogeneity possible in the British parties, a homogeneity that was also promoted by the electoral system in which party splits proved disastrous. In Germany, on the other hand, the exclusion of parties from government responsibility created a greater willingness to engage in party-splitting – a feature equally prevalent among the liberals, whose integrative capacity was limited by a whole series of splits and new party formations.

The differences are even more pronounced when we look at the ability of German liberals to win support among the growing number of working-class voters. Although a Labour Party did not emerge until the 1890s, the British working class had, at a very early stage, a solid network of trade union and cooperative organisations, well organised by trade and by locality. It was organisationally and programmatically independent, but in national elections and the House of Commons it worked together with the Liberals. There was no counterpart in Germany to this 'Lib-Lab' coalition. Attempts to establish such a coalition failed.[31]

The fact that an independent political labour movement had not emerged in Germany as early as the 1860s points once again to the specificity of the formation of the German nation-state, prepared by the liberal-led national movement but carried out 'from above' by the Prussian state. This severly weakened the integrative appeal of the liberals. Unlike their British counterparts, the German liberals were unable to campaign in elections on the basis of their program for government. At the same time, the democratic franchise in Germany meant that their middle-class support carried little weight in the elections.[32]

In the cities, however, the process was reversed. The decline of British liberalism and the rise of the Labour Party began earlier in the cities than at the national level, while in Germany it began at the national level. Protected from the outset by an undemocratic electoral system, German liberals defended the municipal administrations as centres of bourgeois rule, while at the same time instituting an extensive system of social welfare. Social liberalism emerged in Germany at the local level, in Britain at the national level. Both variants attempted to win over the workers to supply political support for middle class liberalism, and both failed. This failure was visible earlier in Germany. After the First World War, however, the differences diminished as both headed rapidly into decline. Bourgeois social circles withdrew from the liberal parties, and they were no longer able to retain or regain the support of working class voters.[33]

Liberal Models

Liberal ideas shaped the nineteenth century, but all attempts to give them some universally valid definition have failed. Books on the history of liberalism generally begin by expressing the hope that, at the end, the reader will understand what liberalism was.[34] This approach is most appropriate because the orientations provided by liberalism were constantly being recast. They were flexibly adapted to different situations, and the spectrum of ideas acceptable within the liberal-oriented community was a very wide one. This very degree of adaptability and tolerance makes liberalism very polymorphic and impervious to definition. This very flexibility, however, helps to explain how it was able to become an 'all-pervasive element in the life structure of the new world' (L.T. Hobhouse). Liberals believed that progress could not be halted and they justified the dynamic of modernity – a dynamic, albeit of small steps and not one of rapid leaps into the future. Progress was to follow a humane standard, understandable and achievable to each individual.

For liberalism, time was the universal friend who irresistibly would bring ever greater happiness for an ever greater number of people. The belief in progress became a liberal passion that rejected the golden age of a dark past, the paradise of a future life and the utopia of a mythical land. Instead, it proclaimed the ideal of a better life for all mankind here on earth, in every community.[35]

At the centre of this theory of progress stood the individual. Liberalism gave a variety of answers to the question of how state and society were to be organised. These answers reflected the changing problems within state and society. The inalienable core of liberal thought always remained; to secure for the individual the freedom of decision, even if this required collective measures such as social welfare. The collective had to take second place to the individual – this fundamental conviction distinguished liberalism from all other ideologies of progress such as nationalism or socialism, in spite of all the rapprochements or amalgamations that may have occurred. When this borderline was crossed and when the collective was given priority, as was the case in the nineteenth century, especially during the imperialist phase of nationalism, liberalism abandoned its identity and became part of another ideology not susceptible to liberal ideas.

This conception of the world, centred on the individual and his freedom, was understood by the nineteenth century as *bürgerlich*. What was meant here was the *Staatsbürger*, the *citoyen* and not the *bourgeois*. During the early decades of the previous century, as the political meaning of liberalism was becoming established, the term 'liberalism'[36] was almost a political synonym for the ideal of 'civil society' (*Staatsbürgergesellschaft*). It stood opposed to everything that limited the freedom of the individual: against absolutism and aristocratic rule, against estatist and confessional privileges. *Staatsbürger* represented the promise of an egalitarian future and was therefore attractive as a program that transcended the boundaries of classes and particular social strata.

In practice, however, the liberal conception was a programme of education in many areas, and one that permitted inequality. Equality before the law, but not political equality was to be put into effect immediately. By means of an unequal franchise, the liberals wanted to graduate participation in the political administration of state and community. The liberal ideal of civil society thus allowed an element of bourgeois inequality to intrude. In the course of the nineteenth century, this element was either eliminated or diminished as European liberals learned to live with the democratic franchise. But they accepted it unwillingly rather than promoted it, and they rejected it whenever possible. Nonetheless, European liberalism gradually expanded its concept of the *Staatsbürger* social, inasmuch as the *citoyen* was given priority over the *bourgeois*.

Women were not included; the active liberals were all men, and they thought of their civil society as a male society. Very few of them demanded voting rights for women, and most liberals accepted this issue only when it was no longer avoidable. Even legal equality for both sexes was something that nineteenth century liberalism rejected.

Contractual freedom, a core notion of the liberal notion of civil society, was to be limited within the family. Liberalism justified this male retreat from its own model of legal equality with the idea of the natural and eternal inequality of the sexes. The great legal works of the nineteenth century such as, for instance, the German *Bürgerliches Gesetzbuch* of 1900, all bear witness to the liberals' intention of giving a patriarchical interpretation to their concept of law.[37]

The main political goal of the liberals was the constitutional state guaranteeing the rule of law and civic participation in the state. They did not develop a universally binding model for the concrete structuring of the constitutional state, but there was general agreement as to the need for a strong parliament that would legally regulate the relation between the state and the citizen. Most liberals also favoured a parliamentary form of government in which the parliamentary majority would determine the composition and policy of the government. Among the major European states, with the exception of autocratic Russia, the liberal desire for a parliamentary form of government was at its weakest in Germany.[38]

With respect to the form of state, European liberals did not have a common line. They tended to favour a monarchic state, checked by parliament but strong enough to function as a kind of 'reserve constitution' for bourgeois society in times of emergency. As the French example demonstrates, they were also willing to come to terms with a republic. The liberals' fear that the republic would allow a socialist overthrow of bourgeois society abated during the course of the nineteenth century, but this was a fear that most of the liberals never lost entirely.

Like its state model, liberalism's social model was *bürgerlich* but not *bourgeois*. Liberalism's civil society would eliminate the barriers to development that existed in the old social order, but it would not replace them with the freedom of unrestricted competition. The broad social base of liberalism was opposed to any social models that completely overthrew tradition. In those cases where social reforms were imposed by the state bureaucracy, as in some of the German states at the beginning of the nineteenth century, in the Habsburg monarchy during the neo-absolutist phase after 1848 and in Russia during the 1860s, the disruptions were greater than in those cases where they were determined or influenced by the liberals working through parliament. Liberal development may have been extended by means of reform from above. However, in those cases where bureaucratic modernisation of society was not accompanied by a liberalisation of political participation, one should not speak of liberal reforms. The desire for the participation of civil society in every kind of reform clearly distinguished societal liberalism from 'governmental' liberalism that modernised without liberalising.

Liberal social models all favoured development and progress, but liberalism did not come into existence as an ideology of industrialisation or as a prophet of capitalist industrial class society. The social vision of early European liberalism was much more directed towards a middle-class society without great differences in the ownership of property, because such differences would conflict with liberalism's desire for social harmony. They would not have been incompatible with liberalism's project of a future civil society of equals. In those societies that had a predominantly agrarian structure, such as Hungary, Spain or Italy, the social models of the early liberals were centred around conceptions of a developing agrarian capitalism. Where trade and industry were highly developed or already dominant, as in Great Britain, Belgium, France or Germany, early liberalism contained within itself a plurality of social models. This included, but was never limited to, the capitalist industrial model.[39]

The early liberal vision of a 'classless civil society' (L. Gall) was, like all liberal models, a long-term reform programme quite capable of co-existing with the reality of a bourgeois class society. Until about the middle of the century, however, it would be wrong to describe this vision as an unrealistic ideology. It became unrealistic only during the industrialisation process of the second half of the century. By then this social model was no longer defended by the liberals. In altered form it had become part of the ideological arsenal of a number of illiberal movements, such as anti-semitism.[40] European liberalism distanced itself from its earlier conceptions of class harmony.

The decline in cooperative programmes, which began very early in France, was an indication of this. The dynamic of industrial development, which brought the era of pauperism in Europe to an end, encouraged the view among liberals that socio-political intervention was no longer necessary. It was now, for the first time, that laissez-faire economics and political liberalism came together making the latter more bourgeois in practice than it had ever been. Even at the high point of Manchester liberalism, however, the mainstream of European liberalism never completely gave up its integrative conceptions. In the era of an expanding franchise, to do so would have relegated the liberals to political irrelevance.

The fact that there was a renaissance of social-liberal models at the end of the nineteenth century was not, however, simply the result of electoral calculation. The 'new liberalism', an all-European phenomenon, was able to relate back to the social *engagement* of early liberalism in its attempt to secure the freedom of the individual through a policy of social welfare.[41] The impulse for the social renewal of liberalism came overwhelmingly from the educated classes, the traditional tribunes of liberalism. They prevented European liberalism from becoming a form of bourgeois liberalism pure and simple, as it attempted to relate its social conceptions to the conditions of industrial capitalism.

Based on the present state of research, it is impossible to make even a hypothetical assessment as to whether European liberalism, in addition to the political and social conceptions that have been outlined, also developed any definite norms of cultural behaviour. *Bürgerlichkeit* as a 'specific type of life-style'[42] existed before the age of *Bürgertum* and liberalism. The work ethic, sense of duty, economic independence, cultural development of the well-formed personality by means of extensive education and absorption of moral values experienced in the family – the nineteenth century inherited rather than created these 'middle-class virtues'. Liberal citizens cherished them not as liberals, but as citizens.

Liberals from south-west Germany like H.E.G. Paulus or Robert von Mohl give detailed descriptions in their autobiographies of how, in the parental home, they learned the virtues of simplicity, moderation, thrift, industriousness and the desire for education, virtues they maintained for the rest of their lives. Their self-esteem and consciousness of their superiority over social strata with a different cultural background were nourished by these virtues. They presented themselves as successful examples of a pedagogy developed in the Enlightenment.[43] But whether this specific lifestyle manifested itself among liberals in a way that would have distinguished them from their conservative fellow-*Bürger* is something we do not yet know.

The behavioural characteristics that Germans still associate with the word 'liberal' – generous and unprejudiced – do not appear to have been specific characteristics of political liberalism. In British, until the nineteenth century, usage of the word 'liberal' referred to the class attributes of a gentleman. Gradually it came to refer more and more to the educated middle class, whose possession of virtues that used to be limited to a specific rank was now seen as a 'product of intellectuality'.[44] How far such an adaptation of an aristocratic code of conduct was common in nineteenth century Europe cannot be determined.[45]

The bourgeois imitation of the aristocracy in Germany may have signified something quite different from what it did in other European states. In Germany, the influence of aristocratic lifestyle on bourgeois society seems to have been mediated through the state. It was for this reason that aristocratic culture in the Prussian-German national state took on a more military form than it did in the other European states.

The extent to which even representatives of a self-conscious liberal bourgeoisie in Germany could be convinced of the superiority and authority of this German state of civil servants and military officials, is indicated by the case of the industrial pioneer of electrical engineering, Werner Siemens: 'Although I have always gained a certain amount of satisfaction from the fact that I owe my position in life to my own work, nevertheless, I have always recognised with gratitude that my path was made easier for me by my acceptance into the Prussian army and thereby, into the state of the great Frederick.' At the beginning of his carer in the 1830s, Prussia had no large-scale industry, so 'there existed no well-off, educated middle class that could have acted as a counterweight to the military, the state officials and the aristocratic landowners. Under these circumstances, it meant a lot in Prussia to belong, as an officer, to court society and thereby to have access to all social circles'. It was as *bürgerlicher Offizier*, i.e. as a reserve officer, and not as a world-famous entrepreneur, that Siemens achieved what for a German *Bürger* was the crown of social repute: acceptance into court society.[46]

The extent to which liberal *Bürgerlichkeit* in Germany took on Prussian-militaristic features and how this compares with the wider European situation are matters we cannot properly assess at this time in view of the inadequacy of available research.

Notes to Chapter 2

1. With respect to general developments in the countries considered here, I will not give a general bibliography since any choices from such an extensive range of literature could only be arbitrary. For a discussion of *Bürgertum*, see in particular the contributions in J. Kocka (ed.), *Bürger und Bürgerlichkeit im 19. Jahrhundert* (Göttingen, 1987), especially M.R. Lepsius, 'Zur Soziologie des Bürgertums und der Bürgerlichkeit', pp. 79–100. I would not have ventured into this comparative European study had I not had the opportunity in February 1987 to organise an international symposium on 'Liberalism in the Nineteenth Century: Germany in a European Perspective', led by J.

Kocka. I am deeply indebted to all the participants in this seminar, even if they do not all agree with the conclusions that I have drawn from their findings. The contribution to this seminar as well as detailed biographies were published: D. Langewiesche (ed.), *Liberalismus im 19. Jahrhundert: Deutschland im europäischen Vergleich* (Göttingen, 1988). For a general survey of European liberalism, see L. Gall (ed.), *Liberalismus*. (Cologne, 1976). For source material, see in particular L. Gall and R. Koch (eds.), *Der Europäische Liberalismus im 19. Jahrhundert*, 4 vols., (Frankfurt, 1981). The interpretation of German liberalism found in this article is based on my book, *Liberalismus in Deutschland* (Frankfurt, 1988), (with sources and bibliography).

2. See the contribution of R. Muhs in Langewiesche, *Liberalismus*; also J.J. Sheehan, 'Some Reflections on Liberalism in Comparative Perspective', in H. Köhler (ed.), *Deutschland und der Westen* (Berlin, 1984), pp. 44–57; W.J. Mommsen, 'Preussen/Deutschland im frühen 19. Jahrhundert und Grossbritanien in der viktorianischen Epoche,' in A.M. Birke und K. Kluxen (eds.), *Viktorianisches England in deutscher Perspektive* (Munich, 1983), pp. 31–48; W.J. Mommsen, *Britain and Germany 1800–1914. Two Developmental Paths Towards Industrial Society* (London, 1986).

3. Cf. K.D. Wald, *Crosses on the Ballot. Patterns of British Voter Alignment since 1885* (Princeton, 1983).

4. For literature on the development of liberalism up to the Third Republic see the contribution by P. Aycoberry, H.G. Haupt, F. Lenger and R. Hudemann in Langewiesche, *Liberalismus*; for the most recent survey, see A. Jardin, *Histoire du libéralisme politique de la crise de l'absolutisme à la constitution de 1875* (Paris, 1985); L. Girard, *Les libéraux francais 1814–1875* (Paris, 1985).

5. According to G. Krumeich in Langewiesche, *Liberalismus*.

6. Cf. the contributions of A. Gergely and I Diószegi in Langewiesche, *Liberalismus*. They also provide a list of the most important literature about Hungary in Western European languages.

7. Cf. the contributions by M. Meriggi and H. Ullrich (also referring to the hidden regional variations) in Langewiesche, *Liberalismus*, which also contains bibliographies; also H. Ullrich, 'Bürgertum und nationale Bewegung im Italien des Risorgimento,' in O. Dann (ed.), *Nationalismus und sozialer Wandel* (Hamburg, 1978), pp. 129–156.

8. Surveys with bibliography in J.J. Sheehan, *German Liberalism in the Nineteenth Century* (Chicago, 1978) (up to the First World War); Langewiesche, *Liberalismus in Deutschland*. On the strong regional differences that existed before the establishment of the Reich, see the contributions by H.-H. Brandt, W. Kaschuba, K. Koch, H. Obenaus, T. Offermann and B. Vogel in Langewiesche, *Liberalismus*.

9. Cf. the contributions by R. v. Thadden, N. Hope and F. Eyck in W. Schieder, (ed.), *Liberalismus in der Gesellschaft des Vormärz* (Göttingen, 1983); also J. Stengers (on Belgium) and R. Muhs (on Britain) in Langewiesche, *Liberalismus*; see also the important work by H. Maier, *Revolution und Kirche* (Munich, 1959). In Holland, liberalism and the church were alienated from each other after the 1860s; see H. Daalder, 'Niederländische Liberale im 19. Jahrhundert – eine herrschende aber unorganisierte Minderheit', in H. van der Dunk and H. Lademacher, (eds.), *Auf dem Weg zum modernen Parteistaat. Zur Entstehung, Organisation und Struktur politischer Parteien in Deutschland und den Niederlanden* (Melsungen, 1986), pp. 37–58, 46ff.

10. This is the very appropriate formulation used by H. Rosenberg, *Grosse Depression und Bismarckzeit*, (Berlin, 1967), p. 123. This is one of the most interesting studies on the breakthrough to 'mass society'.

11. Cf. (with bibliography) D. Beyrau, in Langewiesche, *Liberalismus*.; for greater detail, see G. Schramm, (ed.), *Handbuch der Geschichte Russlands*, vol. 3, (Stuttgart, 1983).

12. Cf. (with bibliography) Langewiesche, *Liberalismus in Deutschland*, pp. 94ff. The Weber quotation that follows is on p. 169.

13. Although there are quite a number of comparative studies of the history of liberal

ideas, there are hardly any devoted to the aspect of its institutional effectiveness. In this respect, see M. Bentley, *The Climax of Liberal Politics. British Liberalism in Theory and Practice 1868–1918* (London, 1987); D. White, *The Splintered Party. National Liberalism in Hessen and the Reich 1867 to 1918* (Cambridge, Mass., 1976), pp. 199–221; H. Pogge v. Strandmann, 'Der nicht-so-merkwürdige Tod der liberalen Partei in England' in K. Rohe, (ed.), *Englischer Liberalismus im 19. und frühen 20. Jahrhundert* (Bochum, 1987), pp. 171–195, 187ff.

14. J.S. Shapiro, *Liberalism and the Challenge of Fascism. Social Forces in Britain and France (1815–1870)* (New York, 1964), quoted from the extract in Gall, *Liberalismus*, p. 27.

15. J. Vincent, *The Formation of the British Liberal Party 1857–1868* (Harmondsworth, 1972), pp. 41f. In addition to big businessmen, the author says there were 8.6 percent local businessmen, including professionals.

16. Cf. A. Gergely.in Langewiesche, *Liberalismus*.

17. Cf. J. Abellan in Langewiesche, *Liberalismus*.

18. Cf. the literature referred to in footnote 7.

19. The data that follow are from H. Best, *Die Männer von Bildung und Besitz. Struktur und Handeln parlamentarischer Führungsgruppen in Deutschland und Frankreich 1848/49* (Düsseldorf, 1990). For Germany, see the data in C. Dipper's contribution in Langewiesche, *Liberalismus*, also in Langewiesche, *Liberalismus in Deutschland*, pp. 49ff. The latter differentiates according to parliamentary groups, which Best does not do.

20. Cf. (with bibliography) M.L. Bush, *The British Aristocracy. A Comparative Synthesis* (Manchester, 1984); also contributions of Meriggi, Muhs and Dipper in Langewiesche, *Liberalismus*. An informative survey of the German nobility in the nineteenth century is to be found in H.-V. Wehler, *Deutsche Gesellschaftsgeschichte*, vol. 2, pp. 297ff.

21. For 1848, see H. Brandt, *Parlamentarismus im Württemberg 1819–1870*. (Düsseldorf, 1987), pp.67ff.; literature on the other German states is to be found in Muhs and in Langewiesche, *Liberalismus*.

22. For the most recent and penetrating survey, see Wehler, *Gesellschaftsgeschichte*, vol. 2, pp. 297ff.

23. Cf. D. Langewiesche, 'Bildungsbürgertum und Liberalismus im 19. Jahrhundert', in J. Kocka, (ed.), *Bildungsbürgertum im 19. Jahrhundert*, vol. 4, (Stuttgart, 1989) which contains further figures and bibliography. See also Langewiesche, *Liberalismus in Deutschland*.

24. Bentley, *Climax*, pp. 27ff. Economic bourgeoisie (*Wirtschaftsbürgertum*) includes local businessmen, which is why these figures are higher than those quoted before. A large amount of data is collected in H. Setzer, *Wahlsystem und Parteientwicklung in England* (Frankfurt, 1973).

25. H. Ullrich, in Langewiesche, *Liberalismus*.

26. Cf. Diószegi, in Langewiesche, *Liberalismus*.

27. Cf. Daalder, *Niederländische Liberale.*, pp. 43ff.

28. For Holland, see S.G. Taal, *Liberalen en Radicalen in Nederland 1872–1901* (Den Haag, 1980); for Italy and France, see Ullrich, Krumeich and Hudemann in Langewiesche, *Liberalismus*; for Germany, see Langewiesche, *Liberalismus in Deutschland*; for Great Britain, see Bentley, *Climax*; Wald, *Crosses*; D.W. Bebbington, *The Nonconformist Conscience. Chapel and Politics 1870–1914* (London, 1982).

29. Cf. (with bibliography) Ullrich, *Bürgertum*; Haupt, as well as Haupt/Lenger, in Langewiesche, *Liberalismus*; Langewiesche, *Liberalismus in Deutschland*, pp. 34ff., 113ff.

30. Cf. Diószegi.

31. Cf. Langewiesche, *Liberalismus in Deutschland*; for Great Britain, see J. Breuilly, 'Liberalismus oder Sozialdemokratie? Ein Vergleich der britischen und deutschen Arbeiterbewegung zwischen 1850 und 1875.', in J. Kocka, (ed.), *Europäische Arbeiterbewegungen im 19. Jahrhundert* (Göttingen, 1983), pp. 129–166.

32. For other important differences, see Breuilly, 'Liberalismus'; C. Eisenberg in this volume; G. Lottes, 'Der industrielle Aufbruch und die gesellschaftliche Integration der Arbeiterschaft in Deutschland und England im viktorianischen Zeitalter', in Birke/Kluxen, *Viktorianisches England*, pp. 61–78.

33. For Great Britain, see Pogge von Strandmann, *Der nicht-so-merkwürdige Tod* (with bibliography); on local liberalism in Germany, see Langewiesche, *Liberalismus in Deutschland*, pp. 202ff.; for post-war developments, see ibid., pp. 242ff.; M. Freeden, *Liberalism Divided* (Oxford, 1986).

34. This is also the case in the most recent general study: A. Arblaster, *The Rise and Decline of Western Liberalism* (Oxford, 1984). Good short surveys are also to be found in E.K. Bramsted and K.J. Melhuish (eds.), *Western Liberalism. A History of Documents from Locke to Croce* (London, 1978); Gall/Koch, *Der europäische Liberalismus*, vol. 1, pp.VIIff.

35. Shapiro, *Liberalism*, p. 30. The quotation from L.T. Hobhouse, *Liberalism* (London, 1911), p.46, is found in Shapiro on p. 20.

36. Cf. R. Vierhaus, 'Liberalismus', in Brunner *et al.* (eds.), *Geschichtliche Grundbegriffe*. vol. 3, (Stuttgart, 1982), pp. 741–785; H. Peterson, 'Liberal im britischen Englisch', in Rohe, *Englischer Liberalismus*, pp. 101–132.

37. Cf. the survey of Germany in U. Gerhard, *Verhältnisse und Verhinderungen. Frauenarbeit, Familie und Rechte der Frauen im 19. Jahrhundert* (Frankfurt, 1978); U. Vogel, 'Patriarchale Herrschaft, bürgerliches Recht, bürgerliche Utopie', in J. Kocka, *Bürgertum im 19. Jahrhundert*, vol. 1, pp. 406–438; U. Gerhard, 'Die Rechtstellung der Frau in der bürgerlichen Gesellschaft des 19. Jahrhunderts', ibid., pp. 39–468; U. Frevert, (ed.), *Bürgerinnen und Bürger. Geschlechterverhältnisse im 19. Jahrhundert* (Göttingen, 1988); D. Blasius, *Ehescheidung in Deutschland 1794–1945*, (Göttingen, 1987). The latter also has a bibliography on developments in Europe.

38. Cf. K. v. Beyme, *Die parlamentarischen Regierungssysteme in Europa* (Munich, 1973), pp. 431ff.

39. Of the studies in Langewiesche, *Liberalismus*; Italy: Meriggi; Hungary: Gergely; Spain: Abellán; Great Britain: Muhs; France: Haupt, Haupt/Lenger and Aycoberry; Belgium: Stengers (all of these studies are accompanied by bibliographies); cf. also D. Langewiesche, 'Gesellschafts- und verfassungspolitische Handlungsbedingungen und Zielvorstellungen europäischer Liberaler in der Revolution von 1848', in Gall, *Liberalismus*, pp. 162–186. On the position of the GDR, see S. Schmidt, 'Politik und Ideologie des bürgerlichen Liberalismus im Revolutionszyklus zwischen 1871 und 1917', *Zeitschrift für Geschichtswissenschaft* 31, (1983), pp. 24–37.

40. For Hungary, see Diószegi; for Germany, see S. Volkov, *The Rise of Popular Antimodernism in Germany* (Princeton, 1978); P. Kennedy and A. Nicholls, (eds.), *Nationalist and Racist Movements in Britain and Germany before 1914* (Oxford, 1981).

41. For Hungary, see Diószegi; for Italy, see Ullrich, 'Bürgertum'; for France, see Krumeich, also W. Logue, *From Philosophy to Sociology. The Evolution of French Liberalism 1870–1914* (DeKalb, 1983); for Great Britain, see M. Freeden, 'The New Liberalism Revisited', in Rohe, pp. 133–154; Bentley; a comparison of Britain and Germany in S.-G. Schnorr and K. Rohe, in Rohe, pp. 223–268, 269–293, see note 13; E. Feuchtwanger, 'The Liberal Decline in Germany and Britain. Peculiarity or Parallel?', *German History*, no. 4, 1987, pp. 3–15; for Germany, see G. Hubinger, in Langewiesche, *Liberalismus*; Langewiesche, *Liberalismus in Deutschland*; cf. also K. Holl, *et al.* (eds.), *Sozialer Liberalismus* (Göttingen, 1986).

42. Lepsius, 'Zur Soziologie des Bürgertums', p. 96; cf F.H. Tenbruck, 'Bürgerliche Kultur', *Kölner Zeitschrift für Soziologie und Sozialpsychologie*, Sonderheft no. 27, (1986), pp. 263–285; P. Münch, (ed.), *Ordnung, Fleiß und Sparsamkeit. Texte und Dokumente zur Entstehung der 'bürgerlichen Tugenden'* (Munich, 1984); L. Gall, '...Ich wünschte ein Bürger zu sein'. Zum Selbstverständnis des deutschen Bürgertums im 19. Jahrhundert' *Historische Zeitschrift* 245 (1987) pp. 601–623.

43. According to an unpublished M.A. thesis by U. Zimmermann, 'Verhaltensweisen südwestdeutscher Liberaler in der ersten Hälfte des 19. Jahrhunderts'.

44. Petersen, pp. 101ff., 128. For Germany, see U. Engelhardt, *Bildungsbürgertum. Begriffs- und Dokumentgeschichte eines Etiketts* (Stuttgart, 1986).

45. A very stimulating but perhaps exaggerated account of 'aristocratisation' is to be found in A.J. Mayer, *Adelsmacht und Bürgertum* (Munich, 1988); cf. H. Kaelble, *Das aristokratische Modell im deutschen Bürgertum des 19. Jahrhunderts. Ein europäischer Vergleich* Typescript (Bielefeld, 1987) ; J. Harris and P. Thane, 'British and European Bankers, 1880–1914: an 'aristocratic bourgeoisie'?', in P. Thane *et al.* (eds.), *The Power of the Past* (Cambridge, 1984), pp. 215–234; F.M.L. Thompson, 'British Landed Society in the 19th Century', *ibid.*, pp. 195–214.

46. W. v. Siemens, *Lebenserinnerungen,* 1893, (Munich, 1966), pp. 298ff.

3 | Nobility and Bourgeoisie in Nineteenth Century Europe: A Comparative View

Werner Mosse

The relations of nobility and bourgeoisie in different European countries, whilst following certain broad patterns, are determined largely by the distinctive characteristics of the two groups in each country. Whilst nature and role of the nobility are mainly the product of political factors, notably relations with the monarchy, the *haute bourgeoisie* (*Großbürgertum*) are above all the product of economic development. With regard to either group there is of course an interaction of political and economic factors.

Initial Theses

Before I turn to the major factors influencing the nature and development of the two groups in the four countries to be considered here, England, Prussia/Germany,[1] France and Russia, I would like to put forward some general propositions:

1. Both the nobility and the bourgeoisie in the nineteenth century were highly structured rather than monolithic groups.

2. The bulk of members of the two groups never met on either a social or a political plane to any significant extent.

3. A relatively small stratum of the *haute bourgeoisie* did meet - and interact with - elements of the nobility.

4. From this interaction there evolved during the course of the nineteenth century a composite elite in which, whilst the originally dominant aristocratic element declined in number and influence, the bourgeois component increased in importance.

5. This new elite, increasingly based on wealth, developed a distinctive culture made up of both aristocratic and bourgeois elements.

6. The values of the new elite found expression in and were trans-

Notes to Chapter 3 can be found on page 101.

mitted by distinctive educational institutions and processes of social-ization.

7. Accordingly, a distinction must be drawn between the (plutocrat-ic) new elite and the bulk of the bourgeoisie, the bourgeoisie proper.

8. Important elements of the nobility – lesser gentry, large parts of enobled officialdom, part of the *noblesse d'épée* and *declassé* – also remained outside the new elite which, was in general, restricted to those with substantial financial resources. Especially from the third quarter of the century, the number of nobles able to afford the entrance fee and subscriptions to 'the club' declined.

9. Equally excluded were the bulk of the bourgeoisie, that is, all those wholly committed, whether from necessity or choice, to eco-nomic pursuits; ideologically conscious bourgeois, drawn largely from entrepreneurial groups; members of religious and ethnic minorities; provincials; first generation parvenus, however wealthy; and all but the elite members of the professions.

10. Accordingly, three elements should be distinguished:

a. a composite elite (we focus on its bourgeoisie component in the present discussion),

b. a large part of the nobility outside it, and

c. the bulk of the bourgeoisie which was also excluded from the elite.

11. In parallel to the new composite elite there developed a politi-cal ruling class, closely related to though not identical with it.

12. With local and chronological variations this model holds good for the whole of Europe, though for reasons to be discussed, it was developed fully only in England, to a lesser extent in Prussia/Germany, and imperfectly – for different reasons – in France and Russia.

13. Though some convergence of aristocratic and bourgeois ele-ments in more or less plutocratic forms is to be observed in most countries, pace and extent differed widely according to economic development, political setting and the peculiarities of the formations involved.

14. Ideal-typically the process of convergence takes place in two distinct phases: The first involves the relatively smooth assimilation into the aristocracy of the urban patriciate of wealthy merchants and bankers. The second stage covers a slower, more problematic and imperfectly accomplished integration of major industrial entrepre-neurs and bourgeois civil servants.

15. The mechanisms of this process of convergence differed in different societies and political settings as, to some extent, did the nature of the 'end product'.

16. The concept of the 'feudalisation' of parts of the upper bourgeoisie is misleading. The 'opulent' life-style indulged in by elements of the *haute bourgeoisie*, allegedly copied from the aristocracy, is essentially plutocratic rather than aristocratic. The bulk of the nobility including the gentry, military nobility, and ennobled officialdom were too poor to afford such tastes. The typical way of life of the nobility was from necessity, of which a virtue was often made, frugal, indeed Spartan. Only a handful of wealthy property owners, in many cases owning and/or exploiting raw materials, developing urban property, or receiving ground-rents, could afford to live 'like princes'.

17. Similarly, the new plutocratic life-style, associated in England with 'the Edwardians', was beyond the reach of the bulk of the bourgeoisie.

18. What in fact passes under the name of 'feudalisation' is essentially the entry of a small group of the *haute bourgeoisie* through a combination of wealth and appropriate socialization into the composite (plutocratic) elite.

19. In the process, this group did, in fact, acquire certain characteristics that could be described as 'aristocratic', such as a tendency to invest in landed estates and to take up at least partial residence in the country. Nevertheless, the new composite elite was essentially urban in outlook.

The Political Setting

The political setting within which relations between aristocracy and bourgeoisie were played out, was determined largely by the relative strength of monarchy and aristocracy. In this respect, the situation differed significantly between the different countries.

England

Here the decisive fact is that in the fifteenth century during the Wars of the Roses, the old feudal nobility (a *noblesse d'épée*) largely exterminated itself. The New Monarchy of the Tudors created a new nobility – largely from commoners endowed with monastic land or lands confiscated from rebellious nobility. The feudal tradition associated with the Crusades and the Hundred Years' War disappeared.

In the seventeenth century the House of Commons representing the lesser nobility (*gentry*) and commercial interests mounted a challenge to monarchical authority. Following the Civil War, Charles I was executed and England became a republic under military rule. With the restoration of the monarchy a new conflict developed between the later Stuart kings – would-be absolutists, Roman Catholic and pro-French – and a number of protestant, parliamentary and anti-French nobles (and elements of the economic bourgeoisie). Finally, after the 'Glorious Revolution' of 1688 England departed from the model of continental monarchy.

During the eighteenth century a small group of Whig magnates, the so-called 'Venetian Oligarchy', shared power with a weak – and weakening – monarchy. The beginning of the nineteenth century saw virtually unchallenged aristocratic rule. Then, under Queen Victoria and Prince Albert, the monarchy, already thoroughly civilian – in contrast to the militarised continental dynasties – underwent a process of *embourgeoisement*. It is against the background of these unique circumstances, that the relations between aristocracy and *haute bourgeoisie* in England in the nineteenth century evolved.

Russia

In the later sixteenth century the old boyar aristocracy was virtually exterminated by Ivan IV, a process reminiscent of what happened in England during the Wars of the Roses. In 1613 Russia acquired a new dynasty, the Romanovs. The Autocracy was strengthened, whilst residual boyar influence went into further decline. The lesser nobility in military service acquired a growing importance.

Peter the Great recast the Russian nobility by amalgamating the new service nobility with remnants of the old aristocracy and by 'bureaucratizing' them by means of the Table of Ranks. Social position henceforth depended on rank attained in the service hierarchy, whether civil, military or at court.

Weak rulers following Peter promoted the emergence as a political force of a new *noblesse d'épée* based on the elite Guards Regiments. However, following the challenge to the authority of the autocratic ruler by Guards officers – the Decembrists – in 1825, the *noblesse d'épée* was eliminated as a political force by Nicholas I. From this moment, Russia like England lacked an influential military nobility. Unlike England however, Russia had a powerful autocratic monarchy and a bureaucratized nobility subservient to monarchy and state.

France

The French nobility was weakened but not exterminated by the Wars of Religion in the sixteenth century. In the seventeenth it was 'tamed' on behalf of the monarchy by Richelieu – an operation completed by Mazarin and Louis XIV. Thereafter, the French aristocracy divided into three groups: the old *noblesse d'épée* (nobility of the sword) became a court-aristocracy dependent on the monarchy; a lesser nobility, the civilian, legalist *noblesse de robe* (office-holding nobility); and the increasingly important *noblesse des hautes fonctions publiques* (holders of high public office). The revolution of 1789 resulted in:

1. the execution of King and Queen. As in England the Restoration was both weak and temporary. The second 'restoration' of 1830 installed a middle-class monarchy comparable to that in Britain;
2. the flight and partial elimination of the *noblesse d'épée*, which progressively lost influence under the Restoration and the July Monarchy;
3. abolition of noble privileges and extensive redistribution of landed property (partly in favour of the new Napoleonic nobility);
4. abolition of the *noblesse de robe*, replaced by a bureaucratic magistrature.

Post-revolutionary France thus had a weak monarchy – after 1830 of doubtful legitimacy. The nobility was weak and internally divided into factions of Legitimists, Bonapartists, and Orleanists. The bureaucracy, which replaced both the *noblesse de robe* and the *noblesse des hautes fonctions publiques*, acquired growing influence in the form of the *fonctionnaires*.

Prussia/Germany

In Prussia/Germany "nothing happened". At no point did the nobility of the sword clash with the holders of power – at least until July 1944. No monarch was expelled or executed. Two attempts – belated by 'Western' standards – to limit monarchical power failed dismally in 1848/9 and 1861–4. In consequence, Prussia/Germany – uniquely – was left with both a strong monarchy and an unimpaired military nobility. In this militarized monarchy, the King (or Emperor), who stood at the head of the military nobility, was also the supreme warlord.

To the two traditional forces of monarchy and nobility of the sword, the eighteenth century added a strong bureaucracy,[2] dominated by the nobility but ready to absorb bourgeois elements and tending towards self-perpetuation. Monarchy, *Schwertadel* and the (civilian) bureaucracy were to become the three pillars of the Prussian state and later also the German Empire. In comparison with England, France, and Russia, the Prussian-German situation differed in crucial respects:

1. there was no civil war after the Thirty Years War;
2. consistent failure of *any* political opposition;
3. no trial and execution of the monarch;
4. a militarised and bureaucratised nobility devoid of corporate organisation and without aspirations to share political power;
5. the fatal 'Obrigkeitsfrömmigkeit' (pious obedience) of the Lutheran church and clergy;
6. lack of militant religious dissidence (like the English Independents, Dutch Calvinists etc.). Instead, as of 1555, the unchallenged principle of *'cuius regio, eius religio'*.

Monarchical institutions enjoyed political ascendancy and a military base only in Russia and Prussia. They were comparatively weak in England, with a balance of power between King (Queen), Lords and Commons. In France, after the Revolution (and especially after 1830), they were weaker still and eventually disappeared.

The position of the nobility in each country considered here had elements both of strength and weakness:

1. In Russia and Prussia it was confronted with and subordinate to a powerful monarchy, under which it played a dominant role in the army and administration (particularly in Prussia/Germany, to a lesser extent in Russia).
2. In England and France by contrast, it benefitted from the relative weakness of monarchical institutions.
3. In England, it had the unique advantage of a 'representative' system tailored to its needs.
4. The attitude of the different monarchies to the admission of non-nobles to senior administrative functions varied substantially in different countries at different times. In general, the steady expansion of military and administrative establishments and the rising demand for 'middle-class' skills – combined with the growing shortage of qualified aristocratic candidates – increasingly necessitated the admission of non-nobles to high military and administrative office. Thus, despite periods of 'aristocratic reaction', the numerical weight of the

nobility in the highest ranks of civil administration progressively declined. A similar trend, if less marked, is to be observed also in senior military positions (except in the elite Guards regiments). The 'technical' arms, on the other hand, artillery, engineering and com-missariat – requiring some mathematical or accounting skills and with low social prestige – had never attracted members of the 'generalist' nobility and soon came to be dominated by commoners.

Thus the political framework into which a rising bourgeoisie had to fit – shaped essentially by monarchy and the nobility (the role of the clergy was less important) – differed significantly in the countries under consideration. Its nature decisively shaped the relations of bour-geoisie and nobility.

Economic Development

Another set of factors influencing the relationship was the chronolo-gy, nature, and extent of economic development. It was this which helped to determine the strength, role, and prestige of important seg-ments of the bourgeoisie. Two major factors influenced economic development in Europe and with it the economic position of both those parts of the nobility which were active in the proto-capitalist sector and of the bourgeoisie (principally the *haute bourgeoisie*):

1. Geographic location. Early capital accumulation was largely a function of overseas (colonial) trade and navigation (in a more limited way, also of long-distance overland and river trade). In this respect, there existed in Europe a West-East gradient from the Atlantic seaboard to the Urals and the Pacific. By the end of the sixteenth cen-tury at the latest, both the Mediterranean and the Baltic had lost much of their earlier commercial importance. Portugal, Spain, England, France, and the Netherlands were well placed geographical-ly, Germany less so (with the Hanseatic League a mere 'flash in the pan'), whilst Russia was to remain cut off from the major arteries of world trade.

2. Geography however, intersects with another factor: as already noted by Montesquieu, successful commercial activity is often (if nei-ther always nor exclusively) the province of religious and ethnic minorities. Independently of this, as is well known, affinities have been noted between the Calvinist (and, to some extent, Jewish) reli-gious ethic and economic motivation and success. Conversely, Roman Catholicism and perhaps to a lesser extent also Lutheranism, Anglicanism, and the Russian Orthdox Church, have been associated

with a rejection of the ethic of economic performance. The existence of commercially-oriented minority groups, a measure of religious tolerance, a ready acceptance of persecuted refugees all helped to promote early commercial development (England, the Netherlands) whereas religious persecution tended to retard it (Spain, Portugal, France). Prussia/Germany occupied an intermediate position with its utilitarian policy of religious tolerance.

If one takes the two major criteria, the geographical and religio-ethnic, then England and the Netherlands, with high scores on both counts, were clearly best placed for commercial (and capitalist) development. Well placed geographically, Spain, Portugal, and France (the Catholic countries) largely nullified their geographical advantage by religious bigotry. Prussia/Germany compensated for its relative geographical disadvantage by the encouragement of economic activity by minorities, refugees and individuals from commercially and industrially more advanced countries. Russia on the other hand, aggravated a 'hopeless' geographic position by extremes of intolerance (despite the somewhat mercantilist attitudes of rulers such as Peter I and Catherine II).

It is in the light of these considerations – the degree of urbanisation, the development of craft-traditions, and the extent of mercantilist state intervention all played a secondary role – that the comparative development of the bourgeoisie and (to a lesser extent) the nobility and the evolution of the relations between them must be seen. The impact of economic factors on the nobility will be considered first.

England

Some individual members of the new (Tudor) nobility displayed commercial initiative in wool production, land reclamation, overseas colonisation and maritime ventures in the late sixteenth and seventeenth centuries. By the eighteenth century important elements of the nobility had embarked on capitalist enterprise. The 'agricultural revolution' of the eighteenth century brought with it large-scale capital investment for purposes of amelioration. Typically, the wealthy magnate leased his land to tenant farmers operating on a substantial scale, reinvesting part of the rent in 'improvements', road- and canal-building, or the exploitation of natural resources found on the estate(s). With early urbanisation, property-development was added in a number of cases. Overall, by the beginning of the nineteenth century, a significant section of the English nobility (especially the wealthier part) was engaged in some form of capitalist enterprise.

France

By contrast, the French nobility left early commercial experiments largely to the mercantilist state. As it emerged from the Wars of Religion and the purges of Richelieu and Louis XIV, the traditional nobility remained a *noblesse d'épée*. Predominantly Catholic, it largely disdained economic activity. A limited *noblesse d'affairs* was to emerge only in the July Monarchy and under the Second Empire. Of the *noblesse de robe* and the *noblesse des hautes fonctions publiques*, the former, concerned primarily with legal matters had, by definition, little involvement in commercial or entrepreneurial activity. The latter on the other hand, notably in the age of mercantilism and again under the Second Empire, activley encouraged (*bourgeois*) economic development, though not participating directly in entrepreneurial activity. Not till mid-century, under the impact of Saint-Simonian ideas, did 'entrepreneurial' nobles emerge. Nor were their activities representative. By and large, the French nobility (interested mainly in military and ecclesiastical careers) remained essentially non-commercial.

Prussia/Germany

The Prussian nobility, in keeping with the sluggishness of German economic development, confined its commercial activities largely to the production of grain, sugar, spirits, and bricks (largely for export). This was in the main primary production (even if directed towards a market), involving relatively little capital investment and little mobile capital. It thus differed in character from the commercial interests of members of the British aristocracy.

When in 1859 the Prussian state abandoned the 'Direktionsprinzip' (exclusive rights of management) in its mining activities, some magnates, notably in Silesia, branched out into coal production with some later diversification (with varying success) into wider commercial activities. The Silesian nobility was also engaged in the food processing industry, particularly in sugar refining. Indeed Silesian landowners have been described as 'industrialised aristocrats' ('industrialisierter Großadel'), but they were to remain a somewhat exceptional group. The bulk of the German nobility continued to look towards military or administrative, rather than commercial careers.

Russia

Since the days of Peter the Great the Russian *dvorianstvo* had been defined as a bureaucratic ('state service') nobility. As such, it had had imposed upon it a rigid hierarchical structure. In the tradition of "public service', it had evolved a system based largely on seniority and routine with an almost total lack of initiative. The desire to avoid responsibility and risk-taking was overwhelming. The low productivity of serf labour, which was not abolished until 1861, impeded economic development even if it did not wholly preclude commercial activities like those of Stroganov and Demidov.

When largely state-sponsored economic development began after the Crimean War, its main protagonists were to be foreigners (i.e. Westerners), naturalized Germans, and members of minority groups, notably Old Believers and Jews. Entrepreneurs were even recruited from among the ranks of the ex-serfs or peasants, as depicted in Checkov's 'Cherry Orchard' or Gorky's 'The Artamonov Business'. In any case, effective economic development was delayed until the last quarter of the century. The *dvorianstvo*, devoid of economic motivation and experience and drawn relentlessly into state service, was never to become a commercially oriented group, though a few of its members started sugar-refineries, distilleries, or glass-works on their estates or traded in timber.

Social Differences

So much for the major differences in the economic position of the nobility in the various countries, necessarily at the level of gross simplification. Certain other social peculiarities of the aristocracy were also of some importance.

England

The British nobility was distinguished from those of other countries by two important characteristics: first, by the strict application of the principle of *primogeniture*. Only the oldest son (or nearest male relative) inherited title and estate. The remaining offspring became commoners (even if for a generation children of the highest nobility might enjoy 'courtesy titles'). The effect of this, was that all offspring of nobility except eldest sons could, without derogation, marry commoners. It was thus entirely possible for sons or brothers of peers to intermarry with the children of the wealthy bourgeoisie. There thus came into existence an extensive network of kinship relations between the nobility and select families of commoners. The descent of all sons except one into the ranks of the 'commons' was one factor preventing the British nobility from becoming a closed caste.

The other distinctive feature was that the lowest effective title of nobility (disregarding the archaic designation of 'gentleman' and 'esquire'), that of 'knight', was non-hereditary. Thus children of knights also reverted to the rank of commoner and readily intermarried with the offspring particularly of untitled landowners. In consequence, considerable elements of the British nobility continuously descended into the untitled and non-noble landed class, the gentry. At the level of the gentry, the line between noble and common landowner was fluid. At the same time, merchants, judges and professional men could enter the gentry class by buying land. By participating in the activities of local landowners, they (or more likely their children) could secure election to Parliament and, in due course, be ennobled. In this way, the lower grades of nobility in particular were open not only to untitled gentry but also to descendants of merchants and eventually also industrialists 'on the make'.

Prussia/Germany

The German nobility was distinguished by marked regional differences.[3] Among the aristocratic families of the South and West the leading dynasties either belonged to the governing nobility of the 'Reichsstände' (Estates of the Empire) or, particularly in the Swabian and Franconian regions and the provinces of the Rhein, were members of the 'Reichsritterschaft' (Knights of the Empire). Another important asset was 'Stiftsfähigkeit', i.e. hereditary participation in the administration of dioceses, monasteries or orders of Knighthood, all of which were potential sources of considerable wealth. In the 'colonial' provinces of the German East, the heartland of the Prussian state, small 'reichsunmittelbare' territories (territories immediately subordinate to the German Emperor) did not exist. 'Stiftsfähigkeit', which was so important in the South-West, also played no significant role here.

Another basic difference between South-Western and Eastern nobility was, that whereas the former tended to limit the size of their families, the latter failed to do so almost completely. The result in the East was the emergence of an impoverished nobility, indeed a 'noble proleteriat'. The shortage of property among the large population of lesser Prussian *Landadel* (the estate of lesser landed nobility) meant that unlike the English or French nobilities only a small minority of Prussian nobility enjoyed a secure economic base. They could not therefore face the monarch as an independent, self-confident estate and were forced to look to the crown for places as officers and officials, which alone enabled them to maintain a noble way of life and avoid a descent into the peasantry.

In general, the structure of the Prussian/German nobility can be seen as the reverse of the British:

1. Though primogeniture with regard to landed estates was widespread, all sons inherited the title. This created a surplus of landless nobility with noble pretensions largely absorbed into the army and, to some extent, the administration. They claimed, and were usually granted, preference in state-employment.

2. Unlike the British nobility, the distinction between noble and commoner was sharply drawn even at the level of the gentry. Such pretensions to aristocratic exclusivity, though not unknown, were far less common in England.

3. Marriage with commoners, though just acceptable with families of non-noble (or recently ennobled) senior officials or officers, was regarded with disfavour and might terminate the career of an aristocratic officer, depending on the status of the wife. Marriage to wealthy non-noble heiresses for economic reasons, though frowned on, was sometimes condoned, except in the case of military officers marrying into Jewish families.

In short, the lines between noble and non-noble were more strictly drawn and more persistent than they were in England.

France

The French nobility resembled the German, in that all legitimate male children inherited the title. However, unlike England and Germany where in the course of the nineteenth century non-nobles acquired property through the land market in a gradual process, easing the acceptance of rich non-noble property owners into rural aristocratic society, the French revolution brought with it the sudden and violent expropriation of many noble estates (only limited quantities of land were returned under Napoleon and the Restoration monarchy). In the post-revolutionary phase parts of the old aristocracy merged with wealthy *parvenu* commoners who had acquired church or aristocratic property during the Revolution. Both groups combined to form the *grands notables* a socially mixed formation of wealthy property owners, supplementing their incomes from ground rent with interest on government loans. The *grands notables* who were usually the largest taxpayers in their locality were in fact predominantly town-dwellers. Their children attended the *grandes écoles* and pursued careers in the military or diplomatic services, or being devout Catholics, entered the hierarchy of the Church.[4] Political differences within this group did not prevent the formation of strong social ties.[5] Accordingly, members of old landowning aristocratic families were absorbed by a new, predominantly landowning elite of notables. As a group the *grands notables* remained a force in French politics into the days of the Third Republic. Their final decline is conventionally dated to the year 1873.

While the geographic base of the notables was basically in the periphery, many Parisian aristocratic families withdrew to the seclusion of the Faubourg St. Germain. Increasingly after the July-Revolution, Parisian society and politics left less and less room for members of the aristocracy, with the exception of the very rich. As the Austrian Ambassador in Paris lamented around the mid-century, the wealthy were in the process of taking the place in public influence and esteem of those who were merely 'well-born'. 'In other countries where everything has not yet been levelled by sixty years of revolution, as it has here in France, there are still, thank God, seperate classes, but here money is everything, and in the sentiments of the nation, the Rothschilds and the Foulds have the precedence of the Montmorencys and the Rohans.'[6]

Thus in France, unlike in England or Prussia, the nobility – and particularly the older aristocratic families – had ceased to be an important social and political force by the middle of the century. The rivalry between Legitimists, Bonapartists and Orleanists, compounded by the strict division between the survivors of the *ancien régime* and the more recent creations of Napoleon and Louis-Philippe helped to further weaken aristocratic influence. In the aftermath of the Revolution the old nobility of the sword and public office (unlike that of England and Prussia) was swamped by a wave of non-noble groups, made up both of new landowners and the newly ennobled. Consequently the nobility lost most of its cohesion, its self-confidence and its influence.

Russia

The Russian nobility – especially since the time of Peter the Great – had a hybrid and amorphous character. It consisted in fact of at least three distinct elements:

1. the *znat*, an elite group of families, normally titled and claiming more or less authentic descent from Riurik or Gedimin. These were in fact descendants of former territorial princes, including a good

sprinkling of Tartars. Usually, they were landed families with ready access to the Imperial court. Which families were included in the *znat*, was a matter to be decided by noble opinion. By no means all titled families were included.

2. a provincial landed gentry, normally without titles, consisting of families entered on the provincial registers of nobility.

3. a proliferating and widely detested bureaucratic nobility, typically of recent lineage, landless and untitled.

4. the 'beggar gentry' (*szlachta*) poor, uncouth (as depicted by Gogol), uncultured, and in many cases almost indistinguishable from the peasantry.

The *dvorianstvo*, which in many important respects resembled the Prussian nobility, was in fact heterogeneous, devoid of corporate identity and incoherent as a social group. The divisions between aristocrats, gentry and bureaucrats were aggravated by the age old rivalry between St. Petersburg, capital of the bureaucrats (*chinovniks*) and Moscow, capital of the gentry. Though constant recruitment of members of other groups took place through the Table of Ranks, the *dvorianstvo* was typically anti-capitalist and disinclined to accept new bourgeois elements. However, in the last decade of the nineteenth century, there was a degree of rapprochement, in opposition to the bureaucracy, between some Moscow aristocrats, factory owners and members of the professions. This purely political alliance unmatched by closer social ties was to develop further during the Duma-period.

In so far as contacts between nobility and the *haute bourgeoisie* were concerned, these were easiest in England due to the peculiar characteristics of the English nobility: the commercial values adopted by many of its members, the common bond created by landownership, the absence of a centralised bureaucracy until the later nineteenth century, the 'localisation' of government, and common socialisation in the universities of Oxford and Cambridge.

Such contacts were more difficult in Germany since the Prussian nobility preserved a stronger caste-spirit than the English. The Prussian nobility was generally poor, militaristic, bureaucratic and, for all these reasons – again unlike the English – basically anti-capitalist. However from necessity, it had come to accept the bourgeois educational values embodied in the *Gymnasium* and shared common membership in the student *Korps*. In any event, the officer corps and bureaucracy alike, increasingly needed replenishing with carefully selected bourgeois elements.

In France and Russia, for opposite reasons, contacts between nobility and the *haute bourgeoisie* were relatively rare, one of the partners being deficient in each case. In France, at least from 1830 onwards, the nobility – isolated in little pockets, whether in 'the Faubourg' or in the Provinces – was missing as an element in public life. The non-noble *fonctionnaire* and the provincial lawyers ruled supreme.

In Russia, on the other hand, it was the commercial bourgeoisie that was under-developed. Nobility and commoners came together in the heterogenous formation of the *raznochintsy*[7] in which *déclassé* off-spring of the nobility (like Michael Bakunin, Peter Kropotkin, Alexander Herzen or Sophia Perovskaya) mixed with the children of the orthodox clergy (Chernyshevsky, Dobroliubov, but also Pobedonostsev), petty bourgeoisie (meshchanstvo), lesser officialdom, and the poorer gentry (Plekhanov) etc. In fact, the main point of contact was in the radical intelligentsia. When, late in the century, a commercial bourgeoisie did emerge from the peasantry and ethnic and religious minority groups, it was scorned by a large section of the nobility – by then head over heels in debt. The Russian commercial class, more so than that of the other countries under comparison, was subject to bitter attack from two directions: the radical intelligentsia on the left, the conservative gentry from the right. There was little overall convergence, other than in the special conditions of Moscow already mentioned and even there it was confined to a purely political level.

Overall, these various preconditions determined the development of relations between nobility and bourgeoisie in the different countries we have discussed. Whilst the basic pattern outlined in the initial theses is visible everywhere (though in France and Russia only as an incipient trend), the details vary. The process of convergence, complete only in England and to a lesser extent in Prussia/Germany, is observable in France and Russia only in embryonic form. Initially, we will approach convergence at the political level.

Details of Convergence between Nobility and the Bourgeoisie

There was a general trend towards the dilution of a predominantly aristocratic ruling class through the progressive entry of non-noble, i.e., almost by definition, bourgeois elements. In this process certain stages can be distinguished. With due caution, it is possible to suggest some correlation with the 'long secular waves' of the 'Kondratiev

cycle'. The restoration period was broadly one of noble preponderance. During the 'liberal' mid-century there was an increasing influx
of non-aristocratic elements into the European political class. The age
of the 'Great Depression' coincided, generally speaking, with a noble
reaction. From the end of the century, bourgeois elements gained the
ascendancy and the trend towards the formation of the new 'composite' ruling class acclerated. Within these general parameters, developments in the different countries show considerable variations.

England

The salient feature in the English case was, that as a result of political
developments in the seventeenth century the aristocracy acquired
political domination. At the same time, as a result of rapid economic
development, many of its members became imbued with a capitalist
spirit.[8] By the mid-eighteenth century, England had become 'a monetary and market economy on a national scale'.[9] In particular, the distinctive agricultural system was already thoroughly capitalistic.
Landownership was essentially concentrated in the hands of a limited
class of very large aristocratic landlords. They leased their land to tenant farmers who hired farm-labourers, servants and smallholders. This
pool of agricultural workers was to become increasingly dependent
on its income from wage labour. Foreign visitors to the country were
struck by the essentially 'bourgeois' and commercial nature of English
society.[10] The ruling class consisted of an oligarchy of landed aristocrats, headed by a tight self-perpetuating peerage of some 200 Lords,
'a system of powerful rich cousinages under the aegis of the ducal
heads of the great Whig families...'[11] Being themselves 'commercially-minded', members of the ruling aristocracy were ready to ally
themselves with – indeed absorb – wealthy and talented representatives of commerce (or their immediate offspring) and even to choose
them as their political leaders. Indeed, the political history of England
could almost be written in terms of the history of the upwardly
mobile descendants of trade and industry, as the history of the Pitts,
Peels, Gladstones, Asquiths, to whose number might be added
Disraeli, offspring of the commercialised intelligentsia.

In the case of the Pitts, a son of provincial clergy had acquired a
fortune overseas in the seventeenth century. He had bought an estate
and so layed the foundation for political activity in the House of
Commons. His son developed aristocratic connections. The grand-
sons made aristocratic friends at Oxford and married into the

Lyttelton and Grenville families, at the heart of the Whig oligarchy. Grandson and great grandson of the original Diamond Pitt were to hold the office of prime minister for almost half a century (with some interruptions). The wealthy Whig oligarchy relatively willingly conceded political leadership to these bourgeois careerists of comparatively modest means. It is perhaps significant that whilst William Pitt the elder was to become the Earl of Chatham, his second son and successor as prime minister was simply William Pitt.

Even more characteristic is the case of the Peels, a farming family from Lancashire, who in the course of the eighteenth century acquired a considerable fortune in the textile industry. Robert Peel the elder (1750–1830) had purchased an estate and a seat in the House of Commons in the late eighteenth century. He had received a hereditary title through the favour of Pitt the Younger. On his death in 1830 he left the enormous fortune of one and a half million pounds. His oldest son received an elite education in Harrow and Oxford and crowned a political career with the office of prime minister which he held in 1834/5 and from 1841 to 1846. What is significant about the career of the Peels, is the ready acceptance by parts of the political elite of the combination of talent and wealth as a qualification for leadership. It is also remarkable to what extent wealth had already become a passport to a polticial career. Aristocratic connections were no longer a necessity. In fact, the second Sir Robert Peel married the daughter of an ennobled officer of the Indian Army.

Finally, let us mention the rise of the Gladstones, a family of scottish bailiffs who moved into the corn trade and proceeded to make a large fortune in the thriving port of Liverpool, trading with the colonies (presumably also in slaves). John Gladstone, MP from 1816–27, was elevated to the hereditary peerage with the help of Peel and left a legacy of 600,000 pounds sterling on his death in 1851. His fifth son, naturally educated in Eton and Oxford, was the famous prime minister. He married into the landed gentry, by a curious coincidence into the family circle of the younger Pitt.

For the Pitts, Peels and Gladstones the path lead from the acquisition of a fortune and estates, via public affairs and the hereditary peerage, to a great political career. Initially this pattern stretched over three generations, but it was to become shorter and shorter until in the second half of the nineteenth century self-made men like Richard Cobden, John Bright, William Forster and Herbert Asquith could rise to an important position in public life and even to the highest offices of state.

In fact, however much landowners and aristocracy dominated the political scene in eighteenth and nineteenth century England, they consistently allowed scope for men from commercial and industrial backgrounds to rise to positions of real power. Consequently, the British ruling class was composed in varying and unequal proportions or representatives of a traditional landed nobility and bourgeois careerists.

France

In France, the ascent of bourgeois elements into the ruling class came not, as in England, through the absorption of suitably qualified individuals into the old nobility, but, instead, through the intermediation of the pre-revolutionary *noblesse de robe*. Under the French system, men of sufficient wealth could, by purchase of appropriate offices, buy their way into the *robe*.

At the same time, in the course of the eighteenth century, a steady convergence occured between the two main branches of the aristocracy. Members of the *robe* not only bought estates, but their children, in many instances, entered alliances of marriage with the *noblesse d'épée*. Whilst some members of the military nobility adopted *bourgeois* attitudes, members of the *robe*, in turn assimilated elements of an aristocratic life-style e.g. duelling, hunting, use of the prefix *de*. The same is true for the third branch of the French nobility the *noblesse des hautes fonctions publiques*. However, at the same time, they retained characteristics that could be described as *bourgeois*: a concentrated work-ethic, sobriety of dress and an insistence on certain educational qualifications.[12] Nearly all the chief civilian officials, an employment largely scorned by the *noblesse d'épée*, were drawn from the two civilian branches of the nobility and these offices became the avenue of access to political influence for members of the bourgeoisie who could either afford the high entrance fee involved in the purchase of office or were able to attract favourable royal attention. By this route, wealth or talent could be converted into political influence. The bourgeois could become – almost – a gentleman. Even under the *ancien régime*, the *robe* and the *noblesse des hautes fonctions* were turning into groups with charcteristics of both the bourgeoisie and the nobility, forming a bridge between the two, relatively open at both ends.

The Revolution, whilst drastically reducing the influence of the *épée*, which under the July Monarchy effectively withdrew from French political life, and abolishing the *robe*, paved the way for the ascendancy of the *fonctionnaire*. The nascent entrepreneurial class, which began to flourish after 1830, disdained both low-paid state employment and political activity and was glad for both these activities to be left to others. Whilst administrative office fell to the *fonctionnaire*, political influence became largely the preserve of the *grands notables*.

Post-revolutionary French politics lacked the aristocratic stamp that shaped English affairs. The French chambers largely lacked the prestige, and hence the appeal for the offspring of the commercial bourgeoisie, of the English Houses of Parliament. So did the political prizes on offer in the kaleidescopic politics of nineteenth century France. Bureaucratic careers by contrast, which in France held out at least the prospect of attractive dowries, held little attraction in anti-bureaucratic England.

In conclusion, in France, more particularly after the July Revolution, relations between bourgeoisie and aristocracy were minimal. Whilst the *patronat* largely disdained participation in public affairs, which was certainly not true for the legal profession, large sections of the nobility had also effectively withdrawn from public life. Competition for political influence – about which we still know relatively little – must therefore have been between the *fonctionnaire*, the provincial lawyers (particularly the *maire-députés*), *normaliens* (graduates of the *école normale*) and the engineer-technocrats – all of them arguably parts of the non-commercial *bourgeoisie*. France, therefore, earlier and more completely then England, became the fief of the *bourgeois conquérant*.

Russia

In spite of the very different general setting, the Russian situation bears some resemblance to that in France. Just as the French *noblesse d'épée* lost its public function between 1790 and 1830, so its Russian counterpart, which had played a major role in the eighteenth century, saw its power as a homogenous estate destroyed after the abortive rising of 1825. Only individual aristocratic families remained, devoid of political influence, together with a debt-burdened and equally powerless landed gentry. After 1825 – if not before – it was Peter the Great's Table of Ranks which determined relations between the bureaucratised service nobility and the other strata of the population. As a rough generalization, until the mid-century the highest grades of the bureaucratic ladder were filled largely (though not exclusively) by members of the landowning nobility. Thereafter, with the advance of officials originating in other classes of society and with a growing tendency to self-recruitment the share of the landed nobility in senior administrative positions, both civil and military, declined. The Russian nobility tended to become 'classless', recruited from the *raznochintsy*, fusing both nobles and commoners at the highest levels into a partly hereditary service nobility.

The economic bourgeoisie, on the other hand, in keeping with Russia's general economic backwardness, developed only slowly during the second half of the nineteenth century. It was numerically small, weakened by being composed largely of members of unpopular minority groups, and too dependent on state support to play an effective part in public affairs before the beginning of the twentieth century when some of its members began to join in a wider movement of the Russian public (comparable to events in other parts of Europe in 1848). Under the pseudo-constitutional Duma-regime its representatives would make themselves felt both in the Progressive Party and the 'Union of the 17th October'. The more significant role played by the professions (lawyers, doctors, teachers, engineers and statisticians) and their cooperation, in the Cadet Party, with a liberal segment of the aristocracy and gentry, cannot be considered here. In the distinctive Russian setting, parts of the educated public, intellectuals, bourgeois and some noble landowners coalesced to form the so-called *obshchestvo*, a coalition directed principally against the bureaucracy and somewhat less overtly, against the autocracy itself.

On the other hand, for a number of reasons the tsarist regime drew its ministers, especially those of finance, education, justice and sometimes communications, the navy and war, in short the technical ministries, from among specialists, who were often university professors or engineers. These could be sons of priests, of officials of various ranks, of landless nobility or occasionally even merchants. Men of different 'non-feudal' backgrounds could thus attain to high ministerial office in Russia (though not acceptance in, let alone marraige into, St. Petersburg society). Political influence and social prestige in Russia, unlike in England, were entirely distinct. As in France, it was virtually impossible to enter the aristocracy which, in any case, enjoyed comparatively little prestige. Accordingly, association with the nobility was not an obvious object of ambition. Arguably the highest reaches of the bureaucracy, with their high-flown titles and style of address, enjoyed greater prestige. Karenin would probably have been more highly regarded than Count Vronsky, not to speak of the likes of Stiva Oblonsky or Konstantin Levin.

In Russia, as in France, a weak residual aristocracy under the aegis of an influential composite bureaucracy had only few points of contact with relatively weak and politically unambitious entrepreneurial groups. The days of the aristocracy were over, those of the bourgeoisie had hardly begun. If, on the other hand, one chooses to view the bureaucracy as part of the bourgeoisie, then tsarist Russia, after 1825, was essentially a state under bourgeois rule, or rather, a society administered by a ruling class of officials drawn from various social classes. From this point of view, it could indeed be argued, that Russia, at an early stage and under a highly bureaucratized system, developed a post-aristocratic ruling class with strong bourgeois characteristics.

Prussia/Germany

Prusso-German development is characterised by some very distinctive features which will here be compared to the very different British model.

1. The Prussian *Schwertadel* (nobility of the sword), unlike its English counterpart, failed to exterminate itself. It was not decimated and its influence was not curtailed as was that of its French and Russian 'colleagues'. Instead, it flourished, never seriously challenged by the monarchy (though it was progressively tamed) successfully beating off threats from other social groups, and skillfully forcing them into compromises advantageous to itself. In the satisfactory compromise it had achieved with the monarchy (and its successors) it maintained its position in the military in an only slightly diluted form until July 1944.

2. As the Prusso-German nobility did not suffice to staff the expanding range of military and civilian positions, it was consistently supplemented (possibly 'diluted') by an influx of bourgeois elements. A number of aspects however, distinguished this process of amalgamation from analogous developments in Great Britain:

   a. The chief reservoir of recruitment for positions of influence was not, as in England, a wealthy commercial bourgeoisie in the process of becoming a landed class. Instead recruits were drawn from the landless 'educated' classes, the clergy, teaching professions and others with university training. These sources were supplemented by a growing element of self-recruitment. In the last quarter of the century, the commercial bourgeoisie also became available as a field for recruitment, a belated approximation to the English pattern.

   b. The British aristocratic ruling class increasingly drew on commercial wealth in the process of developing into a 'new' plutocratic elite. By contrast the predominantly military and administrative nobility of

Prussia/Germany was replenished from strata of society which were not particularly rich and shared the same anti-capitalist tendencies.

c. Whilst both the British and Prussian ruling classes recruited from middle-class elements, they did so on different terms. The British aristocracy, assured of its innate superiority, easy-going, *insouciant*, relatively open-minded, endowed with social and diplomatic skills, and schooled in compromise and the gentle arts of 'discreet charm' was, as a rule, prepared to meet 'newcomers' half-way. The increasing absorption of 'new men' was facilitated by shared commercial values, by the peculiar structure of the British nobility, we have already discussed, and the socializing influence of the public school, country life, and sports. The Prusso-German nobility – moustache, monocle and all – lacked the flexibility of its British counterpart. To a greater extent than in England and perhaps in a more constrained and self-conscious way, the Prusso-German non-noble was obliged to conform to the tone, style and values of his aristocratic colleagues and brother officers. An aristocratic code of honour dominated the officers' mess.

In both England and Germany it was arguably the aristocratic element which set the tone in the progressive formation of a composite elite with the bourgeois element as the junior partner accomodating to aristocratic models. That the eventual 'mix' turned out so differently, may be ascribed to two causes:

a. Whereas the British aristocracy and gentry on the whole gracefully if dilatorily yielded political power within the new elite to the bourgeois or recently ennobled elements, the German nobility instead entered into a politico-economic 'power-sharing' agreement with elements of the industrial bourgeoisie. Under this, the German nobility preserved its identity (marriage into the bourgeoisie remained exceptional) and reserved for itself leading positions in politics and administration, for which the commercial-industrial classes – by and large – did not compete. With the abolition of the purchase of army commissions and of patronage for civil appointments outside the Church of England the *Versorgungsprinzip* (principle of provision for members of aristocratic families) largely ceased to operate in Britain, outside the colonial empire, from the mid-century onwards. Thereafter, the remaining priveleges of the nobility – other than those of general social deference, resting securely on the rock of snobbery – were few.

b. Whereas British society and, with it, the British social elite was deeply civilian, notwithstanding the relatively high prestige of officers in the Royal Navy, continental societies, not least the Prusso-German, were profoundly militarized even in the 'civilian' sector. Once the comparable commission in the militia had disappeared early in the nineteenth century, there was no British equivalent to the German patent of *Reserveoffizier* and the social prestige it conferred. The militarization of society tended to give the aristocracy – trained from youth in the handling of weapons – an ascendancy over 'mere civilians' which did not exist in England. Bourgeois elements entering the German elite readily accepted certain military values associated with the officer corps and rightly or wrongly with the nobility.

As a result of these features, contrary to what happened in England, in Prussia/Germany few men from commercial and relatively few from bourgeois backgrounds appeared at the highest level of politics or administration, at any rate during the period under discussion. The Camphausens, Hansemanns and Mevissens were to prove a short-lived episode as was the handful made up of the Bambergs, Friedbergs, Friedenthals and Delbrücks in the liberal phase of German and European politics. The isolated and uncomfortable careers of Bernhard Dernburg and Walther Rathenau merely go to show that the Prusso-German political system had little room for bourgeois outsiders (even though some of its leading statesmen – Bismarck, Caprivi, Bülow, Bethmann-Hollweg are cases in point – were partly of bourgeois origin).

Notwithstanding the constant incorporation of commoners at lower levels, the German nobility, or rather the new elite in which it continued to dominate, proved largely resistant to bourgeois advance, quite unlike its English counterpart. It was unwilling to give up even part of its political domination (curiously unmatched by cultural predominance). Overall, the contrast with the British composite elite could hardly be greater.

The Socialisation of the New Elite

In all four countries institutions were created for the socialisation and integration of the new composite elite, drawn in varying proportions from nobility and commoners. A common ideology helped to obliterate the differences and remove residual antagonisms between students drawn from the two groups and to fuse disparate elements into a new elite. These new institutions were to prove their effectiveness above all in the realm of civilian public life and only to a much lesser extent in the military, where tensions persisted between aristocratic and bourgeois officers, or in the private realm, where, on the whole, commoners set the tone. Whilst the steady expansion of state activity both civil and military everywhere necessitated the admission of non-nobles into hitherto noble preserves, the socialisation processes designed to achieve this differed both in general ideological content and in certain specific features. The formation of the new composite elite took place in the different countries in different forms and with different cultural connotations.

France and Russia

With respect of such integrational strategies, there are some surprising similarities in the policies pursued in post-revolutionary Napoleonic France and tsarist Russia. In France and Russia alike in the first half of the nineteenth century governments created elite technological or technocratic institutions, designed both to create a network of alumni transcending social origins and to reserve for them privileged access to appropriate branches of state employment. In fact, the *esprit de corps* created among former students persisted to the end of their often distinguished public careers. What held the alumni together was corporate prestige, pride in professional competence and the evident usefulness of an extensive 'old boy' network.

In France, the new institutions created during or after the Revolution (*Ecole Polytechnique, Ponts et Chaussées*) were connected primarily with military engineering, whilst the *École Normale Supérieure*, which had been set up initially to train teachers for secondary schools, specialised in the education of the future administrative elite. The military academy at St.Cyr, devoted to the 'formation' of future staff officers, should also be mentioned in this context.

In Russia, comparable institutions were created for future diplomats and high officials (The Lyceum of Tsarskoe Selo, later the *Alexander-Lyzeum*). For the training of senior officials with specialised legal knowledge the Imperial School of Jurisprudence was set up in direct imitation of the Polytechnique and it was to become increasingly influential in the second half of the century.

Within a generation or two these *grandes écoles* had created in France and to a somewhat lesser extent in Russia a closely-knit 'mafia' of former alumni in certain branches of the state service, and these contacts extended increasingly into the private sector, notably in connection with railway-construction. There was thus constituted a numerically limited meritocracy of specialists with an ethos of competence which bridged differences of social origin.

Whilst such institutions formed the basis for important specialist networks in specific branches of public service, they did not extend across government and administration as a whole. To the extent that these were integrative institutions – their prime objective, after all was the training of competent specialists rather than either a general education in applied social science or broader social engineering – their functions and effects were limited. In both countries, in fact, the need for general integrative institutions was less urgent than in England or Germany. France in the nineteenth century largely lacked a powerful aristocracy, in Russia the bourgeoisie requiring integration through common institutions of socialization was 'missing'. The situation in Prussia/Germany and England was very different.

Germany and England

In Germany, the key institution for the social, cultural, and ideological amalgamation of noble and bourgeois elements into a new ruling elite was without doubt the elitist *Korps* with its strategically placed 'Alte Herren'(old boys).[13] Unlike the *grands corps* of France and Russia, membership of the corporations was neither based on technical abilities nor designed to promote them. Indeed the prevalent ethos was distinctly anti-intellectual. The essential content of *Korps* socialisation, designed to supplement academic study, was integration into social hierarchy and the development of 'character' through the cultivation of courage and self-discipline in the *Mensur* (fencing). Apart from promoting a particular form of sociability, the quaint drinking customs were designed to accustom young men to a generous (though regulated) consumption of alcohol.[14]

Thus, 'education' in the *Korps* had certain 'aristocratic' features, for example, its anti-intellectualism (exemplified by attacks on 'barren knowledge') or at best, non-intellectualism. Its central institutions were the modified and somewhat watered down aristocratic military duel, a distinctive code of honour, and the emphasis on the military virtues of courage, hierarchy and 'character'. The relaxed attitude towards financial and sexual peccadillos was part of the same pseudo-aristocratic codex.

Besides the extensive modification of the hereditary principle, for which the notion of the 'elective' family was substituted, what distinguished the *esprit de corps* from a genuinely aristocratic attitude was the tightly knit corporate structure with its rules, regulations, crude traditions and organised rituals. At the same time, though the great majority of *Korps* members were bourgeois, it is difficult to identify specifically bourgeois aspects – other than the wholesale consumption of beer. Both drinking and musical rituals sprang rather from medieval student traditions. Max Weber, whose opinion must command respect, considered the *Korps* culture as both specifically German and as, in essence, plebeian. In his view what had once been harmless student pranks had become a social nuisance, 'with the pretension to being a means of aristocratic "education", qualifying one for leadership in the state…'[15]

As Weber pointed out, for those desiring it, membership of a *Korps* all but guaranteed a successful career in the public service. Jarausch refering to several sources concludes: 'A list of former *Korps* members reads like a "Who's Who?" of higher German society. The presence of the old *Korps* members is of course heaviest in the ranks of the Prussian general administrative system and diplomatic corps. But they were significantly overrepresented in all the leading offices of state and senior positions in industry. It would not be an exaggeration to state that half the *Regierungspräsidenten* (regional chief administrators) and a large part of the *Landräte* (district senior officials) are in fact old *Korps* members. The *Burschenschafter* by contrast (by this time almost indistinguishable from *Korps* students, W.M.), were concentrated in the judiciary, science and the arts.'[16] It is worth noting, that in 1908 the *Alten Herren* of the *Korps* alone numbered some 30,000 those of the *Burschenschaften* a further 11,000 – in truth, a formidable network. In 1936, the organized *Alten Herren* of the *Korps* alone reached the almost incredible figure of some 180,000![17]

Besides social status and a hereditary element, the principal criterion of membership selection, was the wealth of a candidate's parents. Among the *Korps* there existed a hierarchy of prestige and a degree of segregation between noble and non-noble corporations. However, given the small numbers of aristocrats involved, the overwhelming majority of the *Korps* were basically 'großbürgerlich' (*haute bourgeois*) – as long as one is prepared to include the sons of senior officials in this category, which may not be altogether legitimate.

Thus, both corporations and *Burschenschaften* were in essence institutions designed to socialise elements of the *haute bourgeoisie* by means of 'pseudo-aristocratic' rituals and codes of conduct and so to prepare them for membership in the ruling composite elite. According to Weber, the conventions adopted by those wearing corporation-colours dictated 'the forms and conventions of the dominant strata of Germany: of the bureaucracy and of all those who wish to be accepted in "society" where the bureaucracy sets the tone'.[18] From a political point of view, therefore, the 'German forms' were plainly unsuited to 'serve as a model for the whole nation, down even as far as its lowest classes, to mould and unify it its gesture to form the external habitus of a self-assured "Herrenvolk" in the way both Romance and Anglo-Saxon conventions have succeeded in doing'.[19] In short, the German composite elite was the product of a narrow class-bound sub-culture, perhaps not quite as 'plebeian' as Weber maintained, but based at best upon an impure (not to say bastardized) aristocratic culture.

Weber, of course, was consciously contrasting the German *Korps* with analogous British institutions serving comparable purposes, the public schools and the universities of Oxford and Cambridge. Indeed, it has been claimed, not without some justification, that 'one of the most remarkable achievements of the English in the nineteenth century was to devise a mode of education which gave the the upper middle class some of the traditional qualities of an old governing aristocracy'.[20]

The modern British public school system developed around the mid-century when, following Thomas Arnold's pioneering work at Rugby, many old public schools were reformed along similar lines and a number of new ones were set up. The reformed public schools, like the *Korps*, which were reorganised at about the same time, were to have as a major function the assimilation of the offspring of the wealthy and increasingly land-owning *haute bourgeoisie* into the still largely aristocratic ruling class. Both systems proclaimed as their main objective the formation of 'character' but differed radically in their ways of achieving this common end. It should of course be remembered, that the public school system was designed for school boys, whereas the *Korps* catered for university students. However, with some slight reservations, it can be argued that the ethos of the public schools laid the foundation for study at one of the Oxbridge colleges. There are other similarities: The German 'Fuchs', obeying orders as a precondition for later exercising authority himself, corresponds to the public school 'fag' acting as the servant of the prefect, set in authority over him. The British system with its much more ancient principles of service and authority, starting at a considerably earlier age, and in the setting of a boarding school was more liable to abuse and probably the more damaging of the two.

One generic similarity of the two sets of institutions was that both, in different ways were a continuation and a partial deformation of elements of aristocratic culture. This has already been shown in the case of the *Korps* ethos. Under the British system, the link was formed essentially by the concept of 'gentility' and the educational and moral ideal of the 'gentleman'. Originally, 'gentleman' was a term refering to a member of a specific stratum of the lower nobility collectively known as the gentry. However, under the influence of Arnold's educational reforms, the term had largely become detached from a specific social class. Instead the 'true gentleman' was distinguished by manners and consideration for others, based in almost equal degrees on Christianity and team sport (both the 'Chapel' and 'the playing field' being essential elements of the public school system). Sport in particular added the concept of 'fairness', of what was or was not 'cricket'. The educational ideal derived from Arnold was somewhat sarcastically but not unfairly described as 'muscular Christianity'. Its educational 'character building' component was based on 'the Classics', the emphasis being one suspects on the Latin rather than the Greek authors.

In forming the modern concept of the gentleman, it has been said, 'the old qualities of loyalty and courage were retained but unselfishness and thoughtfulness were added'.[21] As the Earl of Shaftesbury observed in 1844, he preferred a reformed Rugby to an unreformed Eton because the new generation 'must have nobler, deeper and sterner stuff; less refinement and more truth; more rigid sense of duty, not a delicate "sense of honour"; a just estimate of rank and property, not as matters of personal enjoyment and display, but as gifts from God, bringing with them serious responsibilities'.[22]

The ideal involved, at the very least, a major modification of the aristocratic code, which was based on selfishness, not consideration for others, least of all the weak. In becoming divorced from social structure, the term 'gentleman' acquired a certain ambiguity. ' "Gentleman" might mean a man of gentle birth and heraldic status; or a man who in addition to possessing these attributes behaved in a certain way; or a man who lacked these attributes but practised the same habits of life as their posessors'.[23] The ideal of the 'gentleman' as seen by a foreign observer, is described by Hyppolite Taine in his *Notes sur L'Angleterre*, which appeared in 1872. In search of a true understanding of that essential word 'gentleman', that constantly occurred and expressed a whole complex of specifically English ideas, Taine contrasted it with the French concept of the *gentilhomme*: 'Gentilhomme evokes thoughts of elegance, style, tact, finesse; of exquisite politeness, delicate points of honour, of a chivalrous cast of mind, of prodigal liberality and brilliant valour; these were the salient features of the French upper class. Similarly 'gentleman' expresses all the distinctive features of the English upper class, in the first place ... a large private fortune, a considerable household of servants, a certain outward appearance and bearing, habits of ease and luxury ... Add to them for more cultivated minds, a liberal education, travel, information, good manners and ease in society. ... But for the real judges the essential quality is one of the heart; ... a real 'gentleman' is a truly noble man ... a disinterested man of integrity, capable of exposing, even sacrificing himself for those he leads; not only a man of honour, but a conscientious man, in whom generous instincts have been confirmed by right thinking and who, acting rightly by nature, acts even more rightly from good principles'.[24]

On the basis of these self descriptions and external judgements, two major points of difference between Germany and England cannot be emphasized too strongly. In the first place, with certain happy exceptions, the German *Korps-student* was not brought up to be a gentleman. Consideration for others, fairness and indeed chivalry as part of an impeccable moral code did not form a part of his curriculum. Secondly and most importantly, as Max Weber noted, the German 'form' could not be detached from its narrow class base and transmitted to the vast majority of the bourgeoisie. The concept of the 'gentleman' on the other hand – even if Eton, Harrow, Oxford and Cambridge were perhaps more socially exclusive than any German institution – could, and progressively did become the common property of large sections of the population. The scouting movement, a form of public school for the less privileged, extended the common ideal far down into the lower middle and even working classes.

In contrast to the 'patchy' French and Russian elites and institutions with their strictly professional bias, the British equivalent was both comprehensive and unspecialised (or 'generalist') a feature that was soon to reveal its drawbacks. The British system disdained intellectualism, specialisation, to some extent even professional competence. Such professional training as there was, took place at a later stage, after the early processes of socialisation, the moulding of the generalist, dilettante, gentleman and sportsman had been completed. Matthew Arnold, in Culture and Anarchy (1869) had – from the position of the *Bildungsbürger* – described the British nobility as barbarians, the bourgeoisie as philistines. In certain respects therefore, there was a price to be paid for the undoubted virtues of his father's educational system.

Conclusions

In conclusion, in England and Prussia/Germany, less so for different reasons in Russia and France, social and political processes were at work tending towards the formation of a new composite and increasingly non-noble ruling class. In all four countries here considered, there occurred, in various forms, a degree of convergence between elements of the nobility and parts of the *haute bourgeoisie* tending towards the formation of a new composite ruling elite, which, depending on the general evolution of society, could be predominantly plutocratic (England), bureaucratic (Germany), political (Russia) or 'mixed', i.e. composed of trained officials and municipally-based lawyer-politicians (France). In general, where they did not already dominate, bourgeois elements increased in importance whilst noble influence receded.

In the convergence of residual noble values with norms geared to the needs and the tastes of bourgeois society, educational institutions, as has been seen, played a vital part. Their objective function – notably in England and Germany – was to transmit to the new elite, predominantly bourgeois in social origin, residual modified values inherited from older aristocratic society. In a continuing process, bourgeois and noble elements interacted. Members of the nobility, to ensure their economic survival, had to come to terms with the ways of life of bourgeois society. *Haute bourgeois* elements, to legitimize their entry into and positions within the ranks of the old ruling class, had to accept certain aristocratic forms and values. The same process can be observed occuring also in France and Russia, though with less impetus. There, convergence was to be political rather than social with the integrative factor being a shared hatred, whether for the 'Boche' or the *chinovik*.

The ideal-typical description of the process of mutual interaction between noble and bourgeois and its apotheosis in the emergence of a new amalgam comes not from one of the countries examined here and is, placed in a somehat different setting. Giuseppe di Lampedusa in *The Leopard* describes the love-hate relationship between the aristocratic Don Fabrizio, Prince of Salina and the upstart peasant entrepreneur Don Calogero Sedàra, a relationship cemented by the marriage of the Prince's nephew Tancredi to the parvenu's daughter Angelica: 'As meetings due to the marriage contract became more frequent, Don Fabrizio found an odd admiration growing in him for Sedàra's qualities ... many problems that had seemed insoluble to the prince were resolved in a trice by Don Calogero: free as he was from the shackles imposed on many men by honesty, decency and plain good manners, he moved through the forest of life with the confidence of an elephant'.[25]

Don Calgero, in his turn, was affected (in part involuntarily) by his dealings with the Prince: 'Gradually, Don Calgero came to understand that a meal in common need not necessarily be all munching and grease stains; that a conversation may well bear no resemblance to a dog fight, that to give precedence to a woman is a sign of strength and not, as he had believed, of weakness; that sometimes more can be obtained by saying 'I haven't explained myself well' than 'You haven't understood a word'; and that the adoption of such tactics can result in a greatly increased yield from meals, arguments, women and questionners.... It would, nonetheless, be rash to claim that Don Calgero drew immediate profit from all such lessons; he did try to shave a little more carefully and complain a little less about the waste of soap; but from that moment there began for him and his family, that process of continual refining which in the course of three generations transforms rough peasants into defenceless gentry'.[26]

In fact, in several parts of Europe, the lines between nobility and the *haute bourgeoisie* were becoming increasingly fluid, notably in the later decades of the nineteenth century, a process that reached its apogee in Edwardian England.[27] In countries traditionally governed by strong bureaucratic elites and notably in Prussia/Germany, the convergence, instead of creating a new plutocratic elite as in England produced what Otto Hintze aptly refered to as a 'adlig-bügerliche Amtsaristokratie' (aristo-bourgeois nobility of public office),[28] a description also applicable to the tsarist bureaucratic elite of the second half of the nineteenth century. The nature of the corresponding processes in France – notably the evolution of the French nobility under the Third Republic – awaits elucidation.

The formation of the new composite elite marked, arguably, the triumph of the bourgeoisie, the highwater mark of their influence. Ever since the eighteen-eighties they had felt the challenge from 'below'. Finally, the impact of the Great War on the ruling elites of the different countries considered here varied dramatically. However, in one way or another, the outstanding issue of the relations betwen the nobility and bourgeoisie was resolved once and for all.

Notes to Chapter 3

1. This term is used to indicate the preponderance of Prussia within Germany. In addition, the comments on Germany made in this article refer mainly to the Prussian state.

2. H. Rosenberg, *Bureaucracy, Aristocracy and Autocracy* (Boston, 1966), p. 151.

3. I owe the information which follows to Dr. Johannes Rogalla von Bieberstein, University of Bielefeld.

4. A.J. Tudesq, *Les Grands Notables en France 1840–1849* (Paris, 1969), 'The power of the Notables though based in the countryside was effective in the towns and especially in Paris.' (p. 320); 'Mayors, deputies, departmental- and district councillors; predominantly aristocratic and legitimist property owners, bourgeois owning large estates or holding public office; conservative merchants, loyal to the current regime - these are the three constituent groups of the society of the Notables.' (p. 331)

5. *Ibid.*, p. 331: 'The pursuit of material and local interests was of more interest than larger general issues.'

6. As quoted in: E. Conte Corti, *The Reign of the House of Rothschild* (London, 1928), p. 355.

7. People of various origins outside the Russian class structure, the Russian intelligentsia. They are distinguished by at least a secondary, usually a higher education and the fact that they are not employed in state service.

8. E. Hobsbawm, *Industrie und Empire* (Frankfurt, 1969), p. 14: 'In Britain the resistance to capitalist development had ceased to be effective by the end of the seventeenth century. The very aristocracy, by contintenal standards, almost a "bourgeoisie", and two revolutions had taught the monarchy to be adaptable'. As Engels in 1858 wrote perceptively to Karl Marx '...the English proleteriat in fact is becoming increasingly bourgeois, so that this most bourgeois of nations seems to be about to arrive at a situation where *alongside* the bourgeoisie proper it has a bourgeois aristocracy and a bourgeois proleteriat'. Engels to Marx, 7.10.1858, in: *Marx-Engels Werke*, vol. 29 (Berlin, 1973), p. 358 (own translation).

9. Hobsbawm, *ibid.*, p. 26.

10. *Ibid.*, p. 31

11. *Ibid.*, p. 30

12. See J.A. Armstrong, *The European Administrative Elite* (Princeton, 1973), p. 84.

13. Both *Burschenschaften* with their somewhat different origins and Roman Catholic *Verbindungen* with time increasingly assimilated themselves to the strict *Korps* pattern set by the *Kösener Senioren-Convent-Verband*.

14. See K.H. Jarausch, *Deutsche Studenten 1800–1970* (Frankfurt, 1984), p. 61.

15. M. Weber, 'Wahlrecht und Demokratie in Deutschland', in: M. Weber, *Gesammelte Politische Schriften* (Tübingen, 1971), vol.3, p.280 (all translations by the author); see also, pp. 278.

16. Jarausch, *Students*, p. 69; see p. 66 on the insignificant aristocratic membership in the *Korps*, which amounted to only eight percent.

17. *Ibid.*, p. 191.

18. Weber, Wahlrecht, p. 282.

19. *Ibid.*

20. E.L. Woodward, 'The Foreign Service', in: J.E. McLean, *The Public Service and University Education*, London, p. 172.

21. W.L. Burn, *The Age of Equipoise* (London, 1964), p. 259.

22. *Ibid.*, p. 260.

23. *Ibid.*, p. 259.

24. Cited according to W.L. Guttsman, *The English Ruling Class* (London, 1969), pp. 37.

25. G. Tomasi di Lampedusa, *The Leopard*, p. 95 (in the Munich 1984 German ed.).
26. *Ibid.*, p. 97.
27. J. Stevenson, *British Society 1914–45* (London, 1964), p. 30.
28. O. Hintze, *Der Beamtenstand* (Leipzig, 1911), p. 45.

4 | Businessmen and the Bourgeoisie in Western Europe

Youssef Cassis

There is little doubt that businessmen form an important part of the bourgeois world. Indeed, a narrow definition would only consider as bourgeois the owners of the means of production. Even taking a broader view, it is significant that other social categories, such as professionals and civil servants – in Germany the *Bildungsbürgertum* – are usually added to businessmen in order to draw a complete picture of the bourgeois strata, emphasising thereby their key position.[1]

The importance of businessmen increases when one considers the *grande bourgeoisie*. In France, the *dynasties bourgeoises* of E. Beau de Loménie and the mythical *deux cents familles* are made up of the great banking and industrial families and their connections in the social and political sphere.[2] The object of this essay is to consider the specific place of big businessmen within the bourgeois world in Britain, France and Germany in order to evaluate the extent to which this component of the German *Bürgertum* differed from its British and French counterparts and to determine whether these differences, if any, arose from the particular characteristics of the German *Bürgertum*.

This raises the second point which will be considered here: to what extent are concepts such as *Bürgertum* or middle class useful in analysing the inter-relationships of a certain number of socio-professional groups usually described as bourgeois? In order to develop an accurate analysis, it is necessary to distinguish between several bourgeois strata. French historiography, probably because of the more bourgeois nature of French society in the nineteenth century, has gone furthest in this direction. Following Adeline Daumard, historians tend to distinguish, on the basis of the level of fortune as well as social status, and with some adaptations to specific conditions, between an *aristocratie financière*, a *haute bourgeoisie* and a *bonne bourgeosie*, and, at a lower level, a *bourgeoisie moyenne* and a *bourgeoisie populaire*.[3]

Notes to Chapter 4 can be found on page 120.

Such fine distinctions have not been established by students of the British and German examples. In Britain, historians and sociologists divide the middle class into an upper middle class, a middle middle class and a lower middle class. In Germany, a *Großbürgertum* could be isolated from the *Bürgertum* and, at the lower end, the *Kleinbürgertum*, in addition to the specifically German distinction between *Wirtschafts* – and *Bildungsbürgertum*.[4] In the three countries, however, reference is made to the upper classes (in France the *classes supérieures*, in Germany the *Oberschicht*), which, in the period considered, include the upper stratum of the economic bourgeoisie, or part of it, as well as the aristocracy. There is little doubt that, in the case of big business, we are mainly dealing with the upper echelons of the bourgeoisie, which are part of the upper classes.

One set of questions related to the social position of big business-men revolves therefore around their relationships with the aristocracy. It is arguable, however, whether the composition of the upper classes should be analysed in terms of aristocracy and *bourgeoisie*, *Bürgertum* and the like or in terms of socio-professional groups, namely great landowners, big businessmen, senior politicians, senior civil servants and the most prominent professionals and possibly intellectuals. In the latter case, the term of ruling class, or simply of elite, might be more useful than that of *bourgeoisie*, middle class or *Bürgertujm*. The term 'elite' is simply used here to designate the socio-professional groups that are at the top of the social hierarchy and in a position of power in their respective fields. The term ruling class is used to designate a socially integrated group of economic, political and administrative elites.[5] The choice between the broad concepts or that of elites will mainly depend on the strength of the aristocracy within the upper classes. For Britain and France, where, by the turn of the century, the upper classes had become an amalgamation of aristocratic and upper middle-class elements, the notions of elites, or of ruling class, might be more useful, whereas the case is more debatable with regards to Germany.

The position of businessmen at the top of the social hierarchy is ensured by the possession of three main assets: economic power, social prestige and political influence.[6] The combination of these three assets, at their highest degree, was, for example, a characteristic feature of the financial aristocracy in Britain and France in the second half of the nineteenth century: Lord Rothschild and Lord Revelstoke in the City of London, Alphonse de Rothschild or Rodolphe Hottinguer in Paris[7] were certainly in this position, with their immense wealth, involvement in the biggest financial operations of the day, their network of relationships in the highest society and their personal closeness to political power. There could, however, be variations in the degree of economic power, social prestige and political influence, the strength of one asset compensating for the relative weakness of another, such as high social status making up for a declining economic position,[8] other combinations were possible.

The analysis of the social position of the business elite will therefore be considered at three levels:

(1) The economic level refers to the type of firm, the position in the firm as well as to income and wealth.

(2) The social level refers to the degree of integration into the upper classes, which can be perceived through social origins, education, social life and marriages.

(3) The political level refers to closeness to political power, whether in a personal capacity or through the medium of a pressure group.

After examining the economic, social and political assets of businessmen in Britain, France and Germany, I shall return to the two questions raised above: did the social position of the German businessmen differ significantly from that of the British and French? Are the concepts of *bourgeoisie,* middle class and *Bürgertum* useful for this analysis?

Economic power

The first question that arises here is whether the differences in business organisation between the three countries involved differences in the social position of businessmen. It is well known that, by the turn of the century, the concentration of production and the rise of giant firms had reached a higher level in Germany than in Britain and, to an even greater degree, in France. However, the basis for the existence of what we can call big businessmen were more or less the same. In banking, a financial aristocracy, based on old style family partnerships, existed in the three countries. The biggest joint stock banks in Britain, France and Germany were of similar size, with total assets amounting to about £100 million on the eve of the First World War.[9] One would expect to see more differences in industry.

Table 1 (see pp. 106–7) gives the list of the twenty largest industrial employers in Britain and Germany in 1907 – comparable data are

Table 4.1: The Twenty Largest Industrial Employers
in Britain and Germany in 1907

		Britain	
RANK	NAME OF FIRM	ESTIMATED NUMBER OF EMPLOYEES	INDUSTRIAL GROUP
1.	Fine Cotton Spinners and Doublers Association	30,000	Textile
2.	Sir W.G. Armstrong Whitworth & Co.	25,000	Armaments
3.	Vickers, Sons & Maxim	22,500	Armaments
4.	Calico Printers Assoc.	20,495	Textile
5.	John Brown & Co.	16,205	Shipbuilding
6.	Metropolitan Amalgamated Railway Carriage & Wagon Co.	13,868	Vehicles
7.	Cooperative Wholesale Society	13,203	Food, drink, clothing, footwear
8.	J. & P. coats	12,700	Textile
9.	Guest, Keen, & Nettlefolds	12,451	Iron, coal, steel
10.	Bleachers' Assoc.	11,280	Textile
11.	Platt Brothers	10,600	Mechanical engineering
12.	Stewarts & Lloyds	10,000	Iron, coal, steel
13.	United Alkali	9,049	Chemicals
14.	Pilkington Brothers	9,000	Glass
15.	I. & R. Morley	9,000	Clothing
16.	Harland & Wolff	8,500	Shipbuilding
17.	Workman, Clark & Co.	8,000	Shipbuilding
18.	Rylands & Sons	8,000	Textile
19.	G. Kynoch & Co.	8,000	Iron, coal, steel
20.	Palmers Shipbuilding & Iron Co.	7,500	Iron, steel, shipbuilding
—	Bradford Dyers	7,500	Textile

unfortunately not available for France – and shows that differences certainly existed, particularly in the heavy industries of iron, coal and steel, where the size of the German plants – about ten firms employed 20,000 people or more[10] – was not matched by that of the British ones. There were nevertheless twelve metal manufacturing companies in Britain employing more than 4,000 people in the years 1905-1910[11] and the five largest employers of colliery workers in 1913 all had more than 10,000 employees.[12] The case of France is more debatable. However, if following Horn and Kocka and consider as great enterprises those with 1,000 workers or more,[13] then there was undoubtedly a *grand patronat de la métallurgie*; in 1906, twenty-three French metal-working factories employed more than 1,000 workers,

Table 4.1: The Twenty Largest Industrial Employers
in Britain and Germany in 1907 (continued)

		Germany	
Rank	Name of Firm	Estimated Number of Employees	Industrial Group
1.	Fried. Krupp	64,354	Iron, coal, steel
2.	Siemens & Halske-Siemens-Schuckert-Werke	42,866	Electrical engineering
3.	Gelsenkirchener Bergwerks-AG	31,252	Iron, coal, steel
4.	Phoenix	31,000	Iron, coal, steel
5.	AEG	30,667	Electrical engineering
6.	Harpener Bergbau	26,000	Coal
7.	Ver. Königs-und Laurahütte	23,224	Iron, coal, steel
8.	Gutehoffnungshütte	21,657	Iron, coal, steel
9.	Mansfeld'sche Kupferschiefer-bauende	21,283	Iron, coal, steel
10.	Hibernia	19,212	Coal
11.	Deutscher Kaiser (Thyssen)	18,931	Iron, coal, steel
12.	von Giesches Erben	13,291	Iron, coal, steel (zinc)
13.	Hohenlohe-Werke	12,367	Iron, coal, steel (zinc)
14.	Felten & Guilleaume-Lahmeyer	11,760	Electrical engineering
15.	Union AG	11,605	Iron, coal, steel
16.	Oberschlesische Eisen-bahnbedarf AG	11,500	Iron, coal, steel
17.	Kattowizer AG	10,968	Iron, coal, steel
18.	Bochumer Verein	10,867	Iron, coal, steet
19.	Deutsch-Luxemburgische	10,000	Iron, coal, steel
—	Rheinische Stahlwerke	10,000	Iron, coal, steel
—	Schles. AG f. Bergbau u. Zinkhüttenbetrieb	10,000	Iron, coal, steel
—	Borsig	10,000	Locomotives

Sources: For Germany, Kocka, Siegrist, 'Die hundert größten Industrieun-ternehmen', pp. 106–12. For Britain, Shaw, 'The Large Manufacturing Employers', pp. 52–53. State-owned companies, such as the royal Dockyards and the Royal Ordnance Factories (25,000 and 15,651 employees, respectively, and the railway companies, such as the Great Western and the North Eastern, with 17,770 and 10,000 employees) have not been included.

including the two giants Schneider and de Wendel with more than 15,000 workers on the eve of the First World War. This *grand patronat* also existed in textiles, despite the persistence of the family firms, with forty-four factories employing more than 1,000 people.[14]

The position of businessmen in the firm reveals some differences between the three countries, differences in functions as well as in social status. It is always difficult to assess the executive role of company directors because of the many variations from one firm to another or even within the same firm in the course of time.

The situation is the simplest in Germany, because of the co-existence of two boards: the *Vorstand* and the *Aufsichtsrat*. It is generally admitted that the former was the executive organ and in most cases also responsible for the strategic decisions, whereas the task of the latter, often chaired by a banker, was usually advisory, particularly in financial matters and in times of mergers.[15] British and French companies had only one board, whose main duty was to define the strategic options of the firm, leaving the day to day routine to salaried managers. At this general level, the tasks of the British and French boards fell somewhere between those of the *Vorstand* and *Aufsichtsrat*. The British board was as a rule more involved than the French *conseil d'administration* in running the business of the firm and in some cases, particularly in industry, played a role comparable to that of the *Vorstand*. The board of directors of Vickers, the great armament manufacturer, was, for example, very similar to the *Vorstand* of Krupp, both being made up of a mixture of technical, commercial and financial experts, as well as of senior Navy officers and civil servants.[16] On the other hand, the tasks performed by the boards of some of the London joint stock banks were of the same type as those of an *Aufsichtsrat*.[17]

How did these differences express themselves at the social level? In Britain, the separation was quite strong, both professionally and socially, between the directors, who were members of the board, and the managers, including the general manager, without a seat on the board. Most often, the manager of the British firms were recruited outside the circle of the owners and their family. They came from a lower social background, usually lower middle- to middle-class, entered the firm at a young age, usually without a scientific or technical education, and rose step by step to the top of the ladder. However, as long as they were not admitted to the board, which might have happened on retirement as a reward for services, they were not included in the business elite.[18]

In Germany, the members of the *Vorstand* and of the *Aufsichtsrat* enjoyed an equal social status, and members of the controlling families were often to be found on the *Vorstand* : this was the case of firms like Thyssen, Siemens, Hayer or Stollwerck, to give but one example in four different industrial branches.[19] As a result, the business community was more unified and the salaried entrepreneurs were more integrated with the business elite, as in the well known cases of famous salaried entrepreneurs such as Albert Ballin, Emil Kirdorf or Emil Rathenau.[20]

The situation of the French managers – the *directeurs* as opposed to the *administrateurs* – was closer to that of the British manager than to that of the members of the *Vorstand*, with the difference that they were more highly educated than their British counterparts. In industry in particular, most of them were engineers and had graduated from the *grandes écoles*.[21] This could bring them socially closer to the directors. At the Charbonnages d'Anzin, one of the major coal companies, in 1910 both the chairman, Champy, and the general manager, Cuvinot, had been at the École Polytechnique.[22] A common higher education, however, could not entirely offset social differences.

Personal income and wealth are the ultimate measure of the economic power of businessmen. In the three countries, during the period under review, businessmen were by far the richest socio-professional group. In Britain, landowners remained the wealthiest group up to the late 1870s: according to W.D. Rubinstein, they accounted for 80 percent of the millionaires deceased between 1858 and 1879. For the period 1900–1914, their percentage shrank to 27 percent, whereas 72 percent of the deceased millionaires were businessmen and 1 percent professional men and civil servants.[23] The situation was not very different in Germany where, in 1912, 25 percent of the millionaires were landowners and 68 percent businessmen.[24] There are no equivalent statistics for France. However, it can be noted that in 1911, the average estate of a Paris businessman was 1,450,773 francs (£58,031) as against 334,650 francs for landowners and *rentiers*.[25]

If businessmen exceeded landowners in term of wealth, they also became much richer than the other bourgeois categories. In France, for example, senior civil servants were richer than businessmen in the early nineteenth century. By the end of the nineteenth century, the positions were completely reversed: the average estate of a senior civil servant rose from 253,249 to 431,621 francs between 1820 and 1911, that of a businessman from 189,643 to 1,450,773 francs during the same period.[26] Another interesting point to bear in mind is that the level of major fortunes appears to have been quite similar between the three countries, being probably somewhat greater in Britain, where the highest non-landed fortune reached about £11 million in 1914. In Germany, in 1911, four fortunes were worth £5 million or more, whereas in France the peak single fortune rose to over £2 million (50 million francs).[27]

Comparison of differences within the group of big businessmen reveals a predominance of the financial sector. This was definitely true in Britain, where 52.1 percent of the non-landed millionaires and 50.3 percent of the non-landed half-millionaires were merchants or bankers. At the individual level, most of the very largest British business fortunes of the nineteenth century were in commerce and finance. Very few factory owners or 'cotton lords' were immensely wealthy, most leaving not more than £100,000.[28] Surprisingly, the figures are not very different for Germany where, according to D. Augustine, the tertiary sector accounted for 47 percent of the businessmen with a fortune of 6 million marks (£300,000) or more.[29] Bankers (27.1 percent) were the largest single group, and heavy industrialists (12.4 percent) formed a percentage similar to that of their British counterparts (13.5 percent).

Whatever conclusion could be drawn from these figures about the rationality of the behaviour of the iron and steel industrialists, it can be admitted that the effects of the differences in the business structure of the two countries were partly offset by the homogeneity in the wealth of the businessmen. There are unfortunately no equivalent figures for France. However, it can be noted that in 1901, an average 45.7 percent of top businessmen (57.2 percent of chairmen and deputy-chairmen, 38.1 percent of company directors and 14.3 percent of senior managers) left an estate of 2 million francs or more.[30]

A similar hierarchy, as opposed to a classification by economic sector, is likely to be found in Britain and Germany. In Britain, for example, 66 percent of bank general managers but only 22 percent of bank directors left less than £50,000. Finally, considering the concentration of millionaires in Paris and the huge fortunes of some of the *régents* of the Banque de France, mostly bankers,[32] there is some clear indication that banking and finance must have accounted for a large proportion of French millionaires.

Social prestige

An evaluation of the social status of big businessmen can be attempted through the analysis of their social origins, education, social life and marriages. Social origins of businessmen are usually investigated in terms of upward social mobility. For our purpose, it is more relevant to consider whether the family was old or new in business (a not insignificant element of social status) and to establish the frequency of passages from one socio-professional group to another within the

Table 4.2: Social Origins of Businessmen

	BUSINESSMEN	SONS OF: SENIOR CIVIL SERVANTS	LANDOWNERS	PROFESSIONAL MEN
		%		
Britain	59	0	11	7
France	52	10	0	16
Germany	53	9	2	3

Sources: See note 33.

upper and upper middle classes. In the latter case, it is also interesting to consider the extent to which other groups, such as senior civil servants or politicians, were recruited from the ranks of the business classes.

Comparisons are always difficult between countries, because the samples taken and the categories used by the various students of the subject are not always compatible. However, some general trends can be perceived. And they are very similar for the three countries; as can be seen in Table 4.2, between 52 and 59 percent of the businessmen of the generation considered here were sons of businessmen. Of the remainder, about 10 percent in France and Germany were the sons of senior civil servants,;in Britain, which had a much smaller bureaucracy than the two continental powers, none come into this category, although 10.6 percent were the sons of landowners, many of whom were also civil servants. In Germany 2 percent were from landowning families; in France there were none. Sons of professional men were the most numerous in France (16 percent) followed by Britain (7.3 percent) and Germany (3 percent).[33]

It would obviously be very interesting to make comparisons at the level of the various branches and positions in the firm, but this remains impossible in the present state of research. It can however be pointed out that the recruitment of Westphalian heavy industrialists, studied by T. Pierenkemper, and of the British steel industrialists, studied by C. Erickson, shows considerable similarities. At roughly the same period, 53 percent in Germany and 55 percent in Britain were sons of businessmen; 7 percent in Germany and 7 to 13 percent in Britain were sons of landowners; and 27 percent and 15 to 19 percent respectively were sons of senior civil servants and professional men.[34]

This high degree of self-recruitment of businessmen is, however, not very surprising in an age when one's family remained the best way to reach a top position in business. It was even more marked in banking, where 87 percent of the London private bankers were sons of bankers.[35] Equally revealing for our purpose is therefore the degree to which other socio-professional groups recruited their ranks from businessmen.

Let us first consider politicians. In Britain, only 7.7 percent of the Conservative Cabinet ministers between 1900 and 1919 were sons of businessmen, landowners still providing the bulk of the political elite (50 percent).[35] However, the strong links that had been established between landed and business interests should not be underestimated, particularly with respect to financial and overseas enterprises. In France, 26 percent of the ministers of the Third Republic before 1914 were sons of businessmen,[37] as against 11.4 percent in Imperial Germany.[38]

As far as senior civil servants were concerned, in France, 11 to 24 percent, depending on the *Corps*, were sons of big businessmen, 20 to 36 percent if medium-sized enterprises are taken into account.[39] The corresponding figures for Germany are 1.2 and 20.5 percent.[40] There are no comparable data for Britain. The recruitment of other elite groups reveals therefore more differences than the recruitment of businessmen, with a more bourgeois character and a greater circulation of elites in France. However, these figures should not be considered as more than a suggestion of the general trend. In particular, they say nothing about the overlapping zones between the various groups or about the dividing lines within the elite considered as a whole.

Other indicators, such as education, could be of some help. This is mainly the case for Britain, where education at a public school, particularly one of the major public schools such as Eton and Harrow, even more than at one of the two ancient universities (Oxford and Cambridge), may be taken as the criterion of absorption into the upper classes.[41] On the basis of the sample made up of the entries in the first four volumes of the *Dictionary of Business Biography*, 12.7 percent of businessmen born between 1840 and 1869, and 17.2 percent of those born between 1870 and 1899, attended a major public school, while another 7.9 and 12 percent respectively attended a minor public school.[42]

However, the public school criterion enables us to detect some more precise internal cleavages, for example between the City and industry: 74 percent of the members of the banking community between 1890 and 1914 attended a public school, compared with 31 percent of the steel industrialists active between 1905 and 1925, and 68 percent of Cabinet ministers between 1886 and 1916. Even more revealing, out of all the bankers who had been to a public school, 45 percent were at Eton and 26 percent at Harrow; the figures for Cabinet ministers are 51 and 19 percent.[43] Data are not available for steelmasters, which is in itself an indication of a probable 'lower' education. This is of some importance when one is aware of the strong *esprit de corps* uniting former public school pupils and the strength of the 'old boys' network.[44]

Such indicators do not exist for France and Germany. Apart from the fact that they dispensed the same classical education as the British public schools, education at a German *Gymnasium* or at a French *lycée* can hardly be considered as a sign of integration into the upper classes. However, some great Parisian *lycées*, such as Louis le Grand or Henri IV, were certainly very exclusive, as were some private Catholic colleges, and they did increase the cohesion between the future business, political and administrative elites, but in no way as much as the British public schools. In Germany, the various local *Gymnasia* stood on the same footing as the French *lycée*.[45]

University education cannot be considered as a status symbol in any of the three countries. As far as the French *grandes écoles* are concerned, they certainly offered a possibility to reach the top for people with a relative starting handicap, but were quite unnecessary for sons of banking or industrial dynasties. This is probably why only 29.9 percent of a sample of businessmen drawn from *Qui êtes-vous?* in 1901 gave details about their education. Among them 24.3 percent had been to the *École Polytechnique* and 27.7 percent to the *Faculté de Droit*.[46] However, with the growing complexities of business management, members of the French business elite went to the *grandes écoles* less in order to gain a social status than to acquire a necessary professional qualification.

François de Wendel, for instance, head of the famous family firm of steel-masters, had been to the *Écoles des Mines* between 1894 and 1898.[47] It should also be noted that the *grandes écoles* did develop an *esprit de corps* between their students which continued during their professional life: for example the *polytechniciens* or the *inspecteurs de finances*, who were present both in the state administration and the private sector.[48] Nothing similar existed in Germany apart from the student corporations, the *Korps* and the *Burschenschaften*, which provided students who had attended the same university with a national network that included alumni. However, student corporations have so far mainly been studied in terms of certain practices, notably duelling, and of social ideals, rather than in terms of networks of relationships between the various elite groups. In particular, the presence of future businessmen in these corporations has not been clearly assessed.[49]

Social life was directly dependent on where one worked and lived. In that respect, the difference between capital and province should not be underestimated, above all in France. Paris was the home not only of the *haute banque* and other financial institutions such as banks and insurance companies, a seat on the board of which carried much prestige, but also of the almost equally prestigious railway, dock and water companies. The major French industrial undertakings often had their head office in Paris even though their works could be far away in the country, particularly in such industries as coal, iron, steel or shipbuilding. The head office of the Mines de Carmaux, for example, was in Paris, some 600 kilometers from the coal mines;[50] in 1910 its chairman was the Marquis de Solages and its vice chairman Alfred Cibiel, the former a member of the old aristocracy, the latter of a rich merchant family. Whatever their wealth and their local influence, local industrialists were not in the same league.

The division between capital and province in terms of social prestige of the businessmen also applies to Britain, although in a different way. The difference here was more between the City and industry than between London and the country. London has always meant less for the British upper classes than Paris for the French, and living mainly in the country with occasional visits to the capital was perfectly compatible with, and characteristic of, the upper-class way of life. The difference between a national and a provincial bourgeoisie does not of course apply in the same way to Germany. However, although the Ruhr industrialists remained the most prestigious and powerful business group, the new divisions within the business classes created by the growing importance of Berlin as the major business centre of Germany, particularly the concentration of the financial sector in the capital, deserve a thorough examination.

The way of life led by big businessmen could conveniently be described as 'aristocratic' to the extent that some of its most visible aspects were borrowed from the aristocracy, and also in order to distinguish, within the bourgeoisie, the lifestyle of its upper echelon – the French *aristocratie financière* – from that of its lower ones.[51] This 'aristocratic' way of life could only be led in the capital, coupled with a seat in the country. In Paris, the majority of big businessmen resided in the eighth and sixteenth arrondissements; the business aristocracy lived in a *hôtel particulier*. In London, most of the members of the City aristocracy lived in the two most aristocratic areas of the capital, Mayfair and Belgravia; a third of them also had a country house. Most of the Parisian big businessmen (over 80 percent) had a *résidence secondaire*; for 34 percent, it was a *château*. The same phenomenon is noticeable in Berlin, where rich businessmen and the aristocracy lived in the distinguished western areas near the Tiergarten; owning a country house had also become quite common at this level.[52] Provincial bourgeois were also prevented from being part of the fashionable society.

Clubs formed part of this social life, above all in London, where membership of one of the gentlemen's clubs (Carlton, Brooks, Athenaeum, Reform, Travellers etc.) was a mark of upper-class status. Needless to say, only the most prominent of the provincial industrialists were members of a London club, whereas it was common practice for the financial community. Paris also had its clubs, and a distinction can be made between the old clubs (Jockey Club, Cercle de la rue Royale, Cercle de l'Union, etc.), attended by the aristocracy and the *aristocratie financière*, and the more bourgeois clubs (Automobile Club de France, Bois de Boulogne, etc.) attended by the newer businessmen.

As far as Berlin was concerned, there were no such clubs and on the whole Berlin had a less active social life than Paris and London. However, the Berlin financial aristocracy did entertain on a grand scale during the season and mix with the aristocracy.[53] Titled businessmen were received at the court. Nevertheless, despite the persistence of aristocratic prejudice in Britain and even in France, German big businessmen were not so well integrated with the aristocracy as their British and French counterparts.

Of all the types of relationships between businessmen and other elite groups, marriages were undoubtedly the most important; alliances established between families that continued for several generations, creating for the most powerful of them a formidable network of relationships operating at the highest levels of economic, social and political power.[54]

In Britain, the most striking feature was the degree of integration of the City aristocracy and of the landed aristocracy: 35 percent of members of the London banking community married daughters of the aristocracy or gentry; the percentage rises to 60 percent if one adds other groups traditionally bound to the landed interests, such as army and navy officers (12 percent), senior clergymen (10 percent), senior politicians and civil servants (3 percent). A further 3 percent married daughters from professional families and only 1 percent married the daughters of industrialists.

More important than these percentages, it can be observed that a succession of marriages and intermarriages between banking families and families of the landed aristocracy led to a more complete merging and the formation of a renewed elite. Industrialists, at least in the first phase, were on the whole not included in this network of relationships. The Jewish and Quaker minorities, which were prominent in the financial world, developed their own dynasties and networks of relationships, the former within the international Jewish community, the latter with prominent Quaker industrialist families.[55]

In France, according to the figures of C. Charle, 54.5 percent of big businessmen married into the *fractions possédantes* (i.e. into business), 21.8 percent married the daughters of senior civil servants and 10.9 percent the daughters of professionals. Interestingly, 38.4 percent of senior civil servants and 39 percent of ministers also married into big business, thus confirming the greater circulation of elites in France already observed in the case of social origins. However, the most interesting point made by Charle is that, in addition to the well-known strategies of social promotion through marriage for the upwardly mobile, and of social and business consolidation through intermarriages for old established families, there existed a third strategy of diversification into other socio-professional elite groups. At the highest echelons of this diversification strategy, marriages took place in one and the same world. As Charle puts it:

> Les classements professionnels perdent leur sens au profit d'une appartenance générique au monde, voire au 'grand monde'. (Professional classifications become meaningless as the people involved are part of society, indeed 'high society'.)[56]

In Germany, on the basis of the figures of D. Augustine concerning the wealthiest businessmen, it would appear that 12 percent married daughters of the aristocracy, 62 percent daughters of businessmen and 17 percent daughters of members of the *Bildungsbürgertum*.[57] The number of marriages with daughters of businessmen was therefore significantly higher than in the case of the French business and British financial community. But these figures are still lower than those obtained by H. Henning for the most prominent businessmen in Westfalia – those with the title of *Kommerzienrat*: over 85 percent of them married into business families (66 percent into big business and 19 percent into medium-sized and small business); only 9.5 percent married the daughter of a member of the *Bildungsbürgertum*.[58] German big businessmen appear therefore to have been more isolated, whether from the landed aristocracy or from the other bourgeois groups, than their British and French counterparts.

Political influence

The most common way of measuring the political influence of businessmen is probably through their presence in Parliament.[59] Yet this is not always meaningful, for this presence had as much a social as a political significance. Several British bankers, for example, were Members of Parliament as squires of their county rather than as City bankers,[60] and a seat in Parliament was one of the highest social ambitions of the successful British businessman. In the same way, many of the French businessmen who were deputies in the early twentieth century were local *notables*.[61] In Germany, however, the social status attached to the position of deputy seems to have lost some of its prestige in the last quarter of the nineteenth century, and as a result its attractiveness to businessmen declined.[62]

The most characteristic feature common to the three countries during the half-century preceeding the First World War was the general decrease in the number of businessmen in Parliament. In France, the percentage of businessmen dropped from about 25 percent during the Second Empire to 14 percent in 1871 and 12.7 percent in 1893.[63] In the German Reichstag, the percentage fell from 27 percent in 1890 to 17.1 percent in 1918.[64] In Britain, between 1895 and 1906, the number of non-landed millionaires fell from 31 to 22[65] and the number of City bankers from 44 to 22.[66]

The reasons for this decrease were the same for the three countries. Some derived from the development of modern enterprises, which made a business career less and less compatible with a parliamentary activity; others were the product of political changes, in particular the spread of universal franchise and the growth of socialist parties, making the election of big industrialists in constituencies with large working-class concentration increasingly difficult. It is significant that at the beginning of the twentieth century, the two biggest industrialists in Germany and in France, Krupp and Schneider, could no longer secure an election for themselves or for their representative in their respective constituencies of Essen and Le Creusot against left-wing opponents.[67]

However, the main reason for the decrease in the number of businessmen in Parliament is that, whatever the real power of their respective Parliaments, big businessmen had more efficient ways of influencing the economic policy of the country in the direction of their business interests. This is not to suggest that the Parliaments had lost all significance for policy-making in the eyes of businessmen. Simply, businessmen themselves did not need to be present but could use representatives in order to ensure that their interests would be defended. In all three countries, business associations lobbied Parliament and in France and Germany, more than in Britain, the most powerful trade associations disposed of electoral funds with which they financed political parties or individual candidates.[58]

In addition, there were other channels of influence, outside Parliament, ensured direct access to the executive power. In Germany, the large professional associations were in practice integrated with the State.[69] The most powerful of them, such as the *Verein Deutscher Eisen- und Stahl Industrieller*, the *Langnam-Verein* or the *Centralverband deutscher Industrieller (CdI)* were not only consulted, for their expertise, by the state bureaucracy, but were associated with the decision-making process, particularly in such fields as tariff or social insurance policies.[70]

Trade associations were much less developed in France than in Germany,[71] although the most powerful of them, the *Comité des Forges* – the association of the iron and steel industrialists – was extremely well connected in political circles and the higher administration, and extremely influential in matters of tariff policy and social legislation.[72] Besides, French top businessmen were well represented, together with politicians and senior civil servants, in the various consultative commissions and parliamentary committees, particularly in those dealing with economic and social matters, where they were often in a majority.[73] Moreover, the extension of the *pantouflage*, that is, the passage from the higher administration to the private sector, a more highly developed phenomenon in France than elsewhere, strengthened the personal relationships between the business, political and administrative elites.[76] In Britain, personal intervention and consultation were more efficient than the mediation of pressure groups, which were less developed than in France and Germany, probably because of the more cohesive nature of the British ruling class.

However, all businessmen did not have equal access to political power. The stronger influence of the City of London in the shaping of British economic policy was no doubt due to the fact that bankers had a more direct access to Whitehall than industrialists.[75] In Germany, the Ruhr heavy industrialists remained more powerful than the representatives of the newer light industries, whose main association, the *Bund der Industriellen*, was never in a position to challenge the influence of the older CdI which was dominated by the heavy industries; however, they collaborated in the few years preceding the First World War.[76] In France, Parisian big business, both financial and industrial, was certainly the closest to political power.

There was therefore a basic similarity, if not in the form, at least in the essential nature of political intervention by businessmen, which was more 'technical' than 'political'. When businessmen were active in politics, whether personally or through the medium of representatives, they dealt with questions directly connected with their business interests, most often fiscal and tariff issues rather than with matters of 'high politics', such as the general programme of government and international relations. What mattered to them was the most efficient way to achieve these particular claims.

Conclusion

In terms of economic power, social prestige and political influence, German businessmen do not appear, on the basis of this general survey, to have been very different from their British and French counterparts. They might have headed larger enterprises, but they can be considered as possessing the same status. There are no signs that public opinion held businessmen in a significantly higher or lower esteem in one country than in the others. Finally, businessmen had basically the same type of relationships with the political power in the three countries.

There was, however, an area of difference in the relationships with other elites, whether aristocratic or bourgeois. Briefly stated, it can be said that the German business elite married less often into the aristocracy than the British and less often into the other bourgeois elite groups than the French. However, beyond a 10 to 15 percent difference, not statistically significant enough to draw general conclusions, it is the position of the big businessmen in the dominating elite of the country that appears to have been different. In Britain and France, the upper echelons of the business classes merged with other groups to form a dominating elite. In Britain, the merger of the City aristocracy and the landed aristocracy, with the later addition of the biggest industrialists, formed what is usually called the Establishment.[77] In France, the Parisian *aristocratie financière* merged with the *grande bourgeoisie de robe* to form the *classes dominante*, from which the old aristocracy was not absent, even though it was more in the position of the 'junior partner' than in Britain. What characterised these two groups was their profound social unity: their members belonged to the same world and were sometimes related to one another.

No such group seems to have existed in Germany. In particular, there was no German equivalent to the French or British financial aristocracy. In Britain and France, bankers were the first business group to be integrated into the upper classes, whereas in Germany the banking community was largely Jewish and so could not be absorbed fully into the dominating elite. There might have been a new elite in Imperial Germany, but only in the sense that the aristocracy was henceforth sharing its power with the *Großbürgertum*, that they increasingly shared the same way of life, met socially and that inter-marriages were becoming more frequent. The two groups might also have been functionally integrated, although a complete merger, leading to the formation of a single social group, as happened in Britain did not take place. On the other hand, links between German big businessmen and the other bourgeois elite groups were not as close as in France. However, considering the strength, both social and political, of the German aristocracy,[78] closer links would not have been sufficient to form a single dominating elite.

This is not to suggest that French or British big businessmen should no longer be characterised as bourgeois.[79] They were certainly bourgeois, whether through their way of life, even when they were becoming part of 'high society', or through their cultural values, which were shared by an increasing number of social classes and were perhaps better typified by the petty bourgeoisie.[80] However, the debate about the 'feudalisation' of the German *Großbürgertum*[81] is a reflection of the differences in the composition of the dominating elite of each country. This debate has lost much of its significance in Britain and France in favour, at least in France, of a more detailed analysis of the relationships between the various elite groups that were in their great majority bourgeois. This is the reason behind my initial suggestion that the terms *bourgeoisie* and middle class might be less useful than that of elite or ruling class for an analysis of French and British big businessmen, whereas *Bürgertum* remains applicable to the case of Germany.

Notes to Chapter 4

1. For these differentiations in Germany, see for example J. Kocka, 'Bürgertum und Bürgerlichkeit als Probleme der deutschen Geschichte vom späten 18. zum frühen 20. Jahrhundert', in *Bürger und Bürgerlichkeit im 19. Jahrhundert* (Göttingen, 1987), pp. 21–63.

2. See in particular E. Beau de Loménie, *Les responsabilités des dynasties bourgeoises* (Paris, new ed. 1977), 5 vols., which is a controversial interpretation of French history since 1789 in terms of the influence of a group of bourgeois families. See a criticism of the political implications of this analysis in J.-N. Jeanneney, *L'argent caché. Milieux d'affaires et pouvoirs politiques dans la France de XXe siècle* (Paris, 2nd. ed, 1984).

3. Adeline Daumard, *La bourgeoisie parisienne de 1815 à 1848* (Paris, 1963), as well as her chapters in F. Braudel and E. Labrousse (eds.), *Histoire économique et sociale de la France* (Paris, 1976), vols. III/2 and IV/1. For a regional analysis, see J.-P. Chaline, *Les Bourgeois de Rouen. Une élite urbaine au XIXe siècle* (Paris, 1982).

4. For some definitions in the use of the concept of *Bürgertum*, see U. Haltern, *Bürgerliche Gesellschaft. Sozialtheoretische und sozialhistorische Aspekte* (Darmstadt, 1985).

5. The theoretical literature is very abundant on the subject. See in particular, R. Bendix and S.M. Lipset (eds.), *Class, Status and Power* (London, 1967); R. Dahrendorf, *Class and Class Conflicts in Industrial Society* (London, 1961); R. Aron, 'Social Class, Political Class, Ruling Class', *European Journal of Sociology*, I (1960), pp. 260–82; A. Giddens, 'Elites in the British Class Structure', in P. Stanworth and A. Giddens (eds.), *Elites and Power in British Society* (Cambridge, 1974).

6. One could also use P. Bourdieu's terminology of *capital économique, capital social, capital culturel*, etc. See his 'Le patronat', with Monique de Saint Martin, in *Actes de la Recherche en Sciences Sociales*, 20/21 (1978), pp. 3–82; and *La distinction. Critique sociale du jugement* (Paris, 1979).

7. Respectively heads of N.M. Rothschild & Sons and Baring Brothers & Co. in London, and De Rothschild Frères and Messrs Hottinguer in Paris.

8. This was for example the case of the private bankers in the late nineteenth and early twentieth century.

9. In 1913, the deposits of the London City and Midland Bank amounted to £93.8 million, those of Lloyds Bank to £91.5 million, those of the Credit Lyonnais to £89 million and those of the Deutsche Bank to £79 million.

10. See J. Kocka and H. Siegrist, 'Die hundert größten deutschen Industrieunternehmen im späten 19. und frühen 20. Jahrhundert', in N. Horn und J. Kocka (eds.), *Recht und Entwicklung der Großunternehmen im 19. und frühen 20. Jahrhundert* (Göttingen, 1979), p. 55.

11. Christine Shaw, 'The Large Manufacturing Employers of 1907', *Business History*, 25 (1983), pp. 42–60.

12. R. Church, *The History of the British Coal Industry. Vol 3: 1830–1913: Victorian Pre-eminence* (Oxford, 1986), p. 400.

13. N. Horn und J. Kocka, 'Introduction', in Horn, Kocka (eds.), *Recht und Entwicklung*, p. 1.

14. F. Caron, 'Dynamismes et freinages de la croissance industrielle', in Braudel and Labrousse (eds.), *Histoire économique et sociale de la France*, vol. IV/1, p. 263. See also P. Fridenson, 'Die Arbeiterpolitik großer Unternehmen in Frankreich', in J. Kocka (ed.), *Arbeiter und Bürger im 19. Jahrhundert* (München, 1986), pp. 185–201.

15. See O. Jeidels, *Das Verhältnis der deutschen Großbanken zur Industrie* (Munich, Leipzig, 1913). H. Pogge von Strandmann, *Unternehmenspolitik und Unternehmensführung: der Dialog zwischen Aufsichtsrat und Vorstand bei Mannesmann 1900 bis 1919* (Düsseldorf, Vienna, 1978); W. E. Mosse, *Jews in the German Economy. The German-Jewish Economic Elite 1820-1935* (Oxford, 1987).

16. See C. Trebilcock, *The Vickers Brothers: Armaments and Enterprise, 1854–1914* (London, 1977).

17. See Y. Cassis, 'Management and Strategy in the English Joint Stock Banks, 1890–1914', *Business History*, vol. 27 (1985), pp. 301–15.

18. See for example D.C. Coleman, 'Gentlemen and Players', *Economic History Review*, 2nd ser., vol. 21, (1973), pp. 92–116.

19. In 1907, three members of the Thyssen family were on the Gruben-Vorstand of Deutscher Kaiser, Friedrich Bayer was on the Vorstand of the firm of the same name and the entire Vorstand of Gebrüder Stollwerck was made up of members of the Stollwerck family. In 1912, Carl Friedrich von Siemens became Vorstandvorsitzender of Siemens-Schuckertwerke, replacing a salaried manager, Alfred Berliner.

20. See J. Kocka, 'Les entrepreneurs salariés dans l'industrie alemande à la fin du XIXe et au début du XXe Siècle', in M. Lévy-Leboyer, (ed.), *Le patronat de la seconde industrialisation*, (Paris, 1979), pp. 85–100.

21. See André Thépot, (ed.), *L'ingénieur dans la société française* (Paris, 1985). A good example of the roles of the *administrateurs* and of the *directeurs* can be found in J-P Daviet, 'La Compagnie de Saint-Gobain de 1830 à 1939', 2 vols, University of Paris I, doctoral thesis, 1983.

22. Odette Hardy-Henery, *De la croissance à la désindustrialisation. Un siècle dans le Valenciennois*, (Paris, 1984), pp. 74–77.

23. W.D. Rubinstein, 'Modern Britain', in id. (ed.), *Wealth and the Wealthy in the Modern World* (London, 1980), p. 60.

24. H. Kaelble, 'Wie feudal waren die deutschen Unternehmer im Kaiserreich? Ein Zwischenbericht', in R. Tilly (ed.), *Beiträge zur quantitativen vergleichenden Unternehmensgeschichte* (Stuttgart, 1985), p. 171.

25. Adeline Daumard, *Les fortunes françaises au XIXe siècle* (Paris, 1973), p. 148.

26. *Ibid*.

27. W.D. Rubinstein, 'Introduction', in id. (ed.), *Wealth and the Wealthy*, p. 19.

28. W.D. Rubinstein, *Men of Property. The very Wealthy in Britain since the Industrial Revolution*, (London, 1981), pp. 56–116.

29. Dolores L. Augustine-Pérez, 'Wealthy Businessmen in Imperial Germany', unpubl. paper, FU Berlin, pp. 9–10.

30. C. Charle, 'Intellectuels et élites en France (1880–1900)', University of Paris I, doctoral thesis, 1986, p. 449.

31. Y. Cassis, *Les banquiers de la City à l'époque édouardienne, 1890–900* (Geneva, 1984), p. 238.

32. See A. Plessis, *Régents et gouverneurs de la Banque de France sous le Second Empire* (Geneva, 1985).

33. The figures for Britain are from H. Perkin, 'The Recruitment of Elites in Britain since 1880', *Journal of Social History* vol. 12 (1978), pp. 222–34; and for Germany from H. Kaelble, 'Sozialer Aufstieg in Deutschland, 1850–1914, in *Vierteljahrschrift für Sozial- und Wirtschaftsgeschichte*, vol. 60 (1973) pp. 41–71. Both are quoted by H. Kaelble, *Historische Mobilitätsforschung: Westeuropa und die USA im 19. und 20. Jahrhundert* (Darmstadt, 1978), pp. 107–136. For France, see M. Levy-Leboyer, 'Le patronat français, 1912–1973', in id. (ed.), *Le patronat de la seconde industrialisation*, p. 142. For France, I have added the medium-sized (11.9 percent) to the big businessmen (40.3 percent). For a sample of French businessmen in 1901, C. Charle reaches the following figures: sons of businessmen 57.5 percent (big business 43.4 percent, medium-sized 14.1 percent) sons of senior civil servants 14.9 percent, members of the law professions 12.2 percent; 'Intellectuels et élites', pp. 68–69.

34. T. Pierenkemper, *Die westfälischen Schwerindustriellen 1852–1913* (Göttingen, 1979); p. 44, C. Erickson, *British Industrialists: Steel and Hosiery, 1850–1950* (Cambridge, 1959), p. 12.

35. Cassis, *Les banquiers de la City*, p. 116.

36. Perkin 'Recruitment of British Elites', quoted by Kaelble, *Historische Mobilitätsforschung*, p. 142.

37. J. Estèbe, *Les ministres de la République, 1871–1914* (Paris, 1982), pp. 20–21.

38. M. Knight, *The German Executive 1890–1933* (Stanford, 1955), p. 45, quoted by Kaelble, *Historische Mobilitätsforschung*, p. 150.

39. Charle, 'Intellectuels et élites', pp. 68–69. The highest proportion of sons of businessmen was among the *inspecteurs des finances*.

40. H. Henning, *Die deutsche Beamtenschaft im 19. Jahrhundert* (Stuttgart, 1984), p. 54.

41. E. Hobsbawm, *Industry and Empire* (London, 1968), p. 185.

42. Christine Shaw, 'Characteristics of British Business Leaders: Findings from the DBB', paper presented at the Anglo-Japanese Business History Conference, Business History Unit, London School of Economics, August 1986.

43. Date on bankers in Cassis, *Les banquiers de la City*, pp. 121–129; on steel industrialists in Erickson, *British industrialists*, p. 33; on Cabinet Ministers in W.L. Guttsman, *The British Political Elite* (London, 1965), p. 102.

44. See T.W. Bamford, *Rise of the Public Schools: a Study of Boys' Public Boarding Schools in England and Wales from 1837 to the Present Day* (London, 1967).

45. See F.K. Ringer, *Education and Society in Modern Europe* (Bloomington, 1979).

46. C. Charle, 'Les milieux d'affaires dans la structure e la classes cominante vers 1900', *Actes de la recherche en sciences sociales*, vol. 20/21 (1978), p. 87.

47. P. Fritsch, *Les Wendel, rois de l'acier français* (Paris, 1976), p. 139.

48. See T. Shinn, *Savoir scientifique et pouvoir social. L'école polytechnique 1794–1914* (Paris, 1980); E. Chadeau, *Les inspecteurs des finances au XIXe siècle (1850–1914). Profil social et rôle économique* (Paris, 1986).

49. See K. Jarausch, *Students, Society and Politics in Imperial Germany. The Rise of Academic Illiberalism* (Princeton, 1982).

50. Rolande Trempé, 'Contribution à l'étude de la psychologie patronale: Analyse du comportement des administrateurs de la Société des Mines de Carmaux vis à vis des mineurs (1856–1914)', *Le Mouvement Social*, vol. 43 (1963), p. 53–91.

51. This lifestyle could also be described as plutocratic, rather than aristocratic, in order to emphasise the money, rather than the land element. See the essay by W. Mosse in this volume.

52. Cassis, *Les banquiers de la City*, pp. 289–296; C. Charle, 'Intellectuels et élites', pp. 472–485; E. Achterberg, *Berliner Hochfinanz. Kaiser, Fürsten, Millionäre um 1900* (Frankfurt a/Main, 1965), pp. 43–47.

53. See for example F. Stern, *Gold and Iron. Bismarck, Bleichröder, and the Building of the German Empire* (New York, 1977), pp. 159–175.

54. Despite their importance, data on marriages are usually the most difficult to collect. Except for France, there are no statistics of marriages available for a sample of top businessmen of the period that are representative of the various sectors and branches as well as of the whole country. For Britain, the only figures available relate to bankers, whereas for Germany two sets of data are available: one on the wealthiest businessmen, the other on the Wesphalian *Kommerzienräte*. Some important indications can, however, be gathered from this scattered information.

55. Cassis, *Les banquiers de la City*, pp. 241–288, and 'Bankers in English Society in the late Nineteenth Century', *Economic History Review*, 2nd. ser., vol. 38 (1985), pp. 210–29.

56. Charle, 'Intellectuels et élites', pp. 353, 362, 350–394.

57. Augustine-Pérez, 'Wealthy Businessmen', p. 12. The figures have been recalculated in order to eliminate the cases with no or uncertain information, respectively 13.7 and 36.5 percent. If all cases are taken into account, 31.1 percent married the daughter of a big businessman, with another 12.6 percent of fathers-in-law being most probably businessmen, 3.5 percent married the daughter of a big landowner and 8.3 percent the daughter of a member of the *Bildungsbürgertum*.

58. H. Henning, 'Soziale Verflechtungen der Unternehmer in Westfalen 1860–1914', *Zeitschrift für Unternehmensgeschichte*, vol. 23 (1978), p. 13.

59. See for example J. Turner, 'The politics of Business', in id, (ed,), *Businessmen and Politics. Studies of business activity in British Politics, 1900–1945* (London, 1984), p. 3.

60. Cassis, *Les banquiers de la City*, p. 317.

61. Charle, 'Intellectuels et élites', p. 679.

62. H. Jaeger, *Unternehmer in der deutschen Politik, 1890–1918* (Bonn, 1967), p. 102.

63. Charle, 'Intellectuels et élites', p. 678.

64. Jaeger, *Unternehmer in der deutschen Politik*, p. 47.

65. Rubinstein, 'Modern Britain', p. 73.

66. Cassis, *Les banquiers de la City*, p. 321.

67. Jaeger, *Unternehmer in der deutschen Politik*, pp. 91–92; J.A. Roy, *Histoire de la famille Schneider et du Creusot* (Paris, 1962), p. 87.

68. H. Kaelble, *Industrielle Interessenpolitik in der wilhelminischen Gesellschaft. Centralverband Deutscher Industrieller 1894–1914* (Berlin, 1967), pp. 120–123; M.J. Rust, 'Business and Politics in the Third Republic: the Comité des Forges and the French Steel Industry, 1896–1914', Ph.D dissertation, Princeton University, 1973, p. 356.

69. H.-U. Wehler, *Das deutsche Kaiserreich 1871–1918* (Göttingen, 1977), pp. 90ff. (Published in English as *The German Empire 1871–1918* (Oxford/New York, 1985).

70. See F. Blaich, *Staat und Verbände in Deutschland zwischen 1871 und 1945* (Wiesbaden, 1979); W. Fischer, 'Staatsverwaltung und Interessenverbäne in Deutschland 1871–1914', in H.J. Varain (ed.), *Interessenverbände in Deutschland* (Köln, 1973) pp. 139–61; T. Nipperdey, 'Interessenverbände und Parteien in Deutschland vor dem Ersten Weltkrieg', *Politische Vierteljahresschrift* 2 (1961) pp. 262–80; D. Stegmann, *Die Erben Bismarcks. Parteien und Verbände in der Spätphase des wilhelminischen Deutschlands* (Köln, 1970).

71. See G. Lefranc, *Les organisations patronales en France* (Paris, 1976); and R.F. Kuisel, *Capitalism and the State in Modern France* (Cambridge, 1981).

72. Rust, 'Business and Politics'.

73. Charle, 'Intellectuels et élites', pp. 686–91.

74. See C. Charles, 'Le pantouflage en France (vers 1880 – vers 1980)', *Annales E.S.C.*, vol. 42 (1987), pp. 1115–37.

75. See Cassis, 'Bankers in English Society', in G. Ingham (ed.), *Capitalism Divided? The City and Industry in British Social Development* (London, 1984).

76. See Kaelble, *Industrielle Interessenpolitik*; H.-P. Ullmann, *Der Bund der Industriellen. Organisation, Einfluss und Politik klein- und mittelbetrieblicher Industrieller im Deutschen Kaiserreich* (Göttingen, 1976).

77. See J. Scott, *The Upper Classes. Property and Privilege in Britain* (London, 1982).

78. See the paper by H. Kaelble in this volume. This shows how, in contrast to France, the German *Bürgertum* still had to share power with the aristocracy.

79. On the general question of the groups belonging to the *Bürgertum*, see M.R. Lepsius, 'Zur Soziologie des Bürgertums und der Bürgerlichkeit', in Kocka (ed.), *Bürger und Bürgerlichkeit*, pp. 79–100.

80. On the position of businessmen in French society, see L. Bergeron, *Les capitalistes 1780–1914* (Paris, 1978), in particular pp. 143–163. On the French *bourgeoisie* at the beginning of the twentieth century, see A Daumard in Braudel and Labrousse (eds.), *Histoire économique et sociale de la France*, vol. IV/1. Unfortunately a history of the English bourgeoisie or a general social study of British businessmen is still lacking.

81. See H. Kaelble, 'Wie feudal', for the most recent discussion of the question. For bibliographical details, see note 24.

II | THE MIDDLE CLASSES IN GERMANY AND BRITAIN

5 | The Example of the English Middle Class[1]

Eric Hobsbawm

The term 'middle class(es)' established itself in British political and social discourse some time between 1790 and 1830, first as a synonym for 'the middling people', 'the middling sorts', or 'the middle ranks of people', later as an alternative to these terms. Like all class terminology, it was opposed by political and social conservatives, who preferred the traditional language of 'rank', 'order', and 'degree', which stressed the permanence of hierarchical subordination in society and the 'attachment' that linked loyal inferiors to generous superiors. The language of class replaced the language of ranks precisely when the growing distance between social groups and their conflicting interests began to push their supposed common interests into the background. The analysts of political economy reinforced social classification with economic function. By 1834 John Stuart Mill could write that

> they revolve in their eternal circle of landlords, capitalists and labourers, until they seem to think of the distinction of society into those three classes as if it were one of God's ordinances, not man's.[2]

Yet, as the neutral term 'middle class' implies, the old language of rank, order and degree was no longer the reflection of a society ordered into accepted estates or *Stände*, such as the dominated ideal in continental countries. Unlike the German *Bürgertum*, the English 'middle classes' (the term was used in the plural more than the singular) faced neither the problem of liquidating a society of estates, nor of constructing a national state, nor of establishing a market society. By the eighteenth century England was in no sense 'feudal', even in its wealthy, commercially-minded aristocracy.[3] Its economy was in every realistic sense capitalist. To speak of eighteenth century England as an *ancien régime* is to use metaphorical language. To take but one example. The world of the 'Handwerker' had already split

Notes to Chapter 5 can be found on page 147.

linguistically into two. 'Master' became a synonym for 'employer', 'journeyman' now indicated exclusively a skilled wage-worker, 'trade' (*Gewerbe*) among workers meant the apprenticed worker's craft, everywhere else (except in Scotland) a 'tradesman' meant a shopkeeper, generally a retailer. The bulk of the vocabulary of guilds and corporations passed into the vocabulary of organised labour. In England 'the antecedents of the trade union' emerging from the polarisation of guilds into capitalists and wage-workers, have been traced back as far as the seventeenth century.[4]

Perhaps the disintegration of older forms of social classification left room for those situated between the nobility and gentry on one hand, the 'labouring classes' on the other, to form a single intermediate class of their own. For it is only too plain that in pre-industrially structured societies the mere fact of belonging to some middle group is not an adequate basis for common bourgeois consciousness. In feudal (or just ex-feudal) Scotland,[5] for instance, where the terms 'landed classes' and 'labouring classes' or even 'working class' were readily used at the end of the eighteenth century, 'there was as yet nothing commonly used to describe those who lived in towns and lived by employing their brains and their capital and who were not often seen by contemporaries as having anything very significant in common with one another'[6]: lawyers, ministers, merchants, schoolmasters, tradesmen, officeholders or industrial entrepreneurs.

Yet a sense of class did develop in these intermediate groups, and in a patently class-divided Britain it could not but be formulated, since the political system already implied a sphere of public debate and the political organisation of interest-groups. 'Public opinion' under the British constitution was the incubator of middle-class consciousness, initially in conflict with the entrenched 'landed classes' over taxation and economic policy, but later also in recognition of class movements of the labouring strata. Ideologies of more general reform would naturally emerge from, or attach themselves to this class moreover, the 'higher classes' themselves – the phrase seems to have been used in Burke's *Thoughts on French Affairs* (1793) – were aware of the political need to draw the middle class to their side. They 'form the real and efficient mass of public opinion', wrote Earl Grey to the King, 'and without them the power of the gentry is nothing'. But, seen from their own point of view, 'the class which is universally described as both the most wise and the most virtuous part of the community', the 'middle rank' (to cite James Mill's famous *Essay on Government* [1820]) represented more than itself. It was, to quote Sir James Graham, a moderate Whig who became a moderate Tory, 'that numerous class, removed from the wants of labour and the cravings of ambition, enjoying the advantages of leisure, and possessing intelligence sufficient for the formation of sound judgement neither warped by interest nor obscured by passions', neither by the 'interest' of the landed classes nor by the 'passions' of the lower orders. Thus, fortunately for the common good, 'the seat of public opinion is in the middle ranks of life'.[7]

However, both theory and experience suggested an economic definition for this class. Political economy saw the crucial division between the owners of land and capital, whose interests, as Adam Smith knew, differed. Since his day, economic transformations that seemed revolutionary to contemporaries had dramatically increased the role of the business classes:

> Machinery creates wealth, which augments the middle class, which gives strength to public opinion; consequently to allude to the extension of machinery is to account for the increase of the middle class of society.[8]

In short, both analytically and empirically, entrepreneurs, and especially manufacturers in the expanding new industrial areas, were seen as the core of the middle class. The markedly northern orientation of the chief public campaign for economic liberalism, the Anti-Corn-Law League, probably reinforced this identification.

Recent studies have shown that this was misleading. Of the three major components of the 'middle classes', mercantile and financial wealth, largely concentrated around London, was consistently far greater in total and per capita than the wealth of manufacturers. Industrialists were in a minority among the rich in all levels above incomes of £3,000 per annum.[9] In short trade and finance were the heart of bourgeois wealth even when Britain was the 'workshop of the world'. Again, the professional classes of the era before the 1832 Reform Act shared with the landed nobility the spoils of the 'Old Corruption', which middle-class reformers attacked ceaselessly. Seventeen percent of all testaments of more than a £500,000 left between 1809 and 1858, and 32 percent of those worth between £150,000 and £499,000 came from such professionals, soldiers, sailors, public administrators and holders of political and other pensions, places and sinecures, correctly named 'offices of profit under the crown'.[10] This was larger than the corresponding number left by industrialists. Few of them were as wealthy as the common-born Lord Chancellor Lord Eldon (1751–1838), who left £707,000 without counting his landed estates. Moreover, both mercantile-financial wealth and the beneficiaries of 'Old Corruption' – it would be misleading to call them a *Beamtenstand* – were far closer to the landed ruling class and more easily absorbed into it.

It was therefore logical to single out the new bourgeoisie of industrialism as the essential 'middle class'. As (largely provincial) outsiders, its members had more cause to demand attention for their interests and less chances to make personal deals with government. Since they could also mobilise public support more easily as local notables, they became the organised pressure-group for the policy interests – such as Free Trade – which they shared with trade and finance. In the large industrial towns they stood out as the middle class could not in London: far above 'the petty bourgeoisie', which in the view of a German observer (Engels) 'consisted only of grocers and very, very few artisans'.[11]

The professional classes of 'Old Corruption', on the other hand, could have no collective presence as a middle class, being parasitic on the State and estates of the landed interest. In fact, they were part of what rational bourgeois reform wished to abolish, and, in the clean-up of the Augean stables of 'Old Corruption' after 1832, and the subsequent reform of the civil service and the universities, did largely abolish. Thus in 1809–29 fifteen lawyers and judges had died worth between £150,000 and £500,000, but in 1850–69 only four left the same amounts.[12] The middle class was transformed and its centre of gravity shifted toward the business strata for a few decades, until the renewed rise of professions and of the State as a factor in business.

II.

In the absence of classification by rank and estate, the lines that separated the middle classes from those above and below were vague. Two characteristics of the British situation made them even hazier, but one appeared to facilitate a clearer distinction.

The clarifying factor, which had no intrinsic connection with social structure, was the monopoly position of the Anglican Church in the official institutions of England and Wales. (In Scotland Calvinism formed the official national Church.) Minority religions therefore found themselves collectively discriminated against, and though their disabilities were removed after 1828, effective equality of religions in public life was not achieved until the 1870s. Since unofficial Protestantism and Judaism (though not Catholicism) were notable nurseries of business enterprise, this exclusion bonded together the interest of unofficial religion, important sectors of business, economic liberalism and political reform. The mass-meeting of Dissenting ministers organised by the Anti-Corn-Law League is typical of this. Conversely, in the Parliaments of the 1860s, although not all businessmen were religious Dissenters, 'nearly all Dissenters in Parliament were businessmen'.[13]

This was to some extent an optical illusion. Dissenters formed a minority of businessmen, albeit a disproportionately strong one. Most unofficial Protestants – their number multiplied in 1810–1850 – did not belong to the middle classes, however loosely defined. The leadership of the largest such group, the Wesleyan Methodists, was Conservative until the 1880s, though probably most followers were not. The Liberal Party itself, though a stronghold of business, was also a stronghold of the great Whig landed nobility.[14] And yet, until the links between business, dissident religion and Liberalism were attenuated at the end of the century, they helped to reinforce the image of a mobilised bourgeoisie, child of the industrial revolution.

However, the borders of this class were, and had to be, almost indefinable, for two reasons, which may also explain the peculiar British use of the terms 'class' and 'class system' to mean a hierarchy of layers of status and snobbery. Social mobility precluded a sharp separation of the 'middle class' from those rising into it from below. As a French observer in 1911 put it, the middle classes 'consisted essentially of families in the process of rising socially', the 'bourgeoisie' of those who had 'arrived'.[15] Or, as a Unitarian minister and Free Trade campaigner observed in 1835: 'In the middle classes we note an almost universal unfixedness of position. Every man is rising or falling, or hoping that he shall rise, or fearing that he shall sink'.[16] This implied a certain openness of class frontiers, though it could be agreed that actual manual labour, especially for wages, was incompatible with even the most modest levels of middle-class aspiration.

The border between the middle classes and the upper classes was equally permeable, even before the 1950s when 'as a social class of really national significance the upper class has nearly ceased to exist... For practical purposes, the great majority of those who feel they belonged to it...have become merged in the middle classes, and would now think of themselves as "upper middle class".'[17]

Though the traditional upper class of nobility and gentry, defined by birth, landownership and the political and other privileges that went with both, safeguarded its estates until the agrarian depression of the late nineteenth century, it was notoriously open to outside recruitment – the size of the peerage virtually doubled between 1760 and 1832 – and since normally a peerage required prior proof of the required degree of wealth, there was plenty of scope for the ennoblement of self-made men, even Jews such as the financier Sampson Gideon (1699–1762) whose son was created a baronet and Irish peer in 1789.[18] The creation of peers slackened somewhat in the Reform era, but speeded up considerably from the 1890s: from an annual average of four in 1830–68 to ten or eleven in the fifty years after 1895.[19] Moreover, intermarriage between the high aristocracy and the acceptable branches of business became quite acceptable. A quarter of late nineteenth-century London bankers (more than a third if we exclude cases where information is not available) married daughters of the aristocracy, without even feeling the need to retire from active business, as early business entrants into the aristocratic world had been inclined to do.[20] Factories and forges were no doubt less acceptable than banks, but dynasties in which heavy industry inherited land, mines, and finance are hard to disentangle, are common, as in the northeast.[21]

What made this continuum between birth and accumulation easier to establish was the absence of occupational caste-marks among the nobility and gentry. Primogeniture would in any case have made it difficult to exclude younger sons and other non-inheritors of land from non-aristocratic occupations. However, legally the lesser gentry had long since merged with the commoners, and it is significant that the members of peers' families were also all commoners in law, and therefore eligible for the House of Commons.

The English nobility and gentry therefore contained titled and untitled members whose activities were impossible to distinguish from those of non-aristocrats. Moreover, it was surrounded by 'a host of relatives, well-to-do or quite poor, who claimed gentility because of their family connections'[22] and who consequently held aloof from others of middle-class occupation or income. Poor Mrs Marx was not the only Victorian lady who insisted on a remote kinship with the Dukes of Argyll or some other noble house. In short, while established noblemen lost nothing by marrying Americans, Jews or show-girls, large sections of the middle classes were constantly haunted, as Victorian novels make clear, by the terror of losing caste through marriage to someone who was not, or 'not quite' a 'gentleman' or 'lady'. This naturally cut across a sense of middle-class or bourgeois consciousness, all the more so as (in the absence of kinship to someone of blue blood, however distantly related) the most damning occupations and antecedents were precisely those most closely associated with upward mobility, economic or social, with 'new' as against 'old' money or occupations, and with a milieu incompatible with the English landed classes, such as the world of Dissent.

In turn, every stratum of the rising middle class, every new profession, marked the ledge on the rockface of social ascent where it had come to rest by a claim to have acquired some degree of the high status, whose ideal-typical expression was self-confident 'gentility'. Indeed, in the course of the century the word 'gentleman' itself lost all its traditional connotation of member of the hereditary gentry, entitled to a coat of arms. It became the property of anyone whose middle-class standing was unquestioned. So far as one can tell, the word was never applied (except jocularly) to manual workers, and rarely (except for commercial flattery) to the old petty-bourgeoisie.

For most of the nineteenth century we must therefore distinguish between (1) what might be called neutrally 'the middle classes', i.e. the ensemble of groups, however defined, situated between the nobility and gentry above and the lower middle classes, shadowing over into labour, below; (2) particular occupational or other groups within this ensemble; (3) between such groups, as graded according to hierarchies of status, which were largely a function of the group's age, wealth and official recognition; and (4) 'middle-class consciousness' in its various forms.

It cannot be assumed that a single class consciousness is always to be found or that all members of the ensemble under (1) possess any form of it. Nor can it be assumed that all consciously middle-class groups defined their class in the same way. Nevertheless, with rare exceptions, almost all members of 'the middle class' would, until after 1880, share the following characteristics: (1) they did not (except by deliberate choice as a leisure activity) perform manual labour. As for women, manual work or probably any regularly paid occupation debarred them from the status of a 'lady'; (2) they would normally have to possess some property or capital, however modest; (3) they would almost certainly employ others for wages, if only as domestic servants; (4) they would not be employed for wages themselves, except by State or Church.[23] Except insofar as they were receiving a wage from God or the State, (male) members of the middle class were deemed to be engaged in private enterprise, as earners of profit or independent professionals, both profits and professional fees being still bracketed together for tax purposes.

These five basic criteria provided the ensemble of the intermediate strata with socioeconomic coherence, and they incidentally linked all of them except public officials of middle-class status, once the spoils system of 'Old Corruption' had ended, with the ideal-typical capitalist. And the number of state officials of unquestionably middle-class status, i.e. after the reform of the Civil Service (1855–1870), the Administrative Class of the Home Civil service and the equivalent grades in the Indian and colonial services, was extremely modest. The Home service in the 1870s recruited an annual average of ten to eleven administrators, the Indian civil service thirty to forty: but the mean annual increase between 1841 and 1881 in the number of lawyers was 92, of architects 135, of civil engineers 155, and of accountants 180.[24] In short, the purely official sector of the middle class was relatively insignificant. As we shall see, even in retrospect a *Bildungsbürgertum* is not easily discernible.

III.

After about 1880 six developments transformed the composition, situation and ways of life of the English middle classes.

(1) For the first time the bourgeois rich, irrespective of the origins of their wealth, outclassed the elite of the old landed wealth, as the following table shows:

Table 5.1: Number of persons leaving over £500,000 at death, 1809–1914[25]

Source	1809–58	1859–79	1880–99	1900–14
Land	530	282	175	107
Manufacturing, etc.	49	124	208	244

At the same time there was a striking rise in the bourgeois element in the peerage, the House of Commons and the government. Industrialists became more prominent. 'Commerce and industry', though rising after the 1867 Reform Act, only formed 50 percent of MPs in both major parties after 1885. In 1906 they formed two-thirds in both. Aristocrats, always a majority in Cabinets before 1886, were always a minority thereafter.[26]

Consequently there occurred at the top of the social pyramid 'a visible obliteration of the conventional distinction between the aristocracies of birth and money, the oligarchies of manufacture and land'[27] and the formation of a plutocracy including elements of both. The novelty lay not so much in the assimilation of bourgeois elements into aristocracy, which was not new. It lay rather in the systematic shift of the criterion of social importance from land to money, from birth to wealth: from a nobility assimilating some bourgeois to, one might almost say, a bourgeoisie absorbing sufficiently wealthy members of the old nobility. That intermarriage with aristocrats did not imply abandoning active business, has already been noted. Equally significant is the fact that, after the mid-century, businessmen of non-landed background made no serious attempt to crown their wealth by turning themselves into major landowners, as a few had done earlier.[28]

One significant development that occurred after 1880 and – however we interpret its causes – reinforced the fusion of old and new wealth was the split of the Liberal Party, which was eventually to make the Conservatives into the united party of the fusion between capital and land, a process not completed until the inter-war years. For most of the richest and most prestigious nobles, the great Whig houses, now joined their Tory rivals traditionally resting on the larger but economically less impressive body of rural 'squires', and so did most of commercial and financial wealth (the 'City interests') and a significant body of industrialists, although much of provincial manufacturing, especially when linked to religious dissent, remained Liberal until the 1930s.

(2) A second development strengthened class fusion at the top, even though its chief significance was as a means of integrating old and new generations of the middle classes, a road to promotion within these classes, and a common formula for the membership of the 'upper middle class'. This was formal education in private secondary schools and in universities. The number affected by this form of socialisation was modest. In 1900 all British universities together contained a mere 20,000 students or 0.8 percent of the relevant age-groups, while even as late as 1947 Independent and Direct Grant Schools contained only 81,000 pupils.[29] Nevertheless, their role was increasingly important, and they provided the model for the secondary schools attended by the children of local or aspiring members of the middle classes.

In the absence of a public system of secondary education (until 1902) a variety of private schools had been re-formed or founded in the middle decades of the century on similar lines. Most of them (with the major exception of London) were boarding establishments situated in rural areas, most drew their pupils from a wide area – sometimes the entire country – and turned them into the new version of 'gentlemen' by means of an intensive exposure to Anglican religious worship, classical languages, sports and physical exercise and several years' isolation in a strongly hierarchical single-sex community. Though most such schools provided some scholarships, they were essentially designed for those who could pay large fees. Local pupils and those from the popular classes were kept out in order to ensure social exclusiveness. The unconcealed purpose of these misnamed 'public schools' was to train a ruling class using aristocratic confidence to reinforce bourgeois values. As a contemporary work put it (1894): 'Our aristocrats and wealthy classes can obtain an education that will fit them for the great responsibilities which devolve upon them as directors of our great commercial interest and as legislators of our empire'.[30]

Most public schools were pure middle-class establishments. Although several of them were ancient, and some had traditional links with the aristocracy – Harrow with the Whigs, Eton with both Tories and Whigs[31] – they should not be seen as attempts to absorb a new bourgeoisie into an *ancien régime*, but as devices to form a new bourgeoisie into a coherent class. Public schools proved so successful that, towards the end of the century religious groups excluded from strongly Anglican ethos of the schools formed their own schools along similar lines (e.g. Quakers and Methodists), while other schools relaxed their Anglicanism to meet the demand, as when Clifton (founded 1860) established a Jewish 'house'; the school had hitherto been known chiefly for preparing boys for the Army.

After 1880 the practice of sending sons to the school attended by the father also became usual, as did the organisations of 'Old Boys' or former pupils, and the device of the 'old school tie', a badge of social belonging recognisable not only by past and present members of the school but (because of their generic similarity) by anyone who had attended a similar establishment. Both practices are linked to the rise of sport as part of middle-class lifestyle. On the whole, socialisation took precedence over instruction. Indeed, the various attempts made earlier in the century, by Utilitarian Radicals and others, to establish schools providing 'useful' education for professional and business classes, were overshadowed or absorbed by the standard public school model. There is no systematic equivalent in nineteenth-century Britain for the *Realgymnasium* and *Realschule*.

English universities, i.e. Oxford and Cambridge, had closer associations with the nobility and gentry and, in consequence, little educational interest until reformed in the mid-century. Reform, which also broke the Anglican hold, transformed them into a means of socialising a bourgeois elite as well as institutions of major value to science and scholarship. Socially, the reformed ancient universities were more significant than the foundations of the class-conscious bourgeoisie – Utilitarian Radicals in the case of London University, provincial business elites, mainly in the last decades before 1914 – or the four ancient Scottish universities, not to mention the small University of Wales (1893). The easiest way for their graduates to enter the elite was by a further spell at Oxford or Cambridge. We may note that, except for the Anglican clergy, the old English universities played no significant role in the training of the professions, old or new. They were even less relevant to entrepreneurs, who had usually gone into practical business – their father's or someones else's – at the age of fifteen and sixteen. This was true not only of the first-generation of self-made men but of families with long business traditions in communities like the Quakers and Unitarians who had intense concern for education, culture and intellectual matters.

The shift of businessmen to secondary and higher education for their children therefore signified primarily their search for or arrival at recognised elite status. For the bankers, as Youssef Cassis shows, public schools and Oxbridge became usual in the generation born 1821-40 and almost universal for those born 1861–80.[32] For industrialists the shift came later: about 10 percent of the steel industrialists active in 1865 had been to public school, compared with 31 percent of those active in 1909–25.[33] The percentage of major industrialists educated at public schools has risen continuously and markedly in the twentieth century: in the 1960s it stood at 57 percent.[34] Nevertheless, the generation of the late nineteenth century marks a turning-point. In the Quaker chocolate firm George Cadbury (1839–1922) had still joined his father in the business at the age of 15. It was his son Laurance (1889–1982) who took over the firm after going to Leighton Park and Trinity College, Cambridge.[35]

However, if public school and Oxbridge consummated the acquisition of social status for some, it was the means of acquiring it for others. The family of the economist J.M. Keynes is a good example of what could be done over two generations, starting with a successful Baptist commercial rose-grower and a provincial Baptist preacher, through the systematic passing of competitive examinations and a moderate private income. By the time Maynard Keynes emerged from Eton and King's College, Cambridge, all that remained from the grandparents' world of modest provincial Dissent (other than inherited money) was Keynes' pride in belonging to what he later called 'my class, the educated bourgeoisie'.[36] These were the first persons who might be compared to the German *Bildungsbürger*.

(3) The various devices for marking off an emerging plutocracy and an elite 'upper middle class' from the rest of the middle strata were, in part, responses to the considerable growth of the population that could claim, or wished to assert a claim, to belong to the 'middle class'. The size of this class is virtually impossible to estimate realistically, since no attempts to do so were made officially until the eve of 1914, when the actual number of income-tax payers can first be established, and the first attempt was made to divide the population into 'social classes', essentially on the basis of occupations, to which income and status rankings were assigned.

However, an historian's estimate for 1816 (based on income tax under Schedule D)[37] puts the size of the middle classes then at 165,000–175,000 persons, unmarried or heads of families – exclusive of farmers or rentiers or 3 percent of the total male population.[38] In 1864 the number of Schedule D assessments over £100 a year was given by the tax authorities as about 250,000 or 2 percent of the total male population.[39] In 1909–10 the official estimate of total number of tax-payers, 'the most reliable figure that has been obtainable *at any time*',[40] was about 1.1 million, which, in Stamp's figures, appears consistent with the date for 1864. This would correspond to 5.6 percent. Given the uncertainties of the data, such estimates can bear little weight, except to suggest a significant rise in the income-tax paying population. We may also take it that, since the tax was only levied on incomes above £150 a year (£160 after 1894) 'the tax paying class (is) virtually identical with the middle class as commonly understood'.[41] For comparison with later estimates, let us note the calculation of the 1870s which puts the 'upper and upper middle class' at 4.46 percent, the 'lower middle class' at 10.30 percent.[43]

Among the obvious changes we note the rise of salaried managers in the private sector of the economy, though presumably on a smaller scale than in Germany, except in large-scale industry and finance, where concentration was evident (e.g. joint-stock banking). Of the occupied population in 1911, 3–4 percent are taken to have been managers and administrators.[43] There was considerable growth of the professions old and new, which need not be documented. In 1911 they are reckoned to have amounted to over 4 percent, one quarter counting as 'high professions'. We also note a substantial expansion of the state and public services, which in 1911 employed almost one-third of all salaried persons[44] and the striking increase in office and other white-collar employments, all of which would expect at least lower middle-class status. Indeed, the new salaried white-collar workers ('clerks') now took the place of the old petty-bourgeoisie of shopkeepers, independent artisans and small masters in social and political calculations.

Some aspects of these developments deserve comment. Both the numerical growth in the middle strata and the rise of a salaried middle class raised novel problems of definition and class cohesion. The property-owning employer of labour, or independent entrepreneur, could no longer so easily appear as the ideal type of the middle class. Nor could a stratum numbered in hundreds of thousands readily use personal contact or networks of kin or association to establish national group identity, as was possible for smaller or institutionally defined elites such as aristocracy or Quakers. Education and a common type of lifestyle became increasingly central, reinforced, and indeed made possible, by residential segregation in socially homogeneous suburbs.[45] This applied even more to the new lower middle class.

The overwhelming mass of new middle or lower middle-class positions rested on, or required, varying degrees of formal education and training and therefore required the installation of a public primary (1870–91) and secondary school system (1902), as well as the shift of higher professional training to institutions of higher education. Conversely certificates of examinations passed or, as in the public services, competitive written examinations, became increasingly common. The newly extended educational and professional training systems (unlike the public schools, which only served parents with established middle-class wealth or status) provided entry into the middle classes from below, as well as a criterion for admission. The period saw the emergence of 'self-made professionals'[46] such as the journalists, whose numbers rose by 250 percent from 1881 to 1911[47] and who, being classed with 'authors', were firmly assigned middle-class status (unlike 'newspaper publishers', assigned to social class II in 1911). Again, whether accountants were included in class depended on having passed the examinations of their professional association.

The higher professions and technical cadres were, obviously, associated with the rise of an 'organised capitalism' in which large-scale business organisations and the rapidly expanding public administration were intertwined, and tended to inhabit the same mental universe. The two wars, in which government recruited heavily from industry (and later the universities) reinforced this relationship. It produced a new kind of entrepreneurial cadre which was to be characteristic of twentieth century Britain until the Thatcher era.

Thus the greatest of the private industrial corporations, Imperial Chemicals, lived in a 'symbiotic relationship with government'. It 'had and still has a tradition of recruiting Inland Revenue officials'.[48] But these, like Paul Chambers (1904–81), who became its chairman, and H.W. Coates (1882–1963), who became its vice-chairman, were very likely to be 'self-made professionals' who acquired their higher education as part-time students in new institutions of (as yet) little prestige, like the London School of Economics; or even as boy clerks in the civil service who worked their way up, like (Lord) Stamp (1880–1941), another distinguished Inland revenue man who left to become a figure in big business.[49]

Equally characteristic was the road from business into and out of government, as in the case of T.C. (Lord) Catto (1879–1959). This self-made son of the Northern lower middle class – he started as a clerk at the age of fifteen – was, as vice-president of a Scottish-American firm active in Russia, brought into the orbit of government in the First World War, which he ended as head of the British food mission in the USA. This business-cum-governmental activity won him golden opinions in established Anglo-American financial circles. It also won him, via a director of the banking house of Morgan Grenfell, the top job in the major Anglo-Indian merchant house which the bank owned; and later, via these contacts, a directorship in a major insurance company, of which he became chairman. The Second World War brought him back into the field of government, notably as a financial advisor to the Treasury, director and (from 1944 until its nationalisation) Governor of the Bank of England, after which he resumed his business interests.[50] While no quantitative conclusions can be drawn from such cases, they throw light on structural changes within the British entrepreneurial bourgeoisie in this century.

(4) The significance for middle-class identification of residential segregation and the development of a specific middle-class lifestyle, public and private, has already been noted. This lifestyle, while based on 'comfortable' income – the economist Alfred Marshall thought £500 a year was adequate for a professor – did not require anything that would have been considered wealthy by the plutocracy of this period, nor any demonstration of wealth by conspicuous consumption. Indeed, it could be maintained or approached even on a more modest or uncertain income, so long as certain, mainly cultural, status-indicators were displayed. The 'country cottage', which was to

become characteristic of middle-class literary intellectuals, especially between the wars, was an extremely cheap way of living. Like so much about the rural or semi-rural style of middle-class 'villa' and suburb, it was no doubt a much-reduced echo of life in the country house 'in the vernacular style' that became popular among the rich towards the end of the century and made the fortunes of gifted architects like Sir Edwin Lutyens. But its cheapness did not declass its inhabitants. To this extent the new lifestyle provided a potential bridge between the established and prosperous middle class and the aspiring new lower middle class, much as the former might look down on the latter.

(5) Middle-class identification by lifestyle was, in turn, closely linked with the education and emancipation of women, a largely middle-class phenomenon. Emancipation was almost certainly positively correlated with the status of the woman's family, and may well have provided as status-indicator. Of approximately 700 leading suffrage activists in 1913 20 percent had a university education and about 30 percent a telephone.[51] In turn, the opening of both education and non-manual employment both reinforced and created middle-class status.[52] In professions with unrestricted entry, women were already significant. Thus in journalism they increased from 476 or 8.3 percent of males in 1881 to 1756 or 14.6 percent in 1911. The role of women in the transformation of the middle class awaits further research, but it is plainly important enough to be mentioned here.

(6) A final and vital development in middle-class transformation was the emergence, at the end of the nineteenth century, of what came to be seen as a single and conscious 'working class'.[53] The new white-collar lower middle class defined itself by stressing its difference from the workers more than its similarities to the higher strata of the middle class, if only because separation from the proletariat was much easier than acceptance by higher strata. More generally, it would seem that, existentially, the working and middle classes tended to define themselves against each other. Thus in the new area of sports, the middle class, apart from favouring particular games (tennis, golf), made amateurism, i.e. leisure both to pursue sports and to achieve high standards at them, the test of 'true' sportsmen. Professionals were banned (as in the new Olympic Games) or expelled into separate associations (as in rugby), or segregated in recognisably subaltern corners, as in tennis and golf. Conversely, as soon as Association football had been taken over by the proletariat, and consequently professionalised (in the mid-1880s), the bulk of public schools and other mid-

dle-class schools concentrated on rugby, except (characteristically) a few top elite schools (e.g. Charterhouse) which maintained Association football as a means of distancing themselves from the non-elite.

In short, while in the early nineteenth century the middle class had identified itself and its values in the first instance against the landed aristocracy and its system, at the end of the century it did so by stressing its separation from the proletariat. And, instead of stressing the mid-Victorian criteria of independence from employment and property, now the criteria for membership of the middle class came to be seen as a combination of income, occupation, education and lifestyle.

IV.

In the light of these changes, let us consider the first official attempt in 1911 to divide the population into 'social classes' on the basis of occupations.[54] Its object was 'to represent as far as possible different social grades'. Eight classes were distinguished, the last three (textile workers, miners, farm-labourers) being subsequently integrated into what became and has remained a five-class system. Class I consisted of 'the upper and middle class' and was designed to exclude every element of the 'working class', a term – let us note the novelty – consistently used in the singular, unlike the expression 'middle class(es)'. It deliberately excluded 'the artisan, even though his wages may be higher than the clerk's'. Classes III-VIII, consisting of skilled, intermediate and unskilled labour 'as a whole are meant to represent the working class'. Class II was 'intermediate between the middle and working class', its occupations including members of both. Information did not enable employers and managers to be separated, so that 'many men, especially businessmen, belonging to the middle classes' were included among the workers. Quantitatively the 1911 calculations are unreliable, but conceptually they are valuable.

Four characteristics of this schema may be noted. (1) It refused to distinguish between the 'upper' (i.e. aristocratic) and the 'middle' class, grouping both together under I. (2) It clearly attempted to include the entire identifiable middle class under I, for all clerks and teachers were included, as well as 'persons of private means' otherwise unspecified, who were left unclassified in later censuses. This attempt was soon abandoned. By 1921 Class 1 had been reduced to 'the comfortable classes',[55] i.e. an upper middle class, chiefly by transferring clerks, teachers and the like to Class II, thus reducing I from 12.3 percent of the occupied population to 2.3 percent. Simultaneously Class II was given a much clearer middle-class character by the elimination of working-class elements from it, a movement emphasised by transferring the most subaltern members of the lower middle class, e.g. typists, to class III in 1931.[56]

Logically, market and opinion researchers who adopted the five classes divided the swollen class III into a lower middle-class subdivision (C1) and a skilled working-class subdivision (C2). They also tended to recombine I and II into a comprehensive middle-class group (the ABs) and the semi- and unskilled workers into a single group (the DEs). But these were later developments. The following table illustrates the development of these divisions:

Table 5.2: The Five-Class Divsions of British Society (percent of occupied population)[57]

Class		1911	1921	1961
I	(A)	12.3	2.3	4
II	(B)	16.8	20.35	8
III.	(C) (C1) (C2)	27.9	43.47	55
IV–V	(DE)	43.0	33.85	33

Attempts have been made to extend these classifications retrospectively, but they do not seem useful.[58]

(3) The third characteristic of the 1911 classification was a marked insistence on the educational criterion of middle-class membership, shown both by its emphasis on the professions and by the inclusion of about 250,000 'students' in class I, i.e. counting as a potential member of the middle class anyone undergoing some form of post-primary education ('students' were subsequently left unclassified).

(4) Finally, we already noted a certain bias against industry, other than large-scale enterprise. This may be partly due to the difficulty, in 1911, in distinguishing management from workers, but in subsequent censuses the reduction of Class I left bankers, finance agents, insurance officials etc. in the top class, while assigning most of employers and managers to Class II. However, larger or semi-public employers

(e.g. in 1921 shipowners, company directors, proprietors and managers of gas, electricity, bus and tramway undertakings) were included in class I.[59]

The 1911 classification seems to have been intended to represent the political realities of the early twentieth century – the opposition of all sections of the upper and middle classes to the working class – more than the social and economic realities, which would have suggested a sharper separation between middle and lower middle classes, such as was subsequently introduced. However, the fact that the five-class schema has, in however modified a form, maintained itself as the basis of market and public opinion research, suggests that its was not fundamentally unrealistic.

V.

It remains to survey the political and ideological alignments of the British middle classes.

The middle class rarely formed a single block, or rather, when it appeared to do so, this was due to some extent to the greater public visibility of one of its sectors, as well as to the British electoral system which conceals the strength of electoral minorities. Thus Anglican businessmen were less visible than Dissenters, though they were extremely prominent in some industrial areas such as Lancashire and the northeast, because, unlike Dissenters, they had no need to organise as a pressure group. Moreover, even if the Victorian Church of England was, as a political joke put it, 'the Tory Party at prayer', most Anglicans merely conformed inactively to the country's official religion without necessarily sharing its political bias.

Nevertheless, it seems right to distinguish periods when there was major political consensus among the middle classes from those when there was not. Before 1830 the middle classes were divided; while the most dynamic sections converged over reform and free trade, the bulk of the moderate Conservative 'Peelites' eventually seceded to Liberalism. Between 1830 and 1874 the class must be seen as Liberal, even if this impression is reinforced by the Liberal alignment of the great Whig millionaire-nobles and the skilled working class. It seems equally clear tha² from the 1880s Conservatism was on its way to becoming the typical, if not universal political choice of all sectors of the upper, middle and, certainly, the new lower middle classes. However, the period 1886–1922 was one of division and real fusion was not achieved until the collapse of the Liberal Party and Free

Trade in 1931. During periods of consensus the politically dissident middle class could be dismissed as a historic residuum, held together by regional, local, religious or even family traditions. Examples include British Liberals after 1931, the middle-class parasites of the 'Old Corruption' who could be identified with landed privilege, and middle-class supporters of the Labour Party after the First World War who knew themselves to be supporting a party of another class. To this extent there has been, since 1830, a tendency to generate middle-class consensus except in periods of transition. The present political division of the British middle class (40 percent of ABs voted non-Conservative in 1987) will need to be explained by future historians.

However, within the class, sectoral political differences were always evident. The established professions, on the whole, were Conservative, probably even in the era of Liberal predominance, to judge by the vote for university members of Parliament: the old English universities consistently elected Conservatives without opposition or by large majorities, the Scottish universities moved from Liberalism in 1868 (when they got representation) to solid Conservatism after 1885 – and this in a predominantly Liberal country. Only London University, stronghold of the self-made intellectuals, maintained a strong but not dominant Liberal vote.[60]

With some regional exceptions, industry remained Liberal after 1874, when the bulk of the London financial and commercial establishment began to swing heavily to the Tories. The formerly Liberal City of London, with a purely business electorate, voted 75–80% Conservative on the eve of 1914. The body of senior governmental officials, being dominated by its Indian and colonial contingent, was almost certainly Conservative, though the senior Home service, economically committed to liberal orthodoxies and administering an era of social reform, contained a strong Liberal contingent.

Can we as yet discern 'intellectuals' as a group? In spite of debates on this subject abroad (notably in the French, Russian and German socialist movement – the *Akademikerfrage*), and in spite of the Dreyfus Affair, probably not. As most we can begin to distinguish, as in the novels of E.M. Forster, a division within the bourgeoisie between an educated and cultured section (which hints at a *Bildungsbürgertum*) and the pursuers of money and power. However, most of the intellectual middle class remained in or near the Liberal Party.

There was no significant support for socialism before 1914. Indeed, the only parts of the 1911 Class I drawn to the labour movement were the subaltern non-manual workers in the public service, who were also open to unionisation, notably the primary teachers, who in 1910 formed the fifth-largest trade union in the country. The profession was, of course, largely recruited from children of the working class, to the dismay of the middle class whose spokesmen felt that 'the middle class should supply teachers of their own class – men and women free from the bias and envy of a narrow upbringing'.[61]

VI.

Comparisons with the German situation should be clear from the above survey. They need hardly be spelled out. However, a final question may be asked: how far can the British middle classes be regarded as a 'bourgeoisie' and British nineteenth-century society as a 'bourgeois' society?

Britain was, probably more than any other nineteenth-century state, a country dominated numerically by a class of manual labour working for wages, constituting, by general agreement, between 70 and 80 percent of the working population. Until the rise of the white-collar strata, which formed 19 percent of the working population in 1911,[62] it probably operated with a lower proportion of such strata than any other state. The business classes and the much less numerous professions (even without the manufacturers, the business groups were twice as numerous as the professions in 1841) therefore dominated the 'middle classes' and, given the extraordinary domination of the British economy in the world, the business classes were patently the centre of the middle classes. It would be absurd not to see them as a 'bourgeoisie' in the classical sense. The reason why the 'bourgeois' nature of British society has been doubted is not economic but social and political. They have been accused of deferring socially to aristocratic values, and politically, even at the peak of British economic success, to a landed aristocracy which was, moreover, still the richest group in the country. The eventual decline of the British economy has been ascribed to the absence of a sufficiently 'entrepreneurial ' or 'industrial' spirit for this reason.

These arguments need not be pursued here. It is enough to point out that in terms of economic ideology nothing of significance divided the greater landed nobility from the economic bourgeoisie, and in terms of economic policy no further resistance was offered to liberalism after the period of reform. Why there was conflict in the period before the abolition of the Corn Laws, what the nature of that conflict was, and to what extent Britain before 1832 was an *ancien régime* are important questions, but whatever the answers, it is clear that the reforms were adjustments within a society that had chosen the road to capitalism long before. As has been argued here, this enabled the bourgeoisie to adapt, modify and use elements from the tradition of the nobility and gentry for middle-class purposes. The reasons for the decline of the British economy are not to be sought in a snobbish contempt for entrepreneurial values. No doubt, if the German economy had declined, someone would be blaming it on the reluctance of German *Bildungsbürger* and *Beamte* to accept entrepreneurs as their equals.

In short, if nineteenth-century Britain is not a 'bourgeois' society, it is difficult to see where one is to be found. But it was not a society whose bourgeoisie felt the need to complete its effective domination and hegemony by a formal elimination of the aristocratic system. This system was not only no longer dangerous but, on the contrary, helped to control the masses. As the century advanced, it became increasingly clear that the major problem for the bourgeoisie lay in how to deal with the 75–80 percent of the population who belonged to the working class and who had the potential to dominate politics. The British middle class has shown no lack of class conciousness when faced with this problem since its implications were first debated before the Second Reform Act of 1867.

Notes to Chapter 5

1. The case of Scotland is so different that only occasional allusions to that country are made in this paper. For obvious reasons Ireland, North or South, though part of the United Kingdom for most of this period, is omitted.

2. Cited in Asa Briggs, 'The Language of Class in Early Nineteenth-Century England' , in Asa Briggs, John Saville (eds.), *Essays in Labour History* (London, 1966), pp. 43–44.

3. In how many aristocratic societies would commoners like the lawyer John Scott, son of the owner of a Newcastle coal barge, be granted the title, not of a simple baron, but of an Earl (Lord Eldon)? How many untitled kinsmen of lesser gentry could move in three generations from the position of first baron in the lower-ranking Irish peerage to the rank of Duke of Wellington?

4. See George Unwin, *Industral Organization in the Sixteenth and Seventeenth Centuries* (Oxford, 1904), car. VIII.

5. See E.J. Hobsbawm, 'Scottish Reformers of the Eighteenth Century and Capitalist Agriculture', in E.J. Hobsbawm, et al. (eds.), *Peasants in History: Essays in Honour of Daniel Thorner* (Calcutta, 1950), esp. pp. 5–8.

6. T.C. Smout, *A History of the Scottish People 1560–1830* (London, 1969), p. 363.

7. All cited in Briggs, pp. 43–44.

8. *Ibid.*, p. 57.

9. W.D. Rubinstein, 'The Victorian Middle Classes. Wealth, Occupation and Geography', *Economic History Review*, 30 (1977), p. 619.

10. W.D. Rubinstein, 'The End of "Old Corruption" in Britain, 1780–1860,' *Past and Present* 101 (1983), pp. 55–56, gives smaller percentages than those cited form the same author's 'The Victorian Middle Classes', pp. 606–607. Rubinstein has made the most important recent additions to our knowledge of the nineteenth-century middle classes.

11. F. Engels, 'Die Lage der argeitenden Klasse in England,' in Karl Marx, Friedrich Engels,*Werke*, vol. 2 (Berlin, 1976), p. 250.

12. Rubinstein, 'The End of "Old Corruption" ', p. 56.

13. John Vincent, *The Formation of the British Liberal Party, 1857–1868* (Harmondsworth, 1972), p. 73.

14. According to Vincent, p. 41, the parliamentary Liberal Party had the following social composition in the period from 1859 to 1874: 198 large landowners, 151 businessmen, 84 lawyers (men with legal education), 49 unspecified private income, 20 others.

15. Paul Descamps, *L'education dans les écoles anglaises* (Paris, 1911), p. 67.

16. Cited in Norman Gash, *Aristocracy and the People: Britain 1815–1865* (London, 1979), p. 24.

17. G.D.H. Cole, *Studies in Class Structure* (London, 1955), p. 69.

18. His grandson, Sir Culling Eardley Bart (1805–1863) educated at Eton and Oriel College, Oxford, founded the Evangelical Alliance.

19. W.L. Guttsman, *The British Political Elite* (London, 1968), p. 115.

20. Y. Cassis, 'Bankers in English Society in the Late Nineteenth Century', *Economic History Review* 37 (1985), p. 224.

21. Anon., *The Making of a Ruling Class: Two Centuries of Capital Development on Tyneside*, Final Report, Ser. VI (Newcastle-upon-Tyne, 1978), *passim*.

22. G.D.H. Cole, *loc. cit.*, p. 62.

23. The British income tax, reintroduced in 1842, recognised only five general types of income: (a) income from the ownership of land, houses, etc.; (b) income from the use of land; (c) income from government securities; (d) profits from business, etc.; and (e) salaries of officials or from 'public offices'. There is no specific place for other wages or salaries. Where taxable, they could be dealt with under (d) – they only became important enough to be seperately recorded in 1898. But schedule (e) has since been extended to cover them. J.C. Stamp, *British Incomes and Property* (London, 1920) is the standard guide to the nineteeth-century income tax, and a remarkable work.

24. W.J. Reader, *Professional Men: The Rise of the Professional Classes in Nineteenth-Century England* (London, 1966), pp. 96, 211.

25. Based on Table I in W.D. Rubinstein, 'Wealth, Elites and the Class Structure of Modern Britain', *Past & Present* 76 (1977), p. 102.

26. See Guttsman, *op.cit.*, pp. 38, 41, 82–83, 104.

27. T.H.S. Escott, *Social Transformations of the Victorian Age* (London, 1897), pp. 202–203.

28. Rubinstein, 'New Men of Wealth and the Purchase of Land in Nineteenth-Century England', *Past & Present* 92 (1981), pp. 125–147. It has been argued that the legal protection of aristocratic estates would have made this difficult, and also that the absence of primogeniture among the bourgeoisie tended to fragment such large holdings as businessmen might have built up. While this is true it had not prevented some earlier capitalists from buying themselves into the ranks of the great landowners in the nineteenth century. Rubinstein notes perceptively that most of the new landed families were Scottish, Welsh and Irish: 'this perhaps indicates a major difference in status perceptions from the English pattern'. (p. 133).

29. A.H. Halsey, (ed.), *Trends in British Society since 1900* (London, 1972), p. 206; B.R. Mitchell, H.G. Jones, *Second Abstract of British Historical Statistics* (Cambridge, 1971), p. 217.

30. *Hazell's Annuel for 1894. A Cyclopedic Record of Men and Topics of the Day*, Ninth Year (London, 1894), pp. 225–26.

31. The pre-nineteenth-century nobility and gentry were not necessarily much interested in education, and then it depended on tutors rather than secondary schools. Outside Eton and Harrow, aristocrats were not prominent in public schools.

32. Cassis, *loc.cit.*, p. 213.

33. C. Erickson, *British Industrialists: Steel and Hosiery* (Cambridge, 1979), p. 33.

34. Rubinstein,'Education and the Social Origins of the British Elites, 1880–1970', *Past & Present* 112 (1986), pp. 163–207.

35. *Dictionary of Business Biography*, ed. by D. Jeremy, Vol. I. (London, 1985), pp. 547ff, 554ff.

36. Robert Skidelsky, *John Maynard Keynes, Volume I, Hopes Betrayed 1883–1920* (London, 1983), esp. chapters 1–3.

37. See note 23 above.

38. Norman Gash, *op.cit.*, pp. 21–22. We may assume that few women paid income tax on income from trade, industry or professional profits.

39. Cited in Stamp, *op.cit.*, p. 434.

40. *Ibid*, pp. 447–449.

41. Rubinstein, 'Wealth, Elites . . . ', p. 109.

42. S.R.S. Szreter, 'The First Scientific Social Structure of Modern Britain 1875–1883', in Lloyd Bonfield, et al. (eds.), *The World We Have Gained: essays presented to Peter Laslett on his seventieth birthday* (Oxford, 1986), pp. 337–354.

43. The basic source is Guy Routh, *Occupation and Pay in Great Britain* (Cambridge, 1965). See also George Syers Bain, 'Trades Union Growth and Recognition', in *Royal Commission on Trade Unions and Employers' Associations, Research Papers* 6 (London, 1967), Table I, p. 5.

44. Mark Abrams, *The Condition of the British People 1911–1945* (London, 1946), pp. 66–68.

45. See E.J. Hobsbawm, *The Age of Empire 1875–1914* (London, 1987), cap. 7: 'Who's Who or the uncertainties of the bourgeoisie'.

46. See Hobsbawm, 'The Fabians Reconsidered', in *Laboring Men* (London, 1964), pp. 250–271.

47. *Census of England and Wales,* vol. X (1911), Occupations, Table 26 (Parl. Papers, Vol. 78, 1913).

48. *Dictionary of Business Biography*, vol. I, pp. 649, 706.

49. *Dictionary of Business Biography* (1941–1950), pp. 7–20.

50. *Dictionary of Business Biography*, vol. I, pp. 616–620.

51. J. Park, 'The British Suffrage Activists of 1913: An Analysis', *Past & Present* 115 (1989), pp. 147–162.

52. Like the father of J.M. Keynes, his mother was also a pioneer entrant into university education from a provincial Dissenting background: both met at Cambridge.

53. This is dicussed in Hobsbawm, *Worlds of Labour* (London, 1984), chapters 10 and 11.

54. *74th Annual Report of the Registrar General for Birth, Deaths and Marriage in England and Wales 1911*, Parliamentary Papers (1912–1913), vol. 13, pp. XL-XLI. On this see S.R.S. Szreter, 'The Genesis of the Registrar General's Social Classification of Occupations', *British Journal of Sociology* 35 (1984), pp. 522–546.

55. *Registrar General's Decennial Supplement: England and Wales 1921, Part II, Occupational Mortality* (London, 1938), p. 7.

56. *Registrar General's Decennial Supplement: England and Wales 1931, Part II, Occupational Mortality* (London, 1938), p. 7.

57. Figures are heads of families. Source: D.C. Marsh, *The Changing Social Structure of England and Wales, 1871–1961* (London, 1965), p. 206.

58. Cf. J.A. Banks 'The Social Structure of Nineteenth-Century England as seen through the Census', in R. Lawton (ed.), *Census and Social Structure* (London, 1978).

59. There can be little doubt that the primary criteria for inclusion in class I did not include being an employer.

60. See *McCalmont's Parliamentary Poll Book 1832–1918*, ed. by J. Vincent, et al. (Hassocks, 1971); H. Pelling, *Social Geography of British Elections, 1885–1910* (London, 1967), p. 419.

61. H.A. Clegg, *A History of British Trade Unions Since 1889, vol. II, 1911– 1933* (Oxford, 1985), p. 3; W.R. Lawson, 'John Bull and His Schools', (1908) cited in A. Troop, *The Schoolteachers* (London, 1957), p. 147ff.

62. G.S. Bain, *loc. cit.*

6 | Working-Class and Middle-Class Associations. An Anglo-German Comparison, 1820–1870

Christiane Eisenberg

The first step towards the formation of an independent working-class political party in Germany was Ferdinand Lassalle's General Association of German Workers (*Allgemeiner deutscher Arbeiterverein*), established in 1863. The second was the Social Democratic Workers' Party (*Sozialdemokratische Arbeiterpartei*), founded by August Bebel and Wilhelm Liebknecht six years later in 1869. In both cases the initiative came from dissatisfied members of the liberal educational associations (*Bildungsvereine*). These educational associations were designed to provide the opportunity for workers and *Bürger* to meet, and it was hoped that they would help prevent the emergence of an independent labour movement.

In modern historical research this development has been described as 'the separation of proletarian from bourgeois democracy' (Gustav Mayer).[1] Until now, the explanation for this separation has always been in terms of substantive differences that divided the working class and the liberal *Bürgertum*. The coincidence of national social and constitutional questions subjected this relationship to intolerable pressure, certainly in comparison with England in the same period. The fact that in England, the crises of modernisation occurred not all at once, but took place over a longer period of time, made it possible for the workers and the Liberal Party to cooperate on many individual issues and form electoral pacts as late as the second half of the nineteenth century.[2]

Very little attention, however, has been paid to the actual shape of this separation, which manifested itself as the exodus of politically interested workers from bourgeois associations (*bürgerliche Vereine*). German historians have taken for granted that the *Verein* was an organisational form that transcended estates (*Stände*) and classes, that it

Notes to Chapter 6 can be found on page 174.

was, in other words, an organisation of the whole community and not an arena of conflict.[3] It is also true that the emerging labor movement by no means rejected the *Verein* model. After all, Lassalle's first social democratic party was called an *Arbeiterverein*. The trade unions associated with it styled themselves *Zigarrenarbeiterverein* (Cigar Workers' Association) or *Schneiderverein* (Tailors' Association). Producer cooperatives were formed under such names as *Vereins-Weberei* (Association of Weavers), while consumer cooperatives were known as *Produkten-verteilungsverein* (Distributive Associations). If the working class and the liberal *Bürgertum* went their separate ways, it was according to the generally accepted view, in spite of and not because of the fact that they had been, until then, joined together in the *Verein*-type associations.

Within the German context, this argument seems to be a convincing one. Placed in a English-German comparative framework, however, it begins to lose plausibility. The successful cooperation of the working class and the liberal middle class in England was based on their common organisation in *Verein*-type organisations. Organisations like the German *Verein* did exist in England. However, they did not play any central role in the early labour movement or in social life in general. In England, trade unions, cooperatives, provident funds and various pressure groups were much more important than *Verein*-type organisations. Both working-class and middle-class groups were much more actively involved in these organisations than in *Verein*-type associations. Whether this was a factor that promoted the friendly relations between them is a question worth considering.

In view of this contrasting pattern of development in England, I will examine the organisational form in which the 'separation of proletarian and bourgeois democracy' occurred in Germany. Was the fact that German workers, in establishing their party-political independence, broke away from the middle class *Vereine* a secondary phenomenon, a consequence of the many substantial differences they had with the *Bürgertum*? Or was the *Verein* itself an arena for conflict?

In order to answer this question, I will, first of all, give a definition of *Verein* on the basis of which I will be able to describe the development of voluntary associations in Germany and England. I will also establish their relative importance for the working class in both countries and for the middle class respectively. Against this background I will then look at the relations between the two classes in one particular type of association, the *Bildungsverein* or Workers' Educational Association. I will examine both the relations inside the *Verein* as well as its relations with the rest of society.

The Concept of Verein

German historical research into the *Vereine* has given this form of organisation a very broad definition. To the extent that it does not simply follow the legal terminology and treat as a *Verein* all those organisations that come under the *Vereinsrecht* (law on associations), it tends to concern itself with all forms of voluntary organisations that pursue specific goals and are independent of the state.[4] This definition is based on the synonymous use of the German term *Verein* and the English term 'voluntary association'.[5] This definition is not precise enough for the purpose of comparative analysis since it does not offer any criteria by which one could structure the range of associations found in the two countries. In what follows, therefore, I will work with a socio-political definition of the *Verein*, that treats it as a special form of voluntary association, distinct from other types of organisation.[6]

According to this definition, a *Verein* has four main characteristics. Firstly, it organises individuals who, in a formal sense are regarded as equal. Decisions are made on the basis of 'one man, one vote'. This distinguishes the *Verein* from a limited company or corporation (*Aktiengesellschaft*) and from a union or federation (*Verband*) that brings together a number of associations or enterprises. Secondly, the *Verein* pursues only limited goals. This distinguishes it from political parties, which claim an overall responsibility and competence in public affairs. Thirdly, the activities undertaken by members of the *Verein* are, to a large extent, ends in themselves. They are social, cultural and often political but they are not designed to exert ongoing influence on people outside the organisation. At most, the *Verein* is a discussion circle and its influence is that of good example. To the extent that members seek to influence their social environment in an ongoing way, they will find themselves exposed to competition from the world of affairs and politics. In such cases they are forced to behave in a strategic and power-oriented manner and to transform the *Verein* into a cooperative, trade union, lobby or political party. Fourthly, as long as the *Verein* does not undergo this kind of development, then it does not need to formulate or internally consolidate a unified general purpose agreed to by all. For this reason, the *Verein* bureaucracy remains weak and administrative personnel, mostly unpaid, can be recruited from among the members' ranks.

Although there existed historically a large number of transitional forms between, on the one hand, the *Verein* and, on the other hand, trade unions, cooperatives, lobbies and political parties, this definition accurately describes the type of organisation that existed in Germany and that is usually referred to as *bürgerlicher Verein*. Examples of this type of organisation were the choral societies, gymnastic associations, temperance societies, welfare societies, shooting clubs, educational associations, political clubs and reading clubs. The adjective *bürgerlich* (bourgeois) is not only applied to them if their membership was exclusively or mainly *bürgerlich*. Non-bourgeois strata which participated in these associations or who established competing associations as an expression of their opposition to the *Bürgertum*, for instance, the social-democratic choral societies and sports clubs, must accept to be characterised as *verbürgerlicht*.[7]

The phrase *bürgerlicher Verein* is often used loosely. However, this is not an inappropriate term, because it was precisely this type of organisation, as historical research shows, that was the single most important politico-organisational innovation of the *Bürgertum* since the Enlightenment. The *Verein* symbolised the bourgeois demand for emancipation, inasmuch as it gave expression to the principles of equality and individuality, ignored privileges of birth and status, and thereby contributed to the decline of the estates, guilds and traditional communities. Because of its apparently universal utility, it also seemed to be the appropriate means for transmitting bourgeois norms and values to the sub-bourgeois strata, especially to the working class, and for promoting the *Bürgertum* as the 'universal class' (*allgemeiner Stand*).[8]

There is one other reason for the use of the term *bürgerlich* in this context. The principle of formal equality, on which the *Verein* was based, helped to promote the interests of the *Bürgertum* in two ways. It neutralised the privileges of the aristocracy, and what was of long-term importance, it guaranteed the reproduction of the *Bürgertum's* own material superiority vis-à-vis the lower classes. As is demonstrated by the system of civil law, formal equality only leads to a balance or equalisation of interests when it is applied to social relations that are not themselves characterised by material inequalities.[9] As long as property, education and consequently free time (availability) were possessed by the *Bürgertum*, while the workers had very few or none of these resources, the *Verein* was an appropriate organisational form for the stabilisation of bourgeois domination. Given that the *Verein* offered no ways of compensating for this material inequality, even a working-class majority could do nothing to change the organisational or general social relation of forces. For this, other forms of voluntary association were necessary – trade unions, cooperatives, lobbies or political parties. These latter types of organisation suspended competition among their members and established a unified general purpose. Because they tended not to have among their members dignitaries with free time, their general interests were represented to the world at large by paid and sometimes trained personnel. In this way, trade unions defended the interests of the workers as producers on the labour market. Consumer cooperatives represented the interests of consumers, and political parties and lobbies articulated the collective will vis-à-vis the political system. These organisations were capable of mobilising economic, social and political power. The *Verein*, however, simply cumulated existing positions of power.[10]

Class differences continued to assert themselves not only when entrance to the *Verein* was restricted, as has been suggested by many historians, but also when the *Verein* imposed no social restrictions on membership.[11] For an analysis of the relations between working class and *Bürgertum*, it is therefore important to know, if and to what extent, the differences in social power that existed between the classes were compensated for by economic and political organisations outside of the *Verein*. In what follows, I will analyse the historical development of *Verein*-type associations and their relative importance for the relationship between proletarian and bourgeois democracy in Germany and England.

Development of the Verein

In the Prussian province of Westphalia, which in 1841 had a population of 1.4 million, there were 600 *Vereine* in the period up to 1854.[12] If we use this figure to make an estimate for the whole of the German Confederation excluding the Austrian region, then we arrive at a figure of 14,000 *Vereine* by the middle of the nineteenth century. As has often been repeated and is still true today, Germany was clearly the country of *Vereine*.[13]

Although, as has already been explained, it is correct to describe the *Verein* as *bürgerlich*, one ought not to conclude from the successful expansion of this form of association that there was an equivalent expansion of *Bürgerlichkeit* in German society. This was certainly not the case for the decades between 1800 and the foundation of the Reich in 1871. The success of the *Verein* was only partly due to the preferences of the newly assertive *Bürgertum*. It was also linked to state promotion of this particular type of organisation. Germany was a confederation of minor states and economically backward. In this world of enlightened absolutism it was often the state officials themselves who, in the interest of loosening up the established structures, took the initiative in establishing voluntary associations. Without this external impetus, the *Vereine* would have been slow in getting off the ground. Public support was concentrated on associations that promoted agriculture and industry, but also benefited artistic, scientific and reading societies. Although there were important advances in societal capacities of self-organisation, associations were still being founded 'from above' in the period before March 1848.[14] In the context of the pauperism debate, these associations were established increasingly to incorporate the emerging working class. State officials and bourgeois circles cooperated in trying to prevent revolution. The best known initiatives of this type were the Central Association for the Welfare of the Working Classes (*Zentralverein für das Wohl der arbeitenden Klassen*) in Prussia and at a local level, the Berlin Workingmen's Association (*Berliner Handwerkerverein*) and the Hamburg Educational Society for Workers (*Bildungsgesellschaft für Arbeiter*).[15]

Although the authorities by taking these initiatives ensured the growth of associations, they also established a special law (*Vereinsrecht*) and a police authority (*Vereinspolizei*) designed to restrict their activities. The *Vereine* were to be social, cultural or welfare organisations. The authorities aimed to prevent their transformation into any other type of association, such as political parties.[16] The slow development of market integration, the low level of politicisation of public life and the limited scope of other modernisation processes all contributed to this direction of development in Germany in the first two thirds of the nineteenth century. For lack of other competition, the *Verein* remained the predominant form of voluntary association in German social life. Alongside the *Verein*, there also existed the guilds and corporations, chambers, credit institutions and the knightly orders, which had a compulsory rather than a voluntary character, were under control of the local prince and were an integral part of the apparatus of power.[17]

In this social context, the *Verein* acquired an exaggerated ideological significance. Since it appeared to be the most appropriate body, both for breaking up the encrusted social structures and establishing a new form of social integration, many contemporaries, with widely different political convictions, saw this form of association as a hope for the future.[18] By the time of the revolution of 1848, it was clear that the *Verein* model had established a certain dynamic of its own. In this period of absolute freedom of association and coalition, even the most progressive political movements proved unwilling and unable to give up the loose structure of the *Verein* in favor of a more firmly constructed party organisation. Even the democratic March Central Association (*Zentralmärzverein*) which explicitly sought political power and which, therefore, is considered the first political party in the German Confederation, was not able to break with the conception that democracy had to be as direct as it was known in the *Verein* model. Thus the Democrats institutionalised communication between the extra-parliamentary associations and the members of parliament. The latter, however, belonged not to just one but to a number of different parliamentary groups.[19] Other power-oriented types of organisations such as lobby groups, trade unions and cooperatives came into being during the pre-1848 period, and during the revolution, but their numbers were quite small. These types of organisations, as well as political parties, only began to flourish during the period of rapid industrialisation after the middle of the century. The administration of the *Vereinsrecht* was relaxed.[20] The labour movement was a major participant in this breakthrough.

In England in the eighteenth and nineteenth centuries, there were also numerous artistic, scientific and educational societies, political clubs, temperance societies, welfare organisations and similar types of associations. Following the example of nonconformist religious groups, which did not exist to such an extent in Germany, they generally called themselves societies or associations. The English development differed in one essential respect from that in Germany, namely, that these types of associations represented only a part of the much broader spectrum of voluntary associations that existed at the time. From the time of the late seventeenth and early eighteenth centuries, this spectrum included all those political and economic forms of organisation that became established in Germany only in the second half of the nineteenth century. Political pressure groups emerged in England on a large scale with the establishment of the parliamentary system after the revolutions of the seventeenth century.[21] The precursors of modern trade unions and cooperatives developed a little later. They resulted from the economic boom in the eighteenth century, which encouraged the commercialisation of production and the emergence of a modern consumer society. The first high point of the English trade union and cooperative movements as well as the breakthrough of economic pressure groups took place in the 1820s and in the highly politicised period of the 1830s and 1840s.[22] Modern political parties did not emerge, however, until the middle of the nineteenth century.[23]

If there was in fact a dominant organisational form among the English voluntary associations, it was probably the friendly societies. They provided funds against the costs of sickness, old age, burial and other eventualities. In 1800 there were a thousand of these in London alone. An official report speaks of 32,000 societies with a membership of 4 million in 1874.[24] Friendly societies were rooted in the localities, in trades and in places of work. They were administered on a voluntary basis by the members themselves. Their critics complained of excessive socialising. During the course of the nineteenth century some of them grew quite large, extending beyond local boundaries and transforming themselves into professionally managed and, in some cases commercial insurance companies.

Friendly societies were also the only type of association in England to which the government paid any particular attention, because they seemed equipped to relieve the burden of the poor rates. The Rose's Act of 1793 gave certain privileges to registered societies, which made it possible for them to defend themselves legally against embezzlement. Other legal advantages were granted to them in the decades that followed. Other types of associations were given privileges only later, or not at all, but because the state apparatus was relatively underdeveloped, they did not suffer from restrictive legal measures. The Combination Acts, which came into force against the trade unions between 1799 and 1824/25, were a dead letter, and restrictions on the right of association, such as existed in Germany, had no parallel in England.[25]

It would be incorrect to characterise the English associations that I have just outlined as middle class. The membership of the various voluntary associations was not recruited mainly from the middle class, but rather from all social strata; from the aristocracy to the craftsmen and workers. Women were not excluded. Like the *Verein* in Germany, the English voluntary associations were fundamentally different from the corporations of the 'old world', with their hierarchies determined by birth and rank and their lack of division between the private and public sphere. While German associations, however, were consciously constructed as alternatives to the old corporations and were separated from these by their different legal status, the English associations were in many cases the direct descendants of these older organisations. The main reason for this difference is the fact that corporations still existed in Germany at the time when voluntary associations were on the rise. Whereas in England because of the early modernisation of the economy and society in the late medieval and early modern period, these old organisations were no longer significant and had largely disappeared. As a result the English associations, like their corporate predecessors, displayed a relaxed attitude towards the representation of particular interests. Unlike their German counterparts, they were not weighed down by claims of universality or problems of representation. This is true at least for those associations that aimed at or defended positions of power in the economic or political system.[26]

The Working Class and the Associations

It was against this background that there developed in England, not just middle-class, but also working-class interest groups that transcended the *Verein* principle. With trade unions, cooperatives and support funds, the English workers created a variety of organisations that strengthened their power as consumers and wage-earners. They also developed political clubs, book clubs, temperance societies and other *Verein*-type organisations with cultural goals. Unlike in Germany, however, these associations did not play an important role. In the middle of the 1860s, the critical period in the separation of proletarian and bourgeois democracy in Germany, there were quantitative differences between England and Germany.

Firstly, the cooperative movement of the English working class, after a long period of stagnation and decline, experienced a renewed upswing during the mid-1860s. Its first high point had been reached in the 1830s, when supporters of Robert Owen maintained as many as 500 producer and consumer cooperatives. By 1864, they had regained a level of 364 establishments with 130,000 members. And these figures refer to only the cooperatives that had just emerged in the Cooperative Wholesale Service. The real extent of the broader movement is difficult to estimate.[27] In the German Confederation, with twice the population, there were according to the cooperative federation led by Schulze-Delitzsch, only ninety-seven consumer associations that corresponded with the federation: these had 7,700 members. In the minutes for this year, there is evidence of only twenty producer cooperatives.[28]

Secondly, when comparing the growth of trade unions, the discrepancy is even greater. In the United Kingdom at the beginning of the 1860s more than 265 trades were organised. The first (incomplete) *Trades' Union Directory* in 1861 listed almost 2,000 organisational units in more than 400 localities. The majority of them were local, but some of them were branches of regional and national federations.

According to one leading official, the number of organised workers in 1867 was around 800,000.[29] In Germany in contrast, at the beginning of the 1860s, only two trades were organised: the printers and the cigar workers who, in 1863 and 1865, created national federations that grew out of organisations already established during the period of the revolution. In addition, the miners and a few textile and metal workers established local organisations which, we must assume, carried out trade union functions. In 1848/49 more than thirty such associations had corresponded with the *Arbeiterverbrüderung* (Workers' Fraternity). In most of the other trades, however, the help of the Social Democratic and Liberal Parties was needed to get trade unions organised around the end of the 1860s.[30]

In the middle of the 1860s, very few German workers had access to relief funds such as those provided by the voluntary friendly societies in England. Factory workers were, in many cases, obliged to be members of the firm's health insurance scheme organised by the municipal authorities. In some cases the workers were involved in the administration of these health insurance schemes. However, they were subject to the authority of the officials, the guilds or the employers and did not freely dispose of their own funds.[31]

The most important and basically, the only type of association to which the workers had access in the 1860s was the educational association (*Bildungsverein*) under bourgeois patronage. There is evidence that such associations already existed in the 1830s.[32] Most of them, however, only emerged in response to the insurrection of the Silesian weavers in 1844. The *Arbeiterverbrüderung* which tried to coordinate these initiatives during the revolution, corresponded with between 200 and 250 associations.[33] Although it was certainly not the case that all of these Adult Education Associations (*Fortbildungsvereine*), Craft Associations (*Handwerkervereine*) and Trade Associations (*Gewerbevereine*) as they were known at the time were in agreement on political goals, most of them were either banned after the revolution, dissolved themselves or led a shadowy existence in the underground. With the liberalisation of the law on associations after 1859, the movement experienced a revival so that by the middle of the 1860s there were once more at least 225 educational associations with around 20,000 members.[34]

Workers' educational associations under the leadership of the liberal middle class also existed in England. The so-called Mechanics' Institutes which had served as a model for the German associations in the pre-1848 period,[35] existed first in England and on a much bigger scale than in Germany. Before the middle of the 1820s there were 104 such associations in England, Scotland and Wales. In 1841, middle-class promoters listed 261 Mechanics' Institutes, and for the middle of the century the figures given vary from 560 to 677. In 1850, the membership of 677 associations was given as 103,000.[36] On average, therefore, the English educational associations had twice as many members as did their German counterparts. In the world of English associations, however, the Mechanics' Institutes were relatively less important. Their middle-class initiators faced considerable competition. An unknown number of informal circles of Chartists and Owenites meeting regularly in pubs and neighborhoods, as well as friendly societies, cooperatives and trade unions were also devoting themselves to workers' education.[37]

In view of the differences in the social significance of the associations in Germany and England, how were the relations between middle class and *Bürgertum* on the one hand and the working class on the other structured in both countries? What were the effects of the relatively dense network of economic and political organisations available to the English working class? Did the working class and the middle class relate differently to each other there than the working class and the *Bürgertum* did in Germany, where the workers had their *Vereine* but where these associations, as was argued above, could not compensate for the fact that the workers lacked the necessary resources of time, money and knowledge? In the section that follows I will examine these questions using the example of the workers' educational associations (*Bildungsvereine*) sponsored by the middle classes in England and Germany. My view is that the *Verein*-type associations in both countries were pregnant with conflict, but in England, unlike in Germany, this conflict did not extend into the wider social environment, because the associations involving both the working class and middle class had only marginal social significance.

Arbeiterbildungsvereine and the Mechanics' Institutes

The Mechanics' Institutes, workers' educational institutes under middle class patronage, were established in England mainly during the 1830s and 1840s at a time when the working class, through Chartism, was beginning to create its own independent political movement explicitly directed against the middle class. In many places workers

even contested seats on local councils and on school boards. By contrast, the German workers' educational associations emerged not as a
reaction to actual political unrest but saw themselves, rather, as a preventative measure against such unrest. Most of them were created in
the pre-1848 period, during the pauperism debate, at a time when the
labour movement can hardly be said to have existed.

In both countries it was doctors, lawyers, academics, journalists,
petit-bourgeois dignitaries, bankers, merchants and entrepreneurs who
took the initiative in setting up these associations.[38] From the point of
view of political conviction, in England most of them were Liberals,
Whigs and Radicals; some of them were well known nonconformists.
Representatives of the Anglican church were not involved. Nor, in
Germany were the leading figures in the Catholic and Protestant
churches. In fact, from the middle of the century the churches in
Germany had begun to establish their own competing organisations:
the Protestant *Jünglingsvereine* (Youth Associations) and the Catholic
Gesellenvereine (Journeymen's Associations). As a result of government
support for the *Vereine* in Germany, a large number of state and
municipal officials in numerous cities and towns became involved in
workers' education. In England, however, it was often the workers
themselves who set up the educational associations although they welcomed middle-class support.[39]

The educational goals of the middle class in England and the
Bürgertum in Germany were the same: the inculcation of the norms
and values of respectability and the transmission of useful knowledge.
There were some differences, however, in the day-to-day practice of
the adult education movement in both countries. On the whole,
these differences were not fundamental, but they are interesting to
consider because they give us some idea of the concrete circumstances
in which the workers and the middle class or the *Bürgertum* came into
contact with one another.

The first notable difference is the fact that the German *Verein* had a
more proletarian membership. This aspect becomes particularly
noticeable if, as was the practice of contemporaries, we regard only
the industrial or factory workers as belonging to the working class. In
1841, in the forty-one Mechanics' Institutes for which we have
detailed information, only 46 percent were 'mechanics', in other
words manual workers and skilled factory workers. Within this 46
percent it was the higher class of workers, the labour aristocracy,
which was in the majority. The other 54 percent consisted of small
factory owners and merchants, office workers, professional men,

shop-owners with their personnel, young men with no definite occupation and women.[40] In other words, the lower orders of the middle class were strongly represented.

In a survey of *Arbeiterbildungsvereine* concluded in 1864, master artisans were not classified as workers, as they were in England, but as 'persons working for their own account' or as employers. To make the data useful for a comparative assessment, it will be necessary to alter this classification, and regard the master artisans as belonging to the working classes.[41] Having made the necessary adjustments, one arrives at the conclusion that, of the thirty-six educational *Vereine* for which we have data, around 78 percent of the members came from the working class. This was considerably higher than the proportion of workers in Mechanics' Institutes (46 percent). Although only 2 or 3 percent of the members were factory workers, the German associations had a stronger proletarian character than the English institutes.[42] This low number of factory workers also suggests that the contemporary name for these associations, *Handwerkvereine* (Artisan Associations), was more appropriate than the name subsequently adopted by historians. Factory owners, merchants, innkeepers, technicians, doctors, teachers and academics were in a clear minority. Women and young people were excluded, in any case, by the laws regulating the *Vereine*.

These differences in social structure also help to explain the differences in the extra-curricular program of associations. In the Mechanics' Institutes, with their higher proportion of lower middle-class membership, the middle-class backers clearly tried to disseminate bourgeois values and norms (*Bürgerlichkeit*). These efforts manifested themselves, for instance, in lectures 'on elocution', 'on the value of time' and 'on the importance of fine arts in the elevation of the people'. The bigger Mechanics' Institutes organised art exhibitions, which displayed the works of Rubens, Rembrandt and Breughel, which as one German visitor admitted 'could well help to develop taste'.[43] The bourgeois 'friends of the workers' in Germany, however, who were dealing almost exclusively with manual workers, were clearly concerned with keeping their social distance from the membership of the *Verein*. Many still seem trapped in the corporate way of thinking.[44] The cultural syllabus of the German *Verein* was limited essentially to choral singing and poetry reading at festivals and similar occasions. These activities were able to impart to the workers, under bourgeois leadership and within the borders of their own 'estate', a feeling of fellowship and, as a side-effect, helped to discourage political discussion.[45] The art exhibition of the Mechanics' Institutes and other similar initiatives, all of which were directed at the worker as an individual and signified a rupture in the cultural exclusivity of the middle class, had no parallel in the German associations.[46]

A second difference between the countries was to be found in the approach to teaching in the courses, lecture series and individual talks. The subjects offered were similar in both countries. They extended from remedial teaching of basic skills, geography, history, literary history and elocution to the more vocational subjects intended for upwardly mobile workers, white-collar workers and prospective independent producers. Politics and religion were excluded in both countries. I will return to this later. However, compared to the German *Vereine*, the teaching in the Mechanics' Institutes was organised much more efficiently. From the 1830s they were organised in regional federations whose task it was to plan and coordinate the courses and the lecture series. These programs were then taught by permanently employed travelling teachers and were available to all the institutions. In Germany, however, despite the creation of federations, there was no coordination of courses until the late 1860s. Teachers in Germany were, in most cases, the local teachers from the *Volksschule* (primary /elementary school) whose educational qualifications were completely inadequate for any kind of further education. In the larger towns and cities there were plenty of good academics, but they were generally unwilling to work with the educational associations. A system of different classes oriented towards the individual abilities of the students, such as the Mechanics' Institutes introduced in their program of elementary education, did not exist in Germany. 'Students' of all levels of ability were all taught together, if at all.[47]

The curriculum of the Mechanics' Institutes helped to compensate for the shortcomings of the English educational system. Not without justification, contemporary observers explained the wide spread of self-help educational institutions by the fact that public elementary schools were poorly developed. After all, the rate of illiteracy was still 41 percent (compared to 18 percent in the German states) in the early 1840s.[48] Technical training too, was less institutionalised in England than it was in Germany. Whereas some German states, mainly Prussia, had established vocational and technical schools as part of their absolutist promotion of industry and trade, vocational raining in England was still performed exclusively by business firms in the middle of the nineteenth century.[49] Since the Mechanics' Institutes' curriculum for adult remedial education fitted well with the tendency towards professionalisation among scientists and men of letters, self-organised schooling could rely on a sufficient supply of teachers despite the relative backwardness of the public school system. Due to the lack of bureaucratic-absolutist traditions the career patterns of academics in early Victorian England were much less firmly established then in Germany or France. The Mechanics' Institutes and similar institutions were therefore seen as a welcome opportunity to demonstrate professed competence.[50]

In any comparative analysis, this academic character of the Mechanics' Institutes is very striking, because it was completely absent from the German workers' educational associations. An important cause of this trait in the German *Vereine* was the specific tradition of the German guilds.[51] In the period before the revolution of 1848 and during the 1860s the educational associations were strongly influenced by the joiners, tailors, cobblers and other guild-organised trades. According to the 1864 survey already mentioned, 30 percent of the members in thirty associations were masters, while 40 to 44 percent were journeymen. It is well known that master artisans were lacking in elementary and technical knowledge. But, having passed the examination for entry into the guild, the high point of their career, they showed little interest in any kind of further vocational education. Hence it comes as no surprise that in nineteen associations for which we have available data, a small number of artisans attended courses in only five.[52] Against a social background of increasing economic freedom, it seems that the educational associations had some attraction for the master artisans because of the social opportunities that they offered, and the influence that they had achieved at local level held out a promise of greater social prestige.[53] The journeymen, who had a greater interest in further education than did the masters, often lacked the means to avail themselves of the educational opportunities offered. In keeping with the traditional demands of the German crafts, a large number of these journeymen, before 1848 and during the 1860s, were on the road, so a brief visit to the *Verein* was often all that was possible. As one *Verein* committee reported regretfully, it was for this reason, among others, 'that each meeting of the *Verein* and each lecture should be, insofar as possible, a self-contained whole' so that those present at any given time 'would be able to learn and understand it immediately without regard to previous or future education'. Because of the high turnover rate, 'a proper and systematic coordination' was practically impossible.[54]

Internal Conflicts in the Educational Associations

These differences in the day-to-day practice of the German and English associations should not be over emphasised. They were not as significant as the similarities, especially as far as the relations between working-class and middle-class (bourgeois) members are concerned. In the Mechanics' Institutes as well as in the *Arbeiterbildungsverein*, relations between the classes were prone to conflict and markedly disappointing. These conflicts existed on such a scale that the original intention of the initiators to use education as a means of reconciling the lower classes with bourgeois society, must be viewed as having failed. The experiment was a disappointment in particular because the organisational form preferred by the middle classes in both countries, the *Verein*, turned out, in many respects, to have been inappropriate for the working class.

One of the first disappointments for the workers was the fact that the kind of continued education organised for them by the educational association was more than they were able to cope with. In both countries, the workers soon learned that, after a more than ten-hour day, they were hardly able to make the necessary effort. The realisation gradually grew that it 'isn't possible to educate tired workers'. Education was something that really had to be undertaken in childhood and at an earlier age. Both German and English workers, especially around the middle of the century, began to demand that the state should regard it as a 'primary duty' to establish 'proper schools'.[55] The distrust of the state and of its corrupt institutions, an attitude that was very strong in the Mechanics' Institutes, gradually gave way to a realisation among the English workers that self-help in the educational associations had its limitations.

The initial enthusiasm of the workers began to wane. But even more long-lasting in their effects than this disappointing experience were the conflicts that developed around the issues of power and authority. Given their mixed social composition, one might have expected that such conflicts would be slow to develop in the Mechanics' Institutes. After all, a part of the middle class joined the workers on the school bench. It was also the case that in the English institutes the workers seldom came into contact with middle-class representatives who exercised any kind of financial, academic or official authority. This tended to be the case more often in the German *Verein*. Many of the Mechanics' Institutes also attempted to involve more workers in the leadership of the associations.[56] However, in spite of all these factors, the relations between the workers and the middle class in the English associations were, on the whole, no less prone to conflict than between workers and *Bürger* in the German associations. The participation of the workers in the leadership of the institutes had very little effect, and as long as the middle-class members of the leading committees had more time, money and competence coopting the workers served only to give some legitimacy to the associations that remained under bourgeois control. Limited periods of office, full-time salaried officials and other compensating mechanisms, developed within the modern labour movement, were unknown to both the Mechanics' Institutes and the German educational associations. In neither country did the workers have effective control over the steering committees of the associations. In any case, it was the bourgeois patrons who had the final word in any dispute. As soon as the members showed 'any sign of independent action... the material existence of the association was threatened'.[57]

The relations of power between workers and the middle-class members in the Mechanics' Institutes, and those of workers and *Bürger* in the German educational associations became an issue of conflict independently of and prior to the conflicts over substantial issues.[58] It expressed itself in arguments over the contents of courses. Since the associations offered adults only a general education and were unable to make up for the missed opportunities of childhood and youth, the workers insisted on discussing issues that affected their own work, and their own life situation. As many workers complained they wanted to learn 'how to stop the exploitation of the worker' and not 'how many legs a spider has'.[59] The German workers demanded 'real' or 'true education' whilst their English counterparts wanted 'really useful knowledge'. In both countries, this meant the inclusion of political and religious subjects, which the traditional liberal associations wished to exclude.

The middle-class, or bourgeois right to govern became a prominent issue in the associations in both countries, because members and officials were unable to isolate themselves from the debate going on in society over the right to vote. While both the English middle class and the German *Bürgertum* contended that the workers would first have to be educated before they could have the right to participate in politics, the politically minded workers argued exactly the opposite. They maintained that the workers needed the right to vote in order to be able to create the possibility of a proper education for themselves.[60] In the German educational associations these conflicts reached a high point in the 1860s when at the time of the Prussian constitutional conflict the liberal politicians showed their true opinions on the franchise question and in so doing, disillusioned many workers. Up to that point the hegemony of the *Bürgertum* in the associations had been generally accepted without question. In the Mechanics' Institutes, the question of the franchise had been a burning issue from the time the institutes were established in the 1820s, when the reform movement had united the workers and the middle class. The conflict became chronic when, after the Reform Act of 1832, which gave voting rights to many of the well-off, the middle class withdrew from the movement and gave little or no further support to the demands of the working class.

The Educational Associations and Social Conflict

The relations between the middle and working classes in English and German educational associations were characterised in each case by disharmony and conflict. How then can we explain the fact that these internal organisational differences in England remained confined to the associations, whereas in Germany they spilled over into society at large? Why was it only in Germany that a long-lasting break between proletarian and bourgeois democracy occurred?

In this section I will attempt to show that this difference resulted from the creation of alternative models of organisation by the English working class in the 1860s and 1870s. The shape of class conflict between the workers and the middle class was critically determined by the availability of such alternative types of organisation.

As the economist Albert D. Hirschman has demonstrated, dissatisfaction with organisations can lead to two basic types of reaction: 'exit' or 'voice'. While 'voice' often leads to open conflict, with a tendency for this conflict to escalate (since protest up to a certain point becomes more effective as it becomes louder), 'exit' from an organisation can take place without any great unrest. As a form of response, it tends to promote harmony. Hirschman's observation that protest is a more costly option than 'exit' is very relevant to our argument. To voice protest and to be willing to take on the conflict that will ensue, requires commitment, time and money. Whether this will be successful depends on the actual negotiating position of the members of the organisation. If alternative organisations exist that offer similar programmes, then, according to Hirschman, exit will be preferred to protest.[61]

In the light of the history of the voluntary associations in England and Germany described above, it is clear that dissatisfied members of the Mechanics' Institutes had the option of leaving these associations because there was a wide choice of alternative associations at their disposal, namely, the trade unions, cooperatives and friendly societies. Moreover, the supporters of Robert Owen and the Chartists were actively recruiting members. It is equally clear that no such alternative organisations offered themselves to the members of the workers' educational associations in Germany. Their only option was to voice protest. With certain qualifications, the responses in both countries corresponded to Hirschman's two ideal-types.

Of course, some English workers, as well as some of the middle-class representatives who shared their dissatisfaction, voiced criticism of their associations. They were able to make use of the associations' journal, the *Mechanics' Magazine*, as well as other papers to do so.[62] The organisational measures to increase worker participation in the steering committees of the associations must be interpreted as a response by the middle-class leadership of the institutes to the criticism made by the association's members. This criticism, however, was largely confined to matters directly affecting the institutes themselves. They did not become part of a wider agitation directed against the middle class itself. Instead, dissatisfied workers increasingly voted with their feet. Consequently, the proportion of workers in the associations declined.

By 1841, as already mentioned, they made up less than 50 percent of the associations' membership. The banning of Chartist newspapers from the reading rooms and libraries of the Mechanics' Institutes finally provoked a mass exodus, but even this took place in a very unspectacular manner.[63] The conflicts in the Mechanics' Institutes had no effect on the wider social relations between the working class and middle class. Although there was a suspicion that some institutes were working against the unions and encouraging strike-breaking, the English labour movement reacted with conspicuous disinterest rather than open hostility. Describing the situation in 1861, one of the middle-class promoters of the institutes wrote: 'The banquet was prepared for guests who did not come'.[64]

The conflicts within the German workers' educational associations also ended with the exodus of the politically conscious workers. In 1863, dissatisfied members in Leipzig, Hamburg, Berlin and in the

Maingau region organised, in cooperation with Ferdinand Lassalle, a mass exodus from the educational associations and issued a statement calling for the establishment of the alternative General German Workers' Association (*Allgemeiner deutscher Arbeiterverein*). In 1869 a proletarian-socialist wing broke away from the liberal Federation of German Workers' Associations (*Verband deutscher Arbeitervereine*) and, one year later, this group became part of the Social Democratic Workers' Party (*Sozial demokratische Arbeiterpartei*) founded by Bebel and Liebknecht. But unlike in England, many open conflicts developed during the course of this exodus. Many educational associations experienced small palace revolts aimed at toppling the bourgeois committees. Liberal Populist 'friends of the workers' like Hermann Schulze-Delitzsch, were condemned as traitors to the proletarian cause. Together with a minority of bourgeois critics, workers in numerous cities and towns organised public lectures and initiated a national congress movement that would at last, discuss the taboo subjects of politics and religion and shake off bourgeois tutelage.[65]

The protests by the dissatisfied members of the *Vereine* actually did little to resolve the various problems. On the contrary, in numerous associations the open conflict destroyed the basis for any further cooperation. It would be wrong to look only to the workers for reasons for the break between proletarian and bourgeois democracy in Germany, especially since their representatives stated repeatedly that 'bourgeois and academics are always welcome among us, but only if they are honest and serious in their attitude towards the working class'.[66] The German *Bürgertum* also contributed to the split in their failure to make efforts (in comparison with their counterparts in England) to renew cooperation with the workers. In fact, the majority of them approved of using the police and the courts to prevent workers from establishing their own independent organisations.

I cannot discuss here the numerous reasons for this development. Some of the more obvious ones were the Prussian constitutional conflict, Bismarck's establishment of the German Reich with 'blood and iron' and the structural problems of German liberalism. Within the framework of the present article, what is most interesting is the monopoly of the *Verein*-type organisation in German society, which made any alternative response on the part of the *Bürgertum* appear either unattractive or impossible. A comparison with England only serves to reinforce this argument.

Both the liberal segment of the German *Bürgertum* and that of the English middle class attempted to form political parties in the 1860s.

The National Union (*Nationalverein*) was established in 1859. In 1862 the German Progressive Party (*Deutsche Fortschrittspartei*) was founded and it was a breakaway from this party in 1866, at the height of the Prussian constitutional conflict, that the National Liberal Party (*Nationalliberale Partei*) was formed. At approximately the same time, the Radicals and Liberals in England established the Liberal Party. The organisational structure of the liberal parties in both countries was characterised by the fact that the central party committee and the local constituency bodies were relatively independent of each other. The central committee guaranteed continuity between elections. But it was the local parties that mobilised the voters, and this was particularly important in England, where voters had to register before being able to vote.[67] In this context, educational associations for the workers were not just an expression of middle-class or *bürgerlich* concern for social stability, but were also an expression of party political interests. This aspect was particularly important after the electoral reforms of 1867 passed in both countries. The Reform Act of that year in England gave the vote to a majority of male workers. In the North German Confederation, Bismarck established the universal male franchise, which in 1871 was extended to the whole Reich. Given the extension of the franchise, the educational associations in both countries acquired the role of outposts of the local party, since with few exceptions workers were not represented in the local organisations of the party. In Germany leading liberal politicians were responsible for this restriction on party membership. In 1859, when the National Union was established, they introduced membership subscriptions that made it impossible for workers to enroll. Politically interested workers were only accepted as honorary members and were not given any voting rights.[68] Among the English liberals there was not the same kind of resistance to rubbing shoulders with the workers. Nevertheless, whenever representatives of the middle class attended functions with the workers, as they did in the newly-formed Working Men's Clubs, the atmosphere was very strained. English workers consequently kept their distance from the Liberal Party of their own accord.[69]

For the liberal parties of both countries, therefore, the failure of the educational associations meant that there was no longer any institutionalised contact between middle-class and working-class individuals. However, this was a less serious loss for the English Liberal Party than for the Progressives and the National Liberals in Germany, because in England these points of conduct were basically superfluous. Rather than recruit the workers individually with the help of the educational associations, the English liberals preferred to cooperate with the working class through the numerous trade unions, cooperatives and friendly societies. In this relationship, the English liberals had to come to terms with the exercising of collective power by the workers' organisations, which were willing to cooperate with the liberals only on the condition that the Liberal Party take up their demands and represent them in parliament. This form of cooperation benefitted the Liberal Party because it meant that, with the help of labour movement officials, they were able to recruit the workers en bloc,[70] and this compensated for the loss of their freedom to operate as a party of dignitaries.

This elegant solution, serving the interests of both workers and bourgeoisie, was the basis in England for the electoral alliance of the trade unions and the Liberal Party in the last decades of the nineteenth century. It was not applicable in Germany because independent working-class organisations either did not exist there, or remained in an embryonic state.

In the 1860s and 1870s in Germany the *Bürgertum* was faced with the alternatives of recruiting workers individually, or of giving up any attempt to integrate them into the liberal movement. Because of the enormous political effort involved, the first option was as unrealistic in Germany as it was in England. After the breakdown of the educational associations it was difficult for a party of dignitaries to get through to any worker who was not suitably predisposed. So, for the Progressives and for the National Liberals (as for the conservative parties), only the second option remained open.

The abandonment of any attempt to integrate the working class was also easily accepted by those 'broad circles' of civil society who, in the words of the social reformer Freiherr von der Goltz 'willingly accepted the illusion that the social question would disappear from the agenda as long as one spoke about it as little as possible'.[71] Even for those liberal politicians who realised that the emerging labour movement would be an important element in the future, it seemed advisable to treat it as an opponent so that it would remain small and insignificant for as long as possible. Seen from this angle, the attacks on social democracy and the trade unions in the liberal press and the bourgeois approval of official repression were not an expression of the deficiency in *Bürgerlichkeit*, but rather the consequences of a rational strategy for the long-term maintenance of bourgeois positions of power.

Conclusion

Modern German history has interpreted the division of proletarian and bourgeois democracy in the 1860s and 1870s as a milestone on Germany's special path to modernity (*Sonderweg*). According to this view, the political independence of the working class established at the time of the foundation of the German Reich led to division and hostility between those social forces, which had they been able to cooperate, were capable of bringing about a democratisation of the *Kaiserreich*. The *Bürgertum* was weakened as a democratic force because it was forced by social democracy into an alliance with the traditional powers. The German labour movement ended up in political isolation from which it was not able to extricate itself until the end of the *Kaiserreich*. This view suggests that the relations between the *Bürgertum* and the working class in the German Empire would have been less tense and less strained if an independent workers' party had not been established. In this interpretation much significance is attributed to the early or, as some historians would say, premature emergence of social democracy.[72]

In the present article I have attempted to qualify this interpretation. The emergence of social democracy may appear 'premature'. A comparison of England and Germany demonstrates, however, that this was itself a consequence and not a cause of class conflict in Germany. One of the more profound causes of this situation was the social monopoly enjoyed by the *Verein*-type associations. Whether this should be added to the catalogue of German peculiarities is something that cannot be decided in a comparison of just two countries. It remains a fact, however, that with the *Verein* a particular form of organisation became dominant in Germany, which although its membership was made up of both workers and *Bürger*, failed to improve the relations between the two classes. Based on the principle of formal equality, these associations simply reproduced the differences in social power that already existed between the working class and the *Bürgertum*, and contributed to the divisions in German civic society.

The *Verein*-type organisations could, at most, serve indirectly as an integrating force. This was the case at the end of the century when there developed a large number of independent social clubs, choral societies, sports clubs and other cultural associations within the working class. The proletarian milieu in which they developed, accelerated the consolidation of the Social Democratic Party and of the trade union and cooperative movements. Functioning as a support for the formation of independent economic and political organisations of the working class, the associations promoted the organisational differentiation between the working class and the *Bürgertum*, which, as is clear from the English example and from the example of modern German society, is a precondition for cooperation between the classes.

Notes to Chapter 6

1. G. Mayer, 'Die Trennung der proletarischen von der bürgerlichen Demokratie in Deutschland 1863–1870' in G. Mayer, *Radikalismus, Sozialismus und bürgerliche Demokratie* (Frankfurt, 1969), pp. 108–178.

2. Cf. W. Schieder, 'Das Scheitern des bürgerlichen Radikalismus und die sozialistische Parteibildung in Deutschland'. in H. Mommsen (ed.), *Sozialdemokratie zwischen Klassenbewegung und Volkspartei* (Frankfurt, 1974), p. 21; J. Kocka, *Lohnarbeit und Klassenbildung. Arbeiter und Arbeiterbewegung in Deutschland 1800–1875* (Berlin, 1983), pp. 193ff. On the historiographical tradition of this argument, see B. Faulenbach, *Ideologie des deutschen Weges. Die deutsche Geschichte in der Historiographie zwischen Kaiserzeit und Nationalsozialismus* (Munich, 1980), pp. 103ff.

3. According to T. Nipperdey, 'Verein als soziale Struktur im späten 18. und 19. Jahrhundert' in T. Nipperdey, *Gesellschaft, Kultur, Theorie* (Göttingen, 1976), p. 185. See also the essays in O. Dann (ed.), *Vereinswesen und bürgerliche Gesellschaft in Deutschland* (Munich, 1984).

4. Cf. for instance W. Hardtwig, 'Strukturmerkmale und Entwicklungstendenzen des Vereinswesens in Deutschland 1789–1848', in Dann, *Vereinswesen*, p. 11; Nipperdey, 'Verein', p. 174. On the general problem of definition of Verein, see H.-F. Foltin, 'Geschichte und Perspektiven der Vereinsforschung', in H.-F. Foltin and D. Kramer (eds.), *Vereinsforschung* (Giessen, 1984), pp. 4ff.

5. Cf. D.L. Sills, 'Voluntary Associations. Sociological Aspects', *International Encyclopedia of the Social Sciences* 15, (New York, 1972), pp. 362f.

6. Cf. C.W. Gordon and N. Babchuk, 'A Typology of Voluntary Associations', *American Sociological Review* 24, (1959), p. 25; J. Raschke, *Soziale Bewegungen. Ein Historisch-systematischer Grundriß* (Frankfurt, 1985), pp. 234, 238; H.-D. Horch, *Strukturbesonderheiten freiwilliger Vereinigungen. Analyse und Untersuchung einer alternativen Form menschlichen Zusammenarbeitens* (Frankfurt, 1983).

7. Cf. for instance H. Bausinger, 'Verbürgerlichung - Folgen eines Interpretaments' in H. Bausinger and G. Wiegelmann (eds.), *Kultureller Wandel im 19. Jahrhundert* (Göttingen, 1973), pp. 24–49; V. Lidtke, 'Die kulturelle Bedeutung der Arbeitervereine', *ibid.*, pp. 146–159.

8. Cf. Nipperdey, 'Verein'; also the articles in Dann, *Vereinswesen*.

9. Cf. D. Grimm, 'Bürgerlichkeit im Recht', in J. Kocka (ed.), *Bürger und Bürgerlichkeit im 19. Jahrhundert* (Göttingen, 1987), p. 169f.

10. On the basis of these criteria, political sociology distinguishes between 'protective groups' (Realverbände) and 'promotional groups' (Willensverbände). Cf. V.K. Preuss, *Zum staatsrechtlichen Begriff des Öffentlichen, untersucht am Beispiel des verfassungsrechtlichen Status kultureller Organisationen* (Stuttgart, 1969), pp. 170–172.

11. This aspect is generally overlooked in the historical study of the *Verein*. Cf. for instance, Nipperdey, 'Verein', pp. 185–190, in particular, p. 185: 'That the social equality practised within the *Verein* acted as an integrating force for the whole of society, in the sense of creating a new general class of citizens, has not only been accepted by subsequent historians but was accepted also by contemporaries'.

12. Helpful information from Ursula Krey, Bielefeld, whose thesis on associations in Westphalia is forthcoming.

13. Cf. F. Klein, *Das Organisationswesen der Gegenwart* (Berlin, 1913), p. 65; R. Münch, *Die Kultur der Moderne* vol. 2, (Frankfurt, 1986), p. 815: *Verein*-type organisations like those in Germany 'existed nowhere else in Europe on such a scale'.

14. Cf. U. Scheunder, 'Staatliche Verbandsbildung und Verbandsaufsicht in Deutschland im 19. Jahrhundert', *Gesellschaftliche Strukturen als Verfassungsproblem. Intermediäre Gewalten, Assoziationen, Öffentliche Körperschaften im 18. und 19. Jahrhundert.* (Berlin, 1978), pp. 97–121; R. Dietrich, *ibid.*, pp.68ff.; Nipperdey, 'Verein', pp. 32ff.

15. Cf. J. Reulecke, *Sozialer Frieden durch soziale Reform. Der Centralverein für das Wohl der arbeitenden Klassen in der Frühindustrialisierung.* (Wuppertal, 1983); G. Hanf, 'Handwerkerausbildung in Berlin während der Industrielen Revolution (1787–1873). Eine Untersuchung zur Frühgeschichte des beruflichen Schulwesens', Thesis, Technical University, (Berlin, 1985), pp. 174–192; J. Breuilly and W. Sachse, *Joachim Friedrich Martens und die Deutsche Arbeiterbewegung 1806–1877* (Göttingen, 1984).

16. Cf. A Hueber, 'Das Vereinsrecht im Deutschland des 19. Jahrhunderts', in Dann, *Vereinswesen*, pp. 115ff.

17. Cf. Scheuner, 'Staatliche Verbandsbildung', pp. 102, 108.

18. Cf. H. Stein, 'Pauperismus und Assoziation. Soziale Tatsachen und Ideen auf dem westeuropäischen Kontinent vom Ende des 18. bis zur Mitte des 19. Jahrhunderts unter besonderer Berücksichtigung des Rheingebiets', *International Review of Social History* 1, (1936), pp. 22ff.

19. Cf. D. Langewiesche, 'Die Anfänge der deutschen Parteien. Partei, Fraktion und Verein in der Revolution von 1848/49', *Geschichte und Gesellschaft* 4 (1978), pp. 350ff.; W. Boldt, *Die Anfänge des deutschen Parteiwesens. Fraktionen, politische Vereine und Parteien in der Revolution von 1848* (Paderborn, 1971), p. 162. For the democratic-socialist 'Arbeiterverbrüderung', see F. Balser, *Sozial-Demokratie 1848/49–63. Die erste deutsche Arbeiterorganisation 'Allgemeine deutsche Arbeiterverbrüderung' nach der Revolution*, vol. 2, (Stuttgart, 1975), p. 510.

20. Cf. K. Tenfelde, 'Die Entfaltung des Vereinswesens während der industriellen Revolution in Deutschland (1850–1873)', in Dann, *Vereinswesen*, pp. 55–114.

21. Cf. E.C. Black, *The Association. British Extraparliamentary Political Organisation 1769–1793* (Cambridge, Mass., 1963).

22. On the trade union movement, see: C.R. Dobson, *Masters and Journeymen. A Prehistory of Industrial Relations 1717–1800.* (London, 1980); J. Rule, *The Experience of Labour in Eighteenth Century Industry.* (London, 1981), pp. 147ff.; on the cooperative movement see: S. Pollard, 'Nineteenth-Century Co-operation. From Community Building to Shopkeeping' in A. Briggs and J. Saville (eds.), *Essays in Labour History* (London, 1967), pp. 74–112; on precursors in the eighteenth century see: N. McKendrick, et al., *The Birth of the Consumer Society. The Commercialisation of Eighteenth Century England* (London, 1982), pp. 222–226; on economic pressure groups, see P. Hollis (ed.), *Pressure from without in early Victorian England* (London, 1974).

23. Cf. R. Stewart, *The Foundation of the Conservative Party 1830–1867* (London, 1978); J.R. Vincent, *The Formation of the Liberal Party* (London, 1976).

24. Cf. P.H.J.H. Gosden, *The Friendly Societies in England 1815–1875* (Manchester, 1960). The figures for 1800 are from S. Shipley, 'Metropolitan Friendly Societies in the Eighteen-Twenties', M.A. Thesis, University of Warwick, 1975, p. 47; the figures for 1874 are from P.H.J.H. Gosden, *Self Help. Voluntary Associations in 19th Century Britain* (New York, 1974), p. 74.

176 | *Christiane Eisenberg*

176 | *Christiane Eisenberg*

25. Cf. D. George, 'The Combination Laws Reconsidered', *Economic History, Supplement of the Economic Journal*, 2 (1927), pp. 214–229.

26. See the contributions from M. Schlenke and H. Hofmann in *Gesellschaftliche Strukturen* p. 94; also, A.M. Birke, *Pluralismus und Gewerkschaftsautonomie in England. Erstehungsgeschichte einer politischen Theorie* (Stuttgart, 1978), p. 20.

27. Figures for the 1830s are from B. Webb(-Potter), *Die britische Genossenschafts-bewegung* (Leipzig, 1893), p. 44; the figures for 1850 are from Gosden, *Self Help*, p.185; the figures for 1864 are from C.R. Fay, *Co-operation at Home and Abroad. A Description and Analysis* (London, 1908), p. 292. The figures almost doubled by the end of the decade.

28. Figures for the consumer associations of 1848 and for the producer cooperatives are from C. Eisenberg, *Frühe Arbeiterbewegung und Genossenschaften. Theorie und Praxis der Produktivgenossenschaften in der deutschen Sozialdemokratie und den Gewerkschaften der 1860er/70er Jahre* (Bonn, 1985), Appendix A and B; the figures for consumer societies in 1864 are from E. Hasselmann, *Geschichte der deutschen Konsumgenossenschaften* (Frankfurt, 1971), p. 153.

29. Cf. *United Kingdom First Annual Trades' Union Directory, 1861* (London, 1861), reprinted 1968; figures for 1867 are from W.H. Fraser, *Trade Unions and Society. The Struggle for Acceptance 1850–1880* (London, 1974), p. 16.

30. Cf. C. Eisenberg, *Deutsche und englische Gewerkschaften. Entstehung und Entwicklung bis 1878 in Vergleich* (Göttingen, 1986), pp. 234ff., where there is a critical discussion of alternative views.

31. Cf. A. Diercks, 'Entstehung und Entwicklung der deutschen Krankenver-sicherung bis zum Jahre 1909', *Zentralblatt der Reichsversicherung*, vol. 18, (1922), columns 121f.; Eisenberg, *Gewerkschaften*, pp. 119ff.

32. Cf. Hardtwig, *Strukturmerkmale*, p. 43.

33. Figures from H. Schlechte (ed.), *Die Allgemeine Deutsche Arbeiterverbrüderung 1848–1850. Dokumente des Zentralkomitees für die deutschen Arbeiter in Leipzig* (Weimar, 1979) in the index under 'Arbeitervereine' or 'Arbeiterbildungsvereine'.

34. The figure for the number of associations is from T. Offermann, *Arbeiterbewegung und liberales Bürgertum in Deutschland 1850–1863* (Bonn, 1979), pp. 515–522; The membership figures (for 200 associations in Prussia) are from F. Bandow and K. Brämer, 'Die Handwerker-, Arbeiter- und ähnliche Vereine in Preussen' *Der Arbeiter-freund*, vol. 4 (1866), p. 75.

35. Cf. J. Fallati, 'Englische Arbeitervereine für Unterrricht und Vergnügen', *Zeitschrift für die gesamte Staatswissenschaft*, vol. 2/2 (1845), pp. 75–128.

36. Figures from T. Kelly, *George Birkbeck. Pioneer of Adult Education, in which is com-prised a full and complete History of Mechanics' and Literary Institutions* (London, 1851, reprinted 1969), pp. VIf.

37. Cf. H. Silver, *English Education and the Radicals 1780–1850* (London, 1975).

38. For Germany: Reulecke, *Centralverein*; Offerman, *Arbeiterbewegung*; for England: M.D. Stephens and G.W. Roderick, 'Science, the Working Class and the Mechanics' Institutes', *Annals of Science* 29, (1972), p. 351; K. Burkard, 'Zwischen Autonomie und Philanthropie. Zu den Anfängen der Arbeiterbildung in England', *Archiv f.d. Geschichte des Widerstandes v. d. Arbeit*, vol. 2/3 (1980), p. 20.

39. For England: Stephens/Roderick, 'Science', p. 351; J.F.C. Harrison, *Learning and Living, 1790–1960. A Study of the English Adult Education Movement* (Toronto, 1961), pp.59ff. For Germany: Offerman, *Arbeiterbewegung*, p. 281; E. Dittrich, *Arbeiterbewegung und Arbeiterbildung im 19. Jahrhundert* (Bensheim, 1980), p. 138; D. Dowe, 'Organ-isatorische Anfänge in der Rheinprovinz und in Westfalen bis zum Sozialistengesetz von 1878', in J. Reulecke (ed.), *Arbeiterbewegung an Rhein und Ruhr. Beiträge zur Geschichte der Arbeiterbewegung in Rheinland-Westfalen* (Wuppertal, 1974), p. 60.

40. The most important sources on membership structure are discussed in E. Royle, 'Mechanics' Institutes and the Working Classes 1840–1860', *The Historical Journal* 14, (1971), pp. 310ff.

41. Cf. Bandow/Brämer, 'Handwerkervereine', pp. 77ff. On the classifications of master artisans in England and Germany, see E.J. Hobsbawm, 'Soziale Ungleichheit und Klassenstrukturen in England: Die Arbeiterklasse' in H.-U. Wehler (ed.), *Klassen in der europäischen Sozialgeschichte* (Göttingen, 1979), pp. 53–65, and Eisenberg, *Gewerkschaften*, pp. 47ff. This classification has been justified by recent research which has concluded that most of the formally independent masters in Germany had been dependent upon capitalist merchants for some time. See also, F. Lenger, *Zwischen Kleinbürgertum und Proletariat. Studien zur Sozialgeschichte der Düsseldorfer Handwerker 1816–1878* (Göttingen, 1986).

42. Percentage estimates by Bandow/Brämer, 'Handwerker-Vereine', pp. 79–81.

43. Quotation from Fallati: 'Englische Arbeiter-Vereine', p. 97. On the general efforts to bring about a refinement of taste, see Harrison, *Learning and Living*, pp. 87f.; and M. Tylecote, *The Mechanics' Institutes of Lancashire and Yorkshire before 1851* (Manchester, 1957), p. 309.

44. For an example from pre-1848, see J. Fallati, 'Das Vereinswesen als Mittel zur Sittigung des Fabrikarbeiters', *Zeitschrift für die gesamte Staatswissenschaft*, vol. 1 (1844), p. 748. In the 1870s, some *Bürger* still feared that 'too much education' could lead to 'nobody being satisfied any more with their position'. Quotation from 'Bemerkungen zur Bildungsfrage' *Concordia*, vol. 6 (15 December 1871), p. 65.

45. In this context, see Max Weber's comments on the depoliticising function of the choral societies: 'Geschäftsbericht', *Verhandlungen des Ersten Deutschen Soziologentages vom 19–22 Oktober 1910 in Frankfurt* (Tübingen, 1911), pp. 57f.

46. This impression is confirmed in J. Reulecke, '"Kunst" in den Arbeiterbildungkonzeptionen bürgerlicher Sozialreformer im 19. Jahrhundert' in E. Mai, et al, (eds.), *Kunstpolitik und Kunstförderung im Wandel der Sozial- und Wirtschaftsgeschichte* (Berlin, 1982), pp. 84ff.

47. On teaching practice in England see Tylecote, *Mechanics' Institutes*, pp. 308, 310f.; also Hudson, *Adult Education*, pp.175ff., Stephens/Roderick, *Science*, p. 354. On the practice in Germany, see K. Birker, *Die deutschen Arbeiterbildungsvereine, 1840–1870* (Berlin, 1973), pp. 160f., 172ff.

48. Cf. P. Flora, *Indikatoren der Modernisierung: Ein historisches Datenbuch* (Opladen, 1975), p. 65.

49. Cf. R. Schöfer, *Berufsausbildung und Gewerbepolitik in Deutschland. Geschichte der Ausblidung in Deutschland* (Frankfurt, 1981).

50. Cf. T.W. Heyck, 'From Men of Letters to Intellectuals. The Transformation of Intellectual Life in Nineteenth Century England', *Journal of British Studies* 20/17 (1980/81), pp. 158–183.

51. The differences between the German and English craft traditions are dealt with in detail in Eisenberg, *Gewerkschaften*, pp. 26ff.

52. Figures from Bandow/Brämer, 'Handwerker-Vereine', pp. 79, 295 (Table 9). On the master craftsmen's lack of interest for adult education, see K. Bücher, *Die gewerbliche Bildungsfrage und der industrielle Rückgang* (Eisenach, 1877), p. 35.

53. See also the interpretation of G. Trautmann, 'Industrialisierung ohne politische Innovation. Staat, Parteien und "soziale Frage" in Preußen-Deutschland zwischen 1857 und 1878' (PhD Thesis, University of Heidelberg, 1972), pp. 153, 163.

54. P.D. Fischer, 'Der Unterricht im Berliner Handwerkerverein', *Der Arbeiterfreund*, vol. 1 (1863), p. 398. For the 1860s: *Flugblatt vom ständigen Aussschuß des Vereinstags deutscher Arbeitervereine* (7 July 1865, reprinted Berlin, 1980), p. 3; *Allgemeine Deutsche Arbeiterzeitung*, Coburg, no. 144, (12 October 1865), p. 794 (reprinted, Leipzig, 1977). In England the travelling of journeymen was not an obligatory part of their training, but rather a way of dealing with the problem of unemployment. Cf. Eisenberg, *Gewerkschaften*, p. 78.

55. The quotation is from a letter of H. Schob published in *Social-Democrat*, no. 61 (14 March 1889). For England see R. Johnson, 'Really Useful Knowledge. Radical Education and Working-Class Culture 1790–1848', in J. Clarke, et al. (eds.), *Working-*

178 | *Christiane Eisenberg*

Class Culture. Studies in History and Theory (London, 1979), p. 95; also H. Silver, *The Concept of Popular Education. A Study of Ideas and Social Movements in the Early Nineteenth Century* (London, 1965), pp. 293f.

56. Cf. Tylecote, *Mechanics' Institutes*, pp. 61f.

57. Quotation from 'Nationalliberaler Arbeiter-Beglücker', *Demokratisches Wochenblatt* no. 12 (20 March 1869), p. 139 (reprinted Leipzig, 1969). For England see E. Yeo, 'Some Practices and Problems of Chartist Democracy' in D. Thompson and E. Yeo (eds.), *The Chartist Experience. Studies in Working-Class Radicalism and Culture 1830–60* (London, 1982), pp. 345–380.

58. This was confirmed by one of the founders of the ADAV, Julius Vahlteich, who was active in the Leipzig *Arbeiterbildungsverein* in the 1860s: 'The conflicts are not at all about the social question but about this one central question, who should control the association'. J. Vahlteich, *Ferdinand Lassalle und die Anfänge der deutschen Arbeiterbewegung* (1904, reprinted Berlin, 1978), p.18. For England one gets the same impression from the account of the conflicts in Burkard, *Zwischen Autonomie und Philanthropie*.

59. Letter from Gera in *Social-Democrat*, no. 62 (30 May 1869).

60. For Germany: Offermann, *Arbeiterbewegung*. ch. 4; A. Herzig, *Der Allgemeine Deutsche Arbeiter-Verein in der deutschen Sozialdemokratie. Dargestellt an der Biographie des Funktionärs Carl Wilhelm Tölcke, 1817–1893* (Berlin, 1979), pp. 129ff. For England see Johnson, 'Really Useful Knowledge', p. 77.

61. Cf. A.O. Hirschman *Exit, Voice and Loyalty* (Cambridge, Mass. 1970).

62. Cf. Burkard, *Zwischen Autonomie und Philanthropie*.

63. Cf. D. Jones, *Chartism and the Chartists* (New York, 1975), p. 41.

64. R. Elliot, 'On the Working Men's Reading Rooms as Established in 1848 in Carlisle', *Transactions of the National Association for the Promotion of Social Science* (1861), p. 676. The quotation here is from Royle, *Mechanics' Institutes*, p. 305.

65. This is dealt with in detail by Offerman, *Arbeiterbewegung*.

66. Letter from Leipzig in *Deutsche Arbeiter-Halle,* no. 18 (28 September 1868), p. 74. (reprinted Berlin, 1980).

67. For England see Vincent, *The Formation*, pp. 82ff; for Germany see G. Eisfeld, *Die Entstehung der liberalen Parteien in Deutschland, 1858–1870. Studie zu den Organisationen und Programm der Liberalen und Demokraten* (Hannover, 1969).

68. On this episode, see R. Aldenhoff, *Schulze-Delitzsch. Ein Beitrag zur Geschichte des Liberalismus zwischen Revolution und Reichsgründung* (Baden-Baden, 1984), pp. 128ff.

69. Cf. H.J. Hanham, 'Liberal Organisations for Working Men, 1860–1914', *Bulletin of the Society for the Study of Labour History* 7 (1963), p. 7. 'The Working Men's Clubs were the reformed successor organisations of the Mechanics' Institutes. They were established for the purpose of giving working men, and persons of higher social position, the opportunity of becoming better acquainted with each other, and interchanging their views on subjects of great national interest': H. Solly, *Working Men's Social Clubs and Educational Institutes* (London, 1904, reprinted New York, 1980), p. 87.

70. Cf. Hanham, 'Liberal Organisations'; On the practice of cooperation, see R. Harrison, *Before the Socialists. Studies in Labour and Politics, 1861–1881* (London, 1965).

71. Frh. v.d. G(oltz), 'Die Theilnahmslosigkeit der Gebildeten an der Arbeiterfrage', *Concordia,* no. 13 (25 March 1876), p. 51. See also A. H(eld), 'Der Liberalismus und die sociale Frage III', *ibid.*, no. 20 (13 May 1876), p. 80.

72. According to H. Grebing, *Der 'deutsche Sonderweg' in Europa 1806–1945. Eine Kritik* (Stuttgart, 1986), p. 119: 'For Germany it is without doubt conceivable that cooperation between the liberal reform movement and the labour movement during the decade between 1860 and 1870 could have led to a political order in the German law'.

7 | Moral Standards and Business Behaviour in Nineteenth-Century Germany and Britain

Richard Tilly

S tandards of honesty and business behaviour together form a topic which fits easily into the framework of recent research into the *Bürgertum*, research which looks at among other things, "the relations between capitalistic behaviour and *Bürger-lichkeit*.[1] In this chapter I examine the business morals of nineteenth-century German entrepreneurs in order to illustrate interesting aspects of the relationship between capitalism and *Bürgerlichkeit*. For the purpose at hand, 'entrepreneurs' are defined as heads of enterprises, merchants, bankers, industrialists, brokers and dealers; by the end of the period the category includes managing directors and branch directors. By 'business morals' I mean honesty in business matters, the honouring of one's agreements, basically what Werner Sombart called 'business morality', 'solidity' and 'contract fulfilment' (*Vertragstreue*). For Sombart, business morality was part of the wider complex of bourgeois virtues and implied a bourgeois behaviour pattern which conveyed a public image of probity and worthiness. Of decisive importance was that one appears to others and is taken by others to be honest.[2]

Building on these definitions, this paper addresses the following questions:

(1) Did moral standards of business behaviour change during the course of the nineteenth century?

(2) Can one identify different patterns of business behaviour and morals among different kinds of entrepreneurs or among different branches of the economy; and, if so, can one explain them?

(3) Were such long-term changes or differences associated with tendencies toward embourgeoisement or its reversal?

Notes to Chapter 7 can be found on page 201.

179

(4)To what extent were the tendencies observed peculiar to German society? Can this latter possibility be convincingly substantiated by comparison with other countries?

This paper looks closely at German business behaviour during the nineteenth century, and explores aspects of its interaction with non-business social groups. It then makes an attempt to tackle the question of the uniqueness of German business behaviour by comparatively discussing institutions and behaviour patterns in the capital markets of Great Britain and Germany in the 1870–1914 period. It concludes by briefly summarising some of the important, but still unresolved questions.

Business Morality and the New Institutional Economics

The problem of business morals is of general social significance. It has to do with norms of economic behaviour, with questions of growing concern to economists and economic historians researching what has come to be called the New Institutional Economics (or Transaction Cost Economics). In 1981, Douglass North wrote:

> Neo-classical economic theory can explain how people acting in their own self-interest behave....It can explain why, as a result of the free rider problem, people will not participate in group actions where the individual gains are negligible....It cannot....however, explain...behaviour in which calculated self-interest is not the motivating factor....Neo-classical theory is equally deficient in explaining stability. Why do people obey the rules of society when they could evade them to their benefit?...Indeed, a neo-classical world would be a jungle and no society would be viable.[3]

Rather more relevant to our immediate concerns is a statement made in 1979 by a prominent American banker, David Rockefeller:

> A moral foundation is imperative in a free society that affords each individual the latitude for independent thought and action. Without ethical values a free society would become a jungle....Ethical principles are the glue that hold a business system of free enterprise together. Business runs on mutual trust and confidence that others will live up to their word. The marketplace which is the heart of a human society, could not exist without it.[4]

Until very recently, 'full-blooded' economists who have identified with the postulates of 'methodological individualism' and who have busied themselves with questions of political economy would have been likely to regard such utterances as ideological, probably hypo-critical, possibly as a deliberate distraction from obvious, if unstated goals; at best, an appeal to ultimate values. In contrast to such a posi-tion, Alexander Field accepts Rockefeller's statement as an accurate observation about market economics, whose stability is seen to depend upon a broad consensus concerning the norms and rules of economic activity, a consensus that is in itself not explicable in terms of neo- classical individual utility maximisation. Field therefore sees the urgent necessity of explicit reflection on how norms of economic behaviour emerge.[5]

The case of business morals to be discussed here focuses attention on the question of honesty in economic matters, i. e. the fulfillment of explicit and implicit contracts. Honesty has a significant economic dimension, because it generates confidence; indeed, it is the basis of commercial activity generally. The classic theoretical analysis of the problem was presented in 1970 by George Akerlof in his treatment of the American used car market.[6] The critical variables in this 'market for lemons' were product quality differences and an asymmetric dis-tribution of information concerning those differences as between sell-ers and buyers. The sellers' informational advantage create an unfair or dishonest bargaining situation in which – assuming free competi-tion among sellers an buyers – price differences do not correspond to quality or value differences. In the absence of additional behavioural rules, the persistence of a discrepancy between value and price occa-sions sellers of 'good' products to withdraw from the market; the market itself declines and can disappear altogether.

The argument can be applied to historical cases of market develop-ment in which quality has played a significant role, although it is in the nature of things that few traces remain. For sellers whose high-quality products were persistently undervalued will have demanded, just as buyers of inferior products might have, rules governing price and product quality. Where effective rules were not forthcoming, affected sellers and buyers will have ceased transacting business. The normal historical interpretation will therefore stress the development of rules.[7] New Institutional Economics, in any case, suggests a gener-alised interpretation here. It has sellers of high-quality products suffer-ing from reputational losses through being associated with low-quali-ty products, and since reputation is part of a firm's capital (and expected quasi-rents), reputational losses lead to declining investment. Thus generally speaking, investment activity will tend, in a sense, to reflect expectations concerning the maintenance of business rules.

The larger the capital investments, the stronger positive expectations will have been, but also the larger the need for continued protective rules. Business honesty and capital accumulation thus go hand in hand.[8]

European economic history offers some broad, corroborative evidence on the connection between economic backwardness and dishonesty in economic matters. In the seventeenth century Dutch business morals and confidence in contract fulfillment were believed to be superiour to those of England. By the eighteenth century, however, English business standards of honesty were held to be higher and more capable of generating confidence than those of all the Continental countries. Similarly, by the early nineteenth century, the business morals of Hamburg's merchants were observed to be significantly above those of other German regions.[9] For Europe in the nineteenth century generally, Alexander Gerschenkron has spoken about an East-West differential according to which Eastern Europe's economic backwardness could be connected to the 'abysmally low standards of business honesty' which prevailed there.[10] More generally, one might also view the growing importance of fixed capital and rising levels of private saving entrusted to financial institutions over the nineteenth century as strong indicators of confidence in the fulfillment of business contracts, i. e. in the maintenance of high standards of business honesty.

Such evidence, to be sure, represents no more than correlations, and not statements about causality. Moreover, the question of when, how and under what conditions effective norms were developed still remains open. Perhaps the history of law and legal institutions can help provide the answer. For the connection between the development of market-oriented industrialisation, on the one hand, and general acceptance, indeed, state sanctioning of 'bourgeois' legal norms, on the other, was an obvious part of European economic history since the eighteenth century. Norms were not identical with laws, to be sure. Business morals reflected basic notions about business behaviour commonly shared among businessmen, whereas legal norms covered only those value judgements backed by specific legal sanctions – ultimately by the coercive power of the state. It was frequently the case that legalisation of behavioural norms took place precisely when and where the latter could no longer command general acceptance without sanction. Of course, one must recognise that societies and economies did not always generate the appropriate legal norms just when they were needed. Moreover, the bourgeois legal framework by no means encompassed the entire spectrum of individualistic market behavioural norms, and important areas, such as commerce or labour relations, remained open. Nevertheless, the history of law remains an important reference point for any historical treatment of behavioral norms.[11] For many questions, indeed, it supplies the only systematic set of source materials. The connection between legal and actual behaviour norms, and the possible discrepancy between *de jure* and *de facto* morality deserve attention in its own right, because only by means of such an investigation can one test the hypothesis that German legal arrangements positively affected entrepreneurial behaviour, and provide evidence of the extent to which such a propitious context represented a situation peculiar to Germany.

On the Development of Business Morals in the Nineteenth Century

The previous section suggested some reasons for believing that business behavioral norms were an important part of the industrialisation process; but it is not easy to document the point, and only a beginning can be made here. This section, therefore, attempts no more than to formulated theses and illustrate them with concrete examples. These should suffice to indicate the importance of the general question and to identify some of the sources future research might profitably exploit.

First a few words on change over time, on long-term trends in the honesty of business behaviour. As suggested above, I believe in the thesis of a gradual long-term improvement, i.e. a rising degree of honesty in business affairs. With the widening and deepening of market relationships during industrialisation, the area of economic activity governed by common business rules – particularly by the will to fulfil agreements – grew. At least that is the impression one gathers from the (admittedly) scattered and incomplete records available in business histories, chamber of commerce reports or contemporary commentary on business law. Complaints about breach of contracts or fraud show no rising tendency, while 'honest' business practices such as the refund of cash or the exchange of bad merchandise to disappointed buyers, the introduction of fixed prices, brand labels and also longer-run credit agreements, would seem to have become more widespread.[12] One cannot quantify this impression, but a casual review of readily available indicators does confirm the 'optimist' view.[13]

Two related changes contributed to a long-term improvement in business probity. First, the growth in the volume of business led entrepreneurs increasingly to view individual transactions as links in a larger chain of profitable business ventures, as building blocks in a long-run process of capital accumulation, rather than a one-time opportunities to be exploited to the utmost. This changing attitude found quantitative expression in the growing relative importance of fixed capital in the economy and also in the increasing importance of large-scale enterprises.[14] Second, the sustained increase in the volume of business strengthened the interest of the larger established firms in the maintenance or introduction of rules legalising (and thus sanctioning with the coercive force of the state) the standards and practices which had contributed to their own success and which might be threatened by more desperate, upwardly mobile competitors – by 'illicit competition'. Legalisation of existing practice could thus impose the spread of 'good' business standards, though one result was undoubtedly a rise in the recorded number of norm violations.[15]

Reference to mobilisation of the coercive power of the state forces our attention towards one target of entrepreneurial activity which probably grew in importance over the nineteenth century: the state. In addition to the general interest in legal sanctions just mentioned, business honesty can be related to the state in two particular respects: with respect to tax obligations and to the desire for special favours or privileges.

If we look closely at the tax morality of businessmen in the nineteenth century, we must conclude that it is not possible to speak of an improvement or of clearly rising standards. In the 1890s in Prussia, for example, massive cases of tax evasion came to light, and this was by no means a unique discovery. Tax honesty, to be sure, did not necessarily belong to the core of the businessman's virtues, either in Germany or in other bourgeois countries such as Great Britain. Interestingly, the sharpest criticism of tax morals and of tax evasion in Germany emanated from civil servants, i.e. from the socioeconomic group with presumably the smallest opportunity for successful tax evasion.[16]

With the expansion of state activity in the course of the nineteenth century, particularly after 1870, entrepreneurial chances for dishonest mobilisation of state resources grew. Entrepreneurs no doubt exploited these chances, not only at the national level but also and especially at the local one.[17] Documentation of the point is inevitably limited but not so scarce as to doubt its validity. In Germany, thanks to the existence of a well-established and highly respected civil service bureaucracy, opportunities for profitable corruption were doubtlessly more limited than in most industrial countries in this period.

Business moral standards, however, did not change or develop in a continuous manner, nor were the changes evenly distributed across the entire economy and society. There were fluctuations and relapses, so to speak, and it is above all this kind of shift that deserves our attention. Industrialisation and the spread of market relationships which went with it brought hitherto separated groups into more frequent contact with one other: peasant farmers with petty traders, craftsmen with merchants, private savers with bankers, etc.

In this connection Fritz Redlich has written about a 'collision' between different 'Insider Groups' and their respective moral codes.[18] Such collisions provoked controversial discussions, more or less public, of varying degrees of sharpness, which frequently led to the general acceptance or establishment, quite likely through legalisation and state agency, of one set of norms, possibly the norms of the stronger group, possibly a synthesis of disparate codices. No doubt such collisions reflected structural social and economic forces rather than random events. On the one hand, technical innovations could generate new and large opportunities for profits for entrepreneurs in particular branches of the economy, and these could call forth a strong supply response (e. g. an increased supply of financial service). On the other hand, the emergence of such opportunities and increase in supply could coincide with a rapidly rising demand. Failures, business abuses and grievance could emerge and call forth a discussion concerning the institutions, rules, and norms underlying such markets. A few concrete examples may help illustrate the connections I have in mind.

By the eighteenth century, it seems, fraud and dishonest practices in the wholesale trade carried on by the larger German merchant houses had become quite rare, for by now connections between merchants were standardised and 'monitored' (or controlled) by competition.[19] By the nineteenth century wholesale transactions appear to have occasioned relatively little controversy on this score. There were significant differences, however, between large and small-scale trade. In the latter fraud took place more frequently, it seems, partly a result of the uninformed and inexperienced character of infrequent buyers, possibly also a result of the shorter-run profit horizons of sellers operating in such markets. In the East Westphalian yarn trade, for example, small dealers were frequently accused of shady business practices, and in the cattle trade – not just in Westphalia but all over Germany – small traders and fraudulent transactions were believed to go hand in hand.[20]

Retail trade was also marked by repeated complaints about the fraud and deceit practiced by small businessmen, at least until the strong competition offered by the development of brand labels and department stores with fixed prices, or until government intervention, for example against food adulteration, started to become effective.[21] What did happen in wholesale trade, however, was that interregional differences in business practices, especially in the treatment of protested (uncovered) bills of exchange or of payment stoppages, could lead to misunderstandings and conflict. Out of these, then, evolved the concerted effort to established a common, all-German commercial law.[22] Such efforts, to be sure, included attempts by individual businessmen or groups of businessmen to influence the negotiations in the direction of codification of practices catering to their own special comparative advantage – at the expense of other groups of firms and businessmen.[23]

Far more problematic was the situation in those industries organised by merchant capitalists, especially where established entrepreneurs began to feel the competition of small, aggressively ambitious firms. 'Sewing needle manufacturers in Aachen and Iserlohn and yarn dealers in Elberfel-Barmen,' wrote Friedrich Zunkel, 'turned to fraudulent manipulation of the weight and number of their wares in order to "finance" price cuts, and the cloth manufacturers in Gladbach and Elberfeld frequently mixed bad and good quality yarns in the weaving and dyeing processes with the same aim in mind.[24] In the rapidly industrialising Rhenish-Westphalian region of the 1830s and 1840s, we are told, 'a new buccaneering breed of entrepreneur emerged, devoid of any solid mercantile tradition, with no reputation to lose, and willing to fight for a growing share of the market with all means, even illicit ones'.[25] Similar complaints can be heard from industrial Silesia. In 1820 the highly respected Breslau merchant, von Eichborn, noted the following:

> The Silesian linen trade will again recover, for in recent times the English have been responding to the growing competition by cutting prices, weaving bad cloth and delivering shoddy products, whereas one notices that the Silesians, their backs against the wall, have again begun to deliver high-quality wares. One can only hope that their swelling order books will not lead them back to their old careless ways, for then the initiative will again return to the English. All of this confirms my old thesis, that our linen and cloth manufacturers need a collective institution to enforce quality control, for merchants in general tend to be oriented toward immediate profit chances, regardless of long-run consequences, and the conscien-

tious few are not able to prevent an outpouring of poor weaving and shoddy goods.[26]

Still greater tensions marked the collision between the moral code of craftsmen and workers on the one hand and industrial entrepreneurs – largely shaped by mercantile traditions and standards – on the other. The still young area of industrial labour relations was a natural centre of conflict: payment in debased coins, or in commodities – the 'truck system' – could be and was seen as an attempt to conceal wage cutting. Workers saw such practices – which were a way of shifting transaction costs of business on to employee shoulders – as breaches of their unwritten contract and hence as immoral behaviour. In this particular area, government intervention provided a solution: it outlawed the truck system and, more importantly, undertook measures to improve the supply of money suitable for wage payments.[27] What remains unclear is whether the practices mentioned were in fact, as some contemporaries thought, closely associated with new, aggressive, upwardly-oriented businessmen. Some evidence, from the linen industry of Eastern Westphalia, for example, supports this view.[28]

Another older, conflict-laden, problem which came up in the decentralised cottage-type industries, though not restricted to them, concerned wage deductions to match delivery of sub-standard finished goods. Since the deficiencies were not always clearly visible this practice frequently gave rise to the belief that alleged quality defects were being misused as an excuse for wage cuts. Workers, for their part, as early as the eighteenth century, responded in kind by weaving cloth with less yarn than stipulated and appropriating the differences for themselves. This represented a particularly crass form of labour defiance of employers, and it is interesting to note complaints by employers that workers tended to resort to delivery of inferior products with special intensity in boom phases of the business cycle.[29] When considering such cases, one sees that economic interests were mixed with moral issues, for such behaviour *was* 'economic', if opportunistic. A similar ambivalence marks employer attempts to change existing patterns of labour relations, for example by hiring women in place of men, by dismissals of part of their labour force or by wage cuts. These attempts occasionally engendered violent protests. The obvious presence of clear material interests in such disputes did not preclude a collision of different moral standards. For example, the divergent economic interests of putting-out merchants oriented toward world market prices and those of domestic workers oriented towards local food prices could easily confuse and magnify differing views of what was morally right. This was the case in 1821 in Eupen, where wool shearers destroyed their employer's machinery, accusing him at the same time of dishonest practices such as payment in debased coinage. Similarly, the Krefeld silk workers went on strike in 1828 against their employer's collective action to cut wages, which they labelled 'criminal'. And in 1830 violent protests by Aachen cloth factory workers were set off by wage cuts for shoddy work that were seen as unjust and dishonorable.[30]

Two points are important here. First, industrial entrepreneurs had and have an interest in treating their workers fairly, for peaceful industrial relations and high labour productivity have generally gone together. This interest should have motivated employers to set and maintain clear and equitable rules regarding wages, hours and working conditions. Where and when such rules were missing, as was frequently the case during the early stages of industrialisation, labour protest could easily result, as in the above-cited examples. The absence of equitable rules, in turn, could have had a partially rational dimension, for example where unskilled workers were needed or in oversupply. However, one should not overlook the role of employer ideology, above all the industrialist's belief that workers were naturally lax, undependable, opportunistic, and that only the threat of extreme poverty supplied adequate motivation to work. To some extent, employers did believe in the possibility of inculcating bourgeois virtues of effort and thrift in their workers by well conceived disciplinary and educational devices.[31] In both cases, however, a 'class view' dominated, and was hardly likely to encourage a treatment of workers as equal partners. Instead, one might well speculate that the dominant view ensured that some possibly significant chances for an improvement of labour relations and productivity were missed. One may also surmise that larger, long-lived enterprises, particularly those whose operations required relatively large supplies of *skilled* labour, were least likely to have missed such chances, but solid evidence is lacking.[32]

The second point concerns the 'anti-capitalist' attitude of representatives of the government bureaucracy and of the educated middle class – that possibly unique stratum, the *Bildungsbürgertum*. This attitude is identifiable in the Rhenish Wupper valley in the eighteenth century, from the comments of Jakobi a bureaucrat who expressed, despite some lip service to liberal tenets, quite reactionary sentiments in his 'revulsion at the crass behaviour of the merchant class, who concentrated ever-larger shares of wealth in their own hands'.[33]

When in 1828 the fourteen largest Krefeld silk manufacturers agreed upon and announced a collective wage cut, they immediately encountered sharp public criticism, particularly from government civil servants, who saw the measure no only as an unjust instrument of redistribution but also as a criminal act, subject to prosecution.[34] The attitude of civil servants, however, was not historically constant; experience with such conflicts engendered modification and such positions. On the one hand, civil servants appear increasingly to have sympathised with the position taken by employer-entrepreneurs, the logic of whose economic arguments seemed impeccable; in any case, when protest was associated with the threat of violence, the bureaucrats were solidly behind the interests of the propertied employers. On the other hand, civil servants frequently saw and argued that labour-related protest called attention to the need for reforms. There were also business leaders who recognised this, men like Friedrich Harkort, who supported, in the wake of the revolution of 1848, government intervention against the truck system and child labour, an regulation of workers' benefit societies.[35]

A further factor that helped produce a change in the attitudes of industrial employers toward their workers stemmed from the growing power of the German labour movement in the second half of the nineteenth century. In the many confrontations and protests over industrial labour relations in the period conflicts of interest were mixed with divergent ideas of justice. It was the *arbitrariness* of employer actions themselves, that set off protest and strikes, as in the mining strikes of the 1880s, in which the wholly unconciliatory employer attitudes served as an additional irritant. Many other strikes during the *Kaiserreich* appear to have had as their core a strong sense of resentment about unjust treatment. Examples included the failure of construction employers to stick to an unwritten agreement (Augsburg, 1899), the dismissal of a worker because of his union membership, or the introduction of measures against political and trade union activity on plant property.[36]

Industrial employers were in the course of the nineteenth century increasingly willing to deal with their workers as economic partners who had the right to fair and honest treatment. However, this right was quite strictly reserved to the worker as an individual; employers refused to accept the worker's demand for recognition of the collective characters of labour relations and of corresponding collective organizations.[37] This refusal may well have caused 'dysfunctional behaviour' in certain areas of the German economy before 1914, perhaps a contradiction in the system of 'organized capitalism'. In any case, here was an area in which the developing (*bürgerliche*) legal system proved of little help, since most labour market problems remained virtually untouched by law. Interestingly enough, a few attempts to develop appropriate legal machinery *were* made, such as the Prussian attempt to institutionalise 'industrial occupational courts' (*Gewerbegerichte*) in the early period of industrialisation. They proved unsuccessful, however, probably because they were oriented toward the problems of individual labour contracts, while the German workers and the labour movement increasingly sought collective solutions.[38]

Perhaps no field of activity is more suited for investigating the question of business honesty than that of finance, especially the organised securities world, and subject to critical bureaucratic scrutiny, these organised security markets soon attracted the interest of the less well-to-do, the petty bourgeoisie, small businessmen, hopeful of quick and easy gains. As early as the 1830s long lists of middle-class subscribers were reported for many of the railroad share and bond issues.[39] In the so-called 'small enterprise boom' of the 1850s, according to Zunkel, a wild bout of speculation broke out involving Rhenish-Westphalian projects. The actual capital needs and 'true' long-run profit possibilities took second place to the prospects of immediate speculative profits. Many of the intermediaries proved ready to exploit this frenzied pursuit of quick gains and were not loath to resort to deception, insider agreements on sales, and downright fraud. The crash which followed revealed a majority of shaky enterprises, not a few fraudulent constructions, and a number of respected bankers and well-known factory owners among the victims.[40]

This phenomenon was by no means limited to the Rhenish-Westphalian area[41]; indeed, it repeated itself on a broader front in the 1870s, its thrust this time strengthened by the liberalisation of joint-stock company law in 1870. With Eduard Lasker's revelations on fraudulent railroad financing schemes in 1873, a wave of sharp criticism of the stock exchange swept through German public opinion.[42] In 1873 a stock exchange crash followed the boom, and in the long depression which followed, criticism deepened, centering especially on the business morals of financiers. Of special interest is a reflective account of this experience by one of the financial entrepreneurs involved, the Rhenish business leader, Gustav Mevissen.

> These banking circles were and are dominated by a striking, very flexible morality. Certain kinds of manipulation, which no good *Bürger* would in

good conscience accept as proper in the personal sphere, are approved by
these persons as clever, as evidence of ingenuity. The contradiction
between the two moralities is quite irreconcilable. In my experience there
is no laxer morality, no weaker conscience to be found in any group in
Europe than in that of the Haute-Finance. This laxness of moral standards
builds in substantial measure on the adroitness, the skill with which corrupt and fraudulent transactions are concealed, so that the machinations
remain undecipherable to all except themselves; in addition, in executing
their business they employ such a secretive, devious and roundabout chain
of agents and intermediaries that no outsider can perceive the beginning,
nor distinguish between principal and agent. It is rare indeed when an
outsider is able to penetrate this jungle, able to identify and understand
the goals which motivate the Haute-Finance, the means they employ to
achieve these goals, including those by which they successfully deceive
the gullible public. These goals and rules are quite a distance from the
principles of business which dominate industrial production and regular
commerce.[43]

This quote, among other things, draws attention to the exploitation
of outside investors by insiders. Examples of such unethical treatment
were accumulating in this period and beginning to set off a broad discussion of business morality.[44] It is possible to view this discussion as a
specific result of the 'Great Depression ' of the 1870s. The moralising
attention that it generated was derived from the relatively large number of persons negatively affected. Growing criticism of economic
liberalism found, unsurprisingly, considerable support among the
losers. These included share subscribers of newly founded and quickly
liquidated joint-stock companies, bull speculators in the declining
urban real estate market, and numerous promoters and businessmen
who went bankrupt and whose numbers rose in the late 1870s to
about 10,000 per year.

In the early stages of industrialisation insolvency and bankruptcy
were clearly regarded as evidence of immorality. According to
Zunkel, a man who could not pay his debts was seen as an incapable,
morally inferior person.[45] Conventional wisdom saw a disproportionately strong association between suspended payments and failure,
on the one hand, and newly-founded young enterprises, particularly
those founded on the crest of a boom and without sufficient
resources to live through the cyclical downturn, on the other. The
German textile industries of the 1850s are said to have contained
numerous such 'swindler-type' enterprises – carried up by the
euphoric boom of those years.[46] The disproportionate presence of
'young' firms in the lists of the bankrupt is reported as characteristic

of the 'high industrialisation' period of the *Kaiserreich* as well.[47] However, the question of whether the business morality of bankrupt entrepreneurs actually differed from that of leaders of long-lived enterprises remains – owing to insufficient evidence – an open question. In this connection it is interesting to note that Gerhard Hahn's study of business failure in the Rhineland for the 1890-1913 period comes to the conclusion that it was largely poor business judgement or lack of rudimentary business skills such as book-keeping which led to bankruptcy, rather than dishonest practices. Moreover, contemporary businessmen do not appear to have criticised their bankrupt counterparts in negative, moralising terms.[48] It is true, though, that Hahn does record that 'tradition-oriented' businessmen who went bankrupt made greater efforts to satisfy their creditors than did others, and that could be taken as evidence for a stronger attachment to conventional behavioural norms.

At this point it is worth noting that in the course of nineteenth-century Germany bankruptcy laws became less punitive and reduced some of the moral opprobrium traditionally associated with business failure. The legal proceedings themselves were rationalised, speeded up, and the rehabilitation of the bankrupt eased. A noteworthy breakthrough was achieved with the Prussian Bankruptcy Law of 1855, which then served as the basis for the Imperial Bankruptcy Law of 1877. Businessmen, particularly leaders of the mercantile community, took an active role in deliberations leading to the passage of this legislation, but their collective opinions, we are told, were frequently contested by the views of the legally trained civil service bureaucracy, and the end product reflected the participation of both groups.[49] Thus legal norms governing an important sphere of business life represented a mixture of business *and* bureaucratic viewpoints. This was a not infrequent mixture in the *Kaiserreich*.

To round off this survey of possible collisions between the behavioral norms of business leaders and those of other social groups, we move on to briefly consider the relations between traders and bankers (or creditors) on the one hand, and rural producers on the other. During the first half of the nineteenth century this nexus involved the links between creditors and rural producers, not only producers of agricultural commodities but protoindustrial ones as well. Some illustrative materials concerning complaints about usurious lending rates and the development of debt dependency can be drawn from the history of the East Westphalian linen industry.

Special legal sanctions associated with mercantile credit represented a significant limitation on the ability of spinners and weavers to dispose of their own product. According to the guild Control Act of 1791 creditors had exclusive purchase rights to linen produced by their debtors; violation of this regulation called for a fine of 10 Reichstaler or a 'corresponding prison sentence'. And weavers were obligated to sell their goods at the guild market, a rule also designed to secure credit.[50]

It is uncertain whether differing moral standards prevailed. One can observe, for example, that debtors frequently attempted to turn the

> harsh practices of petty credit affairs, the high interest rates, the disadvantageous repayment terms, or the arrangements for property seizure, against he creditors themselves. What more likely form of revenge was available than to take on a large debt with the aim of leaving one's creditors holding a worthless claim?[51]

In the second half of the nineteenth century, industrialisation and urbanisation generated profit opportunities for peasant producers, opportunities whose exploitation called for considerable investment, and for credit to finance it. In many rural areas mobilising such credit involved considerable friction and conflict. From the 1850s on, there are many reports full of criticism of sharp agricultural financing practices and complaints about usurious loan charges. The standard sources – particularly the reports of the *Verein für Socialpolitik* – must be treated with caution, but the basic reproach made toward local credit dealers does seem to have a core of truth to it. These moneylenders, 'quasi-bankers', so to speak, filled a gap in rural credit provision, and they frequently exploited their temporary monopolies without scruple, extending personal credit to peasants, using the resultant debt dependence to compound interest income and, ultimately, to redistribute local land ownership in their own favour.[52] An important collective response to these conditions was the formation of credit cooperatives, especially the Raiffeisen loan offices. The organisation of the rural population into associations with collective liability improved the credit status of individual members. Knowledge of local conditions and each other's credit-worthiness could be pooled, the costs of credit – essentially risk premiums – could be substantially reduced. Positive results were realised in a very short time. As early as 1875 a Prussian investigating commission reported that

> the credit conditions of the small farmers who form the majority of members of the (cooperative) associations, have already brought about a sub-

stantial improvement in the credit conditions, until very recently so deplorable, of the small farmers who form the majority in most of them.[53]

The commission characterised the social structure of the cooperatives as follows:

> As a rule the well-to-do and the educated are the association's leaders. The general assembly, in which the local poor and needy dominate, is usually sufficiently realistic to see that maintenance of the organisation and particularly of its credit depends on voting for a leadership recruited from a well-to-do elite. The local mayor, the pastor, tax collector, the better-off farmers, those who are magistrates or eligible as jurors, together with the schoolteachers, are the persons who run the associations and who grant their credit. As so often here in the countryside, it is the more intelligent and wealthier part of the community which controls affairs, although decisive power formally lies with the general assembly, an organisation which virtually anyone can join since only very few associations demand an entrance fee; most of them accept every membership applicant, and credit-worthiness will only become an object of concern when a member applies for credit. In spite of this rather risky type of organisational or membership structure, we have only heard of one concrete case in which complaints were truly warranted, in an association in which the general assembly voted down the most competent person nominated by the mayor in favour of a man who was lax in controlling debt service and thus quite popular.[54]

The composition of membership and function in these cooperatives seem to have reflected a characteristic mixture of bourgeois and peasant elements. We may view as bourgeois the introduction and enforcement of strict business rules, the fight against usury and the indirect encouragement given to peasant debtors to run their farms in a more efficient, rational matter. Less bourgeois, perhaps, and more attuned to peasant values was the dominant principle of cooperation itself, perhaps also the opportunities cooperatives gave to local elite for additional social control.[55]

Entrepreneurial Behaviour and Collective Norms. A Comparison with Britain focusing on Capital Market Conditions, 1870–1914

Attempts to periodise entrepreneurial behaviour and behavioral norms are difficult and risk easy contradiction, but they are nevertheless useful in historical accounts. In this context it is worth looking at the history of economic fluctuations and considering in particular the special case of the 1870s. Many years ago Hans Rosenberg discussed the social and political consequences of the change of economic climate of those years under the heading 'Great Depression', and more recently Hans-Ulrich Wehler has stressed connections between the economic depression and 'a general de-liberalisation of public life and political affairs'.[56]

During the Great Depression, which Wehler feels to be an important turning point in the history of the Germany *Bürgertum* generally, changes took place in accepted entrepreneurial behavioural patterns which led to new legal norms. Important institutional landmarks were the founding of the Reichsbank (1875), the Imperial Bankruptcy Law (1877), the joint-stock Companies Act (1884), the Introduction of taxes on stock exchange transactions (1881, 1885) and the regulatory Stock Exchange Law (1895). These changes are of interest here, because they mark interventions through which collective norms limiting the freedom of individual businessmen attained legal status.

This 'triumph' of collective norms in the area of business behaviour represent in my opinion a peculiarly German characteristic of the nineteenth century; this point will be further elaborated in the following discussion of capital market changes in Germany and Great Britain. This discussion touches on the familiar story about connections between banks and industrial enterprise, above all the thesis that the great Germany banks maintained closer ties with industry and financed more risky investments than did their British counterparts. Lack of space precludes looking at more than a few relevant points here, and the reader is referred to the still growing body of literature.

One of the main subjects of German discussion in the 1870s was the joint-stock Company Law of 1870 which was seen as too lax and too liberal. Critical reform suggestions appeared as early as 1873, but it was a Prussian government memorandum in 1876 that initiated intensive official deliberations on the matter.[57] From the point of view of the Prussian Ministry of Trade the principal evils of existing practice derived form the fact that 'the promoters of new joint-stock companies saw them merely as means to realise quick profits, and having reached their goals left those companies to their respective fates'.[58] The details of the deliberations and negotiations – which lasted until 1884 – cannot be reproduced here.[59] The main result was important, and covered the following points:

(1) Protection of the investing shareholder through making public all contracts and agreements pertaining to a company's founding.

(2) Protection of shareholders by requiring subscription of all shares and cash payment of 25 percent of all share capital before a company commenced business operations.

(3) Protection of shareholders by strengthening the general shareholders' meeting and by the creation of the supervisory board (*Aufsichtsrat*) and the detailed listing of its duties.

(4) Protection against the threat of 'dubious' companies by setting the minimum share denomination at 1000 marks and forbidding trade in such shares before they are fully paid up.

(5) Securing the continuity of an enterprise and protection of its creditors by a number of further regulations.

A number of points which the Law of 1884 left open were dealt with in the Stock Exchange Law of 1895, which required companies issuing shares for stock exchange trading to first publish a prospectus of their general financial and business condition, the companies' officers were legally liable for the accuracy of this report.

The negotiations between representatives of business and those of the government bureaucracy – whose majority in the meantime had become advocates of a state-sponsored softening, or modification, of economic liberalism – led to a stricter, more conservative, joint-stock company law which made company formation less easy. In the interest of establishing a corporate business environment that would be more stable and less vulnerable to criticism on grounds of social justice, business representatives themselves acquiesced in the tightening of legal rules, even at the price of limiting the freedom of individual entrepreneurs.[60]

In Britain in the period 1870–1914 the relatively liberal legislation enacted between 1856 and 1862 (which codified earlier law) governed joint-stock company matters and was comparable to the liberal North German Confederation Law of 1870. In spite of repeated waves of public and semi-public discussion, however, few steps were in the direction of reform. Not until 1900 did a law enforcing publicity of contracts underlying newly founded companies come into being. And this law, almost immediately felt to be an overly restrictive measure, was soon weakened in the legislation of 1907 and 1908, and the gap between British and Germany legal arrangements widened once more.[61]

A further comparative defect of the British system lay in the organisation of the Stock Exchange, in its system of brokers and jobbers. Virtually all members of the London Stock Exchange specialised exclusively in Stock Exchange business. In consequence, they had practically no interest in the long-run success of their clients outside of the Stock Exchange arena. This attitude was in sharp contrast to those of their German counterparts who combined stock exchange activity with regular banking business.[62]

This had to do with legal arrangements governing the German stock exchanges. Thanks to the stock exchange taxes of 1881 and 1895, the market position of the very large banks was strengthened relative to that of the smaller banks and private bankers, particularly with respect to the financial business of large industrial companies and intermediation between stock exchange and private investors.[63] The key role of the 'great banks' as stock exchange intermediaries, bulwarked by devices such as the proxy voting of deposited shares, secured them positions on the supervisory boards of the companies they helped finance.[64] These intimate connections contributed to a harmony of interests between banker and industrial enterprise: Stock exchange business thus became more than a mass of individual transactions but part of a longer-term, ongoing relationship.

The result of this cooperative development in Germany was a system of industrial finance in which banks supported risky investments and reorganisations (e.g. mergers), particularly those involving large-scale enterprises. One part of this activity was a rigorous trade in company shares having high returns but also high risks. Since the larger banks themselves pursued a policy of diversification, they could in turn offer their own depositors and shareholders diversified investment packages, portfolios in which even relatively risky investment projects would appear less dangerous than they would in isolation. In this way, risky investment projects could be financed that might otherwise have been postponed or abandoned.[65]

In Great Britain we find a very different situation: in the London capital market little attention was paid to shares in domestic industrial enterprises, unlike Germany. The burden of fixed interest obligations was relatively larger than in Germany, which meant that British enterprises had to carry a larger share of their business risks themselves. High-risk industrial sectors were also less strongly represented in the London equity market than in that of Berlin.[66] The classic story of the failure of the British capital market was that of the electrical engineering industry. The new companies created in the 1880s were apparently oriented toward quick speculative profits, failed to develop sturdy organisational bases, and soon collapsed, with the result that the main losers, 'outsider' shareholders, turned away from this branch

of industry, and along with them, the British capital market as a whole. The gap that then inevitably emerged in Britain, was filled by foreign firms.[67] This development mirrored the institutional structure of the British capital market. 'Insider promoters' or company 'founders' and the Stock Exchange dealers they worked with, possessed a considerable informational advantage over potential shareholders. But the promoters rarely followed the aim of developing long-term business relations with the enterprises whose shares they unloaded. They saw these promotions as a 'killing', a 'cow to be milked to the limit'. One could not foresee the future, nor what it might bring. As a result 'promoters, the stock exchange, and investors were prepared to support "mania" waves of flotations in good times, but when the booms were over the firms created, many of them weak ones, were on their own – as were the investors'.[68] Many fraudulent promoters were mixed with the honest, if ill-conceived, projects, and were supported by a relatively corrupt financial journalism.[69] There were no powerful institutions capable of taking a "discriminating, long-run view of enterprise development potential" and for this reason no barrier was erected to keep the many less-promising projects from entering the market. The price of such concentration on short-run Stock Exchange profits, of the absence of banks which combined Stock Exchange activities with long-term business ties to industry, was the non-development of a 'permanent market for industrial securities calling for more than a minimum of risk bearing'.[70]

By contrast, in Germany businessmen themselves demanded and achieved institutions and legal norms which substantially limited the freedom of action of individual entrepreneurs in money and capital market matters. In Britain a much more individualistic laissez-faire ideology remained dominant among business leaders. The trust of these businessmen, and also the trust of parliamentary representatives of the public interest, in the positive powers of individual entrepreneurs and free competition remained, at least until the turn of the century, too strong for change to take place.[71]

The attachment of British entrepreneurs to individualist norms was not limited to capital market affairs, but was a general phenomenon. This attitude has recently been identified by Ulrich Wengenroth as a major cause behind the failure of an effective interest-group organisation to develop in the British steel industry between 1870 and 1914: 'A clear unwillingness to surrender individual entrepreneurial autonomy to collective instruments for achieving market power in the framework of national cartels, represents the real peculiarity of the

British steel industry in the period observed'. The obvious comparison with developments in Germany leads Wengenroth to the conclusion that entrepreneurs in Great Britain, thanks to a relatively satisfactory market situation, at least until around 1900, could justify their interest in maintaining individual autonomy, whereas in Germany the much more precarious position of heavy industry in the 1870s and 1880s made the need for collective, cooperative action seem much more pressing, especially for the large banks which also pushed for it.[72] This differing attitude toward collective norms is thus seen as a characteristic of different paths of industrial growth, very much in the sense of Gerschenkron's 'syndrome of backwardness'.[73]

The comparison between the German and British capital market illustrates a connection between business morality and business behaviour on two levels. First, the willingness of businessmen to accept or even promote collective, cooperative arrangements for handling their business, would seem to have important economic and social consequences; this willingness betrays an apparent contradiction between the bourgeois ideal of individual independence in the structuring of economic relationships and the growing economic usefulness of collective organisation. Second, the strong suspicion that established business leaders played a dominant role in the deliberations and negotiations that produced legal codification of business norms supports the double inference that opportunistic business behaviour, oriented toward short-term, individual utility maximisation is a characteristic particularly marked among new, untried, upwardly striving entrepreneurs, and one that was much more effectively repressed and controlled in Germany than in Britain, whose economic system was much less influenced by institutionalised cooperative rules.

Conclusion

A positive evaluation of economic achievement, of independence, and of free competition is doubtless part of 'business morality', and is at the core of what one may call the bourgeois virtues, or *Bürgerlichkeit*. This set of values implies honesty in business transactions, for otherwise entrepreneurial success would have no general legitimation. Such a morality thus belongs to any comprehensive characterisaton of German capitalist business leaders as a social group. It is more than that, however. Honesty, in the sense of adherence to generally accepted rules of economic behaviour, would seem to be a fundamental prerequisite for the development of market economies, a factor that helps explain how and why industrialisation in 'bourgeois' countries such as Germany came about.

Nevertheless, the notion of business morality raises many questions which remain unanswered, unsolved. For one thing, there is the question of the socially differential effects of a given set of rules of business behaviour. Within the 'bourgeois society' of the nineteenth century significant differentials evolved – and persisted – with respect to the distribution of income and of opportunity. One may well ask whether a given set of behavioral norms might not be recognised as disguised instruments for maintaining social and economic inequality, instruments which ultimately rest upon the coercive power of the state. From this perspective, rules and norms, also business morality, could be seen as means for justifying an unequal distribution of opportunity; it is conceivable that maintenance of nominal *de jure* equality of opportunity could strengthen the maintenance of real *de facto* inequality among social groups. Should one then consider whether business morality, the 'rational' economic core of bourgeois society, is a largely hypocritical ideology? This is not the place for a definitive judgement, but it may not be out of place to at least suggest that, should the answer to our rhetorical question be 'yes', then the contradiction may be part of bourgeois society itself.[74]

Another unresolved problem concerns the obvious fact of international differences and changes over time in the rules of economic behaviour during the Age of Industrialisation, and the reasons for them. Economic development in the countries which generated bourgeois values did not take place simultaneously, but over time with differing structures, and varying degrees of success. In the course of the 'Second Industrial Revolution' in the 1870s, and in association with the emergence of large-scale enterprises and rising state intervention, new rules and norms developed whose 'bourgeois' pedigree or character is questionable. The comparison between Britain and Germany attempted here strongly suggests that German entrepreneurs were much less reluctant to surrender decision-making autonomy to collective rules backed by law than were their counterparts in Britain. One can presume that this had much to do with the stronger tradition of state bureaucracy in Germany. However, present evidence, it remains an open question whether German businessmen were therefore less 'bourgeois' than British ones, or whether German *Bürgerlichkeit* simply implied a greater degree of collective rules and cooperation in business affairs.

Notes to Chapter 7

1. J. Kocka, 'Einleitung' in: J. Kocka (ed.) *Bürger und Bürgerlichkeit im 19. Jahrhundert* (Göttingen, 1987), pp. 7–20, here p. 9.

2. W. Sombart, *Der Bourgeois* (München, 1913), p. 135 ff.

3. D. North, *Structure and Change in Economic History* (New York, 1981), p. 11. See also *Ibid*. and R. Thomas, *The Rise of the Western World. A New Economic History* (Cambridge, 1974).

4. Cited by A. Field, 'Microeconomics, Norms and Rationality', in *Economic Development and Cultural Change* 32 (1984), pp. 683–711, here p. 686.

5. Field, *Microeconomics*, p. 702; also *Ibid*., 'What is Wrong with Neo-classical Institutional Economics. A Critique with Special Reference to the North Thomas Model of pre-1500 Europe', in *Explorations in Economic History* 18 (1981), pp. 174–98; see also North, *Structure*, p. 47.

6. G. Akerlof, 'The Market for Lemons. Quality, Uncertainty and the Market Mechanism' in *Quarterly Journal of Economics* 84 (1979), pp. 488–500.

7. For a pre-industrial case see Avner Greif, 'Reputation and Coalitions in Medieval Trade: Evidence on the Maghribi Traders', in JEH, 49 (1989), pp. 857–882.

8. On this see B. Klein, 'Self-Enforcing Contracts', in *Zeitschrift für die gesamte Staatswissenschaft* 141 (1985), p. 594–600 and esp.H. Albach, 'Vertrauen in der ökonomischen Theorie', *Ibid*., 136 (1980), p. 2–11. Albach argues here that positive experience with good products generating reputation can modify Akerlof's predicted result.

9. Sombart, *Bourgeois*, p. 162, 167–93; W. Ruppert, *Bürgerlicher Wandel. Studien zur Herausbildung einer nationalen deutschen Kultur im 18. Jahrhundert* (Frankfurt, 1981), p. 59, 84.

10. A. Gerschenkron, *Economic Backwardness in Historical Perspective* (Cambridge, 1962), p. 19f., 22. In economically underdeveloped countries of the twentieth century one can observe low standards of business morality reminiscent of Europe's backwards ares of the eighteenth and nineteenth centuries. On this see K. Borchardt, *Europas Wirtschaftsgeschichte. Ein Modell für Entwicklungsländer* (Stuttgart, 1967), p. 13f.

11. D. Grimm, 'Bürgerlichkeit im Recht', in Kocka, *Bürger*, p.149–188. See also the commentary by P.Landau, *Ibid*., p.189–195. The absence of a clear correlation between legalisation of norms and enhanced sanctions, on the one hand, and behaviour, on the other, is one of the most serious weaknesses in the NIE interpretation of history as practiced by North and others.

12. Space limits prevent a comprehensive survey of the literature here. In the following I limit myself to citing relevant bits of documentation. The use of business histories raises enormous and probably unresolvable problems of representativeness; but the statement in the text about trends is probably not dependent upon this feature of the sources surveyed.

13. Some data on what might now be labelled 'white-collar crime' can be brought to bear in this connection. For instance, although it is likely that the share of registered crime was rising relative to the unknown total, the number of cases per 100,000 population (*Vermögensdelikte*) stagnates between 1880 and 1914: an average of 475 in the years 1887–90, and one of 480 in the years 1905–13, while the share of fraud in these totals declined. These figures can be contrasted with the enormous expansion in the annual level of monetary transactions over the period. Taking the Prussian Bank and Reichsbank yearly business turnover per capita as an indicator of this expansion one observes a total growth between 1870–74 and 1910–13 of 563 percent. Over the same period, in contrast, these banks' balance sheet position bad debts – which might arguably serve as an index of dishonest business – declined by about 20 percent *Verwaltungsbericht der Preußischen Bank* 1870–1875; *Verwaltungsbericht der Reichsbank*, 1910–13.

14. See R. Tilly, 'The Growth of Large-Scale Enterprise in Germany since the Middle of the Nineteenth Century', in H. Daems and H. van der Wee (eds.), *The Rise of Managerial Capitalism* (Löwen. 1974), p.145. It is also likely that the average length of employment grew in the nineteenth century, or at least since the 1870s, since the mutual interest in maintenance of a stable relationship is likely to have grown. For evidence on the U.S. see Susan Carter and Elizabeth Savoca, 'Labor Mobility and Lengthy Jobs in Nineteenth-Century America', in *Journal of Economic History*, 50 (1990), pp. 1–16.

15. See among others, J. Molsberger, 'Wirtschaftskriminalität und Wirtschaftsordnungen', in Institut für Wirtschaftspolitik an der Universität Köln (ed.), *Wirtschaftspolitische Chronik* 25 (1976), esp. pp. 182f., 185.

16. F. Meisel, *Britische und deutsche Einkommenssteuer. Ihre Moral und ihre Technik* (Tübingen, 1925), esp. p. 119ff. According to Meisel the 'tax morality' of large landed estate owners was by no means 'better' than that of urban businessmen.

17. Of concern here are not collective aims realised through pressure group activity, but individual gains. For gains related to the armaments business the Krupp history is instructive. See W. Boelcke, *Krupp und die Hohenzollern in Dokumenten* (Frankfurt, 1970).

18. F. Redlich, *Der Unternehmer. Wirtschafts- und sozialgeschichtliche Studien* (Göttingen, 1964), p.191ff.

19. Ruppert, *Bürgerlicher Wandel*, p.50ff., 84f.; A. Hasenclever, 'Josua Hasenclever', in *Rheinisch-Westfälische Wirtschaftsbiographien*, vol. 1 (Münster, 1932), p. 379f.

20. J. Mooser, *Ländliche Klassengesellschaft 1770–1848* (Göttingen, 1984), p. 285; R. Wirtz, 'Sozialer Protest in Baden 1815–1848. Determination, Motive und Verhaltensmuster' in H. Volkmann and J. Bergmann (eds.), *Sozialer Protest* (Opladen, 1984), p. 48.

21. Ruppert, *Bürgerlicher Wandel*, p. 59; K. Bücher, *Die Entstehung der Volkswirtschaft*, vol. 2 (Tübingen, 1920), p. 220, 226, 304f.; F. Blumenroth, 'Leonhard Tietz', in *Rheinisch-Westfälische Wirtschaftsbiographien*, vol. 7 (Münster, 1960), p. 53; H.-H. Teuteberg, 'Der Kampf gegen die Lebensmittelverfälschung', in *ibid.* and G. Wiegelmann (eds.), *Unsere Tägliche Kost. Geschichte und regionale Prägung* (Münster, 1986), p. 371ff.

22. An extended literature is available which discusses these issues in legal history; see v.a. M. Apt (ed.), *Gutachten der Ältesten der Kaufmannschaft von Berlin über Gebräuche im Handelsverkehr*, 3 vols. (Berlin, 1900–1914); G. Meyer, *Der Handelsbrauch, insbes. sein Verhältnis zu den dispositiven Gesetzesbestimmungen* (Erlangen, 1928); V. Pöhls, *Darstellung des gemeinen Deutschen und des Hamburgischen Handelsrechts für Juristen und Kaufleute*, 3 vols. (Hamburg, 1832); H.-H. Graul, *Allgemeine Geschäftsbedingungen und Handelsbräuche* (Halle, 1932); W. Silberschmidt, *Die Entstehung der deutschen Handelsgerichte* (Leipzig, 1894); R. von Ihering, *Gesammelte Aufsätze aus den Jahrbüchern für die Dogmatik des heutigen römischen und deutschen Privatrechts*, vol. 1 (Jena, 1881); K. Goetz, *Handelsgewohnheitsrecht und Handelssitte* (Krefeld, 1913).

23. J. Deparade, *Die Kodifikation von Handelsgebräuchen durch die Industrie- und Handelskammern und ihre Bedeutung für den Handelsverkehr und die Rechtsentwicklung* (Magdeburg, 1927).

24. F. Zunkel, *Der rheinisch-westfälische Unternehmer 1834–1879* (Köln, 1962), p. 38.

25. H. Henning, *Sozialgeschichtliche Entwicklungen in Deutschland von 1815 bis 1860* (Paderborn, 1977), p. 28; P.Borscheid, 'Westfälische Industriepioniere in der Frühindustrialisierung', in K. Düwell and W. Köllmann (eds.), *Rheinland-Westfalen im Industriezeitalter*, vol. 1: *Von der Entstehung der Provinz bis zur Reichsgründung* (Wuppertal, 1983), p. 159, 164; H. Blumberg, *Die Deutsche Textilindustrie in der Industriellen Revolution* (Berlin, 1965), p. 135; W. Köllmann, *Sozialgeschichte der Stadt Barmen im 19. Jahrhundert* (Tübingen, 1960), p. 140.

26. K. von Eichborn, *Das Soll und Haben von Eichborn & Co. in 200 Jahren* (München, 1928), p. 291.

27. Zunkel, *Unternehmer*, p. 41f.; R. Tilly, *Financial Institutions in the Rhineland,*

1815–1970 (Madison, 1966), p. 22f.; R. Strauss, *Die Lage und die Bewegung der Chemnitzer Arbeiter in der ersten Hälfte des 19. Jahrhunderts* (Berlin, 1960), pp. 81–81.

28. Mooser, *Klassengesellschaft*, p. 71.

29. J. Kuczynski, *Geschichte des Alltags des deutschen Volkes, vol. 3: 1810 bis 1870* (Köln, 1982), p. 163ff.; Köllman, *Sozialgeschichte Barmen*, p. 141; K. Ditt, *Industrialisierung, Arbeiterschaft und Arbeiterbewegug in Bielefeld 1850–1914* (Dortmund, 1982), p. 15.

30. D. Dowe, *Aktion und Organisation. Arbeiterbewegung, sozialistische und Kommunistische Bewegung in der preußischen Rheinprovinz 1820–52* (Hannover, 1970), p. 26ff.; R. Tilly, 'Protest and Collective Violence in Germany during Modernization', unpublished manuscript, 1978. See also A. Herzig , 'Vom sozialen Protest zur Arbeiterbewegung. Das Beispiel des märkisch-westfälischen Industriegebietes (1770–1865)', in Volkmann/Bergmann, (eds.), *Sozialer Protest*, p. 253ff.

31. For Great Britain: S. Pollard, 'Die Fabrikdisziplin in der Industriellen Revolution', in W. Fischer (ed.), *Die soziale Frage* (Stuttgart, 1967), p. 159ff. For Germany see: H. Scherer, Fabrikdiszpilin in der Frühindustrialisierung, mit bes. Berücksichtigung der rheinisch-westfälischen Schwerindustrie, Diplomarbeit Universität Münster 1968; W. Köllmann, *Friedrich Harkort*, vol. 1 (Düsseldorf, 1964), pp. 65–68.

32. Scherer, *Fabrikdisziplin*, p. 49ff.

33. H. Kisch, *Die hausindustriellen Textilgewerbe am Niederrhein vor der industriellen Revolution* (Göttingen, 1981), p. 224, 226.

34. See note 29.

35. See H. Volkmann, *Die Arbeiterfrage im preußischen Abgeordnetenhaus 1848–1869* (Berlin, 1968).

36. See the contributions by I. Fischer, 'Maurer- und Textilarbeiterstreiks in Augsburg, 1899–1914', and I. Costas, 'Arbeitskämpfe in der Berliner Elektroindustrie 1905 und 1906', both in: K. Tenfelde and H. Volkmann (eds.), *Streik. Zur Geschichte des Arbeitskampfes in Deutschland während der Industrialisierung* (München, 1981), esp. p. 78f., 83 and 101f.; W. Köllmann (ed.), *Der Bergarbeiterstreik von 1889 und die Gründung des "Alten Verbandes" in ausgewählten Dokumenten der Zeit* (Bochum, 1969).

37. Many sources from the field of business and labour movement history document this point. For example H.-J. Rupieper, 'Die Herausbildung der Industriearbeiterschaft im 19. Jahrhundert. Das Beispiel M.A.N., 1857–1914', in J. Bergmann et al. (eds.), *Arbeit, Mobilität, Partizipation, Protest* (Opladen, 1986), p. 216f.; H.-P.Ullmann, 'Unternehmerschaft, Arbeitgeberverbände und Streikbewegung 1890–1914', in Tenfelde/Volkmann, *Streik*, p. 195. According to this latter view, business employers began in the 1890s to view labour unions as institutions which were here to stay, and began to construct formal employer associations as a counter-device.

38. See the articles 'Arbeitsvertrag' (E. Loening), 'Arbeitsvertragsbruch' (R. Loening), 'Arbeiterschutzgesetzgebung' (von Landmann) and 'Gewerbegerichte', in *Handwörterbuch der Staatswissenschaften* (Jena, 1909), p. 594f., 1165–71, 1176–91, 880–90; L. Puppke, *Sozialpolitik und soziale Anschauung frühindustrieller Unternehmer in Rheinland-Westfalen* (Köln, 1966), p. 4; R. Bahr, *Beiträge zur Entwicklungsgeschichte des Gewerbegerichts* (Leipzig, 1904); K.-H. Schloßstein, *Die westfälischen Fabrikengerichtsdeputationen. Vorbilder, Werdegang und Scheitern* (Frankfurt, 1982).

39. H. Leiskow, *Spekulation und öffentliche Meinung in der 1. Hälfte des 19. Jahrhunderts* (Jena, 1930); S. Spangenthal, *Die Geschichte der Berliner Börse* (Berlin, 1903), pp. 39–41, 55, 88ff.

40. Zunkel, *Unternehmer*, p. 52f., 58f.

41. H. Rosenberg, *Die Weltwirtschaftskrise 1857–1859* (Göttingen, 1974), esp. p. 56, 98f., where he speaks of 'swindles involving even that paragon of solidity and integrity, so often rightfully praised for its virtues, the Prussian bureaucracy ...' The scandals led to doubts concerning the effectiveness of the government's policy of strict concessioning as a control mechanism. See also H. Blumberg, 'Die Finanzierung der Neu-

gründungen und Erweiterungen von Industriebetrieben in Form der Aktiengesellschaften während der fünfziger Jahre des 19. Jahrhunderts in Deutschland, am Beispiel der preußischen Verhältnisse erläutert', in H. Mottek et al. (eds.), *Studien zur Geschichte der industriellen Revolution in Deutschland* (Berlin, 1960), p. 165ff., esp. p. 174, 176.

42. See H. Rosenberg, *Große Depression und Bismarckzeit* (Berlin, 1967), esp. p. 70f.; and G. Mork, 'The Prussian Railway Scandal of 1873. Economics and Politics in the German Empire', in *European Studies Review* 1 (1971), pp. 35–48.

43. Cited in J. Hansen, *Gustav von Mevissen. Ein rheinisches Lebensbild, 1815 bis 1899*, vol.. 1 (Berlin, 1966), p. 781f.

44. *Ibid.*, vol. 2, p. 598ff.; M. Löwenfel, *Das Recht der Actien-Gesellschaften. Kritik und Reformvorschläge* (Berlin, 1879).

45. Zunkel, *Unternehmer*, p.67; Th. Nipperdey, *Deutsche Geschichte 1800 bis 1866. Bürgerwelt und starker Staat* (München, 1983), p. 208.

46. Blumberg, *Textilindustrie*, p. 235.

47. See on this F. Gehrmann, Konkurse im Industrialisierungsprozeß Deutschlands 1810–1913, Diss. Münster 1973, esp. appendix, where individual enterprises are surveyed; A. Wirminghaus, 'Statistik der Konkurse', in *Handwörterbuch der Staatswissenschaften* (Jena, 1909), p. 104f.

48. G. Hahn, *Untersuchungen über die Ursachen von Unternehmermißerfolgen (besonders im rheinischen Industriegebiet)*, Diss. Köln, 1956, p. 49ff.

49. On this see Gehrmann, *Konkurse*, Chapt. II, p. 68ff.; Hahn, *Untersuchungen*, p.24f., 28ff.; W. Uhlenbruck et al. (eds.), *Einhundert Jahre Konkursordnung 1877–1977. Festschrift des Arbeitskreises für Insolvenz und Schiedsgerichtswesen e.V. Köln zum einhundertjährigen Bestehen der Konkursordnung vom 1. February 1877* (Köln, 1977); C. Hahn (ed.), *Die gesammten Materialien zur Konkursordnung und dem Einführungsgesetz zu derselben vom 1. February 1877* (Berlin, 1881).

50. Mooser, *Klassengesellschaft*, p. 293f.

51. *Ibid.*, p. 305.

52. W. Pieper, '*Der landwirtschaftliche Ersatzbankier Süddeutschlands*', in *Bankhistorisches Archiv* 4 (1978), pp. 68–70.

53. *Bericht der Enquête-Kommission über die Raiffeisen'schen Darlehnskassen-Vereine, im Auftrag des Ministeriums für die landwirtschaftlichen Angelegenheiten Preußens (1875)*, Staatsarchiv Münster.

54. *Ibid.*

55. See H. Faust, *Geschichte der Genossenschaftsbewegung* (Frankfurt, 1977), esp. p. 273, 280ff.

56. Rosenberg, *Große Depression*; H.-U. Wehler, 'Wie bürgerlich war das Deutsche Kaiserreich?' in Kocka, *Bürger*, pp. 243–280, here p. 271.

57. See on this the useful documentation by W. Schubert and P. Hommelhoff (eds.), *Hundert Jahre modernes Aktienrecht. Eine Sammlung von Texten und Quellen zur Aktienrechtsreform 1884* (Berlin, 1985). The correspondence, reports and basic data related to the memorandum are in Deutsche Zentralarchiv Merseburg, Rep. 120, II a, A XII 5. They were partially utilised by E. Engel, *Die erwerbsfähigen juristischen Personen insbes. die Aktiengesellschaften im preußischen Staat* (Berlin, 1876).

58. Schubert/Hommelhoff, *Aktienrecht*, p. 9. R. von der Borght, *Die Bewährung der Actiengesellschaften in Deutschland auf den veschiedenen Gebieten ihrer Tätigkeit* (Halle, 1883), esp. p. 11, 16.

59. Schubert/Hommelhoff, *Aktienrecht*, N. Horn, 'Aktienrechtliche Unternehmensorganisation in der Hochindustrialisierung (1860–1920). Deutschland, England, Frankreich und die USA im Vergleich', in Horn and J. Kocka (eds.), *Recht und Entwicklung der Großunternehmen im 19. und frühen 20. Jahrhundert*, Göttingen 1979, p. 123ff.

60. See also N. Reich, 'Auswirkungen der deutschen Aktienrechtsreform von 1884 auf die Konzentration der deutschen Wirtschaft', in Horn/Kocka, *Recht und*

Entwicklung, p. 255 ff. A different judgement: B. Grossfeld, 'Die rechtspolitische Beurteilung der Aktiengesellschaften im 19. Jahrhundert', in H. Coing and W. Wilhelm (eds.), *Wissenschaft und Kodifikation des Privatrechts im 19. Jahrhundert*, vol. 4 (Frankfurt, 1979), p. 249. In addition T. Raiser, 'Sozialer Wandel durch Recht, dargestellt am Beispiel der AG', in M. Rehbinder and H. Schelsky (eds.), *Zur Effektivität des Rechts* (Düsseldorf, 1972), p. 414ff.

61. On this P.Cottrell, *Industrial Finance, 1830–1914. The Finance and Organization of English Manufacturing Industry* (London, 1980), Chap. 3, esp. p. 54ff. The German Joint-Stock Company Law of 1884 is said to have played a role in British parliamentary deliberations in 1899–1900. Interestingly, Edwin Chadwick, a respected and successful company promoter, is reported to have repeatedly, if vainly, pleaded for introduction of stricter legal controls on joint-stock company promotions. See on this Cottrell, *Industrial Finance*, pp. 59–64. This corresponds to the logic of the Market-for-lemons analysis (note 6). See also F. Lavington, *The English Capital Market* (London, 1921), esp. pp. 214–18.

62. Lavington, *Capital Market*, p. 183ff., 213ff.; E.V. Morgan and W.A. Thomas, *The Stock Exchange. Its History and Functions* (London, 1962); R.C. Michie, 'Options, Concessions, Syndicates and the Provision of Venture Capital, 1880–1913' in *Business History* 23 (1981), pp. 147–64; and her 'The London and New York Stock Exchanges, 1850–1914', in *Journal of Economic History* 46 (1986), pp. 171–87.

63. J. Riesser, *Die Deutschen Großbanken und ihre Konzentration* (Berlin, 1910), p. 464 ff.; M. Pohl, *Konzentration im dutschen Bankwesen 1848–1980* (Frankfurt, 1982).

64. In addition to Riesser see also Reich, *Auswirkungen*.

65. W.P.Kennedy and R. Britton, 'Portfolioverhalten und wirtschaftliche Entwicklung im späten 19. Jahrhundert. Ein Vergleich zwischen Großbritannien und Deutschland', in R. Tilly (ed.), *Beiträge zur quantitativen vergleichenden Unternehmensgeschichte* (Stuttgart, 1985), pp. 45–93; Tilly, *German Banking*.

66. Tilly, *German Banking* esp. p. 128ff.; J.B. Jefferys, *Business Organisation in Great Britain 1856–1914* (New York, 1977), Appendix E.

67. W. Kennedy, 'Institutional Response to Economic Growth. Capital Markets in Britain to 1914', in L. Hannah (ed.), *Management Strategy and Business Development* (London, 1976), p. 169 ff.; I.C.R. Byatt, *The British Electrical Industry, 1875–1914* (Oxford, 1979); H.A. Shannon, 'The Limited Companies of 1866–1883', in E.M. Carus-Wilson (ed.), *Essays in Economic History* (London, 1954), p. 385.

68. Cottrell, *Industrial Finance*, p.187, 189; Kennedy, *Institutional Response*; Lavington, *Capital Market*, p. 217f.

69. A.E. Harrison, 'Joint-Stock Company Flotations, 1882–1914', in *Business History* 23 (1981), p. 176 f.; D. Porter, 'A Trusted Guide to the Investing Public. Harry Marks and the Financial News 1884–1916', in *Business History* 28 (1986), p. 1–17; J. Armstrong, 'Hooley and the Bovril Company', *Ibid.*, pp. 18–34. Ernst Terah Hooley was a prototypical, notorious promoter in this period, one who enjoyed considerable success.

70. Kennedy, *Institutional Response*; and his 'Economic Growth and Structural Change in the United Kingdom, 1870–1914', in *Journal of Economic History* 44 (1982), pp. 105–114; R. Tilly, 'Financing Industrial Enterprise in Great Britain and Germany in the Nineteenth Century', in H.-J. Wagener and J.W. Drukker (eds.), *The Economic Law of Motion of Modern Society* (Cambridge 1986), p. 123ff.

71. Cottrell, *Industrial Finance*. A similar reluctance towards stricter government controls – especially in comparison with Germany – can be shown to have characterised the problem of bankruptcy and liquidation of companies. See the critical comments on British Law in *London Economist* in the 1880s and 1890s.

72. U. Wengenroth, *Unternehmensstrategien und technischer Fortschritt. Die deutsche und die britische Stahlindustrie 1865–1895* (Göttingen, 1986), esp. Chap.VI.

73. Wengenroth's findings for the steel industry are probably applicable to other areas of British economic life, for recent contributions to the history of industrial organisations pointing in the same direction: R.P.T. Davenport-Hines, 'Trade Associations and the Modernization Crisis of British Industry 1910–35', J. Turner, 'Servants of Two Masters. British Trade Associations in the First Half of the 19th Century', unpublished papers, Tokyo Business History Conference, Jan. 1987; J. Zeitlin, 'From Labour History to the History of Industrial Relations', in *Economic History Review* 40 (1987), pp. 159–84.

74. See D. Rüschemeyer, *Bourgeoisie, Staat und Bildungsbürgertum*. 'Ideal-types' for comparative research on 'Bürgerlichkeit' are in Kocka, *Bürger*, pp. 101–120.

8 | Honour and Middle-Class Culture: the History of the Duel in England and Germany

Ute Frevert

The Duel in the Nineteenth Century: Feudal Relic or Bourgeois Practice?

The notion of honour today, at the end of the twentieth century, has an archaic ring to it. It is no longer a fashionable word. Recent attempts to reactivate it for political purposes in Germany have not been a success. The attempt to prevent the withdrawal by the Austrian authorities of an invitation to the Bavarian Prime Minister as a slight to the 'honour' of the entire state remained at the level of bathetic rhetoric, while the 'word of honour' given by a late prime-minister of Schleswig-Holstein soon crumbled in the face of investigation by journalists and the police. In contrast, the notion of the duel remains very popular. Almost every day we read in the papers about debating duels, tennis duels and duels between business firms – the range of possible associations are almost limitless. What is meant, in all cases are forms of combat in which two persons or institutions measure their strength against each other and compete for a victory that promises prestige, power or profit. These duels, however, have little in common with the classical duel, since what is at stake is not honour but competition and comparative achievement.

The loss of meaning of the notion of honour is thus matched by the descent into banality of the idea of the duel. When honour is no longer at stake, the 'duel' loses its social significance. The fact that the word is still used so widely indicates that it has maintained, even for the modern person, a peculiar mystique, although no one could or would want to experience the real thing.

I do not intend, in the present article to examine either the changes

Notes to Chapter 8 can be found on page 236.

in the semantics of the terms 'honour' and 'duel' or the socio-historical reasons for these changes.[1] My brief introductory remarks were intended simply to indicate how far removed we are today from the attitudes and patterns of behavior which, a hundred years ago, were taken for granted as an everyday part of German life. In the nineteenth century, known even to contemporaries as the 'bourgeois century',[2] honour and the duel were an established part of social life. Like the Wagner cult and Schiller festivals, they were part of what Thomas Mann called 'bourgeois atmosphere'. To characterise the duel as unbourgeois, or to dismiss it as just another one of those feudal relics that continued as social anachronisms in German society[3] would be to ignore it as a concrete phenomenon and to fail to recognise its significance as a bourgeois convention. It would also be a misinterpretation of 'bourgeois atmosphere' or, to use a more modern concept, 'bourgeois culture', a misinterpretation that ignores the typical ambivalences and contradictions of this culture.

That these contradictions not only characterised bourgeois society as a whole, but also manifested themselves in individuals, is clear from the example of Max Weber. Although he himself was a sharp critic of that particular 'German etiquette' that found its highest expression in *Satisfaktionsfähigkeit* (capable of giving satisfaction, i.e. of fighting a duel) he nonetheless did not hesitate to submit to this practice when his own personal honour seemed to be at stake. He publicly supported duelling, maintained close relations with his student fencing fraternity and was proud of his military rank as a reserve officer. When in 1910 Marianne Weber, an activist in the bourgeois women's movement, was insulted in a newspaper article, he immediately declared that he was prepared to defend 'the honour of his wife' in a duel, and it was only the refusal of his adversary that prevented it from coming to actual combat.[4]

Weber was not only personally attached to these social conventions; he devoted a lot of attention to them in his work. He took it for granted that social groups, classes and strata are not held together merely by material interests, that politics was by no means limited to the rational negotiation of competing needs and that power had more than an economic foundation. He considered the social order based on the *ständisches Prinzip* (the principle of the *Stand* or 'estate') to be on a par with market forces, the former structuring social reality as much as economically-conditioned class relations. This principle manifested itself in the concept of honour, which demanded of the members of an estate a particular conduct of life that distinguished them from other groups. The decisive significance of 'conduct of life' in determining the honour of the estate and in deciding its membership implied, according to Weber, 'that the estates are the upholders of all 'conventions': Every 'stylisation' of life, in no matter what form it manifests itself, either originates in or is preserved by the estate.'[5]

Satisfaktionsfähigkeit, the right to restore one's personal honour by means of a duel, was considered by Weber to be one of those conventions, stylisations or symbols that served to preserve and strengthen *ständisch* honour. The duel was both the purest expression of honour and the final proof of an honourable character and honourable conduct of life. It recognised in honour the highest standard to which individual behaviour had to submit regardless of the consequences. One did not just live for honour; to preserve it, one was willing to die.

Not all estates, however, considered it essential to emphasise and defend honour in this way. According to Weber, it was the officers and the educated classes who created for themselves a code that prescribed the duel and that linked membership of the estate with the individual's right and willingness to defend his honour in this way. For the military and civic elite in Germany, therefore, the duel became a convention that promoted the social integration of this stratum and guaranteed its 'distance and exclusivity' (Weber) vis-à-vis other 'estates'. Whoever wanted to be accepted into this exclusive circle had to accept the rules prescribed by the code of honour. Property and wealth were, of course, essential, but they were not sufficient to ensure acceptance, for honour 'normally contradicts the naked pretensions of property'.[6] Formal military and educational qualifications had to be given substance by a corresponding way of life. It was only this conduct, which involved much more than mere competence and success in one's professional career, that brought with it honour, which elevated and 'ennobled' the collective as well as the individual who was part of it.

As a phenomenon associated with the structure of estates, honour was not something that could be unequivocally attributed to one class. The duelling honour of this elite, capable of giving satisfaction, was not resolved into the social conventions of a class defined only in terms of economic power. In fact, the German middle class, the *Bürgertum*, with its multitude of career and property-owning groups, cannot itself be adequately be described within the Marxian or Weberian model of class. Here, one is forced to make use of non-economic criteria. In the attempt to uncover the inner cohesion and external boundaries of the *Bürgertum* by means of analysis of its culture or lifestyle,[7] its notion of honour and honorable behaviour provide essential starting points.

The present paper, however, is not just a contribution to the study of the *'psychologie bourgeoise'* (Adeline Daumard) in Germany. The comparison with England should also help to establish whether and to what extent the code of honour of the German bourgeois-aristocratic elite was a national peculiarity. After all, from the middle of the nineteenth century the conventions governing 'points of honour' developed quite differently in England than they did in Germany. The task is to explain these differences, taking into account the different social and cultural profile of the elite in both countries.

If one is inclined to view the duel as a feudal relic, then its early disappearance in England will be seen as an indication of the advanced bourgeois character of the English society, whereas the German development will be taken as further evidence for the weakness of bourgeois culture (*Defizit an Bürgerlichkeit*) in that country. This argument was made as early as 1909 by the social scientist Lujo Brentano when he explained the decline of the duel in England as a consequence of the social and political hegemony of the English middle classes and attributed the 'growing recognition' of the duelling principle on the continent to the 'feeble character of the German *Bürgertum*'.[8] This interpretation has also found support in England, where a study of the English opposition to duelling between 1700 and 1850 came to the conclusion that the replacement of the 'code of honour' by a 'code of Christian commerce' around the middle of the nineteenth century was a consequence of the growing self-awareness of the English middle classes.[9] It was this bourgeois self-confidence, it might be concluded, that was lacking in Germany, where as the social democrat August Bebel complained in 1896, it was considered the ' "done thing" to ape the airs and graces of the aristocracy' and to 'fight duels with no less zeal than the nobility'.[10]

Contemporary judgements, however, do not always hit the mark, and there are almost always not just one but a number of historical truths. The enthusiasm for duelling displayed by social circles that stood apart from the aristocracy in nineteenth-century society has raised some doubt as to whether a simple feudalisation thesis can explain these affinities. On the other han..d, the social, political and cultural hegemony of the English middle class is a controversial issue among historians, certainly for the period in mid-century when the duel disappeared from the code of polite behaviour among the English elite.

Before we can use the development of the duel in Germany as evidence for a German *Sonderweg* or for deficiencies in the culture and honour of the German *Bürgertum*, it is essential to examine the phenomenon of the duel more carefully and to situate it in the social and historical context of each country.

The Duel in the Early Modern Period.

When exactly duelling began in England and Germany is unclear, as is its relationship to the various forms of judicial and non-judicial single combat recorded in the Middle Ages. At least by the second half of the sixteenth century the term 'duel' was in use in the English and German language, and there is documentary evidence from the early seventeenth century of the first official bans on duelling.

In England, James I in 1613 prohibited 'private challenges and combats', which as one contemporary remarked in 1606, were happening 'now a day among soldiers and men of honour' and served 'to discharge a man for an injury received'.[11] The king declared this practice to be incompatible with the 'qualities of gentlemen' and referred the combatants to the common law. At the same time he called upon his Attorney General, Francis Bacon, to make an exemplary prosecution.[12] Thus, three years later, Bacon laid a heavy fine and prison sentence on a noble officer, Gervase Markham, for preparing a challenge to a duel. Markham's crime was exacerbated by the fact that he, as a member of the lesser nobility, had attempted to provoke his superior who was a member of the House of Lords, accusing him of lying. Members of the gentry were, according to Bacon, only 'second Nobles' and by insulting a peer of the realm, committed a double crime. In any case, a duel, like any other form of murder, was 'a direct affront of law...and tends to the dissolution of magistracy'.[13]

However, neither royal disapproval, nor the strictness of his public prosecutor were enough to persuade the English nobility to give up the duel. The new code of honour, influenced by the French, seemed to offer a welcome possibility for containing and regulating conflicts. On the evidence of newspaper reports, private letters and official statements, Lawrence Stone has concluded that the frequency with which peers became involved in violent disputes diminished remarkably between 1580 and 1640. At the same time, however, the number of duels and challenges increased significantly. In the first two decades of the seventeenth century, one in every four peer was in danger of losing his life in a duel.[14] The members of the middle and lower nobility also appropriated the new code of honour and used the duel as a means of settling conflicts among themselves and with the upper nobility 'on terms of equality' (Stone) – even though the king and the courts did everything possible to prevent this blurring of social differences.

Duels continued to take place throughout the course of the seventeenth and eighteenth centuries. The diary of the Secretary of the Admiralty, Samuel Pepys, mentions many cases from the 1660s in which the nobility defended their honour with the sword. He also expressed the hope that the authorities might make 'some good laws' against it.[15] In 1713, after a fatal duel between two members of the upper nobility, the House of Commons discussed how best to prevent this practice, but it failed to reach an agreement on the appropriate legal measures.[16] In any case, laws and ordinances remained without effect as long as the social elite subscribed to the code of duelling and regarded it as a mark of cowardice not to respond to an insult with a challenge to a duel. Moreover, the courts were generally hesitant to punish duelling as murder under the common law; even when such a sentence was passed, the king frequently granted a pardon.

The situation on the Continent was similar. In the German states the nobility engaged in duels as a response to attacks, or what they saw as attacks, on their honour, and here too kings and princes issued edicts in an effort to stop this practice. From the time of the late sixteenth century almost all of the German states issued decrees and regulations proscribing both challenges to duels and participation in them.[17] The frequency with which these decrees were repeated is evidence of their ineffectiveness, but also of the interest of German rulers in curtailing the practice of duelling. They took offence at the fact that their subjects, as was said in the *Principality of Württemberg's Edict against Duelling* in 1714, were intent 'on carrying out vengeance for themselves' instead of 'leaving it to us, the highest authority in the land, who have the authority given to us by God and whose task it is to ensure that every person's honour and body and property are preserved undisturbed'.[18] The state's monopoly of force as well as its legal authority were not to be questioned and every form of self-administered justice was regarded as criminal and potentially destabilising.

We know very little about the extent or frequency of duelling in the German states, and there is a similar lack of information about their causes and the participants involved. It seems to have been predominantly nobles who used this means of responding to slights on their honour, although there are a number of edicts and court records (very few of which have been preserved) from the seventeenth and early eighteenth centuries that speak of commoners engaging in duels. In a decree issued in Hamburg in 1660, it is said that 'people of common estate', following the example of their superiors, had begun to take up duelling – 'therefore it was necessary to proceed with even greater seriousness and strictness against this destructive evil'.[19] From the principality of Lippe, the criminal records of 1688 speak of two cases of duelling involving artisans or non-noble officials, while in Bremen in 1769 two barbers' apprentices drew their swords to settle a dispute.[20] Students also took to 'achieving their own satisfaction' as the Saxon Herzog Johann Georg remarked disapprovingly in 1694 with reference to the university city of Jena.[21]

The tendency to engage in duels was strengthened by the ease with which weapons were acquired. In both England and Germany it was originally an exclusive privilege of the nobility – the military estate *par excellence* – to carry arms. In the middle ages, this privilege had been extended to members of the universities, and later, when the state as well as municipal and university authorities tried to take back this privilege, it was stoutly defended by the students. From the sixteenth century, the sword became part of student apparel and was frequently used in order to settle conflicts of honour within the student milieu, as well as conflicts with the citizens of the town (especially journeymen) and with officers. From the second half of the seventeenth century there were fencing schools in all the German universities, where students learned how 'to avoid injury when some reckless fool seeks to acquire vain honour from us by means of wild revenge'.[22]

What in the past would have been part of the education of the sons of the nobility now became accessible to the sons of the *Bürgertum* – a process of social diffusion that the Prussian king, Friedrich II, intent on strengthening the nobility, tried in vain to forbid. His ruling of 1750, which prohibited non-noble students from 'wearing swords at the universities' while allowing the sons of the nobility to continue doing so, was unable to prevent fencing and duelling from becoming an established part of that academic culture that distinguished students from other bourgeois groups, whatever their social origin.

Fencing was also part of student life in the English universities in the seventeenth and eighteenth centuries, although it never acquired the significance that it did in Germany. There was a fencing school in Oxford in the 1770s. According to Jonathan Swift fencing was an essential part of a 'good education' in the first half of the eighteenth century, alongside dancing, riding, the learning of French and travel in Italy.[23] However, the 'noble art of self-defence' went steadily out of fashion in Oxford and Cambridge. Its place was taken by country sports like hunting, riding and rowing, as well as team games like cricket, which became very popular in England after the middle of the eighteenth century.[24] Unlike in Germany, the sword was never part of student dress.

The English aristocracy also gradually ceased to wear the sword as an external sign of their social privilege. When Karl Philipp Moritz travelled in England in 1782, he remarked that no-one carried a sword 'in the public street'. Only in court society, where the aristocracy were among themselves, was it still common practice. Two decades earlier, the Prussian officer von Archenholz had already made a similar observation and added that the English were learning less and less to use the sword, and that pistols had thus replaced the sword as the weapon for duelling.[25] This is corroborated by the appearance of special duelling pistols, which were apparently much in demand.[26] In Germany, at this time, sword duels were still more common.

The Duel in Enlightened Public Opinion

The enormous expansion of newspapers and publishing in the eighteenth century meant that the duel began to receive greater public attention. What previously had been the subject of rumours, sermons or public writs now became a daily theme of discussion in numerous publications, pamphlets and articles as well as in literature. On the stage, where hitherto the duel had been used mainly as a dramatic device, it was now often the centre of action. In the Royal Theatre at Covent Garden, a comedy was produced under the title *The Duellist* in 1773, in which a general and a member of the high nobility were made the butt of ridicule. With his extremely sensitive notion of honour and his duelling mania, he is considered a crazy character even by his peers and a young officer of much lower status puts him in his place: 'A sense of honour does not consist in impatience at just reproof or in the fear of unmerited reproach'. In response to the rhetorical question of the general, 'How is a man of honour at present to support his consequence without having recourse to the duel?', the young officer replies: 'By having recourse to his good-nature, my dear General'.[27]

This play, which was sharply critical of the morals and habits of the aristocracy, was part of a massive public campaign mounted from the second half of the eighteenth century onwards against the duel and its underlying code of honour. It is true that in 1784 William Jackson still considered the duel to be one of the 'universal passions' that demanded respect and that could not be suppressed by any law. Certain offences could only be properly redressed by the person who was offended and who was motivated, in so doing, 'by something antecedent, and superior to all law, and by a desire as eager as hunger or lust'.[28] The majority of his literary contemporaries, however, held different opinions. A cultivated education, argued the university teacher Richard Hay, also in 1784, should serve to suppress every instinct for revenge and substitute a 'virtuous Honour' for the 'selfish and degenerate Honour' that leads a man to reach for a weapon without due cause. An honour based on virtue would need no external instruments of force and would not come into conflict with the laws of society.[29]

That the duel was contrary to law, religion and reason was an oft-repeated commonplace in the critique of duelling in the eighteenth and early nineteenth century, a sentiment that found expression in the encyclopedias of the time. Nonetheless, one finds in *Chambers' Cyclopaedia* of 1788:

> At the same time, it must be admitted that to this absurd custom we must ascribe in some degree, the extraordinary gentleness and complaisance of modern manners and that respectual attention of one man to another, which at present, render the social intercourses far more agreeable and decent than among the most civilised nations of antiquity.[30]

At the beginning of the century, the doctor and polemicist, Bernard Mandeville had agreed in a similar manner in his widely read *Fable of the Bees* that the duel had had an extremely positive influence on the refinement of manners and on the civil behaviour of the upper class. According to Mandeville, the prospect of being called to account for dishonorable behaviour and possibly paying for it with one's life kept those of high society in their place and produced 'thousands of well-mannered and refined gentlemen in Europe who would otherwise have been insolent and unbearable fools'.[31]

The opponents of the duel maintained, however, that the code of honour had with time been refined to such a degree that even the smallest breaches of etiquette could be classified as an offence, thus creating the potential for innumerable duels. This 'false honour' was concerned with externalities and, so it was argued, had little to do with the 'real honour' that found its source within the individual itself. The rationalism of the enlightenment and the earnest inwardness of the puritanical movement combined their critique of the conventions and behaviour of the upper class with a new model of bourgeois honour that was based on rational or Christian virtue and morality and that was beyond the reach of an artificial stylised culture.

The arguments against the duel in Germany drew on similar ideas. According to Georg Friedrich Meier, a preacher and 'public teacher of the wisdom of the world', writing in 1746, honour was ' a shadow of virtue' and could be defended only by virtuous behaviour.[32] He was seconded in 1750 by the political scientist, von Justi:

> Our honour rests in us ourselves and comes only from ourselves, and we maintain our honour as long as we undertake no bad or indecent actions, the duel being one of these; for, whoever wishes to be an honorable man and whoever wishes to be known as such, he must undertake nothing that is against the common peace or the laws of God and of the fatherland.[33]

If the inner honour of a man could not be injured or reduced by the actions of a third party, then attacks on the 'good name' of a virtuous man were to be dealt with by taking the offender to court.

These attempts to define a universal notion of honour rejected any concept of honour that linked it to a particular estate and that, in certain situations, could require a person to become involved in a duel. At most one was willing to admit that officers might have a professionally determined and extremely sensitive feeling of honour that could not be adequately measured against the standard of civilian honour. But the basic position was: 'Every estate has the same claim to honour as any other, the lowest as well as the highest.'[34]

This principle was not always followed in practice. Prussian law of the late eighteenth century applied different standards of honour to its citizens. Offences against 'persons of the peasant estate' or lower ranks of the corporation, the latter including artisans and the professions; were punished less severely than offences against 'persons of the higher bourgeois estates'. Offences against noblemen and top state officials were, in turn, punished twice as hard for the same offence as against the 'higher bourgeois estates'.[35] Underlying these different degrees of punishment, determined by considerations of estate, was a notion that the sense of honour among the upper social strata was more highly developed than among the lower orders. Hence, an insult within the nobility was more serious and of greater import than insults exchanged among peasants and artisans.

It was precisely for this reason that the Prussian legislators refused to treat violent disputes within the *Bürgerstand*, at whatever social level, as duels. A duel was said to exist only in the case where men with a highly developed sense of honour linked to their membership of a particular estate, took up arms in single combat. This kind of honour was conceded only to the nobility and to the officers, to the great annoyance of some middle-class men who claimed this corporate privilege for themselves. In 1791, an anonymous 'academic' declared in an article that it was unsupportable that the bourgeoisie were not considered capable of giving satisfaction to officers or the nobility. The aristocratic-military *point d'honneur* should be either "made common to all estates or got rid of altogether; The general wearing of the sword would tend to promote social behaviour" and would suppress violent assaults by military officers.[36]

On this point there was particular ambivalence in the contemporary debate over duelling in Germany, a debate carried out almost exclusively by men from the 'educated classes'. Although, on the one hand, they rejected the duel for political, religious, moral and rational reasons, on the other they envied the nobility's celebration of their 'self-love' and their 'tender cultivation of self'[37] in the duel, as well as their right to defend without constraint the integrity of their own person. Bourgeois honour and recourse to the courts left little room for the cultivation of such a 'culture of the self'. Situated within the person, bourgeois honour had become a most private affair, and its external expression had been reduced to the possibility of defending oneself in the courts. Concomitantly, the universal definition of bourgeois honour as proposed by the Rhenish merchant, Gustav Mevissen, speaking in the Prussian diet in 1847, abolished all social differences and left no space for the satisfaction of the individual's need for social distinction.[38]

The extent of disunity on this question within bourgeois public opinion is confirmed by a look at the encyclopedias of the nineteenth century. Although a majority of the articles and pamphlets published on the issue of duelling took a negative view, the liberal *Staatslexikon* of 1847 praised the 'good effects' of duelling and emphasised that:

> the dominance of an independent personal honour and an independently established code of honour, combined with a manly courageous character and zeal in defence of this honour, constitutes one of the most wonderful aspects of our whole modern culture and, at the same time, is a strong defence against political despotism...and against the shameful rule of materialism and meanness.[39]

Twenty years later, the conservative *Staats- und Gesellschafts-Lexikon* of Hermann Wagener described the duel as 'the self-defence of honour' and proclaimed confidently:

> We can not and will not allow honour and the right of the individual to be subsumed by the absolute omnipotent state, and we therefore hold firmly to the authoritative right and duty, determined by each person himself, to be the defender and representative of his own realm and his own honour.[40]

In English encyclopedias of the time we find no such apologetics. *Chamber's Encyclopaedia* in 1860 was able to report that 'the practice has fallen into disrepute by the gradual operation of public opinion, and in this country it may probably now be regarded as finally abolished'. In 1877 the *Encyclopaedia Britannica* described the duel as 'obsolete in England'. 'The latest survival of feudalism (had), as a result of the increasing reason and humanity of English society', finally disappeared from the face of the earth, and this was regarded as great progress by comparison with the situation on the Continent.[41] In 1884 a chronicler of the Victorian era interpreted the 'utter discontinuance of the duelling system' as a sign of 'the rapid growth of a genuine civilisation', and he added with pride: 'At the present hour a duel in England would seem as absurd and barbarous as anachronism as an ordeal by touch or witchburning'.[42]

In Germany, this 'victory of civilisation' was viewed quite differently. Heinrich von Treitschke, the most popular and most influential historian of the Empire, wrote in 1894 about the English aristocracy of the first half of the century:

> The old notions of honour and corporate prejudice were dispersed by the power of money, whereas the German nobility remained poor but chivalrous. The wind of commerce blew through the life of the whole nation. That indispensable and final defence against the dissolution of society, the duel, fell out of use and soon disappeared altogether. The horse-whip soon replaced the sword and pistol, and this victory of primitiveness was celebrated as a triumph of enlightenment.[43]

Treitschke blamed capitalism and commerce for deforming the code of honour in England, and his argument paralleled that made by Lujo Brentano fifteen years later. Brentano, however, regarded this 'deformation' as positive and expressly welcomed the triumph of the bourgeois over the aristocratic principle. Whether this explanation stands up to new insights into the structure and mentality of the English upper class is something I will now examine.

English Gentlemen and their Code of Honour

In 1824, a book was published in London with the title *The English Code of Duel. A Reference to the Laws of Honour and the Character of Gentlemen*. The book was directed both towards the general reading public to which it attempted to explain the legitimacy of the duelling principle, and to those social circles in which duelling was in fact, common practice. By laying down the rules of honorable combat, the anonymous author sought 'to preserve to *gentlemen*, in their purity, the rights which have so long remained to them under the recognised laws of honour'.[44] He considered all male members of the nobility, whether civilians or officers, capable of giving satisfaction.

This definition, however, posed some problems which the author himself was not intending to address. The principle of primogeniture meant that in England, unlike in Germany, the nobility lacked clear contours. Although this principle was intended to guarantee the continuity and cohesion of that class, in reality it tended just as much to break down the barriers which separated it from other classes. If only the eldest son alone inherited his father's title and property, his brothers were forced to find a place for themselves outside of their class of origin and earn their living in some other way. From the point of view of values, education and norms of behaviour, however, they were still bound to the social milieu of the family they came from. Among those 'downgraded' sons of the nobility, two different worlds met – the world of the landowning elite and the world of the professionals, officers and religious and public officials.

Obviously, these non-inheriting sons had a claim on the (informal) title of gentlemen, as did the bourgeois merchants and bankers who owed their wealth to their commercial and financial involvement in the big trading firms and banks of the city of London, and who had many links with the landed interests. As the etymology of the word gentry suggests, male members of the gentry, the untitled owners of land, also belonged to the circle of gentlemen. In other words, the title of gentleman was not the exclusive property of a particular class, but rather referred to a particular style of life, to a more or less precise ensemble of social norms, beliefs and patterns of behaviour. Undoubtedly, this way of life required a solid economic foundation – gentlemen needed money and time at their disposal. The lower social orders, as well as a large part of the middle classes, could therefore, not be considered gentlemen. What remained were the well-off landed elite and sections of the middle-class clientele, living in conditions of complete economic security.[45]

Above all, the lifestyle of a gentleman presupposed free time or leisure. Men who, day-in and day-out, had to struggle for a living lacked this free time and consequently were unable to take part in the activities that distinguished a true gentleman: hunting, horse-racing, public office, extended visits to friends as well as many other forms of pleasant entertainment. This aristocratic culture of leisure was held together by a strict etiquette; it was structured by exact rules that the players had to observe with great care. A gentleman who broke these rules was no longer a gentleman. If he failed to pay his gambling debts, he knew he certainly would not be invited to the next game. If, on the other hand, he did not pay his tailor's bill, this was not regarded by his fellow gentlemen as a breach of the rules. The rules of gentlemanly behaviour only applied within their social group, but within this group they had to be upheld to the letter.

Whereas the gentleman might set himself above the details of everyday middle-class life in a generous and masterly manner, he had to pay very careful attention to maintaining his standing among other gentlemen. As one writer said in 1790: 'A person whose situation, but more particularly whose conduct in life, entitles him to the appella-tion of gentleman, cannot exist without preserving his character absolutely unspotted'.[46] A highly sophisticated code of conduct ensured that any 'spots' could be removed in an honorable manner and placed an obligation on the gentleman to behave, among his equals, in a chivalrous and exquisitely polite manner. If he failed to comply, he faced immediate consequences: an improper word to a lady or an insult offered to another gentleman would mean, as a rule, a challenge to a duel.

The duel allowed the offended party to demonstrate that he had the courage and the sense of honour to repel any attack on his personal integrity, even at the cost of his life: he was confirmed as an honor-able man. The offender also had the chance to demonstrate that he was not lacking in love of honour, and that he was willing to assume full responsibility for the full and possibly lethal consequences of his behaviour. At the end of the duel, both parties, if they survived, would have been 'cleansed'. Both had put their character and honour to the test and could now treat each other with the usual respect. There were no winners or losers, and unlike in the old medieval 'divine judgement', the outcome of the combat did not decide the question of rightness or wrongness in the original dispute. Conflicts were not settled in this way. Rather, in the personal interaction of the conflicting parties, they were nullified.

A good example of this complex social framework was the duel that took place near London in 1762 between John Wilkes, member of the House of Commons and newspaper publisher, and Earl Talbot. Talbot had been offended by some remarks in Wilkes' newspaper, which he attributed to Wilkes himself. Wilkes refused to make any statement on the matter, citing his status as 'a private English gentleman, perfectly free and independent'. As such, he refused 'to submit to the arbitrary dictates of a fellow subject...; my superior indeed in rank, fortune and abilities, but my equal only in honour, courage and liberty'. He was prepared to give Talbot satisfaction, however, and to respond to the accusation after the duel, if he survived. And that is what in fact happened. Immediately after the first exchange of shots – no one had been hit – Wilkes admitted that he had been the author of the incriminating article. Talbot, in turn, praised him for his courage, 'and said he would declare everywhere that I was the noblest fellow God had ever made. He then desired that we might now be good friends, and retire to the inn to drink a bottle of claret together, which we did with great good humour and much laughter'.[47]

For Wilkes the affair was an opportunity to defend his personal integrity as a 'private English gentleman' against the challenge of a person of higher rank. In the situation of the duel, both men, of different social standing, showed themselves to be of equal worth. Both acted as men of honour. The act of single combat not only disposed of the offence and restored the honour of the noble lord – it also built a bridge between two gentlemen and created a solidarity that transcended the social differences in rank, wealth and power. In addition, it clearly distinguished the gentlemen from all those other men who were not capable of giving satisfaction, and established a visible symbol of membership in 'good society'.

The danger that these clear lines of demarcation might begin to break down was for defenders of the duel a constant source of concern in the late eighteenth and early nineteenth century. As the officer, Stanton, impressed on men of high social standing in 1790, the duelling principle was 'not intended to descend below those whose situation in life ranks them as gentlemen', and he warned them against entering into a duel with a man who was not a gentleman. The author of the *British Code of Duel* recommended in 1824 that, before a duel was arranged, it should be established that both parties belonged to the class of gentlemen.[48] However, since the definition of a gentleman, as Stanton himself remarked, had less to do with the objective criterion, 'situation of life', and had more to do with 'conduct of life', it was

222 | *Ute Frevert*

possible to use the duel, itself a prominent symbol of this conduct, as a means of acquiring the social position of a gentleman.

In fact, in the 1820s it was no longer exclusively the nobility who gave expression in the duel to their situation as gentlemen. The officer, Gilchrist, who in 1821 drew up a list of the most important duels which had come to public attention between 1763 and 1821, listed only relatively few members of the higher aristocracy among 344 duellists – among them such well-known public figures as the prime ministers William Pitt (1798) and the Duke of Wellington (1829). Most of the duellists were men without titles, officers, journalists, lawyers, doctors, students, church ministers and actors. There were also businessmen in this illustrious circle: in 1784 the bourgeois owner of a brewery engaged in a duel with an aristocrat who, as Ascot accused him, of not paying his debts. In 1820 a dispute in a coffee-house ended with a duel between a merchant and a gentleman of fortune, fought with pistols.[49] In 1812 Lord Ellenborough, a judge who had had to deal with a number of cases involving challenges issued by merchants and tradesmen exclaimed that it was high time 'to stop this spurious chivalry of the compting house and the counter'.[50]

What the aristocratic Ellenborough put down as spurious and imitative chivalry may, in fact, have been attempts by men of the middle classes to establish their membership of the highest social circles. But whether this social diffusion really led to a situation in which, as the *Edinburgh Encyclopaedia* supposed and hoped in 1830, 'the great may be led to renounce a practice which can no longer be regarded as honorable' is more than questionable.[51] After all the position of power enjoyed by the aristocracy in English society until the end of the nineteenth century did not rest on their being an enclosed caste but, rather, on the fact that they demonstrated a degree of openness and adaptability. When 'downwardly mobile' nobles, victims of primogeniture and 'upwardly mobile' bourgeois retained or acquired elements of an aristocratic lifestyle, this only demonstrated the attractiveness and the integrative power of the aristocratic model and helped secure its survival.

The duel, however, unlike many other stylisations of the landed elite, survived only until the middle of the nineteenth century, and then died a rather sudden death. In the second half of the century, bourgeois and noble gentlemen no longer settled their disputes in Hyde Park or on Wimbledon Common, but in the courts. A dispute like that between Oscar Wilde and Lord Queensberry in the 1890s would, fifty years earlier, certainly have ended in a duel.

When Queensberry, who opposed his son's homosexual relationship with Wilde, publicly offended Wilde in a London club, the latter began court action. Although the language in which Wilde's biographer reported the incident in 1918 was the language of the duel – 'challenge', 'mortal combat', 'fight', 'death duel' – single combat between two contestants was no longer an option, even if a duel might have been a more discreet and stylish way to end this affair, which was an embarrassment to both sides, than a scandalous trial in a criminal court. The preliminaries would also have been less crude, a few months before the trial ended, Queensberry threatened Wilde with physical violence if he ever saw him together with his son again. Wilde answered: 'I don't know what the Queensberry rules are...but my rule is to shoot at sight in case of personal violence'.[52]

Such 'rules' no longer had much in common with the classic code of honour. Rather, they call to mind Treitschke's disparaging remark that the whip had replaced the sword and the pistol to the detriment of civilised society. There were English opinions, too, that favoured the reintroduction of the duel as a way of counteracting 'selfishness and ill-breeding...among well-dressed people'.[53] At the same time, however, there was public outrage over the news that the English Vice Consul in Paris had been a second in a duel fought in 1891: the case was discussed in parliament.[54] There was still delight in a professionally staged duel in the theatre, but in real life the duel had lost its legitimacy. The Victorian gentleman had renounced the code of honour and had adopted a more civilian posture. 'Duelling in England died when it became "gentlemanly" ' remarked an English journalist in 1891.[55]

This was, of course, not an explanation but a descriptive comment. The arguments used to explain the death of the duel in England stood, and still stand, on rather weak foundations.[56] Contemporaries pointed either to the weight of public opinion or to the intervention of the Prince Consort who in the 1840s proposed that duels between officers should be discouraged with the help of military courts of honour, according to the German model. Although this proposal was not accepted, some clauses were added to the 'Articles of War' in 1844 that punished a challenge to a duel with dishonorable discharge, and suggested an apology was 'suitable to the character of honorable men'.[57]

As the German example demonstrated, however, stricter punishment had no effect as long as public opinion, especially the opinion of the social group involved, considered duelling indispensable. As long as a gentleman who did not respond to an insult with a challenge was considered a coward and without honour by other gentlemen, and was excluded from 'good society', the threat of harsher punishment could not prevent the practice of duelling from continuing.

Prince Albert over-estimated not just the influence of the law, but also the role of the army in English society. Victoria's husband had German experience in mind when he thought that the disappearance of the military duel would be the first step towards ending the practice in civilian life. In England, however, the army's impact on society was much weaker than in Germany, especially in Prussia. Already in 1782, Karl Philipp Moritz was surprised at the lack of soldiers in the streets of London: 'Officers, when they do go out, dress not in uniform but in civilian clothes, and are distinguished only by the cockade on their hats'.[58] Another traveller in England, Carl Gottlob Küttner, reported in 1792 that the military enjoyed 'little respect' among the population and that they constituted 'no particular estate'.[59] A large part of the army were not, in fact, present in the British Isles themselves, but were stationed in Ireland, in India, or in the other colonies. This was particularly true of the navy, which embodied England's preeminence as the strongest European sea power and consigned the regular army to second rank.

The limited presence of the military in public life, as well as its early incorporation into the civil political system, contributed to the fact that the English officers played, if not a marginal, then certainly not a formative role in 'good society'. The English officer adopted the manners of a fisherman rather than serving as a model himself. The younger sons of the aristocracy who bought their way into the army, brought with them a gentlemanly ideal based on honour and personal integrity, and cultivated it into a code of the aristocratic amateur who was valued more for his honorable character than his professional competence.[60] Undoubtedly, this code was highly compatible with the character traits that an army required of its officers: courage, bravery and the unconditional commitment to lay down their lives for the honour of the nation, king and country. This reciprocal reinforcement helps to explain why English officers often engaged in duels; however, it should not be forgotten that they saw themselves first as gentlemen and only secondarily as military men.

The same holds true for students who, unlike their German counterparts, had no independent tradition of duelling. Whereas German fraternities considered duelling to be part of 'academic freedom', the notion of honour played no major role in English student life of the late eighteenth and early nineteenth century. Although duelling was not unknown in Oxford and Cambridge,[61] the students did not behave differently from their non-academic compatriots in the same class. As members of the aristocratic bourgeois elite, they reached for their pistols when they thought their honour as gentleman was at stake, but there was no notion of a code of honour particular to students.[62]

The basis for the transformation of the code of honour and for the early disappearance of the duel in England must be sought, therefore, in the forms of socialisation typical of the social elite, of those circles that prescribed and followed the unwritten rules of gentlemanly conduct. The fact that this elite included the nobility and the gentry, and that it was, in comparison with Germany, a relatively open and fluid social formation, says in itself very little about the social value of the duel. Acceptance into this social elite was conditional on the new-comer's adopting its culture and standards of behaviour. As long as the hegemony of the landed classes continued, which it did, on the evidence of historical research, until the 1880s,[63] criticism by outsiders of their lifestyle and socio-cultural norms would not have been given a hearing or gained acceptance within the elite itself. It is therefore unlikely that it was the overwhelmingly negative attitude of public opinion towards the duel that brought about the change.

The institution in which the real foundation for change was laid was the English public school system, in which the sons of the high nobility and the gentry, as well as of professionals, church ministers, officers, bankers and rich merchants were educated as gentlemen. These private boarding schools had, in the view of a government commission that prepared a report on them in 1864, 'perhaps the largest share in moulding the character of an English gentleman'. They raised their pupils in a spirit of self-discipline, respect for order as well as freedom, public opinion and public spirit. In addition, they laid great value on 'vigour and manliness of character'.[64] They were less concerned, as a rule, with imparting formal knowledge, education in the technical sense of the term, and were more concerned with inculcating their pupils with the social habits appropriate to their occupation in later life of important positions within politics, society and culture. An investigation into the 'great schools of England' in 1865 described them as the theatres of athletic manners and the training places of a gallant, generous spirit for the English gentleman'.[65]

However, before the English gentleman could put his gallantry and generous spirit to the test in society, he had to go through a long apprenticeship in a hierarchic and strictly organised institution that forced the individual pupils into the common mould of a uniform and disciplined collectivity. In the private schools newly established or reformed after the 1820s, individuality or independence of mind were not highly valued. A complex system of self-management, in which the younger pupils were subordinate and obedient to the older boys, for whom they acted as servants, combined with a merciless ritual of punishment and initiation, encouraged a sense of community and social conformity. The increasingly popular team games, such as cricket and football, also promoted the tendency to regard the individual primarily as part of a larger group, and the individual student became accustomed to subordinating his own interests and individual needs to those of the collective.

The values imparted by this kind of public school education removed the social foundation for the code of honour that culminated in the duel. Single combat fought in defence of honour placed the individual emphatically in the foreground. What was at stake in the duel was the honour of an individual which had been called into question by some other individual and which the former now had to restore through armed combat with the offender. The duel was based on highly ritualised forms of communication, yet what was given expression in these forms was not collectivity, but absolute individuality. The priority of the group or of the collective taught in the English public school system of the nineteenth century, was diametrically opposed to this principle of individuality and was probably of decisive importance in bringing about the observed change in the behaviour of the English social elite.

The more the cult of athleticism was practised in the schools and universities during the second half of the century, with its effects on the social ranking of the pupils and students, the further the image of the gentleman became distanced from the ideal of aristocratic equality that found its most visible expression in the duel. In the duel, unlike in sport, what mattered was not competition or relative achievement, first or second place, but the courage to make a public display of one's individual sense of honour. Feelings of fear or revenge, concern for the family or for the law – these had no place in the duel. The only thing that counted was one's individual presence, not achievement measurable in terms of victory or defeat.[66]

If it is the case that the sense of public spirit and the orientation towards achievement, which were transmitted through the public school system, transformed the code of behaviour of the English gentleman in the nineteenth century and gradually removed circumstances in which the extremely individualistic duelling principle could manifest itself, then the question of whether this process is to be identified with the triumph of bourgeois values and precepts must be posed. The German example suggests caution in presenting a simple contest between 'bourgeois' achievement and 'aristocratic' honour.

The Duel and the German Bildungsbürgertum

In the late eighteenth century the *Bildungsbürgertum* (educated, professional middle class) in Germany began to search for an appropriate theory and practice for its own conduct of life. It distanced itself from the lifestyle and thinking of the old corporate *Stadtbürger* and from the pretensions of the nobility, whose manner was generally rejected as decadent and immoral. It looked askance at the sins of the nobility – their gambling, their gallantry and emphasis on appearance. Nevertheless the nobleman was envied for his self-assurance, cosmopolitan manner and elaborate self-presentation. In spite of all the enlightened criticism, aristocratic culture remained remarkably attractive to the *Bildungsbürgertum*. This attraction found expression, for example, in Goethe's *Wilhelm Meisters Lehrjahre*, published in 1795. In this novel, Wilhelm recounts to his brother-in-law, who is a business man, the advantages enjoyed by the noble for whom 'a universal, and if I may say so, personal cultivation is possible'. Whereas the personality of the *Bürger* is taken up with the world of work the nobleman can and must conduct himself as a 'public person', independent of material motives and concerns. A 'nobleman' produces not commodities, but himself, and in this he achieves a high degree of perfection: 'Since in court or camp his figure, his person, are part of his possessions – and it may be the most necessary part – he has reason enough to put some value on them and to show that he does so'.[67]

This polished display of personality prescribed by the rules of aristocratic behaviour, and by the underlying concept of aristocratic honour was very attractive to the new *Bürgertum*. They too emphasised public life and communication, though in this case this was not to be limited by the boundaries of estates and was to be open to all those who were 'educated'. Moreover, the bourgeois concept of public life incorporated norms and values that eventually allowed its participants to discover themselves as 'personalities' and to give public expression to this feeling. Unlike the nobleman, however, who embodied the forms of fine appearance, the *Bürger* promoted a culture of individuality based on *Bildung* (education) and centered on the individual person in his striving for self-perfection. The bourgeois ideal was the development of the whole (male) personality, an education that enabled him to make fullest use of his talents and abilities. This education clearly encompassed a range of knowledge that went beyond the requirements of one's profession. It also involved a wide interest in cultural, political and economic problems as well as the training of a strong and disciplined body through physical exercise. The neo-humanist conception of education took up this desire for 'perfection' and in the schools and reformed universities of the nineteenth century, gave it an appropriate institutional framework.

While the educated bourgeois individual longed for a 'wholeness' that could no longer be achieved in 'bourgeois conditions', the aristocratic concept of honour, which was 'pure', apparently non-materialistic and rooted in personal self-esteem, seemed to offer an attractive alternative. From the beginning, the bourgeois intellectual resisted absorption into the commercial and social life of the *Bürgertum* and asserted his right to an individuality based on his education and cultured mind. This emphatic claim to individuality was counterposed to the process of economic, technical and social modernisation, which placed a premium on functional differentiation, division of labor and multiplicity of roles.

An insult affected this bourgeois individual not merely in some particular role – as head of a family, as husband, as professional, as citizen – but rather it threatened his entire personality, which had to be defended at any price. When Adolph Wagner, a professor of economics, was challenged to a duel in 1895 by the entrepreneur and Reichstag deputy, Baron von Stumm-Halberg, he was prepared to accept the challenge under certain conditions because the conflict that had prompted the challenge had crossed over from the sphere of politics and opinion into the area of personal differences.[68] This exaggerated but 'honest' emphasis on the individual and personal – experienced daily in social interaction within educated circles and reinforced by the cultural models prevalent among the *Bildungsbürgertum* – did not allow for offended honour to be rehabilitated by a state court. For the privilege of taking himself seriously as an individual and raising 'the level of his whole life'[69] the *Bürger* paid, if necessary with life and limb.

This fascination with duelling was not entirely due to the 'individualistic idea' incorporated in it, but also derived from its obvious relation to masculinity. It is clear from the self-descriptions of duellists and depictions of them by non-combatants, that it was seen as a pre-eminent symbol of manliness. Self-conscious virility implied the willingness to risk one's life for the sake of honour. The duel was the embodiment of bravery, courage, strength, skill, toughness, consistency and self-discipline – virtues that were considered to belong to the inventory of every man's personality. Thomas Mann's novel *The Magic Mountain*, published in 1924, provides a classic formulation of the tense relationship between a personality based on a refined culture of the mind, and corporality. Shortly before the duel with his opponent Naphta, the enlightened humanist hero Settembrini says:

> The essential nature of the thing remains the primitive, the physical struggle and however civilised a man is, it is his duty to be ready for such a contingency, which may any day arise. Whoever is unable to offer his person, his arm, his blood, in the service of the ideal is unworthy of it. However intellectualised, it is the duty of the man to remain a man.[70]

This close relationship between body and intellect, between doing and thinking, was in harmony with the image of the masculine character in whom physical strength and intellectual activity were fused. In the duel, men gave public proof of themselves as men, in a society that was, outside the extraordinary situation of war, increasingly abstracted from physical strength, courage and bravery. This aspect, may have been particularly attractive to 'intellectualised' academics, who were also the firmest supporters of the cult of individuality in German educational doctrine.

Duelling was part of the socialisation of German academics to an extent unknown in England. English tourists were often amazed by what they considered the strange practice of German students of fighting duels amongst themselves. 'Duelling is more prevalent in the universities of Germany than in any other place of the earth. To have passed two or three years at one of these institutions, and not to have fought as many duels, is a rare example of moderation; and so far from being regarded as an honour, is considered by the student as a proof of a want of spirit'.[71] Quite often amazement was mixed with appreciation in the descriptions of a phenomenon that the Englishman, William Howitt, thought in 1843 would 'meet with the most repugnance in the English mind'. Although he himself was far from praising the German students for their love of duelling, he did not fail to detect in German student life a 'poetic charm' that distinguished it favourably from that in England.[72]

Duelling was, in fact, an important part of the 'academic freedom' that German students in the nineteenth century claimed for themselves and which they defended vigorously against the university and state authorities. Duelling had a long tradition in the regional student associations (*Landsmannschaften*) and student fraternities (*Burschenschaften*) which set out to replace the older corporations at the beginning of the nineteenth century, and which held firmly to the duel as a means of maintaining scholarly honour. They did attempt to limit the number of duels by instituting obligatory proceedings before a scholars' court of honour. The court was to decide on the justification for a particular challenge and was linked to an attempt to regulate more carefully both the modalities and the honorable execution of the duel. At the same time, however, the student fraternities were as the American observer Henry Dwight observed in 1829, 'the great nurseries of duelling',[73] inasmuch as they placed an obligation on their members to fight duels and to give satisfaction. In the words of a fraternity member in 1887, the *Mensur* (student duel) developed the student's 'sturdy manliness by elevating and tempering his personal courage'. It helped to inculcate 'manly fearlessness' and 'the superiority of the manly will over brutish cowardice'. The sword stood as a 'symbol of the German student spirit and of his untarnished manly honour'.[74]

When we recall that at the end of the nineteenth century almost every second German student was a member of a student corporation, then we get some idea of the extensive and profound effect of this 'manly honour' and of its manifestation in the duel. However, scholarly honour and the student duel displayed certain features that distinguished them from the practice of duelling outside the universities. They preserved a large element of the baroque tradition that valued the duel as a game, as a kind of cultivated brawl. The *Mensur*, in particular, was viewed as a kind of joust or physical exercise in which, as the pedagogue Friedrich Paulsen remarked in 1902, 'a certain dominance of the will over the physical system' could be demonstrated.[75] The corporate administration of scholarly honour adopted *ständische* definitions and had little in common with the highly individualised and ideologically bolstered notion of honour prevalent among the educated middle-class 'Philistines', as the 'old boys' of the corporations were known. Nevertheless academic culture played an important role in transmitting and reinforcing the practice of duelling. It prepared the ground and instilled the habits, the 'Comment' that guided the future *Bildungsbürger* in reacting to perceived slights on his honour.

In the light of this institutional and ideological background it comes as no surprise that, in the duelling statistics, academics and officers provided the largest contingent of combatants.[76] Many a legal, medical or scientific dispute provided the occasion for a challenge. Irreconcilable political differences could at least be dealt with in an honorable fashion in the dawn light of some forest clearing. When the left-liberal professor of medicine and deputy in the Prussian diet, Rudolf Virchow, cast doubt on the veracity of the prime minister, in 1865, Bismarck challenged him to a duel although neither the diet president nor most of the deputies considered the statement to be offensive.[77] Four years earlier, the head of the Prussian war cabinet Major General von Manteuffel took personal offence at the criticism of his policy voiced by the Berlin court official, Carl Twesten. He demanded personal satisfaction, which Twesten did not refuse. The liberal judge was subsequently sentenced to three months imprisonment by his colleagues. In its judgement the court accepted as mitigating circumstances that Twesten had felt himself unable to withdraw from the duel 'because it was reasonable to assume that, by so doing, he would lose the respect of the other members of his estate'. The *Berliner Volkszeitung* took a very different line and subjected the bourgeois-liberal judge to sharp criticism. Five days after the duel, the paper was of the opinion that

> Above all, we would like to make plain to Herr Twesten, in all seriousness and ignoring for a moment his excellent character, that he has failed to preserve the honour of his estate! It would have been his duty to replay to the provocation with the statement, that it was his honour to belong to the estate of the Bürgertum, which happily has escaped the barbarism of the law of the strongest.[78]

Both judgements, that of the court and that of the journal, referred to conceptions of the honour of the *Bürgertum*, but they arrived at opposite definitions of the 'corporate honour' (*Standesehre*) of the *Bürgertum*. Twesten's colleagues shared his assumption that the other members of the estate (*Standesgenossen*) expected him to defend his honour. The journalist, however, considered his behaviour incompatible with the 'honour of a civilised estate'. The 'estate' was clearly disunited on the question of how its honour was to be defended. This contradiction between the habitus of the enlightened law-abiding *Bürger* and his urge for unconditional self-assertion remained unresolved in the breast of many a male individual.

Political orientation failed to provide a clear guide. The duel was not the exclusive preserve of the conservative heirs to feudal traditions and it was not just romantics who pined for the 'chivalrous' manly virtues of the German middle ages. The liberal and socialist pioneers of modern society also demanded and gave satisfaction in duels. When, in 1896, August Bebel delivered one of his fiery speeches against militarism and the duelling menace, the Prussian Minister of War reminded him that even Bebel's own 'party saint' had died in single combat. Prior to Ferdinand Lassalle's duel fought in 1864 as the result of a love affair, Heinrich Heine, whom no-one could suspect of holding conservative or aristocratic opinions, had exchanged pistol shots with the businessman Salomon Strauss in 1841.

The willingness to restore one's personal honour by means of a duel was not, in the nineteenth century, confined to a particular political viewpoint or to an exclusive social milieu. Whereas the Prussian law-makers of the late eighteenth century assumed that the notion of honour on which the duel was based existed only among the nobility and the officer corps, the judiciary after the 1820s recognised that 'attitudes towards honour and the ability to give satisfaction had changed'. Duels between persons of the *Bürgertum* were therefore dealt with in accordance with the duelling laws rather than being treated and punished as murder.[79] The Bavarian government, which in the pre-1848 period had attempted to regulate the duel legally, was also forced to face the fact that the sense of honour that disposed one to engage in duelling was no longer to be found only among nobles, officers, cadets, councillors and senior officials but also 'among all men of higher education', which comprised county judges and middle-ranking officials as well as doctors, lawyers, mayors, businessmen and artists. Higher education appeared to have become synonymous with an elevated sense of honour and tended to break up the hitherto 'exclusive divisions of estates and orders'.[80]

This de-aristocratisation – or embourgeoisement – of the notion of honour was not confined to the institutions of higher education. The military, which was more visible in Germany than in England and which had a much more significant impact on German society, played an equally important role. As a state within the state, beyond parliamentary control and subject only to the king as commander in chief, the army had a large number of carefully guarded privileges, among which duelling took pride of place. Just before the First World War, the Prussian Minister of War claimed that the duel had a 'thoroughly honorable foundation' and cited it as a proof of courage. He accused the Reichstag, which had persistently criticised duelling of aiming to destroy the army's sense of honour and undermine the corporate identity of the officer corps.[81] Kaiser Wilhelm I announced in 1874 that, he would tolerate in his army neither 'an officer capable of offending the honour of one of his comrades in a frivolous manner' nor 'an officer unwilling to defend his honour'.[82]

Although both ministers and the monarch warned against the exaggeration and abuse of the military notion of honour, they also made it clear that duelling belonged to the officer corps and that it played an important role in ensuring the honorable behaviour of its members. Although forbidden in law and subject to heavy penalties, the military code demanded its due. If an officer withdrew from single combat, or if he refused to issue a challenge, he cut himself off from the circle of honorable men and was obliged to leave the service. If on the other hand he took part in a duel and was found out, he had to face a court martial, though he could be sure of a royal pardon.

The increasing embourgeoisement of the officer corps and in particular the rising number of reserve officers recruited from the *Bürgertum*, ensured that the forms of military honour spread increasingly to bourgeois circles. The lawyers, doctors, editors, officials and professors with military commissions did not hesitate to parade their military honours in civilian life and found plenty of opportunities to do so. Within these social circles the scholarly and military codes of honour formed an explosive mixture, that took its toll in lives, though most duels undoubtedly ended without bloodshed.

Every duel, nonetheless, especially with the increasing use of pistols, represented a very real risk to life. No duellist could be certain that he would leave the field of honour alive and upright. He had let himself in for a dangerous game, the outcome of which, despite the rules and regulations, remained uncertain. This lethal game called for both passion and cool-headedness. It demanded the highest levels of self-discipline, while allowing the participant to set his 'self' as an absolute.

The two encyclopedias published in 1847 and 1867, which defended the duel, pointed to this unconditional assertion of subjectivity typical of the German *Bürgertum*. They praised the duel as a piece of self-assertion on the part of the *Bürgertum* and as a manifestation of the freedom of the individual man to stand up for his own honour rather than handing over another area of existence to state regulation and intervention. In addition, they valued the idealism and personal courage of a man who considered his honour of greater value than life and limb. The duel, in their view, contained an element of resistance to a society increasingly determined by material interests and hemmed in by an administrative corset, constricting the space available to individuality. 'As long as the world remains the way it is' concluded the entry on duelling in Wagener's *Staats und Gesellschaftslexikon* 'war and duelling will be unavoidable and indispensable means of preventing the descent of nations and individuals into the mire of material interests, personal cowardice and mindlessness'.[83]

Bourgeois Society and the Duel

It would be a mistake to describe these defensive pleas as 'unbourgeois'. Obviously *Bürgerlichkeit* meant more than being anti-militarist, civilian, law-abiding and rationalistic. As long as the self-conception of the German *Bürgertum* remained rooted in the conception of *Bildung*, and as long as its model was the individual subject whose values were more ideal than material and whose goal was self-perfection, the bourgeois habitus would remain ambivalent and open to the aristocratic cult of personality. One such element was the duel. With its radical emphasis on the individual, its mediation of the spirit with the corporal, its disregard for external constraints, duelling culture was ideally suited for absorption into the way of life of the *Bildungsbürgertum*. With a solid base in the universities and in the military it was by no means a barren tradition to which one conformed reluctantly. On the contrary, it offered to the male member of the *Bürgertum* the opportunity to prove his personal integrity, his honour and his masculinity, and to do so in an aesthetically staged *fait total*.

What distinguished Germany from England in this respect was above all the dominant role of the formally educated within the middle-class formation, and the special place that *Bildung* had in the *Bürgertum*'s self-awareness and lifestyle. Even though the curriculum of the English public schools was similar to that found in the German *Gymnasium*, and although the classical canon stood at the centre of both systems, the German notion of *Bildung* took on a social, cultural and political significance that it never had in England. The phenomenology of the duel fitted harmoniously into this conception. In addition, the notion of honour associated with duelling found ready acceptance among the German *Bildungsbürgertum* because it corresponded to its estatist group character and particular form of intellectual and social consciousness. Additionally, the close contact with the state and the high proportion of state officials among the *Bildungsbürgertum* gave added impetus to their efforts to acquire a special, more elevated concept of honour that would distance them from other social strata.

In England, there was neither an omnipotent state that ennobled its servants and set them apart from other social groups, nor was there an independent and socially influential *Bildungsbürgertum*. The sociocultural hegemony of the old landowning elite, and its relative openness to the upwardly mobile middle class and non-inheriting nobles, ensured that the middle class strata absorbed by this elite (professional and business classes, including industrialists) would not develop their own bourgeois culture. Instead, they adapted to the standards of the upper class, acquired its cultural style, and reached for the pistol when the question of defending its honour arose. Therefore the duel in England, unlike in Germany, failed to take on an authentic bourgeois profile. The English middle class did not fully incorporate the duel; it merely copied it.

This formal adaptation contributed to the fact that the duel lost its social acceptance in England much earlier than it did in Germany. When the English elite, around the middle of the nineteenth century, agreed on a different concept of honour and a different method of defending it, there was no resistance from the rest of society. The army, in which, as in Germany, the duel had a special place did not have the power to make its own military conventions acceptable in civilian society. Nor did the English universities have a specific student code of honour which, nourished and kept alive by the fraternities, clung to the duel as one of its highest privileges. The two most powerful institutions that kept the duel alive in Germany had in England either a lesser social weight (the army) or a different structure (the university). Thus, the Association for the Discouragement of Duelling founded in England in 1843 did not meet with strong opposition. Just one year later, it counted 349 members, the majority of whom were nobles, higher officers and members of parliament. In 1850, the association was able to report that the duel had largely disappeared.[84]

In Germany an Anti-Duelling League was only established in 1902, and it is questionable whether it would have been successful without the experience of the First World War. Even in the 'civilian' Weimar Republic, there were still challenges and duels between bourgeois officers and professionals. As late as 1934, a history professor in Göttingen felt his honour so impugned by a colleague that he challenged him to a duel.[85]

The amazing continuity of 'duelling society' (Norbert Elias) in

236 | *Ute Frevert*

Germany was not a consequence of the stronger influence of feudal
structures or relations of power, but resulted from the specific forms
of socialisation within the German *Bürgertum*. Unlike in England,
there were two 'ideal types' of duelling culture in Germany – the
estatist and the bourgeois. The genuinely bourgeois emphasis on individual *Bildung* together with the already existing feudal (*ständisch*) traditions in the army and the universities combined to create a potentially explosive mixture. It ensured the survival of the duel, even
when the feudal element in German society declined as a result of
social and political change.

Notes to Chapter 8

1. See for a more detailed account, Ute Frevert, *Ehrenmänner. Das Duell in der bürger-
lichen Gesellschaft* (Munich, 1991), as well as Frevert, 'Bourgeois Honour: Middle-class
Duellists in Germany from the Late 18th to the Early 20th Century', in: R.J. Evans/D.
Blackbourn (eds.), *The German Bourgeoisie* (London, 1991), pp. 255–92.
2. In 1920, Kurt Tucholsky wrote 'The bourgeois age is finished, what will come
now nobody knows.' Kurt Tucholsky, *Politische Texte* (Reinbek, 1971), p.104. Thomas
Mann in 1933 called the nineteenth century 'the bourgeois epoch'. Thomas Mann,
'Leben und Grösse Richard Wagners', in Mann, *Wagner und unsere Zeit* (Frankfurt,
1986), p. 63.
3. According to H.-H. Wehler, *Das deutsche Kaiserreich 1871–1918* (Göttingen,
1973), p. 163.
4. Marianne Weber, *Max Weber. Ein Lebensbild* (Heidelberg, 1950), pp. 473ff.
Weber's attitude to student fraternities and to the German code of honour can be seen
in Max Weber, 'Wahlrecht und Demokratie in Deutschland', (1917) in Max Weber,
Gesammelte politische Schriften (Tübingen, 1958), pp. 266–272.
5. Max Weber, *Wirtschaft und Gesellschaft* (Tübingen, 1972), p. 637.
6. *Ibid.* p. 635.
7. The attempt to define the Bürgertum by means of its culture is not an invention of
modern historians. In 1919 Tucholsky described 'the *Bürger*' as 'a cultural (*geistige*) classification. One is bourgeois by character, not because of birth and certainly not because
of career': Tucholsky, *Texte*, p.87. Most modern studies of the French, English or
German middle classes focus on values, lifestyles and patterns of behaviour. See, for
instance, H. Henning, *Das westdeutsche Bürgertum in der Epoche der Hochindustrialiserung.
1860–1914* (Wiesbaden, 1972); A. Daumard, *Les bourgeois de Paris au XIXe siècle* (Paris,
1970), p. 352; P. Stearns, 'The Middle Class. Towards a Precise Definition', in
Comparative Studies of Society and History 21 (1979), pp. 377–396, especially p. 385. A
more conceptual approach is to be found in J. Kocka, (ed.), *Bürger und Bürgerlichkeit im
19. Jahrhundert* (Göttingen, 1987), especially pp. 42–48; H. Bausinger, 'Bürgerlichkeit
und Kultur', in Kocka, *Bürger und Bürgerlichkeit,* pp. 121–142. See also the commentary
by Nipperdey in the same volume, pp. 143–148.

8. L. Brentano, 'Über die Duellfrage', *Mitteilungen der Deutschen Anti-Duel-Liga* 29 (1909), pp. 2–7.

9. D.T. Andrew, 'The Code of Honour and its Critics. The Opposition to Duelling in England, 1700–1850', *Social History* 5 (1981), pp.409–434, especially pp. 431ff.; H. Perkin, *The Origins of Modern English Society 1780–1880* (London, 1974), pp. 271ff.

10. *Stenographische Berichte über die Verhandlungen des Reichstags IX. Legislaturperiode, IV Session 1895/97*, vol. 3 (Berlin, 1896), p. 1809.

11. L. Bryskett, *A Discours of Civill Life* (London, 1606), p. 65, quoted from F. Billacois, *Le duel dans la société française des XVIe–XVIIe siècles* (Paris, 1986), p. 51.

12. L. Stone, *The Crisis of the Aristocracy 1558–1641* (Oxford, 1966), pp. 247f.

13. *The Works of Francis Bacon*, J. Speeding (ed.), vol. 13 (London, 1872), pp. 103–115. Quotations from pp. 108, 112.

14. Stone, *Crisis*, p. 770.

15. *The Diary of Samuel Pepys*. H.B. Wheatley (ed.), vol. 2 (London, 1893), pp. 299, 311f., quotation from p.312; vol. 7 (London, 1896), pp. 47.

16. R. Baldick, *The Duel. A History of Duelling* (London, 1965), p. 71f.

17. Cf. D. Prokowsky, *Die Geschichte der Duellbekämpfung* (Bonn, 1965), pp. 34ff.

18. Hoch-Fürstlich-Württembergisches Edict, Wider die Duellen, 1714, Hauptstaatsarchiv, Stuttgart, A59 Bü21. This edict was repeated in similar form in 1724, 1736 and 1738.

19. Quoted from Prokowsky, *Duellbekämpfung*, pp. 60f.

20. Staatsarchiv Detmold, L 86 no. 183, 825; Staatsarchiv Bremen. Ratsakten 2-D. 17.c.6.

21. 'Duel Mandat und Verordnung. Woranch alle und jede auf Sr. Fürstl. Durchl. gesamte Universität Jena befindliche Studiosi und sonst männiglich daselbst sich gehorsamst zu achten, Eisenach 1694', Hauptstaatsarchiv Stuttgart, A 202 Bü 2534.

22. Advertisement by a university fencing master 1723, quoted from H.-W. Prahl and I. Schmidt-Harzbach, *Die Universität* (Munich, 1981), p. 66. See also, 'Das Waffentragen auf Deutschlands Hohen Schulen', *Zeitschrift für historische Waffen- und Kostümkunde* 9 (1921), pp. 58–68; R. and R. Keil, *Geschichte des Jenaischen Studentenlebens von der Gründung der Universität bis zur Gegenwart, 1548–1858* (Leipzig, 1858), especially pp. 61ff., 95f., 108ff., 170ff., 250ff.

23. Jonathan Swift, 'A Dissertation On Good Behaviour and Good Education' *The Prose Works of Jonathan Swift*, H. Davis (ed.), vol. VIII, p. 138–139; John Locke remarked in 1690 that 'fencing and riding the great-horse are so generally looked upon as necessary qualifications in the breeding of a gentleman'; 'Some Thoughts Concerning Education', in *The Works of John Locke*, vol. 9 (London, 1823), p. 193.

24. D. Rothblatt, 'The Student Sub-Culture and the Examination System in early 19th Century Oxbridge' in L. Stone (ed.), *The University in Society*, vol. 1 (Princeton, 1974), pp. 247–303, especially pp. 256ff.; V.H.H. Green, 'The University and Social Life', in T.H. Aston, (ed.), *The History of the University of Oxford*, vol. 5 (Oxford, 1986), pp. 309–358, especially pp. 339ff. (Duelling is not mentioned at all).

25. C.P. Moritz, *Reisen eines Deutschen in England im Jahr 1782*, O. zur Linde (ed.), (Berlin, 1903), p. 50; J.W. v. Archenholz, *England und Italien*, vol. 3 (Leipzig, 1787), pp. 45f.

26. J.A. Atkinson, *Duelling Pistols and some of the Affairs they Settled* (London, 1964), pp. 37ff.

27. W. Kenrick, *The Duellist. A Comedy* (London, 1773), p. 80.

28. W. Jackson, *Thirty Letters on Various Subjects*, vol. 1 (London, 1784), new edition: (New York, 1970), pp. 6, 12ff.

29. R. Hay, *Three Dissertations on the Pernicious Effects of Gaming on Duelling and on Suicide* (Cambridge, 1812), pp. 83–176, quotations from pp. 17. See also the extensive discussion on the English critiques of duelling in the eighteenth and nineteenth century in Andrew, Code, v. a. pp. 416ff.

30. E. Chambers, *Cyclopaedia or a universal Dictionary of Arts and Sciences*, vol. 2 (London, 1788), entry: 'Duel'. I am grateful to Ulrike Spree and Willibald Steinmetz for their help with English encyclopedias between 1755 and 1892.

31. B. Mandeville, *Die Bienenfabel (1714)* (Berlin, 1957), pp. 194ff.; quotation from p. 195.

32. G.F. Meier, *Gedanken von der Ehre* (Halle, 1746), pp. 225, 313.

33. J.H.G. v. Justi, *Deutsche Memoires oder Sammlung verschiedener Anmerkungen*, vol. 1 (Vienna, 1750), p. 81.

34. 'Über die Ehre', *Monat.sschrift von und für Mecklenburg* 2 (1789), columns 658–666: quotation from column 663.

35. 'Über Injurien, Hausrecht, Notwehr und Duelle nach preußischem Rechte' (Berlin, 1827), p. 173.

36. 'Besonderheiten des sogenannten militärischen Points d'honneur'. *Journal von und für Deutschland* 8 (1791), pp. 155–57.

37. J.C. Schmid, *Über die Duelle* (Landshut, 1802), pp. 3, 28.

38. Mevissen had attempted to define bourgeois honour as 'general honour of the nation', in terms of its agreement with the law and the morals of bourgeois society. E. Bleich (ed.), *Der Erste Vereinigte Landtag in Berlin 1847*, vol. 2 (Berlin, 1847), p. 202.

39. C. Welcker, Entry: 'Infamie', 'Ehre', 'Ehrenstrafen', in C. V. Rotteck and C. Welcker (eds.), *Das Staats-Lexikon*, vol. 7 (Altona, 1847), pp. 377–404; quotation from p. 390.

40. H. Wagener (ed.), *Staats- und Gesellschafts-Lexikon*, vol. 23 (Berlin, 1867), entry 'Zweikampf', pp. 199f.; quotation from p. 200.

41. *Chamber's Encyclopaedia*, vol. 3 (London, 1860), entry: 'Duel', p. 692; *The Encyclopaedia Britannica*, vol. 7 (Edinburgh, 1877), pp. 511–515.

42. J. McCarthy, *A Short History of Our Time* (1884), quoted in J.R. Reed, *Victorian Conventions* (Athens, 1976), p. 146.

43. H. V. Treitschke, *Deutsche Geschichte im Neunzehnten Jahrhundert*, vol. 5 (Leipzig, 1894), p. 480.

44. *The British Code of Duel* (London, 1824), p. 74.

45. Cf. L. Stone and J.C. Fawtier Stone, *An Open Elite? England 1540–1880* (Oxford, 1986), pp. 164ff., 277ff.; Perkin, *Origins*, pp. 271ff. See also the contribution by E.J. Hobsbawm in the present volume. On the literary presentation of the English gentleman, cf. P. Mason, *The English Gentleman. The Rise and Fall of an Ideal* (London, 1982); also D. Castronovo, *The English Gentleman. Images and Ideals in Literature and Society* (New York, 1987).

46. S. Stanton, *The Principles of Duelling* (London, 1790), quoted from Atkinson, *Pistols*, p. 24.

47. Quoted from J.P. Gilchrist, *A Brief Display of the Origin and History of Ordeals; Trials by Battle; Courts of Chivalry and Honour; and the Decision of Private Quarrels by Single Combat: also, a chronological Register of the Principal Duels fought from the Accession of his Late Majesty to the Present.* (London, 1821) no. 68–76.

48. Stanton, *Principles*, quoted from Atkinson, *Pistols*, p. 23; *British Code*, p. 23.

49. Gilchrist, *Brief Display*, pp. 172ff., 320f.

50. Quoted from Andrew, 'Code', p. 433.

51. *The Edinburgh Encyclopaedia*, vol. 8 (Edinburgh, 1830), p. 181.

52. F. Harris, *Oscar Wilde. His Life and Confessions*, vol. 1 (New York, 1918), especially pp.186ff. I am grateful to Gabriel Motzkin for the information about Wilde.

53. 'Why not revive duelling?', *Evening News and Post* (11 August, 1891), qouted from C.A. Thimm, *A Complete Bibliography of Fencing and Duelling* (1896), new edition (New York, 1968), pp. 471f.

54. Cf. Thimm, *Bibliography*, pp. 457f., 479f.

55. Quoted from Thimm, p. 467.

56. Not only contemporaries had difficulty with these explanations. Later historians

also offer no explanation, in many cases not even recognizing the need for one. Together with O.F. Christie, *The transition from Aristocracy 1832–1867* (London, 1927), pp. 22ff., 130ff., it was W.L. Burn, *The Age of Equipoise. A Study of the Mid-Victorian Generation* (London, 1964) who was one of the first to point to the change in the gentleman-ideal and to the key role played by the duel: 'When duelling ceased to be obligatory on English gentlemen, the conception of what constituted a gentleman was changing' (p. 259). He does not, however, give any reason as to 'why a practice which for centuries had been the particular mark of a gentleman ceased with such suddenness' (p.258). V.G. Kiernan, *The Duel in European History. Honour and the Reign of Aristocracy* (Oxford, 1989), pp. 221f. also offers no convincing explanation. The reference to 'pecuniary satisfaction' (pp. 131, 199). contradicts the concept of a gentleman that is based on non-material values. Perkin, *Origins*, defends the view that the aristocratic ideal of a gentleman (and duelling) was replaced by an 'entrepeneurial ideal', reflecting the real social hegemony of the 'capitalist middle class' (pp. 271–288). Andrew, 'Code' offers a similar argument. Both overlook the fact that the leading sections of the middle clsses (as has been shown by Stone and Fawtier Stone, *Open Elite*) were prepared to adapt themselves to aristocratic culture and that it was only towards the end of the nineteenth century that the entrepreneurs attained social influence.

57. Cf. T. Martin, *The Life of His Royal Highness The Prince Consort*, vol. 1 (London, 1880), pp. 169–172; *Hansard's Parliamentary Debates*, 3rd Series, vol. 73 (London, 1844), columns 811ff.

58. Moritz, *Reisen*. pp. 39, 50.

59. C. G. Küttner, *Beyträge zur Kentniss vorzüglich des Innern von England und seiner Einwohner*, no. 2 (Leipzig, 1792), p. 100; no. 5 (Leipzig, 1793), p. 68.

60. Cf. G. Harries-Jenkins, *The Army and Society 1815–1914* (London, 1980), pp. 1ff; *Parliamentary Debates*, vol. 73, columns 803ff., 824f.

61. This is clear from the frequent references to duelling in the novels of the eighteenth and nineteenth century, the subject matter of which revolved around the student milieu. See, for instance, J.G. Lockhart, *Reginald Dalton. A Study of English University Life* (1823) (Edinburgh, 1846), pp. 331ff.; see also M.R. Proctor, *The English University Novel* (1957), new edition (New York, 1977), pp. 1, 37, 62f., 73.

62. Cf. V.A. Huber, *Die englischen Universitäten* (Kassel, 1840), new edition (Aalen, 1969), vol. 2, pp. 444ff.

63. According to Stone and Fawtier Stone, *Open Elite*, p. 292; E.J. Hobsbawm, *Industry and Empire*. (Harmondsworth, 1969), pp. 80ff.

64. Quoted from B. Simon, *The Two Nations and the Educational Structure 1780 to 1870* (London, 1974), p. 312. See also G. Best, *Mid-Victorian England 1851–1875* (New York, 1972), pp. 162ff., 246ff.

65. Quoted from B. Simon, 'Introduction' in B. Simon and I. Bradley (eds.), *The Victorian Public School* (Dublin, 1975), p. 4; T.V. Bamford, *Rise of the Public Schools* (London, 1967), pp. 59ff.; E.C. Mack, *Public Schools and English Opinion since 1860* (1941); new edition (New York, 1973).

66. This fundamental difference between sport and duelling was overlooked by H. Schöffler, *England das Land des Sports* (Leipzig, 1935). Schöffler maintained that boxing replaced duelling in England in the eighteenth century. This mistake was very influential and has been repeated in a number of modern histories of sport. I am grateful to Christiane Eisenberg for pointing this out to me. On the sporting-cult in English public schools, see J.A. Morgan, *Athleticism in the Victorian and Edwardian Public School. The Emergence and Consolidation of an Educational Ideology* (Cambridge, 1981).

67. J.W. Goethe, *Wilhelm Meister's Apprenticeship*, translated by Thomas Carlyle, (London, 1899), pp. 250–251.

68. A. Wagner, 'Meine Duellangelegenheiten mit dem Freiherrn von Stumm', *Die Zukunft* 10 (1895), pp. 408–427, especially p. 422.

69. R. Scheu, 'Duel und kein Ende', *Die Fackel* 196 (1906), pp. 5–12. Although the piece is a sarcastic one, the author was correct about the 'individualistic idea' of the

duel: 'The leading idea is not the satisfaction that one owes but the importance that one attaches to oneself.' (p. 9).

70. Thomas Mann, *The Magic Mountain* (Harmondsworth, 1979), p. 699.

71. H.E. Dwight, *Travels in the North of Germany in the Years 1825 and 1826* (New York, 1829), p. 49.

72. W. Howitt, *Life in Germany, or Scenes, Impressions and Everyday Life of the Germans* (London, 1849), pp. V–X.

73. Dwight, *Travels*, p. 51. See also, Keil, *Geschichte*, and K.H. Jarausch, *Deutsche Studenten 1800–1970* (Frankfurt, 1984), pp. 38f., 48ff., 59ff.; W. Hardtwig, 'Studentische Mentalität – Politische Jugendbewegung – Nationalismus. Die Anfänge der deutschen Burschenschaft', *Historische Zeitschrift* 242 (1986), pp. 591–628, especially pp. 591ff.

74. G. Pusch, *Über Couleur und Mensur* (Berlin, 1887), pp. 11, 25.

75. Wagner, 'Duellangelegenheiten', p. 424; F. Paulsen, *Die deutschen Universitäten und das Universitätsstudium* (Berlin, 1902), p. 485.

76. See Frevert, *Ehrenmänner*.

77. *Stenographische Berichte des Preußischen Abgeordnetenhauses*, vol. 3 (Berlin, 1865), especially columns 2250ff.

78. Quoted from A. Kohut, *Das Buch berühmter Duelle* (Berlin, 1888), pp. 101, 104.

79. H. Gräff et al., *Ergänzungen und Erläuterungen des Preußichen Criminal Rechts durch Gesetzgebung und Wissenschaft*, first section (Breslau, 1842), pp. 513f.

80. Hauptstaatsarchiv Munich, Staatsmat. No. 579 and 2450; Minutes of the council's session, 24 November 1826.

81. Geheimes Staatsarchiv Berlin-Dahlem, Rep. 84a, No. 8037; Minister of War, v. Falkenhayn, 22 April 1914.

82. Quoted from K. Demeter, *Das deutsche Offizierkorps in Gesellschaft und Staat 1650–1945* (Frankfurt, 1965), p. 290. Duelling was not a monopoly of the Prussian army but was also popular in the Bavarian army, as has been shown by H. Rumschöttel, *Das bayrische Offizierkorps 1866–1914* (Berlin, 1973), pp. 145ff.

83. Wagener, vol. 23 (1867), p. 200.

84 Cf. *Parliamentary Debates*, vol. 73, columns 833ff., 1018; Demeter, *Das deutsche Offizierkorps*, pp. 302f.; *The Fourth Report of the Association for the Discouragement of Duelling* (London, 1850).

85. R.P. Ericksen, 'Kontinuität konservativer Geschichtsschreibung am Seminar für Mittlere und Neuere Geschichte', in H. Becker, et al. (eds.), *Die Universität Göttingen unter dem Nationalsozialismus* (Munich, 1987), pp. 219–245, especially p. 229.

9 | Property Rights and the Status of Women in Germany and England

Ursula Vogel

'The law of servitude is a monstrous contradiction to all the principles of the modern world. . . .There remain no legal slaves except the mistress of every house' (J. S. Mill, 1869, after the abolition of slavery in the United States)[1]

'Conjugal love works to mitigate the necessary *Herrschaft* of the husband over the wife'. (Carl von Rotteck, 1846)[2]

Liberty and Property

Bourgeois Society – a Society of Property Owners

This paper will explore a specific contradiction in the liberal self-image of modern bourgeois society (*bürgerliche Gesellschaft*). The central thrust of bourgeois legal thought, as it evolved from the second half of the eighteenth century onwards, was its radical confrontation with the institutional traditions of 'feudalism'. It stood opposed to the remnants of personal servitude in the manorial system, to the restrictive constitution of the guild system and, above all, to the privilege and public authority enjoyed by the aristocracy. How are we, then, to explain that analogous forms of personal rule (*Herrschaft*) survived, virtually unchallenged, in the sphere of gender relations until the end of the nineteenth century?

The specific forms of this *Herrschaft* which, more than in other domains of modern law, testified to the resilience of germanic medieval traditions, will be examined here by reference to the rights of property. We shall see that, in relation to women, the universal postulates of bourgeois liberty and equality suffered constraints of a more enduring and more fundamental kind than those imposed upon

Notes to Chapter 9 can be found on page 265.

other disadvantaged groups in nineteenth-century German society. We will, therefore, have to ask ourselves whether, and how, this particular contradiction can still be incorporated into the normative model of *Bürgerlichkeit*. Should gender equality be understood as a delayed and yet integral moment in the continuum of emancipatory processes? Can we describe the particular disadvantages of women in similar terms to those affecting dependent wage labourers – as, for example, an 'enclave of unequal right'? Or do we have to consider marriage and family as unique forms of social relationships which by their very nature must impose limits upon the rights of the autonomous individual?[3]

Within the framework established by these questions, the notions of *Bürger* and *bürgerlich* – and, similarly, the meaning of liberty and domination (*Herrschaft*) – are meant to refer to the core premises of liberal political theory in the tradition of Locke, Adam Smith and Kant. The basic presupposition of their thought must be sought in the idea of natural liberty that pertains to all human beings as rational agents. Defined as both a right and a capacity of self-determination, the autonomy of the individual serves, on the one hand, as the methodological starting point from which all forms of social association are derived, from the constitution of marriage to the organisation of the state, the paradigm of contract and consent. This understanding of freedom contains, on the other hand, the evaluative principles by which liberal thinking judges the legitimacy of relations of power and dependence sanctioned by positive law.

In the normative structures of German private law (*Privatrecht*) – which will be the main focus of this paper – the postulate of equal liberty manifests itself in the idea of a universal capacity for rights. Conceived as the entitlement of every human being to be recognised as a legal person, i.e. as a bearer of rights and obligations, this concept was central to the evolution of a modern legal system. As such, it embodied the opposition to a traditional hierarchical order predicated upon hereditary status and ascribed right. This was the meaning that Eichhorn's *Introduction to German Private Law* gave to the word citizen (*Staatsbürger*) in which 'some of the most recent codifications of law refer to the status of a general capacity for rights that extends to all members of a given nation without regard to the modifications of their status by the particular relations of social rank'.[4]

In the bourgeois model of private law, civil society constitutes itself as a sphere free from coercive domination.[5] Whether individuals will succeed in protecting their private autonomy against any form of personal, arbitrary power will depend crucially on the recognition and security of private property. In the universe of liberal values liberty is not only closely connected but, in the last instance, identical with exclusive rights of ownership – rights both in one's person and one's goods.

Here lies the salient point for the following argument: it is the unconstrained freedom to *dispose* over one's property by which liberalism identifies the individual as a citizen, and by which it distinguishes full members of civil society from those who stand in need of rule and protection. Locke, for example, used this very criterion to formulate the distinctive attributes of political power (over citizens) in opposition to paternal and despotic power (over children and slaves): 'Paternal power is only where minority makes the child incapable to manage his property; political where men have property in their own disposal; and despotical over such that have no property at all'.[6]

Similar assumptions defined the status of the legal person (*Rechtsperson*) in German private law. The passive capacity for rights belongs to all human beings as such (including children). But only if this first and basic element is joined by the capacity to exercise these rights, that is, to perform legally valid actions and to incur obligations in one's own name, can the individual lay claim to the status of a citizen (*Staatsbürger*).[7] As we shall see, it is this second element of full legal agency – manifest in the dispositive rights of property – which women lacked.

The comparison of German and English marriage law will help us to understand how the relations of power and dependence between men and women were mediated by inequality of property rights. If we choose the Prussian Civil Code of 1794 as our starting point, this does not mean that it should be considered as the representative example of all German systems of matrimonial property. The complexity and confusing plurality of regional and local customs in the legal constitution of marriage forbids any such generalisation. In some respects, the Prussian code reflects an exceptional concentration of progressive legislative intentions. Taken as a whole, however, it cannot be read as a manifesto of liberal-bourgeois conceptions of law. It is true that it already articulated principles which pointed in the direction of a general concept of citizenship based upon legal equality, but it filled this conceptual framework with traditional notions of differential legal status that transmitted the legacies of a hierarchical social order. Among these differentiations, familial status still served as a major category in determining the rights and obligations of individuals.[8]

That by the end of the eighteenth century women had not yet reached the threshold of equal civil rights does not separate them from other still disadvantaged groups. Rather, what needs to be explained is the curious fact that in liberal reform programmes of the early nineteenth century which aimed at the legal emancipation of those other groups, the subordinate condition of women and, in particular, of married women was hardly ever mentioned. The gradual expansion of civil and property rights after 1807 confirmed the emancipatory potential of liberal ideas. It asserted itself in the abolition of personal servitude, in the defeudalisation of land ownership, and in the integration of Jews and aliens into the legal community. The legal condition of women, by contrast, remained insulated against the process of emancipation until the end of the nineteenth century.

Was the much delayed emancipation of women a peculiar feature only of German society? Does it support the assumption of the special character and development of bourgeois liberalism in Germany? The perspective on the position of women under the English Common Law will cast these questions into sharper relief. We shall find that our comparison accords with a general observation stated also in other chapters of this book: at least with regard to the early nineteenth century, German conditions cannot be described in simple categories of backwardness or of a specific 'deficit of *Bürgerlichkeit*'. On the contrary, the comparison with England points towards a paradoxical conclusion. Here was a society which granted to its (male) citizens a higher degree of political and economic freedom than could be found anywhere else in Europe but which, in its marriage and family law, displayed the virtually undisrupted continuity of the hierarchical order of the Middle Ages.

However, in the second half of the nineteenth century this seemingly paradoxical correlation was to change significantly. In England, a liberal public opinion moved the property rights of women onto the political agenda. That the power relations between the sexes cemented by the laws of marriage reflected badly on the avowed beliefs of liberalism – arguments of this kind were raised not only by the women's movement. They served as a strategic vantage point in the critique of modern civilisation that emerged from the most influential works of liberal jurisprudence and political theory. The understanding of historical progress as a movement 'from status to contract' enabled writers like Maine, Dicey and John Stuart Mill to expose the profoundly anachronistic character of the institution of marriage. And the wider diffusion of individualist values and modes of thought, especial-

ly under the influence of Benthamite utilitarianism and classical political economy, affords further reasons why the archaic constraints on
the married woman's property rights could become a public scandal.[9]

In Germany, by contrast, liberal doctrines remained more closely
bound up with 'conservative' concerns. The prior commitment to
considerations of order was reflected in strong currents of opinion
that aimed at the restoration of the family.[10] As far as the legal emancipation of women was concerned, the standard texts of German liberalism – such as Rotteck's *Staatslexicon* – had little to offer. The
dominant theme of much recent literature on nineteenth-century
German liberalism the coexistence and disparity of progressive constitutional principles, on the one hand, and a backward looking
model of social relations, on the other – could be seen to apply, with
particular force, to liberal perceptions of gender (once, that is, the
issue is included in the expanding field of this research).[11]

We can observe that, virtually without exception, liberal thinkers
in nineteenth-century Germany pursued a strategy which effectively
insulated gender, as but a natural category, against the universalist
implications of individualist principles of law. This pattern was reinforced where liberalism extolled the exemplary meaning of Christian
and Germanic conceptions of marriage and where it affirmed notions
of love and community predicated upon inequality and hierarchy. On
the level of normative analysis, too, we are thus confronted by contradictions that seem intrinsic to bourgeois ideals. Were these contradictions due merely to the historical tenacity of patriarchal traditions
of thought? Was it, at least conceivable that they might be resolved at
a future stage of social progress? Or were the constraints that
obstructed the universal implications of its core principles inseparable
from the normative model of *Bürgerlichkeit* itself?[12]

Ownership and Power

Women's Property Rights in German Private Law

'The rights of both sexes are to be considered equal, unless they have
been modified by specific laws or valid declarations of will'. (ALR, I, 1,
§24)

'The husband is the head of the conjugal society, and his will is to prevail
in the common affairs of the marriage'. (ALR, II, 1, § 184)

Among the codifications of the Enlightenment, the Prussian Civil
Code is the only one to explicitly state the general principle of gender

equality. But the relevant passages of this legal document leave little doubt that here, too, women were in most respects still subject to special laws. The principle of equality was overlayed by the effects of the institution of sexual guardianship (*Geschlechtsvormundschaft*). This institution derived originally from the germanic 'munt' – from that absolute power of a patriarchal lord over all the members of his household which prevailed in the legal customs of many primitive nations. In the course of historical development and, notably, under the influence of Christian doctrines, this patriarchal power had lost its absolute character. Indeed, in relation to the single woman, it had by the beginning of the nineteenth century become a mere formality. It had, however, survived in the marital guardianship of marriage (*Ehevogtei*); and here it had retained elements of its original dual character as a relationship of personal rule and protection.[13]

It is important not to lose sight of the differentiation between the legal status of the married and the unmarried woman, not least because it exposed the increasingly tenuous nature of the argument most commonly cited on behalf of the *status quo*, which ascribed to the whole female sex the attributes of natural weakness and need for protection. In the nineteenth century, different and more sophisticated schemes of legitimation were called for if one wanted to ensure the legal subjection of women in the domain of marriage while conceding to single women full equality of civil rights with men, and if one wanted – in yet another twist – to exclude all women categorically from the rights of political citizenship even when their status of legal independence would have entitled them to the vote.

Conflicting tendencies of a similar kind can already be found in the Prussian code. In those sections that deal in general terms with the rights of persons and property, the text typically refers to 'widows and spinsters'. They are, in certain respects, to be treated like 'male persons', for example as regards their capacity to conclude valid contracts and make testamentory dispositions (ALR, I, 5, § 23). The majority of women could claim such rights only in exceptional circumstances. Thus, in the rules relating to contracts, we find the following statement: 'The contracts of children still subject to paternal power and, similarly, of married women, will be dealt with in their proper context' (I, 5, §§9–25).

The 'proper context' is the marriage and family law. Only here will we find a detailed and comprehensive account of women's civil status. It is premised upon the definition of marriage as a 'society' constituted by *Herrschaft*. The powers that the law conferred on the husband as the head of the conjugal association had the effect of isolating the wife in a special legal sphere of her own. Within this enclave she had, no doubt, certain rights and obligations. But in the world outside (i.e. in relation to third parties) she could exercise such rights only through the representative agency of her husband. It is this contradictory and arbitrary character of the inequality decreed by the law that will be our main concern as we attempt to trace the patriarchal structures of marriage in the rights and obligations of property.

Even that first and indispensable prerequisite of individual liberty – the right over one's person and labour, to freely dispose of one's capacities and resources – was insufficiently secured in the legal formulation of the marriage bond. Tangible restrictions of a woman's freedom derived from the husband's legal power to give or refuse consent as to whether his wife could engage in independent work of her own, and to cancel all obligations that she might have incurred in the respect. If, with his permission, she did work outside the home, her earnings would, as a general rule, become part of his property. Rules like these demonstrate the unique form of unfreedom associated with sexual difference.

They highlight the fact that the exclusion of women (as wives) from membership of civil society and its law was of an altogether different kind from the disadvantages suffered by other oppressed groups. The wage-labourer, for example – in formal legal terms the owner of at least his labour power – was in this regard subject to less stringent restrictions than a wife. She alone faced an absolute barrier that denied her even the formal opportunities of acquiring property in her own right and, with it, the basic requirement of citizen status (a point which has so far received scant attention even from the most outspoken critics of the liberal idea of private property).[14]

As regards the definition of matrimonial property the Prussian code followed two basic models. It distinguished between the so-called 'administrative community' (*Verwaltungsgemeinschaft*), based upon the general presumption of separate property, and the genuine 'community of goods' (*Gütergemeinschaft*) which, in turn, allowed for numerous variations depending on which goods of the spouses were thus joined together.

According to the first scheme (*ALR*, II, 1,§§ 205–344), all the property that a wife brought into marriage came under the control and usufruct of the husband. Although he was debarred from diminishing the substance of certain goods (mainly, immovables) without her consent, he could dispose freely over the income from such property and – an important point – use it against his personal debts. Moreover, he acquired upon marriage the full, unqualified right of ownership in her movables. The same principle applied, as already indicated, to her earnings from any independent work outside the home.

The second system, the community of goods (*ALR*, II, 1, §§ 345–433), united the property of both spouses (or, a substantial part of it) into a single mass placed under joint ownership. In formal legal terms, the wife was in this case a co-owner with equal rights and obligations. This presumption had, above all, the effect of securing her a legal title also to all goods acquired during marriage – a claim which would be realised at the dissolution of marriage by death or separation. As long as the marriage lasted, however, she could not make any decisions with regard to the 'communal' property. At most, her rights amounted to a veto against the alienation or mortgaging of certain goods (such as land).

In both these systems of matrimonial property we can discern the contours of Germanic and medieval traditions which had withstood the reception of the Roman Law and its individualistic notions of ownership. Elements of this legacy still survived in the arrangements of the Civil Code of 1900 (*BGB*). Not only the conservative representatives of German jurisprudence but, as we shall see, the advocates of liberal principles, too, tended to extol in this hierarchical construction of property rights an exemplary form of 'community' capable of counteracting the corrosive tendencies of modern individualism.[15]

We should not forget, however, that in this context the notion of 'community' would be seriously misleading – if we were to associate it with genuinely equal rights or shared responsibilities. Rather, both forms of matrimonial ownership converged in the core assumption (and that applies to most European marriage laws of this period) that, as a consequence of marriage, virtually all of a wife's property passed into the dispositive power of her husband: 'The husband has everywhere a very large power of dealing as he pleases with the whole mass of property . . . *A system of community need not be a system of equality*'.[16]

The defenders of the traditional order of marriage would frequently claim that marital power should be understood as, primarily, a protective relationship and benevolent concession of the law to women as the weaker partner. Demands for securing to a wife full and equal freedom of property management 'no doubt overestimate the competence and the natural inclinations of the German woman'.[17] In many respects, the Prussian code seems to confirm the presumption of a woman's special need for protection. It imposed upon the husband a duty to maintain his wife in appropriate conditions, to defend her person and honour against the world outside, to represent her interest in property transactions and in the courts and even, in special cases, to accept liability for her debts (ALR, II, 1, §§184–204). In those instances where the law aimed to protect a wife's interest against the designs of the husband, it did so explicitly for the reason that she 'should not be disadvantaged or defrauded'(*ibid.*, §20).

The authors of the code, however, did not always or consistently claim the natural weakness and inexperience of the female sex. How else could we explain that they entrusted the wife with a considerable freedom of disposition in form of the *Schlüsselgewalt* (the right to pledge her husband's credit) and, similarly, of the *Notverwaltungsrecht*? The latter term means that in the case of his incapacitation or pro-longed absence 'she was entitled to do everything required for the orderly administration of property' (*ibid.*, §202). The claim of an allegedly natural incapacity becomes weaker still if we consider the concessions made in favour of the so-called 'reserved estate' (*Vorbehaltsgut*). On the basis of special contractual arrangements, either before or during marriage, a wife might assume the full rights of ownership over property of any kind. Without being constrained by the need to seek her husband's consent, she could conclude contracts, engage in litigation and accept liability towards creditors (*ALR*, II,1, §§208f.; 221–230).

If we relate the analysis of property relations in marriage to the general norms that constitute bourgeois society as an association of free and equal individuals we will be left with a complex and highly ambiguous picture. In some respects, the legal status of the married woman bears close resemblance to that of minors under guardianship; in others, it recalls the conditions of feudal dependence – insofar as a husband acquired, together with the control over his wife's property, the rights and obligations normally assigned to the public power. The married woman was thus the subject of patriarchal and paternalist concerns. And yet, under certain conditions, she might be empow-ered to assume full responsibility for virtually all affairs of civil life. This ambivalence of legislative intentions manifests itself most strik-ingly in such special regulations in favour of a wife's independence. The law attempted to create a space for modern needs and interests without challenging the patriarchal foundations of the institution of marriage.

Nineteenth-century legal developments, especially in the domain

250 | *Ursula Vogel*

of jurisdiction, tended to suppress the emancipatory potential of the Prussian code. It was rendered ineffective by a whole web of special rules which separated marriage from the terrain of universalist principles. According to the basic premises of liberalism and its anti-paternalist emphasis, unnecessary power was indistinguishable from illegitimate power. Insisting on the inalienable rights of the autonomous individual, Kant called the benevolent paternalist state 'the greatest conceivable despotism'.[19] With regard to the law of marriage he, too, confirmed the old maxim 'He shall be your lord'.[20]

'A Case of Virtual Slavery'

Matrimonial Property under the English Common Law

> So great a favourite is the female sex of the laws of England (Blackstone).[21]

> Criminals, Idiots, Women and Minors. Is the Classification Sound? (Title of a pamphlet from the English women's movement, 1869).[22]

By relating German marriage laws to their English counterparts, we will be in a better position to address the general question whether conditions in Germany can adequately be described in terms of the delayed historical development of bourgeois society. At the outset, we have to confront a major difficulty. Whether we consider the theoretical construction of legal doctrines or the practice of legislation and jurisdiction, certain fundamental differences between Continental and Anglo-saxon traditions of law would seem to limit the usefulness of such undertaking.[23]

For the sake of brevity, we will summarise the most pertinent features of this disparity. In contrast with the decisive influences and revolutionary innovations which had transformed the legal systems of Continental Europe since the Middle Ages, the English Common Law remained relatively unaffected by the reception of Roman Law and, similarly, by the rationalist doctrines of modern natural law. It lacked those elements of systematic organisation that in Europe had emerged form the alliance between Romanist jurisprudence and the absolute state. Jurisdiction based itself not on abstract rules enshrined in the normative framework of codified law but upon particular instances of historical precedent. This orientation will, in turn, explain the more dominant role of the courts and of the legal profession in the historical development of the Common Law.

Given these characteristics, the English Common Law cannot easily be fitted into a general model of bourgeois law (*bürgerliches Recht*). We will not find exact equivalents to normative categories like '*allgemeine Rechtsfähigkeit*', or '*Rechtsperson*'. Nor can we simple transfer the criteria of historical periodisation by which we commonly identify a distinctly 'bourgeois' phase in the evolution of German society. What we, for example, recognise as a key period of legal transformation and codification in continental Europe corresponds to more than half a century of protracted stagnation in the development of English private law (1760–1830). Moreover, even when in subsequent decades the dynamic of legal reform gathered momentum, it did not refer the claims of hitherto underprivileged groups to universal principles of legal equality. Rather, changes of this kind – and that applies with particular relevance to our theme – evolved in a process that gradually extended the boundaries of previously exclusive privileges: 'We have often had occasion to remark that here in England the law for the great becomes the law for all'.[24]

More than was the case in Germany, the Common Law drew a clear distinction between the status of the unmarried woman (*feme sole*) and that of the wife (*feme covert*). Whereas the latter did not exist as an independent legal person, the former enjoyed the same civil rights as a man. It is true that the single woman, too, remained excluded from participation in public life (i.e. from the suffrage, jury service and public office), but she possessed all the rights and obligations pertaining to property and, thus, the full capacity for valid legal actions. The independence of the *feme sole* was to serve an important function in the reform demands of the nineteenth century, since it demonstrated the experience and acceptability of women's equal rights. This explains why in England the legal emancipation of the married woman could take the form of a gradual assimilation, up to the point when she had obtained the same status 'as if she were a feme sole'.[25]

Moreover, the property rights enjoyed by the single woman could serve as a stepping-stone for demanding equality with men also in the public domain. The more the electoral reforms of the nineteenth century lowered the property barriers of political participation, the more numerous grew the category of women who, in their capacity as property owners and taxpayers, satisfied all the conditions of political rights. J. S. Mill, for example, invoked this already existing equality of property rights when he proposed, in 1867, that the electoral law should substitute the word 'persons' for 'men'.[26] In the same context belong the propagandistic campaigns of the women's movement to assert the universal, generic meaning of 'man' in the courts.[27] In their own time, these efforts may not have been successful, but they did expose the increasingly fragile and arbitrary web of reasons that sustained women's exclusion, as in the notorious case of a judge who pronounced that women were to be considered as persons only in the sphere of the criminal law.[28]

Upon entering into marriage, the English woman automatically lost the status of a legal person. The legal fiction that postulated the identity of husband and wife rendered her, so to speak, invisible. In the eyes of the law she no longer existed.[29] Blackstone, whose systematic reconstruction of the Common Law remained the authoritative interpretation of English legal traditions until well into the nineteenth century, defined this identification in the following way:

> By marriage husband and wife are one person in law: that is, the very being or legal existence of the woman is suspended during the marriage, or at least is incorporated and consolidated into that of the husband: under whose wing, protection and *cover*, she performs every thing; and is therefore called in our law-french a *feme-covert*; is said to be *covert-baron*, or under the protection and influence of her husband, her *baron*, or lord; and her condition during marriage is called *coverture*.[30]

From the representation of marriage in one person derived all further rules. As a matter of principle, the married woman could have no rights and obligations that would have presupposed her separate legal identity. This general premise might have curious implications. Thus, husband and wife were unable to exchange substantial gifts or to enter into contractual arrangements with each other. The husband would, as it were, have made a present to himself and 'to covenant with her would only be to covenant with himself'.

This fiction had the further effect that – by contrast with the more flexible prescriptions of the Prussian code – the English wife could under hardly any circumstances assume the capacity for legal action. The same reasons restricted her liability for criminal offences and torts. The law presumed that in such cases she had acted under duress – under the husband's coercive influence, not out of her own will. When, during the American War of Independence, the property of loyalists was confiscated, this sanction threatened to annihilate also the dower right of the wife (the traditional entitlement of the widow to a share in her husband's estates). In this situation the defending lawyers were able to turn the identity fiction to the advantage of women:

> The real question is whether the statute (against treason, U.V) was intend-
> ed to include persons who have by law no wills of their own . . . Infants,
> insane, femes-covert all of whom the law considers as having no will can-
> not act freely.[31]

In cases like the above, legal practive seemed to confirm Blackstone's
much-quoted formula of the favourable treatment of the female sex
under English law. Yet, by the same token, it demonstrated the
power of a husband responsible for all his wife's actions, 'as a master is
for the acts of his slaves or his cattle'.[32] From Mary Wollstonecraft to
August Bebel, the analogy with the conditions of slavery dominated
all critical accounts of the English marriage laws. Indeed, the extent
to which the English wife was deprived of even basic rights and
obligations conflicted with any modern conceptions of legitimate
authority. While the marital guardianship of the German law, according to which the husband acted as the representative of his wife, contained at least some elements that might be justified by the idea of
community, the Common Law offered no basis for legitimations of
this kind.

Similar differences can be observed in the domain of matrimonial
property.[33] The Common Law recognised no equivalent to the
Continental community of goods (*Gütergemeinschaft*). Since under the
premises of coverture the married woman, as a non-person, could not
partake in any scheme of joint ownership, she had no claims on the
property acquired during marriage. The same principle ruled out, at
least for the majority of cases, contractual arrangements similar to
those that we encountered in the reserved estate (*Vorbehaltsgut*) of the
Prussian code. True, insofar as the property that a wife brought into
marriage consisted of real estate, the husband – here as in all other
European legal systems – acquired only the the rights of administration and usufruct. That is, on the dissolution of marriage, such property, together with all dispositive powers, returned to the woman. In
addition, the dower right (to which we referred above) secured to the
widow a life-long claim upon a certain share of her husband's immo-
bile property.[34]

In the predominantly agrarian societies of the Middle Ages, such
rules afforded reasonable protection to a wife's property. In the much
changed circumstances of a society where the dowry consisted mainly
of movables, they would no longer suffice. For this type of property
(including the right of testamentary disposition) fell to the husband.
As part of his 'right to the wife's services', furthermore, he was pre-

sumed to acquire her earnings as his own property. To these rights corresponded similarly extensive obligations on his part. A husband was liable even for those debts that his wife had incurred before marriage, 'for he has adopted her and her circumstances together'.

If the exclusion of the married woman from the legal order appears more rigidly enforced in England than elsewhere, this is due not least to the fact that here individual property – for example, in the domains of commercial, credit and contract law – had long shed the fetters of feudal constraints. Nowhere else would we find the demands of possessive individualism asserted in such unequivocal terms as in Blackstone's formulation of the 'right of property: or that sole and despotic dominion which one man claims and exercises over the external things of the world, in total exclusion of the right of any other individual in the universe'.[35] Nowhere else, on the other hand, was the principle of individual ownership as severely restricted as in the property rights of the married woman.

Blackstone himself would have found no contradiction in this disparity. He defined the rights and obligations of husband and wife exclusively from the institutional meanings of marriage. The latter had its place among the 'great relations of private life' whose very origins and purposes necessarily implied *Herrschaft*: 'Master and Servant – Husband and Wife – Parent and Child – Guardian and Ward'.[36] The subordination of the wife (postulated in the identity-fiction) stood justified by the primary goal of marriage: to guarantee legitimate heirs through unquestionable bonds of paternity. The nexus between property and family lineage (and its continuity over successive generations) was seen as a necessary condition of social stability. Like many of his contemporaries, Blackstone would have associated the independence of the married woman, above all, with the danger that outsiders, i.e. bastards, might usurp the property rights of legitimate offspring.

For the early nineteenth century our comparison of German and English law will, in each case, reveal noticeable internal tensions between the public and the private dimensions of the legal order. Thus, the absolutist-bureaucratic state had enacted a relatively liberal marriage law. The Prussian code, as we have seen, displayed some tendencies that pointed towards the recognition of women as independent legal persons. England had after 1688 consolidated the institutions that safeguarded the freedom of citizens in the public sphere. Its family law, by contrast, remained enclosed in the hierarchical legacies of the feudal past, which sanctioned the near-absolute power of the husband and father.

The paradox of public liberty and private rule would become even more evident if we were to extend our comparison to include the American development of Common Law traditions. We would find that, even within the newly established framework of a republican polity, marriage preserved the features of the old Common Law.[37] While property laws in general were transformed to suit new demands of economic expansion – manifest, for example in the defeudalisation and mobilisation of land ownership – the distribution of property rights in marriage remained intact until the middle of the nineteenth century.

Everywhere – and not just in relation to the allegedly special case of Germany – we encounter certain contradictions that reflect the process of asymmetrical modernisation in different spheres of bourgeois law. Everywhere, it seems, marriage and family law were left behind by the dynamic of economic and political liberalisation. But for the first half of the nineteenth century we cannot rely on close correspondences between the public and the domestic constitution of bourgeois society. Political liberty and patriarchal despotism could well coexist. Conversely, the authoritarian structures of a political system did not necessarily imply analogous structures in the private sphere of marriage.

The Special Case of England

The Dialectic of Progress and Backwardness

Around the middle of the century the relationship between German and English legal developments began to change its pattern. In Prussia, the political reaction, supported by the conservative disposition of the courts, attempted to reverse the liberal provisions of the civil code.[38] In England, by contrast, we witness the beginning of a reform movement that would eventually, in the 1880s, lead to the legal emancipation of the married woman. These reforms evolved in a manner highly characteristic of the continuity, flexibility – and not least, the backwardness of the English law. That they secured to English women the conditions of personal independence which in Germany and France were to be achieved only in the twentieth century, must to some extent be explained by the defects of an archaic legal system.

In this context, marriage displayed the most conspicuous symptoms of a general crisis. It was particularly affected by the confusions and contradictions that resulted from the division of the legal system into two separate branches – Common Law and Equity. The Married Women's Property Acts of 1870, 1882 and 1893 were propelled by a more general process of rationalisation which culminated in the Judicature Act of 1873. It was largely because they were part of these wider developments – and not because of a strong popular commitment to the cause of female emancipation – that the Property Acts found the support of the legal profession.[39]

'What was it which delayed till well-nigh the end of the Benthamite era a reform which must, one would have thought, have approved itself to every Liberal?'[40] This was the question from which Dicey's classic account of law and public opinion in nineteenth-century England explored the causes of women's delayed emancipation. Of considerable importance in this context was the fact that the wealthiest classes in English society had always been able to circumvent the severity of the Common Law in order to protect the dowry of their daughters against embezzlement by the husband. To be sure, these settlements – defined by the law of Equity as 'reserved estate' – were not aimed at securing the independence of the individual woman. They were meant to safeguard the property interests of her family. The frequent inclusion of the so-called 'restraint on anticipation' – which deprived the married woman of the free disposal over 'her' property – suggests that these interests were to be protected also against the detrimental consequences of female weakness and inexperience – against, that is, a wife's vulnerability to 'the kicks and kisses' of the husband. However, since this privileged property could, as a matter of principle, entail a wife's full dispositive powers, it pointed the way towards conceding to all married women the same privilege of separate rights of ownership.

That demands of this kind did eventually meet with success was due to a variety of factors: to the impact of Benthamite radicalism and its systematic critique of antiquated legal practices; to the capacity of a parliamentary system to draw the needs and interests of minorities into the forum of public debate; and, in no small measure, to the personality and influence of John Stuart Mill.

Not only as the philosopher of modern liberalism but, above all, in his role as a public moralist, Mill shaped the intellectual profile of a whole generation. While he at times expressed strong reservations regarding the participatory demands of the masses, he was absolutely committed to the legal and political equality of the sexes. The *Subjection of Women* (1869) offered a theoretical position that one could not have found in the environment of nineteenth-century German liberalism. The reception of this work in Germany shows very clearly that even those who supported Mill's plea for the extension of educational and occupational opportunities resisted the central claim of his argument: that the legal rights of women – as of men – were to be judged solely by the claims of the autonomous individual, not by their instrumental function within marriage and family.[41]

Among the conditions favourable to women's emancipation, we must also refer to the impact of changing economic and social circumstances. Only by the middle of the century had the number of working wives (around 750,000, or 25 percent of all working women) reached that critical threshold at which the injustices bound up in the institution of *coverture* could emerge as a major social issue. They became visible, above all, in the predicament of a growing number of working-class women who, as a consequence of their husbands' claim on their earnings, were exposed to destitution and who could only maintain themselves and their children by turning to the poor relief system of the state. The women of this group – and the same applied to most women in the middle classes – were unable to avail themselves of the protection offered by the *separate estate* and its expensive contractual arrangements:

> There came, therefore, to be not in theory but in fact one law for the rich and another for the poor. The daughters of the rich enjoyed, for the most part, the considerable protection of equity, the daughters of the poor suffered under the severity and injustice of the common law.[42]

This is not to say that public opinion in England was more sympathetic to the demands for women's equal rights than in Germany. In both countries such demands met with the fear that a wife's claim to separate property and personal independence would lead to the decline of marriage. Here as there the 'stone age argument of physical force', reinforced by the imperatives of militaristic and imperialist expansion, rendered the full equality of the sexes inconceivable.[43] However, in England it was possible, by mere extension of a traditional privilege, to disconnect the property question from the more radical and more comprehensive meanings of women's emancipation. Even the Conservative members of Parliament could be assured that the proposed reforms would not go further 'than give to every married woman nearly the same rights as every English gentleman had for generations past secured under a marriage settlement for his daughter'.[44]

In view of the numerous anomalies that continued to restrict the property rights of wives, it is not clear why both English and German commentators understood these reforms as a definite advance over conditions that prevailed in other European countries at the turn of century.[45] The German Civil Code of 1900 also established the married woman's right to her own earnings and consolidated other concessions that she had gained in previous decades (most importantly, rights of litigation and of access to a number of occupations).

There remained, however, a significant difference insofar as in virtually all systems of matrimonial property available under the Code the husband still retained 'a dispositive power over property not his own' (Wieacker). In relation to the goods that his wife brought into marriage he continued to exercise the rights of administration and usufruct. What in England had developed into a universal right of personal property that automatically accrued to all women upon marriage remained in Germany a special concession which required particular prenuptial arrangements. Under the dominant influence of Germanist jurisprudence the law affirmed, yet again, a patriarchal relationship of fundamental inequality. Marriage was – and remained for another half-century – still exempted from the universal principle of right which a *Bürgerliches Gesetzbuch* claimed as the very basis of its authority.

In the eyes of English reformers the independence of the wife had become inextricably bound up with her right to separate property. As they saw it, the systems of community (*Gütergemeinschaft*) so prominent in Continental civil law proved conclusively that 'communal' property could not be disconnected from patriarchal rule. Judged by economic benefits alone, the community of goods had definite advantages over a system of divided ownership, because it gave women a share in the property acquired during marriage. The balance sheet will look different if we compare the two systems under considerations of the married woman's personal independence. As long as the community was administered and represented by only one of the partners (roughly until the 1970s), it sustained the subordinate position of the wife. From this vantage point the historian of English law might well cast the reforms of the late nineteenth century into a general pattern in which progress was dialectically linked to the very backwardness of English institutions. Precisely because the identity-fiction of the Common Law had for many centuries sanctioned the virtually absolute power of the husband, the idea of legal equality could only take roots in the individualistic conception of separate property:

Elsewhere we may see the community between husband and wife growing and thriving, resisting all the assaults of Romanism and triumphing in
the modern codes. Long ago we chose our individualistic path.[46]

Liberalism and Bourgeois Emancipation

Those people who single-mindedly and oblivious of the laws and boundaries established by nature herself, chase an abstract ideal of equality will
claim far more rights for women than the latter could possibly want to
have. Such people will once again destroy the most sacred and most
enduring foundation of all human and bourgeois (*bürgerlich*) virtue and
happiness. (C. Welcker)[47]

Was it, then, the predominance of individualist values in the political
culture of England which created more favourable conditions for the
emancipation of women? The concluding section of the paper will
consider this question by comparing some of the core ideas of
German and English liberalism. We are concerned with the emancipatory potential that liberal theories of law and state could impart to
cause of gender equality. Which epistemological principles and which
political priorities were capable of transcending the limitations of traditional liberalism? Conversely, which values and argumentative
strategies could be invoked by those who wanted to exempt gender
issues from the avowed universality of liberal postulates?

The appeal to the universal truths of the 'rights of men' which had
once sustained the demands of reformers like Mary Wollstonecraft,
Condorcet and von Hippel, had by the middle of the century lost
much of its credibility. English liberalism, however, could draw new
resources for a radical critique of the *status quo* from the rationalist
ethic of utilitarianism.[49] If the legitimacy of all existing institutions
had to be confirmed before the tribunal of the greatest-happiness
principle, then the disadvantages suffered by women could become
visible as a massive injustice. Moreover, the materialist construction
of 'happiness' and the prior commitment to the elimination of tangible suffering made it possible, in this as in other cases, to expose the
harsh reality of destitution and force behind the facade of legal mysti-
fications. The equality principle could also draw upon the levelling
tendencies inherent in the idea of individual interests. That is, to the
extent that all individuals, without exception, could claim the same
right to the satisfaction of their desire for happiness – and that each
person was to be considered the most competent judge of her interest

– the traditional presumptions in favour of male guardianship stood devoid of legitimacy (and so did, of course, the endorsement of women's special entitlement to protection).

Another powerful drive towards emancipation could be derived from the utilitarian project of a science of legislation and, particularly, from the presupposition that general scientific maxims could be directly and uniformly applied to all – and even the most disparate – human relationships. Some of Mill's most effective criticisms were part of an argumentative strategy that judged marriage by the very same individualist principles as any other business transaction between formally equal partners. From this perspective he was able to expose the special laws to which women were subordinated as so many forms of unjustifiable domination.[50]

At this point we can refer to the very different philosophical orientations in the environment of German liberalism. The latter tended to stress the limited applicability of abstract principles – and nowhere more emphatically than in the sphere of gender relations. It appealed, instead, to the normative force of life's concrete circumstances and constraints.[51] However, the traditional restrictions imposed upon the idea of legal equality were clearly no longer capable of cogent explanation and justification. Older conceptions of civil society as a community formed by heads of households (*Gemeinschaft der Hausväter*)[52] could not meet the demands of legitimation, because the understanding of rights as individual rights was the main thrust of liberalism's constitutional programmes. Moreover, the capacity to claim and exercise rights was, if sometimes reluctantly, recognised in single women. The main difficulty here stemmed from the intention to endorse 'the complete legal equality of women and men'[53] and, at the same time, to ban this idea from the domains of both marriage and politics. The simultaneous commitment to equality and difference could only be sustained by shifting the argument to a terrain of non-legal or meta-legal imperatives. They postulated the incommensurate values of marriage as a community of love and, in a different track, the natural and irreducible complementarity of male and female sexual character.

Such patterns of legitimation were evident in the ways in which love was manoeuvered to support the institution of the community of goods. Considered as a general principle, the idea of collective ownership was anathema for liberals, because it lacked those attributes of individual property that were the necessary safeguard of liberty. For these reasons, nineteenth-century liberals rejected the experiments of socialism as well as the collective customs and rights that had survived in the village commons.[54]

The primacy of individual liberty and independence was, however, suspended when the argument turned to marriage. Here the dignity of the law was inseparably linked to communal property.[55] Only this form of property was said to express the nature of an affective relationship that encompassed the whole existence of two individuals. But behind the screen of love thus celebrated as a purely ethical force outside and above the terrain of formal law, the argument sanctioned a specific legal distribution of property and freedom. It was invariably the wife who was committed, by the very nature of love as total dedication, to deposit her property in a 'community' controlled by the husband.

> Just as she gives herself and her whole person to the man of her choice in order to take part in every aspect of his life, she will not recognise any divide in relation to her property. She submits it completely and without reservation to the discretion of her husband, in which her own interest is enclosed. That in this relationship the wife occupies a subordinate role . . . is but the self-evident consequence of the position accorded to man by nature.[56]

A new appreciation of conjugal love resonant with romantic sensibilities might have been well suited to express, in the idea of marriage, both the unity and the individuality of the two partners. But in our context, the emphasis on love did no longer − as it had done in the utopian projections of early romanticism − voice the desire to liberate both men and women from the fetters of conventional sex roles.[57] Love had become disconnected from the image of marriage as friendship and intellectual companionship. It was joined, instead, to a conservative understanding of community that always presupposed the fundamental legal inequality of the two individuals.

Authors like Gerber and Sybel, no doubt, realised that while the idea of love might support notions of shared ownership it could not, by itself, justify the hierarchical organisation of the community of goods. This deficit of legitimacy may explain why the nexus between love and legal subordination was sealed by a deterministic understanding of sexual nature. The aim was to immunise the inequality of right against any possible challenge by rooting it in the biological difference of sex − 'unassailable by human will, personal talents and the advance of time'.[58] Postulates such as these confirm the retreat from the bourgeois ideal of equality according to which the 'merely physical and moral . . . inequalities whether of bodily strength, health or of mental and emotional disposition' were to be irrelevant to the normative categories of law.[59]

This contradiction, however, could not be resolved by claiming the immutable complementarity of sexual character. The alleged equal value of different, yet necessarily complementary, attributes of male and female nature remained an empty formula, because it presupposed an asymmetrical relationship which, from the perspective of liberal beliefs, embodied qualities of unequal worth. While man was by nature destined to 'autonomous action', woman should be directed towards the values of 'bearing, giving birth, nourishing and preserving'. The exalted notion of femininity may have included numerous virtues. The point is, however, that neither a superior morality, nor purity and dignity, neither the role of the priestess at the domestic shrine nor metaphors like the 'unity of the evergreen with the oak', could possibly count as an equivalent of individual liberty.[60] It was no accident that in the definition of legal categories women – their higher morality notwithstanding – were as usual bracketed together with children and the insane:

> That an electoral law excludes all women in virtue of their sex, even though they may own the required property, is no more an inconsistency than when such a law turns away children because of their immaturity, the insane because of their mental disabilities, or social misfits because of their bad reputation.[61]

Nor was it accidental that the issue of legal entitlements should, in the last instance, be decided on the basis of physical strength:

> Man alone can serve the common good in mastering floods and fires, in struggling with wild animals and human beings, in building roads and trenches, in waging war, etc. It is therefore not true that woman should be able to claim an equal right with regard to public affairs.[62]

A similar shift of emphasis from the postulate of freedom to a nebulous notion of 'dignity' (a term that in Welcker's account of gender relations surfaces no less than forty times!) emerges from the perception of historical progress. This point can best be demonstrated by a comparison with the central concepts in which Maine's *Ancient Law* construed the process and advance of European civilisation. The disconnection of individuals and their property from the collective rule of the sib (kinship), and the substitution of contractual commitments for the natural ties of the family, appeared in Maine's account as a general law of evolution characteristic of advancing societies. The movement 'from status to contract'[63] had gradually eroded the foundations of slavery and servitude as of the father's power over his adult sons. The marriage laws alone had, until present times, preserved relics of those barbaric relations based on physical force. In this context Christianity was charged with a special responsibility for consolidating the legacy of germanic structures of domination. Especially with regard to the married woman's lack of property rights, 'the expositors of the Canon Law have deeply injured civilisation'.[64]

According to the expositors of German liberalism, the threshold between barbarism and civilisation had already been crossed in that early period of history which marked the transition from oriental despotism (polygamy) towards the germanic-Christian constitution of the family – 'that greatest and most hopeful progress in the history of mankind'.[65] The measure of progress was the respect of women buttressed by the monogamous marriage and 'the duties of honour and chivalry incumbent on men'.[66] Against this ideal the elements of force and coercion that sustained the near-absolute subordination of women in germanic law paled into insignificance. Here, too, we can observe that the retreat from the utopian goals of liberalism and the endorsement of the prevailing legal institutions – sanctioned by history and nature alike – tended to obliterate the link between legal inequality and force.

In other social and political confrontations of the time – in the debates about the emancipation of the Jews and the liberation of the peasants from the yoke of personal servitude – the efficacy of liberal campaigns was owed to a strategy that pierced and relativised the claims of natural inequality by referring them to the specific historical origins and cementations of power relations. Both the intention to historicise 'nature' and the equation of personal power with mere force were the central premises of liberalism's emancipatory theories. Why, then, was this critical potential not transferred to the domain of gender relations? It seems that in liberal conceptions of the conditions of social stability, the inequality of the sexes had the unique function of insuring society against disorder. It was the last bulwark against the much-feared uncontrollable eruption of egalitarian demands. The very idea of 'a complete equality of woman and man both in the family and in the arena of public rights and obligations'[67] – those 'decadent theories' attributed to Bentham and Harriet Martineau and, above all, to the French socialists – conjured up frightening images of a general dissolution of the civil order. In a time that already had moved 'in the wrong direction' in satisfying egalitarian demands, the barriers against the full equality of women were left as the only safeguard that society 'would not slide towards the extreme and break down all floodgates'.[68]

What were the concrete experiences that linked the, after all, rather modest demands for women's legal equality to apocalyptic visions of social breakdown? In the first instance, we may remember the hysteria of irritation and indignation in which contemporaries responded to the experiments of the Saint-Simonians – to the 'savage desire of the Communists'[69] to replace the conventional forms of marriage by the excesses of permissive love. In combatting this provocation German liberalism had, at the same time, to defend another front. It had to disprove the allegations made by its conservative opponents that a consistent application of its individualist values would of necessity move beyond the abolition of aristocratic privileges. It was, according to the defenders of the hierarchical order of the past, due to the insatiable demands propelled by the liberal idea of equality that it could not respect any inequalities of property nor, in the last resort, any differences between the sexes.[70] Caught in the middle ground between two battle-lines, German liberals had to preserve the patriarchal marriage as a necessary guarantor of order. At the same time, however, they had to guard against the danger that, as a consequence of thus relativising the norms of bourgeois equality, patriarchal principles would re-assert themselves in the public domain of constitutional law.[71]

The tension between the poles of universalism and constraint characterised the liberal model of bourgeois society at all stages of its historical development. In its projections of a rational order of law, equality was the indispensable condition of freedom. But when applied to the concrete historical environment of liberal theory, this postulate was always followed by a bracket of exclusions (of women, domestic servants, wage labourers, the poor and destitute).[72] Whether the idea of a social order based upon reason and free from domination could retain its credibility despite exclusions of this magnitude depended crucially upon the perception of future social progress.

Classical liberalism has often been credited with a utopian perspective capable of pointing beyond time-bound divisions and constraints. This concession may be valid if we focus exclusively on the barriers of social rank and class. It seems less warranted in relation to the divisions of gender. In this domain nineteenth-century liberalism did not develop an image of future society ('*soziales Zukunftsbild*'[73]) that transcended the conventional structures of power. On the contrary, in defining women by allegedly natural and immutable attributes of sexual character, liberal doctrines deprived them of the constitutive attributes of autonomous agents – of the capacity for freedom and self-development. Women did not belong to the persons addressed by the 'impressive idea of a society that consisted of free and equal citizens capable of governing themselves in public debate and rational decisions'.[74] The claimed utopian dimension of bourgeois ideals is inseparable from the postulate and promise of universal rights. If one half of the human race is subtracted from this promise the ideal itself will only serve ideological functions.

On the other hand, examples like that of John Stuart Mill might still allow us to speak of the egalitarian potential of liberal theory. Here we do indeed find the image of a free society in which the liberty of citizens would no longer depend upon domination in the private sphere, where on the contrary political freedom would be strengthened by the independence and equality of individuals in their personal relationships.[75] But even this vision still imposed definite constraints upon the equality of women. On the basis of equal rights and equal access to the conditions of economic independence, marriage could become a bond of friendship. For the internal order of the family, however, Mill still affirmed the conventional pattern of the sexual division of labour, albeit on the basis of voluntary commitment and without the stigma of legal subordination.[76] In some ways, then, it is precisely this example which has sustained doubts as to whether the equality of women and men could have a place in a society committed to the ideals of *Bürgerlichkeit*.[77]

Notes to Chapter 9

1. J.S. Mill, *The Subjection of Women*, in *The Collected Works of John Stuart Mill*, vol. 21 (London, 1984), p. 323.
2. Carl v. Rotteck, 'Familie, Familienrecht', in C.v. Rotteck and C. Welcker (eds.), *Das Staats-Lexikon. Encyklopädie der sämtlichen Staatswissenschaften für alle Stände*, 2nd ed., vol. 4 (Altona, 1846), p. 598.
3. Cf. K.M. Grass and R. Koselleck, 'Emanzipation', in O. Brunner et al. (eds.), *Geschichtliche Grundbegriffe. Historisches Lexikon zur politisch-sozialen Sprache in Deutschland*, vol. 2 (Stuttgart, 1975), pp. 153–97; D. Grimm, *Recht und Staat in der bür-*

gerlichen Gesellschaft (Frankfurt, 1987), pp. 11–50 [quote on p. 33]; O. Kahn-Freund, 'Matrimonial Property Law in England', in Kahn-Freund, Selected Writings (London, 1978), pp. 163 ff.

4. Quoted in M. Riedel, 'Bürger, Staatsbürger, Bürgertum,' in Geschichtliche Grundbegriffe, vol. 1 (Stuttgart, 1972), p. 705.

5. Cf. Grimm, Recht und Staat, pp. 12ff.; C.B. Macpherson, The Political Theory of Possessive Individualism (Oxford, 1962), chs. 5 and 6; A. Ryan, Property and Political Theory (Oxford, 1984), passim; D. Schwab, 'Eigentum', in Geschichtliche Grundbegriffe, vol. 2, pp. 89ff.; Schwab, 'Arbeit und Eigentum. Zur Theorie ökonomischer Grundrechte im 19. Jahrhundert', in Quaderni Fiorentini per la Storia del Pensiero Giuridico Moderno, no. 3–4 (1974/75), pp. 515ff., 523.

6. John Locke, Two Treatises of Government (London, 1962), p. 410.

7. Cf. G. Beseler, System des gemeinen deutschen Privatrechts, 4th ed. (Berlin, 1885), pp. 217 ff.; R. Huebner, A History of Germanic Private Law (London, 1918), p. 41ff.

8. Cf. R. Koselleck, Preussen zwischen Reform und Revolution (Stuttgart, 1967), pp. 52 ff.; H. Conrad, Individuum und Gemeinschaft in der Privatrechtsordnung des 18. und beginnenden 19. Jahrhunderts (Karlsruhe, 1956), passim.

9. Cf. A.V. Dicey, Lectures on the Relations between Law and Public Opinion in England during the Nineteenth Century (London, 1905), pp. 369–96; H.S. Maine, Ancient Law. Its Connection with the Early History of Society and its Relation to Modern Ideas, 2nd ed. (London, 1863), pp. 157ff. For the first stages of the women's movement in England, cf. L. Holcombe, Wives and Property. Reform of the Married Women's Property Law in Nineteenth-Century England (Oxford, 1983).

10. Cf. S. Buchholz, 'Eherecht zwischen Staat und Kirche. Preußische Reformversuche in den Jahren 1854–1861', in Ius Commune, Special Issue, no. 13 (Frankfurt, 1981), pp. 1–122; Buchholz, 'Preußische Eherechtsreform im Vormärz (1830–1844), in Ius Commune, Special Issue, no. 15 (Frankfurt, 1981), pp. 150–88; D. Schwab, 'Familie', in Geschichtliche Grundbegriffe, vol. 2, p. 291ff; cf. also note 47, below.

11. Cf. W. Schieder, 'Probleme einer Sozialgeschichte des frühen Liberalismus in Deutschland', in Schieder (ed.), Liberalismus in der Gesellschaft des deutschen Vormärz, (Göttingen, 1983), pp. 9–21. Already Gall's programmatic essay of 1975 suggested the relevance of this issue by reconstructing the model of early liberalism out of that of a pre-industrial, ständisch society 'on patriarchal foundations': cf. L. Gall, 'Liberalismus und bürgerliche Gesellschaft. Zu Charakter und Entwicklung der liberalen Bewegung in Deutschland', in Gall (ed.), Liberalismus, 2nd ed. (Frankfurt, 1980), p. 176. Yet, despite the considerable expansion of social and ideological questions in the research of the past decade, gender and its relation to the theory and politics of liberalism has so far hardly received any attention: cf. also the four volumes of selected texts by L. Gall and R. Koch (eds.), Liberalismus im 19. Jahrhundert (Frankfurt, 1981).

12. These questions are discussed in a wider context in U. Frevert (ed.), Bürgerinnen und Bürger. Geschlechterverhältnisse im 19. Jahrhundert (Göttingen, 1988).

13. For the history of marriage and family law in Germany and England, cf. M. Weber, Ehefrau und Mutter in der Rechtsentwicklung (Tübingen, 1907) (reprint, Aalen, 1971); H. Thieme, 'Die Rechtsstellung der Frau in Deutschland', Recueils de la Société Jean Bodin, vol. 12 (1962), pp. 351–76; D. Schwab, 'Gleichberechtigung (der Geschlechter)', in A.R. Erler et al. (eds.), Handwörterbuch zur deutschen Rechtsgeschichte HRG), vol. 1 (Berlin, 1971), pp. 1696–1702; W. Ogris, 'Munt, Muntwalt', HRG, vol. 3, 1984, pp. 750–62; H. Coing, Europäisches Privatrecht, vol. 1 (Munich, 1985), pp. 224–45; U. Gerhard, 'Über die Voreingenommenheit der Jurisprudenz als dogmatischer Wissenschaft', in K. Hausen and H. Novotny (eds.), Wie männlich ist die Wissenschaft? (Frankfurt, 1986), pp. 108–26; F. Pollock and F.W. Maitland, The History of English Law before the Time of Edward I, 2nd ed. (Cambridge, 1968), vol. 2, pp. 363–447. On the Prussian Civil Code, cf. H. Hattenhauer (ed.), Allgemeines Landrecht für die Preußischen Staaten von 1794 (ALR) (Frankfurt, 1970); H. Conrad, 'Die

Rechtsstellung der Ehefrau in der Privatrechtsgesetzgebung der Neuzeit', in J. Engel and H.M. Klinkenberg (eds.), *Aus Mittelalter und Neuzeit* (Bonn, 1957), pp. 253–62; U. Gerhard, *Verhältnisse und Verhinderungen. Frauenarbeit, Familie und Rechte der Frauen im 19. Jahrhundert* (Frankfurt, 1978), pp. 154–89.

14. Cf. the positions quoted in note 5, above.

15. Cf. O.Von Gierke, *Der Entwurf eines bürgerlichen Gesetzbuchs und das deutsche Recht* (Leipzig, 1889), pp. 394, 405ff; cf. also the references given in section 4, below.

16. Pollock and Maitland, *English Law*, vol. 2, pp. 403, 400, my emphasis.

17. Gierke, *Entwurf*, p. 471.

18. At this point we would also have to consider the procedures that prevailed in the system of jurisdiction. In the absence of formal contractual arrangements, the courts tended to decide in favour of the husband's right of administration and usufruct. It is difficult to derive from the available research a clear picture how many women actually made use of the opportunities given in the *Vorbehaltsgut* and whether the latter – as the corresponding English institution of the separate estate – was available only to the propertied classes. Cf. S. M. Okin, 'Patriarchy and Women's Property in England. Questions on some Current Views', in *Eighteenth Century Studies* 17 (1983/84), pp. 121–38.

19. Kant, 'Über den Gemeinspruch: Das mag in der Theorie richtig sein, taugt aber nicht für die Praxis', in W. Weischedel (ed.), *Kant, Werke in zwölf Bänden*, vol. 11 (Frankfurt, 1964), p. 146.

20. Kant, *Die Metaphysik der Sitten*, in *Werke*, vol. 8 (Wiesbaden, 1956), p. 392.

21.W. Blackstone, *Commentaries on the Law of England*, vol. 1 (Oxford, 1765), p. 433.

22. Quoted in L. Holcombe, 'Victorian Wives and Property', in M. Vicinus (ed.), *A Widening Sphere. Changing Roles of Victorian Women* (Bloomington, 1977), p. 273.

23. Cf. A.B. Schwarz, 'Das englische Recht und seine Quellen', in K. Heinsheimer (ed.), *Die Zivilgesetze der Gegenwart*, vol. 2 (Mannheim, 1931), pp. 3–76; H. Peter, 'Englisches Recht', *HRG*, vol. 1, pp. 922–39; F. Wieacker, *Privatrechtsgeschichte der Neuzeit*, 2nd ed. (Göttingen, 1967), pp. 496ff; W. Friedmann, *Legal Theory*, 5th ed. (London, 1967), pp. 515–55.

24. Pollock and Maitland, *English Law*, vol.2, p. 402.

25. For the text of the Married Women's Property Act of 1882, ct. Holcombe, *Wives*, pp. 243–52.

26. Cf. J.S. Mill, *Autobiography*, in *Collected Works*, vol. 1, p. 285.

27. Cf. M. Ostrogorski, *The Rights of Women. A Comparative Study in History and Legislation* (London, 1893), pp. 44ff.

28. Cf. B. Harrison, *Separate Spheres. The Opposition to Women's Suffrage* (Oxford, 1975), pp. 55ff.

29. Cf. N. Basch, *In the Eyes of the Law. Women, Marriage and Property in Nineteenth Century New York* (Ithaca, 1982), pp. 15–79; Holcombe, *Wives*, pp. 18–36.

30. Blackstone, *Commentaries*, vol. 1, p. 430.

31. Quoted in L. Kerber, *Women of the Republic. Intellect and Ideology in the American Revolution* (Chapel Hill, 1980), p. 134.

32. Mill, *Subjection*, p. 284.

33. Cf. Blackstone, *Commentaries*, vol. 2., pp. 433–36.

34. We can assume that, here as everywhere else, the position of a widow was much to be preferred to that of a wife – especially if she had some property and if we take account of the benefits of personal freedom.

35. Blackstone, *Commentaries*, vol.2, p. 50.

36. Blackstone, *Commentaries*, vol.1, p. 410.

37. Cf. Basch, *In the Eyes of the Law*, p. 25ff.

38. Cf. S. Buchholz, 'Savigny's Stellungnahme zum Ehe- und Familienrecht. Eine Skizze seiner rechtssystematischen und rechtspolitischen Überlegumgen', in *Ius Commune*, 8 (1979), pp. 166ff.

39. Cf. M.L. Shanley, 'Suffrage, Protective Labour Legislation and Married Women's Property', in *Signs* 12, (1986), p. 74f.

40. Dicey, *Law and Public Opinion*, p. 382.

41. Cf. H.-U. Bussemer, *Frauenemanzipation und Bildungsbürgertum. Sozialgeschichte der Frauenbewegung in der Reichsgründungszeit* (Weinheim, 1985), pp. 64ff.

42. Dicey, *Law and Public Opinion*, p. 381. Only about 10% of all married women were protected by the provisions of the separate estate.

43. Cf. C. Rover, *Women's Suffrage and Party Politics in Britain 1866–1914* (London, 1967), pp. 28–52.

44. Dicey, *Law and Public Opinion*, p. 387.

45. Cf. Weber, *Ehefrau*, pp. 361–70; Dicey, *Law and Public Opinion*, p. 389ff.; Wieacker, *Privatrechtsgeschichte*, pp. 474ff.

46. Pollock and Maitland, *English Law*, vol. 2, p. 433.

47. C. Welcker, 'Geschlechtsverhältnisse', in *Staatslexikon*, vol. 5, p. 663.

48. Cf. O. Dann, *Gleichheit und Gleichberechtigung. Das Gleichheitspostulat in der alteuropäischen Tradition und in Deutschland bis zum ausgehenden 19. Jahrhundert* (Berlin, 1980), pp. 170 ff., 205.

49. Cf. E. Halévy, *The Growth of Philosophical Radicalism* (London, 1972); Dicey, *Law and Public Opinion*, pp. 63ff. We should emphasise here that neither Bentham nor James Mill explicitly argued for women's emancipation. We are concerned with the general implications and the potential of utilitarianism.

50. Cf. Mill, *Subjection*, pp. 290 ff.

51. Cf. Rotteck, 'Gleichheit', in *Staatslexikon*, vol. 6, p. 47. Welcker, 'Geschlechtsverhältnisse', pp. 665, 669.

52. Cf. Gall, *Liberalismus*, p. 165.

53. Welcker, 'Geschlechtsverhältnisse', p. 670; cf. also K. Brater, 'Frauen', in K.C. Gluntschli and K. Brater (eds.), *Deutsches Staatswörterbuch*, vol. 3 (Stuttgart, 1858), pp. 722ff., 727.

54. Cf. G.F. Kolb, 'Gütergeneinschaft', in *Staatslexikon*, vol. 6, pp. 275–83.

55. Welcker, 'Geschlechtsverhältnisse', p. 670; Rotteck, 'Familie', pp. 598ff. (although with some emphasis on the benefits of the *Vorbehaltsgut*); Bluntschli, 'Ehe', in *Staatswörterbuch*, vol. 3, pp. 203, 211.

56. Gerber, 'Betrachtungen über das Güterrecht der Ehegatten nach deutschem Rechte', in *Iherings Jahrbücher* 1 (1857), p. 257; cf. auch H.v. Sybel, 'Über die Emanzipation der Frauen', (Bonn, 1870), quoted in M. Twellmann, *Die deutsche Frauenbewegung. Ihre Anfänge und erste Entwicklung 1843–1869*, vol. 2 (Meisenheim, 1972), p. 198.

57. Cf. U. Vogel, 'Rationalism and Romanticism. Two Strategies for Women's Liberation', in J. Evans et al. (eds.), *Feminism and Political Theory* (London, 1986), pp. 34ff.

58. Sybel, *Emanzipation*, p. 198.

59. Rotteck, 'Gleichheit', p. 43; cf. auch Welcker, 'Geschlechtsverhältnisse', pp. 661, 664.

61. K. Maurer, 'Familie', in *Staatswörterbuch*, vol. 3, p. 503.

62. R. V. Mohl, *Staatsrecht, Völkerrecht und Politik,* Monographien, vol. 3, 1868 (reprint: Graz, 1962), p. 303, note 1.

63. Maine, *Ancient Law*, p. 170.

64. *Ibid.*, p. 158.

65. Welcker, 'Geschlechtsverhältnisse', p. 667; Bluntschli, 'Ehe', pp. 201ff.

66. Welcker, 'Geschlechtsverhältnisse', p. 657.

67. *Ibid.*, p. 665.

68. Mohl, *Staatsrecht*, p. 303.

69. Bluntschli, 'Ehe', p. 215; cf. also Kilb, 'Ehe', in *Staatslexikon*, vol. 4, p. 180.

70. Cf. Welcker, 'Geschlechtsverhältnisse', pp. 655; Dann, *Gleichheit*, p. 178.

71. Rotteck, 'Familie', p. 607.

72. Cf. J. Kocka, 'Bürgertum und Bürgerlichkeit als Probleme der deutschen Geschichte vom späten 18. bis zum frühen 19. Jahrhundert', in Kocka (ed.), *Bürger und Bürgerlichkeit im 19. Jahrhundert* (Göttingen, 1987), pp. 21–63.

73. Gall, *Liberalismus*, p. 177.

74. Kocka, 'Bürgertum und Bürgerlichkeit', p. 32.

75. J.S. Mill, *Subjection*, p. 295.

76. *Ibid.*, p. 324.

77. Cf. W.C. Krouse, 'Patriarchal Liberalism and Beyond. John Stuart Mill and Hariett Taylor', in J.B. Elshtain (ed.), *The Family in Political Thought* (Brighton, 1982) pp. 145–72.

III | THE MIDDLE CLASSES IN GERMANY AND FRANCE

10 | French Bourgeoisie and German Bürgertum, 1870–1914

Hartmut Kaelble

The social, cultural and political achievements of the French *bourgeoisie* made a profound impression on the Germans in the nineteenth century. In no other European country did the middle classes, at that time still modern and novel, appear to be so highly developed. The French *bourgeoisie* was seen as representing the future of the German *Bürgertum*, even if one regarded such a future with ambivalence or hostility. This aura of modernity surrounded the French *bourgeoisie* not just prior to the Franco-Prussian war, at a time when France was still culturally and economically ahead of Germany. Even at the end of the nineteenth century when Germany had surpassed France economically, the French *bourgeoisie* was still regarded in Germany as a model. Werner Sombart considered France to be 'the birthplace of modern social classes', including the *Bürgertum*. The only concept that he found to be untranslateable was, tellingly enough, the term *bourgeoisie* itself.[1] Modern historians still see France as having been more bourgeois than Germany at the time, and regard France as the 'classical bourgeois nation'.[2] Since the end of the Second Empire and the establishment of the bourgeois Third Republic no other European country has been so strongly regarded as a standard by which to measure the development of Germany, and especially the development of the German *Bürgertum*.

Was the French *bourgeoisie* really so different, and what was it that made it so different? Was it primarily a question of politics, of the greater political power of the French *bourgeoisie*, and consequently of the existence of a more bourgeois state? Or was it rather a question of social structure? Was the French *bourgeoisie* a more closed social class, not threatened so much by inner tensions, aristocratic attitudes and working class aspirations? Or was it more a question of culture, of the bourgeois lifestyle, for which Paris set the example for the rest of

Notes to Chapter 10 can be found on page 298.

Europe? Up to now there has been no reliable answer to this question, because historians have never really compared the French *bourgeoisie* with its highly developed bourgeois lifestyle and culture to the German *Bürgertum*.

In the following comparison of the French and German middle classes, I will not deal with every conceivable aspect of their social history. One of the main issues has been discussed extensively by the *Bürgertum*-Group of the ZiF Research Centre, and consequently reappears in several of the contributions in this book. This is the question of the deficiency of liberal *Bürgerlichkeit* in Germany and the socio-historical reasons underlying it. This question can easily be misunderstood, and must therefore be looked into in greater detail; as other contributions to this volume also make clear, the question is a meaningful one only in relation to other specific Western European countries. In the late nineteenth and early twentieth century these would primarily include France, Great Britain, the Netherlands and Switzerland. If the standard is the whole of Europe, then one cannot speak of a comparative lack of *Bürgerlichkeit* in Germany. Likewise, for certain regions of the Empire that were of lesser importance in the Reich than they are today in the Federal Republic (Baden-Württemberg, Bavaria, the Hanseatic cities and the regions on the left bank of the Rhine), this comparative lack of a liberal *Bürgertum* before 1914 was not characteristic.

This deficiency in bourgeois liberalism in the latter part of the nineteenth century was not the product of what, in comparison with the rest of Western Europe, must be regarded in general terms as a particularly German path of economic and social development. I will attempt to account for this deficiency by looking at some specific and limited differences in mentality and social structure that characterized the middle classes in France and Germany and the underdevelopment of liberalism. My principal goal in this contribution is to examine these differences in detail and, at the same time, to avoid some of the dead ends of the previous debate, for instance, the thesis of the feudalisation of the German *Bürgertum*.

This essay is written from a modern-day perspective, one in which the differences between French and German society have become much less significant. It will attempt to demonstrate that the disunity of Europe through the two world wars and the conflicts of the interwar period, were not simply a product of political miscalculations, but emerged against a background in which European societies – in our case France and Germany – were developing in profoundly divergent directions. An essential element in the social alienation that existed between France and Germany was the development of the French and German middle classes in different ways. I will not attempt to show how these divergent developments affected politics of the period, nor will I attempt to indicate how strongly present-day European societies ressemble each other. In this essay I will simply elucidate the fact of this divergent development.[3]

My primary interest here is the differences between French and German middle classes, so I will deal exclusively with what it was, in this respect, that made France different from Germany. Another basic limitation, of course, is the fact that this discussion only deals with the differences *within* the European middle class. This comparison is concerned with differences that are of a different character and of lesser significance than those that would be essential to a comparison of Europe with Japan, the United States, Poland or Russia. Our comparison, in other words, concerns different types within what is a unique European middle class: what is at stake is not the existence, or non-existence, of a middle class. This limitation is important inasmuch as the comparison takes for granted the basic common features of European middle classes. I do not deal with the common historical roots of the middle class and the *embourgeoisement* (*Verbürgerlichung*) of the industrialising European societies, with the profound changes in the nineteenth century middle classes resulting from professionalisation and big business; nor as I describe the way in which the middle class in each country related to the nobility, the state and the working class, or examine the role of the intellectuals in Europe. A survey of this kind would involve starting from scratch in previously largely unresearched territory, and thereby would involve far too much detail.

Unfortunately, for reasons of space, I will also have to refrain from going beyond a comparison of the two nations to look at the enormous amount of regional variety within each country. This would have been a very interesting undertaking, not only because of the uniqueness of Paris, but because of the similarities that would be found between the southern and western parts of Germany and the northern and eastern parts of France. Research in this area too is not so well advanced that we could summarise it in a few sentences.

In the late nineteenth and early twentieth century, the differences between the French and the German middle class were considerable. In no other epoch were they so different from one another. This is especially true with respect to the following four, closely-related, aspects: (1) The *Großbürgertum* in Germany still shared political power with the nobility and was therefore politically much weaker than the French *haute bourgeoisie*; (2) the *Bürgertum* was deeply divided among itself, while in France the *bourgeoisie* was a more strongly integrated and unified social class; (3) the intervention of the state in the world of the *Bürgertum* was much greater in Germany, causing a greater fragmentation of the middle class than existed in France; (4) the German *Bürgertum* was confronted with a different configuration of other social layers and classes than that faced by the *bourgeoisie*, causing it to be much less liberal than its French counterpart.

The Sharing of Power with the Nobility

The much greater political power of the nobility in Germany before the First World War was one of the first, the most obvious and best-known features that distinguished Germany from France, and made it particularly difficult for the people of the two countries to understand one another. Before 1914, there was not a single bourgeois chancellor, nor was there a clear majority of bourgeois ministers. The same was true for the largest state in the federation – Prussia, where the aristocracy played a particularly dominant role. These aristocrats were not simply straw men representing bourgeois interests. Behind the aristocratic political leaders in Germany stood a powerful bloc of interests: a solid, and for the conditions of the time, highly modern agrarian mass, the *Bund der Landwirte* (Agrarian League). This was largely controlled by the landed aristocracy and the influential conservative parties which the aristocracy dominated as well.[4] The constitution also was radically different from that of the French, with an Imperial Court that was more accessible to the aristocracy than to the *Bürgertum*. The Emperor intervened not only in military affairs, but in most of the central political decisions as well. The government of the Reich was largely dependent on him, and he had more influence on it than the predominantly bourgeois, but weak, Reichstag. The German aristocracy had the greatest amount of political influence that could be imagined within what was, in principle, a bourgeois society.

The German aristocracy also retained privileges for their sons which would have been unthinkable in France. It occupied, to a much greater extent than the French aristocracy, the highest positions in the army and administration. In both Prussia and in Saxony, all leading positions were held by the aristocracy. In Prussia in 1910, seven of the eleven ministers, eleven of the twelve *Oberpräsidenten* (senior officers of provinces), fifteen of the twenty-two chiefs of police and even the majority of the *Landräte* (regional officials) and *Oberamtmänner* (heads of districts) were from the nobility; in many cases, from the old nobility. The majority of generals in the Prussian-German army still came from the nobility. Even in the officer corps the *Bürgertum* were for a long time in the minority. As late as the 1890s, almost half of the officers were of noble blood. Although career demands made on state officials and officers were quite high, recruitment for the top positions was still restricted to men of aristocratic background. In fact, during the two decades before the First World War, there was even an increase in the proportion of nobles occupying these high positions.[5]

One should not exaggerate this picture. In time, the proportion of top jobs going to the nobility declined, partly through a growth in the administrative bureaucracy and partly through the massive expansion of the army before the First World War. It is certainly also true that even in Prussia there were areas where the *Bürgertum* was influential, for instance, in the ministries of trade and industry, in the navy and in the higher courts. The nobility limited itself to the highest political positions in the Empire, provinces, regions and districts, whereas the *Bürgertum* dominated at a second level where specialised knowledge was required. The southern area of the Reich, however, had greater similarities with France. In Bavaria, Württemberg, Baden and Hessen-Darmstadt the local nobility did not occupy leading positions in the administration on the same scale as they did in Prussia. The *Bürgertum* in the south had played a leading role for quite some time. In the territory of what is today the old Federal Republic – a fact that was important for later development – leading positions were not cut off from the *Bürgertum* by a nobility that insisted on its privileges.

Before the First World War, however, these were exceptions. The traditions, expectations and limitations brought by the nobility east of the Elbe, were dominant in German society before 1914. This was also clear to the French. 'German thinking', wrote one of France's most knowledgeable experts on Germany in 1907, 'has always attempted to reconcile itself as best as it could with the powers of the past...Instead of creating a logically integrated and harmonious state, it has continued to bow down to tradition, to prove its respect for monarchic authority, and has done everything possible not to offend traditional rights, nor to rush headlong into democracy'.[6]

The contrast between Germany and France became sharper in the years leading up to the First World War. After the establishment of the Third Republic in 1871 the French nobility lost most of the power that it had regained during the Bourbon reaction, under Louis Philippe, and during the Second Empire of Napoleon III. A royal court to which the nobility had privileged access no longer existed. After the new Constitution of 1875, hardly any of the government heads or ministers came from the nobility. Count MacMahon, elected state president in 1873 by an anti-republican majority, was the only prominant noble who was politically active in the Third Republic. He capitulated before the strengthening Republic, and resigned as President in 1879. Only at a regional level did the French nobility still possess some political influence. At the national level it was the *bourgeoisie* who were dominant. There was no French counterpart to the powerful Agrarian League.[7] The fall of Napolean III and the establishment of the Third Republic was undoubtedly an important turning point in the estrangement of both societies. What the *Bürgertum* lost with Bismarck's military victory over France and the foundation of the Reich, the French *bourgeoisie* won with the defeat of Napoleon III and the Constitution of 1875.

In France, there was nothing of the Prussian monopoly of privileges for the sons of the nobility. This was particularly the case in the army. During the Third Republic the proportion of generals who came from the nobility declined strongly. In 1879, 39 percent of the generals came from the nobility; by 1900 it was only 20 percent. The officers had been bourgeois for a long time, and in fact a significant number of them had petit-bourgeois backgrounds.[8] At the turn of the century the French nobility played a much less significant role in the upper echelons of administration than was the case in Prussia. During the course of the nineteenth century anonymous competitions, in the form of the *concours*, gradually became the predominant means of recruitment. By the 1880s the powerful bourgeois families who, until the Second Empire, had exercised strong control over access to jobs in the administration was no longer effective. The French nobility also had to submit themselves to this form of competition.

However, the percentage of aristocrats in top administrative positions in France was certainly higher at the turn of the century than it is today. There were still some aristocratic preserves, particularly in the foreign and diplomatic service, where the *concours* established itself rather late (1880), as well as in the war ministry and in the ministry for the navy. It is also important to note that with respect to those leading positions that were not visible within the public sphere, such as permanent secretaries or advisory councils, the proportion of nobles in France was essentially similar to the proportion in Prussia. During the Second Empire, 24 percent of the permanent secretaries came from the nobility, a proportion which fell during the Third Republic.

A real contrast existed between both countries with respect to those leading administrative positions involving many public/social responsibilities, and which were 'cleansed' with each incoming regime. Before the founding of the Republic, almost half of the prefects in France came from the nobility; by the eve of the First World War it was only one in ten; the public face, not just of the army but also of the administration of the French Republic, took the form of a bourgeois official. The Prussian army and the Prussian administration, however, not only offered a more influential political role and greater benefits to the nobility, but it was also mainly through the nobility that the army and administration were represented in the public sphere.[9]

There was nothing, on the eve of the First World War, which indicated that the drastic differences in power that characterised the *Großbürgertum* and *haute bourgeoisie* would level out in the forseeable future. There were very few indications that the *Bürgertum* would protest against the division of power with the nobility, or that they would attempt to take the whole of political power for themselves. With the exception of a small left-liberal minority, the *Bürgertum* appeared to accept the status quo in the division of power. It was a situation that guaranteed freedom of entrepreneurial action, secured economic growth and also guaranteed Germany's position in the world. At any rate, these things were not threatened by the delegation of power. Most members of the *Großbürgertum* not only passively accepted this division of power with the aristocracy, they also supported it through their representatives in the Reichstag and through their political alliance with the big estate owners. This political alliance had important political consequences. It guaranteed internal support for Germany's world policies, for the mobilisation against France and England, and later for the war aims of 1914. It contributed to the division within German liberalism, and protected the Reich government from the participation of the largest of the German political parties at the time, the Social Democrats. It also helped to prevent a loosening of the age-old property qualification for elections in Prussia, and ensured that the Reichstag continued to exercise little influence on the government. There were undoubtedly severe crises and conflicts of interest within the alliance between big industry and landed aristocracy at the beginning of the 1890s. These problems continued in the years after 1905 and once again just before the First World War, but all the same, the alliance never collapsed.[10]

This acceptance of the great political influence of the nobility and of its strong presence in the public sphere had a lot to do with the profound crisis of German liberalism after the 1870s. This crisis was further intensified by the conditions particular to Germany in which the nobility had rejected liberalism even before the Empire. This type of profound crisis of liberalism did not exist in France before the First World War. The 1870s were also a turning point in France, but in direct contrast to Germany, this was the period in which the liberals rose to power and the monarchist currents were excluded.

There were a number of different reasons for these contrasting developments which need to be examined in greater detail, but which I cannot go into here. Among these reasons were: the French Revolution as a historical point of departure; the greater ability of the French liberals and republicans to present themselves as representatives of national interests; the opportunity, which did not exist in Germany, for the liberals to mobilise against the Catholic Church; the slower pace of economic and social development in France, which did not create for the professional groups, officials and professors the kind of identity crisis in which the German academics and professionals, the *Bildungsbürgertum*, in Germany found themselves after the 1870s.[11]

The Lower Level of Social Integration of the German Bürgertum

According to post-war historians, social developments in the German *Bürgertum* played an important role in bringing about the alliance of the *Großbürgertum* with the landed aristocracy. The 'feudalisation' of the *Großbürgertum* is seen as having played a key role. I would now like to look in some detail at this socio-historical explanation of the division of power in the Empire.

The 'feudalisation' of the *Bürgertum* describes its purported acceptance of the values and lifestyle of the nobility, rejection of bourgeois attitudes, and the complete fusion of the upper layer of the economic bourgeoisie with the landed aristocracy in a 'feudal-capitalistic' elite. A variety of historical works have been devoted to detailed and extensive examination of this phenomenon. S.ome of them have attempted to show an increasing integration of the *Großbürgertum* and the nobility as a result of bourgeois marriages into aristocratic families. Integration also occurred via the entrance of sons of the *Großbürgertum* into prestigous careers in what were still considered to be aristocratic fields (officers, landowners, diplomats) and also through social contact with the nobility at parties and receptions.

This concept of feudalisation also implied a submission by the *Bürgertum* to a non-bourgeois social hierarchy. This manifested itself through the demonstrative granting of reserve officer commissions to bourgeois figures, the bourgeois desire for ennoblement and aristocratic orders and titles instead of (as had been the case among the *Bürgertum* before the foundation of the Empire) specifically bourgeois honorary positions such as honorary citizen of a town, or honorary doctorate from a university. Other historians have seen feudalisation as a bourgeois imitation of the lifestyles of the aristocracy: the construction of castle-like villas instead of solid bourgeois homes; the purchase of estates; the entrance of bourgeois sons into the aristocratic student corps instead of into the bourgeois *Landsmannschaften* or *Burschenschaften*; the education of bourgeois daughters in elegant finishing schools instead of in regular schools together with other middle-class girls; an expensive imitative lifestyle far removed from the traditional bourgeois values of thrift and solidity.

Historians saw in the tendency towards feudalisation of the *Großbürgertum* not just a general decline of the bourgeois way of life common to most of Europe, but above all they saw this as laying the social foundations for the later political alliance with the landed aristocracy which was to have such momentous consequences. They saw France as the historical counter-example; a bourgeois society that had not adapted itself to the nobility, remained liberal and still risen to full political power.[12]

Recent studies have shown with increasing frequency that this contrast between *bourgeoisie* and *Bürgertum* has long been overstated. On the one hand we have a *Bürgertum* that had only partially ascended the rungs to political power, had collaborated politically with the aristocracy and that was to some extent excluded from top positions in the army and administration. On the other hand we have a *bourgeoisie* that was liberal, had superceded the aristocracy and had full political power in its country. What has been misunderstood, however, was the social background to this phenomenon. Recent studies show that there is very little evidence for a predominant social feudalisation of the German *Bürgertum*, regardless of whether this is seen as a fusion of the economic bourgeoisie and the aristocracy in a feudal-capitalistic elite, or as a submission of the *Bürgertum* to an aristocratic system of social values.

Especially important here are the very rich, the multi-millionaires among the German bourgeoisie, because they were the ones who could best afford to create an aristocratic way of life for themselves. Research on the period before the First World War shows that few of these rich big businessmen married into the aristocracy. This was the case despite the fact that the majority of these multi-millionaires had grown up in millionaire families, and thus would have been attractive marriage partners for the aristocracy when at a marriageable age. Also, the daughters of these few hundred very rich bourgeois families married into the aristocracy to a much lesser extent than has been assumed up to now. Only about one in five of these daughters married into the nobility, and these were often only recently ennobled families, not the old nobility. It also seems that the aristocracy were not inclined to marry into bourgeois circles. The marriage markets of both bourgeoisie and nobility, therefore, tended not to intersect.

The career choices of the sons of these bourgeois multi-millionaires are especially indicative of how little influence the aristocratic model had on bourgeois society. Very few of them, only around one in ten, chose careers that would have been regarded as aristocratic at the time – landowner, officer or diplomat. The vast majority of them followed the bourgeois model and became entrepeneurs as well. If they did not inherit their father's business, they established their own. When they did not become entrepeneurs, they generally chose some other typically bourgeois career, especially in the liberal professions. These liberal professions were chosen with the same frequency as were the more aristocratic ones.[13] Thus contrast with the French *bourgeoisie* is not to be found, as has generally been assumed up to now, in the submission of the German *Bürgertum* to aristocratic norms, nor in the fusion of the big-business families with the nobility.

This does not mean, of course, that the political cooperation of big industry and big landowners came about without any kind of social background. The second essential difference between the French and German middle classes was much more important: the more distinct social isolation of the German businessman within bourgeois society, less in relation to the liberal professions, the doctors, lawyers and architects, than from the professions close to the state – government officials, judges, professors and church officials, and even teachers. This social isolation meant that not only the social links, but also the political solidarity of the German economic bourgeoisie with other sections of bourgeois society never developed as strongly as it did in France. The *Bürgertum* as a whole was not as closed and integrated a social class as was its French counterpart. It was a more divided and fragmented class. Unlike in France, there were no strong social links that might have stood in the way of the political cooperation of the upper layer of the German bourgeoisie with the landed aristocracy.

There was certainly a tendency in Germany, before 1914, towards greater unity and integration of the *Bürgertum*. Traditional educational advantages among highly qualified officials, the liberal professions, teachers in university and higher education were reduced. Business entrepreneurs gained more education. A growing proportion of entrepreneurs had some form of higher education. This was especially true of managers, the majority of whom, before 1914, had graduated from university or an institute of technology. Of even greater significance was the fact that families of entrepeneurs were becoming much more closely integrated with the families of higher civil servants, academics and professionals (*Bildungsbürgertum*). In 1864, only one in twenty-five professors came from a business family, in 1910 it was as many as one in ten. Among top officials in Westphalia during the first three decades of the nineteenth century, only one in thirty came from a business family. At the turn of the century, this proportion had risen to one in five. Depending on the region, between one in three and one in five higher officials and about one in five judges (for example in Saxony) had a similar background. The sons of businessmen in Rhineland and Westphalia increasingly tended to marry into families of officials or families involved in the liberal professions. The dividing line between *Bildungsbügertum* and businessmen at the turn of the century was no longer as strongly drawn as it had been during the first half of the nineteenth century.[14]

In contrast to France, however, the dividing line between the entrepreneurial bourgeoisie and the rest of bourgeois society at the turn of the century was still a firm one. Even at the school and university level, the *Bürgertum* in Germany was much less closed than the French *bourgeoisie*. Especially after the turn of the century the children of businessmen followed an educational path that was different from that pursued by the children of higher officials, doctors, lawyers, pastors, teachers and professors. Businessmen's sons attended the *Realoberschulen* and *Realgymnasien*, and after that the technological institutes (*technische Universitäten*). By contrast, the children of the *Bildungsbürgertum* went to the *Gymnasien*, and afterwards, in many cases, to the philosophical and law faculties of the universities. In France the sons of the *bourgeoisie* tended to intermingle in the same educational institutions. As they tended to go to the *lycée* and then afterwards to the same *grandes écoles*, they were much less separated from one another than they were in Germany.[15] The higher degree of specialisation found in German higher education tended to reinforce these differences.

The difference between the French and German middle classes was further intensified by the one-sidedness of the integration that took place in the German *Bürgertum*. The sons of businessmen may have joined the world of academics and professionals, but the businessmen still remained isolated in German society. There was no reverse movement of the academics and professionals into the world of business. At the turn of the century, only one in ten of the big entrepreneurs came from academic or professional families. This was a similar proportion to what had existed at the beginning of the nineteenth century. On the other hand, in France in 1912 one in every four entrepreneurs came from families of high officials or professionals. The internal integration of the French *bourgeoisie* was, in this respect, much stronger.

It is possible that in Germany there were stronger barriers to marriages across social groups within the *Bürgertum*. Not only the daughters of the business multi-millionaires, for whom a doctor, lawyer or high official might not have been such a good match, but also the daughters of the remaining big business families seldom married into the liberal professions. In Germany in 1914, the business and liberal professions did not live in entirely separate worlds but nonetheless, compared to France, there still existed strong barriers between them. A united middle class did not exist in Germany to the extent that it did in France.[16]

It seems that there are a number of different reasons for this heterogeneity within the *Bürgertum*. One of them had to do with tradition. Much more so than in France, it seems that the top officials and the educated elite were cut off from the values and hierarchy created by industrialisation. They were sceptical of, if not hostile to, the emerging industrial society as well as the profit and growth mentality of the employers, the industrial cities, and the new social hierarchies in which income and economic achievement counted for more than education.

This old bourgeois elite from the period before the industrial revolution lost a lot of social prestige and respect in the new social hierarchy. It also saw industrialisation as bringing about a crisis in its own economic position. A large proportion of the *Bildungsbürgertum*, as a result of the anxiety brought on by this crisis and out of an unwillingness to adapt to it, reacted to industrialisation by cutting themselves off from it, by refusing to change the curriculum in the upper schools and in the universities, by hanging on stubbornly to the classical education on which their own prestige had been built, by demonstrating a social contempt for entrepreneurial values and conceptions, by rejecting modernity and by guiding the career choices of their sons and the marriage choices of their daughters away from the world of business.[17] This exclusion of the economic bourgeoisie by the educated and professional elite in Germany was something remarked upon by French observers of the day. In 1908, Henri Lichtenberger, a professor at the Sorbonne, wrote about his travels in Germany:

> In place of the old hereditary and cultural nobility there is emerging a new entrepreneurial aristocracy that weighs merit and status in terms of business know-how and success. Of course, the ultimate consequences of this still lie in the future, and in the midst of this modern society old social groups continue to exist on the same terms as they always have. Thus the *bourgeoisie* involved in the liberal professions – the intellectuals, the professors, the officials and officers – all remain untouched by this entrepreneurial spirit.[18]

Conversely, German observers remarked on the higher level of closure of French bourgeois society and on the fact that the French educated elite had fewer reservations to relating to the bourgeois economy. The economist Werner Sombart stated that 'the intellectuals in Germany are much more alienated from the bourgeoisie than is the case elsewhere'.[19] One German who was quite knowledgeable about society on the other side of the Rhine at the time wrote: 'In France education and property are more in accord than they are here'.[20]

This closer relationship between academics and entrepreneurs in France had a second, more traditional, basis: the established layer of civic dignitaries, or *notables*, was much more developed in France than in Germany. During the long transition period between the ancien régime and modern capitalist society these *notables* constituted the upper crust especially in the provinces, outside of the big cities, in the countryside and in the small towns. This layer of notables was made up of a number of different social groups – the landed nobility, the earlier entrepreneurs, doctors, lawyers and bourgeois landowners – and characterised by the ownership of property, careers exercised within and limited to the region, and specialised knowledge. Its dominant political influence rested partly on property qualifications necessary for election and partly on the social acceptance, characteristic of a traditional society, of an elite's claim to leadership and power.

This layer of notables, which began to lose its influence in France during the Third Republic but which retained it in many places until the interwar period, was not a modern bourgeoisie, as its dynamic core was not made up of entrepreneurs. The values of the notables were more traditional, and depended more on income from the property they already owned than from entrepreneurial expansion. At the same time, they were not an elite of the ancien régime with ties to feudal rights. They were certainly not promoters of liberal, or even less likely, republican ideas. However, what is decisive in this context is the fact that, from the early nineteenth century, the economic bourgeoisie, academics and landowners were socially integrated within this layer of notables and carried out common political actions. At the same time in important regions of Germany, businessmen, officials and landowners were in sharply divided social groups. The closer integration of the French *bourgeoisie*, therefore, had its background in the strong internal integration of the *notables*.[21]

The greater isolation of the economic bourgeoisie in Germany was further intensified by a very modern development – the emergence of big business. The classical entrepreneur of the industrial revolution in the 1850s and 1860s was, from the point of view of his economic power, still completely rooted in urban bourgeois society. He employed at most a few thousand workers. It was generally a local enterprise with strong links to the town, and its management was a relatively simple matter. The wealth of these entrepreneurs may have been impressive within the confines of their town, but it was not impressive on a national scale. They came from, married within and were still solidly integrated into local bourgeois society. There were museums and the voluntary associations (*Vereine*) where they met with the other members of the urban *Bürgertum* and *Kleinbürgertum*, and with whom they were often active in local political administration.

One cannot overemphasise the extent to which the new *Großunternehmer* (great entrepreneurs) who emerged in the 1880s differed from the traditional entrepreneurs of the industrial revolution. The *Großunternehmer* owned enterprises with many thousands of workers who, along with their dependents, formed a population greater than most German towns. These big businesses were often spread over a number of different places. Thus, their owners were seldom integrated into any local urban society. The task of directing such enterprises was a complex one and not immediately comprehensible to the rest of the *Bürgertum*. From the point of view of their wealth and power, these big businesses now had little in common with the urban liberal professions, or with local officials and teachers. They stood far above them, and belonged to the richest and economically most powerful section of German society.

These *Großunternehmer* constituted a majority of German multimillionaires before the First World War. The growing economic distance between them and the rest of the German *Bürgertum* had the effect of dissolving traditional social ties, disrupting traditional patterns of marriage and career choice and ending once close social contacts. The big industrialists, and later their children, gradually began to develop their own lifestyle which further alienated them from the rest of the *Bürgertum*. Their luxurious castle-like villas, their sumptuous receptions and soirées served to widen their differences with the traditional *Bürgertum*. To interpret this as simply an imitation of the lifestyle of the nobility is to draw, in many cases, a premature conclusion. Frequently the eclectic approach of the new bourgeois elite caused it to distance itself from the nobility as much as it did from the rest of the *Bürgertum*. The same phenomenon existed, no doubt, in France. It seems, however, that in Germany this layer of industrialists expanded more rapidly and on a different scale than it did in France before the First World War. The economic factors that loosened the ties between this new elite and the academics and professionals also appeared to be stronger in Germany.

At first sight, this argument about stronger internal divisions within the *Bürgertum* may sound surprising. The French *bourgeoisie* has always been regarded as having been strongly divided, although in ways that at first glance appear not to have existed in Germany: the division manifested itself between the *bourgeoisie* in Paris and in the provinces and between the Catholic and the lay *bourgeoisie*. In Germany, however, in addition to the completely different type of divisions that separated the economic bourgeoisie from the *Bildungsbürgertum*, there also existed strong religious and social divisions. For example between the Protestant and the Jewish (about which there have recently been some interesting studies) and between Protestant and Catholic sections of the *Bürgertum* (still largely unstudied). There were also strong regional differences, for instance, between Ruhr magnates, Hanseatic merchants and Saxon industrialists, which made it impossible to establish a common organisation to represent their interests in Germany before 1914. There was also the growing prestige of Berlin bankers, university professors, top officials, painters and writers that intensified the differences between the urban capital and the provinces.

These lines of division were often more complex than the simple contrasts that existed in France, but they created divisions in the German *Bürgertum* that went beyond the split between the industrial bourgeoisie and the *Bildungsbürgertum*. These divisions were not so strong that they might call the existence of a bourgeois social class in Germany into question. However, they do indicate that at the turn of the century the middle class in Germany was less unified than it was in France.[22]

The Fragmentation of the Bürgertum by the State

An additional reason for the *Bürgertum* being less well-integrated as a social class than the French *bourgeoisie* was state intervention in bourgeois society, especially in the career world, guiding and regulating the bourgeois social hierarchy. Although the state was not always successful in exercising this control, it did succeed in fragmenting the German middle class to an extent unseen in France.

This regulation by the German state of the bourgeois professions was something that would have been inconceivable in France. This was particularly clear before 1914 in the case of lawyers. Lawyers in Germany were supervised very closely by the state in their professional activities, especially after the law of 1879 that regulated the legal professions. Examinations were administered by a state examinations commission, not by a commission of lawyers or university teachers. They received their training as state *Referendare* (administrative trainees), not in the offices of legal firms. Admission to the profession was decided by administrators from the Ministry of Justice, not by a body of professional colleagues. Their practice was supervised by a disciplinary committee made up of lawyers, but only the state prosecuter had the right to indict someone before this committee. This preliminary investigation had to be carried out by a state judge and appeals could only be made to a state court. Lawyers in Prussia, if they were notaries at the same time, had the same status as an official, and in the occupational census they were simply counted as officials. The legal profession throughout Germany was not really a liberal one.

At the turn of the century, there was only limited opposition among German lawyers to this control by the state. It must be noted that this arrangement also gave certain advantages to lawyers. It protected them from competition, guaranteed them a secure income and gave them a higher degree of social prestige. The regulations of 1879 also gave Prussian lawyers a certain amount of freedom from what had previously been an even more rigid form of state control. In any case, state control over lawyers at the turn of the century meant that their professional activities were determined by regulations that were not common to, and therefore served to divide them from, the rest of the *Bürgertum*.[23]

On a lesser scale, state control also existed in the case of the German medical profession. State control over doctors began to decline strongly after the 1860s, but increased again towards the end of the century. Once again, the majority of the doctors supported this development, and it was also defended by the medical associations. Doctors took their medical examinations from a state commission, not from a collegiate or university body as well. Admission to the profession was decided by state officials, not by any body of professional colleagues. Their practice was supervised by a state disciplinary committee organised in officially recognised professional associations. State control may have been weaker here than in the case of the legal profession, but it too protected doctors from competition, assured them a secure income and gave greater prestige to the profession. As in the case of lawyers, the fact that the profession was regulated by special rules which set doctors apart from both officials and entrepreneurs, created yet another division within bourgeois society.[24]

The sharpest contrast to Germany in continental Europe was provided not by France but by Switzerland, where the state intervened in bourgeois society on a much smaller scale, and where free competition was therefore much more deeply rooted as a principle of professional activity and as a common bourgeois ideology than in Germany.[25] There were also significant differences with respect to how professional activities were organised in France. The greatest contrast was to be seen in the legal profession. Lawyers in France at the turn of the century had much greater independence from the state than did their German counterparts. Examinations were the responsibility of the university, not of state commissions. Training was conducted through an internship (*stage*) in legal firms and organised by law societies or other professional bodies, not by the state. Admission to the profession was decided by a professional collegium, and the disciplinary committee that supervised legal practices was made up of professional colleagues. Only in extreme cases were lawyers indicted before a state court as in cases of expulsion from the profession. Nowhere on the Continent were lawyers more autonomous than in France. In spite of repeated attempts by the French state to exercise greater control over the legal profession, the independence of lawyers, which had existed since the time of Louis Philippe and had strong roots in pre-revolutionary tradition, was successfully preserved during the years before the First World War.[26]

Around 1910, the differences between France and Germany with respect to the medical profession were not so sharp, but they were still significant. Doctors in France were also regulated by the state to a much lesser extent. Training, admission to the profession and medical practice were regulated largely by the medical profession itself. Examinations were a matter for university bodies and admission to the profession was controlled by professional committees in which the state played almost no role. The medical profession in France was to a very large extent autonomous.[27]

In general, the professions in France were much more independent and much less controlled by the state then they were in Germany. Professional training, admission to the various professions and controls over professional practice were largely a matter for the professionals themselves. The Revolution of 1789 abolished all professional organisations, especially the organisation of lawyers, one of the oldest and most developed of the liberal professions, and imposed the principles of the free market, without any control over entrance into the professions or the quality of practice. However under Louis Philippe the lawyers succeeded in establishing powerful professional organisations and thereby re-established the link with the pre-revolutionary period. The lawyer's organisation was the vanguard for the other liberal professions. In sharp contrast to Germany, what remained in France as a legacy of the French Revolution was the French *bourgeoisie*'s rejection of any form of state control. Unlike the Germans, they both defended and wanted to defend the liberal professions against the state. This achievement of autonomy for the professions was a foundation on which a common bourgeois consciousness could develop in France. As this was absent in Germany, what remained was how best to achieve a laborious compromise among the various professional groups.

The German state intervened not only in the professions but also in the bourgeois social hierarchy. This added to the fragmentation of the *Bürgertum* as a social class. The German monarchic state, by means of a policy of complicated decorations and titles, attempted to structure German society and create a number of fine distinctions that would go beyond those differences resulting from wealth and income. A certain role was played here by the practice of ennoblement of bourgeois figures, but this was neither a common practice in Germany, nor did it create an important layer of *Amtsadel* (nobility conferred by office) or *Briefadel* (nobility conferred by letters patent) as was the case in France during the Napoleonic era, during the rule of Louis Philippe and at the time of the Second Empire.

Of much greater importance in Germany was the system of *Ratstitel* (title of honorific counsellor). This title carried with it the right of access to the court. After 1848 and during the 1860s this became a way of exercising political control. It not only promoted a state-selected bourgeois elite, but it also created real divisions within the *Bürgertum*. Every bourgeois profession had its own access to titles: for doctors it was the *Medizinalrat*, for entrepreneurs it was the *Kommerzienrat*, for lawyers it was the *Justizrat*, each of which was conferred by a different ministry.

In addition to this, the German state developed a complex system of honours. Apart from the honorary posts granted by the urban government and the honorary titles granted by the universities, there was also a complex system of political decorations. Prussia alone had four different medals of merit, each of which was further divided into different classes: the Red Eagle, the Black Eagle, the Crown and the Hohenzollern. The other states in the Empire followed the Prussian example. Saxony had three ranks: the Albrecht, the Heinrich and the Medal of Merit. Within all those ranks there was a complex hierarchy. Some were only given to certain types of people. For instance, the Prussian Medal of the Black Eagle was only given to officials and military officers and was linked with ennoblement. The Saxon Medal of Heinrich was only granted to officers. In Prussia, if not elsewhere, the system of commissions in the officer reserve was an important element in the bourgeois social hierarchy.

Altogether, the German state succeeded in covering up economic differences with a complex network of slight differences from state to state. In German public life these state-created social differences often played a more important role than economic achievements or wealth. A contemporary French observer was struck by this phenomenon: 'The love of titles', wrote Jules Laforge, who served for five years as a French reader for the then Empress, 'is one of the characteristic traits of the Germans that is best known in France...The Prussian order of ranks has forty-three categories (a parliamentary representative stands at number forty, behind a low-ranking court officer)'.[28]

In France on the other hand, the system of state decorations and titles was much simpler and did not weaken the unity of the *bourgeoisie* as a social class to the same extent. Ennoblement no longer existed in the Third Republic. Commissions in France were not highly regarded enough to define slight gradations in social distinction. The title of counsellor which divided the middle class into various professional groups, did not exist either. There was just one decoration, the *Legion d'honneur* of which there were five classes. This decoration was, in principle, available to all members of society and was not a divisive element within the *bourgeoisie*.

On the other hand, positions determined by public elections such as town mayor or parliamentary representative, were considered much more important in France than they were in Germany. Such publicly elected officials occupied a leading position in the towns and districts of France. As in Germany, it was not economic achievement and wealth alone that created social differences. It was the distinctions that were a product of positions over which the bourgeois had political influence and decorations that were bourgeois–republican in nature. Honorary positions and decorations in France therefore tended to strengthen the class unity of the French *bourgeoisie*, and did not fragment it as did the decorations, ranks and titles of the *Bürgertum*.

Other Social Structures and Conflicts

Bourgeois mentalities and values at the turn of the century developed differently in Germany and in France because the *Bürgertum* and *bourgeoisie* had differing social structures and were confronted by different social conflicts. The contrasts between them in a European context were much sharper at that time than they had been in 1850 and were a great deal sharper than they are today. They were also much more pronounced than they were between any other European countries at a similar level of economic development. Two features of German society were particularly significant: the weakness of the economically independent petty *bourgeoisie*, and the greater concentration of industrial workers and the impressive organisational strength of the labour movement. Both of those factors explain why the bourgeois model had little attraction, and why bourgeois culture was strongly resisted by both the nobility and the working class in Germany.

The *Großbürgertum* was confronted by a social structure which relegated it to a much more unstable and uncertain social situation than was the case in France. One of the main reasons for this was the fact that the economically independent petty bourgeoisie and the independent farmers in Germany constituted much smaller social strata than they did in France. Only every fourth or fifth economically active person in Germany, in other words a small minority, belonged to these social strata. In France, on the other hand, these strata made up almost half of the economically active population. It is important that in Germany not only the independent farmers but also the trading and commercial petty bourgeoisie of the urban centres who were close to the *Bürgertum* proper (the master craftsmen, the merchants, the landlords and carriers) were numerically much weaker than in France. The main reason for this was that the social stratum of the petty bourgeoisie did not grow at the same rate as the population in general. Their absolute numbers did not decline, but they lost much of their social weight. In France, however, where there was a much slower and more even rate of population growth, the petty bourgeoisie retained their social status.

Of course, only a part of the stratum which the statistical office described as independent really lived an economically secure life. A significant proportion of them, for several different reasons, led a life that was not at all different from that of the workers. Even with this limitation, about which it is difficult to be statistically precise, the fact remains that a significantly smaller number of people in Germany earned their living through independent economic activity. The influence of the mentality and social conventions that are associated with economic independence was therefore much weaker in Germany. The industrial bourgeoisie in Germany did not have the same reassuring safety cushion as the French in the form of a broad stratum of an independent petty bourgeoisie to rely upon.[29]

At the same time, the industrial bourgeoisie in Germany was confronted by a much larger working class than existed in France. Whereas in France only about one third of the economically active population were considered workers, in Germany it was more than half. In both France and Germany a significant number of labourers worked on the land, in urban domestic situations, in small enterprises, in trade and in personal service. It would have been difficult to mobilise these labourers for the workers' parties. Less than half of the German labourers worked in industrial enterprises. In spite of this, the number of industrial workers in Germany at the turn of the century was much greater than in France, and industry played a larger role in

German society. Purely industrial working-class cities like Ludwig-shafen, Gelsenkirchen or Kattowitz were more common in Germany than in France.[30] The gap between the bourgeoisie and the workers was not bridged or lessened by rapidly growing strata of white collar workers and civil servants. There is no evidence to indicate that either the numbers or the rates of growth of these new strata were bigger or more rapid in Germany than in France at the turn of the century.

The industrial bourgeoisie in Germany, partly because of this differ-ent class structure, was confronted with greater – even if not particu-larly more radical – social conflict without having, at the same time, secure political allies. On the eve of the First World War, the socialist trade union movement in Germany had two and a half million mem-bers. One in every six wage earners was a member of this powerful, strongly centralised, and efficient labour organisation. Although not politically radical, it was one of the most effective working class organisations in Europe.

The number of trade union members in France in 1910 is estimated at about one million (the socialist CGT had less than half a million). Less than one in ten workers were organised in trade unions. A simi-lar situation existed with respect to the socialist parties. On the eve of the First World War the verbally radical and strongly centralised German SPD was able to mobilise over four million voters. For Europe at that time this was a very high level of electoral support, and was something which seriously worried the German bourgeoisie. The French SFIO was a much looser alliance of various political currents and before the war was able to win at most one and a half million votes. Thus the German bourgeoisie faced a much more strongly organised opposition than did their French counterparts.

This does not mean that social conflict in France was less severe than it was in Germany. At the height of the wave of strikes that affected both France and Germany before the First World War, and which grew to previously unknown proportions, both countries had as many as half a million workers on strike. Both countries lost an average of of eight million working days per year. Since there were fewer industrial workers in France, this means that level of opposition among French workers was probably higher than in Germany. Repressive measures, the intervention of the police and army, were more widely used by the bourgeois French government than by the German. The German government never had to confront an event on the scale of the Paris Commune, when the French government had to use the military to regain control of the capital.[31]

What really distinguished the situation in the two countries at the turn of the century was the much more solid and thereby threatening organisation of the bourgeoisie's opponents in Germany. It made the German bourgeoisie more inclined to seek out state intervention. It also forced them into more rigid employers' organisations in which individual employers had very little independence. The French bourgeoisie were more successful in resisting this tendency in the pre-1914 era.

The liberal and republican wings of the industrial bourgeoisie in France also had a great level of political support among other social strata. In spite of a number of economic crises, the French petty bourgeoisie maintained its attachment to republican political culture. French white-collar workers were also more liberal. In France before 1914 there was no organisation with a political orientation and weight comparable to that of the *Deutschnationaler Handlungsgehilfenverband* (German National Association of Clerks). Therefore, bourgeois liberalism had more political support in France not only among the industrial bourgeoisie, but also among the middle strata of society.[32]

Conclusion

A socio-historical comparison of France and Germany can only give a partial answer to the question posed by the ZiF Research Group and by this paper, as to whether there was a deficiency of *Bürgerlichkeit* in Germany during the period of the Empire and if so, why this was the case. The comparison with France is essential in dealing with this question.

During the four decades before the First World War there was an undisputed contrast between the stable, liberal French Republic which was able to keep the emerging monarchist, conservative or clerical opposition under control, and the conservative, authoritarian German monarchy in which liberal movements had their place, but did not enjoy power. Of course, this contrast is not simply a product of social differences between the *bourgeoisie* and the *Bürgertum*. Other differences which have been barely touched upon, were also important: the French Revolution as an anchor for liberal movements in France, for which the 1848 Revolution in Germany was only a poor substitute; the earlier establishment of a nation-state in France, and the fact that the German nation-state not only emerged later but was also created by a conservative statesman and thus cannot be viewed as an achievement of German liberalism; the identification of the French army with the liberal Republic. This identity was disturbed although not destroyed by the Dreyfus Affair.

Further differences include: the Catholic Church, against which French bourgeois liberalism was able to mobilise effectively until the end of the nineteenth century, and for which there existed no functional parallel in Germany; the greater importance of intellectuals in French politics and public life, a fact advantageous to French liberalism before 1914; the slower pace of demographic change in France which saved them from some illiberal interventions by the state and gave bourgeois liberalism greater scope for action.

By European standards, the differences between France and Germany were much greater at the turn of the century than they had been earlier in the nineteenth century, and also wider than they were later in the twentieth century. The principal difference resided in the fact that the French *bourgeoisie* had sole political power and controlled all the top positions in politics, administration and in the army. The *Bürgertum*, however, shared power with the nobility and had to accept a system that accorded the sons of the nobility with leading positions in the administration and the army. Only in the universities, in the administration of justice, in local administration and in the governments of the southern German states was the *Bürgertum* able to establish a leading position for itself. This difference was intensified by the fact that the *Bürgertum* cemented the power-sharing arrangement by means of a political alliance with the landed nobility east of the Elbe. The 1870s were years of profound crisis for German liberalism, whereas this same decade saw a strengthening of the liberals and republicans in France.

A second essential difference had to do with the closer social integration and greater social unity of the *bourgeoisie* at a time when the *Bürgertum*'s social relations and lifestyles were splintering off in different directions. A profound split existed in Germany between the economic bourgeoisie and the *Bildungsbürgertum* which weakened the *Bürgertum* as a social class in relation to the nobility, and removed any inhibitions that the *Großbürgertum* might have had about an alliance with the big landowners. It was a division caused partly by the threat that industrialisation represented for the old official and educated elite, and partly by the the absence in German of a layer of traditional *notables*. It had to do with the very rapid economic rise of big business in Germany and the economic distance that separated this upper stratum of big businessmen from the rest of the *Bürgertum*. Another major factor in the fragmentation of the *Bürgertum* was state intervention in the different bourgeois professions and social hierarchies.

Finally, the industrial bourgeoisie in France at the turn of the century had a firm base of support in a broad social stratum that was socially close to it – the self-sufficient and mostly republican layer of the petty bourgeoisie. The bourgeoisie in Germany by contrast, was socially confronted by an industrial proletariat that was not only numerically superior but also better organised and more verbally aggressive than they were. Bourgeois values and lifestyles had a greater force of attraction in France than in Germany, where they were wedged in and restricted by a politically stronger aristocratic culture and by a very highly developed working-class culture.

These differences should not be exaggerated. The French *bourgeoisie* and the German *Bürgertum* were simply different types within the broad spectrum of European middle classes. The differences between them were not as profound as those between, say, Europe and Japan, or between Russia and the United States. It is difficult and perhaps futile to speculate about which of the two variants was the more modern. The French *bourgeoisie* might appear to be more modern because it ended the system of power-sharing with the aristocracy, was a more closed class, and because around 1910 the liberal professions had a more modern understanding of themselves as independent self-organising professions. On the other hand, the German *Bürgertum* had some claims to greater modernity. There was a much earlier decline of family businesses and an earlier emergence of modern large enterprises; career specialisation especially between public administration and the economy was more advanced in Germany as well. Social reforms carried out by the German state and local authorities were more developed and had been accepted much earlier; organisations representing bourgeois interests were more numerous, differentiated and effective. In a number of areas it is difficult to find any significant differences between French and German bourgeois society, for instance in the area of attitudes toward social conflict, the use of the police and the army against social protest and the attitude to free-market competition.

The conclusion remains that at the turn of the century, the middle classes in France and Germany were developing, within the European framework, in different directions. The most important differences were the strength of bourgeois liberalism in France, the greater support there for a fully developed parliamentary system, greater opposition to state intervention and control, more tolerance, greater resistance to anti-semitism and the greater political effectiveness of intellectuals.

Notes to Chapter 10

1. W. Sombart, *Die Deutsche Volkswirtschaft im 19. und im Anfang des 20. Jahrhunderts* (Berlin, 1919), p. 440.

2. H.A. Winkler, 'Bürgertum', in *Sowjetsystem und Demokratische Gesellschaft*, vol. 1 (Freiburg, 1966), p. 949.

3. This article is part of a larger project supported by the Volkswagenwerk Stiftung, which was published in German under the title *Nachbarn am Rhein: Entfremdung und Annäherung der französischen und deutschen Gesellschaft seit 1880* (Munich: Beck, 1991). The conversations, colloquia and conferences of the 'Bürgertum' Research Group at the ZiF in Bielefeld provided a climate of singular intellectual stimulation. It is truly an extraordinary achievement of Jürgen Kocka, the organiser and inspirational force of the group. For their careful study of this article and for their suggestions, I would like to thank Heinz-Gerhard Haupt, Jürgen Kocka and Allan Mitchell.

4. For a general treatment of the role of the nobility in German history, see A.J. Mayer, *Adelsmacht und Bürgertum: Die Krise der Europäischen Gesellschaft 1848–1914* (Munich, 1984), p. 98ff. On the *Bund der Landwirte*, see H.-J. Puhle, *Politische Agrarbewegungen in kapitalistischen Industriegesellschaften* (Göttingen, 1975), p. 68ff; also, by the same author, 'Aspekte der Agrarpolitik im "Organisierten Kapitalismus"', in H.-U. Wehler (ed.), *Sozialgeschichte heute* (Göttingen, 1974), pp. 543–564. On the conservative parties, see W. Ribhegge, *Deutscher Konservatismus seit 1780* (forthcoming).

5. Cf. H. Henning, *Die deutsche Beamtenschaft im 19. Jahrhundert* (Stuttgart, 1984), p.37–52, (contains material on Saxony, Prussia, Baden-Württemberg, Bavaria and Hessen-Darmstadt); H. Reif, *Westfälischer Adel 1770–1860* (Göttingen, 1979); 'Adelsanteile in Preussen',: Stenog. Protokolle des Preußischen Hauses der Abgeordneten, 3. Sitzung, 14 Januar 1911, p. 104 (reprinted in a number of places, among them W. Runge, *Politik und Beamtentum im Parteienstaat: Die Demokratisierung der politischen Beamten in Preussen zwischen 1918 und 1933* (Stuttgart, 1965), p. 170 D. Bald, *Der deutsche Generalstab 1859–1939* (Munich, 1977), pp. 104–113.

6. H. Lichtenberger, *Das moderne Deutschland und seine Entwicklung* (Dresden, 1908), p. 9ff.

7. On the question of the economic and political influence of the nobility in France see the very good summary in M. Agulhon, 'La propriété et les classes sociales' in *L'Histoire de la France rurale*, vol. 3, *Apogée et crise de la civilisation paysanne: 1889–1914* (Paris, 1976), pp. 87–94 (first half of the nineteenth century); on the proportion of the nobility in French cabinets and parliaments after 1871, see J. Charlot, 'Les élites politiques en France de la IIIe à la Ve République', *Archives européenes de sociologie* 14 (1973), pp. 78–92; J. Estébe, *Les ministres de la république: 1871–1914* (Paris, 1982); M. Dogan, 'Les filieres de la carrière politique en France', *Revue française de sociologie* 8 (1967); J.G. Heineberg, 'Personnel of the French Cabinets', *American Political Science Review* 25 (1931), pp. 389–396.

8. Cf. W. Serman, *Les officiers français dans la nation 1848–1914* (Paris, 1982), pp .818;

C. Charle, 'Le recrutement des hautes fonctionnaires en 1901', *Annales* 35 (1980), pp. 380–409; F. Bédarida, 'L'armée et la République', *Revue historique* 88 (1964), p. 151.

9. General works on this subject are: C. Charle, *Les hautes fonctionnaires en France au IXe siècle* (Paris, 1980), p. 27ff., 33f.,61ff.; *Intellectuels et élites en France, 1880–1900*, 2 vol., state thesis (Paris, 1986); 'La naissance d'un grands corps', *Actes de la recherche en sciences sociales* 42 (1982), pp. 3–17. Specialised works include: C. Charle, 'Le recrutement', p. 307; G. Thuillier, *Bureaucratie et bureaucrates en France au XIXe siècle* (Geneva, 1980), p. 334ff., (*concours* and nepotism); on the *conseil d'état* see V. Wright, *Le conseil d'État sous le Second Empire* (Paris, 1973); on the prefects see B. LeClère and V. Wright, *Les Préfets du Second Empire* (Paris, 1973); J. Siwek-Pouydesseau, *Le corps préfectoral sous la Troisième et Quatrième République* (Paris, 1969), p. 128 (prefects during the government of Broglie); 'Sociologie du corps préfectoral (1800–1940)', in Aubert et al., *Les préfets en France: 1800–1940* (Geneva, 1978), pp. 163–172; on the directors of ministries see V. Wright, 'Les directeurs des administrations centrales sous le Second Empire', in *Les directeurs de ministères en France* (Geneva, 1976), p. 44ff., (proportion of nobility); E. Chaudeau, *Les inspecteurs des finances au XIXe siècle: Profil social et role économique, 1850–1914* (Paris, 1986), p. 45 (reduction in the proportion of nobles from 12 percent before 1890 to 9 percent after 1890); L. Bergeron and G. Chaussinaud-Nogaret, *Grands notables du Premier Empire*, 11 vol. (Paris 1978–1984); on the proportion of nobles in high ministerial offices in Prussia, see Henning, *Beamtenschaft*, p. 37ff.

10. Cf. D.Stegman, 'Unternehmerverbände', in *Handwörterbuch der Wirtschaftswissenschaften*, vol. 8 (Stuttgart, 1980), p. 155–170; H.-P. Ullmann, *Interessenverbände in Deutschland* (Frankfurt, 1988); *Der Bund der Industriellen* (Göttingen, 1976); S. Mielke, *Der Hansa-Bund für Gewerbe, Handel und Industrie: 1909–1914* (Göttingen, 1976); H. Kaelble, *Industrielle Interessenpolitik in der Wilhemischen Gesellschaft* (Berlin, 1967).

11. Cf. the articles by H.-G. Haupt, R. Hudemann, F. Lenger, G. Krumeich, J.J. Sheehan in D. Langewiesche (ed.), *Liberalismus im 19. Jahrhundert* (Göttingen, 1988); also, D. Langewiesche, *Liberalismus in Deutschland* (Frankfurt, 1988).

12. F. Zunkel, *der Rheinisch-Westfälische Unternehmer: 1834–1879* (Cologne, 1962); 'Industriebürgertum in Westdeutschland', in H.-U. Wehler (ed.), *Moderne deutsche Sozialgeschichte* (Cologne, 1970), p. 309–341; W. Zapf, *Wandlungen der deutschen Führungsgruppen: 1919–1961* (Munich, 1966), p. 38ff.

13. See H.Kaelble, 'Wie feudal waren die deutschen Unternehmer im Kaiserreich?', in R. Tilly (ed.), *Beiträge zur quantitativen deutschen Unternehmensgeschichte* (Stuttgart, 1985), pp. 148–174; D.L. Augustine Perez, 'Heiratsverhalten und Berufswahl in den nichtagrarischen Multimillionärsfamilien in Deutschland vor 1914.', unpublished MA thesis (FU Berlin, 1983), p. 63ff.

14. Particular pieces of information are from: Henning, *Beamtenschaft*. pp. 111ff.; H. Kaelble, *Soziale Mobilität und Chancengleichheit im 19. und 20. Jahrhundert* (Göttingen, 1983), p. 50, 76, 90 (professors, higher officials); Berger, 'Ergebnisse der Landesverbandstatistik. Allgemeine Lage und Herkunft der höheren Beamten Sachsens', *Amt und Volk* 2 (1928), p. 224 (judges in Saxony, mostly recruited before 1914).

15. F. Ringer, *Education and Society in Europe* (Bloomington, 1979), pp. 157ff.; 'Bildung, Wirtschaft und Gesellschaft in Deutschland 1800–1960', *Geschichte und Gesellschaft* 7 (1981), pp. 262–275.

16. For Germany, see Henning, *Beamtenschaft*, p.122 (marriage); Kaelble, 'Wie feudal', pp. 155ff.; 'Social Mobility', pp. 104, 228ff.; Henning, 'Soziale Verflechtungen'; For France, see M. Lévy-Leboyer, 'Le patronat français 1912–1973', in M. Lévy-Leboyer (ed.), *Le patronat de la seconde industrialisation* (Paris, 1979), p. 142; C. Charle, 'Les milieux d'affaires dans la structure de la classe dominante ver 1900', *Actes de la Recherche en Sciences Sociales* 20/21 (1978), p. 87; Y. Cassis, in this volume; A, Daumard, *Les bourgeois et la bourgeoisie en France* (Paris, 1987).

17. F, Ringer, *The Decline of the German Mandarins. The German Academic Community 1890–1933* (Cambridge, Mass., 1969); H. Mommsen, 'Die Auflösung des Bürgertums

300 | Hartmut Kaelble

seit dem späten 19, Jahrhundert', in J. Kocka (ed.), *Bürger und Bürgerlichkeit im 19. Jahrhundert* (Göttingen, 1987), pp. 288–315; D. Langewiesche, 'Bildungsbürgertum und Liberalismus im 19. Jahrhundert', in J. Kocka (ed.), *Bildungsbürgertum* (Stuttgart, 1989); A. Lees, *Cities Perceived. Urban Society in European and American Thought 1820–1940* (Manchester, 1985), pp. 140ff.,181ff., 196ff., 311; O. v. Simson, *Der Blick nach Innen* (Berlin, 1986); W. Lepenies, *Die drei Kulturen* (Munich, 1987).

18. Lichtenberger, *Das moderne Deutschland*, p. 56.

19. Sombart, *Volkswirtschaft*, p. 450.

20. O.A.H. Schmidz, *Das Land der Wirklichkeit der französischen Gesellschaftsprobleme* (Munich, 1914), p. 225.

21. On the *notables* see: J.-M- Mayer, *Les débuts de la Troisième République 1871–1899* (Paris, 1973), pp. 9ff.; W. Mager, *Frankreich vom Ancien Régime zur Moderne* (Stuttgart, 1980), pp. 195ff.; A. Jardin and A.J. Tudesq, *La France des notables 1815–1848*, vol. 2 (Paris, 1973), pp. 220ff.

22. On the growing importance of Berlin and the city's bourgeoisie before 1914, see the contributions of W. Fischer, M. Stürmer, T. Nipperdey, W. Knopp and J. Kocka in *Berlin und seine Wirtschaft* (Berlin, 1987); on the special features of Jewish bourgeoisie in Germany see W. Mosse, *Jews in the German Economy. The German-Jewish Elite 1820–1935* (Oxford, 1987); S. Volkov, 'Jüdische Assimilation und jüdische Eigenart im deutschen Kaiserreich', *Geschichte und Gesellschaft* 9 (1983), pp. 331–248.

23. See the following works which also contain extensive bibliographies: H. Siegrist, 'Gebremste Professionalisierung. Das Beispiel der Schweizer Rechtsanwaltschaft im Vergleich zu Frankreich und Deutschland im 19. und frühen 20. Jahrhundert', in W. Conze and J. Kocka (eds.), *Bildungsbürgertum im 19. Jahrhundert* (Stuttgart, 1985), pp. 301–331; H. Siegrist, 'States and the Legal Professions. France, Germany, Italy and Switzerland. 18th to early 20th Centuries'; H. Siegrist, 'Die Rechtsanwälte und das Bürgertum. Deutschland, die Schweiz und Italien im 19. Jahrhundert'. in J. Kocka, *Bürgertum im 19. Jahrhundert*, vol. 2 (Munich, 1988), pp. 92–123.

24. C. Huerkamp, 'Ärzte und Professionalisierung in Deutschland. Überlegung zum Wandel des Arztberufs im 19. Jahrhundert', *Geschichte und Gesellschaft* 6 (1980), pp. 361ff., 377ff.; 'Die preußisch-deutsche Ärzteschaft als Teil des Bildungsbürgertums. Wandel in Lage und Selbstverständnis vom ausgehenden 18. Jahrhundert bis zum Kaiserreich', in Conze/Kocka, *Bildungsbürgertum*, p. 379. C. Huerkamp, *Der Aufstieg der Ärzte im 19. Jahrhundert* (Göttingen, 1985), pp. 254ff.; R. Neuhaus, *Arbeitskämpfe, Ärztestreiks, Sozialreformer. Sozialpolitische Konfliktregelungen 1900 bis 1914* (Berlin, 1986); M. Ramsey, 'The Politics of Professional Monopoly in 19th Century Medicine. The French Model and its Rivals', in G.L. Geison (ed.), *Professions and the French State. 1700–1900* (Philadelphia, 1984), pp. 254ff., 269ff.

25. Cf. Siegrist, 'Gebremste Professionalisierung', pp. 314ff.; R. Braun, 'Zur Professionalisierung des Ärztestandes in der Schweiz', in Conze/Kocka, *Bildungsbürgertum* pp. 332–357.

26. Cf. Siegrist, 'Gebremste Professionalisierung', pp. 393ff.; J.-L. Debré, *La Justice au XIXe Siècle. Les Républiques des avocats* (Paris, 1984).

27. J. Lennard, *La vie quotidienne du médecin de province au XIXe siècle*, 2 vol. (Paris, 1977); Ramsey, *Medecine*.

28. J. Laforgue, *Berlin, der Hof und die Stadt* (1887) (Frankfurt, 1970), p. 60.

29. For these figures which are, of course, only approximations, see: P. Flora, *State, Economy and Society in Western Europe 1815–1975*, vol. 2, (Frankfurt, 1987), pp. 498, 514; see also the contribution by H.-G. Haupt in this volume.

30. P. Flora, A. Przeworski, et al. 'The Evolution of the Class Structure in France, 1901–1968', *Economic Development and Cultural Change* 28 (1980), pp. 725–752.

31. See the figures for trade union membership in: Y. Lequin, 'La Montée des antagonismes collectifs' in Y. Lequin, *Histoire des français XIXe et XXe siècles* (Paris, 1983), pp. 455ff.; S. Mielke (ed.), *Internationales Gewerkschaftsbuch* (Opladen, 1983), pp. 342, 445ff.;

H. Kaelble, *Auf dem Weg zu einer europäischen Gesellschaft* (Munich, 1987), p. 84 (In relation to industrial workers the difference between both countries was not particularly great. For contemporaries, however, the absolute number of trade union members was probably very significant.); see the figures for party membership in H. Grebing, *Geschichte der deutschen Arbeiterbewegung* (Munich, 1977), p. 104; see voting figures in T.T. Mackie and R. Rose, *The International Almanac of Electoral History* (London, 1984), pp. 132, 152; for comparisons between the labour movements in both countries see: J. Kocka, 'Die Trennung von bürgerlicher und proletarischer Demokratie im europäischen Vergleich', in J. Kocka, *Europäische Arbeiterbewegung im 19. Jahrhundert* (Göttingen, 1983), pp. 5–20; H.-G. Haupt, 'Staatliche Bürokratie und Arbeiterbewegung. Zum Einfluss der Polizei auf die Konstitutuierung von Arbeiterbewegung und Arbeiterklasse in Deutschland und Frankreich zwischen 1848 und 1880', in J. Kocka (ed.), *Arbeiter und Bürger im 19. Jahrhundert* (Munich, 1986), pp. 219–254; H.-G. Haupt et al., 'Der politische Streik', *Jahrbuch der Arbeiterbewegung* (1981), pp. 13–53; F. Boll, 'Streikwelle im europäischen Vergleich', in: W.J. Mommsen and H.G. Husung (eds.), *Auf dem Weg zur Massengewerkschaft* (Stuttgart, 1984), pp. 109–134; M.-L. Christadler, *Die geteilte Utopie. Sozialisten in Frankreich und Deutschland* (Opladen, 1985), pp. 11–24; F. Boll, 'International Strike Waves: a Critical Assessment', in W.J. Mommsen/H.-G. Husung (ed.), *The Development of Trade Unionism in Great Britain and Germany, 1880–1914* (London, 1985), pp. 78–100; for a very informative account of strikes and trade unions internationally, see, in particular: K. Tenfelde (ed.), *Arbeiter und Arbeiterbewegung im Vergleich* (Munich, 1986); on the effects of the French bourgeoisie, see H.-G. Haupt and K. Hausen, *Die Pariser Kommune* (Frankfurt, 1979), pp. 190ff; for an excellent survey of the French social conflict, cf. P. Fridenson, 'Le conflit social' in A. Burgière and J. Revel (eds.), *Histoire de la France,* vol. 3 (Paris, 1990).

32. H.-G. Haupt, 'Soziale Ungleichheit und Klassenstrukturen in Frankreich seit der Mitte des 19. Jahrhunderts', in H.-U. Wehler (ed.), *Klassen in der europäischen Sozialgeschichte* (Göttingen, 1979), pp. 121ff.; see the editors' 'Introduction' in G. Crossick and H.-G. Haupt (eds.), *Shopkeepers and Master Artisans in 19th Century Europe* (London, 1984), pp. 21ff.; H.A. Winkler, 'From Social Protectionism to National Socialism: The German Small Business Movement in Comparative Perspective', *Journal of Modern History* 48 (1976), pp. 1–18; J. Kocka, *Angestellte zwischen Faschismus und Demokratie* (Göttingen, 1977), pp. 323ff.; H.-G. Haupt, 'Angestellte in der französischen Gesellschaft vor 1914', in J. Kocka (ed.), *Angestellte im europäischen Vergleich* (Göttingen, 1981), pp. 112–141.

11 | The Petty Bourgeoisie in Germany and France in the Late Nineteenth Century

Heinz-Gerhard Haupt

The statement by the journalist Günter Gaus, that he came from a petty-bourgeois (*kleinbürgerlich*) family was corrected by the late Chancellor of the Federal Republic, Ludwig Erhard: 'No, from a proper bourgeois one (*gutbürgerlich*)'.[1]

The problem of the relations between *Bürgertum* and *Kleinbürgertum* (petty bourgeoisie) is manifest in this exchange. Were the latter an independent social group or should we consider them to be part of the *Bürgertum*? What is it that distinguishes the small master artisans and shopkeepers from the propertied and educated *Bürgertum*? What unites them?

I will concentrate, in what follows, on the petty bourgeoisie, a social group characterised by the fact that, as entrepreneurs and traders, they combined ownership of capital with involvement in labour. The master artisan and small trader both worked in their own enterprises; they contributed their own labour to production or distribution, having themselves invested the capital to establish the shop or workshop. Like the industrial bourgeoisie, they owned and controlled the means of production, they belonged to that broad social layer of owners of property and, like them, they were not forced to sell their skills on the labour market. What distinguished them from the industrial bourgeoisie, however, was the importance of manual labour, the size of their enterprise and the level of property.[2]

Apart from these general differences of a class-analytical nature, social historians also have to determine the real extent of similarities and differences and establish whether both social groups lived in a different milieu or whether there were many contacts between them. Of all the possible aspects that one could consider, we are mainly interested here in those aspects which throw some light on particular

Notes to Chapter 11 can be found on page 320.

features of the middle class in Germany and France. What structural features and behavioural patterns typical to these classes manifested themselves in the economic contacts between petty bourgeois and bourgeois ranks, in their political links and their social mobility? This conceptual diffuseness has certain advantages here over a stricter form of definition since it enables us to look at forms and levels of transition that one could easily fail to recognise in a more strictly definitional or systematic approach.

A comparison of Germany and France would lead one to expect to find differences in the relations between upper-middle-class and petty-bourgeois spheres of living. Previous research suggests that, because of the stronger corporate (*ständisch*) character of class relations, the social distances between master artisans and entrepreneurs, between shopkeepers and merchants in Germany were greater than in France where, after 1789, corporate structures had only a marginal existence in the business sector.[3] The more rapid pace of industrialisation in the German states and the tendency towards large enterprises were not without consequences for the small business sector. Although this did not lead only to the destruction of small businesses but also to the establishment of new ones and to the conversion of production in others, nonetheless it had a much greater effect on the master artisans than did the form of capitalist development that occurred in France, based on the small entrepreneurial sector.[4]

The political support of petty-bourgeois organisations for conservative forces, what Heinrich August Winkler described as a policy of 'reinsurance', would seem to point to a close coalition between petty-bourgeois and bourgeois conservatives in Germany, whereas French political culture, less conservative and less shaped by an authoritarian state, offered the possibility of a different political orientation for the French petty bourgeoisie.[5] Therefore, although we begin by looking at the urban petty bourgeoisie and their relations with upper-middle-class circles, we will also have to look at differences between French and German society.

The present undertaking is hindered by the fact that a comprehensive history of the French or German petty bourgeoisie has yet to be written. There are also very few studies of the situation and social behaviour of master artisans in France during the period under consideration, namely, the decades around the turn of the century when the economic threat to the petty-bourgeois sector increased and when, as a result of ever greater state intervention, there was also an increase in the organisational activity of this social group. It is a period in which all the conflicts and alliances between different sections of bourgeois society manifest themselves and can be examined together. By combining local micro-studies with a more general analysis, I will attempt to uncover some of the factors that are essential in determining the characteristic features of the middle class in each country.

Real and Apparent Independence

Independence, guaranteed by property and safeguarded by education, was something enjoyed by both petty-bourgeois and upper-middle-class layers. Until late into the twentieth century, to become independent was also the dream of workers who wanted to escape the constraints of wage labour. However, the independence of the small masters and traders turned out to be more of an aspiration than an experienced reality. Their threatened and limited independence distinguished their status from that of the upper middle classes. They stood in a variety of relations to different sections of the wealthy bourgeoisie who were able, more or less, to control and rule them.

Before 1914, forms of personal dependence still existed in which economic relations formed the basis of the putting-out system of work (*Verlagssystem*) in which the distributor used his access to the market as a means of imposing on the small master, whose production was often family-based, the dictates of his own payment policy and his own often detailed requirements concerning the quality of the finished products. In this system the small-scale producer of commodities was ruled over by a commercial bourgeoisie that had come into being during the early period of industrialisation.

This form of organisation still existed in Germany during the latter part of the nineteenth century, especially in the confectionery industry, in shoe and cigar manufacture and, in the form of middlemen, in the building trade.[6] In France it survived until the First World War in the textile industry as well as in the production of knives, toys and furniture.[7] A part of this distribution activity was carried out by wholesale traders who passed the commodities on to the retailers. This pure market relationship, however, concealed solid and direct relations of dependence.

According to a survey carried out by the Trading Commission of the French National Assembly in 1913 among trading associations and representative bodies, 87.8 percent of shopkeepers bought their own goods individually and bought them, according to 71.3 percent of those questioned, not from the producers but from wholesalers. In 32 percent of cases, dependence on a single wholesaler was typical; in 13 percent of cases, on two. In the opinion of 52 percent of organisations, the shopkeepers were dependent on credit made available to them by the merchants. Their inability to pay for goods at time of purchase and recourse to borrowing tied numerous small retailers, as well as craftsmen involved in the putting-out system, to merchant capital. Only 8.2 percent of those polled suggested that the supplier demanded special privileges in return, 8.7 percent said that the wholesaler demanded a monopoly of supply and 3.5 percent reported that the wholesaler claimed a portion of returns.

In spite of these small percentages, it is clear that the business activities of the shopkeepers were affected by this and their financial and commercial scope for action was restricted.[8] This situation was also underlined by the Chamber of Commerce of Châlons-sur-Marne in northeast France, when it wrote that: 'The wholesalers grant extensions of credit to the small retailers and, as a consequence of this, the small traders no longer have the independence to set better prices'.[9]

It was not just the wholesalers, but also other sections of the bourgeoisie, who were involved in the provision of circulating and starting capital. According to the results of the French survey already mentioned, 17 percent of all correspondents thought that shopkeepers were dependent on nonfamily credit, while 48 percent assumed at least some form of mixed dependence on both family and non-family credit. In the city of Niort as well as in Paris, there was a dense network of financial ties in which the small shopkeeper and the master artisans moved, in which they were partly trapped and which they fell through in times of crisis.[10] Wholesalers, notaries, solicitors, property-owning bourgeois and an obscure world of agents made up the ranks of the money-lenders who were willing to give credit to the small traders; the more uncertain their prospects and the more limited their securities, the more expensive was the credit available to them.

One should not forget the dependence of the petty bourgeoisie on consumer monopolies and local power-groups. For instance, it would have been difficult for the master artisans in Toulouse, who worked for the luxury market, to break out of the client relationship which they had with the families of the local aristocracy. In many of the industrial cities of eastern and central France, the small shopkeepers would have had to worry about their very existence if they supported the activities of the workers. The steel magnates of Lothringen threatened to cut off electricity and water, which they controlled, while the mine owners of Decuzeville tried to buy up the shops of the city so as to cut off the workers from necessary provisions during periods of strikes.[11]

In all such cases the petty bourgeoisie were made clearly aware of their proper place in the bourgeois hierarchy and they saw that relations of exchange were also relations of political domination. Differences in the situation of the petty bourgeoisie and the bourgeoisie, as well as the dependence of the one on the other, became particularly clear during periods of crisis, when the credit margins were narrower and when repayments were demanded. It was not the unity but the opposition of interests of the petty bourgeoisie and bourgeoisie which were manifest in these relationships. It was through such relationships that the petty bourgeoisie, or important sections of this group, came into contact with the different sections of the commercial, property-owning and financial bourgeoisie.

By 1900 the situation had begun to change but these relations continued to affect the lives and business practices of important sectors. Many of these bourgeois groups lived on the margins of the bourgeoisie and sometimes carried on their business behind closed doors, especially when dealing with credit for barely solvent traders and small masters who had very few securities and a small capital base.

But apart from those marginal elements, the petty bourgeoisie also had contact with the forward-looking sections of the bourgeoisie. Relations here became less personal and more businesslike. Among the new groups that the small traders and artisans had to deal with now were the industrial giants, providing plenty of orders for supply industries during boom times but drying up during periods of economic downturn and the department stores and chain stores which recruited members of the petty bourgeoisie to work as branch managers.[12]

The 'Casino' enterprise in St. Etienne, established in 1860 and transformed into a limited company in 1898, with numerous branches in southwestern France and a turnover in 1911/12 of 24 million francs, was typical of this new type of structure. It was such a massive buyer that it was able unilaterally to determine the conditions of contracts with suppliers. This was facilitated by the way in which the food and consumer goods industry was broken up into a large number of small businesses which were unable to counter the company's preponderant share of the market. The freedom of action of the branch manager was even more limited; he was able to decide the quantity but not the range of goods and, in many cases, was not empowered to return damaged or rotten products. He also had to pay a deposit to the parent company on which the latter did not pay interest but which became part of its working capital.[13]

Although relations between the branch managers and the parent enterprise, between industrialists and their suppliers, were, on the basis of contracts, more businesslike and less personal, these modern bourgeois groups with their high levels of capital investment, knew how to exploit the client relationships that existed with the petty bourgeois milieu. In France in 1891, when a parliamentary commission was discussing an increase in taxation, the big department stores in Paris mobilised their small suppliers in the provinces to exert political pressure.[14] Economic and political relations became intertwined and the relations of dependency became clearly visible.

Finally, both master artisans and small shopkeepers, at the end of the nineteenth century, operated in an area which was moulded and permeated by official regulations. This was the basis of their contact with *foncionnaires*, state officials whose task it was to ensure the implementation of the legal regulations pertaining to production and labour rights. This kind of supervision varied according to the period and according to the local political situation. As a general rule, this supervision was very strict in those areas where the officials, supported by the local authorities, had to deal with only a small number of pettybourgeois producers and traders who were breaking the regulations. The supervision was much less strict in those areas where a majority of the local traders and artisans were opposed to the decrees and regulations and where these regulations themselves were a matter of public controversy. In a period of much conflict with workers and other employees, the authorities were not strongly inclined to create another social conflict by undertaking rigorous proceedings against the petty bourgeoisie.

However, although there may have been a certain amount of opportunism in the implementation of official regulations, in Germany as well as in France, there was still a significant amount of conflict between the petty bourgeoisie and the representatives of urban officialdom.[15] It is well known how sensitive they were to official inspection of their milk and wine, how strongly small undertakings fought for their survival, using legal and illegal means, against the implementation of labour-protection laws, such as the prohibition of working on Sunday or at nighttime for women, and how they opposed the visits of the labour and factory inspectors.[16] They did not regard the largely symbolic fines which they had to pay around the end of the century as some small matter. On the contrary, they made very strong protests and appealed to the authorities to bring this dishonourable treatment to an end.

This largely unknown area of social policy and official regulations opens up new perspectives for the study of the relations between the petty bourgeoisie and the state authorities. The generalised implementation of labour-protection laws in the large and medium-sized factories brought the small businessmen into the grip of the regulatory bodies. State power and state regulations were an extremely difficult problem for them. If we take into account the experiences of the petty bourgeoisie and craftsmen in this area of state intervention, then the thesis of petty bourgeois belief in and fixation on the state, a thesis derived from a study of the publications of the various associations of the time, will need to be modified, at least for Germany and France.

Because of all these factors, independence, for important sections of the petty bourgeoisie, proved to be a fiction. Economic relations, sometimes of a personal, sometimes of a business-like character, tied the petty bourgeoisie to the bourgeoisie – made them, in effect, subordinates. Granting or withholding credit, making or cancelling orders, the bourgeoisie became the arbiters of survival or bankruptcy, interfering in the details of business practice and turning economic dependence into political domination when many considered it necessary. From this point of view, therefore, one will have to modify the traditional image of small independent artisans and traders. According to this view, although partly destroyed and in difficulty, small traders and artisans nonetheless possessed a core which, by means of the electric motor and increases in capital, was independent, innovative and capable of survival. The modification is to be made with respect to the traditional image of the prosperous retail shops that offered goods from many countries and drew in the public with their well-stocked window displays.

Of course, the independent, well-off master artisan and the solid well-to-do trader did exist. In his study of Münster and Arnsberg, Adolf Noll has given us a statistically convincing but not vividly descriptive account of this group. Hansjoachim Henning similarly concentrates his study almost exclusively on this oligarchy within the petty bourgeoisie.[17] These studies do not deal with the relations of dependence in which the petty bourgeoisie found themselves. If we measure the independence of the master artisans according to the criteria of whether they could choose between different suppliers in the purchase of their raw materials and whether they could choose among different buyers in the sale of their products, then, according to Alain Cottereau, in Paris at the beginning of the twentieth century less than 2 percent of the active population were independent. To this conclusion we should also add the results of the census of the population and of professions carried out in 1901, according to which 80 percent of all business in France were run by small businessmen, either alone or in conjunction with family members.[18] Against this kind of statistical background, the arguments offered above become even more plausible. At the same time, we can notice a difference between Germany and France. In Germany, the number of independent masters was clearly higher than it was on the other side of the Rhine.

A further difference between both countries has to do with the strength and survival of the putting-out system, which was much stronger in France and had a much greater influence there on the relations between the bourgeoisie and petty bourgeoisie – unless, of course, this impression is a product of the fact that very little research has been done in Germany on the putting-out system at the end of the nineteenth century. It is clear that the importance of bank capital was a special feature of Germany's development. While the German cooperative and commercial banks included the small-business sector within their sphere of operation, in France the master artisans were completely dependent on the credit of their suppliers or other private persons of varying degrees of respectability. In view of the very bad situation that existed in France, legislation concerning the provisional credit for small and medium-sized businesses was proposed in 1910 and implemented in 1917. The cautious policy of the French banks, which were generally afraid of the risks of industrial investment, especially investment in the unstable and crisis-ridden area of small shops and workshops, forced the petty bourgeoisie to rely on the family or on marginal bourgeois groups for financial help.[19]

If one can get to know a social group through economic dealings with it, then there must have been quite a few members of the professional middle class who were familiar with the problems of the petty bourgeoisie. Lawyers and notaries, financiers and managers of savings banks, workshop inspectors and municipal officials, merchant capitalists and wholesalers were able to form some idea of the manner of life and business of the masters and shopkeepers. Among, the *haute bourgeoisie*, however, apart from literary sources, there seems to have been little familiarity with the situation of the petty bourgeoisie. As an example of this one could cite the reaction of the daughter of the president of a higher regional court at the end of the nineteenth century who, on being informed that a relative had married a wholesale merchant in Bremen, 'inquired somewhat timidly and with great restraint in her letter of congratulation whether my sister would have to serve the guests from behind the counter'.[20] It is probably the case that, to the extent that personal dependencies were replaced by more business-like relations, the core of the bourgeoisie had even less insight into the inner structure of petty-bourgeois society and the importance of mediators, such as notaries and solicitors, increased. Of course, for some industrial entrepreneurs the small supplier remained important, just as the small shops remained important for the network of trade. For petty bourgeois and bourgeois alike, independence was a fixed point in their self-definition and aspirations, but this did not provide a bridge between them.

Social Barriers between the Petty Bourgeoisie and the Upper Middle Class

The petty bourgeoisie extends right into the people but still has contact with the *bourgeoisie*, commented the Orleanist, Odilon Barrot, on the eve of the 1849 revolution.[21] This expression, with some reservations, remained valid at the end of the nineteenth century. Quite a number of the best known and most successful entrepreneurs in Germany and France (more in the former than in the latter) gave master artisan or shopkeeper as the profession of their father. Among students in both countries who rose later to official positions, there were sons of craftsmen and shopkeepers. All of these scattered pieces of information, which are, of course, no substitute for systematic analysis, nonetheless indicate that the break between the upper and middle layers of the middle class was not so complete and that ways continued to exist for petty bourgeois individuals to rise above their situation and adopt upper-middle-class lifestyles. Statistics do not give us any indication of the extent of this because they do not cover the whole population of master artisans and shopkeepers.[22] However, if we fit the situation that existed in both countries after 1880 into the larger framework of developments during the whole of that century, it becomes clear that the situation had changed quite a lot from what it had been in 1850. We also gain a better picture of how difficult it was to ascend the path of upward mobility that led into the ranks of the upper middle class.

Few members of the lower ranks succeeded in scaling the heights of the social hierarchy. One of the most common strategies for social climbing in the latter part of the nineteenth century was for the master artisans and shopkeepers to equip their sons with 'educational capital' so they could move up into white-collar jobs or minor official positions. In Bremen this was the preferred route of the master artisans rather than of the shopkeepers, while in Brunswick it was practised more by the merchants than by the master artisans and small shopkeepers.[23] Another method of advance was simply to expand one's business. Reports from Brunswick at the end of the century indicate that retail traders were also acting as wholesalers for particular products, were managing agencies or had installed an outlet for one of the savings banks.[24]

This form of diversification could be characterized as bourgeois since it deviated from the principle of securing a living (*Nahrungssicherung*) and represented an adaptation to the profit mechanism. It could also be interpreted as a variation of the proletarian practice of supplementing wage-labour with independent activity and increasing the family income from a number of sources. Among the many attempts to indulge in more lucrative business beyond the workshop and retail trade, there must have been a certain amount of upward social movement. In most cases, however, the reality would have been a long process of attempts and failures, a process of small steps rather than giant leaps, and only in very few cases would success have been achieved within one or two generations. The petty bourgeoisie was really a transit class, something which one was born into and attempted to leave behind. The ambitious petty bourgeois aspired to membership of the *bourgeoisie* and *Bürgertum*.[25]

Marriage was and remained one of the favourite means of changing one's social position. In the middle of the nineteenth century a grocer in Paris would have had little difficulty in marrying a woman from a bourgeois family. However, by the end of the century, according to all the available information, this happened very seldom. Jean-Pierre Chaline has confirmed that this was the case in Rouen, while studies of Bremen and Brunswick give us a similar picture.[26] A more common practice was for the sons of merchants and, to a lesser extent, of entrepreneurs, to look for wives among the daughters of masters and shopkeepers. The well-known literary example of this kind of social ascent is Theodor Fontane's *Frau Jenny Treibel*:

Ah, her mother, the good Frau Bürstenbinder, always dressed the little babe so smartly. In her womanly wisdom she knew exactly what she was doing. Now the pretty little one has become a commercial councillor and can have whatever she wants, and that includes the ideal, all the time, in fact, a masterpiece of a Bourgeoisie![27]

The daughters of the petty bourgeoisie were attractive for the sons of the upper middle class not only because they were excessively domestic, but also because of their thrift, industriousness and orderliness. For the small traders and masters, on the other hand, this link with upper middle class families also had its own advantages. For instance, in the western French city of Niort, as has been demonstrated by Jean-Baptiste Martin, the creditworthiness of the small shopkeepers depended quite a lot on such connections and upper-middle-class in-laws could be very useful in securing the survival of the workshop or shop.

Whether one can generalise from these examples for the whole of both societies remains to be seen. However, these examples do indicate that, although there was a stronger upper-middle-class resistance to newcomers at the end of the century than there had been around 1850, it was still possible for the petty bourgeoisie to gain entrance into upper-middle-class circles. These possibilities were, of course, quite limited. The petty bourgeoisie adopted the strategies of advancement used by the upper middle class: diversification, expansion of production, education and marriage. The often misplaced raptures of Frau Jenny Treibel about the upper-middle-class ideal is an example of her efforts to adopt the appropriate conversational tone so that her social origins would not be noticed. Although the upper-middle-class principles of advancement were recognised as having general validity, one's petty bourgeois past was often that part of one's biography which required energetic suppression.

The formation of oligarchies within the individual crafts or among small traders could also be interpreted as a form of *embourgeoisment* (*Verbürgerlichung*). Among butchers in Lyon, a trade in which almost 50 percent died at the end of their working life without leaving behind an inheritance, a small group emerged at the end of the century which, by means of house purchases, strict endogamy and inheritance, created for itself the foundations of a butcher dynasty.[28] The formation of a stable core in individual professions, a phenomenon which Henning has also observed in Westphalia,[29] was accompanied by the revival of feudal patterns of social behaviour as well as by the adoption of typical attributes of upper-middle-class success, including the ownership of property.

This adoption of upper-middle-class lifestyles did not mean that the petty bourgeoisie changed their careers; on the contrary, these were continued through a number of generations. Stability and the ability to plan one's future were fundamental features of upper-middle-class existence. These features, now possessed by small groups of masters and tradesmen, made it possible for them to structure their lives, at least in the medium term, and to put themselves forward as spokesmen for the various crafts and for the small traders.

In their relationships with the upper middle class one can distinguish three different groups within the petty bourgeoisie and this threefold division cuts across the individual professions. In the first group, limited but real changes in their economic careers made it possible for them to advance socially, even into the upper middle class itself. The second group is characterised by the fact that, through their upper-middle-class lifestyles, they formed isolated social groups within petty bourgeois society. The third group lived in close proximity with the lower classes with whom it had day to day contact. The first two groups were a minority in both Germany and France. The majority of master artisans and traders found themselves in the third group. Those happy few who were able to make it into the arcanum of the upper middle class or who were able to imitate the latter's lifestyle were a small minority in relation to that vast majority that oscillated between a situation of proletarian labour and a precarious petty bourgeois independence. The first two groups were larger in Germany than in France, which may have been due to the different levels of industrialisation in both countries and to the differences in the public and legal status of the crafts.

An example from Bremen can demonstrate empirically the difference in the degree of social stability between upper-middle-class groups and a section of the petty bourgeoisie. Between 1890 and 1914 on average around one third of all small shops closed after trading for six years, whereas for all trading firms, including branch shops whose conditions of existence were not far removed from those of the small petty bourgeois establishments, the corresponding figure is one seventh.[30] The statistics for bankruptcies and sales of shops in France at the beginning of the century reveal a disproportionately high number of small businesses.[31] Short-term planning and rapid change were characteristic of the economic life of the petty bourgeoisie. There was a higher proportion of newcomers among shopkeepers in Bremen than among businessmen of larger enterprises; the former also moved house within the city or moved away from the city altogether at a much faster rate. This constant search for a new and better place was also an expression of the ephemeral character of their independence, which was always viewed in a transitional or short-term rather than a long-term perspective.

Planning was also made difficult for the small retailer by the fact that income did not increase as one got older. But, as the example of Bremen demonstrates, the incomes of the wholesale merchants either increased with age or remained at an already achieved high level. In both France and Germany, the small shop was seen as a way of avoiding the poverty of old age that was seen among workers and their widows, and this remained the case after the introduction of pensions. The role of families varied, if we can assume that Bremen was typical.

In one-third of the shops in Bremen around 1900 that did not employ external labour, both wives and children worked, making the family the sphere of both production and reproduction. Unlike in the early industrial period, the master artisans and shopkeepers did not have bigger families in order to increase their domestic labour force. In fact, in Malthusian France as well as in Germany, they limited the number of children and concentrated their resources on particular individual careers as well as on continuing the family business. Among wholesale merchants, however, only a small proportion worked without hired help and apprentices. Here the dividing line between family and business had already been drawn. It was this division which, according to Jürgen Habermas, was linked to the creation of a middle-class public sphere and of middle-class values.

Although the distance between the petty bourgeoisie and the upper middle class in both countries was not as great as that which existed between the latter and the workers, nonetheless there were significant differences between them with respect to their social behavior, their attitudes and their future perspectives. Stability and the ability to plan the future were much more in evidence among the upper middle class than among the owners of shops and workshops. They also both occupied different positions in society. Although petty-bourgeois status may have been a social goal for the workers, for those born into that social class it was often a mere transitional stage on the way to upper-middle-class positions. Within the upper middle class there was also, of course, a certain amount of mobility or flux in professional careers, but these changes took place within the same social sphere and there was a much lower proportion of failure, of loss of social position.

Alongside all of these differences, of course, there existed important similarities Master artisans and shopkeepers, like merchants and industrialists, were owners of means of production and property, although not on the same scale and of the same quality. Both made use of the available educational institutions, either for the purpose of giving their children the possibility of a career not based primarily on manual labour or for the purpose of acquiring, in addition to the economic, a certain amount of cultural capital. One should not begin with the assumption that there existed a deep cleft between both groups. In reality, there were a number of routes of passage from one group to the other and a variety of intermediate levels. There remains also, of course, the question of differences within the upper middle class itself and the extent of instability in upper-middle-class careers.

The opportunities for masters and retailers to change their social position were similar in both France and Germany. Judging by the amount of success in rising into upper-middle-class positions, these opportunities were very few in both countries. The number of petty bourgeois who had consolidated themselves and lived in semi-bourgeois conditions seemed to be greater in Germany than in France, where the number of proletarianised and dependent artisans was very high. In both countries craftsmen and shopkeepers practised birth-control and concerned themselves for the future careers of their children. However, Malthusianism was stronger in France than in Germany. All of these comments point to the need for a more detailed comparison based on more precise information.

Embourgeoisement and the Adoption of Bourgeois Values

Those virtues that were an accompaniment to the emergence of bourgeois society appear frequently in the publications of the federations and associations of master artisans and shopkeepers.[32] There is praise of work, thrift, order, family and property and condemnation of laziness, waste, chaos, moral laxity and indigence. One interesting feature of those publications is that they show little interest in the social questions dominating bourgeois thought at the time. One of the possible reasons for this is the fact that the masters and shopkeepers considered their way of life and their methods of production as an exemplary solution to those social problems. Patriarchal relations, the possibility of upward social mobility through business enterprise, educational qualifications: these were the solutions society should adopt to avoid poverty, rootlessness and political radicalism. The words and the images, the fears and the hopes were similar in both countries. In Germany this panegyric was already widespread in the 1880s, but in

France it did not really begin to make a large impression until the beginning of the twentieth century.

Should this adoption and praise of bourgeois virtues be understood as *embourgeoisement (Verbürgerlichung)*? Based on the present level of research, it must remain an open question whether the ideals associated with the development of bourgeois society continued to serve as the basis of the self-awareness and self-justification of the upper middle class or whether the petty bourgeoisie had also, in the meantime, incorporated these values and had made itself into the ideological rearguard of the upper middle class. However that may be, the petty bourgeoisie certainly adopted the upper-middle-class code of conduct, giving it, at the same time, a specific function and bias. It functioned as a means of separating the world of the masters and shopkeepers from that of the lower classes which, because of their living conditions, were not in a position to maintain even the appearance of belonging to the upper middle class.

The thrift of the small independent masters and traders distinguished them from the alleged wastefulness of the proletariat; the friendly interiors of the shops contrasted with the dark corridors of the tenements; the decency of the petty bourgeoisie contrasted with the supposed promiscuity of the lower classes. With the same kind of arguments, one could exclude from the petty bourgeoisie the owners of unstable and short-lived shops and workshops who had neither the education nor the social grounding that would enable them to live a bourgeois lifestyle. In the statutes of the Bremen Association of Shopkeepers we read: 'The decisive criteria for acceptance [into this Association] are the appropriate training or proven ability through the orderly management of the relevant type of business'.[33] In the common view of the time, neither training nor order were to be found in those grocery shops in which the wife managed the shop while the husband was a wage labourer. In this context, therefore, the adoption of bourgeois values can be understood as a means of differentiating between honourable and less honourable forms of business.

The adoption of bourgeois values, however, played a role not only within the class of petty bourgeoisie but also externally, in its relations with the upper middle class. They were able, in other words, to make use of these values against the upper middle class itself.

During this period in which the small independent producers and traders were being courted by associations and political groups, they were also the object of satirical attacks and caricatures. Their parochial attitudes and conformity, their fears and their narrow-mindedness, were constantly being attacked. *Klein* became identified with 'limited', 'locally based', as having 'narrow horizon'.[34] The scale of these attacks has not been studied but their existence is beyond doubt. The view of themselves and of the world, on the basis of which the *Kleinbürger* supported and turned towards the *Bürgertum* can also be understood in this context as a means of defending and asserting themselves against the negative roles ascribed to them. It may be that in defending themselves against such attacks the organised core of the master artisans and small traders won for themselves a stronger sense of their own identity, in a manner similar to the self-discovery of the French labour movement in the middle of the nineteenth century.[35]

In France at the end of the century the confrontation between the petty bourgeoisie and the *bourgeoisie* was quite extensive in the public political sphere.[36] In this confrontation the petty bourgeoisie presented themselves as supporters of the values of the Revolution of 1789, as the heirs of the *bourgeoisie* who, in the meantime, had become part of that aristocracy against which the petty bourgeoisie now had to defend themselves. This confrontation, promoted by the defence organisations of the small traders, extended beyond the petty bourgeoisie itself and was taken up by the working class. When the German *Kleinbürger* assessed the activities of the government and the practices of the *Bürgertum* according to the standards of thrift, industriousness and fair competition, they were making more of a moral than a political accusation.

In applying the model of patriarchal family life or the model of the economically-run workshop or shop to public political life or to the large capitalist organisations, the main criticism of the petty bourgeoisie was being directed against the arrogance of political leaders, their wastefulness and proneness to scandal. This aspect, which David Blackbourn was the first to point out,[37] needs to be studied more carefully in order to discover with which arguments and in what manner the *Kleinbürgertum* defended itself against the *Bürgertum*.

In Germany as well as in France, the petty bourgeoisie was the object of upper-middle-class policy, which fluctuated between absorption and exclusion. In both countries, at the beginning of the twentieth century, there emerged significant movements towards collective organisation which, like the *Reichsverband des deutschen Mittelstandes* (National Association of the German Middle Classes), the Hansa League or the *Association des classes moyennes*, attempted to associate the shopkeepers and masters more closely with the policies and interests of the upper middle class.

This attempt had a specific pre-history. In France, some sections of the urban petty bourgeoisie, since the time of the 1848 revolution, had worked closely with the republican movement and had seen in the Third Republic the form of government that corresponded to their aspirations. It was also easy for them to find a political home in the socialist groups, to the extent that these groups, until 1890, had an orientation to the *peuple* more so than to the working class. It was only during the crisis of the 1880s, when large-scale forms of trade and industry appeared to threaten the existence of numerous crafts-men and shopkeepers, that the political orientation of the petty bour-geoisie began to change and they began to establish their own inde-pendent organisations. During the 1890s, when the break with the socialist parties deepened, the majority of the provincial associations remained close to the radicals, while in Paris conservatives and royal-ists dominated after 1900. Although this development in Paris spread to a few other cities before 1914, the dominant links in France remained with the radical socialists who claimed for themselves the traditions of the French Revolution, who sang the praises of solidarity and who defended the right to private property.

The *Reichsverband* was not the only option in Germany, and there was certainly a division between north German and south German members of the *Mittelstand*. This development, however, took place against the background of a general disassociation of the *Mittelstand* from the liberals, itself a reflection of liberal neglect of petty bourgeois interests. Some sections of the shopkeeper and craft associations were won over to a policy of social protectionism and to anti-democratic goals which corresponded to the interests of a certain section of the *Bürgertum*.[38]

Something else which contributed to the difference between the two countries was the fact that in Germany there was an earlier and stronger attempt by the state, by making both symbolic and genuine concessions to the petty bourgeoisie, to separate them as *Mittelstand* from the working class.

Alongside these attempts to win petty-bourgeois support for upper-middle-class goals, we should not forget the attempts to keep the petty bourgeoisie out of the decision-making process. These attempts were more obvious in elections to the chambers of commerce than in urban political elections.

In France equal voting rights were in force in the cities after 1882 and the petty bourgeoisie often succeeded in obtaining responsibilities in urban government. In Germany, because of property qualifications, grocers and small masters had only limited influence.[39] In both countries a business patriciate opposed any extension of voting rights. In a few German towns such as Bremen and Hamburg small retailers were allowed to establish their own chambers of commerce (*Kleinhandelskammer*), but in other towns like Brunswick and St. Etienne there were frequent conflicts,[40] and the local notables justified the policy of social exclusion with reference to unqualified applicants. In St. Etienne the problem was partially solved by the introduction of a class voting system. The small traders now had the right to participate but the notables still had the final say. In Brunswick where no such system existed, the situation became very polarised politically. Against the chambers of commerce, which opposed any extension of their electorate, the *Schutzverein* (Protective Association) was formed which put forward protectionist and anti-Semitic demands and attached itself to the German Social Party (*Deutschsoziale Partei*). This blocking of political participation and articulation promoted the turn away from liberalism.

A further limit to upper-middle-class influence was to be found in the structure of petty bourgeois society. This was, as I have already said, a highly fluid milieu in which movement was the rule and stability the exception. For example, among the butchers in Lyon who, in general, were regarded as prosperous, one tenth changed address in the city in the last one third of the nineteenth century and one third disappeared from the directories altogether.[41] Of course, not all of these became proletarians; some of them died and some of them may have improved or changed their social position. But the extent of the fluctuation was so large that it resembles the movement which took place in the working class at the same time.

Among the petty bourgeoisie, as among the workers, conditions changed so rapidly that any orientation towards upper-middle-class values, which would have assumed long-term economic stability, was unlikely. Added to this was the fact that incomes, in any case, were inadequate to live an upper-middle-class lifestyle. Around half of Düsseldorf master artisans in the middle of the nineteenth century were not required to pay tax.[42] According to estimates by Karl Bücher, in 1893 60.8 percent of Leipzig craftsmen had an income that was too low to feed their families.[43] Under such conditions, upper-middle-class norms could have made no headway among that section of the petty bourgeoisie close to the working class. The

320 | *Heinz-Gerhard Haupt*

majority of these were master artisans and shopkeepers. It was among this section of the petty bourgeoisie that associations and organisations of an upper-middle-class orientation would have had the least influence.

In spite of economic, social and political contacts, those factors which divided the petty bourgeoisie and upper-middle-class groups were stronger than those that united them. While both classes held property, by the end of the nineteenth century, the petty bourgeoisie were an independent social group, separated from the upper middle class by self-definition, by a higher degree of instability and dependence, by specific differences in the way they led and planned their lives, and, finally, by specific political interest. This overall difference was very strong in both countries. National peculiarities that emerged as a consequence of industrialisation were less pronounced in the area of social relations and contacts, although it is possible that there are gaps in our knowledge here because of inadequate research. These national peculiarities manifested themselves in the different weight of republican traditions in both countries, in differences in the scope of the state's integration policies, and in the different possibilities that existed in both countries for participating in the decision-making process. It is clear that the stability and security, the orderliness and predictability of the middle class have been overemphasised. There are still uncertainties as to the influence of upper-middle-class ideology and where that influence was felt, whether the ideology took hold of the *Kleinbürger* and brought about their *embourgeoisment (Verbürgerlichung)*, or was simply adopted in accordance with their own particular needs. We are not yet able to ascertain the extent of upper-middle-class influence on that section of the petty bourgeoisie that lived and worked in proletarian conditions.

Notes to Chapter 11

1. G. Gaus, *Zur Person. Porträts in Frage und Antwort* (Munich, 1964), p. 49.

2. A summary of the class-analytical discussion is to be found in the introduction to H. G. Haupt (ed.), '*Bourgeois und Volk zugleich'? Zur Geschichte des Kleinbürgertums im 19. und 20. Jahrhundert* (Frankfurt, 1987).

3. There are hardly any special studies of French craftworkers in the second half of the nineteenth century. Only recently has some research been done in this area but it is as yet unpublished.

4. For overall developments, see W. Fischer, *Wirtschaft und Gesellschaft im Zeitalter der Industrialisierung* (Göttingen, 1972), pp. 315ff.; F. Caron, *Histoire économique de la France XIXe–XXe siècle* (Paris, 1984).

5. H. A. Winkler, *Mittelstand, Demokratie und Nationalsozialismus. Die politische Entwicklung von Handwerk und Kleinhandel in der Weimarer Republik* (Cologne, 1972); S. Volkov, *The Rise of Popular Antisemitism in Germany. The Urban Master Artisans, 1873–1896* (Princeton, 1978); for France, see in particular P. Nord, *Paris Shopkeepers and the Politics of Resentment* (Princeton, 1986).

6. See R. Boch, *Handwerker-Sozialisten gegen Fabrikgesellschaft* (Göttingen, 1985); H. Aubin and W. Zorn, (eds.), *Handbuch der deutschen Wirtschafts- und Sozialgeschichte*, vol. 2 (Stuttgart, 1976), pp. 332f.; U. Engelhardt, (ed.), *Handwerker in der Industrialisierung. Lage, Kultur und Politik vom späten 18. bis ins frühe 20. Jahrhundert* (Stuttgart, 1984).

7. See G. Dupeux, *Aspects de l'histoire sociale et politique du Loire-et-Cher, 1884–1914* (Paris, 1972), pp. 563ff.; Y. Lequin, *Les Ouvriers de la région lyonnaise* (Lyon, 1977), pp. 142ff.; see, in particular, the contemporary studies: P. du Maroussem, *La question ouvrière* (Paris 1891–96), vol. 1, *Charpentiers de Paris: Compagnons et indépendants* (1891), vol. 2, *Ebénistes du faubourg Saint-Antoine* (1892).

8. A. Landry, 'Rapport au nom de la commission du commerce et de l'industrie chargée de procéder à une enquête sur la situation du commerce en France et notamment, sur la condition actuelle du petit commerce', Chamber of Deputies, 10th legislature, 1914, no. 3452.

9. Archives nationales, C2498.

10. A. Daumard, *La Bourgeoisie parisienne de 1815 à 1848* (Paris, 1962), pp. 69ff.; J. C. Martin, 'Commerce et commerçants à Niort au XIXe siècle, Les faillites', *Bulletin de la Société historique et scientifique des Deux-Sèvres*, second series, 13 (1980).

11. D. Reid, *The Miners of Decazeville, A Genealogy of Deindustrialisation*, (Cambridge, Mass., 1985), pp. 75ff.

12. Cf. M. Lévy-Leboyer, 'Le patronat français a-t-il été malthusien?', *Le mouvement social* 88 (1974), pp. 9ff.; M. Miller, *Au Bon Marché (1869–1920) ou le consommateur apprivoisé*, (Paris, 1987); F. Faraut, *Histoire de la Belle Jardinière* (Paris, 1987), especially pp. 13ff.

13. For the example of the docks in Rheims, see P. Gemahling, 'La concentration commerciale sans grands magasins', *Revue d'économie politique* 26 (1912), pp. 170–192.

14. Archives nationales, C5498, 26 June 1891.

15. H.-G. Haupt, *Les Petits Commerçants et la politique sociale. Etude sur l'application du repos hebdomadaire en France et en Allemagne avant 1914* (Bremen, 1983).

16. See the examples in F. Raison-Jourde, *La Colonie auvergnate de Paris au XIXe siècle* (Paris, 1976); similar attitudes existed in Germany in the latter part of the nineteenth century in the conflicts between the urban health authorities and the small producers and shopkeepers, as is demonstrated in the conflicts documented in the regional and local archives.

17. A. Noll, *Sozio-ökonomischer Strukturwandel des Handwerks in der zweiten Phase der Industrialisierung unter besonderer Berücksichtigung der Regierungsbezirke Arnsbertg und Münster* (Göttingen, 1975). For Henning, see footnote 29.

18. A. Faure, 'Note sur la petite entreprise en France au XIXe siècle, Représentation d'état et réalité', contribution to the Annual Conference of Economic Historians, Paris, 1980.

19. J. Bouvier, *Un Siècle de banque française* (Paris, 1973).

20. T. Spitta, *Aus meinem Leben* (Munich, 1969), p. 91.

21. O. Barrot, *Mémoires posthumes* (Paris, 1875), vol. 1, p. 209.

22. H. Kaelbe, *Soziale Mobilität und Chancengleichheit im 19. und 20. Jahrhundert. Deutschland im internationalen Vergleich* (Göttingen, 1983), pp. 42ff., 245ff.

23. These are my own estimates for the period 1890–1914, based on directories from Bremen and marriage announcements in Brunswick.

24. For Brunswick cf. Staatsarchiv Wolffenbüttel, 12A Neu Fb 7 a 320 I: inquiry into small retail trade.

25. See G. Crossick and H.-G. Haupt, 'Master Artisans and the Historian', in G. Crossick and H.-G. Haupt (eds.), *Shopkeepers and Master Artisans in Nineteenth-Century Europe* (London, 1984), p. 6f.

26. Cf. J. P. Chaline, 'Les contrats de mariage à Rouen au XIXe siècle. Etude d'après l'enregistrement des actes civils publics', *Revue d'histoire économique et social* 48 (1970), p. 260ff.; see also W. H. Sewell Jr., *Structure and Mobility. The Men and Women of Marseille, 1820–1870* (Cambridge, 1985).

27. T. Fontane, *Frau Jenny Treibel* (Frankfurt, 1984), p. 20.

28. M. Boyer, 'Les mètiers de la viande à Lyons de 1860 à 1914 (une étude sur la petite bourgeoisie)', thesis, University of Lyon, 1985, p. 477ff.

29. H. Henning 'Handwerk und Industriegesellschaft. Zur sozialen Verflechtung westfälischer Handwerksmeister, 1870–1914', in K. Düwell and W. Köllmann (eds.), *Rheinland-Westfalen im Industriezeitalter*, vol. 2 (Wuppertal, 1984), pp. 178ff.

30. These are my own estimates from the directory. See also H.-G. Haupt, 'Kleine und große Bürger im Bremen um 1901', *Bremisches Jahrbuch* 64 (1986), pp. 151–159.

31. *Recensement général de la population*, 1906, vol. 1 (Paris 1911), p. 452.

32. See extracts in H.-G. Haupt (ed.), *Die radikale Mitte. Lebensweise und Politik von Handwerkern und Kleinhändlern in Deutschland seit 1848* (Munich, 1985).

33. Staatsarchiv Bremen, 4, 75/7–VR 235.

34. See the examples in G. Stein, (ed.), *Philister-Kleinbürger-Spiesser. Normalität und Selbstbehauptung* (Frankfurt, 1985).

35. Cf. J. Rancière, *La nuit des prolétaires. Archives du rêve ouvrier* (Paris, 1981).

36. Nord, *Paris Shopkeepers*, pp. 31ff.

37. D. Blackbourn, 'Between Resignation and Volatility. The German Petite Bourgeoisie in the Nineteenth Century', in Crossick and Haupt, *Shopkeepers*, pp. 43ff.

38. Winkler, *Mittelstand*.

39. M. Agulhon, et al., *Les Maires en France du Consulat à nos jours* (Paris, 1986); J. Reulecke, *Geschichte der Urbanisierung in Deutschland* (Frankfurt, 1985).

40. R. Gellateley, *The Politics of Economic Despair. Shopkeepers and German Politics 1890–1914* (London, 1974); J. Lorcin, 'Histoire sociale et attitudes mentales. Les archives de la Chambre de Commerce de Saint-Etienne', in *Actes du 89e Congrès national des Sociétés savantes* (Lyon, 1964), vol. 2, pp. 793–809.

41. Boyer, 'Les métiers', p. 512ff.

42. F. Lenger, *Zwischen Kleinbürgertum und Proletariat. Studien zur Sozialgeschichte der Düsseldorfer Handwerker 1816–1878* (Göttingen, 1986), pp. 33, 240.

43. K. Bücher, 'Eigentumsverhältnisse der Leipziger Handwerker', *Schriften des Vereins für Sozialpolitik* 67 (Leipzig, 1897), pp. 699–705.

12 | Authority Relations in German and French Enterprises, 1880–1914

Patrick Fridenson

The rise of large-scale enterprises in France and Germany during the period between 1880 and 1914 led gradually to the development of a new style of authority in enterprises in both countries. By authority I mean not simply the bipolar relations between entrepreneurs on one side, and workers and employees on the other, but rather the whole command structure of an enterprise – its cohesion, and the alliances and conflicts among the different groups within it. These authority relations existed not only vertically, between the head of the enterprise and the base, but also horizontally, within each work level in the hierarchy. As Max Weber was one of the first to point out, this form of exercise of authority created a specific structure of enterprise with its own rules, norms and procedures.[1] This structure also contributed to a change in the perception and self-image of the economic bourgeoisie, indeed, of the middle class as a whole in both countries.

What we are dealing with here is a complex of relations which is, as yet, largely unknown and which has been examined only in a small number of monographs on particular enterprises, and in the history of particular towns or regions. The small number of works devoted to a general study of the French and German middle class in the nineteenth century ignore almost completely the complex relations between the bourgeois heads of enterprises and the workers in those enterprises, creating the impression that these large firms resembled absolute monarchies.[2] In fact, there is very little reason for making such an assumption.

What I would like to do here, first of all, is to attempt to outline an 'ideal type' of bourgeois rule in the big enterprise and to compare its actual workings in Germany and France.[3] The question I want to

Notes to Chapter 12 can be found on page 343.

pose is this: who were, in reality, the more bourgeois, the French entrepreneurs of the Third Republic or the German entrepreneurs of the Empire? I will then look at a fundamental type of bourgeois authority in both countries: the workshop regulations that came into force and became very widespread between 1880 and 1914. Here I am interested in the hierarchic models that operated inside the enterprise and that determined both the actions of people and the ways in which these actions were justified. Finally, I will look at the paternalism that existed in the automobile industry in both countries. This was a new industrial sector and one which was typical of the second phase of industrialisation that began during this period. Perhaps, in this way, one can introduce into the general debate about the middle class a concept of the enterprise which does not limit itself to strategies, structures and conflicts between entrepreneurs and workers, but also looks at the enterprise as a society in microcosm.

The Bourgeois Character of Entrepreneurship in Germany and France

Non-bourgeois Models

One way of approaching this question of the bourgeois character of entrepreneurship in both countries would be to look at those elements in the various forms of paternalistic authority which were pre-bourgeois or non-bourgeois. The economic bourgeoisie mixed the new with the old. One such pre-bourgeois element was the position of the nobility in the running of enterprises, another was the influence of religion.

The proportion of nobles and their weight in the leadership of enterprises was greater in Germany than in France. The reasons for this are to be found in the generally stronger involvement of the nobility in heavy industry and the latter's pre-eminence in the German economy as well as in the co-operation between the nobility and the bourgeoisie within this branch of industry.[4]

It is much more difficult, in this context, to assess the importance of religion. In some cases religion was used as an element of cohesion within the enterprise. Peugeot, for instance, in the region of Montbéliard, recruited only Protestant workers, many of whom had been recommended by the Protestant pastor himself. When the French coal-mining companies brought in Catholic miners from Poland, they brought in Catholic priests as well. In Germany,

Christian trade unions had many members, although they remained much smaller than the 'red' trade unions, while in France the influence of Christian trade unions was restricted to the layer of Catholic white-collar workers.[5] Under certain circumstances, religion made it easier to accept authority. Of course, the religiosity of the French and German workers declined during the period under consideration. Even for Protestant regions, therefore, it is uncertain whether religion mediated a specific work ethic. Similarly, Social Catholicism did not really succeed in getting a foothold among the Catholic workers in spite of the intensive efforts that were made well before the papal encyclical, *Rerum Novarum*, in 1891.

As for the importance of religion among the entrepreneurs, one must remember that in France, unlike in Germany, Protestantism was in a minority. It is highly questionable, therefore, whether an enterprise run by Protestant entrepreneurs would have had greater influence or power over the workers. A study of the textile industry in northern France, where there were both Catholic and Protestant influences, revealed no significant differences in this respect. A study of (German) enterprises in Alsace, on the other hand, attributed the continuity in enterprise management, the cohesion among the entrepreneurs and the high esteem accorded to education to the fact that the entrepreneurs were Protestants, mainly in the Calvinist tradition.[6] In addition, a minority of the entrepreneurs was strongly influenced by Social Catholicism. This Social Catholicism was promoted in France by leading engineers like Emile Cheysson. Its essential claim was that entrepreneurs could solve the most important labour problems in a peaceful and human manner with the help of religion alone, without the need for trade unions or state intervention.[7]

The leaders of the larger enterprises also borrowed from another non-bourgeois institution: the army. During this period the railways, the mining companies and the big stores structured their command and disciplinary system as well as their system of promotion for staff personnel along military lines. Persons with a military background were also sought to fill posts in the administration of production and personnel. Werner Siemens was influenced strongly by his training in an artillery school. German business experts recommended the army as a complex but effective organisational model. In France, Henri Fayol, who first worked as an engineer and later became an entrepreneur, argued after 1888 in favor of a restructuring of the big centralised firms in which the different business functions would be separated from the top leadership of the firm and handed over to a spe-

326 | *Patrick Fridenson*

cialist staff. Fayol also wanted to introduce military procedures into the enterprises.[8] In Germany, Heinrich Mann portrayed, in his 'Empire Trilogy' (not only in *Der Untertan*, but also in the succeeding volumes, *Die Armen* and *Der Kopf*), a paternalistic model of authority close to that found in the military: the lieutenant became the entrepreneur's 'super-ego'.[9]

Two Bourgeois Models

The most important forms of entrepreneurial authority in this period were based on two specific bourgeois models 'invented' by entrepreneurs or engineers and adopted by economists and sociologists. These models were developed during a period of social tensions; the workers' struggles of the 1880's in France and the miners' strikes in Germany between 1889 and 1891. Unlike the enlightened bourgeois models of the eighteenth century, which saw the middle class on the offensive against the ruling aristocracies, the models of the 1880s and 1890s had more of a defensive character. The middle class was now confronted by a new opposition, this time from the lower classes (the manual and white-collar workers and a section of the middle layers).

The first model corresponded to liberalism in its pure form and advocated the maximum application of laissez-faire principles. The entrepreneur should have the greatest possible freedom of action and his authority should not be limited by any kind of special institutions. Conflicts between the entrepreneur and a section of his workforce, or between the firm and the world around it, should be regulated on the basis of the legal norms valid for the whole of society (in France, the *Code Civil of 1801*). There was a preference for ad hoc procedures appropriate to each particular case. The entrepreneur demanded to be 'master in his own house' or, as the saying was in France: 'Charbonnier est maître chez soi'.

If we take this model as our standard, then the French entrepreneur, who was less hindered by external constraints, would appear to be more bourgeois than his German counterpart. Social policy provides a good example. In 1883 a law was passed in the German parliament dealing with accidents at work and laying down the rules concerning responsibility and compensation. French entrepreneurs, on the other hand, succeeded in preventing the French parliament from passing a simlar law until 1898.[10] During the 1880's in Germany laws were passed that dealt with workers' health insurance, accident insurance, invalidity and pensions. In France, as a result of a strategy of obstruction on the part of French entrepreneurs, it was not until 1928–1930 that laws regulating social insurance were introduced.[11]

This classical liberal model, even in France, did not exist in its pure form. There were at least two exceptions: (1) The regulation of individual conflicts within enterprises (between entrepreneurs and workers, between workers and supervisory personnel, between workers themselves) as a result of a law dating from 1806, came under the control of a special institution, the *conseils de prud'homme*, in which elected representatives of entrepreneurs and workers attempted to settle disputes of this kind.

Where this was not possible, the *conseil* came to a legally binding decision. During the period up to 1914, the number of such arbitration tribunals and the number of cases brought before them increased constantly. The majority of these cases were settled by agreement, even after 1907, when the jurisdiction of arbitration courts was extended to all workers in trade and industry. In every town, where such a court of arbitration existed, the decisions of this court gradually developed into a local labour law. Germany imported these institutions, industrial tribunals and arbitration courts, without giving them the same individual and local character. In Germany these courts operated more in the framework of state law.[12]

The declared goal of the *conseils de prud'homme* was, while maintaining balance and fairness, to stop the turnover of labour and to discipline the workforce, since acts of repression had proven to be futile.

(2) As a result of turbulence in the labour market, many French entrepreneurs in the smaller towns, especially in the metal industry, were forced to abandon their policy of patronage, a policy designed to strengthen the legitimacy of entrepreneurial authority by means of traditional charity. In its place, they pursued a policy of 'proper' paternalism. Because they had to attract and employ hundreds of thousands of new workers, the employers were forced to concern themselves with everything pertaining to the workers' conditions of existence, especially in the case of the skilled workers. This meant, at the same time, the disappearance of the previous independence of the workers, an independence which had rested on the workers' ownership of land. The workers, from now on, were entirely dependent on the employers.

Parallel to this, the employers also established a variety of leisure-time associations and *fêtes* by means of which they created for themselves a new legitimacy that was to protect them against the dissatisfaction of the workers, which expressed itself in strikes, and against the criticisms of the trade union and socialist movement. Unlike the big cities, where the complexity of social relations offered entrepre-

neurs other possibilities for asserting their authority, industrial paternalism in the smaller towns led to the formation of an independent
social world. In some respects, this relatively closed social milieu had
certain liberal features. It demonstrated the unwillingness of the entrepreneurs to leave the initiative in the hands of the state, the communities or local groups, such as the land-owning *bourgeoisie*.[13] The
Bismarckian Empire, in contrast, combined state paternalism with the
maintainance of a system of patronage in heavy industry.[14]

The second model of entrepreneurial rule can be described as
social-liberal. In this model, the freedom of action of the entrepreneur
vis-à-vis his workers is subject to certain constraints, and new institutions are created which implement, within the firm, the principles and
methods of public life, especially the legal protection of the person.
The enterprise becomes a kind of constitutional monarchy.

If we take this model as our standard for defining the bourgeois
character of economic entrepreneurship, then German entrepreneurs,
after the 1880's would appear as unquestionably more bougeois than
their French counterparts. Basing themselves on a number of factors,
among them the role of the workers' committees discussed below,
some authors have even spoken of the 'constitutional factory', of constitutionalism within the enterprise. For Germany, at any rate, this
kind of characterisation is exaggerated. In contrast to public life, the
relations that developed between entrepreneurs and workers did not
involve participation in decision-making. What existed was more of a
formalisation of communication between enterprise management and
personnel. This kind of enterprise management could be taken as an
indication of the bourgeois character of entrepreneurship, but it could
equally well be taken as evidence of the relative weakness of German
entrepreneurs vis-à-vis the interventionist measures of the state and
pressure from the trade unions. German entrepreneurs had not yet
developed the basic elements of an industrial relations policy, and the
comparison with France merely demonstrates that their French counterparts were much less inclined towards the formalisation of authority
relations within the enterprise.

At this point it is necessary to make two remarks about certain
nuances in the contrast between Germany and France. First, the bitter
strikes in France during the 1880's, which were repressed with great
ferocity, led the Republicans to be much more concerned about the
workers as potential voters. They therefore supported laws which
helped to limit the power of the entrepreneurs and which protected
the civil rights of the workers within the enterprises. The law of 1884

gave the freedom of association to both entrepreneurs and workers; the law of 1890, which the employers spent four year attempting to block, gave miners the right to elect delegates to the Safety Commission. These delegates were paid by the employers and maintained a public complaints register which was accessible to every miner. A further law in 1894 abolished the mining companies' control over the sickness and pension schemes by means of which the employers had previously been able to supervise the use of medicines and the nature of the sickness, and the length of sickness leave and to restrict the mobility of the miners. This law placed the administration of the funds in the hands of elected representatives of the miners and laid down regulations for the distribution of pensions at a national level.[15] Earlier, a law of 1880 had extended the republican principles of equality and election to the labour sphere, inasmuch as the president and vice-president of the arbitration courts had to be elected by the members of these courts and all members had to be paid a representational allowance.[16] A law of 1892 made possible 'the arbitration and settlement of collective differences between entrepreneurs and workers'. After 1902, members of parliament drafted laws which defined the legal status of these collective agreements. The main goal of all these laws was to channel demands and complaints in a reasonable manner. In addition, however, they also drew attention to the existence, inside the enterprises, of certain characteristic deficits of modern society, which required better organisation in order to ensure its governability. Many intellectuals at the beginning of the twentieth century dreamed of a 'social constitutionalism' which would regulate the powers of trade union representative bodies in accordance with the model of political representa-tion.[17]

Second, liberal French entrepreneurs did not limit themselves to defending their prerogatives vis-à-vis the state and repressing those actions of the workers who questioned their authority. The situation in the labour market made it necessary for them to consider their behaviour carefully. Some of them, like the Social Catholic Emile Cheysson, favoured a *patronage éclairé* which would give them a certain degree of autonomy. There were others, especially in those regions where the labour movement was strongest – for instance, in the coal mining region of the north who were willing after 1891 to adopt a contractual policy which would include the recognition of the trade unions and the delegation of negotiating rights to local or regional associations of employers. In this way, a certain number of French entrepreneurs pursued a strategy of greater openness towards the workers, a strategy which carried further those changes already introduced by the state.[18] These findings make the differences in development between France and German more relative. At the same time, however, the difference in basic political orientation remained.

National Differences and the Limits of Entrepreneurial Control

In France, as in Germany, entrepreneurial authority rested on the utilisation of new human resources, with the assistance of which entrepreneurs were able to keep up with technical progress and also able to react to social tensions as well as to the mobility of the labour market. It is well known that the management of large firms increasingly required specially trained personnel and that this management was taken over more and more by top-level employees and engineers. We also know that there was an increase in the number of supervisory personnel, at a time when the selection criteria for these posts were becoming more demanding, and that entrepreneurs competed with each other for highly qualified workers and employees. What developed out of this was a enterprise structure which was held together more by an ideology of competence than of output. It is against this background that I would now like to look at the different structures of entrepreneurial authority in both countries, as well as at differences in the composition of the new entrepreneurial stratum.

According to case-studies of particular historical examples, it would appear that the administrative structures of large firms in France were less complex and less varied than was the case in Germany. In such different types of firms as the Albert chemical plant, the Dyckerhoff cement works and the Mannesmann works, there was a clear evolution that led from autocratic management by a single entrepreneur to a polycracy, in other words, to a variety of complementary management functions and personnel. In France there was also a gradual expansion of hierarchic structures in the railway and mining companies, in the metal industry and in the chemical industry, but without the same variety that existed in Germany. German entrepreneurs were also more inclined to delegate part of their authority to employer associations, which were more powerful and more capable of enforcing their authority than were most of similar associations in France. These associations existed initially at the local level and dealt specifically with questions of social policy. Later, after 1904, they existed as national organisations.[19]

Sombart and Wiedenfelt have shown that technicians, as a rule, did not play any major role in the management bodies of big industrial firms in Germany before 1914. In France, on the other hand, the influence of engineers on industrial and commercial policy, even on the social and financial management of large enterprises, grew to such an extent that one of their leading thinkers, the university professor Henri le Chatelier, accused them in 1917 of neglecting production: 'The foreman is king of the factory, the engineer plays only a subordinate role and is more involved in administrative activities, unlike in Germany, which already possesses a developed industrial organisation'.[20] The majority of French engineers had been educated to respect the methods of the army and public administration, and this education did not predispose them to favour polycracy.

How are we to determine the influence of the model of public administration on the authority structures and management methods of large firms at that time? In the case of Germany, historians are not in agreement. Jürgen Kocka believes that the German bureaucratic tradition played the role of catalyst for the development of administrative structures in the big industrial and commercial firms. Robert Locke, on the other hand, defends the view that it was the state bureaucracy which profited from the efficiency of administrative structures in the private economic sector.[21] In France, in spite of a long bureaucratic tradition comparable to that of Prussia, entrepreneurs did not limit themselves to a simple imitation of public administration. It was mainly in the banks and in the railway companies that this kind of imitation occurred. There are three possible explanations for these differences.

First of all, the typical enterprise in both countries was different. In Germany, the big firms were often investment companies, while in France there were a large number of family firms (including firms that were owned by more than one family, as was the case, for instance, with Saint-Gobain). In Germany, the factory owner became a specialist, while in France he remained a generalist.

Second, the education and training of entrepreneurs was different in both countries. The education available in the German *Gymnasium* and in other educational institutions was, as in France, very general and not practically oriented. In Germany, however, during this period, the number of engineers and specialists who were given training in the applied sciences was twice as high as in France. Commercial colleges were also established in Germany, which were financially independent of the state. These commercial colleges did not limit themselves to teaching their students double-entry bookkeeping, but concerned themselves with all aspects of management, brought together systematically in a theory of business administration. Although it was very much theory-oriented, this new subject was also interested in the study of concrete cases. Half of the articles in a new journal devoted to this subject and established in 1906 were devoted to such concrete examples. Nothing comparable existed in France.[22]

Third, the proportion of managerial entrepreneurs, a minority in both countries, was probably higher in Germany than in France. In 1912 around 33 percent of all German entrepreneurs belonged to this category, while in France it was 30 percent. Managerial entrepreneurs had a greater interest in enterprise planning, in the improvement of organisation and in the development of workshop regulations. It is possible that they were more dynamic than the traditional family entrepreneurs.[23] Fayol, the best known managerial entrepreneur in France, possessed all of these characteristics, and he predicted the demise not only of the family firm but also of the joint stock company and an increase in the power of managers.[24]

Having looked at differences in the development of entrepreneurial authority in both countries, I would now like to look briefly at the limits of this authority. Even in the workplace, the control of the entrepreneur was not total. It was mainly the skilled workers who were subject to this entrepreneurial supervision; it affected unskilled workers to a lesser degree. Also, between 1880 and 1914, there developed, in certain branches such as the coal and metal industry, and with the explicit approval of the employers, a relative autonomy of particular groups in the workplace. This development took place at a time of uncontested tightening of factory discipline. In enterprises where management carried out direct supervision, for instance, in the form of Taylorism, a section of the workforce succeeded in reestablishing their autonomy on the basis of manual skill.[25]

As far as the effects of entrepreneurial authority and supervision on the private lives of the workers was concerned, there was a twofold development. On the one hand, there was an increase in entrepreneurial control in those towns which were dominated by a paternalistic firm. The supervision of the workforce would then extend to, for instance, the cleanliness of the workers' living quarters. The large stores in the bigger towns also kept watch over the private lives of their workers. On the other hand, there were quite a number of employers who gave up many of the elements of paternalistic control (restricting trade union and political activity, supervising local traders, occupying local political posts, keeping an eye on religious practices).

There were two reasons for this liberalisation. First, the growing importance of the trade unions and, in France, the consolidation of the Republic, made it opportune for the employers to give up certain elements of entrepreneurial authority that would only have been a hindrance to the efficiency of the firm. Second, a new entrepreneurial attitude became dominant, which saw capital as mobile and no longer tied to a particular town. Linked to this were two other considerations, namely, that a relative autonomy outside of working hours could make the worker more productive and less rebellious, and that the creation of an *esprit de corps* should no longer be seen as a goal in itself but as a product of the effective administration of people.[26]

Workshop Regulations in Both Countries

There are a number of difficulties involved in the analysis of workshop regulations. The first of these concerns the number of available sources in both countries. The French National Library has 600 workshop regulations for the whole period from 1789 to 1914, 360 of which have been published on microfilm.[27] Apart from monograph studies that deal with the big firms, there are, as far as I am aware, only two systematic studies that deal with workshop regulations in Germany. These analyse twenty-six workshop regulations from the periods 1838–1888 and 1880 to 1910 respectively.[28] The second difficulty has to do with the fact that in both countries there were models of workshop regulation which were simply copied in hundreds of cases. These were, in other words, largely formalised documents, influenced in part by legally established regulations, which places a question mark over their role as indicators of the bourgeois character of entrepreneurship.[29]

As a response to objections of this kind, one could point out, firstly, that these workshop regulations were renewed within definite periods of time and adapted by the employers to the local social conditions and, secondly, that it is precisely this element of formalisation and imitation which makes them representative. Finally, one cannot limit oneself to a simple textual analysis. One has to ask whether these factory rules were actually implemented, and it is here that an analysis of strikes and of the decisions of arbitration courts provides us with additional information. While taking due account of this inequality in source material, it would appear that the differences between both countries outweighed the similarities.

The Implementation of Workshop Regulations

The first difference is in the number of workshop regulations. During the course of the nineteenth century in France no general legal framework was established for workshop regulations, except in the case of child labour, where an article of the law passed on 22 March 1841 prescribed that regulations were to be drawn up and published. There were quite a number of laws to limit the disciplinary rights of employers, which were drawn up by left-wing parliamentarians after 1819, but none of these proposals was put into effect. It was not until 1932 that a very timid law placed limits on the levels of disciplinary fines.[30] In Germany, on the other hand, after a law dealing with the prevention of labour accidents was passed in 1891, workshop regulations were obligatory in factories employing more than twenty workers.

The history of the origin of this law underlines the significance of workshop regulations. In view of the extremely high level of public concern caused by the miners' strike of 1889, Baron Hans von Berlepsch, chief minister in the Rhine province and later Prussian minister for industry and trade, came to the view that it was essential to go beyond the 'Berlin Protocol' of 1889, in which the employers and the miners had agreed to the establishment of a committee of elected workers' representatives. What was needed, in his opinion, was an 'organised' system of worker representation. This proposal was then taken up by Kaiser Wilhelm II in the February Decree of 1890. The text, published in the midst of an election campaign, made it the responsibility of the state to determine the form of worker representation in the enterprises, the members of which 'are given the authority to participate in the regulation of matters which are of common concern and to safeguard their interests in relation to the employers and the organs of my government'.[31]

The need for state regulation was confirmed by the failure of the 1890 international conference in Berlin dealing with the regulation of safety at work. Entrepreneurs, however, were opposed to these demands of the state, and one of their spokesmen, the general secretary of the National League of German Industrialists (*Centralverband deutscher Industrieller*), announced in 1890 that the establishment of workshop regulations was 'the right of employers, who alone are responsible for the enterprise'.[32] According to the law of 1891, workshop regulations had to contain provisions for dealing with daily work-time and breaks, the period and manner in which wages had to be determined and paid, the period of notice, the kinds of fines, their level, the way in which they were arrived at and the uses to which the money was put, as well as the use made of forfeited wages.

Since, in France, the establishment of workshop regulations depended basically on the discretion of the employer, it is not surprising that, in the period between 1800 and 1880, such regulations were to be found only in a small number of weaving mills, mechanical spinning mills and in some big enterprises (mining, metallurgy, mechanical engineering). After the 1880s there was a definite increase in the number of workshop regulations. This was a period marked by the second phase of industrialisation, the takeover of government by the Republicans and the growth of the labour movement.

In reality, at least in the period before 1866, the classical liberal model had not worked. Throughout the whole of France, arbitration courts were rejecting workshop regulations established unilaterally by employers and were attempting either to modify the regulations on the basis of agreement between the employers and workers or were trying to limit the power of the entrepreneurs in keeping with conceptions of morality and justice. This had a particular effect on fines. In 1866, two rulings of the appeal court annulled this practice of the arbitration courts and declared that workshop regulations unilaterally established by employers were legally valid. This was the beginning of a new development. The rule of the entrepreneur and the argument from economic necessity stood, from then on, above criteria of justice and fairness. The entrepreneur was granted a kind of private jurisdiction, inasmuch as the sanctions which he imposed inside his enterprise were now legalised.

Did these high court decisions now give an impetus to the liberal model? It is very doubtful. Many of the arbitration courts refused to accept the decision of the appeal court mentioned above and continued their practice of dealing with disputed regulations, or those imposed unilaterally by the employer, according to criteria of justice and fairness. There was also the additional fact that, after 1880, many workshop regulations came into force in the immediate aftermath of labour disputes and were based on negotiated settlements between the employers and workers or on informal compromises. Only a minority of such regulations seems to have been imposed unilaterally by employers, something which happened generally in those cases where the employer appealed to the higher court against a decision of the arbitration tribunal. Workshop regulations of this kind did not appear to contemporaries as either legal or legitimate.[33]

In Germany, as a result of the law of 1891, it was possible for the employer, before issuing new workshop regulations, to meet with an elected workers' committee. Did this signify a victory of the social-liberal model? Quite apart from the fact that this meeting was optional and that a law of 1909 prescribing this kind of consultation was never implemented,[34] it seems that many enterprises did not issue any workshop regulations or, when they did, they failed to consult the workers beforehand. The number of workers' committees that were active also decreased as time went by. In 1905 they existed in only 10 percent of enterprises with over twenty workers. It was also the case that the influence of these workers' committees, established on the basis of the 1891 law, was more limited than that of the committees established by various enterprise owners before 1890.[35]

However, one should not exaggerate these obstacles and difficulties. A detailed study of the M.A.N. works shows that the workers' committee was an institution accepted by all the groups in the firm. It prepared the way for a representation of the collective interests of the workers, provided a practical lesson in the settlement of conflicts and was an important stage in the development of modern industrial relations.[36] In France, on the other hand, apart from the coal-mining companies and, later, the railways, only very few enterprises allowed organised representation of the workforce, and where this did happen, it was mostly a result of strikes or other social conflicts.[37] Even taking into account a whole series of nuances, it seems to be the case that German entrepreneurs were closer to the social-liberal model than were their French counterparts.

The Content of Workshop Regulations

As far as the content of workshop regulations is concerned, there were also clear differences between Germany and France. The legal influences affecting the style of such regulations were different in each country. The workshop regulations in German enterprises were influenced by Austrian and Swiss law, especially the factory laws of 1859 in the Swiss canton of Zurich. In both cases there was a tendency to generalise workshop regulations, to give precise definition to universally binding rules, as well as a tendency to limit or supervise the prerogative of the entrepreneur.[38]

In France, the old practice of 'factory police' had come to an end, a practice which had existed before the revolution of 1789 and which had given representatives of the state the right to be involved in the formulation of disciplinary regulations. In its place, two new influences were now at work. Firstly, workshop regulations, influenced by the law of 1791 and by the *code civil*, underlined the primacy of the individual citizen, in that they destroyed the corporations. Secondly, through the establishment of arbitration tribunals, workshop regulations were adapted to local conditions, while county and city courts also played a role in anchoring legal norms within the enterprises.

The content of workshop regulations, in the narrower sense, also differed in both countries. In France, they tended to be concerned more with technical problems (training, safety provisions), problems which arose especially when new machinery or new products were introduced. This obviously had to do with the fact that technicians and engineers were involved in drawing up the regulations. They were also influenced by French legal decisions regarding accidents at work. This type of regulation occurred much less often in Germany, was less detailed and was not legally prescribed. In Germany it was the social question which stood at the centre – healthcare, pensions and housing. These were issues seldom dealt with in French workshop regulations, which probably had more to do with the specifics of French paternalism than with the fact that French entrepreneurs tried to avoid, wherever possible, any kind of formal regulation of social policy. The biggest difference between both countries was the fact that there was a legal limit to fines in Germany, whereas in France there was none.

Disciplinary regulations, however, were very similar in both countries. In this respect, at any rate, Germany was not less bourgeois than France. The fact that the same disciplinary provisions reappeared constantly between 1800 and 1914 is not evidence of the greater power of entrepreneurs. On the contrary, it demonstrates a certain powerlessness on the part of the entrepreneurs in their attempt to instill into the workers bourgeois rules concerning good behaviour and fair division of roles and tasks. From this point of view, what the increasing variety of workshop regulations demonstrates is neither the breakthrough of a 'technology of power' (Foucault) nor a tightening up of labour discipline. It is evidence, rather, of a continuing tension between regulations and established habits and of the instability of the entrepreneur's power. The attempt by the entrepreneurial bourgeoisie to 'civilise' the workforce remained a dubious undertaking.[39]

Two further similarities relate to the role of white-collar workers and the legal status of workshop regulations. In both countries there were special labour (service) regulations drawn up for white-collar workers, which underlined their special status within the enterprise.

The legal status of workshop regulations remained ambiguous, however, in both countries. Many jurists attributed to them a contractual character and recognised them as an integral part of the labour contract between workers and employers. Other saw them as the 'internal laws' of a particular institution, the enterprise, which was situated between the family as a private and the state as a public institution.

This analysis of workshop regulations confirms, in general, the image of a predominantly classical liberal system of entrepreneurial authority in France, with slight variations that resulted from the intervention of public, mainly local, authorities. The social-liberal character of entrepreneurial authority in Germany was largely due to the influence of the central and state governments, which, in their desire to politically integrate the workers, were obliged to be more liberal than were the majority of entrepreneurs. Around the turn of the century, things began to move. In Germany, a growing number of entrepreneurs were willing to adopt a more flexible policy in relation to social issues and personnel and were more willing to enter into compromises. They attempted to create workers' associations or leisure-time associations in their enterprises. In France, the manager Henri Fayol explained to his board of directors the usefulness of limited forms of worker representation. In his personal notes, he approved of strong trade unions, under the condition that they would not attempt to usurp the prerogatives of management, that they would limit themselves to the problems of wages and work-time and that they would be financially responsible for their actions.[40]

Case Study: The Automobile Industry in Germany and France

In 1912 the German automobile industry employed 35,877 workers. The number employed in France was very similar. In both countries the structure of the industry was also very similar. Alongside a large number of small and middle-sized firms, there were a small number of big firms, and it is these that I will examine.[41]

German Automobile Manufacturers

I will consider two firms in detail: Daimler, originally a family firm but increasingly run by managers, and Opel, led by five brothers. On the basis of what we know about these firms, they are good examples of the social-liberal model of entrepreneurial authority. This form of entrepreneurial authority evolved from simply talking to the foreman in charge of each workshop to a complex, centrally directed production organisation. This happened at Opel in Rüsselsheim in 1906, with the establishment of a central labour bureau, which, led by a senior engineer, coordinated all the manufacturing processes, supervised efficiency and provided every foreman with an instruction booklet.[42] In the Daimler works in Untertürkheim, which for a long time was a proper 'federal system of autonomous foreman-republics', there was a central office which, from 1911, provided every foreman with a piece-rate guide which severely limited the latter's discretion in establishing the amount of wages per worker.[43] In Opel, the powers of the foreman were even more restricted. After 1906 he was equipped not only with a piece-rate guide but also with cards (*Begleitkarten*) on which he had to record the type of work and the time worked.[44] At Daimler the workers were subordinate not only to the departmental engineers but also to those white-collar workers responsible for establishing wages. In 1909, possibly following the example of Opel, the firm introduced a card system which provided managers with information on material at hand, the workforce and its wages. In 1911 an engineer, presumably one of the top people in the central office, was assigned the task of determining wages more precisely.[45]

In 1906, after serious social conflicts, Daimler issued its workshop regulations and established a workers' committee. This committee had the right to offer support to any worker who was dissatisfied with his proposed wage level, although the final decision, of course, would rest with the firm's management. The committee also had the right to appeal to the directors of the firm if a worker received a fine which was considered too high. This committee, which apparently existed before the workshop regulations came into force, was recognised by the firm in 1906 as the representative of the workers in wage negotiations, in place of the German Metalworkers Association (*Deutscher Metallarbeiter-Verband*). There was also an agreement, arising from a demand of the workers, that each section in the plant would be able to elect a shop steward who would deal with the foreman in cases of wage conflict. If this failed to bring about an agreement, the workers' committee had the right to take the issue to the management.

Nevertheless, when there was a conflict later in 1910, the firm's directors paid no attention to the views of the workers' committee, claiming that the latter had merely a consultative function. Outside of the plant itself, the workers benefited from the protection of the industrial court in Stuttgart. In 1911 this court annulled a disciplinary fine which Daimler had imposed on seventy-seven workers who were resisting a change that the management had made in the workshop regulations, shortening the period of notice, and who had imposed an overtime ban as a way of exerting pressure. The court, however, did not annul the change in the workshop regulations which the workers had opposed.[46]

It was always the policy of the Daimler management to negotiate with the workers. There was just one exception: the threatened lockout in 1910, which was done out of solidarity with a decision of the employers' association in the metal industry, the *Verein Deutscher Metallindustrieller*, of which Daimler was a member.[47]

From the point of view of the firm's management, the workshop regulations were an instrument designed to strengthen the identification of the workers with the interests of the firm. The firm did not interfere in the private lives of its workers, although in 1912 it made available part of the necessary capital to buy land so that houses could be built for the workers. They did this in the hope that home-ownership would attract the workers away from Social Democracy and make them into 'solid Bürgersleute'.[48]

Obviously, part of the explanation for the social-liberal policy of the Daimler management was the high level of organisation of its workforce. The situation in France was quite different.

French Automobile Manufacturers

Two spectacular cases symbolise the practice of entrepreneurial authority in France before 1914. In March 1904 workers in the car factory, La Minèrve in Billancourt, destroyed all the machinery in the factory after a foreman had threatened them with a revolver.[49] In the Spring of 1906, because the workers had been on strike for an eight-hour day, automobile manufacturers in Paris decided to remove from the factories all stools on which the workers could occasionally sit and to burn them on the factory grounds.[50]

The policy of the French car manufacturers towards their workers was more autocratic that what was to be found in Germany. Only one firm set up a workers' committee: Delaunay-Belleville. In one other case, a firm (Renault) allowed workers' delegates, but these delegates were not permitted to form a committee. Labour regulations were tightened after the strikes of 1906 and, from this time on, the entrepreneurs resisted 'all factory rights that had become established by custom'. Firms did not usually negotiate with their workers. There are numerous reports of workers being fired as a preventative measure before labour conflicts or as punishment. The required period of notice at Renault was one hour. At Daimler, before 1910, it was fourteen days. As a rule, workers did go on strike to achieve their goals. But whenever entrepreneurial authority was at stake, the employers remained hard. There was such a case in 1903 at Peugeot, when the workers rejected a change in workshop regulations. Similarly, when the workers demanded the removal of a foreman, the reinstatement of a worker, the abolition of piece-rate work or of timekeeping, the entrepreneurs were prepared to let it come to a strike.

French entrepreneurs supervised their workers to a greater extent than did their German counterparts and, in the best paternalistic tradition, they set up a large number of social institutions: housing, consumer-cooperatives, insurance and pension funds, leisure-time associations and, in particular, sporting associations.[51]

Centralised administration, on the other hand, seems to have been less developed than was the case in German firms. It seems that only Renault, from 1912, had a central office that was responsible for the scheduling of operations and issued each worker with instructional sheets. The engineer Ernest Mattern introduced at Peugeot between 1907 and 1914 a complete managerial instrumentarium: promotion policy, instruction manuals, control cards, production plans, as well as graphic representations of stocks inventory. He broke up the usual arrangement between engineers and skilled workers and extended the organisational obligations of management to the sphere of production by linking profitability to acknowledge of production. However, he did not set up a planning office before the war.[52]

Further evidence for the strength of the classical liberal model is the fact that there were few regional agreements among entrepreneurs during times of confrontation with workers. Although contacts were made in Lyon in 1905 and in Paris in 1906, from then on the major employer associations in the automobile industry did not intervene in the relations between its members and their workers. They concentrated instead on relations with the state and on press publications which emphasised the efficiency of enterprise managements.[53] Individual enterprises had a very high degree of autonomy. Evidence of this can be seen in the way that the system of factory delegates came to an end in Renault in 1913. The system had been in existence for only four months and was abolished after a strike. The state and the legislative authorities also kept their distance. The state intervened in conflicts only to the extent that it collected information on the views of both sides or made police and soldiers available to the firm to be used against the strikers.

The adoption of the Taylorist system in seven French car firms between 1907 and 1914 may have been an added boost for the liberal model of authority which became the rule throughout almost the whole of the French automobile industry. In an case, Taylorism contributed to strengthening this model and made available to it the techniques whereby relations between different groups of workers could be devalued and dissolved. In this way, nothing was left for the workers but to adhere to the measurable and unchangeable standards of achievement developed by the bourgeoisie.[54] This breakdown of solidarity among the workers and of their traditional values would, so the entrepreneurs hoped, put an end to the trade union movement and to socialism.

Conclusions

The evolution of entrepreneurial authority in France and Germany between 1880 and 1914 brought to the era a new model of legitimacy and a new form of behaviour within companies characterised by impersonal and general rules[55] and by a strong emphasis on entrepreneurial efficiency which went beyond considerations of purely financial profitability. In this process, the position of the foreman declined in importance and his authority was severely limited. Engineers and white-collar workers, on the other hand, attempted to take advantage of this development to strengthen their own positions within the enterprise. The workers demanded a collective representation of their interests either within the factory or at local level, a demand which corresponded to their desire for self-management. The importance of pre-industrial models declined. Enterprises like M.A.N., where the workers wore uniforms and saluted in military fashion, were an exception.[56] Gradually, at least in the large firms, a bourgeois entrepreneurial *modus vivendi*, influenced in many ways by the state and by local conditions, won the upper hand. In Germany this had more of a social-liberal, in France, more of a liberal stamp.

Of course, there were differences within each country, depending on the region, the branch of industry, the size of the enterprise and the period.[57] Further evidence could be found in the architecture of new factories and in the ostentatious style of the residences of many factory owners.[58] At this point, however, we must content ourselves with the impression of a difficult compromise between, on the one hand, the liberal reinforcement of entrepreneurial prerogatives and the establishment of generally binding regulations and, on the other hand, the implementation of many individual rights that were to the advantage of the enterprise workforce. This contradictory structure cannot be compared to the bourgeois social order as it existed in the public sphere. Obviously, bourgeois forms of authority in the enterprises were still in the process of development at the time of the First World War.

Notes to Chapter 12

1. M. Weber, *Wirtschaft und Gesellschaft* (2nd. ed., Tübingen, 1972), vol. I, ch. 10.

2. Cf. A. Daumard, *Les Bourgeois et la bourgeoisie en France depuis 1815* (Paris, 1987), pp. 189–193.

3. For the sake of consistency, I restrict myself to the territory of the Federal Republic of Germany and Alsace.

4. J.-M. Flonneau, 'L'Etat et grande bourgeoisie industrielle en Prusse des années 1840 aux années 1860', *Le Mouvement Social*, 26 (1986), pp. 59–61.

5. Y. Cohen, E. Mattern, 'Les automobiles Peugeot et le pays de Montbéliard avant et pendant la guerre de 1914–1918', thesis, University of Besançon, 1981; P. Pierrard, *L'Eglise et les ouvriers en France* (Paris, 1984).

6. D. Landes, 'Religion and Enterprise. The Case of the French Textile Industry', in E. C. Carter et al. (eds.), *Enterprise and Entrepreneurs in Nineteenth and Twentieth Century France* (Baltimore, 1976); M. Hau, *L'Industrialisation de l'Alsace, 1803–1939* (Strasbourg, 1987), pp. 395–430.

7. On E. Cheysson, see the supplement to *Milieux* 8 (1987), no. 27.

8. J. Kocka, 'Industrielles Management. Konzeptionen und Modelle in Deutschland vor 1914', *Vierteljahrschrift für Sozial- und Wirtschaftsgeschichte* 56 (1969), pp. 332–372; D. Reid, 'Genèse du fayolisme', *Sociologie du travail* 28 (1986), pp. 82–87.

9. I would like to thank Paul-Michael Lützeler for this information.

10. J. Stone, *The Search for Social Peace. Reform Legislation in France 1890–1914* (Albany, 1985); F. Ewald, *L'état-providence* (Paris, 1986).

11. D. Simon, 'Le patronat face aux assurances sociales 1920–1930', *Le Mouvement Sociale* 27 (1986), pp. 7–27; H. Kaelble, *Auf dem Weg zur europäischen Gesellschaft* (Munich, 1987), pp. 73–82.

12. A. Cottereau, 'Cent quatre-vingts années d'activité prud'homal', *Le Mouvement Social* 28 (1987), pp. 3–8; W. Eberwein and J. Tholen, *Belegschaften und Unternehmer*, 4 volumes (Bremen, 1982–1984).

13. G. Noiriel, *Les Ouvriers dans la société française XIX–XX-siècle* (Paris, 1986), pp. 77–80, 89–92 (published in English as *Workers in French Society in the 19th and 20th Centuries* [Oxford/New York, 1990]); D. Reid, 'Industrial Paternalism. Discourse and Practice in 19th- Century French Mining and Metallurgy', *Comparative Studies in Society and History* 27 (1985), pp. 579–607; S. Elwitt, *The Third Republic Defended* (Baton Rouge, 1986), pp. 114–169.

14. P. de Rousiers, 'Le paternalisme allemand', *La Science Sociale* 31 (1901), p. 408; M. Nolan, 'Economic Crisis, State Policy and Working-Class Formation in Germany, 1870–1900', in I. Katznelson and A. R. Zolbert (eds.), *Working-Class Formation* (Princeton, 1986), p. 360ff.

15. D. Reid, 'The role of Mine Safety in the Development of Working-Class

344 | *Patrick Fridenson*

Consciousness and Organisation. The Case of the Aubin Coal Basin, 1867–1914',
French Historical Studies 12 (1981), pp. 108–110; D. Reid, *The Miners of Decazeville*
(Cambridge/Mass., 1985), pp. 132–139. See also Jürgen John, ' "Autoritäre" und
"Konstitutionelle" Fabriken im Deutschen Kaiserreich', *Zeitschrift für Geschichts-
wissenschaft* 35 (1987), pp. 589–600.

16. M. Kieffer, 'La législation prud'homal de 1806 à 1907', *Le Mouvement Social* 28
(1987), pp. 18ff.

17. P. Rosanvallon, *La Question syndicale* (Paris, 1988), pp. 97–108, 246–248.

18. G. Noiriel, 'Du "patronage" au "paternalisme". La restructuration des formes de
domination de la main d'oeuvre ouvrière dans l'industrie métallurgique française', *Le
Mouvement Social* 29 (1988).

19. H. J. Fiedler, 'Entwicklungen von Organisations- und Autoritäts-Strukturen bei
deutschen Großunternehmen', thesis, Frankurt University, 1978; C. Dufour, 'Le
patronat ouest-allemand. Une centenaire polyactif', *La Note de L'IRES 5*, no. 14
(1987), pp. 42–44.

20. M. Leclerc, *La Formation des ingénieurs à l'étranger et en France* (Paris, 1917), p. 95.

21. J. Kocka, 'Family and Bureaucracy in German Industrial Management, 1850 to
1914. Siemens in Comparative Perspective', *Business Historical Review* 45 (1971), pp.
133–156; R. Locke, *The End of the Practical Man* (Greenwich, 1984), pp. 249ff.

22. Locke, *The End*, pp. 155–241.

23. J. Brockstedt, 'Family Enterprise and the Rise of Large Scale Enterprise in
Germany (1871–1914). Ownership and Management', in A. Okochi and S. Yasuoka
(eds.), *Family Business in the Era of Industrial Growth* (Tokyo, 1984), p. 260; M. Lévy-
Leboyer, 'The Large Family Firm in French Manufacturing Industry', in
Okochi/Yasuoka, *Family Business*, p. 230; H. Kaelble, 'The Rise of Managerial
Enterprise in Germany, c. 1870 to c. 1930', in K. Kobayashi and H. Morikawa, (eds.),
Development of Managerial Enterprise (Tokyo, 1986), p. 79.

24. Reid, 'Genese'.

25. Reid, *The Miners*, pp. 124–127; Eberwein/Tholen, *Belegschaften*, vol. 3.

26. Noiriel, *Les Ouvriers*; F. Faraut, *La Belle Jardinière* (Paris, 1987); Reid, 'Genese'.

27. Cf. A. Biroleau, *Les Règlements d'ateliers 1798–1936* (Paris, 1984).

28. W. Hromadka, *Die Arbeitsordnung im Wandel der Zeit am Beispiel der Hoechst AG*
(Cologne, 1979); B. Flohr, *Arbeiter nach Mass* (Frankfurt, 1981).

29. H. Schomerus, *Die Arbeiter der Maschinenfabrik Esslingen* (Stuttgart, 1977);
Biroleau, *Les règlements*, pp. 48, 51, 63.

30. A. Cottereau, 'Les reglements d'atelier au cours de la Révolution Industrielle en
France', in Biroleau, *Les Règlements*, pp. 5,21.

31. H. J. v. Berlepsch, *"Neuer Kurs" im Kaiserreich? Die Arbeiterpolitik des Freiherrn von
Berlepsch 1890 bis 1896* (Bonn, 1987).

32. Flohr, *Arbeiter nach Mass*, p. 21.

33. A. Cottereau, 'Les règlements intérieure devant les prud'hommes au XIX siècle.
Des épreuves de légitimité', contribution to Paris conference, 20–22 January, 1988.

34. The optional character of the committees was approved by the Social Democratic
as well as by the Conservative parties. It was only in mining that a hearing of the committee was obligatory between 1900 and 1905.

35. Eberwein/Tholen, *Belegschaften*, vol. 4 (1984), pp. 1904, 1906–1922.

36. H. J. Rupieper, *Arbeiter und Angestellte im Zeitalter der Industrialisierung* (Frankfurt,
1982), p. 152.

37. J. Rückert and W. Friedrich, *Betriebliche Arbeiterausschüsse in Deutschland,
Großbrittanien und Frankreich im späten 19. und frühen 20. Jahrhundert* (Frankfurt, 1979); P.
Fridenson, 'Die Arbeitspolitik großer Unternehmen in Frankreich und ihre Auswirk-
ungen auf die Arbeiterschaft 1880–1914', in J. Kocka (ed.), *Arbeiter und Bürger im 19.
JahrhundertI* (Munich, 1986), p. 200.

38. Hromadka, *Arbeitsordnung*, pp. 4ff.

39. H. Zwahr, 'Ausbeutung und gesellschaftliche Stellung des Fabrik- und Manufakturproletariats am Ende der Industriellen Revolution im Spiegel Leipziger Fabrikordnungen', in W. Jacobeit and U. Mohrmann (eds.), *Kultur und Lebensweise des Proletariats* (Berlin, 1974), pp. 85–136; Rupieper, *Arbeiter und Angestellte*, p. 98; Cottereau, *Les Règlements atelier*, pp. 18ff.

40. Reid, 'Genese', pp. 90ff.; Eberwein/Tholen, *Belegschaften*, vol. 4, pp. 1915ff.

41. For a study of a smaller car factory in Germany, cf. S. Chopp, 'Une entreprise: Mathis', thesis, University of Strasbourg, 1986.

42. A. Kugler, 'Von der Werkstatt zum Fließband', *Geschichte und Gesellschaft* 13 (1987), pp. 319–321.

43. B. Bellon, *Mercedes in Peace and War* (New York, 1990), p. 38.

44. Kugler, *Von der Werkstatt*, p. 320.

45. Bellon, *Mercedes*, pp. 43–44.

46. *Ibid.*

47. *Ibid.*

48. *Ibid.*, pp. 76–80, quote p. 78.

49. L. Berlanstein, *The Workers of Paris 1871–1914* (Baltimore, 1984), pp. 175ff.

50. P. Fridenson, 'Die Arbeiter in der französischen Automobilindustrie 1890–1914', in D. Puls (ed.), *Wahrnehmungsformen und Protestverhalten* (Frankfurt, 1979), pp. 228–261.

51. J. L. Laux, *In First Gear* (Liverpool, 1976); Fridenson, 'Arbeiter'.

52. Cohen, 'Ernest Mattern', pp. 119, 129f., 137, 140–143, 154ff., 167, 179.

53. Archives of the Chambre Syndicale des Constructeurs d'Automobiles, Paris, 1909–1914.

54. P. Fridenson, 'Une tournant taylorien de la société française (1904–1918)', *Annales E. S. C.* 58 (1987), pp. 1034–1036.

55. J. Kocka, 'Capitalism and Bureaucracy in German Industrialisation before 1914', *Economic History Review* 33 (1981), p. 459.

56. Rupieper, *Arbeiter und Angestellte*, p. 99.

57. For Germany, cf.: W. Ruppert (ed.), *Die Arbeiter* (Munich, 1986); H. Steffens, *Autorität und Revolte* (Weingarten, 1986); E. Glovka-Spencer, *Management and Labour in Imperial Germany. Ruhr Industrialists as Employers, 1896–1914* (New Brunswick, 1984); H. Junkers, 'Entwicklung und Wachstum der Stahl- und Hüttenwerke Oberhausen und Neu-Oberhausen 1880–1890, Beispiele unternehmerischer Entscheidungen in der Gute-Hoffnungs-Hütte', thesis, Heidelberg University, 1970; V. Hentschel, *Wirtschaftsgeschichte der Maschinenfabrik Esslingen AG 1846–1918* (Stuttgart, 1977); G. Schulz, *Die Arbeiter und Angestellten bei Felten und Guilleaume* (Wiesbaden, 1979); S. H. F. Hickey, *Workers in Imperial Germany. The Miners of the Ruhr* (New York, 1985).

58. K. Herding, 'Industriebild und Moderne. Zur Künstlerischen Bewältigung der Technik im Übergang zur Großmaschinerie 1830–1890', in H. Pfeiffer, et al. (eds.), *Art social und art industriel. Funktionen der Kunst im Zeitalter des Industrialismus* (Munich, 1987), pp. 424–468.

13 | Bourgeois Liberalism and Public Health: A Franco-German Comparison

Allan Mitchell

After the French Revolution, it is clear, liberalism displayed a Janus-face. Looking back at the monarchical absolutism of the eighteenth century it appeared as a progressive constitutional movement that supported political freedom and human rights, but looking forward to the rising popular democracy of the nineteenth century it revealed itself as a tenaciously conservative force that sought to maintain the existing social order. A certain decadence of the liberal tradition can thereby be observed, as is often the case with sociopolitical ideologies: after an initially innovative conception has become established, it slowly loses its reformist traits, becomes a defender of prevailing circumstances, and protects itself against new impulses.

Thus it was with liberalism, the elaborate *Weltanschauung* that was so characteristic and formative for European history during the nineteenth century. Indeed, the temptation is considerable to designate the period between Napoleon Bonaparte and the First World War altogether as the liberal era. Yet precious little is thereby conveyed unless we are able to give liberalism a general definition, recognise its nuances, and describe its various ramifications. To accomplish this task in a brief essay is scarcely possible. But through a delimited and pointed inquiry we may perhaps cast a somewhat sharper light on that liberal Janus-face and better gain our bearings within this enormous problem.

The following comparison between France and Germany begins with the assumption that during the nineteenth century both countries were involved in an irrepressible process of *embourgeoisement* (*Verbürgerlichung*). Hence the character of the two societies was increasingly and importantly determined by the *bourgeoisie* (*Bürgertum*),

Notes to Chapter 13 can be found on page 361.

although the German development was somewhat slower because of tardy industrialisation and delayed national unification. Only when bourgeois elements were strong could the liberal ideology make headway. In that sense the liberal era was also the bourgeois era. This observation might seem to be a patent banality, but in fact it requires a careful examination. For that purpose the question of public health in France and Germany should serve to help us focus closely on the rich texture of theory and practice.

The Unity and Diversity of European Liberalism

If we begin in the middle of the nineteenth century, we find ourselves directly in the classical age of European liberalism.[1] Before we consider national differences, it would be well first of all to grasp the common characteristics of this intellectually and politically decisive current of opinion. In view of the inexhaustible complexity of liberal apparitions, many historians regard a general definition to be hopeless. German liberalism alone produced a bewildering range of chronological and regional variations that are hardly to be categorised. The introduction to an anthology of pre-1848 liberalism consequently ends with this lapidary sentence: 'The unity of the liberal movement in Germany emanated only from its diversity'.[2] That might be true, but it sounds like a pronouncement about the doctrine of the Holy Trinity. Despite the unavoidable limitations inherent in framing any conception, such vague characterisations are insufficient if 'liberalism' is to be deployed at all as an analytic category. Insofar as we intend to deal with this formerly influential historical phenomenon, we cannot avoid the effort of establishing its basic principles. Three of them are especially prominent.

Liberalism was above all a philosophy of self-help. Nothing was more important for the true liberal than the individual. The world turned on single persons or patriarchal families who controlled their own destiny. That was at the same time their right and their duty. From the fatherland of liberalism, from England, came the authentic gospel of the liberal conviction that individual rights and personal freedom were the inalienable possession of humanity. In his brilliant essay 'On Liberty' (1859), John Stuart Mill captured the indestructible core of this viewpoint in a single oft-quoted sentence: 'Over himself, over his mind and body, the individual is sovereign'.[3] From this were derived all such liberal demands as freedom of speech, freedom of the press, and freedom of the ballot, under the assumption that the human being was also capable of exercising these basic rights. To that extent liberalism was decidedly optimistic, because it professed that the individual thinks and acts by 'rational free choice'.[4]

In the first half of the nineteenth century liberal aspirations were closely linked with demands for a constitution. It was not simply a matter of articulating some principles of law but also of securing them textually and unmistakably within a political framework.[5] From the outset this objective had two components, one explicit and one implicit. Clearly enunciated was the intention to limit the arbitrary power of absolutism. Another goal, at first subliminal but ever more obvious, then appeared: to avoid the radical excesses of democracy. Absolutism and democracy as political poles represented a permanent danger for the liberals. Their relative weight shifted in the course of the century; the restoration of a tyrannical rule seemed less menacing to the liberals, particularly after the Paris Commune, than the revolution of a dissatisfied populace. Still, the basic tenets of individual liberty remained carefully profiled and passionately defended. Differences no doubt existed from time to time and from place to place, but individualism nonetheless remained as the coveted ideal of all genuine liberals.[6]

Liberalism represented a defense against the interventionist state. One cannot say that the liberals were hostile to the state.[7] On the contrary. The liberal state assumed numerous duties and was not basically at odds with traditional forms of European governance. Of course, it should not insouciantly interfere with private or family life, which would have countermanded the declared liberal principle of individualism. In this respect liberalism was a doctrine of the *juste milieu*. It espoused the view that the state had a legitimate role to play in some circumstances but not in others. A constitutional guarantee of individual rights and personal liberty was not altogether sufficient, because all humans must live and interact in society, even when two or more private interests come into conflict. In cases of doubt the state might therefore exercise a 'negative' or defensive function. It would be legitimate to protect the individual and also the community, which justified the police and the courts as well as the army and diplomacy.

Thus in theory the liberals were prepared to make extensive concessions to the constituted political authority. Yet this ostensibly flexible stance had its (often rather imprecise) limits, because in the liberal view the state possessed no specifically 'positive' function. It should not attempt by its intervention to alter the existence of an individual regardless of whether that person approved such action or not. For that reason, initially, charity was a mostly private matter and not a function of the state.[8]

In the economic sphere there was likewise a shared theoretical position among liberals, which was, however, frequently accompanied by divergent practices. The famous liberal slogan of *laissez faire, laissez passer* was quite controversial in early liberalism and nearly as often ignored as proclaimed. But with time the situation became clarified: liberalism opted for free trade, formally acknowledged in 1860 with the Cobden treaty between England and France, to which the German Customs Union was soon joined. This alignment became even clearer when Europe stumbled into an economic crisis in 1873. Now being liberal meant an attachment to free trade. When Bismarck dismissed his liberal colleague Rudolf von Delbrück in 1875, this was an obvious signal that in Germany a rejection of liberal economic policy was in the offing.[9]

To be liberal also meant to economise. The liberals usually supported a monetary policy of *petit budget*. The ideal state should remain limited in its finances as well as in its functions. It should appropriate no more than a minimum from the possessions and earnings of the citizen, and certainly not place the 'natural' distribution of wealth into question. The liberal of the nineteenth century was consequently no partisan of a progressive income tax, which seemed necessary neither in the present nor in the future. After all, the social order already existed in its broad outlines, even though its details might perhaps be imperfectly implemented. It was not the prerogative of the state, in any event, arbitrarily to shake the structure of society.[10]

Liberalism was closely integrated with the bourgeoisie. Liberal philosophy and bourgeois social status were not totally identical, and the concept of 'bourgeois liberalism' is therefore to be employed only with caution and qualification,[11] for two immediate reasons. In the first place, liberal ideas were not a monopoly of the commercial bourgeoisie, as is suggested by expressions and phenomena like 'administrative liberalism', 'bureaucratic liberalism', or 'cabinet liberalism'. There was even an 'aristocratic liberalism', of which Alexis de Tocqueville, among many lesser known names, was an outstanding example.[12] Whether it makes sense to speak similarly of a 'proletarian liberalism' can be left aside; it is demonstrable, at any rate, that liberal conceptions exercised a certain attraction for the growing labour movement, so that a 'radical liberalism' without clear boundaries of social ranking became evident.[13] Such manifest complexity cannot be ignored by scholars of liberalism, and it complicates any attempt to identify liberalism with the bourgeoisie.

The second reason is as compelling as the first. It is undeniable that the bourgeoisie was not unified and did not represent a single cluster of identical interests.[14] One especially relevant facet of this extensive theme can be briefly mentioned here: namely, the difference between large and small enterprises that became conspicuous everywhere in Europe. Managers of large firms with many employees and their own bureaucracy could afford, as a practical matter, to adopt state-sponsored social security or insurance measures. For big business and factory owners the expenditure of money and paper was not overwhelming. The real problem of social legislation in the nineteenth century lay with the smaller trades and commercial enterprises, for which such measures were incomparably more time-consuming and costly. Because there were so many reluctant small enterprises until 1914 and beyond, especially in France but also in Germany, their negative attitude toward interventions by the state remained of enormous importance for the entire society. We can thereby recognise how liberalism was variously conceived and why it was advocated with degrees of enthusiasm by different bourgeois types.[15]

Despite these rapidly suggested reservations, liberalism did represent many bourgeois interests and lifestyles. It was surely no accident that the liberal era coincided chronologically with the extension of bourgeois social dominance. If the concepts of bourgeoisie and liberalism are not always identical, historically they were largely compatible.[16]

German and French Divergences

By 1866, shortly after the founding of the North German Confederation, France and Prusso-Germany resembled each other in many respects and stood apart in virtual parity. Their population, their territory, their form of government, their economic capacity, and their military strength were nearly equal, although many contemporaries assumed that France, as an already established power, held a slight advantage. In that circumstance it seemed plausible that these two great continental powers would continue to develop simultaneously and similarly. We now know that things turned out otherwise, because politics and above all war decided in favour of Germany.[17] These familiar events can be cogently summarised in order to sketch the development of liberalism on opposite sides of the Rhine.

Germany

The war of 1866 was extremely problematical for the German liberals. Many of them abhorred a military conflict between Prussia and the Habsburg monarchy. In the Prussian Lower House the liberal majority expressed its misgivings with a refusal to ratify the military budget. Great critical orations rang out, which were soon to be regretted. Outside of Prussia it was sometimes more than a matter of words: the liberal opposition in Saxony and Frankfurt, for instance, was forced to confirm to the new order.

The campaign of 1870 against France and the subsequent unification of the Reich extracted further concessions from the liberals. Even if many liberals from Baden or Bavaria joined the national cause only with much skepticism, yet they finally did so, and they thereby accepted a bargain that was not entirely to their liking.

The Great Depression of 1873 struck a lethal blow to liberalism. Business, whether big or small, became traumatised by the economic crisis and was therefore incapable of preventing a transition to protectionism. Apart from the fact that Bismarck thereupon left his former liberal allies in the lurch, they were no longer united among themselves. The National Liberal movement, hitherto the main prop of the political regime, was shattered, allowing the chancellor to rule henceforth with a new coalition and without needing to pay undue attention to liberal principles. Thus, in the course of the decade and a half after 1866, German liberalism took early leave as a decisive political force. Beyond 1880 there no longer existed for the German *Bürgertum* at the national level a coherent, reliable, and dynamic parliamentary representation. Instead, the national interventionist state evolved in full command and dominated the German nation until November 1918.[18]

France

The absolutist pretentions of Napoleon III had never been totally convincing, and they were already compromised in 1866, especially in the wake of the Mexican fiasco. His indecisiveness during the Austro-Prussian war and his dithering in the Luxembourg crisis unleashed a merciless critique by his liberal opponents. His foolish decision to allow the escalation of a conflict with Prussia over succession to the Spanish throne was doubtless attributable to his political weakness vis-à-vis the liberals.

With the lost war of 1870 Bonapartist etatism henceforth disappeared as the dominant force of France. It was replaced by the liberal opposition, which was more or less decidedly republican. A struggle over the definitive form of state was conducted in the 1870s, ending with the electoral defeat and resignation of the conservative Marshal MacMahon. Therewith the way was opened for an opportunistic, republican, liberal, and predominantly bourgeois consensus that dominated French politics continuously until 1914 and, actually, until 1940.

Meanwhile French liberalism enjoyed a long and resilient life. It clearly grew stronger after 1866 and proved able to guide the social development of the country and to restrict state interventionism. The peculiar course of the French nation was thus substantially different but no less striking than that of Germany.[19]

Public Health Compared

Although the tempo varied, all western European states in the nineteenth century undertook the long journey to an industrial society. Sooner or later they stood unavoidably before the same national problems of poverty, urbanisation, and epidemic disease. How did the French, in comparison to the Germans, react to this severe challenge? And what does that have to do with the nearly simultaneous but divergent elaboration of bourgeois liberalism? Three examples should serve to answer these questions: social insurance, smallpox vaccination, and the mandatory declaration of tuberculosis. Differences in national performance and their effects can best be compared through such concrete sociopolitical measures.

Social Insurance

The development of social insurance in Germany derived mainly from a tradition of artisanal confraternities and coalmining cooperatives. The usual form of this kind of social assistance was the voluntary insurance group (*Hilfskasse*), which entirely conformed to liberal principles because the individual worker joined of personal volition. In several enterprises and districts, however, the problem of an obligatory group (*Zwangskasse*) was posed; yet the Prussian commercial code of 1845 basically prescribed the principle of voluntary membership.

For the period between 1848 and 1870 it is possible to speak of a muffled duel between voluntarism and obligation. The Prussian regime as well as others, particularly in northern Germany, distinctly tended toward obligation, but they encountered resistance from both the liberals and also the workers themselves.[20] It was a phase of co-existence: the number of *Zwangskassen* doubled in Prussia, yet under liberal aegis the voluntary *Hilfskassen* also increased. The Schulze-Delitzsche movement, among others, supported the latter. This uncertain situation was perpetuated by the new Prussian commercial code of 1869, under which workers retained the right to choose their social insurance. The liberals continued to encourage the model of voluntary *Hilfskassen* primarily because they wished as far as possible to thwart initiatives by the state.[21]

The German empire thereby began with an open conflict between two structural principles of social insurance. This struggle sharpened during the 1870s as long as the liberal influence survived and aided the *Hilfskassen*. The advantages of the *Zwangskassen*, however, gradually became evident: a broader membership meant more efficient administration and better compensation. Hence the state's pressure to impose obligation increased, whereas the *Hilfskassen* were considerably hindered by the anti-Socialist laws of 1878.[22] Accordingly, the liberal opposition lost ground while the National Liberals suffered heavy electoral losses and were expelled from the ruling coalition by Bismarck. Local resistance was not strong enough, and already by 1881 the *Hilfskassen* were numerically outstripped by the *Zwangskassen*. Thus the Bismarckian social legislation of the 1880s actually continued a long line of development for which a state-oriented insurance program was fundamental. Conclusion: 'The conflict between voluntary and obligatory insurance was definitively decided in favor of obligation'.[23]

At the national level German liberalism was thereby defeated in the struggle over insurance. The *Hilfskassen* stagnated and slumped into relative obscurity, whereas with state support and incomparably greater funding the *Zwangskassen* flourished. Without further pursuing here the unfolding of the obligatory principle, let the enormous expansion of social insurance before 1914 be noted. By that time virtually a quarter of the German people was directly insured against illness, accident, and invalidity. Indirect compensation for families was additional, so that more than half of the total population was covered.[24]

In contrast to the intensively researched area of German social legislation stands the scarcely investigated field of French *sécurité sociale*, whose historical parameters and administrative details still remain rather blurred.[25] Yet a general comparison is possible in which, unlike Germany, the lack of intervention by the French state before 1914 is evident.

In the case of France it is first of all necessary to recall the steady growth of the *sociétés de secours mutuels*. These voluntary groups developed from older corporative and religious organisations. But their real history begins with the Restoration and leads, as in Germany, into the muddle of the revolution of 1848. Like the German *Hilfskassen*, the French *sociétés de secours mutuels* regarded it as their main assignment to insure workers against illness and invalidity. Before 1870 the (Bonapartist) state retained a similar interest in fostering these objectives and in exercising control through government agencies, as two decrees of March 1852 testified.[26] A basically different development occurred under the Third Republic, however, because the new regime after 1879 preferred to dismantle state regulation. Thereupon the French *sociétés* experienced their liberal springtime: by 1889 their number increased to 10,000 (there had been fewer than 5,600 in 1866) with more than two million members.[27]

Meanwhile the mutualist movement had become organised and had announced 'undeniably liberal' demands at its first national congress in Lyon in 1883.[28] Unfortunately, the legislative proposal adopted by the congress, which foresaw a voluntary *prévoyance associative*, could not gain immediate approval by the conservative Senate but had to await 1889 for passage. The trajectory was nevertheless fixed: expansion of the principle of voluntarism without any obligatory insurance.

Incidentally it must be added that the expansion of insurance opportunities was accepted only grudgingly by many mutualists. They were rather more interested in limiting the membership and financial obligations of the voluntary organisations. The need for medical care was not nearly covered by French social insurance before 1914, since it reached but roughly 5 million persons, that is, barely a tenth of the French population.[29]

Although an increasing medicalisation of the populace could be observed on both sides of the Rhine after 1870, this evolution displayed fundamental national differences. The far more pervasive intervention of the state in Germany cannot be overlooked, which in daily life assumed the tangible form of the *Zwangskassen*. Instead, republican France retained the liberal *mutualité*, which resisted strict etatist controls. Thus there remained a fundamental distinction in conception and administration between the German social insurance agencies and the French mutual societies. As we shall presently observe, the consequences of these divergent circumstances soon became apparent.

Smallpox Vaccination

By 1880 at the latest, statistics demonstrated with certainty, if not always with precision, that smallpox (*variole* in French) could be not only combatted but almost entirely vanquished. The kingdom of Bavaria had already by 1807 promulgated a programme of obligatory vaccination. Several other German states and cities attempted the same in the course of time, yet their measures remained insufficient, as might be expected before national unification. In the war of 1870 Prussia entered the fray with an immunised army, although the Prussian civilian population was not yet subject to mandatory vaccination. At the same time neither the French people nor its army was obligatorily and systematically protected against smallpox. As a result, during the siege of Paris in the late autumn of 1870, the Prussian army lost fewer than 500 men through smallpox, while the Paris garrison reported more than 23,000 *variole* victims.[30]

The Prussian forces returned victorious and proud to their homeland. But some of them as well as hundreds of French prisoners of war, carried smallpox in their packs. The sequel was a terrible epidemic in Prussia from 1871 to 1873 that killed many thousands of Germans. The new German nation-state drew the logical conclusion: in 1874 obligatory vaccination was introduced throughout Germany by an national law, with the result that in three years the German fatality rate from smallpox fell to almost zero.[31]

In view of this statistic, soon internationally known and confirmed, one might have presumed that France would immediately adopt parallel measures also to protect its population against outbreaks of smallpox. Yet until 1902 nothing occurred in this critical sector of public health, i.e. smallpox vaccination was made obligatory in France thirty years later than in Germany. In this period approximately 10,000 French citizens died annually of smallpox.[32]

Why was that so? An explanation is offered by the rhetorical duel between two prominent French physicians of the late nineteenth century. On one side appeared in 1891 Dr Paul Brouardel, dean of the medical faculty at the Sorbonne, who asserted that each year 30,000 French persons unnecessarily died of infectious diseases, especially smallpox and typhus. According to Brouardel, these 30,000 could be saved by the adoption of Germany's obligatory vaccination.[33] He was contradicted by a prestigious member of the Parisian Academy of Medicine named Léon Lefort, who gave a speech before his colleagues that filled thirty-seven pages of printed transcript.

We can excerpt from it only a few quotations. To introduce obligatory vaccination, declared Lefort, would be 'a severe blow against personal liberty'. Vaccination was currently voluntary and should remain so. The statistics of smallpox were still inexact: 'We know nothing, absolutely nothing'. The populace was not convinced of the necessity of mandatory measures, and many physicians did not wish to be forced to travel into the countryside merely to administer vaccinations. Moreover, it would be a 'flagrant injustice' to decree obligatory vaccination without first having made all indispensable preparations for the execution of a programme.[34]

Up to this point Lefort's caveats were largely of a professional nature. But the ideological gist of his statement followed: 'Prussia is repeatedly cited, and because vaccination is accepted in Prussia one imagines that it would be precisely the same in France. That is a gross error.... You have no more right to baptise my child against my will in the conviction of saving his soul than you have a right to vaccinate him against my will with the intention of protecting his body'. At the conclusion of his observations Lefort accurately predicted that the French parliament would still refuse for a long time to ratify mandatory vaccination, because this would stand – as he emphasised in reference to his preferred example of England – 'in contradiction to the liberal genius of the nation'.[35]

In this discourse we can easily uncover the classical principles of late liberalism. The state should restrain itself from the private domain of the individual in order not to endanger personal liberty, even when it was only the liberty to die miserably of an epidemic disease. Apparently this attitude was shared not only by the medical elite but also in bourgeois society altogether and among its political representatives. If the estimated statistics are approximately correct, nearly 300,000 of the French were left to die of smallpox in the three decades after 1875 before the political leadership adopted another standpoint. The 'liberal genius' of the Third Republic was reluctant to relent.[36]

Conversely, the prompt and comprehensive effect of the national vaccination law in Germany should give pause to those who stubbornly insist that the state-sponsored and scientifically engendered medical practice of the nineteenth century was of only 'marginal' significance for public health.[37] Like the creation of the *Zwangskassen*, the introduction of obligatory vaccination was only possible in an atmosphere in which a tendency toward state intervention already existed. The law of 1874 was a first step in Germany, of which many others eventually followed, in the direction away from liberal principles. By comparison, the situation in France stood in striking contrast because the liberals there maintained their political influence. France marched to a different drum not by chance but because the drummers quite consciously pounded out a different beat.

Mandatory Declaration of Tuberculosis

Tuberculosis presented, medically and sociologically, a considerably more complicated problem then smallpox. To begin with, the statistics remain controversial. We can only be sure that many more Europeans died of tuberculosis in the nineteenth century than from any other disease. An analysis by social class is practically impossible, although it is certain that lung illness occurred far more frequently among the indigent lower orders than in the middle class or aristocracy. One cannot be much more precise, particularly because it was not uncommon that the ill themselves did everything to hide the awful truth such as the *grande dame* who responded haughtily to an unfavourable diagnosis of her family doctor: '*Nous sommes trop nobles pour être tuberculeux*'.[38]

In the early nineteenth century it had been generally assumed that tuberculosis was hereditary. This opinion changed, but slowly and never completely, after Robert Koch proved in 1882 that the sole source of the disease is a bacillus. Only gradually did the scientific view prevail that tuberculosis is avoidable and curable, and that it is therefore worthwhile to promote sanitary and medical measures.[39] We may hence pose the question: under these conditions, how did Germany and France react to the obvious danger of a tuberculosis epidemic?

The German campaign against tuberculosis cannot be separated from the social legislation of the 1880s. Theoretically, and to a considerable extent practically, every German labourer was insured against illness, and the family of an incapacitated patient had the right to a state subsidy. In accordance with the prevailing principle of obligation, insurance agencies were for their part required to support the henceforth unemployed worker, if necessary for a long time. Tuberculosis, however, was an insidious and stubborn disease that often evaded a total cure. The patient meanwhile represented a permanent menace of infection for those in the vicinity. As a result, the directors of German insurance companies acknowledged that it would be much more cost-efficient for their firms to participate financially in the construction of popular sanatoria, and to send tuberculosis victims there, rather than to leave them at home where they would only consume their monthly compensation checks and infect their family. Thus the number of sanatoria in German significantly increased.[40]

This brief survey should not mislead to the assumption that the movement for popular sanatoria was uniquely responsible for an improvement in public health. To that one could object that tuberculosis mortality was already somewhat declining before the 1890s, when the movement experienced its great impetus. This single measure, moreover, cannot be disaggregated from others, for example municipal sanitation or improved nutrition. Moreover, even the many newly constructed sanatoria were inadequate to meet the need of the entire population.[41] Yet the popular sanatoria symbolised the German counterattack against tuberculosis. They were not without success within the context of a specialisation of scientific medicine that was broadly conceived and heavily financed by the state. The mortality rate in Germany in the quarter of a century before the First World War receded importantly (by about 30 percent). Although the curative value of sanatorium treatment was occasionally exaggerated, at least the prophylactic effect proved to be positive in the long term.[42]

In order to achieve a further amelioration of public health, however, it was desirable to encourage the mandatory declaration of the disease by doctors to administrative officials. Even in the relatively state-oriented German empire, such an obligation had many hurdles to overcome. The 1900 national law on epidemics was silent on this delicate question and left it to the member states of the Reich. Many of these regimes, including that of Prussia, joined in the campaign for mandatory declaration but were able to obtain it before 1914 only in a weakened form, namely in cases of death. Even though this was but a partial victory, the course was thereby set for a social policy of state interventionism.[43]

During the prewar period the combat against tuberculosis in France proceeded quite differently. There mortality caused by tuberculosis remained virtually constant before 1914; altogether somewhat more than 100,000 persons died annually of the disease. In Paris alone, week-in, week-out, over 200 individuals died of pulmonary tuberculosis, relatively twice as many as in Berlin. According to a popular saying, cholera was responsible for 400,000 fatalities in France during the nineteenth century, war for 2 million, and tuberculosis for 9 million.[44] Although such round numbers sound dubious, they fairly reflect a realistic picture and offer at least a notion of the relentless gravity of the epidemic.

'At this time', according to a prominent French expert, 'only Germany had found a solution to the problem through its system of social insurance'.[45] But why did comparatively little occur in France in this decisive area of public health? There may be many answers to that question, but a basic explanation is perhaps to be found in this logical sequence of propositions: in France there was no sanatorium movement and no advanced specialisation of medicine because the support of large insurance companies was lacking; there were no large insurance companies because there was no equivalent to the German *Zwangskassen*; there were no French *Zwangskassen* because an obligatory social legislation was lacking; and there was no such legislation because a dominant ethic of state intervention was lacking. Thereby we have regained our point of departure.[46]

To enlighten ourselves still further, we may enter the Rue Bonaparte in Paris and listen to the debate there at the Academy of Medicine. The assembled elites of the medical profession, and hence the appropriate representatives of bourgeois society, are agreed that tuberculosis is by far the deadliest of epidemics. Would it not be reasonable to contain the illness, then, by placing tuberculosis on an official list of contagious diseases and by demanding its obligatory declaration? Let us eavesdrop on the (here abridged) discussion:

Louis Hardy: 'It is the normal duty of the physician to remain silent.' At least he should act 'according to his conscience'.

Germain Sée: To report individuals means to condemn them to 'eternal exclusion'. Mandatory declaration is tantamount to a 'summary execution'. It only brings the 'greatest confusion' into family life without achieving 'the slightest benefit for the patient'.

Victor Cornil: 'If tuberculosis is omitted from the list, that is manifestly for non-medical reasons.... It is feared that the sensibility of families will be offended by reporting a disease they want to hide'.

Augustin Gilbert: If tuberculosis is placed on the list of diseases subject to mandatory notice, that regulation would become a 'dead letter'.

Joseph Grancher: 'For sentimental reasons' strict measures are avoided. 'In families there has been an implicit agreement that tuberculosis is a disease from which one dies without calling it by name. And physicians, as accomplices to this hypocritical lie, have dared neither to speak nor to act'.

Raoul Brunon: When the question is asked why France has not created so many sanatoria as Germany, the answer is: 'This man is too poor; that one cannot abandon his family; the relatives of another cannot bear to be separated from him'. In the face of such patients one cannot even utter the word 'sanatorium'.... And everyone says the same thing: 'I will not be forced. I will not be locked up'.

Alphonse Laveran: Obligatory measures would be 'great illusions' and hence 'bothersome and useless'.

Albert Robin: 'An absolute system should not be imposed on everyone.... It is our duty to profit from the experience of others, but only to adopt for our purposes whatever is appropriate to the national genius of each people'. It is moreover a question of money. 'A steady increase of the French national budget is being primarily caused by new social institutions'. The state cannot afford to care for all the patients. 'Therefore the economic factor remains an absolute obstacle to mandatory declaration'.[47]

Such citations from the prewar years could be augmented by others at will. But these suffice as evidence that the spirit of liberalism lived on in France and exercised a decisive influence in concrete issues of public health. Not until July 1913 did the Academy of Medicine vote for the introduction of mandatory declaration by the narrow margin of forty-five to forty-three, a feeble result that could only abet the already existing indecision of the French parliament.[48]

Bürgerlichkeit and Embourgeoisement

The foregoing analysis of the relationship between liberalism and public health in the late nineteenth century draws attention to two hypotheses that have emerged from the now slowly dwindling debate over the peculiar course (*Sonderweg*) of German history. That altercation need not be reiterated here, particularly as it is probably best seen as the prelude to a serious comparative social history, for which there have heretofore been only inadequate attempts.[49]

The first hypothesis proceeds from the assumption that the *bourgeoisie* in France was fundamentally distinct from the *Bürgertum* because the former possessed a revolutionary tradition absent in Germany. National differences are thereby deduced mainly from already existing social distinctions. This view explicitly places an emphasis on research in social history. It opens new perspectives, seems fresh and flexible, and serves at the same time as a polemical instrument against traditional historiography with its primacy of foreign policy.[50]

A critique of that position underscores the similarities rather than the differences in the basic tendencies of western European society, including Germany. This version stresses above all a general *embourgeoisement* in Europe during the nineteenth century, which of course occurred unsimultaneously and somewhat idiosyncratically in various countries, depending on their national tradition. Thus, in a certain sense, the social differences are derived from national distinctions, and not vice versa. This is by no means an inadvertent lapse into the old historiography, but rather an altered emphasis that places several of the major postulates of the German *Sonderweg* into question.[51]

These contradictions can be resolved by the simple axiom that each nation-state underwent its own peculiar development. Furthermore, the theory and practice of various nations must be measured by specific practical problems, such as public health. In this regard France and Germany had clearly differentiated experiences in the late nineteenth century. The liberal component was strengthened in the French case, whereas German liberalism became weaker as it joined the victorious military and political parade of the nation-state and altered its character through ideological compromises.

It can surely be maintained that the German populace, including the liberal *Bürgertum*, was able to gain concrete social advantages through the development of state interventionism. Measures of public health in the French Third Republic visibly limped behind. Yet in a long term the interventionist state contained a great danger. Precisely because the German imperial regime brought measureable advances in healthcare to many individuals, bourgeois as well as proletarian, the German people in the overwhelming majority offered great support. Their continuing willingness to accept, indeed to approve, the German interventionist state in the waning nineteenth century was comprehensible, but in the early twentieth century it then proved to be catastrophic.

Notes to Chapter 13

1. For overviews see G. Ruggiero, *The History of European Liberalism*, 2nd ed. (Cambridge Mass., 1948); A. Bullock and M. Schock (eds.), *The Liberal Tradition from Fox to Keynes*, 2nd ed. (London, 1966); D. Sidorsky (ed.), *The Liberal Tradition in European Thought* (New York, 1970); L. Gall (ed.), *Liberalismus*, 2nd ed. (Königstein, 1980); and A. Arblaster, *The Rise and Decline of Western Liberalism* (London, 1984).

2. W. Schieder, 'Probleme einer Sozialgeschichte des frühen Liberalismus in Deutschland', in Schieder (ed.), *Liberalismus in der Gesellschaft des deutschen Vormärz* (Göttingen, 1983), pp. 9–21. A chronologically specific definition of liberalism is advocated by D. Langewiesche, 'Gesellschafts- und verfassungspolitische Handlungsbedingungen und Zielvorstellungen europäischer Liberaler in den Revolutionen von 1848', *ibid.*, pp. 341–62.

3. J. S. Mill, *On Liberty* (Harmondsworth, 1974), p. 68.

4. Sidorsky, *Liberal Tradition*, p. 2.

5. See L. Gall, 'Liberalismus und 'bürgerliche Gesellschaft'. Zu Charakter und Entwicklung der liberalen Bewegung in Deutschland', *Historische Zeitschrift* 220 (1975) pp. 324–56. But also see the critique by W. Mommsen, 'Der deutsche Liberalismus zwischen "klassenloser Bürgergesellschaft" und "organisiertem Kapitalismus". Zu einigen neueren Liberalismusinterpretationen', *Geschichte und Gesellschaft* 4 (1978), pp. 77–90.

6. See Arblaster, *Rise and Decline*, p. 15.

7. The anti-etatist tendency of liberalism is overstated, for example, by J. Droz, *Histoire des doctrines politiques en France* (Paris, 1963), p. 72. More to the point: D. Grimm, 'Verfassungsrechtliche Anmerkungen zum Thema Prävention', *Kritische Vierteljahresschrift für Gesetzgebung und Rechtswissenschaft* 1 (1986): pp. 38–54.

8. H. K. Girvetz, *From Wealth to Welfare. The Evolution of Liberalism* (Stanford, 1950), pp. 43–47; C. Sachsse and F. Tennstedt, 'Krankenversicherung und Wohnungsfrage', in G. Asmus (ed.), *Hinterhof, Keller und Mansarde* (Hamburg, 1982), pp. 271–97.

9. See I. N. Lambi, *Free Trade and Protection in Germany, 1868–1879* (Wiesbaden, 1963); H. Böhme, *Deutschlands Weg zur Großmacht. Studien zum Verhältnis von Wirtschaft und Staat während der Reichsgründungszeit 1848–1881* (Cologne, 1966); and above all H. Rosenberg, *Große Depression und Bismarckzeit* (Berlin, 1967).

10. See M. Frajerman and D. Winock, *Le vote de l'imptôt général sur le revenu 1907–1914* (Paris, 1972); and G. Krumeich, 'Der politische Liberalismus im parlamentarischen System Frankreichs vor dem Ersten Weltkrieg', in D. Langewiesche (ed.), *Liberalismus im 19. Jahrhundert. Deutschland im europäischen Vergleich* (Göttingen, 1988), pp. 353–66.

11. On the dispute over this conception see U. Haltern, *Bürgerliche Gesellschaft. Sozialtheoretische und sozialpolitische Aspekte* (Darmstadt, 1985), pp. 60–63. Much too categorical is the flat assertion by J. Droz: 'Liberalism is, in the final analysis, an expression of the economic interests of the French bourgeoisie' (Droz, *Histoire des doctrines*, p. 69). An opposing opinion is expressed by J. J. Sheehan, 'Liberalism and Society in Germany, 1815–49', *Journal of Modern History* 45 (1973) pp. 583–604.

12. Schieder, 'Probleme', pp. 15–19. R. Muhs, 'Zwischen Staatsreform und politischem Protest. Liberalismus in Sachsen zur Zeit des Hambacher Fests', in Schieder, *Liberalismus*, p. 210ff.

13. See T. Offermann, *Arbeiterbewegung und liberales Bürgertum in Deutschland* (Bonn, 1979), pp. 158–88.

14. Now available with selected bibliography: J. Kocka, 'Bürgertum und Bürgerlichkeit als Probleme der deutschen Geschichte vom späten 18. zum frühen 20. Jahrhundert', in Kocka (ed.), *Bürger und Bürgerlichkeit im 19. Jahrhundert* (Göttingen, 1987), pp. 21–63.

15. This theme is especially well delineated by H. Hatzfeld, *Du paupérisme à la sécurité sociale 1850–1940* (Paris, 1971), pp. 263–320.

16. Some German historians tend to equate liberalism and bourgeoisie, as for example H. A. Winkler, 'Liberalismus. Zur historischen Bedeutung eines politischen Begriffs', in Winkler (ed.), *Liberalismus und Antiliberalismus. Studien zur politischen Sozialgeschichte des 19. und 20. Jahrhunderts* (Göttingen, 1979), pp. 13–19; and H.-U. Wehler, *Das deutsche Kaiserreich 1871–1918*, 5th ed. (Göttingen, 1983). They have been sharply criticised by D. Blackbourn and G. Eley, *Mythen deutscher Geschichtsschreibung*

(Frankfurt, 1980), somewhat expanded in an English edition: *The Peculiarities of German History. Bourgeois Society and Politics in Nineteenth-Century Germany* (Oxford, 1984).

17. Briefly summarised by A. Mitchell, *Bismarck and the French Nation, 1848–1890* (New York, 1971); and amplified in *The German Influence in France after 1870* (Chapel Hill, 1979); *Victors and Vanquished. The German Influence on Army and Church in France after 1870* (Chapel Hill, 1984); and by the same author *The Divided Path. The German Influence on Social Reform in France after 1870* (Chapel Hill, 1991).

18. Beyond the already cited writings of L. Gall, see primarily H. A. Winkler, *Preußischer Liberalismus und deutscher Nationalstaat* (Tübingen, 1964); J. J. Sheehan, *German Liberalism in the Nineteenth Century* (Chicago, 1978); and G. A. Ritter, 'Entstehung und Entwicklung des Sozialstaates in vergleichender Perspektive', *Historische Zeitschrift* 243 (1986), pp. 1–90.

19. The historiography of French liberalism is less satisfactory. Elements of a comprehensive treatment may be found in G. Burdeau, *Le libéralisme* (Paris, 1979); W. H. Logue, *From Philosophy to Sociology. The Evolution of French Liberalism, 1870–1940* (De Kalb Ill., 1983); A. Jardin, *Histoire du libéralisme politique de la crise de l'absolutisme à la constitution de 1875* (Paris, 1984); and L. Girard, *Les liberaux français 1814–1875* (Paris, 1985). Also now compare: A. Daumard, *Les bourgeois et la bourgeoisie en France* (Paris, 1987), pp. 183–240.

20. See F. Tennstedt, *Soziale Selbstverwaltung*, vol. 2: *Geschichte der Selbstverwaltung in der Krankenversicherung* (Bonn, 1977), pp. 13–22; and U. Frevert, *Krankheit als politisches Problem 1770–1880* (Göttingen, 1984), pp. 151–84.

21. Frevert, *Krankheit*, p. 176.

22. See G. Stollberg, 'Die gewerkschaftsnahen zentralisierten Hilfskassen im Deutschen Kaiserreich', *Zeitschrift für Sozialreform* 29 (1983), pp. 339–69.

23. Frevert, *Krankheit*, p. 182.

24. F. Tennstedt, *Sozialgeschichte der Sozialpolitik in Deutschland* (Göttingen, 1981), pp. 165–74; and C. Huerkamp, *Der Aufstieg der Ärzte im 19. Jahrhundert* (Göttingen, 1985), pp. 194–240.

25. In addition to the mentioned work of Hatzfeld, one may expecially consult the many studies by J. Léonard: among others, *Les médecins de l'Ouest au XIXe siècle* (Paris, 1978); *La médecine entre les savoirs et les pouvoirs. Histoire intellectuelle et politique de la médecine au XIXe siècle* (Paris, 1981); and *Archives du corps. La santé au XIXe siècle* (Rennes, 1986). See the penetrating critique by M. Ramsey, 'History of a Profession, Annales Style. The Work of Jacques Léonard', *Journal of Social History* 17 (1983), pp. 319–38.

26. J. Bennet, *La mutualité des origines à la révolution de 1789* (Paris, 1981); J. Gaillard, 'Le mutualisme au XIXe siècle', *Prévenir* 9 (1984) pp. 9–15; and B. Gibaud, *Mutualité/Sécurité sociale. Le rendez-vous manqué de 1945* (thèse à l'université de Main, Le Mans, 1984), pp. 120–69; and A. Mitchell, 'The Function and Malfunction of Mutual Aid Societies in Nineteenth-Century France', in Jonathan Barry and Colin Jones (eds.) *Medicine and Charity Before the Welfare State* (London, 1991), pp. 172–89.

27. O. Faure, 'Le rôle de la mutualité dans l'essor des soins (1850–1914). Premier aperçu', *Prévenir* 9 (1984) pp. 69–74; and 'La médecine gratuite au XIXe siècle. De la charité à l'assistance', *Histoire, Economie et Société* 4 (1984), pp. 593–608.

28. M. Rebérioux, 'Premières lectures du Congrès de 1883', *Prévenir* 9 (1984), pp. 75–85.

29. See Faure, 'Le rôle', p. 70 ff; Gibaud, *Mutualité*, p. 192; and A. Gueslin, *L'Invention de l'économie sociale. Le XIXe siècle français* (Paris, 1987), pp. 167–212.

30. P. Darmon, *La Longue traque de la variole* (Paris, 1986), pp. 358–66.

31. C. Huerkamp, 'The History of Smallpox Vaccination in Germany. A First Step in the Medicalization of the General Public', *Journal of Contemporary History* 20 (1985), pp. 617–35.

32. Darmon, *La Longue traque*, pp. 366–71.

33. *Bulletin de l'Académie de Médecine*, 11 November 1890.

34. *Ibid.*, 13 January 1891.

35. *Ibid.*

36. Darmon, *La Longue traque*, pp. 381–85.

37. Thus argues G. Göckenjan, *Kurieren und Staat machen. Gesundheit und Medizin in der bürgerlichen Welt* (Frankfurt, 1985), pp. 10–26, 53–58, 133–36, etc. On the latest German research on the history of medicine, see P. Weindling, 'Medicine and Modernization', *History of Science* 24 (1986), pp. 277–301.

38. J. Grancher, *Tuberculose pulmonaire et sanatoriums* (Paris, 1903), p. 25.

39. See E. Rist, *La tuberculose*, 3rd ed. (Paris, 1954); and O. Gesell, 'Tuberkulose und Pneumologie im Wandel 100 Jahre', *Praxis der Penumologie* 31 (1977), pp. 333–37.

40. P. Weindling, 'The Campaign against Tuberculosis and it Impact on Domestic Hygiene in Imperial Germany', lecture for the Zentrum für Interdisziplinäre Forschung (Bielefeld, 1986).

41. Göckenjan, *Kurieren und Staat machen*, p. 49–58; and R. Spree, *Soziale Ungleichheit vor Krankheit und Tod* (Göttingen, 1981), pp. 36–41, 47–48.

42. Tennstedt, *Sozialgeschichte*, p. 186ff.

43. See a publication sponsored by the Prussian Ministry of Public Welfare, *25 Jahre preußische Medizinalverwaltung seit Erlaß des Kreisarztgesetzes* (Berlin, 1927), p. 208–24. A universal obligatory declaration of tuberculosis on a national basis was first introduced in 1935.

44. E. Aron, 'Le déclin des maladies traditionnelles', in M. Sendrail et al. (eds.), *Histoire actuelle de la maladie* (Toulouse, 1980), pp. 397–422. Among contemporary accounts see L. Landouzy, *La tuberculose, maladie sociale* (Paris, 1903); and G. Artaud, *Tuberculose et sanatoriums populaires* (Paris, 1914). Recent French research is incorporated by I. Grellet and C. Kruse, *Histoires de la tuberculose. Les fièvres de l'âme 1800–1940* (Paris, 1983); and particularly by P. Guillaume, *Du désespoir au salut. Les tuberculeux aux 19e et 20e siècles* (Paris, 1986).

45. Guillaume, *Du désespoir*, p. 259.

46. For more detail see A. Mitchell, 'Obsessive Questions and Faint Answers: The French Response to Tuberculosis in the Belle Epoque', *Bulletin of the History of Medicine* 62 (1988) pp. 215–35; and 'An Inexact Science: The Statistics of Tuberculosis in Late Nineteenth-century France', *Social History of Medicine* 3 (1990), pp. 387–403.

47. These citations are gathered from the *Bulletin de l'Académie de Médecine*, 1889–1913.

48. See Gullet and Kruse, *Histoire de la tuberculose*, pp. 235–78; and Guillaume, *Du désespoir*, pp. 309–25. Mandatory declaration of tuberculosis was approved by the French parliament in 1963, exactly 50 years later, after the epidemic had already been checked through antibiotics.

49. For balanced commentary and bibliography see H. Grebing, *Der 'deutsche Sonderweg' in Europa 1806–1945* (Stuttgart, 1986).

50. The classic rendition is Wehler, *Kaiserreich*; this is somewhat more moderately stated in his 'Wie "bürgerlich" war das Deutsche Kaiserreich?' in Kocka, *Bürger*, pp. 243–80.

51. See Blackbourn and Eley, *Mythen deutscher Geschichtsschreibung*. The debate is summed up by Kocka, 'Bürgertum', pp. 48–54, 62ff.

IV | SPECIAL PROBLEMS AND PERSPECTIVES

14 | The 'Verbürgerlichung' of the Jews as a Paradigm

Shulamit Volkov

I.

L ooking at the period of the Weimar Republic, it seems quite clear that Jews, both men and women, were considered to be *Bürger*. They were overwhelmingly urban, occupied above all in commerce and in the free professions. From our perspective there is no doubt that German Jews at that time were *Bürger* according to both meanings of the term: they were citizens of the state, its *Bürger*, and they belonged to a specific social stratum within it – the *Bürgertum*.

If we go back in time to the *Kaiserreich*, the situation is not quite so clear, but apart from some *de facto* restrictions on entry into the bureaucracy and in matters of serving as officers in the reserve corps, Jews had full citizenship rights. By 1871 a great majority of them were undoubtedly a part of the German *Bürgertum*, if commonly accepted criteria – such as a minimum of *Bildung* (education) and *Besitz* (property) – were applied to them. They constituted an urban, mainly commercial group, well-educated and ostensibly well-off.

As one moves still further backward in time, the scene becomes more complex. The juridical status of Jews prior to the establishment of the *Kaiserreich* varied from one German state to another. It was only after the legislation of the North German Federation on July 3, 1869, which had abolished all restrictions and disqualifications based on religious affiliation, and was later applied to the entire empire, that Jews became full and equal citizens, full *Bürger*, in Germany.[1] At that time, large segments of the Jewish population were also considered *Bürger* in the other sense of this word, as they clearly belonged to the *Bürgertum* even by then.

Two of the Jews' traditional characteristics tend to somewhat obfuscate our perception of their social transformation. Traditionally,

Notes to Chapter 14 can be found on page 387.

Jews were considered overwhelmingly urban, though in fact they were often allowed into villages or small towns only.[2] They were strongly associated with money-lending and commercial activities, indeed proverbially so, though more often than not this only meant that they barely eked out a miserable existence as *Trödler* and *Hausierer* (hawkers and peddlers) and could by no means be considered a part of the emerging city bourgeoisie. At the end of the eighteenth century, it was estimated that about 80 percent of the Jews living in Germany belonged to the lowest strata, 'living from hand to mouth'.[3] Jacob Toury concluded that, all local variations notwithstanding, some two-thirds of the Jewish population in Germany at that time were so placed as to make the gap between themselves and the German *Bürgertum* practically 'unbridgeable'.[4]

Apparently, then, between about 1800 and about 1870, the Jews seem to have bridged that gap, to have, as it were, 'made it'. After a prolonged debate and repeated delays, they finally acquired full citizenship-rights; within two or three generations, though individual families sometimes achieved it even more rapidly, a great majority of them were securely bourgeois. How did they do it? What do we know about the process of their *Verbürgerlichung*?

In fact, we know a great deal. Although the process was extraordinarily complex, probably more so for the Jews than for other individuals or groups ascending the social ladder during that time, we are relatively well-informed as to its prerequisites, its stages, its dynamics and the agonies associated with it. What immediately seems unique for the Jews, and what makes their case, therefore, particularly instructive, is the degree to which their social access was made intentionally and consciously. Entering bourgeois society, being integrated into it, assimilating oneself within it, these were for many Jews during the nineteenth century, though certainly not for all, the major goals in life. For many, accomplishment in this area was the one and only test for success or failure. Furthermore, the *Verbürgerlichung* of the Jews was, aside from its effects on the individual, a group phenomenon. It was a collective project, repeatedly discussed in private and in public. The new Jewish *Öffentlichkeit* (public sphere), rapidly developing since the late eighteenth century, was almost exclusively preoccupied with tracing this process, commenting upon it, arguing the advantages and disadvantages of its various tactics, taking pride in the individual members of the community who had accomplished it successfully and castigating those who found themselves left at the wayside.[5]

The terminology used at the time was very confusing. One talked of emancipation, but also of *Annäherung* (getting closer), of *Anpassung* (adaptation), *Eingliederung* (integration), or *Identifizierung* (identification). One was using interchangeably *Verschmelzung* (merging), *Aufgehen* (absorption) or *Auflösung* (dissolving). Occasionally there was talk of *Anbürgerung*, too.[6] But this use of words, in itself indicative of the mixed intentions of the participants, should not blind us to the main characteristic of the process. What was at stake was clearly and above all entry into the German *Bürgertum*. Despite the terminological and conceptual lack of clarity, the process of Jewish *Verbürgerlichung* remained a particularly clear-cut example of a group's upward mobility and its entry into the middle class. It was considerably easier to follow, to document and to analyse than has otherwise been the case, and it may, therefore, serve us tentatively at first as a model. In the following discussion an attempt will be made to ascertain the nature of Jewish *Verbürgerlichung* and to examine its potential as a paradigm for the general study of this process from the late eighteenth to the late nineteenth century.

The analysis of aspects of German Jewish history as symptomatic for the state of German society as a whole is no novelty in the historiography. There have been recent discussions concerning the indicative character of policies and attitudes towards minorities, and the general significance of the concept of emancipation has been explored extensively.[7] Let us, therefore, leave aside this problem, related to *Verbürgerlichung* in its legal-formal and political sense, and concentrate instead on *Verbürgerlichung* as a social process through which Jews who had overwhelmingly belonged to the 'lower orders' managed to 'enter' the German *Bürgertum* and become a part, though often neither an integrated nor an indistinguishable part, of it. What did the Jews have to do in order to ascend the social scale? What was required of them by the surrounding society, and how did they approach the task themselves? Who defined the criteria for 'entrance', how dynamic were they, how and by whom were they transformed? Clearly, a full, detailed answer to these questions cannot be provided here. What follows is only a sketch, a suggestion for further thought and research.

II.

First, it must be remembered that the criteria for measuring upward social mobility, used by virtually all studies, are usually defined by two factors: economic well-being determined mainly according to tax records, and the occupation of heads of families, as listed in various municipal and state archives.[8] Though the latter includes matters of social status, level of education, etc., the final judgement as to an individual's place in the social hierarchy was clearly based on an assumption concerning the amount of property he owned and the level of his income. While this is unavoidable, it is not unproblematic. In fact, my argument would be that a minimum of economic well-being was no more than a prerequisite for entry into the *Bürgertum*. Such a minimum was a necessary but not of itself a sufficient condition for *Verbürgerlichung*.

The story of Jewish entry into bourgeois society, it is my contention, supports Jürgen Kocka's claim that the *Bürgertum* was neither an estate, typical of the ancien regime, nor a class in the Marxist or the Weberian sense, but a culture, widely conceived as a system of norms and values, a 'general and at the same time a specific pattern of meaning and assessments, mentality and culture'.[9] *Verbürgerlichung* was above all a process of acculturation, and belonging to the *Bürgertum*, or the final entry into it, could not be decided according to economic criteria, certainly not according to such criteria alone. It is therefore possible that our estimates of the degree to which Jews entered the *Bürgertum* in Germany, based as they are on economic indices, are far from accurate. They probably provide an exaggerated view of Jewish 'accomplishment' in this regard.

Nevertheless, to continue to rely on Kocka's argument, the German *Bürgertum* was 'not a class, but neither was it indifferent to class'.[10] One needed a permanent, above-the-minimum income in order to maintain a bourgeois lifestyle. The particular culture of the bourgeoisie, as much as the previously dominant culture of the aristocracy, with which it had to compete, was just as dependent on economic well-being, perhaps even more so. Maintaining the required financial standard was continuously a source of tension for *Bürger*, certainly for newcomers, who were often plagued by feelings of anxiety and insecurity.[11]

Two examples, a century apart, demonstrate this point. Rahel Levin, better known as Rahel Varnhagen, was born to a family of well-to-do merchants in Berlin. Her famous salon in the 1790s was financed by the income she was sharing with her mother, paid regularly by one of her brothers, Markus, who had inherited the family business. The salon was, without doubt, very costly to maintain. In addition, Rahel was travelling, extensively and in style, to other cities and to various resorts, associating there with the 'best circles', with aristocrats and the local artists. She was constantly living above her means, until finally, with her mother's death in 1809, her fortune sank so low that she was forced back onto the limited and exclusively Jewish contacts of her brothers. With a couple of notable exceptions, the circle of her correspondents – previously so brilliant – was now 'reduced' to include Jews only.[12]

For Rahel, sensitive if somewhat pretentious, this meant considerable hardship, disappointment and pain. But she could not have been surprised. Even at that early point in time, the rules of the game were quite clear: a semi-neutral society, which was then ready, though with no great enthusiasm, to accept Jews, indeed even Jewesses, did not offer them any special terms.[13] Impoverished aristocrats may have been allowed to keep their place, but certainly not impoverished Jewesses. In many ways this society was only partially bourgeois; it was still primarily the aristocrats who determined its standards. This was the world of hierarchy, described by Goethe in his *Wilhelm Meister*, and for newcomers wealth was of paramount importance. 'Every Jew knew that economic security, if not wealth, was the first and indispensable prerequisite of any assimilation', wrote Hannah Arendt in her biography of Rahel: 'There was assimilation only and exclusively for wealthy Jews'.[14] And by 'assimilation' here she could only have meant the very minimum of being passively accepted.

Let us now look at another case, taken from a later period, the case of Gerson Bleichröder. After the establishment of the new *Kaiserreich* in January 1871, we are told by his biographer Fritz Stern that Bleichröder returned triumphantly to Berlin. He had been present at the creation of the Reich, and returned decorated with the Iron Cross. 'He was Berlin's most renowned private banker and one of its wealthiest citizens; he was Bismarck's adviser and the counsellor of much of the elite.' But, as Stern rightly comments, even at that time 'it was easier for a poor man to become rich than for a rich man to become honorable'. For Jews it was practically impossible.[15] Like Rahel, Bleichröder aspired to enter not merely the *Bürgertum* but the highest social circles in the land: a mixed elite, where not only Jewish but also many Christian *Bürger* were considered parvenus. Nevertheless, the limited efficacy of wealth in German society throughout this period, even at this late stage, is clearly demonstrated by the Bleichröder dilemma: wealth was indispensable, but was definitely not enough.

This was apparently commonplace in Berlin of the late eighteenth century. Among its Jews, it was not, for instance, Daniel Itzig, minter and banker, who received extensive privileges in the city as early as the 1760s and was formally naturalised a full Prussian citizen in 1791, who was made an object of admiration and pride, but Moses Mendelssohn, an observant Jew from Dessau, who had arrived in Berlin in 1743 with the most modest means but later become a veritable 'star' in the world of German *Bildung*.[16]

As the ghetto walls, real and imagined, were beginning to crumble, the primary target of *Annäherung* for Jews with ambition and talent was the *Bildungsbürgertum*. The truly rich continued to follow the brilliant example of the court Jews, but this became an increasingly narrow path. Others, beginning to sense the relative openness of a changing society, sought entry where this openness was most clearly manifested, indeed made into an ideology. The old *Stadtbürgertum* was traditionally closed to the Jews; the emerging commercial bourgeoisie was socially dependent on the aristocracy, and its standards of entry were very stiff. The only door that was not entirely closed to newcomers, Jews included, was that which led to the *Bildungsbürgertum*. At that time this was an emerging social group in the process of formation, and Jews strove to join it together with others. In a way, their efforts only exemplified – admittedly with some peculiarities of their own and as if under a magnifying glass – a far more general social process.

The clearest way to appreciate the demands placed on Jews, but also upon all other would-be social climbers into the *Bürgertum*, is to observe the conditions presented to them en route to becoming full and equal citizens of the absolutist state. These were explicitly defined as the minimum prerequisites for entry into the *Bildungsbürgertum*, by then in a process of being itself gradually emancipated, and were articulated by state-bureaucrats who, in Prussia as well as in the Habsburg territories and in southwest Germany, represented the avant-garde of the Enlightenment in its special mix with etatism. They spoke the language of their time, using the idiom of their social milieu. They were an integral part of the new *Öffentlichkeit*, influencing, but above all influenced by the *Bildungsbürgertum*. At that time and on these matters, they were its voice, setting up its standard of values. According to them, it was the new *Bildungsbürger* who alone among the underprivileged deserved to join the ranks of free and active citizens and have a say in decisions made for and by the state. Jews, as the more progressive among them were ready to admit, could be included if they underwent the necessary process of improvement and proved adaptable to the intellectual and ethical ideal of the reformers.

Christian Wilhelm Dohm's book published in 1781, *Über die*

Verbesserung der Juden, is no doubt a classic of its kind. It was a work infused with the 'unshakeable educational optimism' of the time and with a strong belief in the beneficial effects of an enlightened environment.[17] Other bureaucratic blueprints for the bourgeois 'improvement' of the Jews were equally infused with this spirit. They were all plans for making the Jews acceptable to the Bürgertum; only then could they aspire to achieve full emancipation.

III.

Four demands were set before the Jews as preconditions for their eventual emancipation and their immediate Verbürgerlichung: reforming the community's occupational structure, acquiring and using the German language, adopting the ideal of learning (Bildung) and absorbing the newly forming bourgeois ethos and pattern of moral behaviour (Sittlichkeit). In the historical literature much has been made of the demand for Produktivierung, namely the challenge set before the Jews to take up so-called 'productive occupations' and to relinquish their traditional role as small traders. This, however, was a relatively unimportant element in the program for improvement, especially as far as the Jews themselves were concerned. Significantly, it was never actually pursued by the various German governments as a realistic policy, though it was a prominent feature of legislation at the time. Central to the process of Verbürgerlichung, for the Jews as well as for the reformers at the Habsburg court, in Prussia and in Baden, was the use of the German language and the provision of secular education for Jewish children. In fact, both the reformers and the reformed believed that even Produktivierung could eventually be achieved only through Bildung.[18]

The matter of language is particularly interesting and symptomatic. As early as 1739 Jews in the principality of Hessen-Kassel had been ordered to use German – and not Hebrew or Yiddish – in their business transactions. Yiddish in particular, by then the normal colloquial language among Jews, was apparently held suspect by the authorities, long before the issue of emancipation had ever been raised.[19] Indeed, until well into the nineteenth century, it was often seen as a secret language for traders and thieves.[20]

Joseph II's first Toleranzpatent for Jews, promulgated in 1791 for his Bohemian territories, stipulated that Jews were to adapt the German language within two years, and similar articles were later introduced into all other Toleranzpatente. In that drafted for Galicia, Jews were in addition explicitly forbidden the use of the Polish language.[21] In Baden, the success of the constitutional edict of 1809 concerning the Jews was primarily, though not exclusively, measured by the degree to which Jews in the Duchy were taking on German family names and using German colloquially and in writing.[22] Finally, this was also a central theme in the Prussian edict of 1812, and was reintroduced unchanged in the 1833 legislation concerning the status of Jews in the province of Posen, where it was made a condition for naturalisation and for being granted the crucial right of emigration.[23]

Yiddish was no more popular among Jewish *Maskilim* (followers of the Enlightenment) than among German bureaucrats. As early as the 1750s, efforts were made to publish reading material for Jews in a language 'very close to High-German', though at first primarily in Hebrew letters.[24] The circle around Moses Mendelssohn in Berlin was unwavering in its opposition to the hated 'corrupt jargon', concerned as it was no less over the decline of correct Hebrew among the Jews than over their failure to use German. The employment of mixed, impure language was vehemently condemned because it was felt to be somehow 'indecent'. Significantly, efforts were first made to revive Hebrew and not to introduce German.

Ha'Measef ("The Collector"), a Hebrew monthly, was published beginning 1784 first in Königsberg, then in Berlin, and finally between 1794 and its closure in 1797, in Dessau.[25] Even Mendelssohn's translation of the Bible, presenting the original Hebrew text and the new German translation, printed in Hebrew letter, in parallel columns on each page, was no less intent on bringing about an improvement in the Jewish community's use of Hebrew than on the introduction of German.[26] But towards the beginning of the nineteenth century this ambivalence was no longer felt. German, High-German and often hyper-correct, was to be the language of the Jewish *Bildungsbürgertum*.[27]

The use of Yiddish among German Jews, however, never entirely disappeared. Continuous immigration from Posnan, Silesia, Galicia and Russia persistently revived it. Moreover, its use never ceased to be a matter of embarrassment for the local Jewish *Bildungsbürgertum*. Jacob Wassermann, in early twentieth-century Vienna, was no less irritated by the Yiddish of many of his co-religionists than was Moses Mendelssohn a century and a half earlier. While Yiddish was a mark of 'otherness', particularly resented by the acculturated Jews, the problem has much wider dimensions.

It was only in the second quarter of the eighteenth century that a common literary language became the norm in Germany, and *Hochdeutsch* became the spoken language espoused by the educated middle class even later. Traditionally it coexisted with a multitude of dialects and local vernaculars. Only gradually did it become the common tongue, clearly marking, outwardly as well as inwardly, the individual's belonging to the nation.[28] Using *Hochdeutsch* in writing and in speech was first of all a statement about membership in a social stratum, the *Bildungsbürgertum*, and then about belonging to a nation, the emerging German *Kulturnation*. Dialect, in turn, was both the sign of lower social status and of pre-acculturation, its use particularly noticeable in northern German. As late as the 1830s Jung-Deutschland idealists attacked the use of *Plattdeutsch*, using arguments similar to those applied by Jews to discredit Yiddish.[29]

Furthermore, the use of language was a prerequisite for entrance into precisely that type of culture created by the *Bildungsbürgertum* and considered the essence of the nation: a 'spoken culture'.[30] Participation in the discourse about science, art and public affairs, all carried on in a common language, was at that time made the highest expression of belonging. The Jews, as well as many other lower and often rural social elements in Germany, had always been outside the limits of this discourse, not only because of the language barrier but also because the whole world of reference and communication associated with it was entirely beyond their horizon.

Entering this world was the essence of *Verbürgerlichung* and the Jews epitomised the efforts of outsiders to accomplish it. We have some reports of Jews visiting the theatre or getting involved in setting up public libraries, literary societies and the like during the early eighteenth century. It could then only have been the concern of a few individuals. By the end of the century, however, efforts to acquire the German language, in its purest form, and avid consumption of literary and artistic products became a real passion for a whole generation of German Jews. This was no longer a marginal phenomenon.[31]

The well-to-do took on private tutors. However, as early as in 1781, David Friedländer, one of Mendelssohn's closest associates, established a 'free school' in Berlin, intent on providing secular education, in addition to religious instruction, for children of the poor. Similar schools were then set up in Frankfurt, Breslau, Dessau and Hamburg, though these were no longer intended as charitable institutions. They constituted a new type of school for children of the rising Jewish *Bürgertum*, training a generation of integrating Jews and preparing the gifted for entry into the *Gymnasien* and the universities.[32] The *Toleranzpatent* in the lands under Habsburg rule ordered Jews either to open new schools for themselves or to send their children to general schools, while these were, likewise by order from above and often in the face of widespread opposition, made open and available to them. Later, teaching German was considered the main purpose of the new Jewish schools. In 1822 even the traditional *Talmud Torah* in Hamburg, established in 1805, introduced German language evening classes for its students.[33] Thus, particularly for Jews, the importance of acquiring a common language as part of the process or *Verbürgerlichung* cannot be overestimated.

IV.

There was a great deal of debate among enlightened Jewish educators during the early period of *Verbürgerlichung*. But they all agreed on the language issue and were convinced of the necessity to care for the improvement of Jewish habits and manners. Here was another aspect of the acculturation process, crucial for the group as a whole, on which all enlightened reformers, Jews and non-Jews alike, easily found a common platform. Like the use of Yiddish, this too remained a relevant issue well into the twentieth century, kept alive by the continuous immigration of Jews from the East and the waves of migrants from villages to towns.

The first German-language Jewish newspaper, which began to appear in 1806, clearly reveals the striving of German Jews to acculturate. *Sulamith* never tired of exhorting Jews to adopt German *Bildung* and *Sittlichkeit*.[34] Its professed goal was the development of the Jewish capacity for *Bildung* and to this the encouragement of correct behaviour seemed absolutely central. In 1807 the paper examined the condition of Frankfurt Jews, judging their enlightenment by the standards of their cleanliness and according to the 'correctness' of their personal manners and sexual attitudes.[35] In repeated sermons, too, the new standards of behaviour, conforming to those recently normalised by the emerging bourgeois society, were urged upon a willing audience.

Sittlichkeit, like the use of language, was not only a matter for the individual. In the process of *Verbürgerlichung* the community as a whole had to learn to conform. Thus appeals for more respectable praying habits, and especially for a stop to swaying and all outward expressions of passion during religious services – were made part of the general communal exertion to 'adjust'. In Sachsen-Weimar-Eisenach a government edict forbade improper behaviour in synagogue, but liberal reformers of all persuasions agreed in decrying such habits, too, while Jewish reformers like Leopold Zunz found it necessary to urge the end to 'wailing'.[36] Here, again, the convergence of the ideal of the enlightened bureaucracy and of various Jewish and non-Jewish reformers was clearly demonstrated. It was a convergence based on an emerging common culture, and Jews were asked to conform to its norms and values perhaps only somewhat more explicitly and vociferously than others.

The new standards of behaviour, manners and mores, which apparently only a prolonged indoctrination could have inculcated in the minds of the traditionally-oriented Jews, were new and forbidding not only to them, but to others as well. The peculiar behaviour patterns of the *Bürgertum* were taking final shape only in the latter half of the eighteenth century. Some manners were inherited form the aristocracy through a long process of adjustment, but the *Bürgertum* greatly elaborated this heritage. Beyond the development of a more or less outward code of behaviour, it also developed an ethos of its own, 'based on frugality, devotion to duty, and restraint of passion'.[37] Everyone attempting to become part of the new bourgeois culture had to learn to abide by the rules dictated by this strict ethos. It was a particularly difficult task, both because it often required a radical departure from previous patterns of behaviour and because the prescribed rules were never really fixed. They remained continuously fluid, developing a dynamic of their own. Up to the twentieth century the parvenu was criticised for not fully conforming, no matter how hard he tried, and the lack of clarity regarding the rules always made such claims appear credible enough.

Thus there were always remarks about Jewish 'intonation', even though their use of German was beyond reproach. There were likewise always complaints about improper Jewish manners, though possibly no other group tried so hard to conform. In both the case of language acquisition and in that of applying correct manners and mores, the demands of bourgeois society were fully internalised by the Jews themselves. Nevertheless a measure of unease about the use of German can still be detected in the words of men like Fritz Mautner or even Franz Kafka. Accusations about improper Jewish behaviour disturbed some of Schnitzler's and Georg Hermann's Jewish characters.[38] Such concerns were not limited to liberal Jews only. For the adherents of neo-orthodoxy as well, proper, even exemplary behaviour received the acclamation of '*Kiddush Ha'shem*' (the sanctification of God's name) as it presumably contributed to honoring 'our brethren and our religion' in the eyes of non-Jewish (bourgeois) society.[39]

Finally, two additional issues may illustrate the process of acculturation experienced by the Jews on their way into the Bürgertum: the relatively simple problem of dress – clothing and head-cover – and the more fundamental issue of theological and religious adaptation. The story of the bourgeois hat has been recently discussed by Hermann Bausinger.[40] For the Jews the problem was particularly vexing. Head-covering is a religious custom, and the sophisticated hat-on-hat-off manners of the Bürger was bound to create considerable complications for Jews. The need 'to pass' in such matters of outward appearance, however, was so pressing, that even orthodox Jews gradually changed their habits. Early in the century, they began to give up head-covering in offices or in the city cafés; they maintained the custom at home where it could be continued unobserved, or in the street, where it luckily coincided with common practice. By the second half of the nineteenth century, the uncovering of the head in all roofed spaces, in accordance with bourgeois habit, was everywhere the rule even among non-reforming Jews. Some rabbis even allowed bare-headed oath-taking in court, if this was "categorically demanded by the judge."[41] Here again, we have a problem of accomodation to new customs, not unique to the Jews, but more complicated in their case and more explicitly and openly discussed, even debated, by them.

The other important, and difficult, area of transformation was that of religious reform. The Verbürgerlichung of Judaism, which had been in progress since the late eighteenth century, consisted of a two-fold process: a shift of emphasis from the community to the individual, and from ritual and law to concepts of duty and morality.[42] The early Haskalah (Jewish Enlightenment) attempted changes within the confines of Judaism, either by absorbing secular notions into it, as had been Mendelssohn's life-long effort, or by a parallel revival of a separate, secular, Jewish-national culture.[43] By the beginning of the nineteenth century, these two alternatives seemed equally inadequate. Judaism then underwent a process of transformation very similar to that being experienced by both Catholicism and Protestantism in Germany.[44]

For Catholics, overcoming the gap between religion and the emerging German national culture was a major problem. The introduction of Bildung into the church and the development of Catholicism away from dogma, institution and authority in the direction of humanism and 'inwardness' were all central to an ongoing

Catholic debate. Similarly for Protestants, the search for an acceptable synthesis with the Enlightenment became a leading theme during the early nineteenth century. The emphasis on revelation was transferred to piety and morality, and the Protestant tendency to stress the importance of the pious heart, the inner feeling, the experience of sin and repentance, was made ever more predominant. Schleiermacher's romantic solution to the dilemma of religion in the 'Age of Reason' influenced almost a century of Protestant theology. But while his ideas were still debated among Christians, they were already heavily relied upon by Jewish reformers and applied not only by Leopold Zunz, an advocate of reform, but also by Samson Raphael Hirsch, the founder of neo-orthodoxy.[45] For Judaism, the stress on the inner faith of the individual and the predominance of ethics was novel, indeed. But in parallel to developments in the Christian church and as a response to the demands of *Verbürgerlichung*, the adoption of Schleiermacher's approach seemed inevitable. The reforming Jewish preachers often listened to his sermons, as he had occasionally followed theirs.[46] Judaism was in this way made palatable to a whole generation of Jewish *Bildungsbürgertum* and was thus fundamentally transformed in the process.

While changes in the Jewish community and Judaism itself paralleled those taking place in the wider society, they present us with a particularly extreme case. Judaism was considered at the time a legalistic religion par excellence.[47] The traditional adherence to Talmudic law lay at the basis of this indictment. Reform in the spirit of *Bildung* was thus considered a far more radical break with the past for Jews than for both Catholics and Protestants. For some of the early reformers and those who acted under their influence, the dilemmas presented by this confrontation eventually led to conversion.[48] For others, who stayed within the fold, it meant a life-long inner struggle. On the whole, however, German Jews in the process of *Verbürgerlichung* managed to preserve their own separate Jewish identity. They created a new version of Judaism, to fit their new life as German *Bürger* of the Jewish faith. They created their own mix of *Bildung* and *Sittlichkeit*, their own brand of confessional religion, or some would even argue, their own particular subculture. The minimum prerequisite for its existence was its fundamental affinity with the increasingly more dominant culture of the German *Bürgertum*.

V.

The initial process of Jewish *Verbürgerlichung*, it has been argued here, was in many ways similar to and even paradigmatic for the one pursued by other upwardly mobile social groups in late eighteenth and early nineteenth-century Germany. But despite the parallelism, it also had its unique features. Jews had particular advantages and disadvantages in accomplishing the sensitive business of 'entry'. They encountered formidable obstacles but occasionally also found themselves in particularly favourable starting-points, and with unexpected advantages.

Jews, it must be remembered, had been outsiders in European, Christian society for centuries. Entering non-Jewish society during the Middle Ages and at the time of the ancien regime normally required the abandonment of Judaism – both in its religious and in its social-communal sense. Emancipation, however, made entry without prior conversion possible for the first time and therefore posed an entirely new challenge. A new need arose to achieve a synthesis, a creative combination of Jewish and non-Jewish cultural elements mixing advantageous traits from both cultural arsenals. In their efforts to materialize the potentialities of this situation, Jews were faced with an immense task. But some specific ethnic and religious traditions, which at the outset seemed to pose the greatest difficulties, proved with time to be of considerable positive value.

Jewish experience in the world of finance and commerce was undoubtedly of importance in enabling their rise into the *Bürgertum*. It did not matter that *Produktivierung* was never seriously attempted by them at a time of rapid development in commercial activity, with new and promising opportunities for the well-trained and well-placed. But other, less immediately obvious characteristics of traditional Jewish society also turned out to have beneficial effects on the process of *Verbürgerlichung*.

It is not necessary to take Julius Carlebach's extreme position and argue that the corpus of Jewish religious tradition included 'all the basic norms and values which eventually became the universally accepted ideology of West-European *Bürgerlichkeit*'.[49] However it certainly included a number of them; others were developed during centuries of life in the Ghetto. It is difficult to ascertain the actual importance of moderation, modesty, frugality, cleanliness or industry in the Jewish lifestyle of the pre-bourgeois era. It can, however, be argued that because such norms were religiously prescribed for Jews, they had already been at least partially implemented, so that later demands set by the standards of bourgeois life, echoing these rules in a variety of ways, could have been accepted and internalised with relative ease.

In some areas the effectiveness of certain aspects of the Jewish way of life can be seen clearly.[50] It is interesting to observe that Jewish child mortality was consistently lower than that of the surrounding population in pre-modern times. The new attitude toward children, gradually established by bourgeois mores was in line with pre-existent Jewish practice. The traditional emphasis on the education of children was similarly useful for Jews in the process of *Verbürgerlichung*. Paradoxically, it was precisely the old-fashioned Jewish religious school, the *Cheder*, vehemently attacked and rejected by enlightened reformers, Jews and non-Jews alike, which had made possible the high level of literacy among Jewish children for generations, and provided them with some solid learning-habits and a basic respect for the learned.[51]

Scholars are divided as to the similarities between Jewish and bourgeois values of family life. In any event, traditional concepts would in many cases have provided no obstacle to the adaptation and assimilation of new norms. During the third quarter of the nineteenth century Jewish family life was considered exemplary and was celebrated by both Jewish and non-Jewish spokesmen of the *Bürgertum*.[52] Old habits and old styles thus contributed to the *Verbürgerlichung* of the Jews. It made them, indeed, bourgeois 'par excellence'.[53]

But the Jews also faced particular obstacles. The increasingly outspoken patriotism of the host culture was perhaps the most formidable of them. Enlightened cosmopolitanism notwithstanding, 'love of the Fatherland and a patriotic spirit' were placed high in the order of bourgeois virtues as early as the mid-eighteenth century.[54] George Mosse has argued that patriotism and nationalism were indispensable for the development of bourgeois values, because emotional and sexual energies were safely channelled through them from the area of personal passion to the sphere of collective enthusiasm and public pathos.[55] In any case, as the nineteenth century progressed, nationalism played an increasingly important role in the self-awareness of the German *Bürger*, and of the *Bildungsbürgertum* in particular.

This proved problematic for Jews from the outset. Mendelssohn's patriotism was less than pronounced, and enlightened Jews of his generation placed their faith in the brotherhood of mankind and the universality of reason. But after the experience of the Napoleonic wars and with the advent of Romanticism, just as Jews too were beginning to adopt the spirit of German nationalism, the newly developing concept of the nation was becoming ever more exclusive. From its earliest formation, the *Bildungsbürgertum* considered itself a national collectivity, striving to overcome the divisiveness of particularism but also fighting off any measure of pluralism. As upward social mobility became identical with assimilation into the nation any failure of Jews to accommodate to the rigour of bourgeois standards was immediately diagnosed as a further indication of a defective national sense. No amount of self-sacrifice seems to have been sufficient to prove their undivided loyalty. The final blow came with the so-called Jewish census (*Judenzählung*) of 1916, presumably designed to examine the Jews' participation in the war-effort, but seen by them as the 'indelible, most shameful insult ever hurled at our community'.[56]

The *Bildungsbürgertum*, the only social group genuinely open to talent and potentially ready to accept Jews, was from the outset ideologically so constituted that it could in fact only partially welcome them. Under the influence of Humboldt's idea of the nation and as a result of the work of the brothers Grimm, local village dialects, for instance, acquired new dignity as the building-blocks of a higher national language. An entire popular culture was accepted as complementary to bourgeois culture, considered outmoded perhaps, but still part of the national heritage. On the basis of this new nationalism, the transformation of values in the process of creating bourgeois society was no longer considered a social and cultural revolution, and was increasingly seen as an evolutionary, historical process.[57] Yiddish, on the other hand, continued to be mercilessly derided; the observance of traditional Jewish law – categorically rejected. Despite the attempts of Jewish intellectuals to create a parallel 'science of Judaism' and to follow the German lead in this regard, too, Jewish ethnic characteristics were never legitimised by this version of historicism. The sense of Jewish group solidarity and a shared Jewish past collided with the requirements of German nationalism. This may not have seemed so major an issue in the late eighteenth century, but it certainly became one by the end of the nineteenth.

VI.

Verbürgerlichung after all meant not only the assimilation of bourgeois lifestyle and ethos. It meant living *like* others and also living *with* them. Becoming similar was, for them, merely a prerequisite to joining in. The *Bildungsbürgertum*, which seems to have set the terms for *Verbürgerlichung* at least until the mid-nineteenth century, defined them precisely: those who wished to enter had to become *Bildungsbürger* themselves, and could only then hope to be accepted. Moreover, the *Bildungsbürgertum* also established the institutional structure, into which all who assimilated must fit.

The new bourgeois society was composed of associations, clubs and a multitude of half-public gatherings.[58] Jews, who were never allowed into the old type of social organisations, based on the principles of the guilds and the *Stände*, made every effort to join these new bodies.[59] Sources on this matter are scarce, but they leave no doubt as to the severity of the obstacles that they encountered. The best available research deals with the position of Jews in the European masonic lodges.[60] Here, religious tolerance was considered a major tenet, but the entry of Jews was rarely accomplished without protracted controversy and not only in Germany. During the late eighteenth century Jews sometimes managed to enter the new literary societies, so typical of the emerging *Bildungsbürgertum*. Indeed, Jews and Jewesses were part of the Berlin salon society at the turn of the century; but this phenomenon, though truly impressive, remained marginal. On the whole, the world of bourgeois associations was only partly open to even the most 'learned' Jews.

This too is paradigmatic. Bourgeois associations, mainly based on *Bildung* and often on a measure of shared nationalism, were principally open – but in practise almost always restrictive. Confessional barriers were everywhere very significant for the *Bürgertum*. Social distinctions, likewise, were strictly kept. In the second half of the eighteenth century and the early nineteenth, literary societies normally excluded lower-class elements, though only rarely as explicitly as in Aschaffenburg, where 'individuals of lower rank (stand)' were statutorily not allowed.[61] Women, too, were systematically excluded from all participation in the various bourgeois associations.[62] As in the case of Jews, exceptions were occasionally made, but these did not herald any fundamental change.

The situation was never entirely unambiguous. Rifle clubs, sports clubs, singing associations and the like had no consistent policy with regard to Jews. On the whole, entry was more difficult during the patriotic wave at the time of the Napoleonic war than during the heyday of the Enlightenment. And later, in relatively more liberal times, as for instance during the 1840s, or in the 1860s, doors seemed to open with greater ease. Finally, growing nationalism after the

1880s made full integration once more almost impossible.[63] By that time the alternatives were clearly at hand. Indeed, as early as 1800 there were three types of literary societies in Frankfurt am Main: mixed, for Christians only, and for Jews. During the nineteenth century Jews established associations of every kind, primarily in large cities but also in smaller towns and in villages. Bourgeois society, despite its rhetoric, proved increasingly restrictive. Unattached individuals, who managed to amass a minimum of property and the necessary *Bildung*, were accepted; but members of a group, identified as such, had to make do with second best: a 'negative integration'[64] based on emulation and not on a real, shared sense of community.

The Jewish case is, once again, not unique. Both women and workers reacted similarly to the barriers erected by bourgeois society. They established parallel sets of associations, through which they further internalised the values of the *Bürgertum* without becoming active or equal members of it.[65] All in all, it appears that the need to develop alternative routes of integration was indeed symptomatic of the nature of bourgeois society. The *Bürgertum* was extraordinarily adept in making its standards accepted by a whole range of social groups without losing its selective, increasingly elitist and, in many respects, strictly homogeneous character.[66] Although the rationale for not allowing Jews in was different from that used against the entry of women or workers, the problems it eventually presented and the solutions that had to be devised were typical for this kind of society and reflected its nature.

The strategy of 'negative integration' was used by Jews and non-Jews throughout the nineteenth century, even as the defining borders of the *Bürgertum* were changing, its entry-requirements transformed and its 'leading sector' re-composed. As late as the mid-nineteenth century, the financial entry requirements of the *Bildungsbürgertum* were still rather low. Even the formal educational requirements were relatively modest. Upwardly mobile families could hope to enter without undue effort. But after 1848, the links between the *Bildungsbürgertum* and the *Wirtschaftsbürgertum* were strengthened, and both the property and the educational prerequisites for prospective newcomers were raised considerably. The so-called *bürgerliche Gesellschaft* became highly differentiated, complex and diversified. Groups and sub-groups were competing over leadership and the borderlines between and among them were continuously shifting.[67] The behaviour of Jews once more reflected these transformations. They seemed to be particularly well attuned to current social change, and

they quickly reacted in order to preserve and improve their laborious-
ly acquired status.

Until mid-century, the tendency was to provide Jewish boys with
the best educational facilities and then direct them towards business
activity. In later years, study at university and taking up professions
became a wide-spread phenomenon. Occupational statistics bear out
this fact. By 1895, about 7 percent of the Jewish workforce was in the
category of 'liberal professions and officialdom' as against 6.4 percent
in the general population, and their movement into these occupations
is ever more apparent later on, especially in large towns and above all
in the capital city of Berlin.[68] It must, moreover, be remembered that,
even at that later date, Jews were only rarely able to enter the bureaucracy, so that their share in the free professions within this statistical
category was correspondingly far higher.

Jews were clearly over-represented in institutes for higher learning,
even when their relative economic well-being is taken into account.[69]
Realising the new significance of professionalism and university training for a modernising bourgeois society, they entered those frontier
areas with full energy. Once again, they were not alone. University
enrollment figures for the last quarter of the nineteenth century prove
the intensity with which elements of the *Kleinbürgertum* were pushing
in the same direction.[70] Women's changing aspirations are also a case
in point. By the late nineteenth century it was apparently no longer
enough to display perfect manners, or to show fluency in a foreign
language and some knowledge of art or music. Women began to
strive for fuller, formal education, for the permission to take the
Abitur and to study in the universities, for greater freedom of occupational choice and for more equal professional opportunities.

The efforts of marginal groups reflect both the changing nature of
the *Bürgertum* and the dynamics of *Verbürgerlichung*. For the Jews,
however, ultimate goals were also changing with time. From about
mid-century, but more emphatically after the final granting of equal
rights in the new *Kaiserreich* and the immediate social disappointments
associated with it, Jews seemed to reformulate their individual and
collective ambitions. Further social ascent, faster modernisation and
ever greater achievements, especially in the cultural sphere, now
became independent objectives, regardless of the usual demands of
bourgeois life. In some areas Jews began to set up new standards, to
be later adopted by non-Jewish members of the *Bürgertum*. Jewish
Bürger were pioneers in the area of girls' education, the reduction of
marital fertility and of the intensive use of professional medical care.

386 | Shulamit Volkov

Their own society of clubs and associations was also undergoing a process of differentiation and their sense of solidarity was being radically reformulated. There is no room here to deal with the extent and the implications of their growing self-reliance.[71]

***

For a whole century, the main motive force of Jewish life was the effort to achieve full *Verbürgerlichung*. Studying this history has provided us with a unique view of the meaning and effort involved in this task. Some elements of the analysis deserve to be repeated in summary as they may be considered paradigmatic:

First, the significance of acculturation is paramount: the predominance of a common bourgeois language, shared habits and manners, the adoption of the ideals of *Bildung* and the standards of *Sittlichkeit*. Within this context the role of the *Bildungsbürgertum* in general and the officialdom in particular is important as they were defining the parameters of acculturation, allowing these parameters a measure of fluidity and manipulating them for their own purposes.

Second are the effects of tradition, highlighted by the Jewish example. Seen as a starting point for *Verbürgerlichung* the advantages and disadvantages that the various components of traditions carry with them proved crucial for the speed and intensity of Jewish *Verbürgerlichung*. They were most probably of equal significance for others, too.

Third, the restrictiveness of bourgeois society is given concrete meaning by viewing Jewish efforts to 'enter'. The mechanisms that this society has developed for upholding both a measure of its integrative potential and a proper degree of exclusiveness are likewise made apparent through this perspective.

Fourth, nationalism, as a central criterion for defining the borders of the *Bürgertum*, must receive proper attention when the Jewish situation is reviewed. Its significance for the process of *Verbürgerlichung* as a whole should not be underestimated.

Lastly, the dynamism that characterised the bourgeois sense of priorities, its changing self-definition and the transformation of its leading sector are all reflected in the assimilating efforts of the Jews. It also defined the limits set upon these efforts.

From the late nineteenth century, the concept of *Verbürgerlichung* no longer suffices for the analysis of Jewish collective behaviour in Germany. The usefulness of studying their development as a paradigm is, therefore, also terminated. From the early twentieth century such unique features as their reaction to growing anti-Semitism, the development of a separate Jewish nationalism and the problems of immigration and emigration become predominant. The National Socialist takeover finally made their absolute uniqueness within German society more apparent than ever and brought with it not only the end of emancipation, *Verbürgerlichung* and assimilation, but the end of German-Jewish history altogether.

Notes to Chapter 14

1. For a full description of this process, with a clear table presenting the legal positions in the various German states up to 1871, see J. Toury, *Soziale und politische Geschichte der Juden in Deutschland 1847–1871* (Düsseldorf, 1977), pp. 334–361, 384–389.

2. See J. Toury, 'Der Eintritt der Juden ins deutsche Bürgertum', in *Das Judentum in der deutschen Umwelt*, H. Liebeschütz and A. Paucker, eds. (Tübingen, 1977), pp. 139–140. Also S. M. Lowenstein, 'The Rural Community and the Urbanization of German Jewry', in *Central European History* 13 (1980) pp. 218–236. Interestingly, up to 1861 Jews in Bavaria were allowed into towns only in restricted numbers. Cf. S. Schwarz, *Die Juden in Bayern im Wandel der Zeiten* (München, 1963).

3. See the summary of this situation in M. Richarz, 'Jewish Social Mobility in Germany during the Time of Emancipation (1790–1871)', in *Leo Baeck Institute Yearbook* 20 (1975), p. 69.

4. Toury, *Der Eintritt*, pp. 149–150,

5. There is as yet no comprehensive study of the Jewish *Öffentlichkeit* in Germany of the nineteenth century. An important beginning is Jacob Toury's study of the Jewish newspapers in Austria. See his: *Die Jüdische Presse im Österreichischen Kaiserreich. Ein Beitrag zur Problematik der Akkulturation 1802–1918* (Tübingen, 1983). See also the comments in H. Wassermann, 'Jews, *Bürgertum* and *Bürgerliche Gesellschaft* in a Liberal Era (1840–1880)', Thesis, Jerusalem, n.d. pp. 109–115. On another form of the new *Öffentlichkeit*, the weekly synagogue-sermons, see A. Altmann, 'Zur Frühgeschichte der Jüdischen Predigt in Deutschland', in *LBIY* 6 (1961), pp. 3–59, and D.J. Sorkin, *Ideology and Identity: Political Emancipation and the Emergence of a Jewish Sub-Culture in Germany 1800–1848*, Diss., Berkeley, California, 1983, pp. 107–160.

6. See J. Toury, 'Emancipation and Assimilation. Concepts and Conditions' [Hebrew], in *Yalkut Moreschet* 2 (1954), pp. 167–182.

7. See S. Jersch-Wenzel, 'Die Lage von Minderheiten als Indiz für den Stand der Emanzipation einer Gesellschaft', in *Sozialgeschichte Heute. Festschrift für Hans Rosenberg zum 70. Geburtstag* (Göttingen, 1974), pp. 365–387; and R. Rürup, *Emanzipation und Antisemitismus. Studien zur "Judenfrage" der bürgerlichen Gesellschaft* (Göttingen, 1975), pp. 11–36, 74–94, 126–132. For the development of the use of the term emancipation, see the entry in *Geschichtliche Grundbegriffe*, vol. 2, especially pp. 162–169, 178–185; and J. Katz, 'The Term "Jewish Emancipation": Its Origins and Historical Impact', in his *Emancipation and Assimilation. Studies in Modern Jewish History* (Farnborough, Hants., 1972), pp. 21–45.

8. See the figures and the sources in Toury, *Der Eintritt*, passim. And now also A. Barkai, 'Sozialgeschichtliche Aspekte der deutschen Judenheit in der Zeit der Industrialisierung', in *Jahrbuch des Instituts für deutsche Geschichte* 11 (1982), pp. 237–260; and 'The German Jews at the Start of Industrialisation – Structural Change and Mobility 1835–1860', in W. Mosse et al. (eds.) *Revolution and Evolution. 1848 in German-Jewish History*, (Tübingen, 1981), pp. 123–149.

9. See Kocka, 'Bürgertum und Bürgerlichkeit als Problem der deutschen Geschichte vom späten 18. zum frühen 20. Jahrhundert', in Kocka (ed.), *Bürger und Bürgerlichkeit im 19. Jahrhundert* (Göttingen, 1987), pp. 42–48.

10. *Ibid.*, p. 46. See also T. Nipperdey, 'Kommentar: "Bürgerlich" als Kultur', in Kocka, *Bürger*, p. 143.

11. This important aspect of bourgeois existence has been rightly emphasised in R. Vierhaus, 'Der Aufstieg des Bürgertums vom späten 18. Jahrhundert bis 1848/49', in Kocka, *Bürger*, pp. 66–67.

12. For the details of Rahel Varnhagen's life See H. Arendt, *Rahel Varnhagen. Lebensgeschichte einer deutschen Jüdin aus der Romantik* (München, 1981), first published in English (New York, 1958).

13. On the 'semi-neutral society' see the works of J. Katz, who coined this phrase, especially his *Out of the Ghetto. The Social Background of Jewish Emancipation, 1770–1870* (Cambridge, Mass., 1973), chapter 4.

14. Arendt, *Varnhagen*, 168. See also her *The Origins of Totalitarianism* (Cleveland, 1958), pp. 56–67.

15. See F. Stern, *Gold and Iron. Bismarck, Bleichröder, and the Building of the German Empire* (New York, 1977), pp. 164–165.

16. On Itzig and other economically successful Jews in Berlin during the second half of the eighteenth century see Toury, *Der Eintritt*, p. 155. On the mythology which had developed around Mendelssohn's personality see Sorkin, *Ideology*, pp. 112–115, and A. Altmann, 'Moses Mendelssohn as the Archetypal German Jew', in J. Reinharz and W. Schatzberg, (eds.) *The Jewish Response to German Culture. From the Enlightenment to the Second World War* (Hanover, 1985), pp. 17–31.

17. The quoted expression is from Vierhaus, 'Aufstieg', p. 66. See Dohm's *Über die bürgerliche Verbesserung der Juden* (Berlin, 1781). On Dohm and his work in the context of his time, H. Möller, 'Aufklärung, Judenemanzipation und Staat. Ursprung und Wirkung von Dohms Schrift über die bürgerliche Verbesserung der Juden', in *Deutsche Aufklärung und Judenemanzipation*, Beiheft 3: *Jahrbuch des Instituts für deutsche Geschichte* (Tel-Aviv, 1979), pp. 55–93.

18. See especially J. Carlebach, 'Deutsche Juden und der Säkularisierungsprozeß in der Erziehung', in H. Liebeschütz u. A. Paucker (eds.), *Das Judenthum*, pp. 55–93.

19. See Toury, *Der Eintritt*, p. 177. See also his 'Die Sprache als Problem der jüdischen Einordnung im deutschen Kulturraum', in Beiheft 4, *Jahrbuch des Instituts für deutsche Geschichte* (Tel-Aviv, 1982), pp. 75–95. Compare also P. Freimark, 'Language Behaviour and Assimilation. The Situation of the Jews in Northern Germany in the First Half of the 19th Century', in *LBIY* 24 (1979), pp. 157–177.

20. See, for instance, A.F.Thiele, *Die jüdischen Gauner in Deutschland, ihre Taktik, ihre Eigentümlichkeiten und ihre Sprache*, 2 vols. (Berlin, 1840).

21. See J. Karniel, 'Die Toleranzpolitik Kaiser Josephs II.', *Schriftenreihe des Instituts für deutsche Geschichte*, Tel-Aviv University, vol.9, (1986), p. 399–418, 429–449.

22. For Baden see R. Rürup, 'Die Emanzipation der Juden in Baden', in his *Emanzipation*, pp. 37–73, especially p. 49.

23. For the Prussian legislation see I. Freund, *Die Emanzipation der Juden in Preußen unter besonderer Berücksichtigung des Gesetzes vom 11. März 1812*, 2 vols. (Berlin, 1812). There is no modern, comprehensive analysis of the 'Germanisation' of the Jews in Posen. A basic summary can be found in J. Jacobson, 'Zur Geschichte der Juden in Posen', in G. Rhode (ed.), *Geschichte der Stadt Posen* (Neuendettelsau, 1953), 243–256.

For a useful summary of the legal situation in Germany see the Introduction in M. Richarz (ed.), *Jüdisches Leben in Deutschland. Selbstzeugnisse zur Sozialgeschichte 1780–1871* (Stuttgart, 1976), pp. 19–26.

24. Toury, *Die Sprache*, p. 77. ('dem Hochdeutsch sehr nah').

25. On *Ha'Measef* see M.A.Meyer, *The Origins of the Modern Jew. Jewish Identity and European Culture 1749–1824* (Detroit, 1967), pp. 115–119. For the intellectual background of this periodical see Stern-Taubler, 'The First Generation of Emancipated Jews', in *LBIY* 15 (1970), pp. 3–40.

26. See Carlebach, *Deutsche Juden*, pp. 73–76. Carlebach's interesting interpretation departs from much of what has been written about this translation in the past.

27. See Freimark, *Language*, p. 176.

28. See Vierhaus, 'Aufstieg', p. 71 and Freimark, *Language*, pp. 158–160.

29. *Ibid.*, p. 165.

30. See T. Nipperdey, 'Kommentar', p. 147. For this discussion see also his *Deutsche Geschichte 1800–1866. Bürgerwelt und starker Staat* (München, 1983), pp. 255–271.

31. On the early Enlightenment among German Jews see A. Shohet, *Die Wende der Zeiten. Der Beginn der Aufklärung im deutschen Judentum* [Hebrew] (Jerusalem, 1960); and J. Katz, *Tradition and Crisis. Jewish Society at the End of the Middle Ages* [Hebrew] (Jerusalem, 1968), pp. 284–297.

32. On Friedländer, see Meyer, *Origins*, pp. 57–84. On the new Jewish schools and Jewish education: M. Eliav, *Jewish Education in Germany during Enlightenment and Emancipation* [Hebrew] (Jerusalem, 1961). A shorter German version is in *Bulletin des Leo Baeck Instituts* 3 (1960), pp. 207–215.

33. Freimark, *Language*, pp. 169–70.

34. A full analysis is in Sorkin, *Ideology*, pp. 83–106. See now the excellent discussion in G.L.Mosse, 'Jewish Emancipation between Bildung and Respectability', in Reinharz and Schatzberg (eds.), *The Jewish Response*, pp. 1–16.

35. Mosse, 'Jewish Emancipation', p. 4. On the links of *Sittlichkeit, Bürgertum* and sexual norms as a general cultural phenomenon, see also his *Nationalism and Sexuality. Respectability and Abnormal Sexuality in Modern Europe* (New York, 1985).

36. Mosse, 'Jewish Emancipation', p. 6. On Zunz see also Meyer, *Origins*, pp. 144–182.

37. Mosse, *Nationalism*, pp. 4–5.

38. Compare the fuller discussion in my 'Selbstgefälligkeit und Selbsthaß: Die deutschen Juden zu Beginn des 20. Jahrhunderts', in *GWU* 1 (1986), pp. 1–13, and 'The Dynamics of Dissimilation: Ostjuden and German Jews', in Reinharz and Schatzberg (eds.), *The Jewish Response*, pp. 195–211.

39. See Sorkin, *Ideology*, p. 151, who quotes from S. Herxheimer, *Sabbath-, Fest- und Gelegenheits-predigten* (Bernburg, 1838), pp. 231,236. More generally on the approach of Neo-Orthodoxy compare also M. Breuer, 'Neo-Orthodoxy – Old and New Aspects'[Hebrew], in *Zehut* 2 (1982), pp. 31–39.

40. See H. Bausinger, 'Bürgerlichkeit und Kultur', in Kocka (ed.), *Bürger*, pp. 124–130.

41. See M. Breuer, *Jüdische Orthodoxie im deutschen Reich 1871–1918. Sozialgeschichte einer religiösen Minderheit* (Frankfurt-am-Main, 1986), pp. 21, 232–234.

42. This analysis relies heavily on Sorkin, *Ideology*, pp. 5–9, and on G.L.Mosse, 'The Secularization of Jewish Theology', in his *Masses and Man. Nationalist and Fascist Perceptions of Reality* (New York, 1980), pp. 249–262.

43. For Mendelssohn's exposition of his views on the matter, see the first part of his *Jerusalem oder über religiöse Macht und Judentum* (Berlin, 1783), in *Gesammelte Schriften*, G.G.Mendelssohn (ed.), (Leipzig, 1843–45), vol. 3, pp. 255–362. On Mendelssohn's position see A. Altmann, *Moses Mendelssohn: A Biographical Study* (Philadelphia, 1973). See also Meyer, *Origins*, pp. 22–56, and the interesting essay by A. Funkenstein, 'The Political Theory of Jewish Emancipation From Mendelssohn to Herzl', in *Jahrbuch des*

Instituts für deutsche Geschichte, Beiheft 3 (1979), pp. 13–28. On the national trend and its most explicit representative at that early stage, Herz Wesseley (1725–1805), see Sorkin, *Ideology*, pp. 57–61; Eliav, *Jewish Education*, pp. 44–51; Stern-Taeubler, *First Generations*, pp. 29–33.

44. For a full and concise summary of this changes see Nipperdey, *Deutsche Geschichte*, pp. 406–440.

45. On Zunz see Meyer, *Origins*, pp. 44–182; on Hirsch, Sorkin, *Ideology*, pp. 202–232 and Breuer, *Jüdische Orthodoxie*, pp. 61–90.

46. On the preachers, see Sorkin, *Ideology*, pp. 107–160.

47. Especially by Kant. See his *Die Religion innerhalb der Grenzen der bloßen Vernunft*, Karl Voländer, ed. (Hamburg, 1961), passim. See also N. Rothenstreich, 'Kant's Image of Judaism' [Hebrew], in *Tarbiz* 27 (1957–58), pp. 388–405.

48. See Meyer, *Origins*, pp. 85–114; also C. Cohen, 'The Road to Conversion', in *LBIY* 6 (1961), pp. 259–279, and Katz, *Out of the Ghetto*, Chapter 7.

49. See J. Carlebach, 'The Forgotten Connection: Women and Jews in the Conflict between Enlightenment and Romanticism', in *LBIY* 24 (1979), pp. 115–118. The quote is on page 116.

50. For details on what follows see my 'Erfolgreiche Assimilation oder Erfolg und Assimilation: Die deutsch-jüdische Familie im Kaiserreich', in *Wissenschaftskolleg zu Berlin, Jahrbuch*, 1982/83, pp. 373–388, and 'Soziale Ursachen des Erfolgs in der Wissenschaft. Juden im Kaiserreich', in *HZ* 245 (1987), pp. 315–342.

51. See the comments in Carlebach, *Deutsche Juden*, p. 66.

52. See Wassermann, *Jews*, pp. 124–136 on the image of Judaism and Jewish life in the *Gartenlaube*.

53. See F. Stern, 'The Integration of Jews in Nineteenth-Century Germany – Comments on the Papers of Lamar Cecil, Reinhard Rürup and Monika Richarz', in: *LBIY* 20 (1975), p. 81.

54. The classic treatment of the transition from cosmopolitanism to nationalism is, of course, F. Meinecke, *Weltbürgertum und Nationalstaat*, (München, 1907). On the patriotism of the rising *Bildungsbürgertum* see Vierhaus, *Aufrtieg*, pp. 65–66.

55. See Mosse, *Nationalism and Sexuality*, pp. 10–20.

56. Quoted from the *Monatsschrift für Geschichte und Wissenschaft des Judentums*, vol. 63 (1919), p. 8; by E.G. Reichmann, 'Der Bewußtseinswandel der deutschen Juden', in W.E. Mosse, (ed.) *Deutsches Judentum in Krieg und Revolution 1916–1923* (Tübingen, 1971), p. 516.

57. On Humboldt see Meinecke, *Weltbürgertum*, chapter 3. On the language issue from this perspective, Toury, *Die Sprache*, p. 80; Freimark, *Language*, p. 158. On *Volkskultur* see the comments in Bausinger, pp. 135–136.

58. See T. Nipperdey, 'Verein als soziale Struktur in Deutschland im späten 18. und frühen 19. Jahrhunderts', in his *Gesellschaft, Kultur, Theorie. Gesammelte Aufsätze zur neueren Geschichte* (Göttingen, 1976), pp. 174–205; also the comments in his *Deutsche Geschichte*, pp. 267–271. Compare now also Kocka, *Bürgertum*, p. 33.

59.The only partial exception to the exclusion of Jews from old-style corporations can be seen in their occasional acceptance into the municipalities, usually under the authority of the local feudal lords. See J. Toury, 'Types of Jewish Municipal Rights in German Townships. The Problem of Local Emancipation', in *LBIY* 22 (1976), pp. 55–80.

60. See J. Katz, *Jews and Freemasons in Europe* (Cambridge, Mass., 1970).

61. See M. Stützel-Prüsner, 'Die deutschen Lesegesellschaften im Zeitalter der Aufklärung', in O. Dann (ed.), *Lesegesellschaften und bürgerliche Emanzipation. Ein europäischer Vergleich* (München 1981), p. 77.

62. See U. Frevert, *Frauen-Geschichte. Zwischen bürgerlicher Verbesserung und neuer Weiblichkeit* (Frankfurt-am-Main, 1986), pp. 35–36. Published in English as *Women in*

German History. From Bourgeois Emancipation to Sexual Liberation (Oxford/New York, 1989).

62. For this and the following discussion see Wassermann, *Jews*, pp. 71–96.

64. The term is taken from Dieter Groh's analysis of Social Democracy. See his *Negative Integration und revolutionärer Attentismus: die deutsche Sozialdemokratie am Vorabend des Ersten Weltkrieges* (Frankfurt-am-Main, 1973). A similar view in G. Roth, *The Social Democrats in Imperial Germany: A Study in Working-Class Isolation and National Integration* (Totowa, N.J., 1963).

65. On women associations see now the concise summary in Frevert, *Frauen-Geschichte*, pp. 72–80, 104–128, and the bibliography in her notes.

66. The process by which the middle class made its own standards into those shared by the whole society, while preserving its exclusivity as a social element, particularly in England, is brilliantly discussed in H. Perkin, *The Origins of Modern English Society 1780–1880* (London, 1969), pp. 271–340.

67. See H.-U. Wehler, 'Wie bürgerlich war das Deutsche Kaiserreich?', in Kocka (ed.), *Bürger*, pp. 246–257.

68. See U.O. Schmelz, 'Die demographische Entwicklung der Juden in Deutschland von der Mitte des 19. Jahrhunderts bis 1933', in *Zeitschrift für Bevölkerungswissenschaft* 8 (1982), p. 64.

69. See N. Kampe, 'Jews and Antisemites at Universities in Imperial Germany (I) – Jewish Students: Social History and Social Conflict', in *LBIY* 30 (1985), pp. 357–394.

70. See, K.H. Jarausch, *Students, Society and Politics in Imperial Germany* (Princeton, 1982), pp. 114–134; F. Ringer, 'Bildung, Wissenschaft und Gesellschaft in Deutschland 1800–1960', in *Geschichte und Gesellschaft* 6 (1980), pp. 5–35.

71. For a fuller treatment of this theme see my 'Erfolgreiche Assimilation', and the various essays in W.E. Mosse (ed.), *Juden im Wilhelminischen Deutschland 1890–1914* (Tübingen, 1976).

15 | German Bürgerlichkeit after 1800: Culture as Symbolic Practice

Wolfgang Kaschuba

Reading this newspaper always gave me the feeling of being in the best society, that society which represented German culture in Europe and beyond.'[1] This dramatic sentence was written in 1869 by the author Heinrich Laube, as he looked back on his life in the 1830s. The newspaper he was referring to was the *Augsburger Allgemeine Zeitung*, considered at the time to be the best newspaper in Germany, and published in Stuttgart by the major publisher Johann Friedrich Cotta. The readers of this newspaper may well have felt that they were the appointed bearers and guardians of a culture that incorporated the best of German refinement and civic spirit. If the subscription list of the *Augsburger Allgemeine* had survived, it would have provided a reasonable Who's Who of German bourgeois society at that time.

This list does not exist, and in any case, the historical equation is not as simple as it might seem. It is true that all of 'better' society read the *Allgemeine*, but its readership spread far beyond bourgeois circles. For anyone who wanted to be well informed and to show that he was able to keep up with the discussions and controversies that went on in the inner bourgeois circles, even if not himself a member of them, the subscription price of the *Allgemeine* was an altogether sound investment. The *Allgemeine* reader not only wanted to have the feeling that he 'belonged', but also to be able to create the appearance of belonging. He wanted to demonstrate, at least with respect to his educational and cultural horizons that he was *bürgerlich*. Nevertheless, this equation did not work out. Being a reader of the *Allgemeine* was not, in fact, a reliable sign of *Bürgerlichkeit*, because it had become a generally fashionable status symbol, and thereby found its symbolic value much reduced.

This example points to a fundamental problem: *Bürgerlichkeit*, then and now, is anything but a systematic category; rather, it has a

Notes to Chapter 15 can be found on page 420.

descriptive or associative quality. The term refers to attitudes and cultural factors and does not lend itself to clear sociological categorisation. *Bürgertum* and *Bürgerlichkeit* (bourgeois mentality, culture and lifestyle) are not congruent. The delineation of a social field cannot simply be transferred to a cultural one. The semantic difficulties were already evident in the early nineteenth century when the term *bürgerlich* began to be extended beyond its original juridico-political context, and into the sphere of sociocultural values. *Bürgerlichkeit* no longer signified simply legal status, but developed into a complex concept referring to social status, a concept based on a variety of different criteria ranging from property to career, and from taste to education in such a way that all of these qualities had to come together in an appropriate expression of bourgeois culture and lifestyle.[2]

If we think of *Bürgerlichkeit* as a historically developing cultural praxis, then we have to alter the way in which we approach a study of this phenomenon: we cannot begin with a pre-defined social structure and then attempt a systematic attribution of cultural values and patterns. Rather, we have to begin with those social situations and configurations in which bourgeois cultural praxis manifested itself as a framework of concrete social action. In such situations, culture defines its own 'bourgeois quality', and establishes its own particular social profile. Who, under what circumstances, and with what justification could describe himself as *bürgerlich*?

Nowhere is historical bourgeois self-awareness reflected more clearly than in the flood of autobiographies and letters written around the end of the eighteenth and the beginning of the nineteenth century. They are a kind of 'subjective testimony', reflections of bourgeois life, and examples of its characteristic self-admiration. In a certain way, the fact that as memoirs they were written some years after the events they describe, makes them even more valuable as sources. Without ignoring the problems of memory and retrospective interpretation, it is this perspective that brings the autobiography as both a literary genre and an essential feature of bourgeois culture, into the foreground: social self-presentation and self-stylisation as an aesthetic practice.

It is revealing that written memoirs consist, for the most part, of descriptions of scenes and situations in which the themes, the actors and their behaviour are portrayed as having taken place within very definite patterns. Consciously or unconsciously, the recollection of familiar facts, social occasions, career situations or public events reflect the inner structure of the bourgeois *Lebenswelt* (life-world). What is

important is not the authenticity of the event but the subjective perception of it: history recalled through the prism of life that is remembered, re-interpreted and formed according to the bourgeois model.

Certainly, these sources will not provide us with a statistically representative image of bourgeois life in the first half of the nineteenth
century.[3] However, this kind of group-biographical approach can,
unlike socio-structural studies, lead to many more profound insights
into the field of bourgeois cultural styles. I use the word culture here
in its twofold meaning: the bourgeois cultural tradition in its narrow
historical sense as well as the broader modern sense of culture as
everyday praxis, as the totality of the bourgeois lifestyle.

Between the Revolutions: Bourgeois Awakening

In a historical perspective, the period at the beginning of the bourgeois nineteenth century appears as a period between two revolutions.
Behind it lay the French Revolution of 1789, a revolution that placed
on the agenda the problem, in Germany as well as in France, of building a society that was at least post-absolutist. Ahead of it lay the
German revolution of 1848 in which the barely initiated experiment
of a 'civil society' (*Bürgergesellschaft*) was confronted with the preco-
cious demands of the masses and consequently abandoned in favour of
a form of bourgeois-pragmatic Realpolitik. These were two lines
drawn through European history, between which crucial ideas were
born and social-historical processes set in motion, that would lead to
the future class-oriented and class-organised German bourgeois society.

Still not completely free of the old order of estates, but transforming it in many respects, the new economic, social and cultural profile
of bourgeois existence began to form itself. Karl Marx speaks of the
class conditions which were being established step-by-step at the time
by the German bourgeoisie. In using this term, he did not exclusively
mean the relations of production, but also the conditions of social and
cultural life. With respect to culture, this meant a fundamental transformation of the (*Lebenswelt*) and lifestyles of the urban bourgeois
groups which no longer fit the old stereotypes of the old-fashioned,
conservative (*Pfahlbürgerliche*) patricians and notables.

One gets the impression that the two to three decades that separate
the final years of the German enlightenment and early Biedermeier
were a period of real bourgeois 'experimentation'. New career and
educational strategies were developed, new forms of public and pri-

vate life were sought, new family models and gender roles were test-
ed. In the way they lived their lives, we can very clearly see the
extent to which the horizons and expectations of the generation born
around the turn of the century differed from those of the generation
of their parents and grandparents. There is a tangible sense of a
widening in the space of bourgeois experience and life-plans through
the 'discovery' of childhood and youth as important periods of individual development through new forms of sociability, new educational possibilities, political ideas and new social values.[4]

Initially, of course, this was true only of small, relatively privileged
bourgeois groups: manufacturers and merchants, educated officials in
public administration, the schools and universities, professionals such
as writers, journalists, lawyers and artists.[5] It is also true principally for
men and male social roles. The opportunities for a woman to structure her own career and private life were distinctly modest in this
new bourgeois world. This made them all the more sensitive to the
contradictions between their positive expectations and hopes on the
one hand, and their negative experiences on the other. In a situation
dominated by new bourgeois ideas of emancipation, the women of
the younger generation must have been much more sensitive to the
roles imposed on them than the generation of their mothers must
have been. Therese Huber, author, wife, mother, and after 1816 editor of the *Stuttgarter Morgenblatt* (morning paper 'for the educated
classes') wrote with resignation to a friend: 'I always knew that
women should be quiet when men spoke, and could never talk about
politics except in intimate circles'. Somewhat later she wrote with a
touch of sarcasm: 'Tell the public that I am better at knitting socks,
and would rather do that, than edit a newspaper'.[6]

After 1819, however, and the Wars of Liberation and the first constitutional successes in southern Germany, but also after the Karlsbad
Decrees, this enthusiasm to experiment and search for new paths
seemed to weaken. In the changed circumstances of Restoration politics and Biedermeier culture bourgeois life began to adapt itself to a
non-bourgeois society. Initially satisfied with what had been
achieved, the *Bürgertum* now directed their main efforts towards legally and socially securing the positions they had gained, and did not
strive to reach the far shores of bourgeois aspiration. When 1848
arrived, the attempt was made only half-heartedly.

Although there are obvious qualifications that one would have to
make, it does seem that this period between the revolutions was a
period – perhaps the only one – in German social history in which

the term bourgeois had unambiguously positive connotations. Two or three young generations of the *Bürgertum* grew up with a self-aware-ness that was anti-absolutist and anti-estatist, with ideas and programs for a new and modern society. Their own bourgeois interests and ideas linked together to form the basis for certain fundamental politi-cal and social attitudes: the principles of public life, individuality, dis-course, public well-being and progress. These were ethical and moral values, which at the time were still free from the suspicion of being empty ideological formulas. They still described bourgeois values and aspirations; they did not as yet bear the burden of proof that went with their being the 'dominant' social norms.

The optimism and the naive empathy with which they pursued progress are illustrated by a list of the topics discussed by a bourgeois student association in Freiburg in 1818:

> In a monarchic or representative state should there be an estate (Stand) that acts as an intermediary between the sovereign and the people? Do the Germans have any taste? Why has no pantheon been erected in Germany until now? Is the male or female nature more sensuous? Does a regent have the right to execute a subject? On the true and misguided education of the mind, an essay on the cultural history of the German people.[7]

Bürgerlichkeit as a Cultural Habitus

These themes were characteristic of the bourgeois discussion of human and social progress that took place everywhere in Germany in the *Vormärz* period (the period before 1848). It was part of everyday bourgeois custom to converse, exchange ideas and 'reason' with busi-ness colleagues, acquaintances and like-minded people. The local social elite were part of this discourse, as were in many cases the pros-perous master artisans and lower ranking officials. They participated as *Bürger* among equals; their ideas were listened to and respected. But were they really among their 'equals', and even with their enthusiasm for bourgeois ideals, did they already belong to bourgeois circles?

The difficulty in determining who was, and who was not, accepted in bourgeois circles, and what the dividing lines were, is illustrated by a scene from the memoirs of the jurist and later diplomat, Robert von Mohl. From a good bourgeois family himself, in his memoirs he describes dancing lessons in Stuttgart in 1815/16 which he shared with 'girls who were from, if not the best families, then certainly from very decent families...daughters of officials, merchants and the like'. They practiced together on the dance floor. However: 'After the lessons one could never accompany these girls on their way home. To speak to them or walk with them if, for instance, one were to meet on the street, was completely out of the question'.[8] For this could have led not only to emotional complications, but also and more importantly, to irritations. Although 'decent', they did not belong to 'good society'. It was at the exclusive and rather formal evenings and balls that von Mohl would meet appropriate partners from the 'first families'. The ladies from the dancing class were excluded from such occasions.

Constellations of this kind were, at the time, the favourite material of light fiction in which the happy ending provided what life itself denied. The scenario, however, did reflect social reality. Against the background of urban society as a whole, these 'decent' families did indeed represent a bourgeois milieu. In certain social situations, and in comparison with other social groups, they were acceptable and were allowed to feel that they belonged. In other social and sociable situations where what mattered was long-term relationships, marriageability, higher education or good taste, they were excluded.

Again, it is difficult to draw general lines of social division. In different situations the attribute *bürgerlich* could express different things, and could be used more or less extensively in literary life, in social entertainment, and in political discourse. The attempt to attribute a particular culture and a particular social status to the *Bürger* fails when confronted with historical reality, because bourgeois culture was not socially formative in many areas, nor bound exclusively to one particular social group. It appeared in general social situations, contexts and interactions in which, quite often, the *Bürgertum* may have played the central role but in which, in most cases, they were not the only participants and they by no means constituted a homogeneous social group.

This is a distinguishing feature of bourgeois culture that separates it from the cultural models of older social groups, for instance, that of the aristocracy or the pre-industrial artisans. Cultural practice and social formation were for them, to a large extent, congruent. Furthermore, the repertoire of cultural practices and the social circles within which they found their validity were regulated by precepts and prohibitions. Well known examples for this period are the regulations which governed clothes, funerals and festivals, as well as all the other rules of everyday life that were concealed in the accepted group standards of *Sitte und Brauch* (manners and customs).

On the other hand, in terms of bourgeois self-conception, the promotion and spread of one's own values and norms of conduct throughout the rest of society was a central function of culture. As a style of life and code of conduct, bourgeois culture claimed universal social validity for itself. It saw itself as the point of reference for all other social groups. It developed not on the basis of its own inner continuity and exclusivity, but exhibited its greatest vitality in its dialogue with other group cultures and in the constant change and exchange that this involved. Paul Pfizer, the liberal politician, thoughtful critic and fascinated eye-witness of this 'bourgeois breakthrough into society', wrote in 1831:

> It is no longer the state, church or family, but rather society that is everything, demands everything, engulfs everything. Society is our fate, our nemesis, our necessity. To do violence to one's own nature, to change one's temperament, to renounce one's innate inclinations and one's whole character if they do not fit into the social model – nowadays such a requirement is considered perfectly reasonable.[9]

Even in such cases as the dancing lesson, where the claim to universality is restricted in the interest of maintaining a certain amount of bourgeois exclusivity, this is not mediated by any kind of formal prohibition, but rather by cultural practice and its symbolic language. Whoever, as a child, has not taken the first steps in the direction of poetic creation would have difficulty later on in letters and in conversation, in finding the melancholy timbre to give expression to their sensitivity. Whoever did not grow up in a household with music would be lacking in the talents necessary for bourgeois salon culture. In short, whoever had not mastered the cultural rules was excluded by them. The congeniality of sensitiveness and the cultural ability to give expression to them – this determined whether the culture acted as a unifying bond or as a practice of social distinction.[10] A 'sketch' of the cultural history of Kassel in the 1820s tells us that apart from the nobility, it was possible to distinguish 'two social strata':

> The higher stratum was made up of those with a university education, especially high-ranking officials, the 'higher arts', officers and others of similar rank. Only a few individuals from trade and industry were considered part of this social class, and these were individuals who had achieved prominence through education, family connections or some special talent. The second stratum consisted of the great mass of those involved in trade and industry, who were joined by lower-ranking officials, mediocre artists and so on. Anyone outside of these two strata was not considered part of society.[11]

This was, then, the social structure of urban *Bürgertum* and of these two social strata only the first one could call itself *bürgerlich*.

Bürgerlichkeit, understood as a socially determined but culturally formed habitus, was a cultural model, multi-layered and variable, but in its basic principles a binding cultural model that contained the decisive elements of social identity within itself. It mediated bourgeois self-understanding and consciousness, defined through the use of material goods, the acceptance of ideal values, the adherence to certain cultural patterns of conduct, all of which, taken together, constituted a complete *Lebenswelt*. It embodied the second nature of the bourgeois, habitualised the appropriate norms and forms, and established for 'culture' a dual function: as identity model and as means of distinction.

Its second function, as means of distinction, acquired a special importance at the beginning of the nineteenth century. This alone made it possible for bourgeois groups, in spite of the renunciation of status privileges and the absence of formal barriers, to preserve limits and distances within society, enabling them to establish a public identity, both as individuals and as a social group. Language and education, clothes and physical deportment, dining habits and domestic decor, family forms and notions of honour, form a very broad spectrum of everyday conduct that functions as a kind of signal system. Its effectiveness is based on 'social signs' and 'symbolic forms' that express a certain association with a material and intellectual culture in which certain patterns of style and taste act as signets of *Bürgerlichkeit*.

Because of its limited social/political influence and its social and territorial disunity, this process of cultural constitution was more important for the German *Bürgertum* than it was for the upper middle classes in other comparable western European countries. With respect to politics, the press and the economy, career opportunities in the civil service and in their general ability to influence public life, the bourgeois groups of France and England had a much wider scope for action, and were in fact closer to being organised as a class. In Germany, on the other hand, it was only in cultural terms that bourgeois inhibitions and identities could be given common expression, finding self-confirmation in a shared approach and access to art and literature, education, history and aesthetics. This cultural practice should not be understood merely as a compensatory model for socio-political weakness. The new bourgeois elite in fact coined a positive new program of social abilities and talents. *Bildung* (education) also meant training for advancement, and middle-class historical con-

400 | *Wolfgang Kaschuba*

sciousness provided a guide in contemporary political constitutional discourse.

What was new in this conception of 'culture' was the appreciation of the manifold utility of bourgeois cultural patterns in all areas of life. These were no longer mechanical rules of conduct derived from corporate culture and firmly inscribed on a static social horizon. This new bourgeois culture was more of a transverse link connecting previously divided groups, sub-cultures, career and confessional groups. With its common ideas and interests, it established new transitions and bonds, often long before these shared elements took on an established social form. Music, literature, art or philosophy are, first of all, elements of communication and discourse around which more stable forms of sociability may gradually crystallise and eventually, in the form of circles or associations, become permanent structures of bourgeois public life.

'New Society' – Bourgeois Groupings and Configurations

For contemporaries, the differences between this period and the late eighteenth century were also evident. In the free imperial cities, provincial capitals and medium-sized towns of the late eighteenth century, bourgeois life reflected the corporate, territorial and confessional fragmentation of Germany and signified, in most cases, a limited horizon bound to professional status and mired in traditional ways of thinking. Bourgeois public life did not exist and the few 'secret societies' or the early reading circles, lacking a corresponding cultural or communicative environment, constituted only small islands of future German *Bürgerlichkeit*.[12]

Andreas Wilhelm Cramer, a professor from one of Kiel's best families wrote of the 1790s: 'There were as yet no clubs, restaurants, confectioners...one could count on an industrious career and private life, on a wife who perhaps knew nothing of embroidery, languages and card playing but who was all the better at mending and knitting, the kitchen and the cellar'.[13] There were few, if any, traces of bourgeois salon culture in Kiel. Ernst Münch, son of an official, paints a similarly meagre picture of small-town life in Baden: 'Although there was very little in my hometown in the way of refinement or fine social circles...nonetheless, from time to time there were quite charming social evenings and ladies circles, often involving amateur theatrical performances'.[14] Whoever was counted among the pillars of 'good society' in Rheinfelden received an invitation. Karl Friedrich Klöden recalled his spartan school years in Prussia: 'From a literary point of view the town was a veritable desert. Apart from the Bible, hymn-book and schoolbooks, there were very few books to be found'.[15]

The change in bourgeois *Gesellung und Gesellschaft* (sociability and society) after 1800 is immediately apparent from the contrast in the lifestyles described in the autobiographies of the younger and older generations. Careers and group formations changed within the generation of the children. New bourgeois milieus and new social relations emerged on the basis of shared cultural practice. New forms of both organised and informal sociability blossomed, transforming the lives and environment of the *Bürgertum*. Birthdays, children's parties, walks on the newly erected promenades, excursions into the countryside, music evenings in the home, balls, visits to the coffee house, evenings at the museum associations – were all forms of this new bourgeois sociability, many of which had been previously unknown. Organised events like the children's birthday parties and unorganised leisure activities like promenading were real novelties. Otto Elben describes what could almost be modern leisure activities when recalling his time as a bookseller in Koblenz. He writes about regular walks and excursions, gymnastic exercises after work, swimming with friends, music evenings in the homes of friends or as part of the choral society, small parties and feasts.[16]

Of course, not everything was completely new. Some of these activities betray aristocratic origins, others are extensions of previous forms of bourgeois social activity; the reading groups and literary circles of the late eighteenth century, the lodges and orders of the freemasons and illuminati, the café and tea-house clubs (in Gotha, a *Theegesellschaft* with a practically unchanging membership of twenty-seven bourgeois families existed continuously from 1778 to the 1820s.)[17]

It was only in the nineteenth century, however, that these forms of sociability began to incorporate everyday bourgeois culture, and manifest themselves as patterns of social behaviour that extended to, and put down roots in, wider society. Amateur theatres and informal circles of theatre-goers were established. Social circuits for young bourgeois ladies and men soon made their appearance in every small German town. Ladies' circles sprang up. The coffee house became a 'daily meeting place...elegant and comfortable from every viewpoint, with a nice garden, a friendly host and an even friendlier cousin who was in charge of the buffet'.[18] Quasi-scientific societies for the study of nature, ethnology and history publicised their activities. The veritable wave of pre-1848 associations (*Vereine*) began as early as the 1820s, starting with the choral societies, gymnastic clubs and the art associations.

These associations soon became the most important institution of bourgeois social and political life. Alongside the small circle of family and relations, the associations offered new possibilities for the *Bürgertum* to bring together bourgeois circles that previously had been socially and regionally separated. They thereby created a proper bourgeois network.

In the autobiographies we find remarkably many early examples of membership in choral societies and gymnastic clubs. In the 1820s and 1830s, the future publisher Otto Elben was a member of the gymnastic club in Stuttgart. This club was mostly made up of graduates of the *Gymnasium*, along with their parents. As a young man in this club, he got to know half of Württemberg's officials, professors and political elite of the pre-1848 period. He met more than two dozen 'good names' with whom he remained close friends, even in later life. When, in connection with his studies he moved to Koblenz, he made immediate contact with local bourgeois society through the gymnastic club and organised choral activities.[19] Heinrich Laube gives us a similar description of his arrival in Halle. Friends he had made in the swimming club helped him to gain access to student and bourgeois circles in the town. Wilhelm von Kügelgen describes having similar experiences in Dresden.[20]

This fusion of the different bourgeois groups into common organisations with mutual cultural styles and attitudes created a new pattern of a 'common bourgeois culture' that became, in fact, the only freely convertable coinage: it formed a kind of national bourgeois currency. The common language of the *Bildungsbürgertum* and of their everyday culture gradually overcame the barriers between the local and regional bourgeois enclaves: it incorporated this national bourgeois currency. Bourgeois society in Hamburg now began to resemble and follow the same basic rules as bourgeois society in Gotha or Karlsruhe. Whoever knew the basic model and was practised in its use now had a ticket of entry into proper bourgeois circles everywhere.

Heinrich Laube, a Silesian, praises his positive experiences in the 1830s: 'Hardly anywhere else can one find such a profound culture among the educated, such refinement in knowledge and taste, as here'.[21] As an art student, Kügelgen, himself a guest in Dresden, introduced a fellow student after only a brief exchange of views and very discreet probing, into the town's 'society': 'With pride I introduced my new friend Ernst Förster, from the *Burschenschaft* (student association) in Jena to the art club, and he was as heartily received as if one already knew that he would soon become a painter and excellent writer on art, and the universally loved son-in-law of the universally loved Jean Paul Friedrich Richter'.[22] It is clear from the experiences reported from other towns that this openness was by no means restricted to the academic milieu of German university towns.

The existence of an urban middle class, an urban milieu and a certain urbanity of social life, was of course a precondition for this development. *Bürgerlichkeit* presupposed an urban environment not only because larger groups of the bourgeois elite were concentrated in the town, or because the town offered unrivalled career opportunities, and not only because in this experimental space relatively free of state control the historical foundations and cultural traditions of bourgeois thought provided fertile ground.[23] Of much greater importance was the fact that it was only in an urban environment that one could find the appropriate concentration of culturally mediating social forms and institutions making it possible for *Bürgerlichkeit* to constitute itself as a cultural entity: secondary schools, theatres, newspapers, publishers, societies, associations, gyms and promenades. In the density of this urban *mélange*, these constituted a precondition for the emergence of forms of public life without which bourgeois culture could not have developed. This new bourgeois culture separated the old Goethe-reading small-town pastor or chemist from a new class of *Bürger* whose *Bürgerlichkeit* was no longer exhausted by particular attitudes to education or style, but availed itself of every note along the whole length of the cultural keyboard.

Robert von Mohl's comparison of the university towns of Tübingen and Heidelberg in the 1820s is very informative in this respect. In Tübingen, with its conservative theological tradition, its horizons limited by its role as training ground for provincial civil servants, as well as by its Protestant ethic, bourgeois life had a 'most peculiar coloration'; it was narrow-minded, limited, small-town and petit-bourgeois. 'Even among the professors in Tübingen there was no kind of refined social life. Life here was the life of real Swabian *Bürger*-families'. Mohl missed the informal visits of friends, the house parties, the musical entertainments, the tea houses, hospitality and restaurants ('in the evenings everything was hermetically shut') – all those things he was to find when he moved to Heidelberg. 'Instead of the narrow bourgeois life of the Swabian provincial town, here was a more liberal, more refined social life and etiquette', which he associ-

404 | *Wolfgang Kaschuba*

ated quite rightly with the 'modern' scientific management of Heidelberg University, 'run by jurists, for jurists'. The atmosphere in the university and in the town was completely different, the result of *haute-bourgeois* and aristocratic influence. Jurisprudence was a very fashionable subject and attracted foreign as well as German academics, students and other interested people, so that the town acquired an atmosphere not unlike that of a spa resort town. Life here, further down the Neckar, seemed to Mohl to be 'so luxurious and relatively refined'.[24] This fine distinction between 'rough and *gemütlich*' and 'luxurious' had ultimately to do with cultural styles and forms. What existed in Heidelberg and Tübingen were two distinct models of urban society.

Social life à la Heidelberg also operated its own social selection. In view of the significant differences in income and property among the different bourgeois groups, the Heidelberg example gives us an approximate idea of the kind of economic basis or degree of existential security required to be a *Bürger*, in the sense of having a definite cultural style and moving in certain social circles. We cannot express this, of course, in absolute figures, because what matters is not just nominal wealth, but rather a combination of a certain level of a material standard of living and a morally-culturally determined lifestyle. Thus, to be a *Bürger* meant not just being relatively free from want, but in addition being in a position to bear the costs of certain bourgeois forms of social life and social responsibility. If one had the prerequisite education but lacked the necessary means to pay for the afternoon in the tea house, the excursion, the balls, the dinner parties or the membership in the association then one was excluded. Without 'a decent bourgeois income',[25] there was no prospect of sharing in this *Bürgerlichkeit*, either socially, in one's career or in politics.

Here we see the social self-regulating mechanism that functioned on a day-to-day basis to draw a line between what was bourgeois and what was not in operation, in such a way that the selective operation of economic, social and cultural hurdles took on the appearance of being something completely natural. Ernst Dronke gives a very expressive description of how 'high-bourgeois culture' in Berlin protected itself behind a socioeconomic wall of household servants, high-level careers, fashion and the subscription to the theatre. In describing the residences, coffee houses and clubs, he provides us with an account of the sociable and social infrastructure of big-city life in Berlin: in the Café Kranzler at lunchtime, the 'officers and fashionable young people'; in the Königstadt Konditorei, the 'businessmen and men from the stock exchange'; in Café Unter den Linden, the students; in the Stehéli near the Gendarmenmarkt, a mixture of privy councillors, opera stars, 'educated gentlemen' and officers.[26] To be present in any of this company meant having a confident appearance, enough money and disposable time. What was demonstratively displayed here was free time, or the leisure time to devote to culture and entertainment. In the afternoons, recollected the industrialist Werner von Siemens, 'fine society' met for a promenade in the Tiergarten and Unter den Zelten.[27]

Signs of Engagement: Political Emblems of Everyday Culture

On a relatively smaller scale, many basic aspects of future bourgeois society were already reflected in these various forms of sociability. One noticeable aspect is the way in which an attempt was made to bridge the gap between areas of experience and activity that had previously been separate, to break through the old borders and segmentation of cultural practice. Serious educational work was combined with pleasurable activities, aesthetic enjoyment with political discourse, intellectual activity with physical recreation. Human individuals and their needs were to develop and experience as a totality and universally. Their bourgeois character was to be displayed publicly: their concepts of pleasure, education, career and politics. What was emerging here was bourgeois public life establishing the contours of its 'community of attitudes and ideas',[28] and through its forms and structures of social life, simultaneously organising and formulating its political demands in what was still a half-absolutist state and society. Madame de Stael praised 'sociable Berlin': 'As a result of the freedom of the press, Berlin, on the other hand, has become in recent years the association of intelligent men and the general spread of knowledge of German language and literature, the real capital city of a new and enlightened Germany.[29]

The student *Burschenschaften* began to assert a more prominent presence in public life around 1817–18. With their 'clubs' they gave demonstrative expression to a 'common German character' directed against local 'philistinism' and small-town authorities. 'We had contempt for the *Landsmannschaften* (regional associations of students) in which the Saxons met only Saxons, the Westphalian dealt with other Westphalians and the man from the Brandenburg March associated only with his March fellows. The stronger the *Landsmannschaften* were represented among us the prouder we were of our greater German *Landsmannschaft*.[30]

Even the externally modest choral societies and gymnastic clubs saw themselves explicitly as part of national German history and national German culture and had a considerable influence on the political conceptions of the pre-1848 bourgeois elite. What was perhaps more important, they extended their influence beyond bourgeois circles into society at large, acting as propagandists and promoters of bourgeois values and ideas. In many cases, this was how these values and ideas first became part of public awareness and gained widespread political impact throughout society. Heinrich Laube was proud of his own bourgeois generation: 'It is a mistake to think that German patriotism and the desire for a united Germany go a long way back in history. This way of thinking and this aspiration are modern'.[31]

From now on, bourgeois social life also meant public life and politics. It was no accident that the first 'national' celebrations and festivals to commemorate the Wars of Liberation held after 1814 were supported by the precursors of the later gymnastic clubs and choral societies, and that these devoted a great deal of attention to the discussion and dissemination of the idea of the nation-state and to the development of historical awareness. Sometime before the Wartburg festival of 1817, those typical forms of the national German festival began to develop, and would continue into the pre-revolutionary period in the form of Goethe and Schiller festivals. At the same time, patterns of national mythology and national cults were developed whose symbolism reached into everyday bourgeois life. Once again Madame de Stael wrote, this time with gentle mockery: 'The women try to arrange their lives as a novel, the men theirs' as history'.[32]

This attitude was given its most pregnant expression in the sub-culture of 'post-1813 youth'; when after the Wars of Liberation fought against Napoleon, young men displayed their love of the Germany of the Middle Ages by wearing loose fraternity coats, long hair and a black and red cap. Laube reported how everywhere in Silesia one came across 'gymnastic fervour, old-German costumes, Jahn's folklore and fierce songs against foreigners'.[33] Ludwig Uhland wrote to his parents from Stuttgart in 1816: 'Everyone is talking about gymnastic events and national costumes'.[34] Kügelgen had similar experiences in Dresden, and in 1814 even the later bitter and ironic Ludwig Börne was able to write that: 'We want to be free Germans, free in our hatred, free in our love...But we are sons of the sword and iron is our gold'.[35] For the first time, democratic visions of society and nationalist-militaristic dreams of the fatherland come dangerously together.

Culturally and politically, these phenomena were very significant because they manifested, for the first time in this form and to a great extent a political 'frame of mind' (*Gesinnungshabitus*). Quite specific forms of expression and stylistic means were used to express definite social and political convictions and to express them in society at large, not just in small, bohemian, inward-looking circles of artists and literati. The sources give frequent indications of how these signs and symbols were becoming part of everyday 'normal' bourgeois life: the cultivation of expressly 'political' circles of friends, symbols of allegiance to a *Burschenschaft*, clothing styles and forms of greeting, and key quotations from cult books such as Schiller's *Die Räuber* or Novalis' *Heinrich von Ofterdingen*.

These forms of symbolic participation in German history and politics were something qualitatively new. They were an essential contribution to the political coloration of everyday bourgeois culture which was now something visible and palpable for every contemporary and which was, no doubt, partially inspired by French and English models. That these demonstrative political gestures were more than a transitory fashion, that they represented a general extension and refinement of cultural praxis in the dimension of the political precursors of modern political mass culture was confirmed during the years leading up to the 1848 revolution. This was achieved when political symbols and emblems acquired increasing significance in everyday bourgeois life. The symbolism was perhaps not as overt as in the case of the other veteran of 'liberation', but it was equally unmistakeable. A certain type was being presented, perhaps a 'liberal' or a 'democrat', who pursued a definite aesthetic or stylistic pattern symbolised by the newspaper he read, the cut of his beard, his vocabulary or his clothes. There were also forms of demonstrative group behaviour: the 'free thinkers' in Freiburg met in the Museum,[36] 'the writers of the radical political party' met in the Café Stehéli in Berlin.[37] Of course, this does not mean that the use of such political symbols was obligatory for the pre-1848 *Bürgertum*. However, a knowledge of this political symbolic code and the observance of its rules were now part of the cultural qualifications of the male construction of *Bürgerlichkeit*.

Bildung as 'the Culture of the Educated'

The central axis around which bourgeois life turned remained, undoubtedly, the canon of bourgeois *Bildung*. It was a unifying factor creating a stronger cultural community than had been the case in earlier generations. In its basic features it was already a 'modern' model of education in which early childhood was seen as a kind of pre-schooling in the parental home. In the very first reading and writing exercises there were regular introductions to the literary canon and even small scientific experiments and didactic games. In spite of the freedom in the choice of children's reading material and games, the educational goals are transparent when, for instance, books are recommended from the parental library, when songs are learned, when small collections of minerals are made available, when toys with magnetic or electrical effects are given as gifts, or when, after a family excursion the children are made to compose an account of the trip for the father.[38]

Then came the elementary or *Bürgerschule*, complemented generally by instruction in the home by parents, relatives or home tutors. What is remarkable here is the extent to which the children were already being prepared for their later roles in public life. In family and other intimate circles they were encouraged to recite poetry, play the piano, or even to present their own poems or ideas. There was, at the same time, a clear preparation for specific gender roles. The girls were more often than not 'companions in attendance' at their brother's lessons, and they themselves tended to be instructed in leisure activities and handicrafts. In more educationally ambitious families the girls were also given lessons in literature.

In the autobiographies one finds a very graphic recollection of these educational experiences in the home from the early age of three or four. This underlines the degree to which this early acquisition of a common fund of intellectual and imaginative material was such a formative experience: formative for the childhood experience of a new generation, but also for the later adult community's shared horizons in matters of taste, historical understanding and perceptions of the world. Already in early childhood, with the as yet hardly conscious absorption of material from reading and study, bourgeois education began to assume the role of 'creator of collective style'. What shaped the childhood experience of the young bourgeois child was no longer the peculiarity of the regional or professional environment of the parents, but rather the common aesthetic and pedagogical features, the shared educational structure of the bourgeois *Lebenswelt*.

Finally, there were – for the sons – the years at the *Gymnasium* and university during which time a great deal of attention was devoted to enabling the boy or young man to develop his own independent outlook and follow his own interests. A particular feature of this education was the way it combined the classical-humanistic canon with a study of the natural sciences and development of character – the latter being supplemented by studies in religion, ethics and philosophy. Schools were chosen with these criteria in mind. Finally, with this solid general education assured, parents were happy to have their sons in the schools and universities try out subjects across a whole range of faculties. Not everything had to be 'turned to account' immediately; what seemed more important, in many cases, was the formation of a versatile and useful 'educational capital'.

'While we were still children our parents decided that at the end of our university studies we should undertake a long journey to complete our education.' This pause at the end of one's studies, a period of orientation, was made possible for Robert von Mohl and his brothers by means of a travel grant from their parents.[39] Such a period of travel was an important turning point in the lives of many young bourgeois men. Long journeys, visits to other families, as well as voluntary or practical work in a variety of business and career environments marked the transition from the life of youth and education to the life of maturity and career.

At the same time, these travels (*Wanderjahre*) were a conscious and extended period of observation, of testing oneself before the final career decision; they were also a period devoted to the development of one's character. Although autobiographies tend to be selective and to indulge in a certain amount of self-glorification on this point, it does seem that careers were, in many cases, chosen independently. The family context created predispositions and the parents did guide the final decision, but career and life paths were no longer prescribed. The son chose not to follow in the father's footsteps with increasing frequency; in fact, from the autobiographies it is clear they did so in only a minority of cases. Even Heinrich Laube, whose parents were unable to finance his studies, made his decisions independently to the extent that he had the material means to do so.[40]

These similarities in educational background brought the younger generation of the different bourgeois groups closer together and increased the number of things they had in common. The education of the sons of the *Bürgertum* was being restructured and developed on the basis of new forms of socialisation and mediated by correspondingly common models of experience; at a similar age one lived in a similar manner and underwent similar experiences. Games, toys, school friendships, piano lessons, reading Goethe, attempting to write, the young 'tobacco clubs', the group culture of the *Primaner* (students in their eighth or ninth year of secondary school), the student *Burschenschaften*, the whole peer-group structure of the young which extended right into later career life – all of these things took their proper place as stations in a bourgeois *rite de passage*. There belonged to each of these stations quite definite gender and age-specific aesthetically-ordered values and behavioural norms which had to be instilled and re-created in the common praxis of bourgeois education. Sensitivity was experienced as something particular to one's personal make-up. However, at the same time it reflected conventions and models of a cult of lofty feelings cultivated, in particular, in arabesque friendship rituals and letter-writing styles. 'You inquire concerning what is happening to my psychic and physical self' began (not only) one letter from the year 1818,[41] an example at the linguistic level of the aesthetic 'distance from the world projected into even one's own personal relationship'.[42]

It would be a mistake however, to believe that in the biographical sequence of such educational stages one has discovered the individuality of a historical bourgeois curriculum vitae. What these incorporate is rather, a comprehensive model of *Bürgerlichkeit*. These biographical sequences no longer describe a singular trajectory, as was still partly the case in the parental generation, but are rather images of a 'generation keeping in step'. Many of the autobiographical self-presentations have uniform group-biographical structures, although each author was, of course, always convinced of the uniqueness of 'his' particular path. It is seldom that one finds an author like the Kiel jurist, Andreas Wilhelm Cramer, who looks back on the 'golden moderation' of his life[43] and sheds an ironic light on the bourgeois ideal of individuality. The new possibilities to freely structure one's life often ended up, in reality, in what was a normal, 'average' bourgeois life.

These educational strategies had two goals. On the one hand, there was the narrower interest in educational and career qualification; but there was also a recognition of the special value of that 'culture of the educated' which functioned as a kind of bourgeois passepartout, the absence of which could not be fully compensated for by either wealth or career qualifications. The economic bourgeoisie – the manufacturers and the big merchants, also tried to participate in this educational process. They sought membership in the artistic societies, the salons and circles in which this 'more refined' *Bildung* was nurtured and mediated. This style was irreverently caricatured by a contemporary:

Only with a pen and paper in his hand is the German of today a being capable of human expression and activity. Take these away, and he is robbed of his power of thought. Only in the opera and the theatre can he recognise the way of the world and the laws of history, and only there does he become aware of his ethical principles and intellectual freedom.[44]

The conscious attention given to this *Bildungsprozeß*, in the way in which it was observed and critically examined, is indicated by the self-assessment of his development made by Robert von Mohl at the end of his student days. He wrote this as part of his memoirs, but he is obviously referring to his diary from the year 1824:

> I was almost twenty-five years old. Of this time, I had spent twelve years at the Gymnasium, three and one half years at the university and three years travelling...My power of imagination was adequate enough to perceive the consequences of new ideas in a science, or of improvement in the conditions of life. I possessed no poetic gifts; of inclination to metaphysical speculation or even of respect for it, there was not a trace. My limit was the inductive discovery of the laws of existent reality. My education was essentially a modern one.[45]

Although not particularly original, this self-characterisation is in accordance with a quite definite model of *Bildung*. It illustrates the extent to which individual experiences and ambitions were already part of a pattern in which self-perception, aesthetic patterns and personal careers were following norms that 'standardised' and 'nationalised' them. The bourgeois subject had become the 'object' of its own observation and concern. It had an analytical interest in its own process of formation, almost as if it were looking at it from the outside. All these phenomena that we group together in the concept of *Bürgerlichkeit* seem centered around this complex concept of *Bildung*, which projected a quite definite socio-cultural practice, in the sense of a system of values and forms of conduct. In any case, this 'culture of the educated' permeates the autobiographies, weaving a thread of individual experience into the fabric of a bourgeois group biography.

Bürgerlichkeit as Modernity: Signals and Signets

Bourgeois notions of progress and modern life existed in infinitely rich variety after 1800, and these were notions that contemporaries discussed with great enthusiasm. Undoubtedly, the attitude toward new things, new ideas and new forms of behaviour was a test of bourgeois style and taste, for it was precisely here, in the space between modernity and fashion mania, that the world of 'distinctions' asserted itself.

One very revealing area is the attitude to technology. New means of transport, like the steamship and the train, new techniques of industrial production and the factories themselves as new production centres were, if not yet part of the real environment, at least visible on the horizon. Small technical novelties, in particular, began to play a prominent role in everyday bourgeois life: the telescope, enamelled tinware, the glass harmonica, the alarm clock, lithographic prints, the walking stick umbrella, technical toys like electrical-shock gadgets, toy trains and building blocks. The panoramic peep-show, with its coloured and illuminated views of cities or battles, fascinated children and adults alike.

Like an early form of television, it was teaching a new way of seeing things: things that were in fact far away, strange and exotic were extending bourgeois vision and bourgeois horizons.[46] Fontane said that it was due to the dazzling pictures of the peep-shows he experienced as a child that the 'historical events of the 1820s' like the wars of Greek independence left an indelible impression on his mind.[47] One by one, Ernst Münch invited all of his classmates to his house to marvel at Merian's copperplate engravings in his father's peep-show. He recollects, that as a result of this experience he formed 'in my small head', a wholly novel 'way of looking at things, old and new'.[48]

Both aspects were important: the possession of technical objects and the ability to handle them which amounted to the demonstrative ability to manage 'technology in everyday life'. Many things were systematically instilled into the small children as a result of unforeseen situations, such as when the children discover that grandfather, by means of the telescope, is able to keep an eye on them from a distance while they play. Thus found out, he has to explain to them the secret of his extended vision, and teach them the principle of the telescope. The way in which adults learned was not all that different from their children: pausing on a Sunday promenade in order to get a closer view of approaching acquaintances with the help of the pocket telescope was a much-loved and acceptable way of demonstrating this new way of seeing – until the point was reached where too many imitators had turned this into a general fad, whereupon it turned into a sign of improper obtrusiveness.

The telescope is a good example of how the fascination with technology was not incompatible with the bourgeois critique of civilisation and longing for nature. This fascination was also capable of showing how the enlightened 'disenchantment of the world' (Max Weber) was also capable of creating compensatory 'magical effects'. In any case, the telescope was very useful in giving a more detailed view of the alpine panorama of peaks and valleys, structuring the visual experience into an exciting movement between totality and partiality, all the while allowing one to observe with pleasure 'the beauty-spots of nature'.[49]

The contemporary discussion of new roles and 'modern' forms of family life opened up further areas. The issues at stake were the borders between the public and the private sphere, changed relations between parents and children, new male-female and female-mother role models, as well as the general issues of 'gender characteristics'.[50] To choose just one example: during the first two decades of the nineteenth century it appears to have been not altogether unsual for (educated) bourgeois fathers to involve themselves more actively in the emotional aspects of the care and education of their children. Wilhelm von Kügelgen describes the temporary division of his family into male and female halves when the mother and daughters went on a longer visit to a spa resort, while the father stayed at home with the two boys. 'Our life together was arranged in such a way that was quite exceptional for fathers and sons'. He reports playing games together and very emotional conversations in the evenings;[51] in other words, emotionally open and intimate situations that would hardly have been imaginable in the later period of reaction or in the Wilhelmine period. The law professor, Cramer, wrote in a similar vein about the first years of his marriage: 'No years could have been happier than these, when I rocked the cradle with one foot, and at the same time copied ridiculous extracts from dusty manuscripts'.[52]

These examples, of course, do not disprove the general validity of the bourgeois family and gender roles that were in the process of formation at the time. It is interesting, however, to see how in this transitional period other possible behavioural models were being probed, before Biedermeier and the pre-March period began to prescribe the script for bourgeois family roles. In this script, both literally and metaphorically, the corset triumphed.

This relative openness and willingness to experiment was, perhaps, an expression of the bourgeois search for identity at the beginning of the nineteenth century. By contrast, intellectual immobility and unambitious mediocrity were seen as explicitly unbourgeois characteristics. The petty-bourgeoise or the nobility, each in their own way, might be conservative, but the *Bürgertum* were on the lookout for new horizons. At the level of such basic ideologies, the differences are clear. Unlike the nobility, the *Bürgertum* did not interpret the present through the past, but saw in the present the pre-history of what was to come. Unlike the petty-bourgeoisie, they did not glorify the historical and local worlds as the best of all possible worlds but rather, casting their vision far and wide, and willing to be self-critical, they made comparisons with history as well as other countries. Modernity was not a passive quality; it did not just mean swimming with the tide of change. Rather, it gave substance to concrete bourgeois interests and wishes, and inquired into the needs of development, as well as the hindrances to progress. It was this conception that was expressed in the term *Mittelstand* which, at the time, was not yet a sociological model but the image of a society around whose bourgeois centre the world turned as it did on its axis.

The autobiographies can be read as reflections on the themes of modernity and progress:

> I accustomed myself from youth onwards to the fact that the old things became new, and what had hardly been established was again changed. I saw the great world events, at least in their beginnings, and in the people who were their agents, but this did not cause me any pain. On the contrary, it was a pleasing spectacle for me. Under such conditions a pious respect of the old and the established was as inappropriate as a fear of great change.[53]

Of course, such attitudes did not imply a complete break with history and with the past. What they did was to open a new perspective on the present as a stage between the historic past and the future. They offered a clear orientation towards the past and established a firm individual and group-biographical perspective. One gets the impression nonetheless, that it was only in certain areas that this new bourgeois generation was willing and able to engage in social and cultural experimentation. In spite of the emphasis on activity, achievement, individuality and the demands for social modernisation derived from these concepts, the adherence to the ethical-moral canon of old bourgeois virtues remained strong, especially in public life. Even the economic bourgeoisie and the professionals exercised self-discipline in this respect, keeping a distance not just from a display of luxury and excessive consumption but also from any suggestion of bohemian fashion.

This was certainly not a result of any pious respect for abstract traditional values. A certain reserve seemed prudent in view of the fact that the economic and social status of the new elite was still, in many respects, quite insecure and still depended on their being a part of the broader bourgeois social spectrum. And this demanded a proof of solidity, a sense of duty as well as of a sense of honour, and extended to one's personal conduct of life. Interestingly, this is also the message of the autobiographers to their own children whose life-span reached well into the second half of the nineteenth century: the autobiography itself was a mediator of the social continuum of values linking together the old and the new, ensuring the continuity of values from one generation to the next.

The newspaper editor, Otto Elben, outlined his father's attitude to modernity in terms of his editorial concepts for the *Schwäbische Kronik* in the 1820s. The newspaper was to take up such novel items as:

> lively descriptions of the festivals, from the first Cannstatt people's festival to the song festival, the Schiller festivals and scientific conferences; reports on industrial exhibitions; descriptions of factories; the national awards for wine, an important part of the national economy; essays on the national economy; effective support for the construction of railways by means of educational and propagandistic articles; the introduction of sections dealing with ethnography and geography.[54]

This demonstrated an attitude to tradition and progress, the balanced nature of which very much impressed the son, and which he adopted as his own.

Bürgerlichkeit appears in this context as a form of confidence in the path of progress. This confidence was based on the *Bürgertum's* belief in their own capacity for modernisation, as well as on the exemplary influence that this would have on the rest of society. Of course, bourgeois self-definitions were often contradicted by everyday bourgeois practice in this balancing act. For instance, the liberal standpoint was hardly compatible with the much sought-after 'ennoblement' that was readily accepted by both officials and industrialists as a reward for their services to the state. The democratic notion of liberty co-existed uneasily with the creation of nationalist myths. The anti-authoritarian impetus of the individual often ended with his bidding for government contracts, or with his building a career for himself as an official. Bourgeois values demonstrated their pragmatic or ambivalent character when demands for general social progress translated themselves almost unnoticed into plans for individual bourgeois advancement.

In this respect, bourgeois autobiographies are real works of art in ideological history. They constantly return to this theme of a contradiction between theory and practice only in order to resolve it in figures of biographical self-legitimation. Social adaptation and political compromise are justified as essential bourgeois qualities in what is still a 'pre-bourgeois' environment. They like to describe their own behaviour as 'moderate' or 'modest'. Progress and modernity are presented as ideal imperatives which then cannot, of course, be implemented all at once and thus have to be brought into harmony with the real social and political environment. One's biography and one's own success are then presented as the final proof of the rightness of this 'middle way'.

Journey into Modernity

Although one is familiar with the usual images of the 'mobile' nineteenth century, it is still amazing how often the travel motif appears in the autobiographies and how rich a spectrum the bourgeois idea of travel presents. The travel agenda contained not just regular family excursions lasting some days, visits to relatives, group excursions for young people and business journeys, but above all, visits to spa resorts. One author saw nothing at all unusual in reporting his thirty-seventh visit to Karlsbad, or another in reporting an annual stay in the 'Nordseebad Wyk auf Föhr'.[55] Robert von Mohl describes, with a certain amount of mischievousness, an official 'whose greatest achievement was that, for fifty years in a row, he visited the baths in Teinach, for which a memorial was erected in his name'.[56]

What is also astounding is the number of journeys undertaken for the explicit purpose of improving one's education. Among some authors, this 'travel fever' occurs so often and with such regularity that it emphasises, once again, the new relationship between the *Bürgertum* and leisure. Leisure and free time, or at least large amounts of free time, were as decisive a precondition for these bourgeois travels as they were for bourgeois education in general. This too was part of the new 'economy of time', a notion that is inadequately and one-sidedly described by the principle of effective and rational time-measurement. It also included that other, and more relaxed, principle of *Bildungszeit* (time for learning).

Of course the older models of bourgeois travel were still used by families after the turn of the century: those 'sentimental journeys' for instance, in the footsteps of Goethe, 'enjoying, revelling in and observing nature', especially in Switzerland, that 'Mecca of nature travellers' with its classical routes and 'panoramic views' which were to educate and aesthetically form the *Bürgertum's* love of nature.[57] In his memoirs, Reichardt already described this type of journey as 'an established article of fashion',[58] and the standard formula 'My first trip to Switzerland' turns up in the memoirs again and again.

Travels devoted to the history of art also continued into the nineteenth century and were seen as encounters with antiquity and with the classical period. In the travel literature and travel guides, the educational experience is described and prescribed with great precision, including practical information about where to stay overnight, and where one could have one's initials engraved for posterity in places of honour. Goethe himself did exactly this on the tower of the Strasbourg cathedral.[59] This was all part of the ritual of the *Bildungsreise* (educational journey). The journey was properly staged as an experience-model and as model-experience. It was ostensible proof of openness to a practical *Weltanschauung* and of a will to *Selbst-Bildung* (self-formation).

According to the old model, practically the only appropriate form of travel was the coach, which would only stop at 'good' inns. Travellers also liked to stop over for some time with relatives or friends. Although the travel area expanded geographically, it remained culturally restricted. Bourgeois travel signified a movement within the tried and trusted social forms, at the accustomed social level and with the right distance from the strange or foreign everyday life. Even abroad, one looked for the old and familiar.

The new model broke with this cultural isolation. Visiting and acquiring insight into distant art and culture with which one was already familiar from reading and from general education was replaced by the search for dialogue with foreigners and with things foreign. This new programme included culture, technology, politics, history, science, literature, art and everyday life. One could almost give it a certain typology: the *tour d'horizon* in the art, history and science of other cities and countries remained obligatory. The visits continued to the museums, churches, theatres, opera houses, universities and archives. The social programme with friends and acquaintances in private homes, cafés and ballrooms continued as well.

All the same, something new was added: the journey 'into modernity'. This journey began with two new means of transport: the steamship and the railway. A technological tour brought the traveller to see new factories, bridges, machinery, warships, new harbor constructions and new railway stations in order to study progress first hand and to experience it with one's own senses. 'Along the way we saw a beautiful steam engine and a coal mine', wrote one Belgian traveller in his diary in 1828.[60] No one now travelled to England or France anymore without having such visits as an important part of their program.

There was also a political *Bildungsreise*. Even before the visits to the museums of Paris, one often went to the places of the Revolution, to the 'original sites' of the battles and executions. The July barricades of 1830 arrived just in time to add new attractions to the hackneyed tour of Revolutionary locations. The visitor to Leipzig seldom missed an opportunity for an excursion to the battlefield of the Völkerschlacht, while the visitor to London who had not visited Parliament and listened to a debate was seriously missing out on something. These visits to the historic sites, to the shrines of great national events, were all part of the search for bourgeois identity.

Finally, there was a kind of inland-ethnology: the search for the *Volksleben* (life of the people) and for what was peculiar in one's own society. Heinrich Laube thought he found this Volk in the Prague cellar-bars of the 1830s: 'I wanted to get to know their simple pleasures, and in the evening I looked for a dance hall'. A similar interest took him to the popular festivals in Vienna.[61] Other visitors, pursuing similar goals, visited the Tivoli of Copenhagen, or the night-clubs and theatres of Paris – no longer by coach, but on foot.

Modern travel consisted in 'moving among the people' and keeping only an internal, but not an external, cultural distance. One travelled through London on the bus in order to see this great metropolis and experience first-hand 'the hustle and bustle of a world-class city'. To widen one's social perception, one visited the docks, the railway stations and even the asylums and prisons. Many of the descriptions read like reports of expeditions to the unknown interior of a country, for instance, in describing a walk though the different sections of Manchester, including 'the poor and filthy areas where the industrial workers lived'. However, there were also pleasant surprises: 'In the vicinity there were also beautiful squares and monuments. The railway lines built above the streets and houses were very interesting'.[62]

Many aspects of foreign society and culture were now seen in a broader framework, from different points of view and with a more open mind. The choices within the travel model were now very broad indeed, and from these, the individual traveller was able to choose different types of travel in different combinations. The emphasis depended on circumstances, on individual interests and educational needs, but generally attempted to include as wide a variety as possible, creating a *mise en scène* of contrasting experiences and counterpoints: art and technology, churches and scenes of revolutionary events, the ballroom and the asylum, hiking and rail travel. Herein lay a distinctive element of bourgeois praxis: tourist travel was no longer an exclusive class privilege. The great works of art and technology were now accessible to all. The railway line and the footpath were open to everyone. All the individual elements of travel appeared to be structured in an 'egalitarian' manner, apart from small differences in price. However, the model of travel as a 'bourgeois adventure' remained the exclusive property of those whose cultural patterns and ways of seeing had been prepared for this kind of *Weltanschauung* by means of the appropriate literary and aesthetic education.

To demonstrate the extensive horizons and the capacity for cultural synthesis involved in this kind of travel programme here is a brief outline of the travels undertaken by the liberal publisher Otto Elben in 1846. His first destination was a German-Flemish song festival in Cologne. He left Heilbronn on a steamship, went down the Neckar and then the Rhine on what was a 'wonderful, poetic journey'. He met some bourgeois choral groups who boarded the ship along the way and heading for the same destination. Arriving in Cologne, he delivered the first of many festival speeches ('the song festivals became a speech school for me'), participated in the nationalistically coloured musical and choral events and went on tours and excursions ('Real popular assemblies were organised on the Drachenfels and in Godesberg'). Then he returned with the choral groups on the steamship as far as Mainz. From there he went by express to Leipzig where he toured the site of the Völkerschlacht before continuing by train to Dresden where his programme included art exhibitions, a visit to the university, coffee houses and an excursion into 'the countryside of the Saxon Switzerland'.

From Dresden he took the train to Berlin where his busy schedule included: the opera and theatre, experiencing Gneist and Ranke 'live' at the university, Potsdam, Charlottenburg, visits to newspaper editors as well as friends from his native region. This was followed by a three-day walking tour to Rügen, a longer visit to Copenhagen which included a look at life in the Tivoli, tours of museums, different types of steamships and the Danish navy and fortresses. He returned on the night boat to Kiel, whence he travelled by train to

Rendsburg in order to participate in meetings and discussions concerning the 'German question' in Schleswig-Holstein.

Finally he travelled by coach and train through Hamburg to Belgium for a song festival in Brussels where he was introduced into various societies, casinos, book clubs, and toured museums as well as electrical telegraph installations. This was followed by some months in Paris, London and Scotland, a long sea voyage to Portugal and Africa, returning fifteen months later through Italy to his home town. Six months later, the publisher got married. The date was March 2, 1848, the very day on which freedom of the press was declared in Württemberg.[63]

This was a bourgeois journey through time which, after encounters with nature, technology, his own fellow nationals and exotic strangers, with social life, politics, science, art and warships, with friends and acquaintances finally ended in modernity. He returned home in the midst of the upheavals brought about by the German bourgeoisie of 1848. These were the same *Bürger* who then settled down to 'moderate progress' and later wrote their autobiographies: the story of their life as an 'apprenticeship' in German *Bürgerlichkeit*.

Notes to Chapter 15

1. H. Laube, 'Erinnerungen: 1810–1840', in H.Laube, *Gesammelte Werke* edited by H.H. Houben, vol. 40 (Leipzig, 1909), p. 157f.

2. On the concept and its history, see M.Riedel, 'Bürger, Staatsbürger, Bürgertum', in O. Brunner et al. (eds.), *Geschichtliche Grundbegriffe. Historisches Lexikon zur politisch-sozialen Sprache in Deutschland*, vol. 1 (Stuttgart, 1972), pp. 672–725.

3. As historical sources I have used thirty memoirs by mainly male authors with different career and social backgrounds born in the period 1790 to 1805. I have also made use of published letters and contemporary writings on culture. Although I did not systematically choose a representative group, the selection does actually reflect the real structure of the historical *Bürgerwelt*. The careers most frequently found among the autobiographers were, in fact, the biggest and socially most influential bourgeois groups, i.e. university professors, factory owners, writers and high-ranking officials. These incorporate the type of bourgeois for whom it was a cultural habit, almost taken for granted, that they would give an autobiographical account of themselves to not only family and friends, but also to the wider public. Memoirs written by artists, art dealers, doctors or women were an exception. To that extent, therefore, the authors chosen do present a kind of group biography of the *Bürgertum* during the period between the turn of the century and the 1848 revolution.

4. See H.H. Gerth, *Bürgerliche Intelligenz um 1800. Zur Soziologie des deutschen Frühliberalismus* (Göttingen, 1976). This was first published in 1935, and is still well worth reading.

5. For a more detailed sociological survey and social profiles, see R.M. Lepsius, 'Zur Soziologie des Bürgertums und der Bürgerlichkeit' in J. Kocka (ed.), *Bürger und Bürgerlichkeit im 19. Jahrhundert* (Göttingen, 1987), pp. 79–100.

6. Quoted from G.König, 'Therese Huber', in *Baden und Württemberg im Zeitalter Napoleons*, published by the Württembergisches Landesmuseum, Stuttgart, vols. 1 and 2 (Stuttgart, 1987), p. 1126f.

7. E. Münch, *Erinnerungen, Lebensbilder und Studien aus den ersten sieben und dreißig Jahren eines deutschen Gelehrten*, vol. 1 (Karlsruhe, 1836), p. 316.

8. R. von Mohl, *Lebenserinnerungen, 1799–1875*, vol. 1 (Stuttgart, 1902), p. 82.

9. *Briefwechsel zweier Deutscher*, edited by P. Pfizer (Stuttgart, 1831), quotation from the 1832 edition, p. 112.

10. On the concept of social distinction, see P. Bourdieu, *Die feinen Unterschiede. Kritik der gesellschaftlichen Urteilskraft*, (Frankfurt, 1982), especially pp. 405–499.

11. O. Bähr, *Eine deutsche Stadt vor 60 Jahren. Kulturgeschichtliche Skizze* (Leipzig, 1884), p. 157.

12. See R. v. Dülmen, *Die Gesellschaft der Aufklärer* (Frankfurt, 1986), p. 81ff.; M. Prüsener, 'Lesegesellschaften im 18. Jahrhundert', *Börsenblatt für den Deutschen Buchhandel* (Frankfurt, edition no. 27, 1972), pp. 189–301.

13. A.W. Cramer, *Haus-Chronik, meinen Anverwandten und Freunden zum Andenken gewidmet* (Hamburg, 1822), p. 15f.

14. Münch, *Erinnerungen*, vol. 1, p. 69.

15. K.F. Klöden, *Von Berlin nach Berlin. Erinnerungen 1786–1824* (Berlin, 1978), p. 116.

16. O. Elben, *Lebenserinnerungen. 1823–1899* (Stuttgart, 1931), p. 29ff.

17. Cf. H.A.D. Reichard, *Seine Selbstbiographie (1751–1828)*, edited by H. Uhde, (Stuttgart, 1877), p. 92.

18. Münch, *Erinnerungen*, vol. 1, p. 312.

19. Elben, *Lebenserinnerungen*, p. 28ff.

20. Cf. Laube, p. 54f.; W. v. Kügelgen, *Jugenderinnerungen eines alten Mannes (1870)* (Berlin, no date), p. 339f.

21. Laube, *Erinnerungen*, p. 78.

22. Kügelgen, *Jugenderinnerungen*, p. 356.

23. J. Reulecke, *Geschichte der Urbanisierung in Deutschland* (Frankfurt, 1985), p. 17.

24. Mohl, *Erinnerungen*, p. 103ff.

25. F.C. Dahlmann, *Die Politik auf den Grund und das Maß der gegebenen Zustände zurückgeführt*, edited by O. Westphal (Berlin, 1924), p. 14 (reprint of the second edition of 1847).

26. E. Dronke, *Berlin (1846)*, edited by R. Nitsche (Darmstadt, 1974), p. 46ff.

27. W. v. Siemens, *Lebenserinnerungen* (Leipzig, 1943), p. 65.

28. W. Hardtwig, *Vormärz. Der monarchische Staat und das Bürgertum* (Munich, 1985), p. 26.

29. A.G. de Stael, *Über Deutschland (1814)*, edited by M. Bosse (Frankfurt, 1985), p. 110.

30. Laube, *Erinnerungen*, p. 56.

31. *Ibid.*, p. 51.

32. de Stael, *Über Deutschland*, p. 637.

33. Laube, *Erinnerungen*, p. 10.

34. *Uhlands Briefwechsel*, edited by J. Hartmann, Part 2 (Stuttgart, 1912), p. 25.

35. L. Börne, *Gesammelten Schriften*, vol. 2 (Berlin, no date), p. 125.

36. K.A. Varuhagen von Ense, *Denkwürdigkeiten des eignen Lebens*, vol. 2 (Berlin, 1971), p. 340.

37. Dronke, *Berlin*, p. 48.

38. Elben, *Lebenserinnerungen*, p. 10.

39. Mohl, *Lebenserinnerungen*, p. 119.

422 | *Wolfgang Kaschuba*

40. Laube, *Erinnerungen*, p. 54.
41. Münch, *Erinnerungen*, vol. 1, p. 326.
42. W. Lepenies, *Melancholie und Gesellschaft* (Frankfurt, 1969), p. 100.
43. Cramer, *Haus-Chronik*, p. 21.
44. Pfizer, *Briefwechsel*, p. 113.
45. Mohl, *Lebenserinnerungen*, p. 39.
46. See for instance, the exhibition guide to Baden-Württemberg.
47. T. Fontane, *Meine Kinderjahre* (Leipzig, 1959) p. 127.
48. Münch, *Erinnerungen*, vol. 1, p. 39.
49. K.W. Kolbe, *Mein Lebenslauf und mein Wirken im Fache der Sprache und der Kunst* (Berlin, 1825), p. 9.
50. See what is still the basic historical outline of the problem: K. Hausen, 'Die Polarisierung der 'Geschlechtscharaktere' – Eine Spiegelung der Dissoziation von Erwerbs- und Familienleben', in W. Conze (ed.), *Sozialgeschichte der Familie in der Neuzeit Europas* (Stuttgart, 1976), pp. 367–393; also U. Frevert, *Frauen-Geschichte. Zwischen BürgerlicherVerbesserung und Neuer Weiblichkeit* (Frankfurt, 1986), especially pp. 15–80.
51. Kügelgen, *Jugenderinnerungen*. p. 380ff.
52. Cramer, *Haus-Chronik*, p. 19.
53. Mohl, *Lebenserinnerungen*, p. 73.
54. Elben, *Lebenserinnerungen*, p. 3.
55. Laube, *Erinnerungen*, p. 179.; C. v. Tiedemann, *Aus sieben Jahrzehnten. Erinnerungen*, vol. 1 (Leipzig, 1905), p. 141.
56. Mohl, *Lebenserinnerungen*, p. 49.
57. According to R. Prutz, *Schriften zur Literatur und Politik*, edited by B. Hüppenauf (Tübingen, 1973), p. 37f.
58. Reichard, *Seine Selbstbiographie*, p. 50.
59. *Ibid.*, p. 207.
60. *Reisebericht eines westfälischen Glasindustriellen*, edited by H. Vollmerhaus (Dortmund, 1971), p. 70.
61. H. Laube, *Reise durch das Biedermeier* (Hamburg, 1965), p. 299, 257.
62. Elben, *Lebenserinnerungen*, pp. 84f.,91.
63. *Ibid.*, pp. 64–112.

16 | The Italian 'Borghesia'

Marco Meriggi

In the early 1930s the liberal philosopher Benedetto Croce complained that a misleading use of the word 'borghese' was becoming common in Italian. For Croce, 'borghese' was a historical category, which could be applied accurately only to the medieval and early modern periods as a way of locating the estate of the 'burghers' in the feudal social structure. Hence the modern usage was contradictory and imprecise, particularly when economically and functionally differentiated strata of society were grouped together into a single social unit labelled 'borghese'. How, Croce asked, could the owners of the means of production be placed in the same social category as self-employed professionals, scientists, and the 'educated classes'?

As one of the last major representatives of that prestigious layer of Italian intellectuals, who had for decades occupied a dominant position in what was a predominantly rural society, Croce preferred to locate the Italian *borghesia* within a framework of political values. Rather than seeing it as a class defined by a position in a particular set of relations of production, he viewed the *borghesia* as a 'middle-class', representing by virtue of its 'central' position, the general interests of society. In the contemporary misuse of the phrase 'borghese', Croce thought he detected the result of a misguided aristocratic or proleterian polemic against the values of the modern world.[1]

Shortly after Croce, the fascist journalist Nello Quilici published a book on the Italian *borghesia*, dedicated to 'the citizen of tomorrow' the 'bearer of progress and modernity'. However, in contrast to Croce, his vision of the 'ideal bourgeois' was of the 'tireless producer, constantly investing and reinvesting the profit of his initiative and effort in the expansion of national wealth'. In the new climate of 'imperial consciousness awakened by fascism', he predicted, this 'bourgeois spirit' would soon flourish and spread.

Quilici's *borghesia* was above all a class of economic producers closely associated with the corporate and authoritarian state. The

Notes to Chapter 16 can be found on page 437.

'bourgeois of yesterday', so dear to Croce, Quilici refers to scornfully as a 'load of bureaucrats', an 'arrogant and inconsequential class of functionaries, who look down upon the farmers, industrialists and merchants'. After the war of independence 'borghese' had come to be synonymous with the liberal professions: lawyers, doctors, and men of letters, whose humanist culture made them the enemies of modern technology. Quilici concluded laconically: 'If one is to identify "borghese" (in its economic sense) with "liberalism" (in the political sense), then…'the borghese' is fated to extinction'.[2]

These contradictory views held by Croce and Quilici are echoed by a survey of dictionaries and encyclopedias, which accurately reflect the historical process of transformation the concept of 'borghese' underwent in this period. As late as 1875 the entries under *borghese/borghesia* emphasised the traditional legal definition of the medieval bourgeois estate. In the last quarter of the nineteenth century social and economic aspects began to acquire a new importance: the term now referred to the 'middle class' (*ceto medio*), which began to force itself between the aristocracy and the rest of the population. According to one contemporary author, what was now meant was 'that class of borghese (*cittadini*) who claim to be members of the borghese estate (*civile condizione*) even if they are completely without means'. For Carpi the 'middle-class' is 'the heart of the nation; source of the most brilliant talent in jurisprudence, letters, the arts, science, commerce, the military and politics'. However, things had begun to change: the generation of the fathers had been active 'in the counting houses, workshops and on the land', whereas their sons devoted themselves to advocacy, literature, the civil service and higher offices of the state.[3]

The *borghesia* was increasingly distancing itself from a role in production and was instead exploiting its specific 'intellectual skills' in new roles and functions. However, it lacked the necessary means and style to follow the example set by the landowning, aristocratic rentier in giving external expression to its social position. Virtually all the dictionaries agreed that 'bourgeois ' also implied 'simplicity, lacking in beauty and refinement, common'. At the same time they mentioned economic and political characteristics which sharply distinguish this estate from 'the populace'. Connotations of class also began to acquire more weight. In 1912 a dictionary stated that 'bourgeois' meant 'for the socialist – not always precisely defined – that class, which enjoys certain privileges over the proleteriat, the workers or the working class'.[4]

Only after the Second World War does a further semantic extension of the concept of the *borghesia* begin to appear in Italian dictionaries, which in general tended to lag behind actual developments in usage. Alongside the traditional explanations refering to ethics, culture and income, we begin to find new interpretations. However, the *borghesia* remains the 'layer of society between the proleteriat and the aristocracy made up of the self-employed, salaried employees, merchants and small property owners'. We do now find references to a *haute bourgeoisie* (*grossa borghesia*) to which belong industrialists and bankers.[5] The Dictionary of the Italian Language published in 1971 lays most weight on the economic role of the *borghesia*. The classical definition in terms of politics and culture has now receded. The *borghesia* is defined as 'that social class made up of individuals who earn their living in commerce, in industry, as self-employed or in leading positions in public office or in the private sector'.[6] A dictionary which appeared in 1983 defines the *borghesia* as the social stratum consisting of owners of the means of production, together with those other groups who share their way of life, goals and ideals.[7] Meanwhile, the conservative, originally aristocratic, criticism of the 'common bourgeois' has largely been replaced by the left-wing critique of the progressive role of the *borghesia*: according to which a member of the *borghesia* is defined as someone 'who seeks to defend and strengthen his own social position by conservative opposition to rapid change'.[8]

These lexicographical-semantic changes reflect the material development of the Italian *borghesia* in the period between the French Revolution and the First World War. Three crucial stages of development can be distinguished: In the course of the first, the *borghesia* parted company with the aristocracy, a process in which professional skills and persistence were more important than economic potency. The *borghesia* then proceeded to acquire an unchallenged position of political power. Finally, in the last stage, which was completed only in the 1930s, the *borghesia* focused its attention on industrial development.

In ideal-typical form, these three stages trace a path from Croce's to Quilici's *borghesia*. 'Bourgeois' in this context includes property owners, self-employed professionals (referred to as the *borghesia umanistica*) and entrepreneurs. These components were mixed in varying proportions in the course of the nineteenth century and should not be considered to be either consecutive formations or exclusive of other formations. Each one of these three basic groups was able to present itself for a time as the symbolic representative of the bourgeois class.

The State and the Borghesia

How does one explain the predominance of a definition of the nine-teenth century Italian *borghesia* which emphasises its position 'in the middle' of the social structure rather than its productive or economic role?[9] The fact is that, outside the agricultural sector, the methods of production in Italy experienced only limited and slow change in the course of the nineteenth century, the so-called 'century of the bour-geoisie'. By comparison with Germany and other European countries Italy entered the twentieth century as a predominantly agricultural society.

Table 16.1: Occupation according to sector in Italy and Germany[10]

| | YEAR | PERCENTAGE EMPLOYED | | |
		AGRIGULTURE	CRAFTS AND INDUSTRY	COMMERCE AND SERVICES
Italy	1871	61	23	16
	1881	62	25	13
	1911	56	27	17
Germany	1849	56	24	20
	1882	43	34	23
	1907	35	40	25

By the end of the nineteenth century industrialisation in Italy had proceeded to a level equivalent to that reached in England a century earlier and attained by Germany some fifty years earlier.

Political-institutional factors rather than industry or the economy are the main driving forces of social change in nineteenth century Italy. In two stages they completely transformed the country. In the first phase (1800–1815), the introduction of the Napoleonic-French legal code did away with the remains of the feudal order whose hold over the patrician-urban aristocracy of northern and central Italy had anyway become weak. At the same time a modern centralised state administration came into being which both undermined the socio-political power of the aristocracy and encouraged the rise of a highly educated *borghesia*.

However, the Napoleonic era did little to change the relations of property and production. Large-scale landholding remained confined to the aristocracy, though as a result of the sale of church property they were joined by a handful of landowners of non-noble stock. Agriculture, employing large amounts of capital and modern techniques in the north, but remaining very primitive in the south, continued as the most significant economic sector. Particularly characteristic of this first phase was the marked independence of the political executive vis-à-vis the dominant strata of society. The moment of change appeared in the shape of foreign armies in the protection of which a new bourgeois layer of property owners and legal professionals emerged, groups which were further strengthened by the new legislation and the repeal of the laws regulating the trades.

The second phase of important change (1859–1871) falls in the period of national unification under the leadership of Piedmont-Sardinia, in which the various regional social elites were reconciled with one another. This process at first strengthened the executive; however, the important role played by parliament also helped to give new influence to the *borghesia umanistica*. In this phase, the various bourgeois groups – property owners, professionals, civil servants and entrepreneurs – began to form a network of close contacts, in which there was a definite shift in weight from the large landowners and members of the liberal professions, who dominated the scene up until the 1880s, to the *borghesia umanistica*, which ascended to political and social leadership of the new nation state.

In some regions the aristocracy had lead the movement for national unification, though in fact its central concern – particularly in Lombardy and Tuscany – was independence from the Habsburgs. The nobility was accustomed to seeing itself as an oppositional rather than a ruling estate and after unification it preferred to take on the role of a social elite, rather than becoming directly involved in political leadership. The aristocracy of central and southern Italy which had distanced itself from, or even opposed, the nationalist movement was even less prepared to take part in the running of the new state. The Piedmontese nobility was the exception. With its well-established tradition of participation in public service and loyalty to the monarchy, it came to play a major role in the political elite of the new nation state and its members occupied powerful positions in parliamentary politics, the military and the administration.

Piedmont, which in the process of national unification played a role similar to that of Prussia in Germany, was too small a region to dominate the nation state. Facing a situation of internal weakness and external insecurity, the Piedmontese elite was thus forced to rely on the support of other regional elites to give the new state a minimum of governability. This dependence virtually guaranteed the eventual decline of the Piedmontese aristocracy. This trend was symbolised by the relocation of the capital from Turin to Florence and then later (in 1871) to Rome, which was better placed geographically and permitted a more balanced mixture of regional elites. Since the aristocratic property owners of the south were on the whole opposed to the new order, the political class was largely recruited from among the liberal professions, particularly the law. If in the first phase of the Italian monarchy landowning, aristocratic politicans had still played a comparatively significant role, they were soon to be replaced by the professions, who entered into a particularly close relationship with the public authorities.

Table 16.2: Social and occupational background of Italian cabinet ministers from 1861 to 1903 (in percentages)[11]

	1861–1876	1876–1903
Aristocratic	43	16
Non–noble	57	84
Landowners	21	3
Military	23	15
Self-employed and intellectuals	45	59
Civil Servants	11	22

No other European parliament, including even that of France, drew its membership so heavily from among the ranks of the self-employed professions and in particular from the law.[12] Bourgeois professionals were also heavily represented in other public offices and had begun to gain ground even in traditionally aristocratic institutions such as the army. By 1872 only 9 percent of Italian officers were of aristocratic origin (against 48 percent in Germany). By 1887 their share had declined to three percent, whereas as late as 1911 a third of German officers and half the generals were titled. Of the Italian generals in 1904 only one sixth were aristocrats.

In a country like Italy in which the state played a crucial role in the process of modernisation, the bourgeois strata was for a long time defined as a class associated primarily with the state (borghesia burocratica). The degree to which it was able to set the tone of public life is even more surprising if one considers that it exerted this influence within a constitutional monarchy whose founding charter emphatically restated the rights of the monarch. In contrast to the experience of the German empire or the Austro-Hungarian monarchy this contradiction between the principle of royal sovereignity and the parliamentary system was softened in practice. The 'bourgeois' parliament exercised its control over the executive by what amounted to a process of osmosis between the political arena and the administration. At least until the 1890s senior officials in government or the civil service were recruited from active parliamentary politics or other areas of public life (e.g. the universities) rather than from the professional civil service. The bureaucracy was therefore an extremely flexible but transient organisation which accurately reflected the flux of parliamentary majorities. Until the 1880s the franchise and the circle of politically active citizens were both tightly restricted. Though the Italian parliament was able to mount an effective liberal opposition to the neo-absolutist and authoritarian temptations of the monarchy, 'from below' it must have appeared as the instrument of an exclusive aristocratic-bourgeois dictatorship.

Prior to the extension of the franchise in 1882 the entitlement to vote and the right to stand as a candidate for election were conditional on meeting the requirements of an economic census and the attainment of a certain degree of education. The requirements were so strict that not only the lower classes, but the entire 'old' and 'new' *piccola borghesia* (in all, 98 percent of the kingdom's population) were excluded from the franchise. Only wealthy property owners, university-trained professionals (e.g. notaries, architects, apothecaries), brokers, priests and members of academies and chambers of commerce, civilian and military civil servants, were permitted to vote. It was within this system that the social formation known in the Italian literature as the *borghesia umanistica* acquired its stamp of peculiar political legitimacy. The *borghesia umanistica* came to dominate public life, from which the most wealthy aristocratic and landowning classes increasingly withdrew. The political and administrative role of the 'educated classes' further strengthened the social dominance they had long enjoyed. This combination of political and social power was to characterise the Italian *borghesia* into the 1890s.

The Borghesia and Society

Although this thin layer of the *borghesia*, the Italian political class par excellence, had early on won its battle against the landowners and the aristocracy, it had for a long time accepted their cultural and social values. The mentality inherited from the agrarian and aristocratic world was widespread among the professional classes. They viewed their skills and training as a property which generated an adequate if not always generous income, sufficient at least to support a lifestyle that distinguished them from the lower classes and *piccola borghesia*. Consumption of white bread, beef and fine wines together with the employment of domestic servants set them clearly apart as a separate class.

In a society that was on the whole very poor and in which even the upper classes hardly qualified as wealthy by international standards,[13] property ownership was invested with a special symbolic significance. Together with government stocks it was the dominant form of capital ownership. Both were forms of investment characterised by low risk and low returns. Above all, they conformed to the pervasive philosophy of the rentier and provided the basis for strategies of social distanciation and distinction vis-à-vis rival groups. The backwardness of parts of the aristocracy and the *borghesia* allowed the *borghesia umanistica* to take on a role as political and social intermediaries.

The dominance of this fraction of the *borghesia* was based on its academic training, and its monopolisation of legitimate culture in a country that was otherwise agrarian and characterised by both material and cultural poverty. The illiterate masses were not only excluded from the vote; they also lacked the elementary competences that were essential in dealings with public institutions.

Table 16.3: Illiteracy in Italy and Germany 1870 to 1900 (in percentages)[14]*

| | RECRUITS | | MARRIAGE REGISTER | |
	1870	1900	1870	1900
Italy	59	33	m59	34
			f78	48
Germany	2	0	m	0
			f	1

*m = male   f = female

These catagories refer to the people who when entering military service or when signing the marriage register, were not able to write their own name.

In such a society the importance of 'intermediary' groups is perhaps less surprising. The *borghesia umanistica* monopolised the knowledge necessary for the organisation of society and helped to bind a culturally underdeveloped and divided civil society to a nation state intent on expanding its functions and sources of power.

Lawyers and doctors were the most respected groups in this 'intermediary' class, to which also belonged teachers, civil servants, notaries, apothecaries and, in the north at least, engineers. Priests who for a long time were politically opposed to the new state occupied an ambivalent sociopolitical position. These occupations constituted a social stratum with shared moral and political values; a class composed of all those who, according to Benedetto Croce, shared an interest in, and felt themselves responsible for, the 'public good'.

How extensive was this *borghesia umanistica* and how was it made up? Counting all those involved in the transmission of knowledge (including priests), about 1,5 percent of the population qualified for membership in this group in 1881, a figure which corresponds roughly to the size of the electorate. Despite its high rate of illiteracy, Italy registered a relatively large number of university students in the second half of the nineteenth century (more than Germany in the 1890s). This disproportion was echoed in all other walks of life: In proportion to the total population there were far more university graduates in Italy than in Prussia.

Table 16.4: Doctors and lawyers for every 1,000 of the population in Italy and Prussia in the year 1901[15]

	Doctors	Lawyers
Italy	0.68	0.74
Germany	0.51	0.12

This image of Italy as a country with an enormous head balanced on a puny body is reinforced if one examines the situation in the south. In these economically retarded regions there was one lawyer or doctor for every thousand of the population and the ratio of students to the population was much higher than in the north. Wherever a modern economy was lacking, the *borghesia* resorted to formal education and professional careers to ensure its reproduction.

The *borghesia umanistica* was not a homogeneous unit, rather, it was made up of disparate local power groups held together only by their participation in public life. Social organisations such as clubs or associations were rare, lacked national coordination and were limited to the north. The state was therefore able to acquire even more importance in the area of interest representation. The 'deficiencies' of the *borghesia* and the 'retardation' of bourgeois society found further expression in the lack of modern parliamentary political structures. In parliament the 'right' and the 'left' were represented by shifting and fragile coalitions of regional and local interests. Given the absence of sharp ideological divisions, the relations of patronage typical of societies fractured along lines of region and locality were the dominant form of political organisation. In these clientele relations, the legal profession – central to the *borghesia umanistica* – acquired further prestige. The parliament chamber was transformed into a courtroom for the settling of conflicts of interest between whole localities and regions, an arrangement which on the whole accurately reflected the characteristic social relationships of southern Italy.

The Breakthrough of the 1880s

From the mid nineteenth century onwards the tell-tale symptoms of the process of modernisation that was affecting other regions of Europe began to become visible in northern Italy; the profit motive of the industrial age came increasingly to the forefront and the engineer began to displace the lawyer and the doctor in the scale of prestige. From the 1880s the economic and technical *borghesia* began to assert itself more and more vocally, though it was to become a truely decisive force only after the turn of the century.

Domestic and foreign political factors encouraged this process of social change. In 1882 the franchise was extended to all literate males.[16] This measure tripled the size of the electorate, which benefited the north and the large towns. It also helped to undermine the system of patronage and weakened the political bloc made up of the professionals and landowners. The intensifying imperialist competition between the European nations and Italy's own efforts to make good its colonial claims lead to further changes in the structure of society and the state. The bureaucracy expanded dramatically, which helped to satisfy the expectations of the unemployed southern intellectuals. It also appeared to be a necessary response to the increasingly assertive non-bourgeois fractions in parliament. The balance of power shifted decisively in favour of the bureaucracy and executive and against the legislature.

This changed power constellation also strengthened the position of the state in the economy, a new situation exemplified by the conversion from free trade to modest protectionism in 1878 and a complete system of tariffs after 1887. The etatist drive for industrialisation, based on a policy of granting privileges and public contracts to particular firms in the hope of stimulating investment and innovation, was aimed at increasing the competitiveness of a country, whose economic structure was so retarded and agrarian that it was increasingly unable to compete in the struggle for colonial acquisitions.

This externally driven process of economic modernisation contributed to the retention of pre-modern attitudes among the Italian industrial *borghesia* and its failure to challenge the rentier mentality of the proprietory and professional *borghesia*. Its organicist and paternalist approach to the organisation of production continued to betray agrarian roots. The Italian industrial bourgeoisie thus lacked a consciousness of its wider social role, and its political programme hardly even considered the possibility of the general transformation of society by the process of industrialisation. Instead, by exploiting the underdeveloped condition of the rest of society and the protection of the state, the industrialists hoped to reap profit without incurring the risks of entrepreneurship.

The extension of the scope of executive action and the increasing influence of the administration curtailed the power of the parliament. The parliamentary deputy increasingly found his role as a mediator between clientele and bureaucracy being taken over by the bureaucrat himself who seemed better suited to the management of relations between the state and organised social interest groups. Civil servants who had made up an important part of the bourgeois political class in the 1860s were able to further increase their influence in the 1890s. With increasing salaries they were in a good position to differentiate themselves economically and in everyday life from the lower middle classes and the formalisation of career paths strengthened their autonomy vis-à-vis the parliament. By the first decade of the nineteenth century they had begun to take on the characteristics of a caste, rivalling the ascendant industrial *borghesia* and its interest groups in the political process of decision-making and policy formation. In both politics and society at large, technical and authoritarian elements acquired a new importance whereas the mediating elements became increasingly less significant.

These developments coincided with the emergence of a militant factory proleteriat which from the 1890s dominated the political scene with its mass meetings. Social interest groups were organised in the form of labour unions, professional associations and employers' federations. Socialist and Catholic mass political parties came to play an increasingly important role both in parliament and society in general. The structural conflict between bourgeoisie and proleteriat was conducted in the form of open class warfare which displaced the traditional opposition between *borghesia umanistica* and the 'uneducated populace'. The old order of the notables had begun to disintegrate and the educated *borghesia* was to discover that its old methods of patronage had lost their effectiveness under the new conditions. The extension of the franchise brought new actors onto the political stage and legitimised new social forces. The oligarchic-liberal power structure which had left its imprint on the first two decades of the newly united Italy had reached its limits.

In the years 1890–1914 the social complexity of the Italian peninsula increased dramatically. The industrialised regions of the north steadily increased in importance by comparison with the underdeveloped southern areas. The character and organization of relations of political power in Italy began to resemble those of Germany.

In 1898 political freedoms were temporarily suspended in Italy. On the model of the German constitution the 'monarchical principle' was to be placed above the rights of the parliament. However, this 'bourgeois coup d'etat' was reversed within the space of a few months; an outcome to which divisions within the *borghesia* contributed significantly. In the following fifteen years the *borghesia* accomodated to the political reality of the organised working class and there were the first tentative initiatives for social reform. At the same time the autonomy of the administration and the other centres of power (e.g. the military) continued to increase vis-à-vis parliament, which appeared increasingly unable to provide a guarantee for the maintenance of bourgeois order.

However, the backing for this authoritarian turn, which took full effect during the First World War, came not from the aristocracy and it would be wrong to see it as a reassertion of traditional values. Rather it was the policy of a restructured Italian *borghesia* which had come to a new understanding of its class interests. This redefinition occured under growing pressure from the non-bourgeois classes, particularly the class conscious industrial proleteriat, which, in contrast to the *piccola borghesia*, was neither eager nor able to adopt middle-class values.

Comparative Issues

Almost forty years ago Gaetano Salvemini compared the political history of Germany and Italy in the period from 1814 to 1870.[17] He was most interested in the problems of national reunification common to both, but also touched on social issues. He pointed out that though Italy's political structure was far less fractured than Germany's – prior to unification there were only eight states in Italy compared to Germany's thirty-two – it was a much more heterogeneous society. Italy lacked ancient federative structures such as the Holy Roman Empire or more modern institutions such as the German Federation (Deutscher Bund) or the Zollverein. The cohesion of the regional aristocracies was correspondingly loose.

The German and Italian aristocracies were also dissimilar at the cultural, social and ideological levels. The German nobility drew on a monarchical and feudal tradition and saw itself as the preserver of values of authority and exclusivity. It was closely identified with the ruling dynasty and the late-absolutist power structure. It had a dominant position in the administration, the military and the diplomatic corps. By contrast the Italian aristocracy with the exception of that of Rome and the south was patrician and urban in character. It harboured republican sentiments and was very open to intermarriage with the propertied *borghesia*. In northern Italy feudal structures and legal forms had lost all authority centuries earlier and certainly did not provide a solid base for the local aristocracy. Since large parts of the country were governed by foreign powers the nobility lacked experience of public office. Unlike its German counterpart it was a social stratum defined by property and status rather than a political governing estate. This helps to explain why the Italian aristocracy departed the political stage so much earlier than the nobility of the German *Kaiserreich*.[18]

By contrast with the Prussian nobility, which was clearly more powerful than its peers from the other states of the new Reich, the dynastic aristocracy of 'little' Piedmont, whose territory made up only an eleventh of the whole peninsula, had to remain open to other regional and social elites. In the course of this process of amalgamation, a group of notables acquired power, influence and prestige, which recruited its membership from among the aristocratic and bourgeois property owners and the educated, economically inactive *borghesia*. The 'humanist' fraction of the *borghesia* usurped the position of the aristocracy whilst remaining open to its culture and values. Through the jobs market this *borghesia umanistica* monopolised the intermediary positions in politics and in the apparatus of the state, mediating functions which were crucial to the project of national unification. As a result, the Italian monarchy took on a parliamentary character and gave wide political scope to the propertied and educated *borghesia*. Finally, the retreat of the aristocracy from the executive and the legislature gave the bureaucracy a significance as a dynamic factor greater even than in Germany.

For the *borghesia* of both countries the relationship to the state was a central element in their understanding of their own position and power base. However, while the German *borghesia* was 'colonised' by the monarchist-authoritarian state, the Italian state acted as an instrument of legitimation and self-defence for the Italian *borghesia*, an instrument which it used in its attempts to define an independent class identity and as a means of defining the boundaries of the *borghesia* as a class (franchise restrictions). The Italian *borghesia* had achieved the colonisation of the monarchy and control of the state: in fact, the *borghesia was* the state.

As we have seen the *borghesia* for a long time was in fact an 'upper middle class', i.e. a group defined in political, moral and cultural terms rather than by its position in the relations of production; a *borghesia* that shared the agrarian ethos of the rentier and viewed the profit motive with scepticism.

Does that make it a *Bildungsbürgertum* (educated middle class) in the German sense? This question can be answered in the affirmative, though some important differences remain to be considered. Within the German *Bildungsbürgertum* the authoritarian civil servant was such a dominant figure that even the liberal professions were drawn into the orbit of the state. Within the Italian *borghesia umanistica* these power relations were reversed. The self-employed professionals of the peninsula derived their *raison d'être* from the material and cultural poverty of the rest of society and enjoyed the privilege of belonging to a class with the rights of political expression. They took advantage of the situation of flux and created a modern state whose political and administrative relations henceforth remained under their control. By contrast with the German *Bildungsbürgertum*, appointed by the centralised authoritarian monarchy, the *borghesia umanistica* of Italy maintained an independent identity. Its hegemony was ultimately based in the poverty, decay, underdevelopment and depoliticisation of the rest of society.

In terms of economic and social modernisation Germany was definitely in advance of Italy. The continuing dominance of the *Junker* did not in itself hamper this modernisation process. The rate of industrial growth was twice as high as in Italy, social legislation was introduce significantly earlier, the network of associations was much tighter and the party system, in which anti-bourgeois forces were represented, was more modern. In Italy on the other hand the quasi-dictatorship of the *borghesia umanistica* resulted in economic stagnation and the conscious retention of a social model based on the ideology of the rentier. Though the Italian model sought to avoid the painful social consequences of a rapid 'leap' into modernity, it also helped to ensure the survival of antiquated social relations of patronage and paternalism. This is the point at which the limitations of that commitment to the 'public good' which Croce emphasised as the most prominent characteristic of the Italian *ceto medio* become visible. The belated commitment to modernisation was motivated more by concern for Italy's position in the European power system than by any interest for the well-being of Italy's own population. If Gaetano Salvemini had extended his comparison beyond the simultaneous foundation of the *Kaiserreich* and the Italian state, he would probably have come across new and unexpected similarities or at least signs of a convergence that had appeared remote in 1871.

With the extension of the industrial *borghesia* and the factory system the peninsular was not spared an authoritarian period. The industrial bourgeoisie was soon confronted with organised opposition: the militant factory proleteriat finally disposed of the trappings of the ideologically subordinate *piccola borghesia*. Italian liberalism on the other hand began to develop militarist, colonialist and 'illiberal' tendencies. The property owners and the liberal professions, so highly valued by Croce, conceded pride of place in the ranks of the *borghesia* to the entrepreneur and the bureaucrats of the new corporate state. It was to be the hyperbole of fascism in which these tendencies found their fullest expression.

Notes to Chapter 16

1. B. Croce, 'Di un equivoco concetto storico: la borghesia', in B. Croce, *Etica e politica* (Bari, 1931), p. 321–338.
2. N. Quilici, *La borghesia italiana* (Milan, 1942), vol.2, p. 432, 360, 419.
3. L.Carpi, *L'Italia vivente. Studi sociali* (Milan, 1878), p. 14, 299, 305, 309.
4. P.Premoli, *Il tesoro della lingua italiana* (Milan, 1912).
5. S.Battaglia, *Grande dizionario della lingua italiana* (Turin, 1961).
6. G.Devoto and G.C.Oli *Dizionario della lingua italiana* (Florence, 1971).
7. N.Zingarelli, *Vocabolario della lingua italiana (1917–1922)* (Bologna, 1983).
8. Devoto/Oli, *Dizionario*.
9. In this contribution I draw on recent Italian research on the subject of the *borghesia*

without making detailed references. Particularly relevant are. G. Baglioni, *L'ideologia della borghesia industriale nell'Italia liberale* (Turin, 1974), P. Macry and R. Romanelli (eds.), 'Borghesie urbane dell'Ottocento', in *Quaderni Storici* 56 (1984), p. 333–612; A. Caracciolo, *Stato e società civile. Problemi dell'unificazione italiana* (Turin, 1972); P. Farneti, *Sistema politico e società civile* (Turin, 1971); P. Frascani, 'Les professions borghesees en Italie à l'époque libérale (1860–1920)', in *Mélanges de l'École Française de Rome – Moyen age, Temps modernes* 97 (1985), p. 325–340; P. Macry, 'Notables, professions libérales, employés', *ibid.*, p. 341–359; R. Romanelli, 'La bourgeoisie italienne entre modernité et tradition. Ses rapports avec l'État après l'unification', *ibid.*, p. 303–323; P. Macry, 'Sulla storia sociale dell'Italia liberale. Per una ricerca sul "ceto di frontiera"', in *Quaderni Storici* 35 (1977), p. 521–550; G.Melis, 'La cultura e il mondo degli impiegati', in S. Cassese (ed.), *L'amministrazione centrale* (Turin, 1984), p. 301–402; E. Ragionieri, 'La storia politica e sociale', in *Storia d'Italia Einaudi*, vol.4 (Turin, 1976); R. Romanelli, *L'Italia liberale (1861–1900)* (Bologna, 1979); P. Sylos Labini, *Saggio sulle classi sociali* (Bari, 1974); P. Villani, 'Gruppi sociali e classe dirigente all'indomani dell'Unità', in *Storia d'Italia Einaudi – Annali*, vol.1 (Turin, 1978), p. 881–978.

10. W. Fischer et al. (eds.), *Handbuch der europäischen Wirtschafts- und Sozialgeschichte*, vol.5 (Berlin,1985), p. 126.

11. P. Farneti, 'La classe politica della Destra e della Sinistra', in I. Zanni Rosiello (ed.), *Gli apparti statali dall'Unità al fascismo* (Bologna, 1976), p. 285–301.

12. P. Turiello, *Governo e governati in Italia*, 2 vols. (Bologna, 1882); see vol.2, p. 297. In the 1870s the Italian parliament had 170 members who were lawyers, the French parliament 48, the House of Commons 30 and the Reichstag only 10.

13. In 1914 per capita income in Germany was 6,400–7,000 French Francs, in Italy it amounted to only 2,570 Francs; see V. Zamagni, 'The Rich in a Late Industrialiser. The Case of Italy 1800–1945'; in W.D. Rubinstein (ed.), *Wealth and the Wealthy in the Modern World* (London, 1980), p. 141. In 1911 the number of inheritances worth more than 1 mill Lire was 1,500 in Italy; 30,000 in England; 1,500 in France; 11,000 in Germany; see A.M. Banti, 'Les richesses borghesees dans l'Italie du XIXe siècle. Exemples et remarques', in *Mélanges de l'École Française de Rome – Moyen age, Temps modernes* 97 (1985), pp. 361–379.

14. Fischer, *Handbuch*, p. 138.

15. M. Barbagli, *Disoccupazione intellettuale e sistema scolastico in Italia* (Bologna, 1974), p. 38.

16. Universal male suffrage was introduced only in 1911.

17. G. Salvemini, 'Germania e Italia dal 1814 al 1870', in G. *Salvemini, Scritti sul Risorgimento* (Milan, 1961), pp. 441–453.

18. See the contributions by H. Kaelble and by W. Mosse, in this book.

17 | The Development of the Hungarian Middle Class: Some East-West Comparisons*

Györgi Ránki

A t the time of the first census in Hungary in 1787, out of a total population of 8.5 million, there were 500,000 nobles and 190,000 *Bürger*.[1] These figures alone indicate the backwardness of this country at the time of the French Revolution, when Hungary was still part of the Habsburg monarchy. All of those factors that in Holland, for instance, had promoted the emergence of a bourgeois class during the eighteenth century – urban traditions and urban autonomy, the guilds, a growing stratum of public officials linked to the absolutist state, Enlightenment ideas – were also present in Hungary, but their strength and influence were incomparably smaller. In the fifteenth century, a period of strong monarchic rule, urban development in Hungary already lagged far behind that in Germany,[2] and this was before the Turks, who established their rule in Hungary after struggles that lasted for 150 years, had wiped out most Hungarian towns at the end of the sixteenth and the beginning of the seventeenth century. Where the towns did survive, they existed in the shadow of an increasingly stronger aristocratic power and an ever more strictly enforced serfdom, so they were unable to play any significant role, either numerically or politically. Although a more lively trade in commodities halted the decline of towns in the eighteenth century and, in many cases, led to an urban revival, the numerically small *Bürgertum*, whose political rights were extremely limited, did not constitute, either economically or socially, a significant force. It was also a section of the nobility rather than the *Bürgertum* that was affected by the ideas of the Enlightenment.[3]

---

*Györgi Ránki died in 1988. He did not have the opportunity to read the English version of his paper. The term *Bürgertum*, which he had used in his German text in reference to the Hungarian middle class, has therefore not been translated.

Notes to Chapter 17 can be found on page 454.

440 | *György Ránki*

The *Stadtbürgertum* who had their own urban traditions and civic rights,[4] were, to a large extent, ethnically non-Hungarian and German-speaking, a fact which did not exactly facilitate the process of bourgeois emancipation. Of the 2,354 persons granted citizenship rights in Pest between 1687 and 1790, 44 percent had not been born in Hungary but came from Austria (30 percent) or Germany (14 percent).[5]

These patrician bourgeois, whose life and work were regulated by the rules of town and guild, increased rapidly in number during the nineteenth century, at a time when the urban population in general was increasing at a much faster rate than the rural population. Between 1787 and the middle of the nineteenth century, when the general population increased from 8.5 to 13.2 million, an increase of 55 percent, the urban population doubled. Budapest, where the population increased as much as threefold during this period, became in 1855, with 139,000 inhabitants, the biggest city in Hungary.[6]

The *Bürgertum* in these towns was by no means at the forefront of the struggle for the political transformation of the country, a transformation which had been so emphatically placed on the agenda by the French Revolution. The towns, with only two representatives in the Hungarian parliament, did not even recognise, much less dominate, the new economic trends and market relations. The patricians, who placed a high value on security and social status and whose economic base was either the guild crafts or trade – the latter limited both regionally and in the variety of commodities involved – were increasingly less able to compete with the newly emerging and prospering entrepreneurs. These entrepreneurs, whose social position had previously been marginal, were more open to modern forms of business and had a better grasp of the new possibilities offered by the western European market.[7] Foreign trade in agricultural products such as beef, tobacco and leather had expanded following the Napoleonic wars, but the merchant sector of the *Stadtbürgertum* had no part in this because it was largely in the hands of the Jews who were, in their majority, excluded from the towns.

This functional transformation within the economic bourgeoisie of the nineteenth century was by no means a Hungarian peculiarity but also occurred in countries with much more developed bourgeois traditions. In a register of bourgeois entrepreneurs from the late nineteenth century, we find only a few of those names which, only decades previously, had been the leading names in economic life. This functional change was an expression of the new demands of modern capitalism. In those countries in which capitalist trade developed in the seventeenth and eighteenth centuries on the basis of a longer, more organic process of urban development, there was undoubtedly a stronger continuity and a higher proportion of traditional property-owners and merchants among the leading modern manufacturers.

In France, as in Germany, this functional change within the bourgeoisie was more or less closely linked with the emergence of a Jewish *Bürgertum* after the emancipation and its incorporation into the non-Jewish national *Bürgertum*. In Hungary, where the traditional *Bürgertum* was numerically, socially, politically and economically far behind the native nobility, the leading role and high proportion of Jews in the newly emerging bourgeoisie was even more pronounced. Since, in addition, the old Hungarian nobility played hardly any role in the new economic life, modern capitalist businesses and institutions were almost completely in the hands of a new, predominantly non-Hungarian bourgeoisie, a Jewish and German bourgeoisie which had come to Hungary not more than one or two generations earlier. In the first half of the nineteenth century the number of Jews rose from 78,000 to 250,000, the main reason for this increase being, besides a relatively high level of fertility, the increase in immigration. Jewish merchants from Bohemia and Moravia had already settled in Hungary in the eighteenth century, encouraged by Joseph II's edict of tolerance. The economic boom during the Napoleonic period and the increases in agricultural production on the big estates provided favourable conditions for their economic success.

When the traditional *Stadtbürgertum* attempted to restrain this rise of the Jews, the Hungarian nobility took the part of the Jews, precisely because of their increasing economic power.[8] Although the first Jewish businessmen and entrepreneurs had already acquired wealth and social status in the 1830s and 1840s, the majority of the Jews at that time still suffered from legal restrictions. A Jew could not inherit property or belong to a guild; he could not be a state or local official and was also excluded from the liberal academic professions. It was not until 1840 that Jews who had been born in Hungary, or who had been given official permission to settle there, were given the right to live in a town, to engage in trade or crafts and to buy property. It was not until 1852 that Jews could become lawyers.

On the whole, the *Bürgertum*, around the middle of the nineteenth century, were still too weak to challenge the economic and political leadership of the nobility. Within the nobility, however, there were influential, nationally-minded forces that considered it necessary to adapt the political, economic and institutional order of the country to the western European model. The social revolution of 1848/49, which abolished serfdom and abrogated feudal laws and institutions, took place under the leadership of the liberal nobility and met with sympathy, often active support, from the *Bürgertum*.

After the revolution of 1848 and Hungary's subsequent defeat in the liberation struggle against Austria, and within the framework of the Austro-Hungarian accord (*Ausgleich*) of 1867, a bourgeois social order with the appropriate legal and institutional system was established, although some material and legal remnants of the feudal structure remained, for instance, in the distribution of land.[9] The bourgeois principle of profit maximisation was now no longer limited to a small urban minority. Although the dominance of the latifundia continued, as did the aristocratic mentality with its emphasis on consumption and lifestyle, land now became, in fact, part of business, sometimes in the hands of the previous owners, sometimes through the extension of capitalist land-purchase. Capital and labour now had freedom of movement, the exception being the farm-labourers working on the estates.

Other characteristic features of the bourgeois social formation – for example, legal equality, publicity and non-intervention by the state in the market, soon established themselves as features of Hungarian society. In a manner not altogether different from France and Germany, Hungary also witnessed a rapid increase in the liberal academic professions, which came to play an increasingly greater role within the *Bürgertum*. There were, in addition, some striking parallels to Germany's pattern of development in the political-constitutional sphere. The Hungarian *Bürgertum* were, nonetheless, significantly weaker than their German counterparts, and it was not until the end of the nineteenth and the beginning of the twentieth century, at the earliest, that they achieved a position of significant political power.

Although, in what follows, I will outline the development of the Hungarian *Bürgertum* during the nineteenth century in terms of the characteristic features of bourgeois society (*bürgerliche Gesellschaft*), I would like to emphasise not so much the similarities with the countries of western and central Europe, which are undoubtedly present, but rather Hungary's own national peculiarities.

II

The basis for the development of a bourgeois society and class in Hungary was the development of the Hungarian economy which, of course, did not take place independently of the trends operating in western Europe.[10] Until well into the twentieth century it was the agricultural sector which remained dominant, a fact which manifested itself not only in the strong economic and leading social and political role of the owners of the big estates but also in the numerical preponderance of the peasantry, which, as late as 1940, still made up 50 percent of the Hungarian population. The manufacturing sector, on the other hand, developed only very slowly, and it was only later that efforts were made to reduce the country's dependence on imports by speeding up industrialisation.

This late and relatively weak industrialisation was very closely bound up with the particular structure of the Hungarian *Bürgertum*. The core of the top layer of the modern bourgeoisie had its roots in the trade in agricultural products. This, in turn, was linked to the economic rise of the Jews, protected by the landowning nobility, and to the economic boom that developed after the 1860s largely on the basis of agricultural exports. At the centre of this economic boom stood Budapest,[11] the country's capital city, where the population between 1855 and 1869 rose from 139,000 to 270,000. From the point of view of social structure, one of the most important consequences of this large increase in population was the emergence of a new *Bürgertum*. The old corporatist town *Bürger*, who were only partly able to live up to the demands of a modern economy, played an increasingly marginal role. With the loss of their previous privileges and with the emancipation of the aspiring Jewish *Bürgertum*, only relatively very few of the old town *Bürger*, mainly those involved in the building trade, were able to turn their wealth, consisting mainly of property in land and houses, to economic use. Of the 1,072 Budapest citizens who paid the highest taxes in 1873, only one in four had possessed the rights of citizenship before 1848. The majority of them came from the rapidly prospering trade in commodities.

Within a few decades a distinct merchant stratum had established itself,[12] consisting of altogether 150 families, very well off and mainly Jewish. A small number of entrepreneurs, mainly of Austrian origin, attached themselves to this group. From the 1860s, this upper stratum of the bourgeoisie, which had acquired its wealth in commodity trading, turned its attention to the greater prospects offered by industrialisation. Although, at the beginning, they maintained a close link with their previous spheres of economic activity – for instance, the milling industry now processed what had previously been the most important article of export, grain[13] – they very soon and very rapidly invested in other branches of industry.

By the end of the century these industrialists were already playing a major role in the banking sector. The banks, in turn, were linked symbiotically with foreign capital, the second major driving force of Hungarian capitalism, and the bankers, most of them Jewish, formed an influential part of the Hungarian bourgeoisie. They were both leading bank managers and powerful entrepreneurs. Behind them stood not only their great personal wealth but also the accumulated mobile capital of the big credit institutions and foreign financial consortiums.

In relation to this upper bourgeois stratum, two other groups now ranked only in second place: these were the traditional owners of property and real estate, some of them descendants of the old patrician families, and the manufacturers, who were to be found more frequently in the western parts of the country and who had their origins in the craft guilds. This is reflected, once again, in the Budapest tax records. Among the 700 largest taxpayers at the end of the century, there were 224 bankers and factory directors, 178 merchants and 148 house and property owners. In 1888 only 10 percent of these top taxpayers were members of the old patrician families.[14] Altogether there were in Hungary, around 1900, between 800 and 1,000 families that comprised the top layer of the bourgeoisie: between 3,000 and 4,000 families made up the middle ranks.[15]

This economic bourgeoisie increased its wealth very rapidly during the two decades before the First World War, on the crest of an unparalleled economic boom. In 1897, two-thirds of the top taxpayers paid less than 1,500 crowns. In 1912 not a single one of the top taxpayers paid below this amount, although inflation throughout this period was less than 30 percent.[16] It is true that individual taxes were becoming an increasingly questionable index of income and wealth, as the big banks transformed themselves into industrial enterprises in the legal form of joint stock companies.[17] Nonetheless, it is clear that the economic bourgeoisie, by means of the amalgamation of property, manufacturing industry, banking and trade, was becoming an increasingly important part of Hungarian society.

According to the census of 1910, in a population of 18,264,533 there were 11,223 persons (including dependants) who owned factories with more than twenty workers, while a further 42,089 persons were manufacturers employing between five and twenty workers. Of 400,000 merchants, 10 to 15 percent were part of the economic bourgeoisie; the rest were petty-bourgeois. To these can be added the 43,760 home-owners and the top echelon of white-collar workers in the private sector who were on the fringes of the *Bürgertum*.[18]

The wealthier members of the bourgeoisie, along with the nobility, constituted a new plutocratic elite in Hungarian society, whose lifestyle was distinctively aristocratic. The rich families from the upper stratum of the Hungarian bourgeoisie were linked to the big landowners in three ways: through marriage, through the purchase of land and through the acquisition of coats-of-arms and titles. A few bourgeois families of the first generation, who had acquired a large amount of wealth even before industrialisation, had made almost simultaneous use of these three methods of integration and had become perfectly 'assimilated'. These families then played no role in the industrialisation process and, in the list of important capitalist entrepreneurs at the turn of the century, their names no longer appeared. The acquisition of landed property was still considered to be 'good form', although it was no longer valued simply as a symbol but as an important part of capitalist enterprise.

With industry and credit becoming the most important areas of activity for the economic bourgeoisie, a particular layer of bourgeois pushed themselves more and more to the forefront, a layer for whom assimilation into the nobility was no longer such an important goal, who tended to marry in their own circles and maintained their own system of values. But this bourgeois layer did not reject noble titles when they were offered, and they were always happy to have people from the best families sit on the board of directors of the bank.

Hungarian historians, have therefore spoken of a general feudalisation of the Hungarian *Bürgertum* and point to the symbiosis of both leading strata, the aristocracy and the aspiring bourgeoisie, as a characteristic feature of modern Hungarian society. One important indication of this feudalisation, it is said, was the increasing rate of ennoblement of bourgeois individuals. Of the 346 Jewish noble families, eight were ennobled between 1824 and 1859, 118 between 1860 and 1899 and 220 between 1900 and 1918.[19] Of these 346 families, 202 named Budapest as their permanent place of residence and 70 percent attributed their wealth to commercial enterprise, even if, at the time of their ennoblement, they were engaged in a different activity. The fact the 346 Jewish families were raised to the ranks of the nobility is seen as decisive evidence for the feudalisation thesis. Further confirmation of the thesis is seen in the fact that in 1893 there were, among the 1,000 most important estate owners, 43 Jewish nobles.

The vast majority of Jewish noble families, however, were active in the economy, and it was here that they played a leading role. Between 30 and 35 percent of the men active in the Budapest stock exchange, in the chambers of industry and commerce, in the Federation of Industry and in the boards of directors of the leading big banks came from Jewish noble families. Apart from the bank directors, the men who filled these posts were recruited in their majority from the Jewish bourgeoisie. Among 152 leading posts in the banking sector, 19 were filled by representatives of foreign banks, 31 by the Hungarian nobility, 23 by individuals from the non-Jewish bourgeoisie, while 79 were in the hands of the Jewish bourgeoisie.[20]

It was precisely in the banking sector, which had a dominant position in the Hungarian economy at the beginning of the twentieth century, that the class-symbiosis of the nobility with the Jewish and non-Jewish bourgeoisie manifested itself most clearly. But whether this symbiosis should be interpreted as feudalisation is very questionable. Most of the ennobled Jewish families, after all, were part of the world of industry and banking. And even if, in a superficial manner, they adapted themselves to the lifestyle of the nobility and, for instance, acquired landed property, they made economic use of this in keeping with their own bourgeois principles. Rather than develop this feudalisation thesis any further, what is really needed, in the case of Hungary, as in the case of Germany,[22] is to investigate whether there were parts of the nobility that adapted themselves to bourgeois practices and lifestyles. Did this lead to the formation of a new plutocratic elite in which the upper strata of the bourgeoisie and of the nobility merged?[23] In any case, the thesis that the Hungarian bourgeoisie did not assume political leadership of the country in the early twentieth century because they had, to a large extent, become part of the nobility or, in some other fashion, had become feudalised, has to be re-examined in a fundamental way.[24]

III

A re-examination of this kind would require, in addition, a more precise definition of the concept *Bürgertum* and a clearer differentiation between, on the one hand, the academic and professional elite (*Bildungsbürgertum*) and, on the other hand, the economic bourgeoisie (*Wirtschaftsbürgertum*).[25] It is certainly the case that many of those 346 Jewish nobles were part of the academic and professional elite and most of the more than one thousand ennoblements that took place between 1824 and 1918 involved public officials, officers and prominent intellectuals.[26]

Nonetheless, it is perhaps necessary in the case of Hungary to emphasise an altogether different line of division than that between academics and professionals and the economic bourgeoisie. In view of the fact that the Hungarian political elite, as well as the upper levels of public officials, came from the ranks of the nobility, at least until the end of the nineteenth century, one has to pose the question about the extent to which this rapidly expanding group can be considered part of the *Bürgertum* and about its relations to the industrial bourgeoisie. It is a well-known fact that the traditional elite, the influential owners of the big landed estates, as well as those noble families whose financial powers were on the wane, had a great aversion to any form of business activity.[27] Rather than become involved in the world of business, they preferred to choose a career in the service of the state and were thus able to draw a dividing line between themselves and the *Bürgertum*.

Whereas, in western Europe, state officials were mainly of bour-

Table 17.1: The Social Compostion of Hungarian Public Officials in 1890 and 1910[28] (percentage)

	ARISTOCRACY		GENTRY		BÜRGERTUM		OTHER	
	1890	1910	1890	1910	1890	1910	1890	1910
Prime Minister	–	4.1	67.5	50.0	23.2	37.6	9.3	8.3
Interior Ministry	1.8	–	64.1	47.6	24.5	42.8	9.6	9.6
Ministry of Trade	1.2	3.5	51.6	47.4	39.2	40.1	8.0	9.0
Finance Ministry	6.6	6.5	43.8	38.6	40.0	45.3	9.6	9.6
Average	2.4	3.5	56.8	45.9	31.7	41.5	9.1	9.1

geois origin, in Hungary they belonged principally to the middle ranks of the nobility, the gentry. In the half-century after the Austro-Hungarian *Ausgleich* of 1867, the number of officials in the public service grew very rapidly. If we do not count local officials and consider only those among the employees of the state who were genuine state officials, then in 1870 we find that there were 9,503 officials, which rose in 1899 to 36,845 and in 1909 to as many as 50,253.[29] In Hungary the proportion of state officials in the working population was much higher than in England or in Germany. By international standards, however, what was remarkable about the Hungarian situation was not the large number of officials, nor was it their importance to the state, which should not be underestimated; this was a state that intervened in the economy and in society to a much greater extent than was the case in other countries.[30] What was really peculiar about Hungary was the social origin and composition of this state official-dom.

Right from the beginning it was taken for granted that state officials were to be recruited mainly from the ranks of the aristocracy and gentry. This was, to some extent, a consequence of the backwardness of the Hungarian urban *Bürgertum*, of the fact that this social stratum did not provide an adequate number of educated candidates. The peasantry also did not provide an adequate basis for recruitment, whereas, among the nobility, there had been for some considerable time a great number of young men who no longer found an adequate income on their family estates and who were therefore seeking a new career. A position in the service of the state was, alongside the owner-ship of land, the only kind of economic activity appropriate to their social status, and the attractiveness of state service for members of the land-owning class was increased by the fact that such positions were surrounded by the glory of power. This 'officialisation' of the nobility appeared almost as a political strategy insofar as, in terms of social ori-gin, mentality and family ties, it provided a guarantee that the bureau-cracy would identify with the traditional landowning nobility. Many of the officials were themselves landowners.

Although the proportion of nobles among state officials declined with time, their leadership role vis-à-vis officials of non-noble origins remained unchallenged. The latter were recruited mainly from the ranks of Hungary's German *Stadtbürgertum*. Although this traditional group had, for quite some time, been unable to keep step with the tempo of modern economic life, and although the new Jewish *Bürgertum* was now a much more important group, it was in a good position, through its culture and education, to fill highly qualified positions in officialdom.

The social rise and assimilation of these German burghers had more to do with their careers in the service of the state than it did with their involvement in trade and industry. Although between 93 and 97 percent of state officials, judges, etc., described themselves as Hungarian, a brief glance at their family names reveals that as many as a quarter of ministerial officials may have been German. In the finance ministry, it was as high as 40 percent.

In view of their social origins alone, it would be plausible to assume that there was a strict separation, if not confrontation, between the bureaucracy and the economic bourgeoisie. What was more serious and more decisive for the special affinity between the state apparatus and the middle ranks of the nobility was the mentality of state officialdom, described by a contemporary observer in 1917 in the following manner:

> Even after the birth of bourgeois Hungary in the revolution of 1848, the Hungarian bureaucracy maintained its feudal character. Public offices are still treated in Hungary today as fiefs. Official positions in the state are still regarded as *nobile officium*; they are part of family inheritance or are granted as reward for public service....The local administration still recruits its officials from one or two noble families; it is still the biggest landowner in the regime who nominates the local judge, notary and mayor. There are still today unpaid posts in the ministries for which only the sons of the nobility may apply. In other words, public office in Hungary was never regarded as a source of income but as a means of ensuring the security of the state power.[31]

The Hungarian bureaucracy can only in a very remote sense be described in Weberian terms as an apparatus based on expertise. Personal relationships were the decisive factor here, alongside of or instead of expertise. In view of this situation, one should regard Hungarian officials as a social class quite distinct from classical *Bürgertum*, and very often antagonistic to it. In spite of all its modern functions and activities, this bureaucracy acted in all political and economic conflicts as a support for the major landowners. The Hungarian *Bürgertum* therefore was at best a part of the state power but never conquered it. Instead of sharing power with the nobility, it was confronted by a state apparatus that was dependent on the landowning nobility and defended the interests of these landowners both institutionally and politically.

This confrontational model, however, has to be modified in two respects. First, this state officialdom was not just an instrument of power in the hands of the nobility. It also assumed responsibility for practical measures in the area of public welfare and in the construction of an infrastructure. It is well-known that the state in Hungary and in the rest of eastern Europe played a much greater role in this kind of activity than was the case in western Europe.[32] Secondly, this legal and institutional system that existed before the First World War not only protected the interests of the big landowners (by leaving almost half of the land in their hands), but also responded to the needs of the increasingly stronger economic bourgeoisie. The state apparatus did not therefore act against the interests of the bourgeoisie but corresponded in many respects to the requirements of bourgeois society. This does not mean that there were no conflicts. There were indeed conflicts, sparked off by officialdom's assertion of its own independence and by its development into a political class.[33]

It is also very difficult, if not impossible, to maintain a strict and unambiguous dividing line between the officials and the intelligentsia. Many members of the intelligentsia were active as lawyers, engineers, doctors or teachers, in other words, as officials. As the role of the state expanded, there was also an expansion in the number of academically educated officials who carried out modern civil functions. With respect to personnel, it was very difficult to make an absolutely clear distinction between officials and experts. The number of academic posts increased rapidly in Hungary in the nineteenth century.

In the earlier part of the century these positions were filled by the Catholic clergy, who still possessed high social status and authority. Before 1848, there were also quite a few lawyers among officials of the absolutist state and in local government – there were around 5,000 men in Hungary who held a diploma in law. As part of the 'official' intelligentsia, one also has to include the professors in the legal and medical faculties of Budapest University, in the Mining Academy and in the teacher-training colleges (approximately 1,000), as well as the teachers in the school network established by Maria Theresia in the latter part of the eighteenth century (approximately 10,000). There were also around 2,000 doctors.

Among lawyers and jurists it was the sons of the traditional nobility who dominated.[34] These professions were, in fact, open to non-nobles as a result of the ordinance of Joseph II at the end of the eighteenth century. However, it was only in the second half of the nineteenth century that bourgeois notables were able to make their presence felt, after all legal barriers in the fields of education and career had been abolished and at a time when an academic career opened a path of social ascent.[35] Initially it was the impoverished sons of the gentry who turned to an academic career. Their main interests apart from the maintenance of an upper-class lifestyle and participation in jurisprudence, were engineering, medicine and a professorial career.

There was also an increasing number of sons of the *Stadtbürgertum* who were now turning to academic life, particularly sons from Jewish families. The majority of upper-level pupils in the schools of Budapest in the 1850s came from Jewish bourgeois families. In all of Hungary, the proportion of upper-level pupils of Jewish origin rose from 11.26 percent in 1870 to 22.13 percent in 1898/99.[36] There was also an increase in the number of Jewish students in the universities; at the end of the 1850s one in every three medical students was Jewish.[37] At the beginning of the twentieth century between 30 and 35 percent of academics were Jewish, equal to the proportion that came from the gentry. Between 40 and 45 percent of Budapest doctors and lawyers came from the Jewish economic bourgeoisie.

The remaining 40 percent of academically educated people came from the *Stadtbürgertum*, from the group of German or Bohemian officials who had settled in Hungary between 1849 and 1867, from the ranks of the aspiring petty bourgeoisie and, only very seldom, from the peasantry and working class. A very small number of assimilated, ambitious sons of non-Hungarian families living in Hungary (Slovaks, Romanians, Serbs) succeeded in rising to the ranks of the educated middle class. Even if all of those non-Jewish bourgeois officials and intellectuals lacked the appropriate 'bourgeois ethos',[38] they cannot be left out of any structural analysis of the Hungarian *Bürgertum*.

From the early twentieth century the capitalist economy increasingly began to produce its own intellectuals. In the banks and credit institutions, in manufacturing industry and in commerce, there was a rapid growth in the number of careers that required technical and economic expertise. Engineers, factory managers, banking experts and even lower-ranking salaried employees constituted a broad stratum of white-collar workers within the economic sector. Before the First World War this stratum contained some 50,000 persons. Whereas officialdom was more the monopoly of the gentry (40 percent), with the Jewish *Bürgertum* having only a very small presence (5.5 percent), among white-collar employees in the economic sector the situation was reversed. Almost two-thirds of all bank officials and half of industrial white-collar employees were Jewish. This was the beginning of a development in which, unlike in the nineteenth century, when it was a person's independence which determined his bourgeois status, this status was now determined by the level of a person's income linked to the kind of conditions in which he worked.

IV

What distinguished the Hungarian *Bürgertum* from similar social formations in western Europe? This question is not so easily answered in the absence of fundamental detailed analysis. If we focus on the relationship of the Hungarian *Bürgertum* to the state power, or on cooperation with the major landowners or links to the state apparatus, then the thesis of aristocratic hegemony and bourgeois abstinence from power, a thesis developed in relation to Germany, can be even more appropriately applied to Hungary.[39] It would be more fruitful, however, to approach this question from a different direction and to examine the *Bürgertum* from the point of view of its long-term interaction with economic development.

What we would need to look at, in this kind of study, would be such things as the distribution of different social layers across the main sectors of the economy, the proportion of the *Bürgertum* involved in trade or manufacture, and which sectors of the *Bürgertum* were the most dynamic in promoting development and change. It would also be necessary to examine the differences between burghers in Budapest and those in the provinces. Did the development of modern large-scale enterprise and of finance capital bring about a polarisation inside the *Bürgertum*, with the wealth and power of the top bourgeois stratum increasing dramatically while the middle-bourgeois strata disintegrated and moved down into the ranks of the petty bourgeoisie? Or did technical and commercial innovations, from the combustion engine to the slowly developing service sector, strengthen the petty bourgeoisie and offer them new sources of power?

It is by no means adequate here to preserve the traditional classifications of the career and social system, such as independent person, white-collar worker or official. We need to find new categories that can adequately encompass the structures of *Bürgertum*. It would also be essential to differentiate, within the *Bürgertum*, between the various economic sectors, since some offered more possibilities than others. Geographical facts as well as market relations in the different regions would be particularly important since these set the limits to the *Bürgertum's* scope for action and influenced the relations of forces within the *Bürgertum* as a whole. We began by inquiring into the similarities and differences in the development of middle-class formations in different countries but, in the case of Hungary, what we end up with is a rather extended research project.

Rather than venture an answer to the more general question, what I would like to attempt at the end of this essay is to establish the figures for the size of the Hungarian *Bürgertum* in the early twentieth century. According to what was officially admitted to be a somewhat generous reckoning, there were altogether 734,426 *Bürger* which included all independent businessmen, merchants and traders, intellectuals with an academic degree, officials in the state and in local government, even messengers in the civil service and policemen. Of the 4,322,960 men over twenty years of age who lived in Hungary at that time, something like 17 percent could therefore be reckoned as belonging to the broad grouping described as bourgeois. With the help of taxation statistics we can distinguish various different strata. Among those with wealth and a high level of income, we can distinguish:

—6,411 independent businessmen with at least five employees;
—30,136 independent traders who paid 20 crowns profit tax;
—62,716 intellectuals (doctors, lawyers, teachers, priests);
—30,913 officials with a tax levy of at least 18 crowns;
—31,058 other officials;
In total, 161,234 persons.

According to these statistics,[40] 22 percent of these belonged to upper or middle layers of the *Bürgertum*, whereas the rest belonged to the petty bourgeoisie. If the classification for independent craftsmen had been three workers instead of five, which would have been a more sensible limit, then the overall number would be increased by between 10,000 and 15,000; this would not, however, fundamentally alter the overall picture. These statistics do not include the 112,950 independent women who, according to the census of 1900, were involved in crafts, mining and transport. But these, in the majority, would have been part of the petty bourgeoisie. The 12,860 women who were officials and white-collar workers were also excluded, because it was not to be expected that women, for whom the possibility of study had only existed since the turn of the century, would be in leading positions.

It was statistics of this kind that prompted G. Rácz, a member of the radical intelligentsia in the early part of the twentieth century, to point, quite correctly, to the numerical weakness of the Hungarian bourgeoisie and to conclude that:

> As far as social structure is concerned, the Prussian kingdom in 1867 was already as much an advanced industrial state as Hungary was in 1900. The proportion of independent people involved in industry in Prussia at that time was 35.9 percent of the overall working population, while in Hungary at the same time it was only 19.9 percent.[41]

Notes to Chapter 17

1. Nobles who owned a house in the town or who were engaged in trade or manufacture were also regarded as bourgeois (*Bürger*). *Magyarország története*, vol. 5 (Budapest, 1980), p. 433.

2. J. Szücs, *Vázlat Európe három történelmi régióiaról* (Budapest, 1981); J. Szücs, 'The Three Historical Regions of Europe', *Acta Historica* 29 (1983), pp. 131–183.

3. D. Kosáry, *Culture and Society in Eighteenth Century Hungary* (Budapest, 1987), pp. 29–33.

4. E. Deák, *Das Städtewesen der Länder der ungarischen Krone (1780–1918)*, vol. 1 (Vienna, 1979).

5. *Budapest története*, vol. 3 (Budapest, 1975), p. 133.

6. K. Keleti, *Hazánk és népe* (Budapest, 1873), p. 48.

7. V. Bácskai and L. Nagy, 'Market Areas, Market Centres and Towns in Hungary in 1828', *Acta Historica* 26 (1980), pp. 1–25.

8. More details in K. Vörös, 'Ungarns Judentum vor der bürgerlichen Revolution', in K. Hitchins (ed.), *Studies in East European Social History*, vol. 2 (Leiden, 1981).

9. The central features of bourgeois society are dealt with in H. Kaelble's contribution to the present volume.

10. I. T. Berend and G. Ránki, *The European Periphery and Industrialisation 1780–1914* (Cambridge, 1982), pp. 21–28.

11. The founding of Budapest as a result of the legal unification of Buda, Pest and Obuda took place in 1873.

12. K. Vörös (ed.), *Budapest története*, vol. 4 (Budapest, 1978), pp. 222f.

13. I. T. Berend and G. Ránki, *A Century of Economic Development* (New York, 1974), pp. 24–40.

14. K. Vörös, *Budapest legnagyobb adófizetöi* (Budapest, 1979), p. 76.

15. P. Hanak, *Ungarn in der Donaumonarchie. Probleme der bürgerlichen Umgestaltung eines Vielvölkerstaates* (Vienna, 1984), p. 362.

16. Vörös, *Budapest legnagyogg adófizetöi*, p. 102.

17. I. T. Berend and G. Ránki, *Magyarország gyáripara 1900–1914* (Budapest, 1955), pp. 142–172. 75 percent of Hungary's industrial production was carried out by joint stock companies and 55 percent of all manufacturing enterprises were controlled by the five leading banks.

18. *A szociologia elsö magyar mühelye*, vol. 2 (Budapest, 1973), pp. 11–14.

19. W. O. McCagg, 'Hungary's "Feudalized" Bourgeoisie', *Journal of Modern History* 44 (1972), pp. 65–78 (these figures are from the table on p. 67).

20. W. O. McCagg, *Jewish Nobles and Geniuses in Modern Hungary* (Boulder, 1972), p. 136.

21. Berend and Ránki, *Magyarország gyáripara 1900–1914*, pp. 116–142.

22. On the earlier ideas concerning the feudalisation of the German *Bürgertum*, cf. E. Kehr, *Der Primat der Innenpolitik* (Frankfurt, 1976) and the study by Hans Rosenberg, 'Die Pseudodemokratisierung der Rittergutsbesitzerklasse', in H. Rosenberg, *Probleme der deutschen Sozialgeschichte* (Frankfurt, 1969), pp. 7–49. For more recent ideas on this subject, cf. D. Blackbourn, 'Kommentar', in J. Kocka, (ed.), *Bürger und Bürgerlichkeit im 19. Jahrhundert* (Göttingen, 1987), pp. 281–287; also H. Kaelble, *Das aristokratische Modell im deutschen Bürgertum des 19. Jahrhunderts* (Zentrm für interdisziplinäre Forschung, Forschungsgruppe 'Bürger, Bürgerlichkeit und bürgerliche Gesellschaft', Preprint no. 2, 1986/87), pp. 9ff.

23. Cf. the essay by W. Mosse in this volume.

24. McCagg, *Jewish Nobles*, p. 66.

25. J. Kocka, 'Bürgertum und Bürgerlichkeit als Probleme der deutschen Geschichte vom späten 18 zum frühen 20. Jahrhundert', in J. Kocka, *Bürger*, pp. 21–63, especially pp. 21–28.

26. Hungarian historigraphy does not use the concept *Bildungsbürgertum* (educated and profesional middle class). In the German translation of a work by P. Hanák, which was published in 1984 (Nahák, *Ungarn*), this term was used in the heading of one section (pp. 369–374). In the original Hungarian text, however, (*Magyarország Története*, vol. 7, [Budapest, 1978]) the phrase used was 'officials and intellectuals' (p. 452).

27. G. Szekfü, *Három nemzedék. Egy hanyatló kor Története* (Budapest, 1920), p. 215; 'The one-time privileged classes held on rigidly to the old "aristocratic" careers and preferred to fall down the social ladder rather than take themselves out of the old accustomed milieu and enter into the service of trade or industry'.

28. A János, *The Politics of Backwardness* (Princeton, 1983), p. 110.

29. I. Hollós, *A Közszolgálati alkalmazottak nyugdíjkérdései és a megoldási lehetöségek* (Budapest, 1926), p. 12.

30. I. T. Berend and G. Ránki, 'Die Rolle des Staates in der wirtschaftlichen Entwicklung des 19. Jahrhunderts', in J. Schneider (ed.), *Wirtschaftskräfte und Wirtschaftswege. Festschrift für H. Kellenbenz*, vol. 3 (Stuttgart, 1978), pp. 325–346, especially p. 340.

31. J. Hesslein, *A köztisztviselöprobléma* (Nyugat, 1917), p. 439.

32. Berend and Ránki, *European Periphery*, pp. 59–73.

33. János, *Politics*, pp. 121–126.

34. *Magyarország története*, vol. 5, p. 595.

35. K. Vörös, 'A modern értelmiség kezdetei Magyarrszágon', *Valóság* 10 (1975), pp. 1–20.

36. J. Mazsu, *A hazai értelmiség feilödésének néhány sajátossága* (Degrecen, 1984), pp. 301ff.

37. *Magyarország története*, vol. 6 (Budapest, 1979), p. 596.

38. Hanák, *Ungarn*, p. 374.

39. A. J. Mayer, *Adelsmacht und Bürgertum. Die Krise der europäischen Gesellschaft 1848–114*; H. Kaelble, *Auf dem Weg zu einer europäischen Gesellschaft. Eine Sozialgeschichte Westeuropas 1880–1980* (Munich, 1987), p. 30.

40. *A szociológia elsö magyar mühelye*, vol. 2 (Budapest, 1973), pp. 7–33.

41. G. Rácz, *A magyar osztálykapcsolás gazdasági alapjai és demokráciánk feilödesi lehetöségei* (Huszadik Század, 1909), p. 364.

Notes on Contributors

Youssef Cassis (b.1952) teaches History at the University of Geneva. He is author of *Les banquiers de la City à l'époque édouardienne, 1890–1914* (1984). His major field of research is the history of banks and entrepreneurial elites in England and Switzerland during the nineteenth and twentieth centuries.

Cristiane Eisenberg (b.1956) teaches History at the University of Hamburg. Her publications include *Deutsche und englische Gewerkschaften. Entstehung und Entwicklung bis 1878 im Vergleich* (1986). Her research has covered modern English and German social history and has focused on the evolution of trade unions and sports from a comparative perspective.

Ute Frevert (b.1954) is Professor of History at the University of Konstanz. She has published widely in the field of modern German social history emphasising gender relations. She is author of *Women in German History* (1989) and of *Ehrenmänner. Das Duell in der bürgerlichen Gesellschaft* (1991).

Patrick Fridenson (b.1944) is Professor at the École des Hautes Études en Science Sociales, Paris. His research has emphasised the social and economic history of France in the nineteenth and twentieth centuries. His numerous publications include *Histoire des usines Renault* (1972) and The French Home Front, ed. (1992).

Heinz–Gerhard Haupt (b.1943) is Director of the European Institute, Florence. He has published widely in the field of modern French social history and the history of the European petite bourgeoisie. He is author of *Sozialgeschichte Frankreichs seit 1789* (1989) and has edited *Shopkeepers and Master Artisans in Nineteenth-Century Europe* (1984).

Eric J.E. Hobsbawm (b.1917) is Professor emeritus at Birbeck College, University of London. He has published countless articles and books on European social history. Among them are *The Age of Revolution. Europe 1789–1848* (1962), *The Age of Capital, 1848–1875 (1975)*, and *The Age of Empire, 1875–1914* (1987).

Hartmut Kaelble (b.1940) is Professor of History at Humboldt University, Berlin. He has done extensive research in the field of European social history emphasising a comparative perspective. Among his books are *Social Mobility in the 19th and 20th Centuries. Europe and America in Comparative Perspective* (1985) and *Auf dem Weg zu einer europäischen Gesellschaft. Eine Sozialgeschichte Westeuropas, 1880–1980* (1987).

456

Wolfgang Kaschuba (b.1950) teaches History at the University of Göttingen. His main field of research is modern German social and cultural history. He is author of *Volkskultur zwischen feudaler und bürgerlicher Gesellschaft* (1988) and is coauthor of *Dörfliches Überleben. Zur Geschichte materieller und sozialer Reproduktion ländlicher Gesellschaft im 19. und frühen 20. Jahrhundert* (1982).

Jürgen Kocka (b.1941) is Professor of History at the Free University of Berlin and permanent fellow of the Wissenschaftskolleg zu Berlin. He has published widely in the field of modern social and economic history, including *White Collar Workers in America, 1890–1940* (1980) and *Facing Total War. German Society 1914–1918* (1984).

Dieter Langewiesche (b.1943) is Professor of Medieval and Modern History at the University of Tübingen. His main research interests are in German history of the nineteenth and twentieth centuries, his publications include *Europa zwischen Restauration und Revolution, 1815–1849* (1985) and *Liberalismus in Deutschland* (1988).

Mario Meriggi (b.1955) teaches Modern European History at the University of Trento. He has recently written a book on *Voluntary Associations and the Birth of Civil Society in Nineteenth-Century Milan* (1992).

Allan Mitchell (b.1933) is Professor of History at the University of California, San Diego. He has published widely in the field of modern German and French history, including *Bismarck and the French Nation, 1848–1890* (1971) and *Victors and Vanquished. The German Influence on Army and Church in France after 1870* (1984).

Werner Mosse (b.1918) is Professor emeritus at the University of East Anglia (Norwich), Chairman of the Leo Baeck Insitute, London, and Fellow of the Royal Historical Society, London. He has published numerous books on modern European history and the history of German-Jewish relationships. His most recent ones are *The German-Jewish Economic Elite, 1820–1935* (1989) and *Perestroika under the Tsars, 1855–1915* (forthcoming).

György Ránki (1930–1988) was Professor of History at the University of Budapest and Director of the Historical Institute at the Hungarian Academy of Science. His research emphasised economic and social history of East-Middle Europe during the nineteenth and twentieth centuries, leading to many books and articles including *The European Periphery and Industrialization, 1780–1914* (coauthored with Ivan Tibor Berend 1982) and *The Hungarian Economy in the Twentieth Century* (1985).

Richard Tilly (b.1932) is Professor of Economic and Social History at the University of Münster. He has published widely in the field of German and

Western European history, including (jointly with Charles and Louise Tilly) *The Rebellious Century, 1830–1930* (1975) and *Kapital, Staat und sozialer Protest in der deutschen Industrialisierung* (1980).

Ursula Vogel (b.1938) teaches history at the Department of Government of the University of Manchester. Her research has focused on the history of political theory and the changing legal status of women in the eighteenth and nineteenth centuries. Her publications include *Konservative Kritik an der bürgerlichen Revolution* (1972).

Shulamit Volkov (b.1942) is Professor of Modern History and Director of the Institute for German History at the University of Tel Aviv. She has published widely in the field of modern German and European social history emphasising the history of German–Jewish relationships. She is author of *The Rise of Popular Antimodernism in Germany. The Urban Master Artisans, 1873–1896* (1978).

Index